TRANSITIO

GW00649316

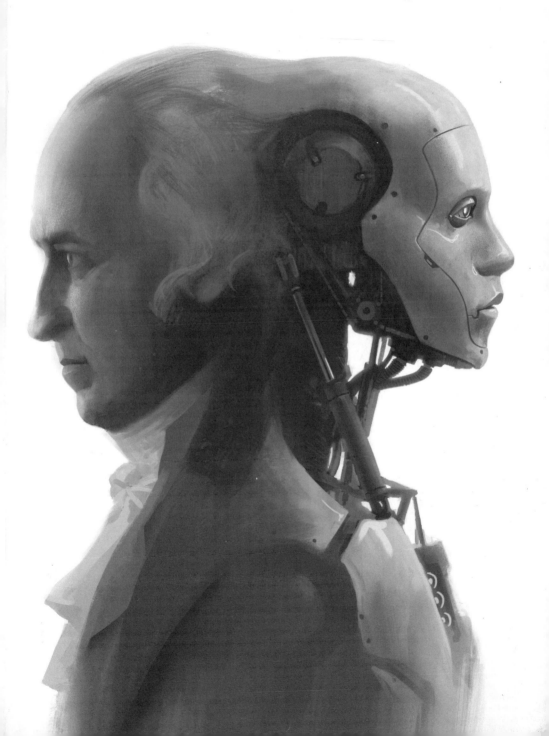

TRANSITION POINT

FROM STEAM TO THE SINGULARITY

SEAN A. CULEY

Matador
9 Priory Business Park,
Wistow Road, Kibworth Beauchamp,
Leicestershire. LE8 0RX
Tel: 0116 279 2299
Email: books@troubador.co.uk
Web: www.troubador.co.uk/matador
Twitter: @matadorbooks

ISBN PB: 978 1789014 853
HB: 978 1789014 884

British Library Cataloguing in Publication Data.
A catalogue record for this book is available from the British Library.

Printed and bound in the UK by TJ International, Padstow, Cornwall
Typeset in 11pt Calibri by Troubador Publishing Ltd, Leicester, UK

Matador is an imprint of Troubador Publishing Ltd

To Helen, Taylor and Pierce

Contents

Acknowledgements   ix
Introduction   xi
Cover Design and Interior Artwork   xv

Part One
Engines of Revolution   1

1   Time, Testosterone and Technology   3
2   From Producers to Consumers: The West Takes Off   28
3   A Quite Extraordinary Series of Events   42
4   Exploration, Enlightenment and Entrepreneurism   69
5   Revolution! The World Takes Off   85
6   Gallifreyan Economics and the Art of Creative Destruction   104
7   Understanding Innovation: Gradually, Then Suddenly   128
8   The End of the Industrial Age   150

Part Two
The Sixth Wave   169

9   The Automation of Labour   171
10   The Automation of the Knowledge Worker   212
11   Convergence! The Automation of the Value Chain   245

Part Three
Evolution or Endgame?   261

12	New Wave, New Paradigms	263

Sixth-Wave Business — 283

13	A New Business Mindset	285
14	A Copernican Business Revolution	310

Sixth-Wave Science and Technology — 333

15	Science Fiction Becomes Science Fact	335
16	The Death of Privacy	363
17	AI Unleashed	380
18	Retaining Control	408

Sixth-Wave Economics — 425

19	The Time of Keynes' Grandchildren	427
20	A Revolution for Me, But Not for Thee	458
21	Levelling the Field	480
22	The Potential for a New Golden Age	521

Sixth-Wave Society — 539

23	All Empires Fall	541
24	Cracks in the Foundations	553
25	Chaos by Design	575
26	Basic-Income Bread and Virtual Circuses	596
27	The Mother of All Cultural Lags	606
28	Brave New World or Big Brother?	628

Beyond the Sixth Wave — 649

29	Battle of the Gods	651
30	A Tale of Two Species	670

Conclusion	685
References	687

Acknowledgements

First and foremost, thanks to my wife and soulmate for the last thirty years, Helen, without whose support this book would have never been written. The last five years have created a financial rollercoaster on which you did not ask, nor want, to ride. I couldn't have done this without the support of someone who believed in both me and this project, and I am eternally grateful for having you in my life.

Secondly, thanks to my sons Taylor and Pierce, for their patience with a father who was mentally distracted by this project during critical years. Also, thanks to my parents for teaching me the virtue of responsibility and effort.

Finally, thanks to all those who have over the years encouraged me to write this. In no particular order, these include: Niels ('Don't write a book, write *the* book') van Hove, Dr Heather Skipworth, Professor Richard Wilding OBE, Professor Alan Waller OBE, Clive and Jenny Froome, Sharon Burton, Gretchen Becker, Sandra Lam, Raphael Rottgen, Lawrence Corr, Nigel Price, Steve Connell, Mark Tattum, Karim Sayani, Nameer Khan, Peter Wilkins and Daniel McMurray.

Introduction

This history behind this book starts back in the summer of 2012, when I was chairperson for a European supply chain conference in Madrid. During the two-day event I listened to various speakers excitingly talk about new technologies that were being developed, ranging from big data analytical tools to warehouse robotics, and it dawned on me that no one was considering what would happen when these were all applied. At the end of the day I sketched out a picture of an end-to-end supply chain and overlaid the different technologies and the areas they would automate. I quickly realised that we were facing a wave of technology that had some very disruptive potential.

A couple of months later I took the ideas from this sketch and wrote an article for *The European Business Review* called *Transformers: Supply Chain 3.0 and How Automation will Transform the Rules of the Global Supply Chain*. It proved popular. I then received a call from the organiser of an event I was speaking at, who had an urgent request: could I prepare and deliver a second presentation at short notice as the last speaker of the day had just dropped out? I stated that I had just written an interesting article that I could easily convert into a presentation. He agreed, I did it, and the audience loved it, with the Q&A session going on so long that the organiser had to come in and shut things down. It had touched a nerve, but intriguingly, the questions from the audience were not so much about the technology, but about their social and economic impact. Questions such as 'What does this mean for our jobs? For society? For our children's futures?'

I was increasingly asked to speak at events in locations ranging from Asia to Africa, the Middle East to Eastern Europe, as well as private sessions for companies who wanted to shake their teams out of complacency. To ensure it stayed relevant, I constantly updated both the content and the style of delivery. Then, in autumn 2013, I decided that this would make a good book. I agreed with my wife that I would take three months off work to transform this material into a short book that should be finished by Christmas. That proved to be ridiculously naive. It quickly became apparent that while my observations identified connections that few had noticed, it was also somewhat incomplete. Like the vast majority of books, blogs and opinion pieces, it was just detailing what was happening, but contained little explanatory insights. Everyone agrees that the world is changing at a breathtaking pace, one that is leaving many people dazed, businesses struggling, economies floundering and societies fracturing. But why?

Establishing the answer to the 'why' question requires an understanding of not only the nature of technological change, but also of the social, economic and political factors that enable and suppress it, plus those that are impacted by it. Suddenly the rabbit hole starts to look deeper than one would expect. Exploring how deep constitutes Part One of this book.

It gets worse, for once you understand the concept, cause and impact of technological change, and the waves that drive it, then further questions emerge. What stage are we in now? What types of technologies does the current wave contain? Which areas will it impact? The truth is that we are about to experience a period of technological change on a par with the introduction of electricity. And like electricity, it will power new production capabilities, create new consumer products and develop entirely new ways of living. Exactly how these technologies are primed to automate every aspect of the business world, from digging things out of the ground to the sale and delivery of finished products, creating a more personal, automated and local supply chain, constitutes Part Two of the book.

Finally, the really big question – so what? What are the likely issues, challenges and opportunities that will arise as a result of all of this disruption? What impact will all this technological change have on business, the economy, our society and our evolution? As the 19th-century Danish philosopher and social critic Søren Kierkegaard observed, life can only be observed backwards, but it must be lived forwards. What lessons can we extract from Part One to ensure that progress is both possible and positive? To be clear, I don't have all the answers – no one does – but I hope I'm able to frame and connect some of the most important and thought-provoking issues and questions. One thing became clear; to discuss technology without investigation into the socio-economic impacts would have been like discussing Christianity without talking about God. These areas are intrinsically linked, and as a result, geopolitics also comes into the discussion, for that tries to control both our economic and our social activities, and technology now provides new ways to do that.

Part Three, therefore, examines six key areas that will be impacted by this current wave of transformative change: our paradigms, our business practices, our scientific and technological explorations, our economic models, our society and our world views. In the business section I explore how capitalism has morphed into corporatism, and how corporate leaders need to adopt a longer-term and more entrepreneurial mindset to adapt to the demands of a new wave, ensuring not just their survival, but also the creation of a more sustainable, customer-centric business model. In the science and technology section I explore the rise of genetic engineering, the dystopian potential for technology to erode our freedoms and privacies, and the potential dangers of artificial intelligence. In the economics section, I explore the changing nature of work, the threat of mass technological unemployment, the need to recalibrate the economic model to ensure a level playing field, and the case for a universal basic income. The society section is perhaps the most interesting – and the most controversial. In this I examine how Western society is currently unravelling, struggling to adapt to rapidly changing technological forces, but taking totalitarian steps just to retain a semblance of order. I examine how some of this chaos is being driven by ideologues, and how their attempts to undermine the foundations that led to the progress defined in Part One is bearing fruit. Finally, the last two chapters explore what happens after this wave. This includes an explanation as to why our world views and the deities we worship will determine our future, and why this may be the beginning of the end for Homo sapiens as the dominant species on the planet.

In places I propose suggestions: ways to improve businesses to deliver more value to more people, ways to ensure technology does not take over, ways to recalibrate our economic models and ways to ensure society works for everyone. I cover some major topics that have been turned into books all on their own, but rather than simply sensationalise, I try to show how, as with the first industrial revolution, the choices we make and the freedoms we allow will determine the society we end up with. However, make no mistake – dystopian outcomes are still viable, and they are much easier to achieve than the utopian ones, for in many cases they simply require doing nothing.

I never intended this to be such a big project, nor such a large book. But the further I went down the rabbit hole, the more I realised that technology, society and the economy are intrinsically linked, and I was unaware of anyone bringing these elements together in a way that highlights both the historical causes and the future implications of this interrelationship. While tempted to split this into separate books; one on technology, and another on the social and economic impacts, I ultimately felt that the power came from explaining their connection, and that if I separated them, then the impact would be lost. The reader would learn 'how' and 'what' is happening, but not 'why'. I've frequently questioned the logic of undertaking such a large and ambitious project, questioning both my right to do it and whether I was being selfish in pursuing it. The time it has taken me to produce this work, mostly due to my family's fondness for food and their aversion to homelessness, has also been frustrating, for since I started many other books have been published on similar topics. It has also been interesting to watch potential events that I had written about actually unfold. As we will explore, the transition period between technological and economic waves is a dangerous, divisive and disruptive time. To then watch the European migration crisis, Brexit and the US election, the nuclear sabre-rattling between the US and North Korea, the escalation of tensions between the West and Russia and the polarisation of Western society was quite a thing. As was watching many of the radical new technologies transform from being mere ideas into implemented solutions.

I hope the extensive journey of exploration and discovery I've been through over the last five years researching and writing Transition Point translates well. In places it may make you concerned and fearful, in others inspired and hopeful. But most of all I hope it makes you think. In places I have not shied away from being controversial, for I believe that when honesty and freedom of speech dies, society dies with it. I hope that this book challenges you to think carefully about some of the decisions that are currently being made, that we do not sacrifice too much in our pursuit of progress, and that we can work together to ensure that the future is a positive experience for everyone.

Best wishes and thank you.

Sean A. Culey

Cover Design
and Interior Artwork

The three images that feature on the cover and at the start of Part One and Part Three are reinterpretations of the Roman god Janus, the god of beginnings and transitions, and of doorways and endings. As such, Janus is the perfect guide, for this is a story of beginnings and transitions, and from this transition could come new beginnings or endings – or both.

On the cover, Janus's two heads are represented by James Watt, the inventor of the steam engine that powered the industrial age; and an android representing the forthcoming artificial-intelligence age. I name this image *Transition Point: From Steam to the Singularity*.

The version of Janus that opens Part One again uses James Watt, but this time his partner is Sergey Brin, the co-founder of Google, wearing a pair of Google Glasses which in 2014 were the epitome of wearable technology. The image is named *Engines of Revolution* for these two individuals were the primary inventors of the two engines that powered two revolutions – the steam engine and the search engine.

The final Janus transition image opens Part Three of this book, called *Evolution or Endgame?* Janus now represents a juxtaposition between a utopian Pollyanna and a dystopian Cassandra vision of the future. Pollyanna Janus becomes female in form, representing the rise of women across industry and the workplace. She is augmented, representing a future where we merge with technology, constantly on and constantly connected. A world of technological advancement and abundance. Her dystopian Cassandra alternative represents the nightmare sci-fi scenario of runaway

AI, where technology, not humanity, becomes the prevalent force on the planet, where our hubris has led to human decline.

I commissioned the artwork in the summer of 2014, and they were all completed by a wonderfully talented young US artist called Houston Sharp, who I'm delighted to announce has since gone on to become an in-demand concept artist/illustrator working on Hollywood blockbusters such as *Wonder Woman, Rampage* and *Dark Phoenix*. I wholeheartedly recommend checking out his portfolio of work at https://houstonsharp. deviantart.com/gallery/

Part One

ENGINES OF REVOLUTION

1

TIME, TESTOSTERONE AND TECHNOLOGY

The farther backward you look, the farther forward you are likely to see.

Sir Winston Churchill

Picture a child sat playing with two toy dinosaurs, a ferocious meat-eating *Tyrannosaurus rex*, and a plant-eating, spiky-tailed, plate-covered *Stegosaurus*. Got it? Good. Now consider the fact that the child is 18 million years more likely to have met a real *Tyrannosaurus* than a *Stegosaurus* would have done, as Rexy and Steggy lived 83 million years apart. Life has been around far longer than we have, but nothing has had the same impact. To understand how little time humans have played a role in this planet's story, an often-used analogy is used: imagine the history of Earth was converted to a single calendar year. Anatomically modern humans only made an appearance at 11.58pm on the 31st December; just 150,000 years ago. Believed to have originated in Africa (although recent findings indicate that it may have been Europe[1]), for most of their existence humans have lived unremarkable lives, foraging for food and focusing on not being eaten by predators or killed by other groups of similarly uncommunicative upright apes. We only discovered how to magic up fire around 125,000 years ago, but while we could now warm ourselves, for 65,000 years the fireside

3

conversation was somewhat lacking, as it was only 60,000 years ago that we attempted speech. These early conversations were pretty unremarkable, which is probably why no one bothered to write any of them down. The eventual transition from grunts to words had profound side-effects, enabling the development of more complex thought processes, cultural creativity and other attributes that separated us from other mammals. For this achievement we bestowed these ancestors the honour of being called anatomically and behaviourally modern humans (*Homo sapiens sapiens*).

Homo sapiens wasn't the only upright, bipedal, talking humanoid on the scene, and if gambling had been a thing back then, you would have almost certainly put your shiny stones and favourite shells on Neanderthals emerging as the dominant species, given their larger brain, better eyesight and substantially more powerful physique. Their large muscular frames enabled them to be successful ambush hunters, as well as helping them cope with the cold of the Ice Age better than *Homo sapiens*. Strong, smart, aggressive and capable of communicating as well as humans, Neanderthals should have been invincible. Yet like the dwarves in Middle Earth, while their physique made them well suited for short bursts of speed and close combat hunting, they were not the best at long-distance running, balance or throwing. They were also pretty antisocial, probably due to them producing so much testosterone that they could win Mr Olympia simply by following the Jane Fonda workout. High levels of testosterone in the presence of competition fuels dominance, whereas high testosterone in times of low threat or competition creates fierce protectiveness.[2] These traits probably resulted in Neanderthals – especially the males – not playing well with others, particularly those they deemed competition for food or females, explaining why they formed small and very close-knit family groups.[3] This unwillingness to mingle probably resulted in some serious *Game of Thrones*-style interbreeding, limiting their genetic diversity.[1] *Homo sapiens*, on the

---

[1]   While mating with *Homo sapiens* did occur, proven since we established that our DNA is 2 per cent Neanderthal, it was probably likely to have been initiated by the Neanderthal, and probably not consensual, if you get my meaning. Interestingly, in 2015, UK Biobank conducted a study of 500,000 Caucasian people and identified 112,338 individuals with white European ancestry whose genomes contain Neanderthal DNA. They then used this data to identify which traits are influenced by Neanderthal genetic variants. The results were that those with Neanderthal DNA present were likely to be night owls, and/or suffer from depression, mood disorders and loneliness.

other hand, experienced a gradual reduction in their testosterone level, developing more 'feminised' features than their Neanderthal cousins, such as a reduction in brow prominence and a more rounded face.[4] Reduced testosterone levels have been linked to the development of language and social skills, which explains why females demonstrate a higher level of social interaction skills than males. Male humans are also hardwired with a genetic honey trap that lowers testosterone after they have children, especially when they are around family groups.[5] This makes them less competitive and sexually aggressive when they become fathers, and thus more likely to stick around after mating. It also makes them more sociable and willing to work with other males.

The Neanderthals' small groups and testosterone-fuelled antisocial behaviour were not a problem in the forests of Europe where they lived during the Ice Age. However, when the climate warmed, the forests where they hunted receded and transformed into wide open spaces, and their inability to run long distances or work together in large groups severely limited their hunting effectiveness. Neanderthals and humans competed for the same food, and while Neanderthals formed small, exclusive family units, Homo sapiens formed larger and more inclusive tribes, developing a social fabric that helped keep them all warm, safe and fed. The security and support of the group also allowed them to travel further to find food, working together to overcome different climates and terrains, increasing their adaptability and widening their resources.[6] In a world of open plains, hunting down massive beasts like mammoths required collaboration, cooperation and networking over considerable distances – plus a willingness to share the spoils. This was where modern humans were more genetically and socially able. It is believed (it's hard to know for sure as evolution isn't a spectator sport) that the Neanderthals' inability to collaborate with others and form large groups made it harder for them to overcome the difficulties of their harsh Eurasian environments, restricting their ability to compete for food in the open spaces. Despite their obvious physical advantages and the fact that they had a 150,000-year head start, we survived, and the Neanderthals' did not. Homo sapiens' more inclusive nature was the difference. Our ability to work together and find common purpose, identity and unity enabled our ancestors to overcome hardships and achieve goals bigger than they could as individual units. Without this, it is unlikely that we would have developed beyond simple hunter-gatherers, and we certainly wouldn't have become the industrialised nations we are today.

Interestingly, the impact testosterone has on social structures can be seen in great apes such as chimpanzees and bonobos. While chimps and bonobos are from the same taxonomical genus – *Pan* – and look somewhat alike, slight differences in genetics make a huge amount of difference socially. Both live in stable social groups and have a relatively long lifespan. However, male chimpanzees have high testosterone levels and, as a result, are incredibly strong and competitive, creating patriarchal hierarchies where issues are often resolved through violence, whereas male bonobos have much lower testosterone levels and, as a result, female bonobos rule the roost and most disputes are settled with sexual contact. Bonobos make love, not war, so to speak, and are pansexual, caring little about the age or gender of their sexual partners. Life in a bonobo tribe is akin to acquiring permanent residency at Caligula's palace. While chimps operate in packs of males to deliberately hunt out, attack, kill and often eat any chimpanzees that stray into their territory, an unknown bonobo that inadvertently walks into another group's territory will receive a much more, ahem, 'pleasant' reception. The bonobos' survival relies totally on the existence of the Congo River, which caused the evolutionary split between them and chimpanzees around a million years ago. As apes are unwilling to cross wide stretches of water, the river has served to keep them apart. This has allowed the bonobos to develop an ape utopia, a never-changing lifestyle safe in the protection of the fruit-laden trees that make up the humid Congo Basin, whereas their relatives north of the river had to adapt to more open, changeable and hostile environments, and their strength and aggressive nature were essential to ensure their survival. Had chimpanzees ever learnt to swim and crossed into the Congo Basin, then we would be learning about bonobos from history books rather than nature programmes. The bonobos would be ill prepared for the velocity and ferocity of the violence that would befall them if their respective groups were to meet. The only way bonobos would survive a chimp attack would be if they managed to figure out how to craft their environment to develop protective shelters and weapons. Yet despite millions of years of advantage, regardless of their propensity for love or war, neither bonobos nor chimpanzees have figured out how to create fire, build structures and invent new things.

Approximately 9,000 years ago the victorious *Homo sapiens* expanded their Paleo diet by learning how to cultivate and irrigate the land to grow crops like wheat. Then, around 6,000 years ago, we learnt that by domesticating and feeding other species such as cows and oxen we could use them for their meat, muscle, manure and milk. The relative newness of this knowledge from an evolutionary perspective explains why so many people have problems digesting wheat, gluten and milk products, as our digestive system evolved long before we introduced these into our diet. Around this time the first human civilisation emerged in the fertile crescent – Mesopotamia – and people started to gather together in large urban areas, creating the first city states. Records of trade were captured by the Sumerians around the same time in the form of cuneiform writing and hieroglyphics, ushering in the period we now call 'recorded history', allowing an insight into how they lived. The emergence of both writing and trade represented the first real economic shift, enabling a more sophisticated exchange of value than just barter. Around this time the wheel also made an appearance, indicating the rise of the first machines and our ability to use other species to supplement our own muscle. From then on progress started to speed up. The Bronze Age overlapped with the age of the Ancient Egyptians, a period that lasted an astonishing 3,000 years, which meant that for the first 1,000 years both mammoths and the pyramid-building Egyptians coexisted. The Great Pyramid of Giza, the last of the Seven Ancient Wonders of the World, was built between 2560–2540 BC, and was the tallest man-made structure in the world for over 3,800 years.[2]

The Bronze Age civilisation collapsed around 1100 BC, ushering in a period known as the Greek Dark Ages, a time where the skill of literacy was carelessly misplaced. The Greek Dark Ages did have their upside, for as well as losing the skill of writing, the old Mycenaean economic and social structures, strict class hierarchy and hereditary rule were also forgotten. The Dark Ages lasted until the 9th century BC, when the Greeks remembered how to write, but this time instead of using the Linear B script used by the Mycenaeans, they adopted and modified the Phoenician alphabet to create their own. Written records from this time indicate that a mercantile class arose in the first half of the 7th century, and coinage appeared around 680 BC. New sociopolitical institutions arose around the 5th century BC, and over in Athens the concept of a democracy was born. Then, in 146 BC,

---

[2] Progress was not limited to Eurasia, as over as in Ancient China, written records from as far back as the Shang Dynasty in 1500 BC have been found

the Greek city state of Corinth came under Roman rule, consolidating the Roman hegemony of Greece. Under the Romans, Europe was transformed. The Roman Empire spread across most of Europe, developing a common language (Latin – although not the first language of most of the empire's inhabitants), central and local government, military, economic trade and commodities, currency, banking, improvements in infrastructure, transportation, organised labour, occupations and trade guilds, great feats of architecture and engineering, sculpture and arts, etc. Which I guess answers the famous question, 'What have the Romans ever done for us?' There was also one key discovery: owning slaves enabled the elites to spend their time concerned not with hard, physical activities but with affairs of a more intellectual, philosophical and leisure-centric nature. However, to ensure the elites could relax and enjoy these privileges, methods of control and entertainment were needed to keep both slaves and plebeians in order, else they could rise up and overthrow them. Hence bread and circuses became the order of the day.

One would think that the Roman era would be when humanity really started to take off, but as we now know, it was not to be. A society based around slaves has no need to industrialise, and slave owners have no need to change the status quo. So they didn't. The Western Roman Empire, an area that spread from Northern Africa all the way to Britannia, finally collapsed in the 5th century AD, and as their provinces regressed the foundations established by the Romans fell into disrepair and ruin. As historian Ian Morris highlights, in the 1st century BC the Emperor Augustus[3] boasted that he had transformed Rome from a city of brick into one of marble. After the fall of the empire, Rome and all the other towns and cities across Europe then reverted to a world of wood.[7] This period became known as the Middle Ages, a period covering a thousand years from the 5th to 15th century AD which is more renowned for great plagues and famines than progress. It is often referred to as the Dark Ages, a period of intellectual 'darkness' between the extinguishing of the 'light of Rome' and the Italian Renaissance in the 14th century. Yet despite this moniker, certain great advances were made, one of which was the second economic shift – the introduction of double-entry bookkeeping and the ability of businesses to keep track of debits and credits.

---

[3]   When not banging his head against a wall and demanding that his now-decapitated friend Quinctilius Varus return his slaughtered legions and sacred eagles...

This period also saw the introduction of new ethnic groups into Europe and the rise of the modern religions: the expansion of Christianity, Buddhism, the rise of monasticism and the birth of Islam, all of which unified people behind common belief structures. Religion has both unified us and divided us – but it has also held us back. The ability to question mankind's place in the universe was deemed completely out of bounds because it challenged the established order of things. In 1633, Galileo Galilei was put on trial by the Catholic Church because he dared to question their geocentric belief that everything, including the sun and the heavens, revolved around the Earth. Despite being found guilty of being 'vehemently suspect of heresy' and forced to spend the rest of his days under house arrest, Galileo fared better than the Dominican monk Giordano Bruno (1548–1600), who was burned at the stake by the Roman Inquisition for the crime of heresy, including believing in heliocentricity. The Inquisitors could have looked through his telescope and seen the evidence for themselves, but they preferred to keep to their beliefs, much to the misfortune of Bruno and Galileo.

This closed world view started to change in the West when a series of paradigm shifts set off a chain reaction of knowledge acquisition. These events are referred to as 'ages' to reflect the enormity of what they represented:

- **The first age redefined our image and knowledge of the world.** The age of Exploration, a period between the 15th the 16th century that bridged the period between the Middle Ages and the modern era, a time when the New and Old Worlds were reconnected, when Europeans discovered and explored Africa, the Americas, Asia and Oceania. This period redefined the shape of the known world and created the expansion of European countries as they raced to explore and claim these new lands.
- **The second age redefined our image of society.** The age of Enlightenment, a period starting in the 17th century following the discoveries of new lands that had challenged the traditional view of the world, opposed superstition and intolerance. Its purpose was to reform society through reason and individualism, challenge ideas grounded in tradition and faith, and advance knowledge through the promotion of scientific thought and method, scepticism and intellectual interchange. Up until the Middle Ages the practices of

episteme (the philosophical investigation into the causes of things) and *techne* (the application of knowledge in order to do things, such as farming, crafts and industry) were separate and distinct. Science was philosophical in nature, concerned with establishing mankind's reason for being, our *telos*, and as such the domain of the elites, whereas *techne* was the tool of uneducated craftsmen. The second age brought these two areas together and created a willingness for science to interact with practical affairs as well as philosophical ones, helping to solve real-world problems of production. A new attitude towards science arose that placed pragmatism before idealism.

- **The third age redefined our image of the economy.** The results of the previous two ages created the perfect foundations for the most influential age of all — the age of Industry. The creation of new trade opportunities through the age of discovery and of a new type of society through the age of enlightenment led — specifically on one windswept island in the Atlantic Ocean — to the creation of a new model, one built on industry and economics. During this time *techne* and science combined to form 'technology', creating a series of cyclical technological revolutions, each building on the foundations of the previous. Revolutions that bent the curve of human progress upwards to such an extent that it makes a mockery of all of the chaos and conflict that went before.

Fire Up the Engines

To demonstrate the impact this revolution had on the rate of human progress, imagine we had the capability to travel back through time and select a lucky individual from Britain to transport one hundred years into the future.[4] Any chosen time travellers, from the start of recorded history right through to the 17th century, would have had only minor problems adapting to this leap forwards, as the ways of working, trading, cooking, communicating and travelling would still be relatively familiar. This includes disruptive periods such as during the 1st century AD when the Romans

---

[4] Same location, just one hundred years forward.

conquered Britain. However, from the beginning of the 18th century our time travellers would find adjusting to this new world increasingly difficult. A 19th-century time traveller would notice a significant transformation in every aspect of society. To comprehend the amount of change they would have to absorb, consider the following paragraph taken from the front page of the *Warren Mail*, printed on Tuesday 3rd February 1880:

What has been accomplished since the 19th century dawned is marvellous... Eighty years ago, Whitney's cotton-gin had hardly begun to work, and the spinning mule was not yet born. But these two have clothed the world. Eighty years ago, men were dreaming of the steamship, which Fulton invented in 1807. His thought has brought China nearer to us than England was when he built his first boat. Fraunhofer taught the young century spectrum analysis, and Fresnel the polarization of light, and all the arts and sciences now owe them a debt beyond measure. Eighty years ago, Jenner was stoutly battling against derision for the idea which, when the century was still young, subdued its first great scourge.[5] To-day there is scarcely a science or useful art that is not constantly indebted to photography, but when the century was born the photograph, which Arago rightly styled "a gift to the whole world" was unknown. Iron bands have almost annihilated distance, and a capital far exceeding the entire wealth of any nation in 1800 has been expended in making this the age of railways, but the century was already thirty years old when the first railroad was opened. The use of anthracite in making iron, and the Bessemer process for making steel have each revolutionized the world; modern civilization would be simply an impossibility if iron could still be treated only in the ways known when this century was young. The sewing machine has brought blessing and comfort to the mother of every household and has saved much to every wearer of clothes, and yet the oldest patent of that nature is not forty years old. Into the cottage of the humblest and poorest, the oil-well has sent light, but petroleum is one of the latest children of the century. And the grandest of them all, the telegraph, which enables London and New York to whisper to each other day and night, and brings news of the industry and commerce of the whole world to the breakfast table of

---

[5] Smallpox

every merchant or workman or employer, has been at work only thirty-six years. Of its thousand appliances and modifications, each a miracle, the signal service and the telephone are among the latest and most marvellous. But who can guess what the new year may bring forth? It is no longer true that "Science moves but slowly, creeping on from point to point." For centuries science crept; then it marched, then ran, and now it flies on the wings of the lightning.

Yet despite 19th-century technology flying on the wings of the lightning, our time traveller would still have been able to adapt to this future world, and after a few weeks, probably find gainful employment and survive. A 20th-century time traveller, on the other hand, would be completely and utterly lost. Consider someone living in London in 1918, at the end of the First World War, being transported to 2018. They would find themselves in an alien environment. They would recognise us as people, but not the society within which we live. Everything around them, including the sheer volume and variety of people, would be new and intimidating. The methods of transportation and communication devices we use, the food we eat, the work we do and the leisure activities we undertake would all be completely alien. One of their biggest challenges would be understanding what we said. They would recognise the language, but not the terms. They would, to all intents and purposes, be unemployable and after twenty-four hours probably unhinged by the experience.

The Great Transformation

The last century has seen dramatic changes to the very nature of Western society. Our time traveller would be amazed at the number of different races, sexual orientations and cultures that walk the streets; the mobility, lifestyle and freedoms people enjoy; the unbelievable amount of information people can access and the sheer number of things they can buy. The basics of modern living, such as central heating, electric lighting, fridges, freezers, vacuum cleaners, microwaves, dishwashers, televisions, radios, computers, games consoles and most recently, intelligent home hubs like the Amazon Echo, would all seem amazing. They would find that people now live longer, are healthier and have more disposable income than ever before.

They would also be amazed at how little time people spend on chores, and how much time they spend on leisure. In fact, the whole concept of an entertainment industry would be a new experience, as it didn't exist one hundred years ago. While 20th-century advancements in technology enabled us to affordably traverse the world and see places we were never able to before, 21st-century advancements have done the opposite and brought the world to the individual. The ability to access a wide variety of media, watch events occurring on a different continent as they happen, and listen to music recorded decades ago are all available to everyone regardless of social standing. No longer are people limited to single sources of news, nor just the local gossip – we now nearly all carry devices that bring the news, events and entertainment of the world to us whenever we want. To our time traveller, the concept of being able to access virtually the combined information of the world via a device that fits in your pocket; one that recognises your face, knows where you are, contains a map of the world so detailed that it can visually and verbally guide you from place to place, answers spoken questions, captures moving and still images, plays music and films and which allows you to instantly see and speak to anyone else who has a similar device, regardless of their location, would seem, as Arthur C. Clarke once declared, like magic. They are more likely to believe that you are a wizard who has control over a tribe of tiny Borrowers that live inside the rectangular device, rather than in some mythical creation called 'computer technology'. They would almost certainly be unable to grasp the concept of the Internet because they would have no point of reference or context with which to associate it. People's pre-occupation ensuring availability of something that you couldn't see, touch or smell would seem delusional. They would struggle to understand or accept your description of it because they simply couldn't visualise what you were describing. What could you use for reference? A computer? They'd have no idea. Television? In 1918, these were still nearly a decade away. Now imagine trying to explain Pokémon Go to them.

Our time traveller would also find a world where the success of humanity is visible through our numbers, our health and our wealth. The world population quadrupled from 1.9 billion in 1917 to 7.5 billion in 2017, while the level of poverty decreased – dramatically. In 1910, 83 per cent of the world's population was living in poverty (on an income of less than $2 per day) and 67 per cent was living in extreme poverty (income of less than $1 per day). This was not some isolated, so-called Third World phenomenon, but a worldwide one, affecting even those living in the birthplace of the industrial revolution. Studies by the Quaker, Seebohm Rowntree, in 1901 found that one third of the population of British cities such as York, now a prosperous and picturesque cathedral city bustling with cafés, restaurants and designer shops, *had total earnings [that] are insufficient to obtain the minimum necessities for the maintenance of merely physical efficiency.* Rowntree's description of 'merely physical efficiency' clearly defines how poor people really were: *A family living upon the scale allowed for in this estimate must never spend a penny on railway fare or omnibus. They must never go into the country unless they walk. They must never purchase a halfpenny newspaper or spend a penny to buy a ticket for a popular concert. They must write no letters to absent children, for they cannot afford to pay the postage. They must never contribute anything to their church or chapel, or give any help to a neighbour which costs money. They cannot save, nor can they join a sick club or Trade Union, because they cannot pay the necessary subscriptions. The children must have no pocket money for dolls, marbles or sweets. The father must smoke no tobacco, and must drink no beer. The mother must never buy any pretty clothes for herself or for her children, the character of the family wardrobe as for the family diet being governed by the regulation, nothing must be bought but that which is absolutely necessary for the maintenance of physical health, and what is bought must be of the plainest and most economical description. Should a child fall ill, it must be attended by the parish doctor; should it die, it must be buried by the parish. Finally, the wage-earner must never be absent from his work for a single day.*[8]

Winston Churchill was famously influenced by Rowntree's report, stating that reading it *made [his] hair stand on end* and that the revelations of the study regarding poverty were a *terrible and shocking thing*, expressing sympathy with *people who have only the workhouse or prison as avenues to change from their present situation.*[9] While poverty and homelessness still exist in York, as in all places, they are nothing like what Rowntree described just over a century ago. The creation of the welfare state in the United Kingdom has provided a safety net to ensure that no one lives in those awful conditions, and the last 100 years has seen York move from 28 per cent of the population not having the funds to post a letter, to none. This elevation out of poverty is a global not local phenomenon, as more of the world's population manages to rise above the bottom levels of Abraham Maslow's hierarchy of needs and do more than just survive. According to calculations by Max Roser, an Oxford University economist who runs a demographic site called Our World in Data,[6] every day sees 325,000 more people gain access to electricity, 300,000 gain access to clean drinking water, and the number living in extreme poverty dropping by 217,000. Despite an ever-rising population, in 2015 the number of people living in extreme poverty worldwide fell below 10 per cent for the first time ever, as shown in Graph 1.

Graph 1: Percentage of World Population Living in Extreme Poverty. [10]

The world has also experienced an explosion in education. In 1917, the world literacy rate was 23 per cent, as most poor and working-class people stayed within the confines of their village or town, and if you could read, information was limited to papers, a few books and public notices. Fast-forward one hundred years to 2017 and the literacy rate had leaped to 86.3 per cent.[11] Two thirds of the world's Internet users are now from developing countries, a sign of the power of market forces and how fast the world

---

[6] https://ourworldindata.org/

is becoming technologically advanced. The poor now have the means to instantly access almost the entirety of human knowledge, something that the wealthy of 1917 couldn't have even if they pooled all their collective wealth.

All the technologies that we now take for granted – from aluminium foil to antibiotics, and from refrigerators to radios – were science fiction a hundred years ago. Every new generation has more rights, more wealth, better health and a longer life expectancy, as well as vastly increased levels of education and entertainment, than the previous. I had a better childhood and significantly more opportunities than my parents, who were born at the end of the Second World War and both left school at fifteen. My parents, even though they were both brought up by working single mothers in rural England, experienced more freedom and opportunities than their parents. Likewise, my children have 24/7 access to information, entertainment and a whole host of amazing and rapidly advancing technology that my generation couldn't even imagine at that age. I grew up in a Britain where many people still only had black-and-white TVs that only broadcast three channels, all of which shut down before midnight every night with a rendition of *God Save the Queen*. You could only buy stuff when shops were open, and most closed at 5.30pm, 1pm on Wednesdays and all day Sundays. All knowledge was locked away in books and the twenty-volume *Encyclopaedia Britannica* was the equivalent of the Internet – if you could afford it. Telephones were hardwired and if you wanted one you had to wait six months until you were connected. Compared to the current 'on-demand, whatever you want to watch/read/listen to, whenever you want it, on whatever device you want it' world, it was pretty rubbish. Yet despite all of this technological advancement, we fail to remember how far we've come, protesting even the slightest disruption in its availability. For example, if the in-flight entertainment system stops working people are quick to moan, forgetting the sheer majesty of the fact that they are watching TV while seated in an armchair that is flying through the air in a metal tube.

As a litmus test of whether this technological revolution has been a good thing for mankind, one only needs to consider travelling back in time to live in any previous era. I would struggle to find many people in the West who would give up the lifestyle and technologies of today for those that existed previously. Life without the Internet, twenty-four-hour entertainment, mobile phones, cars, planes, air conditioning, microwaves, electricity and refrigerators sounds OK until you have to experience it. While many people romanticise over a paradise lost, harbouring nostalgic thoughts of a more honourable, respectful time and of landscapes that look like Constable paintings, they would almost certainly balk at having to live a life without antibiotics or any other worthwhile form of medicine or pain relief. A world without medicine, flushing toilets or computers is one of ignorance, illness and a short life expectancy. The past was also not such a great time to be female. Despite the obvious social issues around a lack of suffrage and limited influence on the running of things, issues such as childbirth were significantly more problematic, mostly due to a lack of pain relief, and caesarean sections were generally not elective, mainly due to their habit of killing the mother.[7] So while nostalgia is a wonderful thing, take off the rose-tinted glasses and the harsh reality of life in bygone ages quickly dawns and opinions rapidly change.

This time travel thought experiment demonstrates just how unprecedented this period of change has been. We have reshaped every aspect of our environment more in the last hundred years than we did in the previous 10,000 – and this is just the beginning. A time traveller from 2020 who is transported to 2120 is almost certainly not only going to be unable to recognise the environment in which people now live – they probably also won't recognise most of its inhabitants. But what caused human advancement to suddenly take off in Britain in the 18th and 19th centuries? Why did our progress suddenly go from linear to exponential? The answer is our ability to innovate. The last 250 years have not just witnessed the age of industry, but also the age of innovation – a new world where we continually seek new and improved ways to do things. A world where economics and the power of creative destruction rule. In 250 years we have moved from steam engines to search engines, from modes of transport powered by hay, to those powered by electricity. We're also just getting started. The futurist and inventor Ray Kurzweil suggests that progress is speeding up so much that the last twenty years have contained as much technological advancement as the previous hundred, and that the 21st century will contain a thousand times more progress than the 20th. If that's the case then if we were to travel to 2118, it would feel as alien to us as the present day would

---

[7] In Great Britain and Ireland, for example, the 1865 survival rate for women unfortunate enough to have to go through a caesarean was just 15 per cent. No one was talking of being 'too posh to push' in the 19th century.

to someone from before the industrial revolution. Future generations will probably balk at our ownership of motorcars that depreciate wildly and spend 85 per cent of their time lying idle in the same way as we look back at people who used to pay for horses and live-in servants.

Not Magic

Humans have one defining feature that distinguishes us from other biological forms – the ability to imagine and invent things that do not yet exist and use them to solve problems. Ever since our ancestors picked up bones, rocks and flint to pound, cut and kill, we have consistently sought to find new ways to improve our well-being and ensure our survival. Our innovative capability has proven to be the most powerful force that has been unleashed on this planet, taking us from hunter-gathers to spacemen. It has brought us everything from the first stone tools, the ability to harness fire, the knowledge to combine copper and tin to make bronze, all the way to the recent development of machines that can understand us and provide us with instant information. We have used our inventiveness to tame the wild, farm the land, build monuments to celebrate ourselves and our gods, and create civilisations. Regarding which is mightier, the mind or the muscle, history has shown that the mind wins every time.

The pre-Socratic Greek philosopher Democritus once declared, *no power and no treasure can outweigh the extension of our knowledge.* Democritus highlights an important concept and one which has consistently demonstrated the extraordinary ability of humans; our infinite ability to think of new solutions to problems and innovate ourselves out of trouble. The pursuit of progress has created a complete re-evaluation of man's place in the world; a transformation caused not by changes in external factors, but by one that we have created ourselves. Ancient society was far from free. People were bound by family and clan or tribal ties, by honour and pride, by ancestor worship and mythical gods. We had to understand that the supernatural is not in control, and that thunder was not caused by Thor's hammer nor floods by Poseidon, in order to believe that natural forces could be tamed, controlled, improved. As the comedian Tim Minchin once quipped, *Throughout history, every mystery ever solved has turned out to be... not magic.*

The evolution of civilisation and technology become intertwined, a conjoined story about our ability to constantly redefine the art of the possible. Our own inventiveness, not mysterious forces, have changed the world we live in. The main drivers behind this inventiveness have been the desires to understand the world around us, to make life easier, work more productive and activities more efficient – and to find new and innovative ways to kill each other. These intellectual drivers; war, wisdom and wealth – the crafts of exploration, economics and elimination – have created enormous expansions in our knowledge and technological capabilities:

- War is driven by our desire to protect what we have, stop something nasty from happening to our people, eliminate threats or take over neighbouring lands and resources.
- Wisdom is driven by the need to understand, and includes the fields of scientific and geographic research, the quest to know the unknown, to answer the questions, 'I wonder why this happens? What's over there? Is there a better way of doing this?'
- Wealth drives the economics of profit and production efficiency. It is driven by entrepreneurs asking, 'Can I make life easier? How can we do this better and cheaper? Can I use my time to make something people value?' and finally, 'Can I make money from this?'

For most of human history, it is the art of warfare that has driven innovation. While war naturally destroys both human lives and material goods, it also stimulates the introduction of technological innovations and political reforms. The threat of conflict creates urgent demand for technological advancement and has been a constant driver throughout history, especially in Europe, generating significant advancement in both armament and architecture. All major empires, from the Roman to the British, became that way due to their knowledge and ability to use superior firepower to overcome, subdue or replace a technically inferior one. The introduction of new machines of war such as cannons and guns brought together scientific practices such as chemistry, mechanics and engineering to develop bigger and better ways to suppress whatever opposition you are facing – or to intimidate them into not fighting in the first place. Despite their obvious negative outcomes, from a long-term perspective wars have been the catalysts of social progress, because the victors were usually societies that operated a more efficient model of organisation and better utilisation of material and human resources. The victor also tended to appropriate any new ideas from the vanquished, and the newly acquired territories provided a rich source of new materials and resources to be traded, and often a new market with which to colonise and develop.

The nature of warfare has changed dramatically due to advances in technology. The development of castles with moats, saw the development of trebuchets and siege engines to attack moated castles. From biplanes that dropped bricks, to flying fortresses that dropped bombs, then *the* bomb, all the way to the modern-day development of autonomous drones and missiles that fly and guide themselves, the history of warfare has predominantly been a catalogue of victories by the side with the most advanced technology.[8] Whenever a less sophisticated culture clashes with a more technologically advanced one, regardless of whether it is Neanderthals versus *Homo sapiens*, the hunter-gatherer societies facing European colonists, or the Japanese against the nuclear-armed Americans, it generally turns out badly for the less advanced side. Jared Diamond's bestselling book *Guns, Germs and Steel*[12] highlighted one of the greatest examples of the unfair advantages technology provides in war. Diamond details how the Spanish conquistador Francisco Pizarro and a small unit of only 169 soldiers defeated the Inca leader Atahualpa and his army of 80,000 warriors using a lethal combination of subterfuge, surprise and technological superiority. Atahualpa had seen the Spanish coming, but had decided that such a small number were no threat to him and his massive army, so he invited them to his camp, expecting to capture them easily. He had, however, not understood the power and fear that their steel blades, cannons and strategies could produce. The Spanish captured Atahualpa within a few minutes of the battle commencing, and then utterly defeated his men, killing thousands of them without losing a single soldier. Atahualpa's freedom was promised in exchange for enough gold to fill a room twenty-two feet long, seventeen feet wide and eight feet high. The Spanish received the bounty, but Pizarro executed Atahualpa anyway, just to make a point.

---

[8]　There are exceptions. Strategy and tactics have, on occasion, proven to overcome a technologically superior foe, such as Hannibal's victory over a superior Roman Army at the Battle of Cannae (50,000 troops versus the Romans' 86,000), where he executed a double-envelopment tactic that resulted in the destruction of the Roman forces, leaving only 10,000 Romans alive at the end of the battle.

Despite a constant drive to advance our military capabilities, wisdom and wealth have now become the primary drivers of innovation. Wisdom, especially in the sciences, tends to leap forward when pressure is applied, usually from war, wealth or both. The desire to excel at warfare can also create scientific breakthroughs which sometimes have commercial viability, creating wisdom *and* wealth. On their own, the sciences have traditionally not been a disruptive force, because they have, in some way, simply been about discovering what was already there, with most scientific discoveries resulting in uncovering and understanding the world around us better. This is important, for understanding how things work is the precursor to being able to control and ultimately improve them. What caused the rate of innovation to explode was the alignment between scientific discovery, industrial endeavour and financial reward. A series of technological revolutions have occurred since the men of invention, industry and investment joined forces, each one building on the knowledge and information generated from the previous, laying the foundations for the next. As our time traveller would have experienced, the inventions of the last two centuries have altered nearly every aspect of society. We have replaced muscle with machine, horses with automobiles, and pens and paper with computers. Seemingly innocuous inventions such as the shipping container have transformed the logistics industry and enabled an explosion in global trade. Our inventiveness has enabled the developed world to progress from purchasing the essentials of life – food, fuel and clothing – through to ever more desirable consumer products. Our ability to invent defines us as a species, for our ability to think beyond our immediate survival has allowed us to both appreciate and preserve the past while simultaneously striving to create a better future. We continue to make numerous discoveries that make previous certainties now seem absurd, causing us to reconsider how much we actually know about the world around us. Old ways of thinking, old formulas, dogmas and ideologies are tested, proven to be untrue and replaced by new ideas and concepts with increasing regularity. This mindset drives us forwards and challenges all our assumptions. Even ideas based on previously sound scientific basis are continually being shown to be false, from the inner workings of our bodies to the number of planets in the solar system. It is a mindset that has led us to a place where many believe we will soon be able to transcend our biological limitations, reverse the signs of ageing and even prevent death. We have progressed to this stage of dominance not through our physical abilities, but through our cerebral ones. Our future is intrinsically linked to that of science, technology and our confidence in our ability to think and innovate.

Turtles all the Way Down

It is important to note that despite sharing similar innovative capabilities, the different groups of human settlements and cultures across the world developed technologies at different rates and of varying degrees of complexity. There is a reason why great technological leaps occurred in some societies, but not in others. An environment had to exist that freed the individual from beliefs and social structures that had previously held them back for centuries. To create an explosion in innovation the size of the first industrial revolution, social foundations needed to exist that would allow ideas to be shared, innovations to be developed, and the outputs to be kept.

So how did the West end up developing such foundations? Western Europe had, for much of its history, lagged far behind the more culturally advanced and equally literate civilisations of India, China and the Mediterranean. If anyone was likely to develop a revolution in industry, people would have placed money on it being one of these cultures. So what enabled Britain to make this technological leap while others could or would not? What were the crucial differences? The answer lies with its political, religious and legal foundations, and in the world view that arose because of them. Throughout history, from hunter-gatherer cultures to the nations of the East, the dominant world view was that a person's role was primarily as a member of a group, where their extrinsic qualities and their value to the tribe were what mattered. They accepted their position within the natural order of things, seeing their relationship with the world around them as being passive; mere pawns in a game over which they had little control. As Joseph Campbell wrote in *Changing Images of Man: According to this image nothing is to be gained, either for the universe or for man, through individual originality and effort. The individual, rather, is to play the role into which he has been born – as do the sun and the moon, the various plant and animal species, the waters, rocks and stars.*[13] Historically, when we believe something to be outside of our control we do not seek to understand it nor improve it, and instead relinquish power to something otherworldly. While the accepted view is that everything is exactly as it should (and will always) be, then any incentive to understand, control or change things is somewhat dampened. Theories of history were supernatural in nature, for the divine ruled time. You didn't dream too big nor sail too far, lest you disappeared off the turtle's back. If the present was different from what went before it was usually considered worse, and the reason for this was that it was a supernatural response to the ever-growing sins of mankind. The promise of an afterlife, be it in Mount Olympus, Valhalla or Heaven, was there to provide both guidance and hope to the impoverished masses. Guidance as to what behaviours were valued, and hope that by following them you would be rewarded by being granted permission to enter a better place. That the sufferings you endured or braveries you displayed would be rewarded after you died, providing meaning to a life often described as *solitary, poor, nasty, brutish, and short*.[9] Hope is a very human emotion, not one shared by other species. The other emotion that was continuously exploited was much more animalistic – fear. Fear of judgement and retribution in this life or the next was used to keep people in check; 'Don't do this or else you will upset the god(s) and they will damn you and your family for eternity.' Hope and fear; two very powerful emotions. Emotions that were used to bind cultures together, but which also held them back. As a result, our technological progress was painstakingly slow and almost invisible.

Things changed rapidly when we learnt three fundamental lessons. Firstly, while we still appreciate that we cannot control what we do not understand, nor improve that which we cannot control, we have now realised that understanding is a possibility, resulting in a desire to understand, control and ultimately improve as much of the world around us as possible. Secondly, we have progressively understood how ignorant we really are and how little we actually know about ourselves and the universe within which our spinning home resides. Since Nicolaus Copernicus first came up with his heliocentric theory around five hundred years ago and identified that we are in fact not the centre of the universe, it's been one long story of continued relegation. But while our opinion of our planet's importance decreased, our perception of our position in it has increased. In the West people came

---

[9] Originally defined by the 17th-century philosopher Thomas Hobbes in 'Leviathan' to describe life during the English Civil War. Hobbes' life ironically wasn't brutish or short, as he lived to ninety-one.

to realise that they were not pawns in some supernatural game plan but the individual masters of their own destiny, their own reality and their own happiness. These lessons are all relatively new, but it was the last that truly freed us and set us on the path forwards. The understanding that we are not bound by forces outside our control, and that our worth is based on our individual actions not our group identity, led to the development of a societal model structured around rights designed to protect individuals, not control them, and of belonging to the land, not those in power. Which, as we will explore, proved to be a fundamental element in the exponential progress of the last 250 years.

The Greeks were probably the first culture to develop the concept of the individual as more than simply a member of the community, tribe or race, but rather a separate entity. They encouraged the development of a self-improvement mindset based around acting from a secular sense of duty, not necessarily towards others but rather inwards, of working on the pursuit of what the Greeks called *arete*, or excellence.[14] During the time of Socrates, Plato and Aristotle, when the concept of the city state emerged, laws and ethical rules were sought beyond individualism for the regulation of conduct, but it was not to the gods that the Greeks looked but to nature, specifically human nature.[10] This meant that by the 2nd century BC, although the Greeks had developed the necessary knowledge to establish a commanding science-based technology, it did not materialise. While the Greeks recognised the individual, their world view was limited by the fact that they viewed the acquisition of knowledge as being reserved for the aesthetic or spiritual enjoyment of the citizens, and not to make routine labour more efficient. That was, after all, what they had slaves for. While advanced in comparison to other civilisations, the Greeks and Romans still didn't manage to affect things that would have made the most difference to their people, such as the prevention of diseases, any extension of lifespan or an increase in the ability to feed the population. Their mindset around resources remained subtractive rather than additive in nature. Supply was finite, and any expansion and growth arose because of removing land, people and possessions from other nations or tribes, rather than through increasing the overall output, wealth, wisdom and well-being of your

---

[10] Though the Greeks, like many slave-based economies, only held these views for the citizens, and not for the slaves.

people. These were also exclusive rather than inclusive cultures. If you were not one of the elite, you were pretty much no one – and if you were no one, then your ability to influence the world around you was severely limited, and your life's mission was survival. Outside of the weapons of war, any technological progress was mostly restricted to small, incremental pieces of wisdom passed down from father to son, and from mother to daughter.

Taking Control

It was the only with the arrival of the Semitic and Christian belief systems in the West that we really began to appreciate the possibility that we were capable of being more than passive planetary guests. Joel Mokyr, Professor of Economics and History at Northwestern University, explains why: *What happened in Europe, in particular in Western Europe, is that slowly but certainly people came to the realisation that in fact the manipulation of the physical world is nothing to feel guilty about. In fact, if you manipulate nature you are only illustrating the glory of the Creator. If the Creator in his infinite wisdom has created something and put us in the middle of it and put it at our disposal, this is a deep Judaeo-Christian presumption reflected in the Book of Genesis. And people I think truly believed it. I think our technological success is in large part due to the fact that we believe that this entire physical environment is ours. We can do with it whatever we want and we can manipulate it for our own benefit.*

This unique perspective of man being superior to nature has exerted an incredible influence on the Western world view and was almost certainly a precursor to our revolutions in agriculture, industry and science. This perspective enabled people to progress from using human slaves, through to domesticating and enslaving other species of animals, and finally to manipulating and controlling the natural forces of wind and water power, all to make their lives easier. They sought to control and exploit nature to seek new ways to increase efficiency and reduce human effort because they thought by doing so they were demonstrating God's will that man should have dominion over the rest of his creations. This mindset is a significant contrast to the world view of other, more spiritual lands, where the natural systems such as the falling of water and the blowing of the wind would be simply viewed as representative of the power and beauty of divine forces. In

Europe, these forces were viewed very differently, as something that could be controlled and manipulated. Once a society begins to think of nature as just another engineering system and identifies natural forces as potential sources of power, productivity and profit, it becomes self-evident that they will then try to control and manipulate them. Declares Mokyr, *The essence of sustained technological progress is the disruption of harmony with nature. We want to keep disrupting it; that is the Western way of doing things.*[15]

There is another unique difference in European cultures. Judaeo-Christian belief systems contain a sense of linear time, of things following one another, whereas other societies thought of time as cyclical, returning to earlier stages and starting over again. This understanding of time had an instrumental effect on their concepts of work, progress and 'the future'. In comparison to the Western mindset, the native Indians of North America, the tribesmen of sub-Saharan Africa and the Aborigines in Australia, three hunter-gatherer civilisations that were continents apart, all developed societies based on tradition, the spoken word and harmony with nature. Without outside intervention, they would probably still be in that state of evolutionary stasis. Some civilisations were even less advanced. Tasmania, an island off the southern coast of Australia, holds the record for the longest isolation period in human history. Humans are thought to have originally crossed into Tasmania approximately 40,000 years ago during the last glacial period, via a land bridge that linked the island to mainland Australia. However, once the sea levels rose and flooded the area known as the Bassian Plain, the bridge was lost, and the Tasmanian people were isolated on the island until Europeans arrived in 1803. During all this time, the small Tasmanian population developed almost no technological advances. They lacked knowledge of how to develop tools of metal or bone, clothing, barbed spears, boomerangs, hooks, sewing and the ability to start a fire. Without these tools, they could not fell large trees, hollow out canoes, carve bowls or sew clothes. The Aboriginal Tasmanians, alongside another group of islanders called the Andamanese, were quite simply the simplest race of people on Earth.[11]

These tribal societies may have been happy places to live, free from the modern curses of consumerism, jealousy and greed, but they were also

---

[11] The Andamanese people occupy the Andaman Islands in the Bay of Bengal. They also did not know how to make fire until contact with outsiders in the 19th century.

materially poor places to live; constantly exposed to the whims of Mother Nature. In a harsh winter some would starve and the old and weak would perish, whereas in a good summer the tribe would prosper. In contrast, people in the West managed to find a way to break free of their subservience to nature. They developed the ability to affect the environment to suit their needs, rather than simply learning how to adapt to changing environments deemed outside of their control. Mokyr highlights this difference well: *If you are going to live in harmony with nature you may be happy, but you are going to be poor. If you are going to be like the West then you are continually disrupting nature, you are continuously causing ecological imbalances, and that is a high price to pay. But it is a price that until now we have been willing to pay and we are still paying.*[16]

2

FROM PRODUCERS
TO CONSUMERS:
THE WEST TAKES OFF

Nations rise and fall, flourish and decay,
by what they believe in and by what their culture stands for.

Ifeanyi Enoch Onuoha

In his seminal book *The Third Wave*, Alvin Toffler details three cultural paradigms that he believes have dominated human habitation on Earth: the agricultural revolution, the industrial revolution and now the information revolution. The progression from hunter-gatherers to farmers represents the first wave of civilisation, for wherever agriculture arose, a form of civilisation was established. Across the connected land masses of Europe and Asia people became part of an agrarian society, but there were still communities, especially on the isolated land masses such as North America and Australasia, where a hunter-gatherer lifestyle remained. According to some historians, this transition from hunter-gatherer to farmer didn't bring universal benefits. Israeli professor Yuval Noah Harari believes that the agricultural revolution created a *Faustian bargain between humans and grains,*[17] the results of which were an inferior diet, increased hours of work, greater risk of starvation, congested living conditions, increased susceptibility to disease (mostly through exposure to domestic animals), new forms of insecurity and a hierarchical system that served the needs of the few over the many. Declares Harari, *The Agricultural Revolution was history's biggest fraud... a handful of plant species, including wheat, rice and potatoes... domesticated Homo sapiens, rather than vice versa.*[18] And for the longest time, he was right.

Life for most of the population was harsh, spent languishing in the lowest sections of Maslow's hierarchy of needs. People didn't worry about psychological problems such as cognitive dissonance because they expected little and were rarely disappointed. Your personal emotional needs were irrelevant; feeding yourself and your family was your primary concern and not having your goods taken off you was your secondary. Religion flourished because it provided purpose and meaning to a population whose life was filled with hardships. The conventional wisdom was that there was a finite amount of everything. To expand your resources, you needed more environment. If you didn't have enough, then you either took from someone else or you went without. Significant amounts of time were consequently spent on developing weapons to defend what little we had or in trying to increase it through acquiring the lands, goods and resources of others, explaining why this has also been the driving force behind many wars and conquests. More land equates to more resources, more resources support more people, more people enable the building of bigger armies, and bigger armies can both protect resources more effectively and help to acquire new ones.

Since food production was only slightly over the level required for biological survival, even small and temporary environmental fluctuations could have a devastating effect on the supply of food and water, with disastrous consequences for the population. This effect was popularised by Thomas Malthus in his 1798 work, *An Essay on the Principle of Population*, in which he wrote, *The power of population is so superior to the power of the earth to produce subsistence for man that premature death must in some shape or other visit the human race. The vices of mankind are active and able ministers of depopulation. They are the precursors in the great army of destruction, and often finish the dreadful work themselves. But should they fail in this war of extermination, sickly seasons, epidemics, pestilence, and plague advance in terrific array, and sweep off their thousands and tens of thousands. Should success be still incomplete, gigantic inevitable famine stalks in the rear, and with one mighty blow levels the population with the food of the world.*[19] Malthus claimed that as the world's food supply grows arithmetically (1, 2, 3, 4, 5...), the population grows geometrically (1, 2, 4, 8, 16...), quickly outstripping the agricultural output of the land needed to provide for it, resulting in starvation. This concept has become known as the Malthusian Catastrophe. In pre-modern Europe (i.e. before 1600) this would seem to be an inevitable conclusion, and Malthus himself stated that it was almost an unavoidable result of population growth. *The great law of necessity which prevents population from increasing in any country beyond the food which it can either produce or acquire, is a law so open to our view... that we cannot for a moment doubt it.*[20]

While this Malthusian Catastrophe was proven to be true elsewhere in the world, keeping population numbers low due to food scarcity, in the 18th century, Western Europe managed to overcome this restriction. What we now know, but Malthus didn't, is the extent to which advancements in science and technology would change the very nature of agriculture and food production. Our ability to create new means of production that could supplement muscle with machine and replace scarcity with surplus, enabled us to circumvent the Malthusian factors that had previously kept population and life expectancy in check. Innovation, driven by the desire of entrepreneurs for economic profit, created new industries and improved crop production. The increase in crop production and methods of harvesting released the populations from their traditional ties to the land, freeing them from the constraints of a Malthusian tragedy so they could collectively work towards launching the most influential period of mankind's short time on this planet.

In the mid to late 18th century two revolutions took place separated by just thirty miles of water. On one side a very bloody revolution changed the course of a nation; on the other, a much less violent one changed the course of the world. Starting in the north-west region of a windswept island in the North Atlantic, the industrial revolution kick-started a series of events that has allowed mankind to substantially grow its wealth, health and numbers. The social, technological and economic foundations for this transformation had been laid in the agricultural, scientific and glorious revolutions that went before. The agricultural revolution was possible because of the sense of enquiry arising from the scientific revolution. As Joel Mokyr argues, *it was the emergence of a belief in the usefulness of progress, and a turning point when intellectuals started to conceive of knowledge as cumulative.*[21] In the early 17th century, Sir Francis Bacon helped to transform the very mechanism for the acquisition of knowledge; knowledge that would be used to develop tools that allowed people to recreate or control the forces of nature. Prior to Bacon, scientific enquiry was linked as much to philosophy as to any other source; an ancient yearning to take hold of the mysteries of nature, to control them according to will. The philosophical investigation into the causes of things, and the application of this knowledge to achieve things – the drive to understand and the drive to control – were deemed separate areas of enquiry. Bacon's method relied on recording the results of experiments to eliminate alternative theories. In 1605, he wrote that, *If a man will begin with certainties, he shall end in doubts; but if he will be content to begin with doubts, he shall end in certainties.*[22] Bacon's notion was truly revolutionary at that time and led the way for men such as Descartes and Galileo Galilei to expand on his approach. It was Galileo's publication of *Two New Sciences* in 1638 that finally ushered in the age of empirical science, a time known as the scientific revolution, which opened up a world of investigation and opportunity. Rather than limiting thought by adhering to beliefs that we simply accepted to be true, the world was now viewed as a mystery to be solved, a black box with unknown contents, contents that man had uncovered through logic, not superstition.

Before the scientific method mankind had no discernible method upon which to develop our understanding. It wasn't through lack of trying. Records of ancient attempts at empirical research have been uncovered that date as far back as the early Egyptians. The Edwin Smith Papyrus, an Egyptian medical textbook, demonstrates that the concepts of examination, diagnosis, treatment, prognosis and disease remedies existed as far back as 1600 BC. In the 11th century the Islamic Arab Alhazen conducted research in optics, mathematics, physics and medicine, and in doing so demonstrated a systemic and methodological reliance on experimentation and controlled testing in his scientific enquiries. However, it was the development of the scientific method that transformed our understanding of the world around us, by providing a basis against which we could test the validity of ideas and hypotheses. The knowledge that flowed out of this new empirical approach proved to be a major advantage to the new inventors, helping them to take a more rigorous and experiential approach to their craft. As Bacon famously declared, *Knowledge is power*,[12] and he believed that scientific knowledge would hold power over nature.

It was only during the 18th century that the practices of science and technology came together, fuelled by the intellectual and philosophical movement known as the age of enlightenment. People came to realise that more things were within their capability to control than they had previously realised. Things that were deemed unmanageable in previous generations, such as the quality of the harvest, suddenly became something that could be influenced, addressed through an understanding of the sciences and application of this knowledge in agriculture. Awareness of nitrates, crop rotation and livestock management created improved crop yields, a greater diversity of wheat and vegetables, and the ability to support more livestock. This rise in agricultural productivity enabled the British population to break their bonds to the land, creating a new urban workforce. The industrial revolutions from 1760 caused a large-scale switch from the agricultural world – where everything was made by human or animal muscle – to the mechanised world, where gasoline, steam engines and electricity created new machines that used artificial power. Toffler states that the industrial age – what he called 'The Second Wave' created: *a situation in which the overwhelming bulk of all food, goods, and services was destined for sale, barter, or exchange. It virtually wiped out of existence goods produced for one's own consumption... and created a civilization in which almost no one, not even a farmer, was self-sufficient any longer. Everyone became almost totally dependent upon food, goods, or services produced by somebody else.*[23]

The industrial revolution was a tipping point. We learnt how to manipulate Mother Nature, her resources and her power to create everything from mechanisms to medicines; developed ways to power the factory and the home; built new industries and new economies; and freed humans from significant limitations and ailments of the previous eras. This new level of intellectual capability has allowed us to overcome Malthusian

---

[12] Personally, I have always had issue with this statement, for knowledge isn't power unless it is applied. If I am knowledgeable of next week's winning lottery numbers, it doesn't make me a millionaire unless I use this knowledge by purchasing a ticket before the deadline for doing so and claim my winnings before the ticket's validity period expires. Knowing the numbers does nothing for me unless I do something with that knowledge.

constraints and sustain a population far greater than was thought possible. It has allowed us to grow exponentially.

From Deceptive, to Disruptive

To explain what is meant by exponential growth, the story of the origins of chess is often used. Around 1260 AD, Ibn Khallikan, a Kurdish historian living in the Abbasid Empire,[13] wrote an encyclopaedia that contained a story about an ancient Indian mathematician called Sissa ben Dahir, who invented the game of chess. Sissa allegedly presented the game as a gift to his king, Shirham, who was so pleased that he ordered that it should be declared a glory, preserved in the temples, and used to train generals in the art of war. In gratitude, the king asked Sissa to name his prize. Sissa replied that he didn't want any reward, but the king insisted. Finally, Sissa said that he would accept the following: one grain of wheat on the first square of the chessboard, two grains on the second square, four grains on the third square, and so forth, doubling the amount each time. The king was surprised and slightly offended at how little was asked for, but accepted Sissa's request, ordering his treasurer to count out and hand over the wheat to the inventor. When the treasurer hadn't returned after a week, King Shirham demanded to know why. The treasurer then explained that despite their initial confidence at how little wheat they would have to collect, they soon found that as each new square contained more wheat than all the previous squares combined, Sissa's reward required more wheat than existed in the entire kingdom, some 18,446,744,073,709,551,615 grains of wheat (18 quintillion, 446 quadrillion, 744 trillion, 73 billion, 709 million, 551 thousand and 61), which, if put in a pile, would stand higher than Mount Everest.[14]

The chessboard story describes the *deceptive* and *disruptive* nature of exponential change. During the early phases, when one grain became two, two became four, and four became eight, the doubling seemed trite and

---

[13] Now known as Iraq.

[14] There are two versions of what happened next. In the first, King Shirham was so impressed by Sissa for both his invention and the ingenuity of his reward that he made him Grand Vizier. The second version has the king having Sissa executed for making him look a fool.

insignificant. Even by the tenth square, where 512 grains were claimed, the treasurer would still not fully understand what was to come. By the time the twentieth square is reached, these deceptively small increments have become significant, reaching over half a million grains. By twenty-five squares, we are up to nearly 17 million. But it's the second half of the board where the numbers go fuzzy, and unfeasibly large numbers get added to other unfeasibly large numbers to create a *really* unfeasibly large number. That's when the deceptive nature falls away and the disruption becomes evident to all.

To see what deceptive and disruptive exponential growth looks like, you only need to examine the change in human population since the industrial revolution. By any measure of success – how many people existed, how long they lived, how healthy they were, how wealthy they were – nothing really changed across the vast period since behavioural modern humans arrived. The human population had grown at a slow, linear rate since around 10,000 BC, reaching around 500 million in 1500. From the 18th century population suddenly started to rise, reaching 1 billion in the early 1800s. We entered the 20th century with 1.6 billion of us and despite two world wars that decimated the stock of young men, we left the century with those numbers reversed at 6.1 billion, reaching 7 billion in 2011 and at the time of writing the population is 7.5 billion and rising.

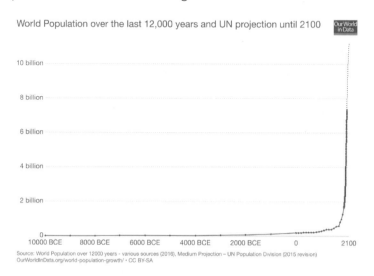

Graph 2: Historical World Population.[24]

What caused this sudden rise? Two factors. The most impactful has been the dramatic reduction in childhood mortality, meaning more of us make it to adulthood. In 1800, 43 per cent of children died before their fifth birthday. In 1960, child mortality had dropped significantly but was still 18.5 per cent, meaning that almost one out of every five children died in childhood. But the last fifty years has seen child mortality plummet, dropping to just 4.3 per cent in 2015. Secondly, an increase in longevity that means that when we make it out of childhood, we tend to stay around for longer. Since 2000, there has been a 43 per cent increase in the number of US citizens living to see their one hundredth birthday,[25] and in the UK the number of centenarians has quadrupled in the past thirty years. The Japanese currently have the highest life expectancy at 86.61 years for women and 80.21 years for men, and the last records in 2014 identified that Japan had 58,820 centenarians.[26] While life expectancy in the West has increased substantially since 1950, it has risen roughly twice as fast in the emerging nations. In 1950, the life-expectancy gap between developed and still-developing countries was twenty-five years. It is now down to thirteen years, and that gap will shrink even further as more countries embrace market economics.

Had Malthus been correct we should now be burying people by the tens of millions due to the land's inability to produce enough food to feed them. Yet the opposite has happened: for industrialisation has not just allowed mankind to survive, but to thrive. It has enabled our numbers to progress into the second half of the chessboard, and in doing so created an exponential growth in not just our population, but also our productivity and wealth. In pre-capitalist societies, producers had direct access to the means of production – the arable land – but only had to concentrate on providing goods for themselves and their families. Survival was the driving force, not providing goods for others, and as a result productivity was stagnant throughout this time.

Up until 1000 AD, economic growth per capita (as well as population growth) was non-existent. In fact, growth remained constant right up to the 19th century, taking 3,000–4,000 years for a doubling in economic well-being per capita to occur. For centuries prior to the industrial revolution, Gross Domestic Product (GDP) growth in the UK averaged around 0.01 per cent per year, meaning that each generation was only around 0.3 per cent better off than their parents; a barely noticeable improvement. Then, suddenly, it exploded. Since the industrial revolution, GDP per capita has risen consistently

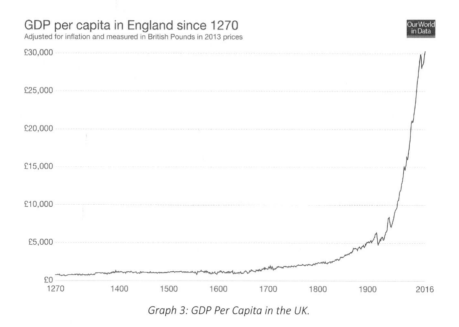

Graph 3: GDP Per Capita in the UK.

at an annual average rate of 1.2 per cent per year. In parallel, UK Total Factor Productivity (TFP) has consistently averaged 0.8 per cent per year since 1750, meaning that since the industrial revolution, GDP per capita has doubled approximately every sixty-five years and productivity roughly every eighty-five years. This exponential rise in GDP per capita in the UK is shown in Graph 2.

The implications for living standards have been profound. Each generation since the industrial revolution has been around 25 per cent better off than their parents. This is a story of improvements in living standards and innovation going hand in hand. UK living standards, as measured by GDP per head, have risen roughly twentyfold since 1850, a huge gain. How much of that gain can be attributed to higher productivity? If productivity had been flat over the period, then UK living standards would have only doubled and we would be experiencing life circa the late-Victorian period. In 1930, the economist John Maynard Keynes wrote in his article: *Economic Possibilities for our Grandchildren* that, *In spite of an enormous growth in the population of the world, which it has been necessary to equip with houses and machines, the average standard of life in Europe and the United States has been raised [by capitalism], I think, about fourfold. The growth of capital has been on a scale which is far beyond a hundredfold of what any previous age had known.* Keynes was highlighting the fact that the period from 1870 to 1890 had been witness to the greatest increase in economic growth ever recorded. This growth brought with it a corresponding improvement in living standards for these newly industrialised countries, bolstered by the falling prices of goods due to the increases in productivity from automation. Yet this period was nothing compared to what was to come. The hundred years from 1901 to 2002–3 saw citizens of the United States experience a sixfold increase in real income, while at the same time the share of income that had to be spent on necessities dropped from 85 per cent to 55 per cent.[27] These gains relied on a revolution of industry, economy and technology. They could only have come about in a society that permitted it.

The Bottleneck is Always at the Top

The success of a nation is not determined by its location, its geology or its soil. It is determined by the rules under which its citizens are kept, and how they relate one to another. In their 2013 bestseller *Why Nations Fail,* Daron Acemoglu and James Robinson detail the impact the political establishment has on a nation's ability to progress. The authors theorise that political institutions can be divided into two kinds – *extractive* institutions, where a minority focus their efforts on developing a system that exploits the rest of the population; and *inclusive* institutions, where the majority are included in the process of governing, hence ensuring that the exploitation of the population is either attenuated or absent. Whereas an inclusive society strives to both recognise and care for all its citizens, an extractive society is designed to support a kleptocratic agenda of keeping a minority in power and the majority in line. This requires conscious choice on the part of the nation's leaders, even in the most basic extractive societies, for a decision must be made as to who to include and who to exclude. Once that decision has been made, the organisational structure needed to enforce this exclusion needs to be defined. Extractive societies expend time and effort on preventing the entirety of their populations from progressing, rather than enabling them to do so. Focus is on control, not creativity; on constraint, not contribution. This mindset is summed up nicely by the German publicist and statesman Friedrich von Gentz (1764–1832): *We do not desire at all that the great masses shall become well off and independent... How could we otherwise rule over them?*

This is why the constant attempts to export Western democracy usually fail

– the civic and political infrastructures needed to support the development of a free society are just not there, and probably never have been. It is incredibly difficult for a non-democratic society to be economically successful in the long term, since prosperity is generated by entrepreneurs, investors and innovators evaluating risks, and these entrepreneurs must have a credible reason to think that their efforts will not simply be plundered by those in power. Conversely, the less power the government has over its people, the wealthier, more equal and freer their people will be. Extractive societies are usually those where the national wealth comes from the resources of the land, and not the industrial efforts and taxes of the people. This means that a small group of elites can easily control and siphon off the wealth of the nation, requiring no need to provide democratic rights or freedoms for the population.

To demonstrate the difference in results that can be achieved in an inclusive political system and society versus an extractive one, consider Zimbabwe and Botswana, two neighbouring countries that both achieved independence from the United Kingdom within a year of each other. Zimbabwe transformed into a top-down, extractive country under the rule of President Robert Mugabe and his ZANU-PF Party, while Botswana has developed a more bottom-up, inclusive society with a representative, democratic political system whose people are protected by the rule of law. At the point of independence, Botswana was one of the poorest countries in the world, with a GDP per capita of about US$70 per year, whereas the newly independent Rhodesia (as Zimbabwe was known until 1980), was sub-Saharan Africa's agricultural and economic powerhouse, often referred to as the breadbasket of the continent. In 1980, President Julius Nyerere of Tanzania reportedly said to Prime Minister Robert Mugabe that *You have inherited the jewel of Africa, please take care not to spoil it.*[28] But spoil it he did. While Botswana has transformed itself into one of the fastest-growing economies in the world, Mugabe's Zimbabwe experienced widespread political corruption, an economic collapse, hyperinflation (in November 2008 the inflation rate was 79,600,000,000 per cent and the Zimbabwean bank was issuing one hundred trillion-dollar notes), the ethnic cleansing and murder of white farmers, and mass starvation. Despite Zimbabwe having a labour force five times the size of Botswana's, the GDP of both countries is now almost the same. However, the real impact becomes apparent when you compare the unemployment rate, poverty figures and GDP per capita of the two styles of leadership. In Zimbabwe, approximately 94 per cent of the population is unemployed, 80 per cent lives below the poverty line and the GDP per capita is a measly $600. Across the border in Botswana, unemployment is 17.7 per cent, 20 per cent lives below the poverty line and the GDP per capita is $17,042 – twenty-eight times more than Zimbabwe's. There is almost zero incentive for any foreign business to invest in Zimbabwe, and a similar amount of incentive for locals to invest their time and money on entrepreneurial ventures. As the white farmers found, in the minds of Mugabe and his followers, what's yours is theirs and what's theirs is theirs. The statements and banners of these political systems always claim victim status and involve declarations of being 'for the masses, not the minority', but the net result always seems to be the same. A tiny minority at the top benefit greatly, but the majority do not. It's not just that people are poor – it's that the system in place prevents them from proactively changing that situation by their own efforts and endeavours. So people don't try. They also don't protest, for people who disagree with the methods or approach used to sustain this system usually find themselves disavowed or worse, disappeared.

The novelist F. Scott Fitzgerald once declared, *The test of a first-rate intelligence is the ability to hold two opposed ideas in the mind at the same time, and still retain the ability to function.* Extractive, totalitarian societies don't want you to hold two opposed ideas in your mind at one time. They want you to have only one idea; their idea. They want to control the psyche of the population. This is behind the blocking of social media sites such as Twitter, Facebook and YouTube[15] in extractive, unfree countries. They don't want the population to move around, meet other people – either physically or virtually – and share ideas. When people share and debate ideas, there is a very real danger that their minds will be opened, their knowledge enhanced, and their beliefs changed. To the leaders in extractive societies this is an incredibly dangerous threat to the security of the world view they perpetrate, and the exclusivity of the society they have developed. To quote Joseph Stalin, *ideas are more powerful than guns. We don't let our people have guns. Why should we let them have ideas?* The leadership of extractive societies spend an enormous amount of effort on controlling the information people can access, enabling them to indoctrinate the population into accepting their propaganda. Information then goes from being an appreciating asset to a

---

[15] Worryingly, it is also driving those companies to behave in totalitarian ways, demonetising and blocking creators whose opinions and viewpoints they don't share or who challenge their ideological belief system. More on this in Part Three.

depreciating one, because it is usually out of date, biased to the agendas of the elite, and used to keep people misinformed.

The leaders of extractive states hold a very different view of what social structure needs to exist, and how much power the individual can hold. As a result, our ability to innovate, one of our few infinite resources, is suppressed and not utilised to anything like its full potential. This in turn changes the economic model that exists in these countries, which in turn affects the level of innovation. Scientific and technological developments are almost exclusively limited to those elements that support the state, such as the armed forces and protection of the borders, rather than for personal or business benefit. Secondly, if innovation is allowed, people are usually poor and lack the capital to operationalise their inventiveness, or the market to sell the outputs to. Finally, because the outcome of any innovation is likely to be claimed by the elite, the population decides that there is little point. Why invent a new way of doing something simply to have it – or its output – taken by someone else? The net result is that our most common and infinite resource, the ability to innovate, becomes sparse and finite.

In contrast, inclusive, democratic societies view the status quo as the enemy, for it denotes stagnation, regression and decay. Innovation and progress, specifically those that uncover new ways to drive economic efficiencies or new market opportunities, become the focus of society and its economic, technological and scientific practices, and you, as an individual, are perfectly entitled to indulge in these practices and profit from the resultant goods and services you produce. These societies provide the ability to trade freely, as well as legal support around the rights of the entrepreneur to protect their intellectual and physical property. This ensures that entrepreneurs deem it worthwhile to invest time and money on developing new innovations and new ventures. Inclusive societies support the free flow of information, freedom of movement and open lines of communication, and promote the welfare and education of their citizens. Once the acquisition of knowledge is both allowed and encouraged, an inclusive and innovative society then needs to set up the incentives to reward those who take the risk to acquire and apply this knowledge. The development of a market-based economic system that rewards the producers of new ideas, thus encouraging more ideas to be created, is a cornerstone of an innovative society. One that allows for entrepreneurial activities and promotes the investment of time, effort and capital for future social and monetary reward. The unknown merely becomes a challenge to be solved, and if there's a buck to be made in solving it, then a race develops to solve it first.

Inclusive societies take this infinite resource (our ability to innovate) and encourage its use through the development of a market-based economy and invention patent laws. The combination of these two elements creates a multiplying environment whereby the forces of invention, industry and investment come together to create products and services that are both protected from being immediately re-engineered and copied, giving the creators protection from wasting their efforts, and able to be sold for a profit, providing them with a potential return on their investment. The freedom to communicate allows inclusive societies to spread their ideas, and this diffusion of ideas amplifies its effect through encouraging others to build on this innovation, once the demand for it is proven. Inclusive societies also need to ensure that there is internal and external market competition and strive to prevent monopolistic situations from arising that may create an uneven playing field. Monopolies are another form of extractive institution, one that kills the innovation golden goose through self-interest.

The Western economic model of free market forces has unlocked the innovative capabilities of people worldwide, freeing them from closed minds and closed markets and allowing them to dream up things that people are prepared to pay for. This unleashing of mankind's innovative ability is responsible for virtually all our progress and growth to this point, bringing us everything from food, crockery and clothing, to virtual-reality gaming devices. It is therefore important that we understand how the conditions for this most transformative environment came about. What choices were made that influenced the type of society that developed, and why did the choices other cultures made differ? How did an isolated, wet and exclusive England become an inclusive and innovative United Kingdom? As we will explore, a combination of tragedy, unintended consequences, historical development and citizen freedoms arose to create a societal model that was radically different from the closed and centralised regimes that were the accepted norm for most of recorded history. A society where rulers were subject to the law and the law belonged to the people, not the state; where collective rights did not trump individual rights; where these rights were inherited, not passed down by governments; and where citizens had the ability to create and keep their own wealth. These principles led to a revolution that continues to transform the world.

3

A QUITE EXTRAORDINARY SERIES OF EVENTS

The measure of a society is not only what it does but the quality of its aspirations.

Wade Davis, anthropologist[29]

Following the decline of the Roman Empire, the small and relatively insignificant windswept island of Britannia was a pretty grim place to live, lagging far behind other cultures such as the Chinese Yuan Dynasty and the Eastern Roman Empire of Byzantium.[16] The last years of Roman occupation had seen their stranglehold on the country weaken, and the commander of Britain, Magnus Maximus, abandoned the troublesome north and west regions, leaving them in the control of local warlords. Germanic marauders were constantly invading the island, raping and pillaging the local folk, and the Roman towns and villages were constantly blighted by raiding parties from the northern Picts and the Scoti of Ireland. Desperate, in 411 the British Roman leaders requested assistance from Rome. To their dismay, the Western Emperor, Honorius, informed them, via what is known as the Rescript of Honorius, that he could not spare the troops and that they were

---

[16] Which, although in decline, was still the most powerful economic, cultural and military force in Europe.

on their own. This marked the end of Roman rule and occupation, and the despondent Roman legions crossed the channel for a final time. Empty of forces to defend it, Britain then witnessed a mass migration from Northern Europe, creating a new society made up of a mix of these invaders and the indigenous population, now known as the Anglo-Saxons. The infrastructure left by the Romans slowly fell into disrepair and their cultural norms faded away. Except one: slavery. The enslavement of humans to serve as forced labour was an embedded practice in Britannia as it was across the rest of the Roman Empire. The Germanic tribes also practised slavery, and naturally the Anglo-Saxons continued the system, sometimes in league with Norse traders who sold people that they had captured on their escapades to the Irish. There were also established slave-trading routes through Bristol to Ireland and across Europe to Rome and on through Venice to the Byzantium, and later to the emerging Muslim world. As you would expect, a slave's life was an unenviable one. They could be branded or castrated, treated like animals and punished by mutilation or death. A famous passage written by Aelfric, a late 10th-century abbot of Eynsham, near Oxford, imagined the pains of an unfree ploughman: *I go out at daybreak, goading the oxen to the field, and I join them to the plough; there is not a winter so harsh that I dare not lurk at home for fear of my master. Throughout the whole day I must plough a full acre or more... I must fill the stall of the oxen with hay and supply them with water and carry their dung outside. Oh, oh, the work is hard. Yes, the work is hard, because I am not free.* Slavery was a major barrier to industrialisation, for people in servitude are more concerned about the fact that they are not free than they are about inventing spinning jennys, steam engines and motor cars. Even if they did invent anything, any reward from their endeavours would belong to their masters, not them. Masters of slaves were not that interested in inventing labour-saving devices either, mainly because they had slaves to do the work for them.

Anglo-Saxon Britain was split originally into seven kingdoms – Northumbria, Mercia, East Anglia, Essex, Kent, Sussex, and Wessex – but was unified under King Æthelstan in 927. It developed a somewhat paradoxical society, with 10 per cent of the Anglo-Saxon population believed to live in servitude, while also putting in place a relatively democratic system based on law and council, rather than a monarchic dictatorship. In contrast to elsewhere, the concept of the law of the land existed. Anglo-Saxon kings could not, except in exceptional circumstances, make new laws, and the first act of any new conquering king was often to assure his subjects that he would uphold their ancient privileges, laws and customs. Criminal acts were not just an injury to the victim, but a crime against the English nation. Kings were advised by the witan,[17] an advisory council containing the land's most powerful and important people, ranging from archbishops to earls and thegns. They gathered to discuss matters of both national and local significance and to advise the king on the administration and organisation of the kingdom, dealing with issues of taxation, jurisprudence, church affairs, defence and the law. Crucially, the witan also had the responsibility of selecting the next king. The witan is therefore seen by many to be an early, less structured forerunner to the current Parliament.

The Anglo-Saxons also treated their womenfolk more equally than in other societies. While still living in a mostly patriarchal society, Anglo-Saxon women enjoyed considerable independence, and were able to own property, decide who they married, and even rule. Widows had inheritance rights, custody of their children and authority over dependants, and any personal goods, including lands, that they brought into a marriage remained their property. The system of primogeniture (inheritance by the firstborn male) was not introduced to England until after the Norman Conquest, so Anglo-Saxon siblings, regardless of their sex, held more equal status than over in the Continent. The history of the Anglo-Saxons is a tale of the establishment of British cultural identity: not only its language, but also its cherished institutions, such as shires and boroughs, and the instinctive tendency towards freedom, fair play and democracy. The permanency of laws and customs and the presence of an advisory council prevented a totalitarian society from emerging, and, alongside the 6th century emergence of Christianity, formed the basis of British culture.

Then came the Normans.[18] The Normans were Vikings who had conquered Northern France in the 10th century and possessed advanced military capabilities in the form of the armoured knight, although their victory over Harold in 1066 owed as much to good fortune as it did to military power. They were not gracious victors, and their arrival was more massacre than migration. As conquerors, they butchered and tormented their way across

---

[17] Also referred to as the witenagemot.
[18] ...from whom I am descended, for in the Domesday Book is listed Hunfrid de Cuelai, who settled in Norfolk where I grew up.

the country, crushing any last traces of rebellion within the Anglo-Saxons and native Britons. Their leader, William I (known as William the Conqueror), saw the country as his to do with what he wanted, issuing a great survey in 1086 (called the Domesday Book, or 'Book of Judgement') to ensure that every scrap of land and animal hide was known to the king, so taxes could be paid on it. The assessors' reckoning of a man's holdings and their values was dispositive and without appeal. As Henry II's High Treasurer, Richard FitzNeal, wrote in 1179, *That is why we have called the book 'the Book of Judgement'... because its decisions, like those of the Last Judgement, are unalterable.* The invasion of the Normans did not result in a mass replacement of the Britons; just the establishment of a different elite class. They were estimated to be no more than 8,000 in number, so to reinforce their power and to ensure subjugation of the vanquished population, the Normans built a series of great castles across the country in places such as York, Lincoln, Warwick, Windsor, Kenilworth, Nottingham and Cambridge. The local people were not welcoming of their new oppressors, and William was particularly furious at the resistance, especially in York where in the summer of 1069 the native people burnt down two castles and killed the Normans who occupied them. In retaliation, William's forces travelled north to York that very same winter, retook and repaired the two castles, and then, using the city as a base, commenced what became known as the Harrying of the North, a widespread campaign of terror that involved the utter destruction of not just the rebels, but also their loved ones, livestock and land. The 12th-century chronicler John of Worcester wrote that food was so scarce in the aftermath of the harrying that people were reduced to eating not just horses, dogs and cats, but also human flesh. The Anglo-Norman chronicler, Orderic Vitalis, stated that the Normans *arrogantly abused their authority and mercilessly slaughtered the native people like the scourge of God smiting them for their sins.*[30] Some were so shocked by the brutality of these new Norman rulers that they were reluctant to even talk of it. So William became king. *What treatment he meted out to those who managed to survive the great slaughter, I forbear to tell,* sighed Eadmer of Canterbury at the turn of the 11th century.[31] The island of Britannia was now under the complete control of the Normans, and in the words of Orderic Vitalis, *The English groaned aloud for their lost liberty and plotted ceaselessly to find some way of shaking off a yoke that was so intolerable and unaccustomed.* But while the Normans now ruled, the concept of the law of the land and the yearning for individual liberty would remain in the hearts of the English, dormant but not subdued, awaiting the right circumstances to rise and flourish again.

While the natives got used to wearing the yoke of oppression, somewhat perversely, there was one group who benefited greatly from the Normans' presence – the slaves. While slavery still existed in Christian countries, under the Normans the enforced enslavement of humans virtually disappeared as a practice in England. In 1070, William the Conqueror ousted the elderly pre-conquest Archbishop of Canterbury, Stigand, and replaced him with Lanfranc, a leading light of the Christian reform movement and William's own moral tutor since boyhood. The new archbishop was soon urging William to abolish the slave trade – and the Conqueror complied. William introduced a law preventing the sale of slaves overseas,[32] and in 1080 passed a decree forbidding the sale of Christians to foreigners or heathens.[33] According to the 1086 Domesday Book census, one in ten of the population of England were still slaves. However, in 1102 the Church Council of London, convened by St Anselm of Canterbury, issued a decree: *Let no one hereafter presume to engage in that nefarious trade in which hitherto in England men were usually sold like brute animals.*[34] This decree highlights two key points that were instrumental in the development of the mindset capable of leading to an industrial revolution nearly seven hundred years later. Firstly, it demonstrated that the interpretation of Christianity in England now saw the enslavement of its own people as abhorrent and wrong in the eyes of God. [19] Secondly, it highlighted, through the 'sold like brute animals' comment, the existence of a world view that saw mankind as being above the other animals that inhabit the Earth, entitled to exploit them as beasts of labour. By 1200 the enslavement of humans was almost non-existent in the British Isles. In its place the Normans had introduced a new form of slavery called serfdom, one that tied people to a different kind of master – the land.

It's a Hard Knock Life

While the domestication of animals and advances in agriculture had increased food output for Europeans, the effort involved and the lack of variety of crops had, as Yuval Noah Harari explains in *Sapiens*, made people's

---

[19] Something that wasn't necessarily the case elsewhere.

lives worse than when they lived a more frugal but collaborative existence as hunter-gatherers. *The average farmer worked harder than the average forager, and got a worse diet in return.*[35] In Europe, the effort involved in turning land into food was an all-consuming task. As Alan Macfarlane, the Professor of Anthropological Science at Cambridge, has highlighted,[36] Western and Northern Europeans had a much harder time than those living over in Asia. For centuries in the East, the primary form of grain consumed has been rice. Rice is both labour intensive and produces far more grain per head than the hard grains of Europe such as barley and wheat. The more you worked the rice fields, the more rice was produced, so any increases in population also led to an increase in output of rice, creating a virtuous cycle. They also had a culture of slavery and thus no shortage of people to use to work the paddy fields. Once the rice crop is successfully harvested, the rest is relatively easy – remove the outer husk, boil it and eat it. The Asia people built their agricultural industry around this very simple but very effective crop, enabling them to develop and feed higher populations than Europe.

While more technically advanced than the 'poor but happy' hunter-gatherer societies in the world, in 14th-century Europe, the masses were both poor *and* unhappy. The climate was unsuitable for rice, so hard grains such as barley, oats and rye were grown for the poor, and wheat for the governing classes. Compared to rice, these grains all required significantly more effort to farm. The wooded European landscapes needed to be cleared of forest, the heavy soil had to be tilled, the grains harvested and the cereal milled and ground into flour before it could be transformed into edible food such as bread, porridge, gruel and pasta.[37] This presented Europeans with three major challenges not faced by their Asian counterparts: firstly, the land produced far less output per person working on it; secondly, the work demanded much more effort than human muscle is capable of; and thirdly, the milling and grinding process required the development of some form of technological innovation in order to make it a feasible practice. These three challenges, combined with the abolishment of enforced slavery, created a desire within the European people to find a way to make the production of food easier. Harvesting grains like wheat and corn required the combined efforts of many people, and without slaves one must do it oneself or find another way. As it was hard physical labour, it was not long before the people looked to utilise the extra muscle that animals could provide. This would not have been deemed a consideration without the existence of a world view where man was both superior to nature and able to use the natural world as he pleased. They first used oxen, then they moved to horses harnessed to metal ploughs with wheels, then they forged iron agricultural tools and used waterwheels and windmills. The Europeans needed to develop a civilisation based on engineering and the use of non-human power just to survive. As McFarlane states, the industrial revolution *is really the final effect of something that started hundreds of years earlier, and has led to people thinking deeply about how you can use natural forces to help human beings survive in a difficult environment.*[38] This is a very different world to what was developing in the rice fields of the East. While Europe created an industrial revolution to make life easier, over in the East the hard-working Asians were living through an industrious revolution.

Medieval life was framed by two economic realities. Virtually all wealth was in the form of land, and land could not be sold. Land ownership therefore represented the preponderant display of wealth, social stature and political power. It also meant that unless you were born rich, your chances of becoming rich were virtually nil. As the construction of power sources such as windmills and watermills were expensive and required significant capital outlay, it was only the rich European landowners who could afford to build them. That landowner would often be the lord of the manor, who would provide wood and the labour from his estate to build the mill. In return for providing this capability, he would expect all the serfs in his manor to use it. This was not some philanthropic gesture; it was a means of gaining control of the population. Once the mills were built the lord would ban the use of hand-milling equipment (called quernstones) in the villages in his manor, obtaining a monopoly on the milling and grinding of grain, effectively binding the serfs to his land just to survive. The investment in the construction of power sources such as windmills and watermills helped to introduce into the social ecosystem the practice of making significant investments of capital in the development of labour-saving devices, simply to centralise production, create a monopoly and make a profit. This was the start of the capitalist system that was to prove instrumental in the development of an industrialised society.

As well as cultivating their own small plots, the serfs were required to tend communal land for the population of the village, and the lord's land for his personal benefit. It was a totally one-sided relationship. The serfs owed the lord their crops, their labour and their commitment to take up arms in his defence, and in return the lord provided protection and some food, but little else. The entire feudal system was geared in favour of the landowner, for the serfs had effectively become bound both to the lord of the manor and to the land he owned. The system also constrained the freedom of movement: some serfs were born unfree and could not leave their manors to work elsewhere without the local lord's consent, while others had to accept limitations on their freedom as part of the tenure agreement for their farmland. Boys were, almost without exception, compelled – often by force – to remain on that land and practise their father's trade. And things would likely have stayed like this for centuries, had it not been for some very unfortunate events with very disruptive outcomes.

The Cursed Continent

From 950 to 1250 AD Europe benefited from three hundred years of beneficial weather. Known as the Medieval Warm Period, it provided bountiful harvests that enabled its population to grow to levels that would not be obtained again until the 19th century. The following years saw temperatures cool, but in 1257, Europe was gripped by abnormal and cataclysmic weather conditions. A Medieval monk documented the time: *The north wind prevailed for several months... scarcely a small rare flower or shooting germ appeared, whence the hope of harvest was uncertain... Innumerable multitudes of poor people died, and their bodies were found lying all about swollen from want... Nor did those who had homes dare to harbour the sick and dying, for fear of infection... The pestilence was immense – insufferable; it attacked the poor particularly. In London alone 15,000 of the poor perished; in England and elsewhere thousands died.*[39] At the time the only assumption would have been that this was some punishment from God. In fact, it wasn't until 2012 that the cause of this famine was identified: the eruption of the Indonesian Samalas volcano, part of the Rinjani Volcanic Complex on Lombok Island. This was the largest volcanic eruption for 10,000 years, blocking out sunlight, altering atmospheric circulation patterns and cooling the Earth's surface. It caused crops to wither, bringing famine, pestilence and death. Mass burial pits from this time have been found all over Europe, including one in London containing the remains of 15,000 people, nearly a third of the city's population.

While the atmosphere and climate recovered after the Samalas eruption, from around 1280 the yield ratios of wheat (the number of seeds one could eat per seed planted) started to decline, causing food prices to climb steadily. In years with good weather the yield ratio could be as high as 7:1 (for every seed planted, seven seeds were harvested – six for the future year's seed, and one for food), while during bad years it could be as low as 2:1.[40] The 14th century marked the end of the Medieval Warm Period, making way for a twenty-year period between 1310 and 1330 where the winters were severe and the summers cold and wet, resulting in extremely poor crop yields. These agricultural problems reached a peak in 1315 with the onset of unusually heavy rain across Europe that led to a longer catastrophic period called the Great Famine. This torrential rain inevitably caused flooding, leading crops to rot and livestock to drown in the waterlogged fields. What farm animals remained starved as the straw and hay could not be dried and cured, resulting in no fodder for them to eat, causing the price of food to double in England. Salt, which was the only way to cure and preserve meat, was also difficult to obtain due to the wet weather, and wheat prices increased by 320 per cent, meaning the peasants could no longer afford bread. Stores of grain for long-term emergencies were limited to the lords and nobles, and people became desperate and began to harvest wild edible roots, plants, grasses, nuts and bark in the forests. By the spring of 1316, the continuing rain resulted in a European population that was deprived of both energy and the food to sustain it.

All segments of society were affected, but it was the peasants, who represented 95 per cent of the population, who suffered most as they had no reserve food supplies. Any concern for the future was forgotten as in desperation animals were butchered, the next year's grain was consumed, children were abandoned to fend for themselves,[20] and some elderly people voluntarily refused food to ensure that the younger generation could eat and survive.[41] There were even many reported incidents of people resorting to cannibalism, such was their desperation. The famine reached its peak in 1317, but as so much of the seed stock had been consumed

---

[20] This situation was portrayed in the Brothers Grimm fairy tale, *Hansel and Gretel*.

and the population was severely weakened by diseases such as pneumonia, bronchitis and tuberculosis, it was not until 1325 that the food supply returned to normal and the population began to increase. It is estimated that in many Northern European cities and towns the Great Famine resulted in the death of 10–25 per cent of the population. Yet this death toll was nothing compared to the next crisis to hit Europe, for travelling along the Silk Road from Asia came the *Yersinia pestis* bacterium, causing a pandemic that was to become known as the Black Death.

Peaking in Europe in the years 1346–53, the Black Death struck a Europe that was finally beginning to regain its numbers following the Great Famine. This increase in population had led to crowded cities and villages, providing an optimal environment for a disease that proved to be a terrifyingly efficient contagion. People who felt perfectly healthy when they went to bed at night could be dead by morning. In 1348, the plague spread so rapidly that before any physicians or government authorities had time to reflect upon its origins, about a third of the European population had already perished. It was especially bad in the crowded cities where contact with the disease proved hard to avoid. As fear and death spread rapidly throughout the Mediterranean and Europe, people fled to the country to try and avoid it, but their lack of knowledge and understanding resulted in attempts to control the plague that varied between worthless and barbaric.[21] This included the massacre of the entire Jewish population of Strasbourg, who had been falsely accused of trying to cause the disease by poisoning the city's wells. The 2,000-strong Jewish population was given a choice between converting to Christianity or being burned alive. Although Strasbourg had not yet encountered the plague, the nine hundred Jews who refused to convert were herded into wooden houses and, over six days from 14th February 1349, systematically burnt alive. The plague arrived anyway, claiming approximately 16,000 lives.[42]

The plague also had a very instrumental effect on Northern Europe's relationship with religion. As the mechanism behind infection and the transmission of diseases was not understood in the 14th century, many

[21] We received an insight as to what that must have been like from the news images of the spread of Ebola throughout the crowded slums of the West African nations, and the fear and mistrust the poor and uneducated have for the authorities and the amount of denial regarding the existence of the disease, despite all evidence to the contrary.

people believed only God's anger could produce such horrific displays of death. In a society where the final recourse for all problems had been religion, and where Roman Catholicism was the only tolerated faith, the fact that no amount of prayer was effective against either the famine or the plague led to the start of the decline of the institutional authority of the Catholic Church and the rise of the Protestant faith.[43] The church hadn't helped its cause, for in its ignorance it had declared the cause of the Black Death to be the impropriety of the behaviour of men; only to watch horrified as its clergymen perished in higher numbers than the general population. The irony wasn't lost on the common folk, for if the plague was a judgement passed upon the sinful, and the men of the cloth were dying in droves, then God had surely judged them and found them wanting. This was the final straw in England where the corruption within the Catholic priesthood had been angering the people for some time. They now didn't believe that the clergy or the church as an institution represented the will of the people or the will of God. This wasn't a loss of Christian faith; it was the people rejecting the corruption of organised religion and instead beginning to long for a more personal relationship with God. And this transition laid the foundations for a much more influential shift in England's relationship with the church.

Due to a lack of truly accurate records, the exact death toll of the Black Death is unknown, but it is estimated to have wiped out 30–60 per cent of Europe's population, resulting in the deaths of an estimated 75 to 150 million people.[44] English soldiers unknowingly carried the disease from France to England, starting an especially devastating round of plague in the British Isles that is estimated to have killed as much as 75 per cent of the population in many areas.[45] To show the impact the Great Famine and Black Death had on the population, during both these events life expectancy fell to 29.84 and 17.33 years respectively. Did I mention that life in Britain was grim?

A Basic Economic Problem

The combined effects of the Great Famine and the Black Death inadvertently created the conditions for a new relationship with religion, a new societal model, new mindsets and a scientific and agricultural revolution that laid the foundations for the industrial revolution. The dramatic fall in population meant that there were far fewer people to work the fields, which led to an increasing pressure to look at new ways to increase the productive output of the land. The serfs, aware of their current rise in value, were for the first time able to exert pressure on landowners and demand better terms and wages due to the shift in their favour in the balance of supply and demand. Afraid of this power shift and needing to control the price of labour, in 1351 the nobility responded by passing the Statute of Labourers, which placed a maximum on the wages of serfs and limited their mobility. This legislation was, however, poorly enforced and did not stop the demands for a rise in wages. Tensions between the peasants and nobility continued, culminating the English Peasants' Revolt of 1381 when a wide spectrum of rural society, not just peasants, rose up in protest against the punitive taxation being levied on them to fund the Hundred Years War. The rebels sought a reduction in taxation, an end to the system of unfree labour known as serfdom, and the removal of the king's senior officials and law courts. This protest claimed a series of initial successes, such as the taking of the Tower of London and forcing the then 14-year-old King Richard II to sign a treaty abolishing the practice of serfdom. While the revolt was finally crushed, the treaty revoked and 1,500 of the rebels caught and executed, the balance of power had been shifted forever. The serfs were now aware that their services carried a high value, that they had leverage and that they could rise in unison when pushed too far. Those in power knew this also. Rural wages continued to increase, and lords increasingly sold their serfs freedom in exchange for cash or converted traditional forms of tenure to new leasehold arrangements.[46] Wages in England and across Western Europe rose to the point that in 1450 they reached a level that would be unmatched again until the 19th or 20th century.[47]

Over the course of the 15th century, the institution of serfdom, brought across from the continent with the Norman invaders in 1066, vanished forever in England. English commoners would no longer be serfs, bound to the lord and the land. They would have the right to negotiate their wages, to buy or rent land, to settle where they chose and to sell the food they grew for a profit. By the end of the century this new breed of tenant farmer could earn their own money in direct proportion to the amount and quality of food they brought to market. People could become traders as well as farmers, and for the first time working harder and more efficiently had a direct benefit on the workers' well-being. This increased the agricultural output of the land, as well as the output of other goods that the farmer was now free to sell, like wool.

The breaking of the bonds to the land and the removal of labour obligations to the lord created a society that was far more open than elsewhere. The English farmer could freely move about the country to sell his goods, whereas French farmers (for example) were bound by direct and indirect taxes, tariffs and other kinds of restrictions. This resulted in most English farmers becoming commercial people, able to produce yields of crops and foodstuffs to sell in urban areas. This freed them from reliance on the lord for their family's well-being and allowed them to raise their own funds, move around the country and pursue other methods of income. It created an environment where men felt free to pursue ways to improve their families' situation and look for ways to increase the crop yield to create a surplus quantity that could be traded for profit. It was the start of the creation of a market-based economy.

England had become a nation with an entrepreneurial mindset. The power of the lords over the population was waning and the practices of slavery, unfree servitude and serfdom were at an end. A new type of inclusive society was being developed; one where people could combine effort and entrepreneurial enterprise for financial gain and, in doing so, secure their survival. The development of the desire to improve the productivity of the land created a revolution in agricultural practices. This revolution constituted a period of scientific experimentation, understanding and technological invention within the agricultural industry that allowed English farmers (and their Dutch counterparts) to create previously unobtainable levels of productivity. Farmers were continually adopting new methods of farming, experimenting with new types of vegetables and grains, and learning about manure and other fertilisers. Innovators like Thomas William Coke (1754–1842) proposed the utilisation of field grasses, new types of fertilisers and greater attention to estate management. Jethro Tull (1674–1741) invented a horse-drawn seed drill in 1701 that economically sowed the seeds in neat rows, and later developed a horse-drawn hoe. A contemporary of Tull's, Charles 'Turnip' Townshend (1674–1738) stressed the value of turnips and other field crops such as clover in a four-field rotation system of planting. The clover introduced nitrates to the soil and turnip was used to feed livestock, while the wheat and barley were mostly for export and domestic use, replacing the previous practice of simply leaving the land fallow to recover.

The development of these new innovations and the potential for increased agricultural output had further unintended consequences. The open-field system of crop rotation that had been practised for centuries suddenly became an obstacle to the potential of increased agricultural productivity, and the solution was to enclose the land, which meant enclosing entire villages. This became known as the Enclosure Movement. Landlords knew that the peasants would not give up their land voluntarily, so they appealed by petition to Parliament. The first Enclosure Act was passed in 1710 but was not enforced until the 1750s. This opened the floodgates, and between 1750 and 1760, more than 150 acts were passed, and between 1800 and 1810 Parliament passed more than nine hundred acts of enclosure. While enclosure ultimately contributed to an increased agricultural surplus that was necessary to feed a population that would double in the 18th century, it also brought disaster to the countryside by dispossessing peasant farmers of their land. These workers, freed from servitude to a lord and from any ties to the land, were now desperate to find a way to provide for themselves and their families. The end of feudalism, combined with improved farming techniques and a rise in automation, fully freed them from the land, allowing people to travel elsewhere and pursue other trades such as merchants, craftsmen and professional soldiers. The need – and ability – to find new ways to make money to survive started to change the mindset of the entire population. Having successfully progressed from a hunter-gatherer lifestyle to a farming-based one, and in doing so learnt to domesticate animals and harvest and maintain the land, the people of Europe now had to find new ways to make a living. This large displaced population unknowingly became the perfect workforce for the new revolution in industry that was emerging. Without the enclosure movement, the population would have stayed focused on their agricultural smallholdings, but now, free from serfdom and any ties to the manor, they headed towards the new factories that had begun to spring up in their thousands in towns and cities.

The Roots of Liberty

At the same time as the Agricultural Revolution was taking place, another revolution was brewing – one that would also prove pivotal. A seemingly unrelated series of events would end up synergistically creating the cornerstones of a democratic system capable of fostering an industrial revolution: the protection from oppression, the constitutional rights of the individual, and the devolution of power from a single monarch to an elected body.

The first of these events, the signing of the Charter of Liberties, was undertaken by William the Conqueror's youngest son Henry I on his accession to the throne in 1100. This treaty effectively started the process of recognising the rights of landowners by protecting the property of barons and earls after their deaths, ensuring that ownership would transfer to their surviving family rather than being opportunistically grabbed by the ruling monarch. The Charter limited the power of the monarch while also reinforcing their responsibilities such as the maintenance of forests and essential common land, creating a stable and peaceful foundation upon which the country could prosper.

Then, in the late 12th century, Henry II's reforms of the court system greatly expanded the role of royal justice in England, producing a more coherent legal system and enforcing a more general Common Law to replace the smorgasbord of local and canon laws that previously existed. Predictability in legal proceedings emerged, and those not lucky enough to be born into a family of wealth and influence suddenly had rights and could obtain a fair trial. In 1215, the Magna Carta was sealed under oath by King John to proclaim certain liberties and to protect the rights of the feudal barons. King John, after angering the barons by breaking feudal custom and raising taxes without their consent to support his failing war efforts, was forced by the barons to accept a further limiting of his powers in exchange for their continued support. The Magna Carta contained sixty-three clauses and focused on ensuring that, *the English Church shall be free, and shall have its rights undiminished, and its liberties unimpaired* (Clause 1), while also reinforcing the customs and rights of the people of England, such as, *the city of London shall enjoy all its ancient liberties and free customs, both by land and by water. We also will and grant that all other cities, boroughs, towns, and ports shall enjoy all their liberties and free customs* (Clause 13). The main purpose of many clauses was to protect the feudal barons' property, ensure that the king's will was not arbitrary, and clarify that no freeman could be punished except through the law of the land. One of the most important clauses was Clause 39, defining rule of the law of the land and the right of individuals to freedom: *No free man shall be seized or imprisoned, or stripped of his rights or possessions, or outlawed or exiled, or deprived of his standing in any other way, nor will we proceed with force against him, or send others to do so, except by the lawful judgement of his equals or by the law of the land.* Unlike elsewhere in the world, in England, the law was being designed not to enforce control over the individual, but to ensure their freedom.

The events of the 14th century, notably the Black Death, significantly weakened the stranglehold of the representatives of the Catholic Church on the people of Britain (and most of Europe), changing the population's perspective on religion and resulting in a more personal relationship with God. This weakened the power of the Catholic Church in England, something that was to be fractured completely in the 16th century. After an unsuccessful appeal to the Pope (Clement VII) in 1527 for an annulment of his dynastic marriage to Catherine of Aragon, King Henry VIII established himself as the Supreme Head of the Anglican Church of England, outlawing Catholicism in England and Wales and effectively separating England from the papal authority of the Catholic Church[22] and setting in motion the Dissolution of the Monasteries. This act, known as the English Reformation, was in part associated with the wider process of the European Protestant Reformation, a religious and political movement that affected the practice of Christianity across most of Europe during this time. Prior to this break with Rome, it was the Pope and general councils of the church that decided doctrine. Church law was governed by the code of canon law with final jurisdiction residing in Rome, all church taxes were transferred straight to Rome and the Pope had the final word on the appointment of bishops. The split from Rome changed this, making English monarchs the Supreme Governor of the English Church by Royal Supremacy, thus acknowledging the Church of England as the established church of the nation. All doctrinal and legal disputes now rested with the monarch, and the papacy was deprived of both revenue and the final say on the appointment of bishops.

The side effect of King Henry's actions was that as well as creating a new religious English state, he severed the ties with both Rome and the Catholic world view, releasing England from the papal suppression of new ideas and scientific insight that would blight people such as Bruno and Galileo. Over the coming decades, this break also helped to enable a new

---

[22] The original Brexit – or given it was England not Britain, perhaps just Exit.

sense of nationalism within England and continue to strengthen the new perspective of the relationship between individuals, the Bible and God that had arisen during the time of plague. Over the course of the 16th century Protestantism became intimately associated with English national identity; while Catholicism, especially as embodied in France and Spain, was viewed as the nation's enemy. A deep-seated fear of 'popery' spread across Stuart England, manifesting itself as a widely held conspiracy theory that Catholics were actively plotting to overthrow the Church of England and once again impose the Rule of Rome. This theory of religious conspiracy was given real credibility by the existence of genuine Catholic subterfuge, manifesting in the Gunpowder Plot of 1605. Which goes to prove that just because you're paranoid doesn't mean they aren't after you.[23]

The fear of a Catholic resurgence was not helped by the then-heir apparent, Charles I, deciding in 1625 to postpone Parliament to prevent any opposition to his planned marriage to the fifteen-year-old Roman Catholic French Princess Henrietta Maria.[24] Following his marriage, and after numerous clashes with Parliament over his attempts to levy taxes without their consent, on the 26th May 1628 Parliament adopted a Petition of Right, calling upon the king to acknowledge that he could not levy taxes without Parliament's consent, nor impose martial law on civilians, nor imprison them without due process, nor quarter troops in their homes.[48] Charles assented to the petition on 7th June,[49] but by the end of the month he had prorogued Parliament and reasserted his right to collect customs duties without their authorisation. For the next eleven years Charles ruled England without a Parliament, a time referred to as the Personal Rule or the Eleven Years' Tyranny. Charles believed in the divine right of kings and thought he could govern according to his own conscience. But Parliament perceived his actions to be those of a tyrannical absolute monarch, ultimately resulting in the three English Civil Wars that cost the lives of 3.6 per cent of the population[50] and led to the creation of Parliament's New Model Army and the execution of Charles I in 1649. The conflict also resulted in the abolishment of the monarchy, the House of Lords and the established Church of England, and in their place a new Republic was established, the Commonwealth of England,

---

[23] Joseph Heller, *Catch-22*.

[24] Charles knew many members of the House would be concerned that he would lift restrictions on Catholicism and undermine the official establishment of the reformed Church of England.

under the control of Oliver Cromwell. This period had the potential to turn England into a military dictatorship, and in Scotland and Ireland Cromwell's forces put down any rebellion with extreme force, something that the nations would remember with bitterness for generations. England was also at war with Spain, so during this entire period all attention was focused both inwardly and outwardly on matters of war. Cromwell's death in 1658 left England in political turmoil that would both end the Republic and result in the return of the Stuarts to the throne of England. After the restoration of Charles II in England, and the termination of the Anglo-Spanish War in September 1660, Parliament restored the Church of England to its previous form. However, enforcing the encompassment of all the people of England into one religious organisation, a concept taken for granted by the Tudors, had to be abandoned. This would prove to be important.

The religious landscape of England assumed its present form, with the established Anglican Church occupying the middle ground and Puritans, dissident Nonconformist Protestants (such as Congregationalists, Baptists, Quakers and later Methodists) and Roman Catholics now having to continue their existence outside the national church rather than controlling it. The development and tolerance of these Nonconformist Protestant variants would prove to be a crucially important element in both the evolution of free thought and individualism in society. These religious variants removed the need for priests to be the middlemen between the individual and God, promoted individual reading and interpretation of the Bible, and corrected distortions of original Christian thinking. They were also a clear rebellion against centuries of abuse of power and privilege by the church. Not for them restrictive religious doctrines and enforced educational dogmas. They saw faith differently to other religions, viewing life holistically and your goodness as something demonstrated more by your actions than by your attendance at church. The Protestant world view and work-ethic, with its emphasis on individual conscience, personal Bible-reading and industriousness, was a key factor in the rise of Northern and Western Europe's mercantile culture. It was also vitally important in the development of a society where people could ultimately choose the extent to which they invested in religion. Nonconformist movements like the Quakers also had a particularly important perspective when it came to progress, always encouraging people to look for a better way forward rather than accepting the world as it was. The Quakers' view stemmed from their belief that you should follow the divine light within you. This made Quakers willing to challenge accepted practices and to find new and innovate ways to do things, differentiating them from other religious beliefs. The rise of the Nonconformist religions also coincided with the rising tide of a radical political movement of the period, starting during the Civil War with the Levellers, who published their manifesto *Agreement of the People* which advocated popular sovereignty, extended voting suffrage, religious tolerance and equality before the law. In stark contrast to situations elsewhere in the developed world, the stage was being set for the creation of a society which was, for the majority, free from oppressive religious doctrine or centralised agendas.

A Bloodless Revolution

Charles II tried to reintroduce Catholicism to England, but aware of the ever-present fear of a Catholic tyranny he had to play a careful game. He secretly made a promise to the Catholic King Louis XIV of France that he would convert to Catholicism, at an unspecified future date, in return for his support in the ongoing Anglo-Dutch Wars. Charles also attempted to introduce religious freedom for Catholics and Protestant dissenters with his 1672 Royal Declaration of Indulgence, but the English Parliament forced him to withdraw it. Shaken by the thought of once again coming under the rule of Rome, Parliament took preventative measures by introducing, in 1673, the Test Act, declared as *an act for preventing dangers which may happen from popish recusants.*[51] This served as a religious test for public office designed to ensure that only members of the Church of England could hold office, with specific measures to safeguard against Catholics and Nonconformists holding influential positions. In 1678, in an attempt to exclude Catholics from both houses, the Test Act was extended to peers and members of the House of Lords, but the Lords resented this intervention, delaying passage of the act and weakening it by including an exemption for the future James II, effective head of the Catholic nobility, at whom it was largely aimed. Then, in 1679, Titus Oates' revelations of a supposed 'Popish Plot' sparked the Exclusion Crisis when it was revealed that Charles' brother and heir to the throne, James, Duke of York, was a Catholic. The crisis saw the birth of the pro-exclusion Whig and anti-exclusion Tory parties.

Upon Charles II's death in 1685, the Protestant nobles feared that under the rule of his son, James II, who had converted to Catholicism, England would finally become a Catholic tyranny, ruled as a satellite state of Rome under the control of an all-powerful Catholic monarch, King Louis XIV of France. Members of the Anglican establishment could see that in France the king ruled in an absolutist, not pluralistic, way, and they wanted none of it. A movement quickly gathered strength to avoid such a form of monarchy developing in England, with people growing increasingly worried that all the bloodshed of the previous seventy years would be for nothing. Fearing an absolutist Catholic takeover, Whig politicians, led by the Earl of Shaftesbury, actively began promoting exclusion bills designed to prevent the now-Catholic James II from succeeding to the throne. James was forced to make numerous promises designed to both defend the existing government in church and state and reassure those who were concerned by his recent conversion to Catholicism. These promises allowed him to ascend to the role of king in February 1685. However, they also proved to be short-lived and empty, for the new king wasted little time in trying to secure not only freedom of worship for Catholics, but also the removal of the Test and Corporation Acts so that Catholics could occupy public office and secure his religious objectives using prerogative powers. In May 1686, James also decided to obtain from the English courts a ruling which affirmed his power to dispense with Acts of Parliament. He then dismissed judges who disagreed with him on this matter, as well as the Solicitor General, Heneage Finch. In 1687, James prepared to populate Parliament with his supporters so that he could manipulate the repeal of the Test Act and the penal laws, instituting a wholesale purge of anyone in office who opposed his plan. James was doing exactly what the Anglican establishment had feared; he was turning England back into an absolute monarchy. The reaction to this turn of events would prove to be pivotal.

The crisis reached its tipping point with the birth of King James' son, James Francis Edward Stuart. The birth of a boy immediately changed the existing line of succession by displacing the heir presumptive, James' Protestant daughter Mary. Britain was now facing the possibility of not only having a Catholic king but becoming a Roman Catholic dynasty. These fears started to become real in 1687 when James issued the Declaration of Indulgence, an act that promoted religious freedoms, but which many understood to be designed specifically to remove the penal laws against

Catholics. In May 1688, James issued an instruction that this declaration be read from every Anglican pulpit in England, outraging the Church of England and its staunchest supporters. On 8th June, James had the Archbishop of Canterbury, William Sancroft, imprisoned in the Tower of London for refusing to proclaim it. Now fearing an imminent Catholic takeover, on 30th June 1688, seven English peers including the Earls of Danby and Halifax and Henry Compton, Bishop of London, contacted the Protestant Dutch leader[25] William III of Orange, who was also the husband of King James II's daughter, Mary. They pledged their support to him if he brought a military force into England to overthrow James II; a plan William accepted on the provision that both he and Mary would become joint heirs to the throne of England. This became known as the Glorious Revolution.[26]

William landed at Torbay in Devon in November 1688. James, fearing for his life and believing his army was populated with Protestants who were likely to turn against him, fled to France, and in doing so effectively abdicated the English throne. In January 1689, William summoned Parliament, which duly passed the necessary legislation to name both him and his wife Mary as joint monarchs of England. England's separation from Rome was now complete. The Whig and Tory parties that supported the ascendance of William and Mary had sought the support of Protestant Nonconformists such as the Quakers, Methodists, Baptists and Congregationalists, and promised them that in return for their support and oaths of allegiance they would be allowed their own places of worship, and to be their own teachers. This Act of Toleration would be granted in the outcome of a successful revolution. While James II had also issued an act of toleration, the Nonconformists believed that this was purely to open the door to Catholicism, and not to Nonconformist Protestant beliefs. They therefore decided that their future would be much more secure if the sovereign was a Protestant and pledged their support to the revolutionaries. This decision had a bigger impact than many realise.

It seems ironic to say that the Glorious Revolution represented a new era of religious freedom, given that its main purpose was to prevent Catholics from assembling and praying in England, but given the previous persecutions and conspiracies it represented the beginning of a period of calm and the

---

[25] Called a stadtholder; head of state of the crowned republic of the Netherlands.
[26] Also known as the bloodless revolution.

start of a change of focus for the country. Unlike other coups throughout history, James had been dethroned not by violence but by the decision of a legitimate Parliament. It was also a vindication and victory for the concepts laid down by influential philosophers such as John Locke, such as the separation of church and state, the idea that civil society was created for the protection of property, and thus the divine rights of kings works against this.

Other acts had also taken place during this period to enshrine the rights of people and limit the powers of any future rulers. In 1679, the *Habeas Corpus* Act was passed, designed to protect the liberty of the individual by ensuring that they could not be detained without due cause, and requiring that any person arrested by the authorities be brought before a court of law so that the legality of the detention might be examined. Then, to ensure this removal of the threat of a Catholic monarchy was permanent, a series of legal acts were passed, including the Bill of Rights (1689), the Mutiny Act (1689), the Act of Toleration (1689), the Act of Settlement (1701) and the Act of Union (1707). The passage of the Bill of Rights prevented any future movement towards absolute monarchy and reasserted the nation's 'ancient rights and liberties', set limits on the powers of the monarch and established the rights of Parliament. The bill included clauses to prevent the monarchy from dispensing with Acts of Parliament, raising money without Parliament's consent, suspending laws, levying taxes, making royal appointments or maintaining a standing army during peacetime without Parliament's permission. It also ensured the free election of MPs, legally established the constitutional right of freedom of speech in a Parliament that acted as the centre of all policymaking.

Keeping Royal Fingers out of the Nation's Wallet

Parliament then enacted another revolution, this one financial. Almost immediately after being crowned, William (now King William III) declared war with France, and for the next twenty-five years (apart from one five-year truce) England was engaged in a long and expensive war with its neighbour across the Channel. The House of Commons deliberately kept William III underfunded, ensuring that he and his successor Anne had to keep Parliament almost continuously in session to obtain the necessary war funds. In 1690, the Commons established a Commission of Public Accounts to monitor how the revenue was being spent by the Crown, inserting appropriations in its supply bills to establish the purpose of any raised revenue. This increase in the ability of Parliament to control the nation's revenue helped to ensure the success of the Bank of England, created by statute in 1694 to act as the government's banker and debt manager, so investors in the bank could be confident that their loans to the government would be repaid by parliamentary taxation appropriated for that purpose.

The final piece of the financial revolution which altered the relationship between Crown and Parliament was the creation of the Civil List in 1698. This was the assignment by Parliament of a set annual amount of Crown revenues to the monarch to meet the costs of running the government and royal establishment. The annual amount assigned to King William and his household was £700,000, an amount that did not change until the beginning of the reign of George III in 1760. From this point onwards, the Crown was totally reliant on Parliament's control of revenue for its day-to-day running. England was not only free from a Catholic takeover, but also from any future monarch seizing control – they simply wouldn't have the power or the finances to do so. An elected Parliament was now in control, effectively placing democratic power into the hands of the people of England, preventing an extractive oligarchy or absolutist monarch from taking control.

A New Union Emerges

The Act of Settlement in 1701 ensured that anyone who converted to Catholicism, or who married a Roman Catholic, was disqualified from inheriting the throne. While the church still held an incredibly important role in Britain, the country was now free from the dogmas of Rome and the Inquisition. The Act of Settlement also had an unintended but critical consequence, becoming in many ways the major reason for the union of Scotland with England and Wales to form the Kingdom of Great Britain. Scotland, a predominantly Catholic country, was unsurprisingly not in favour of an act designed to prevent a Catholic leader. In a desperate bid to create financial independence from England, in 1698 the Scots launched an ambitious attempt to colonise Panama, called the Darien Scheme, in order to dominate transoceanic commerce. Members of Parliament, public bodies, town corporations, landed gentry and thousands of citizens all sank their life savings into the scheme, investing between 25 and 50 per cent of the available wealth of Scotland. However, an inhospitable terrain, new diseases, lack of trade and, fatally, conflict with competing Spanish settlers caused the colony they established – Caledonia – to collapse. Most settlers died from fever, dysentery and malaria, with only a few hundred of the 2,500 that set off from Scotland surviving. Scotland was now in dire financial straits, and the Parliament of England decided that, to ensure the stability and future prosperity of Great Britain, full union between the Scottish and English Parliaments and nations was essential.

In 1702, James II's Protestant daughter Anne became queen after the death of William III. Parliament needed to secure the throne against any future Catholic takeover before Queen Anne's death, and so on 1st May 1707, under the Acts of Union, two of her realms, the kingdoms of England and Scotland, united as a single sovereign state. The Kingdom of Great Britain was created, the English and Scottish Parliaments were merged, and Westminster became the central Parliament of Great Britain. Crucially, the Acts of Union enabled Scotland to keep its unique legal system (Scots' Law) and its own church with its own state religion; the Protestant Reformation movement called Presbyterianism.[27] This union calmed down the long-running dispute between England and Scotland, enabling Scotland to financially and intellectually prosper. By 1750, the major cities in Scotland, specifically Edinburgh and Glasgow, had created an intellectual infrastructure of mutually supporting institutions such as universities, reading societies, libraries, periodicals, museums and Masonic lodges. From there the principal architects of the industrial and economic revolutions would arise; people such as James Watt and Adam Smith.

The Inclusion Acts also enabled the continued development of the Nonconformist Protestant religions. Had James II not been dethroned, Catholicism would have been the only form of worship allowed. Now Nonconformists were permitted to meet and discuss ideas, but due to the Test Acts they were still excluded from holding civil or military office or attending university. This led to them funding their own private dissenting academies. The decision to permit the practising of Nonconformist

---

[27] The English weren't going to make the mistake of telling the Scots what prayer book to use again!

religions was to become an important factor in the development of social and economic freedom and inclusiveness in Britain and beyond. The British campaign to abolish the slave trade is generally considered to have begun in the 1780s because of the Quakers' anti-slavery committees and their presentation to Parliament of the first slave-trade petition in 1783. They protested that it was both duplicitous and shameful that a society that viewed itself as the bastion of inclusiveness, freedom and democracy should be practising and profiting from human misery. In 1785, English poet William Cowper emphasised this when he wrote that, *We have no slaves at home – then why abroad? Slaves cannot breathe in England; if their lungs receive our air, that moment they are free. They touch our country, and their shackles fall. That's noble, and bespeaks a nation proud. And jealous of the blessing. Spread it then, and let it circulate through every vein.* The Hull-based Anglian Nonconformist and politician William Wilberforce led the campaign throughout what would become a twenty-year struggle, making it his purpose in life to suppress the slave trade, which was finally achieved in 1833 with the passing of the Slavery Abolition Act.

Whereas the 14th century forever changed the relationship between the serfs and the landowners, creating a new form of freedom for the poor and the ability to operate as tenant farmers, the 17th century changed forever the balance of power in Britain. A century blighted by religious intolerance, fear of tyranny, battles for supremacy between Parliament and monarch and civil war left its mark on the country. This had not been a time of progress for England; but a time of civil war and disagreement. But it also represented a tipping point; one where it could easily have ended up an absolute monarchy, a papal state, a military dictatorship, or a society based on parliamentary rights, individual liberty and freedom. The deliberate decision to act; to define the respective powers of Parliament and the Crown in England and to invite foreign monarchs to rule the country specifically to ensure the retention of the natural rights of its people, was unprecedented. Any change of leadership by force usually involves bloodshed, something England had had its fill of. While this bloodless revolution was not truly democratic, for most common folk at that time still had no say in Parliament, it ensured a constitutional rather than an absolute monarchy and enshrined the sovereignty of Parliament. The monumental outcome of this action was not known at the time but represented a clear decision on the type of society England – and later Britain and the United States – wanted to become. One where the nation, its laws, its people and its freedoms were sacrosanct, and more important than any king or religion.

The aforementioned treaties and actions all played their part in ensuring that a ruling monarch acted in the best interests of their subjects, while also protecting the rights of landowners from the possibility of a centralised, unelected body simply exerting their will upon them. They represented the laying of social foundations upon which the framework of a modern democratic state could be built, one that recognised and protected the rights of the individual and the limitation of power. The concept of the law of the land now enabled all people to maintain their status as free citizens, to own property without fear of it being seized, and as such represented a key differentiator between Britain and the rest of the world. The law belonged to the land, and unlike elsewhere did not change due to political shifts, change of leader, or shifts of state religion. It was not a tool to be wielded simply by those in power, preventing even a king from entering the house of a common man and arresting him without due process. Freedom had become the default state for the population and this freedom was guaranteed by the law. The government and the monarchy were all servants of the law and as subject to it as every other citizen of the country. These inalienable rights protected the citizens of England, except for a short period of totalitarian rule after the Civil War, from the horrors of group-based collectivist ideologies being enforced upon them. It also protects its citizens from failures in alternative democratic models practised in Continental Europe where freedom is granted to the people by the state through certain rights. For example, a Frenchman has rights, but when any new activity is presented, the state intervenes to decide whether it or not it deems it legitimate. A British citizen, on the other hand, is free to do anything that is not specifically forbidden. This distinction is often forgotten, but it was crucially important for it allowed the development of a society where people were permitted to experiment with new techniques, discuss new entrepreneurial ventures and personally profit from their inventiveness and industry, free from worry that the state (or ruling body) would suddenly declare their activities illegal and requisition the results of their endeavours. The British were free to explore and experiment, while overseas it was best to check. The law of the land also ensured that existing laws could not be changed on the whim of a ruler or new government, being designed, as previously stated, to ensure individual freedoms, not suppress them.

A series of seemingly unconnected events ranging from foreign conquests to disasters, selfish intents and bloodless revolutions had unknowingly laid the legal and social foundations of a far bigger and more influential revolution – one that would change the world.

4

EXPLORATION, ENLIGHTENMENT AND ENTREPRENEURISM

The great question which, in all ages, has disturbed mankind, and brought
on them the greatest part of their mischiefs... has been, not whether be
power in the world, nor whence it came, but who should have it.

John Locke, *An Essay Concerning Human Understanding*, 1689

England had now become Britain. It had a monarchy, but not an absolute ruler. It had a Parliament, but not a military dictatorship, nor a republic. It had political balance and constitutional guarantees that England would never again be ruled by proxy from Rome. England was now the most stable and united nation state in Europe. While it might appear oxymoronic to align the exclusion of Catholics to the development of an inclusive society, their exclusion was to prevent an absolute monarchy, the repression of liberalism and the oppression of the established church, rather than to create these conditions – and intent matters greatly. The treaties and bills between Crown, State and People enabled the development of more inclusive, pluralistic political institutions, and were all necessary steps to enable the creation of a society that supported the cultural movement known as the 'age of enlightenment'.

Living on a small island ensured that the English did not suffer the intellectual hubris that blighted the leaders of places such as China, who believed that all worthwhile knowledge could be found within the boundaries of their huge nation. The English knew that there was a large, undiscovered world out there, for strange inhabitants from unknown places – from Romans to Vikings – had frequently appeared from the sea mist, raiding their villages and occupying their land. They had always believed that vast swathes of knowledge lay beyond their shores, waiting to be discovered. This mindset and ideological warrant was crystallised in the 17th century by the Lord Chancellor Sir Francis Bacon, who not only declared that *Knowledge itself is Power*,[52] but also that *Many shall travel and knowledge will be increased*. This was the inscription across the front cover of his 1620 work *Novum Organum Scientiarum*, translated as 'New Instrument of Science'. The cover shows a galleon passing between the mythical Pillars of Hercules that were alleged to have stood either side of the Strait of Gibraltar, marking the exit from the well-charted waters of the Mediterranean into the Atlantic. The symbolism Bacon was intending was clear: with the discovery of the Americas, the pillars – the boundary of the Mediterranean – had been broken through, opening a new world for exploration. He was hoping that his work would likewise break through barriers in human understanding. As American historian Carl Lotus Becker proclaimed, *a philosopher could not grasp the modern idea of progress... until he was willing to abandon ancestor worship, until he analyzed away his inferiority complex toward the past, and realized that his own generation was superior to any yet known*.[53]

Bacon also questioned how man could ever enjoy perfect freedom if he had to labour continuously merely to supply the necessities of existence. His answer as to what form this help took was clear – machines. Machines, labour-saving devices, would liberate mankind. These glorious products of science and invention began to revolutionise the idea of progress itself. If a simple machine could do the work of twenty men in a quarter of the time, then could the new Jerusalem be far behind? The concept of progress took hold and captured the imagination, allowing people to strive forever forward, forever upward. This optimistic and progressive vision was meant man was going somewhere, that his life had direction and could be altered and self-determined. It was a revitalisation of a more stoic mindset, where people could stand up and make something of themselves if they took responsibility for their actions and worked from a premise of reason not emotion. It reinforced the world view that man was superior to nature and not subservient to it, that they had independent agency and self-direction, and bolstered the pervasive idea that the history of human society is one of progress. Heaven on Earth seemed a reality and human happiness, improved morality and an increase in knowledge were now within man's reach.

The Reformation and the Glorious Revolution revitalised the freedom of individual learning and expression, enabling a mindset of independent and liberal thinking, civil liberties and religious tolerance, replacing the previous world view that, to quote historian Jonathan Israel, was *based largely on a shared core of faith, tradition and authority.*[54] John Locke was one of these new liberal thinkers. In his famous *Second Treatise*, published just after the Glorious Revolution in 1689, he develops many notable themes, including a depiction of the state of nature wherein individuals are under no obligation to obey one another, but to be their own judge of what the law of nature requires. His work also covers conquest and slavery, property, representative government, separation of the realms of church and state, and the right of revolution. Locke, while a deeply religious man, greatly understood that the church had no right nor need to press itself upon civil liberties and society. Locke's influence on the development of Western civilisation was great, with an entire passage from the *Second Treatise* being reproduced verbatim in the United States Declaration of Independence. Thomas Jefferson wrote, *Bacon, Locke and Newton... I consider them as the three greatest men that have ever lived, without any exception and as having laid the foundation of those superstructures which have been raised in the Physical and Moral sciences.*[55]

In his famous 1784 essay *What is Enlightenment?* the German philosopher Immanuel Kant answers the question in the first sentence: *Enlightenment is man's emergence from his self-incurred immaturity.* He also describes it as *man's release from his self-incurred tutelage,* 'tutelage' being defined as the *inability to make use of his understanding without direction from another.* Kant was highlighting that in Europe, man was allowed to consider himself freed from the constraints of perceived uselessness and able to affect his own future in positive ways. To choose his own destiny. The purpose of the Enlightenment movement was to reform society using reason, not faith or power. It advocated the challenging of ideas that were grounded in tradition and faith, and the advancement of knowledge through the scientific method. It promoted scientific thought, scepticism and intellectual interchange. Kant declared that it was necessary that all church and state paternalism be abolished, and people be given the freedom to use their own intellect and think for themselves. As he observed, *a revolution may well put an end to autocratic despotism... or power-seeking oppression, but it will never produce a true reform in ways of thinking*.

The Enlightenment was nothing less than a complete revolution in human thought. This new way of thinking declared that rational thought begins with clearly stated principles, uses correct logic to arrive at conclusions, tests the conclusions against evidence, and then revises the principles in the light of the evidence. This was more than mere ideas, but the development of a set of values upon which society should be developed. At its core was a critical analysis of traditional institutions, customs and morals, and a strong belief in rationality and science. The Enlightenment created a a period of profound optimism, a sense that through science and reason – and the consequent shedding of old superstitions – human society would improve. This mindset was instrumental to the development of the scientific revolution, and the discoveries of this period challenged many traditional concepts and introduced new perspectives on the world and man's place within it. Combined, they developed a new world view of progress and of a bright future, one which mankind's ability to think with logic, reason and fairness would enable them to control. Mankind was finally emerging from the darkness of prescribed thought and beliefs, ready to take on the world.

While the Enlightenment was a European-wide phenomenon that arose from French, German and English thinkers such as Voltaire, Kant and Locke, the effect it had on British society and the freedoms it provided was especially crucial. British society had, since the days of the Magna Carta, been slowly developing the foundations of a world view that increasingly valued the rights of the individual and minimised the power of the state to take those rights away. The development of a bottom-up, secular nation where the state enforced neither political or religious control was a rare thing indeed; something that is easy to forget. Across the Channel the French revolution was required to break the long-standing, top-down absolute monarchy and the fixed dogmas of the Roman Catholic Church. Only after much blood was shed did the foundational principles of individual liberty and religious tolerance emerge – only to see the country swiftly move from revolution to military dictatorship under Napoleon, resulting in twelve years of conflict and conquest, only to end in defeat.

Group Rights vs Individual Responsibilities

The British mindset spread across the water to the Americas, whose revolution was also about individualism. The French Revolution, despite being inspired by the American Revolution that it had supported and heavily financed, was much more collectivist in nature. For example, the third point in the Declaration of the Rights of Man of 1789 was that *The principle of all sovereignty resides essentially in the nation. No body nor individual may exercise any authority which does not proceed directly from the nation*. The collective – the group – rules over the individual, and group justice is more important than individual justice. The US founding fathers were keen to emphasise that democratic systems based on group justice were not their aim in setting the constitution, and why they favoured a representative, not a pure democracy. James Madison, in Essay No. 10 of the Federalist papers declared that: *Pure democracies have ever been spectacles of turbulence and contention; have ever been found incompatible with personal security or the rights of property; and have in general been as short in their lives as they have been violent in their deaths*. The problem with group justice is that it requires a shared, utopian vision to exist regarding what the ideal world looks like – and it generally seeks to identify and remove those that don't share that vision. Individuals are either deemed tools of the regime, or they are obstacles to the regime. It's a mindset that ends up with millions of individual rights being removed 'for the greater good'.

The difference between these two mindsets applies not just to rights but also to responsibilities. In Britain (and ultimately anywhere that adopted British values) the individual is responsible for their own actions, their own life and their own behaviour. Britain thrived because, as Daniel Hannan articulates in *How We Invented Freedom and Why it Matters*, a society arose whose starting point was that you are free to do what you want unless told otherwise. Conversely, societies based around group responsibilities start from the opposite premise – that you shouldn't do something unless told that you could. The latter approach promotes social responsibility, placing all emphasis on the state to legislate for undesirable scenarios, creating a society where people become well versed in their individual rights, but not their individual responsibilities. If the law doesn't insist that I have to do something, then I won't.[28] Conversely over in Britain people could freely try things without checking, and only if told otherwise would they stop. This created the need for an informal social agreement between citizens based around individual responsibility and respect – which is why the British adherence to systems like queuing seem so peculiar to those without that mindset. It works because people who queue jump break an unwritten but well-accepted contract to behave in a way that is fair. In societies that don't promote individual responsibility, queuing become free-for-alls, with limited consideration for fairness or whether anyone was there before you, because you owe them nothing and queue-jumping is not illegal. One society is based around individual freedom and responsibility, the other about regulation and rights.

The difference of mindset in Britain compared to Europe (especially France) became obvious to those who were exposed to both. When the great Enlightenment writer Voltaire was exiled from France to Britain for nearly three years, he became intrigued by Britain's constitutional monarchy and the country's greater support of the freedoms of speech and religion in contrast to the French absolute monarch and Catholic rule. In 1733 he published his views on British attitudes toward government, literature and religion in a collection of essays in letter form, entitled *Letters Concerning the English Nation*. The next year they were published in French as *Lettres philosophiques*. Voltaire regarded the British constitutional monarchy as more developed and more respectful of human rights (particularly religious tolerance) than its French counterpart, something that didn't go down well with his countrymen. The French publication of *Letters* caused a

---

[28] A good example is the attitude to picking up dog mess. In countries that prioritise individual responsibility such as the UK and the US, the attitude is 'Your dog, your job.' In countries that based on social responsibility, such as France and Spain, the mindset is 'Your [the state's] pavement, your job.' This is highlighted by global pet company Beco Pets, which reports sales of 1.85 million poo bags annually in the UK, but only 3,600 in France. According to those who try to combat the dog poo problem in France, the attitude from the dog owners is 'I pay my taxes – you pick up my shit.' Data Source: Daily Telegraph, *'Sacre bleu! French dog owners least likely to clean up after their pooches'* 08/03/2015

huge scandal, the book was banned, copies burnt, and Voltaire was forced again to flee. France, it seems, was not yet ready for such free thought, demonstrating instead a rather ironic intolerance of being described as intolerant, and in doing so perfectly proving Voltaire's point.

The Enlightenment introduced critical ideas such as the centrality of freedom, democracy, and reason as primary values of society, replacing the divine right of kings or traditions as the ruling authority. It effectively created the beginnings of democratic society as we know it today; a fundamental element needed to ignite a revolution in innovation as entrepreneurism requires freedom and liberty. However, what really lit the fire of intellectual and industrial endeavour was the ability to read, digest and share ideas. Something as transformational as the age of enlightenment could only occur in a society that allows its people to freely access information, meet with other members of society to discuss this information, and work together to develop and publicise their own inventions and concepts.

The First Information Revolution

It was trade that drove the creation of the written word through the need to record transactions, and it was the written word that drove the creation of the printing press. Until this point all information was scribed onto parchment by hand, which was incredibly slow and expensive. In 1215, a single sheet of parchment would cost a ploughman two weeks' wages, which explains why the writing on these parchments is so small and the pages filled from edge to edge. The invention of the printing press, credited to the German goldsmith and later printer, Johannes Gutenberg, in 1439, transformed the ability to mass-record, store and share ideas, displacing the earlier singular methods of printing such as block printing or hand-copying that were undertaken in the monasteries of Europe. Printing soon caught on and rapidly spread from Germany to over two hundred cities in a dozen European countries. The first book to be printed in English emerged twenty-five years later in 1475. By 1500, printing presses in operation throughout Western Europe had already produced more than 20 million volumes. In 1534, Henry VIII granted a Letters Patent to the University of Cambridge, enabling them to set up their own publishing operation, and it has been operating ever since, distributing the ideas of great minds such as John Milton, Isaac Newton and Stephen Hawking. It is both the oldest publishing house in the world and the oldest university press, second in size only to the second oldest university press: Oxford. Henry VIII's continuation of the Reformation movement also created demand for the printing press as he decreed that from 1536 every parish in the country should have its own copy of the Bible so parishioners could develop a more personal relationship with God. In the 16th century, with presses spreading further afield, their output exploded tenfold to an estimated 150–200 million copies per year.

The printing press generated an explosion of information about the sciences, religion, weaponry, inventions, trade and economic systems; elements that together formed the foundations of the modern world. Author Ramez Naam summarises its impact well: *the... type printing press, captured no additional energy, grew no additional crops, and cured no diseases. But it did something more important – it accelerated the spread of ideas. It intensified the web of connections between minds. In so doing, it amped up the Darwinian process of idea evolution, accelerated the process of innovation, and thus, indirectly, it increased our access to energy, increased our ability to grow food, and accelerated the development of medicine, science, and all the other domains of human knowledge that have enhanced our lives.*[56] The ability to retain and communicate ideas allows people to learn, experiment and improve upon those ideas in order to create new ones. The creation of a method of mass-producing information and distributing it created a production line for knowledge, spawning an innovation explosion and the world's first information revolution. The printing press changed the conditions under which information was collected, stored, retrieved, criticised, discovered and promoted, which had important causative effects on the Reformation, the Renaissance and the scientific revolution. The importance of printing as a beacon of modern achievement enabled the so-called Moderns to rival the wisdom of the Ancients, in whose teachings much of Renaissance learning was grounded. Elizabeth Eisenstein's book, *The Printing Press as an Agent of Change*, highlights the fact that before the printing press was developed, ideas recorded in only a few manuscripts were always in danger of being forgotten or lost by the intellectual community. Put those same ideas in hundreds of identical printed copies, and they were much more likely to spread and endure. For example, without the printing press, the 1453 fall of Constantinople to the Ottomans and the loss of its extensive collection of classical texts would have been disastrous for humanity.

The developments in religious tolerance and the freedom of movement, thought and ideas in Europe, especially in England, came together to create a society where ideas could freely diffuse and flow. Although the printing press itself did not immediately transform society, this is probably because the books and printed material were still too expensive for the average person. While better than monks scribing by hand, printing was predominantly limited to the sharing of ideas amongst the wealthier classes. But while the pool of participants in the first information revolution may have been small, it was enough to start a revolution in science and thought. The printing press became the disruptive technology of the age of reason; the force multiplier of the Enlightenment. Then, in the 18th and 19th centuries, the combination of mechanical presses and the production of innovative, cheaper 'pulp' paper created an explosion in the availability of information, newspapers and works of literature, allowing for the mass production of books for education; meaning schools could affordably share the written word with their pupils. This mass production and mass distribution of books helped endorse the concept of individualism, changing people's perceptions of themselves by allowing individual enquiry and intellectual activity, rather than group indoctrination. The Protestant world view and its emphasis on individual conscience, personal Bible-reading and industrious behaviour helped to facilitate the rise of the merchant culture like nothing before.

The industrial revolution increased both the demand for and supply of information. An increased population with the ability to read, combined with increased production capabilities, led to an audience eager to digest books, pamphlets, newspapers and journals, which transmitted ideas and attitudes in the same way as YouTube and Facebook have diffused and spread ideas in the 21st century. Libraries soon appeared, lending out their material for a low price, as well as bookstores that would offer a small lending library to their patrons. This allowed even those who could not afford to purchase books to access, read, learn and internalise the ideas contained within them. It is hard to imagine just how the Renaissance, the Reformation, the scientific revolution and the industrial revolution could have happened without printing, and here lies a clue. In countries that didn't adopt the printing press, they didn't happen. Books are dangerous instruments because they contain ideas, and Nonconformist ideas are threatening to the ruling elite. If your society is based around a top-down extractive structure rather than a bottom-up inclusive tone, then the concept of knowledge and ideas being printed and shared is bad news, for it feels like a threat to your power. The oral transmission of information retains the power of knowledge with those who have the right to dispense it, such as religious leaders. The printing press presented leaders with a choice: do you embrace the freedom of information and an increase in knowledge, education and innovation throughout your society, or fear and suppress it?

A Third Place: Caffeine, Clubs and Capitalism

Historian Alan Macfarlane believes that England had one crucial and unique element in its inclusivity arsenal, which helps explain why it was the first country to industrialise. *If you are going to have an industrial or scientific revolution which is immensely complex, you need a social organisation which will encourage a blend of two things. On the one hand you need individuals who are thinking hard, competing. On the other, you need co-operation, collaboration, trust and mutual solidarity, so that the ideas can be shared and generated together... What the English developed, and had now spread over much of the world, was a way of bringing these together.*[57]

Although the British are famous for their vast consumption of tea, it was the 17th-century introduction of another hot beverage, coffee, that had a surprisingly large impact on the spread of Enlightenment values and the scientific and industrial revolutions. Innovation requires more than ideas; it requires an environment where people can connect to freely discuss these ideas and their development and distribution. Enter the coffee house. England openly embraced the concept of the coffee house; a place to buy, sit and drink this new brew. A third place between home and work. Entrance to coffee houses was permitted to anyone who wore good clothes. Books and papers were made available and a penny would rent a table for the day. This increased consumption of reading materials of all sorts was one of the key features of the 'social' Enlightenment.

Some people frequented coffee houses so often that they used their local establishment as their postal address. Coffee houses soon became immensely popular, differentiated from the often-inebriated patrons of the inns, and by 1675, there were more than 3,000 coffee houses in England. The establishment soon became concerned by the explosion in places where people met and discussed the topics of the day, as coffee houses became hotbeds of political scandal-mongering and intrigue. Charles II tried to suppress the London coffee houses, issuing a proclamation in 1675 which ran: *His Majesty hath thought fit and necessary that coffee houses be (for the future) put down and suppressed, because in such houses divers false, malicious and scandalous reports are devised and spread abroad to the Defamation of his Majesty's Government and to the Disturbance of Peace and Quiet of the Realm.*

The newly empowered people of England were now accustomed to not taking their monarch's instruction as the word of God, and Charles' proclamation was so unpopular that it was almost instantly withdrawn, reinforcing how 'bottom-up' English society had become. By the time England had become Britain, in the reign of Charles' daughter Queen Anne, the coffee-house club was a firmly established feature of England's social life. The power of the coffee houses was that they brought about something that had never happened before: they brought the social classes together. They broke down barriers, creating a sense of inclusiveness as people from different backgrounds and upbringing met and shared information and gossip. Coffee houses were open to all and indifferent to social status, and as a result became associated with equality and republicanism. They also became very popular with a certain growing group of people, the bourgeoisie, making available to this new political class a place to contact like-minded, aspirational thinkers.

Coffee houses soon became centres of art and literary criticism, and gradually widened to include even economic and political disputes as matters of discussion. Perhaps the best-known frequenters of coffee houses were literary figures such as Samuel Johnson and Adam Smith, who worked on the drafts of *The Wealth of Nations* at the British Coffee House in Cockspur Street. The coffee houses became the very embodiment of the public sphere. They offered not only a forum for self-expression, but one for airing one's opinions and agendas for public discussion. They provided a window into a nation with a new sense of inclusiveness, one which allowed people to meet, mingle, read and debate almost anything they wanted without the paranoia that plagued other European countries.

Like Voltaire, visitors from France were struck by this sense of openness, inclusiveness and unrestricted opinion and sharing of information. A place where people could joke and make fun of political and religious figures without fear of retribution.[29] To one French visitor, Antoine François Prévost, coffee houses were liberating, a place *where you have the right to read all the papers for and against the government,* and which formed the *seats of English liberty.*[58]

Coffee houses also performed an important economic service, becoming meeting places where business could be partaken of, news exchanged and the *London Gazette* (government announcements) read. They were also the catalyst for the establishment of such famous institutions as the Stock Exchange and Lloyd's Insurance (so called because it was founded in a coffee house run by Edward Lloyd, a location where underwriters of ship insurance met to do business). The coffee house continued to grow in popularity throughout the 18th century, providing the people with an informal meeting place, one where the proprietor often provided books, journals and sometimes even popular novels for their customers to read. Some reading material was not only digested and discussed on the premises, it was produced there as well. Two influential periodicals sold from 1709 to 1714, *The Tatler* and *The Spectator*, were closely associated with coffee-house culture in London, being both read and produced in various coffee establishments in the city.

Gradually, those in the higher echelons of society craved a meeting place that was less crowded and where discussions were more civilised, and to satisfy that need they created their own gentlemen's clubs. Clubs in Britain provided the new bourgeoisie with a structured and controlled social framework to meet, discuss and catch up on events. One of the original clubs was simply called The Club. This political dining club, whose 18th-century members included Samuel Johnson, Charles James Fox, Adam Smith, Edmund Burke and Edward Gibbon, met one evening a week at the Turk's Head in Gerrard Street to debate the issues of the day. The Club, one of many established meeting places that arose, expanded in the 19th century, and over the years included esteemed members such as Richard Owen, Samuel Wilberforce, William Gladstone and Alfred Tennyson.

---

[29] These famous 'freedoms', including the ability to speak freely and tell jokes without fear of the establishment knocking at your door, are something which, as we will explore in Chapter 24, the British government is ominously retracting.

The growth of these, and clubs of all kinds, is a crucial part of the 'X factor' that explains why the industrial revolution happened in Britain. They provided a meeting place for the Nonconformist Protestant groups who had pledged their support in the Glorious Revolution in exchange for the passing of the Act of Toleration in 1689. Kept out of public life by their religion, the Quakers, Methodists, Baptists and Congregationalists found outlets for their talents in trade and commerce, and the coffee houses, clubs and societies of England proved ideal meeting places for them to do this. As Alan Macfarlane explains, *We now live in a world that has millions of clubs, and we all take it for granted that this is the kind of thing humans can do. But in most civilisations, clubs have been a political threat to the State; because they often encouraged free thinking, they've been a threat to the Church, and so they have been banned or people have had their primary loyalties to their family or their village.* The rise and acceptance of clubs and coffee houses in Britain were in sharp contrast to other nations, where both were banned as they were deemed a place where people would gather to plot. For example, coffee houses in Mecca were deemed such a concern that imams banned them, and coffee, from Muslim life between 1512 and 1524. In Constantinople, the sultanate of Murad IV feared that coffee houses had become a place for 'mutinous soldiers' to meet, so in 1633 he banned coffee and decreed that all coffee houses be torn down. Britain, a country that had increasingly embraced belief in individual activity, responsibility and freedom from state or religious intervention, became the heyday of clubs and the societal gatherings they enabled. Alan Macfarlane again: *It's only when you get separate individuals with all of their skills, all their different backgrounds, to come together trustingly, to work together and to share their knowledge and information and skills, that you can build something as complex as an industrial civilisation. One person can't do it. You need all of the accumulated skills of writers, academics, politicians, businesswomen, craftsmen, put together to make this new kind of civilisation. And the British Club made this possible.*

Here was the 'X factor' in action, a crucial element that differentiated British society and set in place an industrialised, inclusive, capitalist society that would change the world. These clubs and coffee houses were places where men of invention, investment and industry could meet and freely discuss their ideas and agree to join forces for mutual gain. Partnerships were formed across class lines in a manner that was unique to Britain and critical to the development of the engines that drove the industrial revolution. States Macfarlane: *in the Lunar Club in Birmingham, Josiah Wedgewood the potter would talk problems in pottery, to which Joseph Priestley, the chemist, would offer his solutions... James Watt, the inventor of the modern steam engine, would be there, and he would talk about problems with the steam engine, and how you were going to distribute it and make it. And Matthew Boulton, the greatest eighteenth-century ironmaster, was a member of the society. He'd say, "Well, why don't we go into partnership then!"*[59]

Industry was also a magnet for the second (and third, fourth, etc.) sons of wealthy families. Back in 1066, the Normans introduced to England the practice of primogeniture, the common-law right for the firstborn son in a family to inherit the entire estate. This left him with inherited wealth, but any subsequent siblings with nothing. As Adam Smith wrote, *When land was considered as the means, not of subsistence merely, but of power and protection, it was thought better that it should descend undivided to one... To divide it was to ruin it, and to expose every part of it to be oppressed and swallowed up by the incursions of its neighbours.*[60] Daughters were expected to find a rich husband; and non-firstborn sons to find a new means to riches. While primogeniture ceased to be practised elsewhere in the world, in England it was still customary, despite the Statute of Wills being passed in 1540, which permitted the oldest son to be cut off entirely from his inheritance. Land was therefore retained by the same family and in the same quantity, rather than being equally divided between children. This fact can be easily observed when flying over English rural landscapes, as land ownership follows natural boundaries such as hedgerows and rivers, compared to the Continent where land is divided into man-made, straight-lined, segments. Primogeniture meant that for subsequent sons a fear of poverty provided the impetus for action; industrial endeavours provided the outlet and the coffee houses and clubs often provided the conversations and the contacts.

Britain now had relative stability, property and contract rights, the rule of law, a relatively democratic political system and an increasingly liberal society that both encouraged individualism and the sharing of ideas and opinions. It had both ensured the sovereignty of the nation and the sovereignty of the individual; a state of affairs that set it apart from almost every other country. It also had an expanding population that created a market for mass-produced products. A glance at the events in the century leading up to 1830 has shown some reasons why Britain had the edge over its near neighbours. The Germans could not have imagined a market beyond their nobility. The French may have had gifted inventors, but they could not strike the right balance between man and machine. They were also diverted by a small matter of revolution and the terrors it brought with it. Innovation exploded in Britain because of the increasingly inclusive societal model that developed. As Daniel Hannan explains: *The three precepts that define Western civilization – the rule of law, democratic government, and individual liberty – are not equally valued across Europe... Democracy, too, is regarded as a means to an end – desirable enough, but only up to a point... As for the idea that the individual should be as free as possible from state coercion, this is regarded as the ultimate Anglophone fetish...*[61]

Britain had developed a bottom-up societal model that allowed men of invention, industry and investment to freely come together and share information, develop mutually beneficial contracts, and trade amongst themselves. Uncovering new ways to create new market opportunities become the focus of society and its economic, technological and scientific practices, driven by a cultural and legal framework that allowed independent citizens to both partake in these practices and profit from any resultant goods and services. In this environment the unknown becomes a challenge to be solved, and if there's a buck to be made in solving it, then a race develops to solve it first. For every successful businessman and inventor there were many more who failed, but British society allowed people the freedom to dream that success was possible, and that the only thing standing in their way was themselves. It's this mindset that drove people to board ships and travel across the Atlantic, to new lands where they could pursue what became known as 'the American Dream'.

The economic model of capitalism provided everyday people with the incentive to work hard, take risks and strive to develop new technologies. People swarmed to the numerous public lectures on new scientific inventions, drawn by the prospect of hearing something new that they could then use to make money. Abu Talib, an Indian Muslim visitor to late 18th-century Britain, commented on the fascination of the British for mechanisation: *The British were endowed with a natural passion for technical innovation. They possessed inventive skills and preferred to perform even minor routine jobs with the aid of mechanical instruments rather than manually. They had such great passion for the use of technical instruments that they would not perform certain tasks unless the necessary instruments were at their disposal.*[62] Joel Mokyr describes how this mindset led to the development of James Watt's steam engine in his book *The Lever of Riches*: *Watt's work, which combined inventive genius with a desire to cut costs, minimise wear and tear, and extract the last drop of duty from the last puff of steam in his engine was paradigmatic of the kind of mind that helped to make the Industrial Revolution.*[63]

The age of industry had arrived, and the world would never be the same again.

5

REVOLUTION! THE WORLD TAKES OFF

Little else is requisite to carry a state to the highest degree of opulence from the lowest barbarism, but peace, easy taxes, and a tolerable administration of justice.

Adam Smith, 1755

No other revolution can be said to have had such an impact as the first industrial revolution. This was much more than a mere revolution in industry; it was a complete structural change in the socio-economic organisation of the Western world. Unlike other revolutions that altered their country's direction, the explosion of innovation and industry that started in Britain changed the trajectory of the entire human race. Its impact made a mockery of all the chaos and conflict that went before, affecting almost every aspect of daily life for the inhabitants of the countries that embraced it. It created a complete rupture in the old central relationship between landlords and unfree peasants, transforming it into one between capital owners and property-less wage labourers. Mercantilism made way for a new model of free market economics, one which enabled people to pursue ways to better their lives, and in doing so created record levels of growth and prosperity. However, economic models cannot develop without the right societal model to support them. Britain showed that the potential of the nation could be unleashed by giving its people something incredibly powerful – freedom and choice – even if that meant they used that choice to not follow the official religion, nor vote for the government at the polling booth. What Britain discovered, and others quickly followed, was that if you allow the population to have free will, then they will want a free market and, as we found out, the combination of free markets and a free society created the perfect conditions for the generation of innovations and wealth that over the long-term benefited every class in society.

Much has also been made of the geographic benefits Britain enjoyed, being an island state with a relatively temperate climate and an abundant source of fossil fuels. But the existence of these natural advantages is of no benefit to its citizens if they lack the freedoms, world view or the economic capability to make use of them. Merely saying, 'Well, Britain had lots of coal near lots of ports' disregards the real differentiator. Geographic benefits, despite being an important supportive factor, are not the main reason behind why the industrial revolution happened in Britain.

No African nation came close to creating a society capable of developing an industrial revolution, despite being populated tens of thousands of years before Europe[30] and being blessed with a wealth of natural resources such as oil, diamonds, salt, gold, iron, cobalt, uranium, copper, bauxite, silver, timber and petroleum. China, a more culturally advanced nation than any in Europe for the first half of the last millennium, has large sea ports and is also rich in coal. Whereas England was mired in serfdom in the 13th century, China was the richest, most advanced and most populated country on the planet, and would have appeared to be the civilisation most likely to drive technological progress and settle in America and Australia, rather than the inhabitants of a small, backward island in the Atlantic. The Chinese had already invented paper, wood-block printing, gunpowder and banknotes, and were hundreds of years ahead of Europeans in the working of iron. They also had a standing army and a navy. With the exception of the period of the Roman Empire, China had been wealthier, more advanced and more cosmopolitan than any place in Europe for thousands of years. Geographically, China's massive land mass allowed for the population to grow, the abundance of easy-to-grow rice helping to avoid any Malthusian

---

[30] Allegedly. New evidence has suggested that this might not have been the case.

Catastrophe to the point that China maintained a population of more than 100 million, far more than Europe's 50–60 million. So why didn't the Chinese invent the steam engine?

To be clear, the reason why Britain was able to industrialise when China (or anywhere else) did not has absolutely nothing to do with race or any perceived genetic exceptionalism. It does, however, have everything to do with the mindset of its leaders and the political, legal and social framework that was in place, for these controlled the beliefs, freedoms and aspirations of its population. For much of its history, China considered itself to be the centre of the world; the Middle Kingdom. This hubris led to its leaders believing that they did not need to look outside their own borders for knowledge, for they already knew everything worth knowing. It consequently became very restrictive in its teachings, focusing on the ability to remember and regurgitate existing concepts and ideas rather than exploring the unknown. Conformity and adherence to rules was everything. This narrow focus resulted in China concentrating its efforts on adhering to its own dogmas, and not the growth and wealth of the nation and its people. China was not interested in individualism, free thinking or the printing of any ideas that were contrary to what already existed. These things were at best frowned upon, but more likely strongly restricted or banned. There was no likelihood of China allowing a dissident section of society like the Quakers or Methodists to develop.

Alexis de Tocqueville, the 19th-century French political writer, makes the comparison between the freedom of the society in England and that in China. Tocqueville greatly admired the harmony and freedom of thought in England, writing in his memoirs that the *union of all the educated classes, from the humblest tradesman to the highest noble, to defend society, and to use freely their joint efforts to manage as well as possible its affairs. I do not envy the wealth or the power of England, but I envy this union. For the first time, after many years, I breathed freely, undisturbed by the hatreds and the jealousies between different classes, which, after destroying our happiness, have destroyed our liberty.*[64] In comparison, Tocqueville was convinced that the bureaucratic nature of Chinese society had stifled all originality and innovation. He summed up the situation as follows: *China seems to offer the classic example of the sort of social prosperity with which a very centralised administration can provide a submissive people. Travellers tell us that the Chinese have tranquillity without happiness, industry without progress, stability without strength, and material order without public morality. With them society always gets along fairly well, never very well.*[65] *The Chinese, following in their fathers' steps, had forgotten the reasons which guided them. They still used the formula without asking why. They kept the tool but had no skill to adapt or replace it. So the Chinese were unable to change anything. They had to drop the idea of improvement. They had to copy their ancestors the whole time in everything for fear of straying into impenetrable darkness if they deviated for a moment from their tracks.*[66]

The top-down control of the country determined the rate and nature of growth; if the emperor was interested in an aspect of scientific investigation, then progress would be made. If not, it wouldn't. This differed greatly from the model in England where inventiveness and innovation were allowed and encouraged; undertaken by industrious individuals whose actions were not monitored nor clamped down on by an all-powerful leader and an army of bureaucrats. If no one in England was interested in your invention, you could simply go elsewhere, either to other European countries or to the New World. Not so in China. If the emperor was not interested, then you continued at your peril. In China the possibility of the urban merchant classes coming to anything like the position of decisive influence that they achieved in many European countries was unlikely. China lacked both a free market and institutionalised property rights, its laws designed to control individuals, not free them. The Chinese state was always interfering with private enterprise, taking them over, prohibiting or preventing their activities, manipulating prices or exacting bribes. At various times the government was motivated by a desire to reserve labour to agriculture, control important resources (such as salt and iron) and disapprove of any form of self-enrichment – except by officials of course, giving rise to abundant corruption and rent-seeking. [31] China's dominant social ethos was also that of Confucianism, which disapproved of matters of trade and commerce, caring more about things such as prestige, honour, culture, arts, education, ancestors, religion or family piety. Making money came far down the list. Maritime trade was also restricted, seen as a diversion from imperial concerns, a source of income inequality, and worse, an opportunity to leave. Confucius had specifically declared that it was wrong for a man to make a distant voyage while his

---

[31] Which, as we saw in the previous chapter, is one of the main causes of a lack of innovation and entrepreneurship in a society, due to the punitive effect this has on potential profits and the increase in effort required simply to start up a business.

parents were alive, and condemned profit as the concern of 'a little man'.

So, despite their ingenuity and inventiveness, which, if allowed to flourish, would have enriched China and probably brought it to the threshold of modern industry, its stifling state control killed technological progress. China's culture of routine, traditionalism and immobility prevented its people from attempting any innovation that was not sanctioned in advance. Its restrictive top-down structure, closed mindset and closed borders prevented its transformation to an industrialised society, not its location or natural resources. The Chinese, we are told, had a proverb: *He who does not go forward will go backward.*[67] As David Landes wittily writes in *Why Europe and the West? Why Not China?* the saying was apparently as much an observation as prescription. While the Europeans suddenly became heirs to a vast flow of new knowledge, acquired through the trade routes and the explorations and discoveries of new lands, those in the East had closed themselves off or were simply not interested.

The Japanese also followed a very similar, exclusive trajectory to the Chinese. For nearly a century, Japan had been a spectacular success story for European missionaries, with approximately 500,000 Catholics by the early 1600s. Although Japanese politics at first favoured the European missionary effort, the imperial regent Toyotomi Hideyoshi (1536–1598) launched an anti-foreign policy that banned Christianity and killed a number of Christian missionaries that lived in Japan, believing that the religion was a threat to the traditional Japanese way of living and thinking. To ensure that no further intrusions of foreign ideas made it into Japan, a series of edicts called *sakoku* were issued in the 1630s by Shogun Iemitsu, that closed the country and effectively prohibited any contact with the outside world. The Japanese people were now forbidden to leave the country, or return if they did leave, under pain of death. Europeans were expelled from the country, and the only exceptions to this rule were people associated with the Dutch East India Company, and they were limited to the man-made island of Dejima in Nagasaki harbour. Trade continued between China and Japan and other parts of Asia, but for the next two centuries the East was effectively closed to the West. The measures Iemitsu enacted were so powerful that it wasn't until the 1850s that Japanese ports were finally opened up, Westerners were allowed to settle, and the Japanese were free to venture overseas.

It wasn't just the East that was afflicted by this mindset. Despite Islamic society being the early leader in the pursuit of scientific knowledge and the keeper of the writings of Aristotle, Plato and other Greek and Roman philosophers that had been lost to Europe after the fall of Constantinople, the Ottoman Empire also hit a technological brick wall. Again, this was a direct result of their own decisions, the most devastating being the Ottoman sultans' actions to suppress the spread of ideas and freely written words. The Turks had known about the printing press since the 14th century, but only adopted it in the 18th century due to religious conservatives who were sceptical of European inventions and their perceived evil effects on society. In 1483, Sultan Bayezid II prohibited any printing in Arabic script within the Ottoman Empire, an edict that was continued until Sultan Ahmed III gave permission for the establishment of the first legal printing house in 1727. Even then, this freedom was limited to the printing of secular works in Arabic script, resulting in printing not taking off until the 19th century, nearly four hundred years after it had in Europe. For all this time the ability to record and distribute ideas, critical to the development of an open, innovative, entrepreneurial society, had been quite simply not allowed on pain of death.

It is perhaps understandable to see parallels between the protectionist decisions made by China, Japan and the Ottoman Empire and the Glorious Revolution's exclusion of Catholics from holding positions of influence, as in both cases the desire was to protect their society from outside forces. However, look deeper and you see that both the objective and the outcome were very different. England feared an erosion of its freedoms and a return to more authoritarian, top-down absolutism. China, Japan and the Ottoman Empire, on the other hand, wanted to reinforce their top-down culture, and in doing so limit the freedoms of their people. And as discussed, people trapped in countries whose leaders chose exclusion over inclusiveness, control over freedom and restriction over openness simply did not innovate and experiment. As Alexis de Tocqueville declared, *The nation [China] was a hive of industry; the greater parts of its scientific methods were still in use, but science itself was dead.*[68]

The Appliance of Science(s)

It is unlikely that a country will industrialise without first experiencing a scientific revolution. As historian Joel Mokyr explains,[69] the Chinese could not have had an industrial revolution without first having the foundations of enlightenment thinking and scientific understanding. For Thomas Newcomen to develop the atmospheric engine may not have required him to understand the laws of thermodynamics – which weren't understood for another 150 years – but he did have to understand that the Earth is surrounded by an atmosphere. The discovery and understanding of atmospheric pressure led to scientists being able to develop the barometer, which led to people running up and down mountains to demonstrate that the pressure went up and down dependent on their height above sea level. This understanding led to man's desire to control the effect of atmospheric pressure, which led to the creation of Savery's 'Miner's Friend', then Newcomen's atmospheric pump, and finally Watt's steam engine. To paraphrase Mokyr, you couldn't have constructed a steam engine without first knowing about atmospheric pressure, any more than you could build a nuclear reactor without understanding atomic theory. It is also not possible to conceive and create something like a stationary steam engine unless you have an exceptionally good and carefully engineered control device at the top of the pump. To create this device requires skills in precision engineering, and the accurate and precise manipulation of metals at a miniature level – like those developed for the clockmaking industry. To undertake precision engineering also requires the ability to see both clearly and precisely. This required the development of glass. Without clocks and glass there would therefore have been no steam engine. The European invention of the mechanical clock also enabled the organisation and control of labour using time.[32] Clocks were initially used to control the daily cycle of monastic life, and it established a concept of people coming together at set times to do group activities. This developed both the behaviours and the mindset needed to support a capitalist, industrialised society; one where a person's time was a commodity that could be bought and sold.

But what about glass? Glass is a strong, malleable, visible substance, which was also used to create three other key inventions instrumental to the industrial revolution – magnifying lenses, spectacles and glass vessels. The development of magnifying glass allowed people to work with precision, visibility and control, which were indispensable elements for the new sciences. It also enabled people in the West to see two things others couldn't: the microcosm and the macrocosm. Tiny things can be

---

[32] It is no accident that this process is still known today as 'clocking on'.

viewed via microscope lenses, and very distant things such as stars and planets using telescopes – both instrumental to the scientific revolution. The manufacture of lenses was both the most demanding and precise technique by several orders of magnitude, requiring more sophisticated technology than anything else around at that time, while also being the invention that allowed for very precise workmanship. The creation of spectacles extended the usefulness of workers by correcting failing eyesight that would normally end their working life. Glass therefore enabled people in the West to both see things that other cultures couldn't, and to see them for longer. The scientific practices of chemistry and physics, instrumental to the development of industrial machines, also relied on the invention of glass. Glass containers allowed scientists and industrial inventors to see and monitor the movement and behaviour of steam, air and processes that extinguish fire. Glass, through its transparency and strength, enabled the new practitioners of science, and thus the practitioners of industry, to understand vacuums and the air pressure, volume and temperature relationship. These air pumps played a key role in the technology that led to the construction of both Newcomen's atmospheric engine, and of course Watt's improved version. The steam engine required an understanding of feedback and control systems from the development of clocks, precision engineering, explosive power from cannons and warfare, airflow and air pressure from the sciences, and boilers from brewing and distilling. Its creation enabled water to be pumped from mines, allowing men to extract coal which was used to power more engines, driving industrial machines that powered a revolution.

This interdependence of conditions creates a problem when one attempts to delineate them, and thus the industrial revolution was not simply about new developments in technology, power or transportation – it was about all of them combined with the social and economic environment to enable these innovations to bear fruit. Simply exporting the concept of a capitalist democracy to countries that lack the basics such as individual freedoms of movement and thought, the ability to share ideas and the right to keep what you create always seem to end in failure. Countries that attempt capitalism but do not have foundational elements in place, especially individual freedoms and protections such as property rights, fail, because unless you have clear title to the outcomes of your endeavours, it can be taken from you. Land is the most basic of commodities, but a surprising 70 per cent of the world's land is still unmapped and the people who work it lack any form of land documentation or proof of ownership. This means that farmers in places such as Ghana can have their land taken off them at any time, or simply repossessed when they die, leaving their family with nothing. They have no property rights, and therefore no security, and in this situation are unlikely to invest what time and money they have on any long-term focused activities.

In contrast to top-down, autocratic societies where wealth flowed directly into the hands of the nation's rulers, or those without basic freedoms and rights, Britain had – through a mix of deliberate acts and unintended consequences – created a bottom-up, aspiration nation, where people were protected from having the results of their efforts taken from them. As William Pitt the Elder declared in 1763, *The poorest man may in his cottage bid defiance to all the forces of the Crown. It may be frail; its roof may shake; the wind may blow through it; the storm may enter; the rain may enter; but the King of England cannot enter – all his force dares not cross the threshold of the ruined tenement!* As the Adam Smith quote that opens this chapter declares, if a government provides its people with physical security, a fair legal system and enforceable property rights, people will prosper. It is upon the rights allowed to the individual – the ability to live a private life, to speak and meet freely, to decide for yourself what endeavours you will undertake, and to keep the efforts of these endeavours – that the success or failure of this great transformation lies. Because these ideas are now the well-established foundations of most developed nations, we often forget just how exceptional they were at the time.

These fundamental prerequisites are still not available in many extractive countries, even today. Currently Venezuela has an estimated $14.3 trillion worth of natural resources, including the world's largest oil deposits, more than even Saudi Arabia, but half its children are malnourished and 60 per cent of the country's businesses have shut down in the last five years.[70] Food shortages have resulted in some citizens resorting to eating pets and zoo animals, and the Venezuelan President even announced a 'Rabbit Plan' that encouraged people to breed rabbits for food.[71] Countries that put freedom first feed their people, whereas those that prioritise other goals, regardless of their location or level of natural resources, tend to go hungry.

Industry and Integrity: Uncommon Bedfellows?

It is currently fashionable to perceive all of the 18th- and 19th-century industrialists and entrepreneurs who embraced and launched the worldwide spread of the capitalist model as uncaring profiteers on the exploitation of others. However, history doesn't bear this out. The aim of Adam Smith's promotion of free trade was to open the markets, so all could benefit, not just the wealthy. Rather than the capitalist anti-hero many have made him out to be, he in fact railed against the restraints of trade that were part of the Mercantilist movement, the regulations, special privileges and subsidies that business people were able to cajole out of the government, as well as the more widely known lavish public spending schemes and high taxes. Smith believed that these things worked to conspire against the working classes, creating a cabal of merchants more powerful than the government, who strove to keep prices high, and whose activities deliberately hindered the working man from being able to prosper under his own effort and initiative. In Smith's mind the best way to help ordinary working people was to sweep away the regulations and restraints on commerce, as well as the protections developed to benefit these cartels, so that markets were open, competitive and as fair and inclusive as possible.

One of the more overlooked facts about this period was that the mindset of corporate social responsibility was actively practised and promoted by many industrialists, especially those with Nonconformist beliefs such as the Quakers. The Victorian age was the heyday of paternalistic capitalism, and many large employers considered that it was to their moral and corporate benefit to utilise a certain amount of resources in caring for their workers.[72] The first crop of industrialists was renowned for their philanthropic activities; men such as Watt's business partner, Matthew Boulton. Boulton sponsored the production of music festivals in Birmingham from September 1768 to provide funds to build a local hospital, and a General Dispensary where outpatient treatment could be obtained. He served as treasurer, and wrote, *If the funds of the institution are not sufficient for its support, I will make up the deficiency.* The Quakers, those Nonconformist Protestants who went into business due to the restrictions included in the Test Acts back in the 17th century, also used their business as a tool of social improvement. The products they manufactured, such as soap and chocolate, were specifically made with the poor in mind, to help them stay clean and to provide an affordable alternative to alcohol. Quakers succeeded in business thanks to their faith-inspired integrity, insisting on fair pricing, paying off debts and behaving in honourable ways. Their beliefs stretched to their employees as well, driving them to build beautiful factory towns for their workers and to provide them with schools, churches, recreational areas and plenty of green spaces. For example, the Rowntree family built a model village just a mile north of their factory in York to give local people alternative accommodation to inner-city slum dwellings. Joseph Rowntree also set up four charitable trusts, one to lobby for parliamentary reform, another to run the model village, one to make charitable grants and a fourth to investigate the causes of poverty. In 1893, George Cadbury bought 120 acres of land close to his Birmingham works, and at his own expense planned and built the model village of Bournville to *alleviate the evils of modern, more cramped living conditions*. Likewise, the model village of Port Sunlight in the Wirral was founded by William Lever in 1888, named after Sunlight, the brand of soap made there, which itself was produced to alleviate hygiene issues in Victorian Britain. Port Sunlight was an exercise in profit-sharing, designed to *socialise and Christianise business relations and get back to that close family brotherhood that existed in the good old days of hand labour.* Rather than give their employees additional money directly, they instead invested it in the village. *'It would not do you much good if you send it down your throats in the form of bottles of whisky, bags of sweets, or fat geese at Christmas. On the other hand, if you leave the money with me, I shall use it to provide for you everything that makes life pleasant – nice houses, comfortable homes, and healthy recreation.'* Which they did. Like Cadbury, the Levers built a beautiful green village space, with nice houses, free schools, recreational areas, art galleries and swimming pools for the workers to enjoy, alongside a generous pension scheme. It is worth viewing images of these villages, especially Port Sunlight and Bournville, to see how different these places were compared to the houses in typical 19th-century, back-to-back inner-city slums.

An Empire made of Entrepreneurs

While most people are familiar with the names of the key architects of the physical side of the industrial revolution, men such as Watt, Wedgewood and Brunel, this period also saw an explosion in the numbers of small entrepreneurs such as shopkeepers and merchants, who were necessary to both transport and sell the fruits of industry and empire.[33] Adam Smith, in *The Wealth of Nations*, highlighted both the importance and the apparent dichotomy of this new class: *To found a great empire for the sole purpose of raising up a people of customers may at first sight appear a project fit only for a nation of shopkeepers. It is, however, a project altogether unfit for a nation of shopkeepers; but extremely fit for a nation whose government is influenced by shopkeepers.*[73] As the British Empire spread, the trade routes and related overseas trade fuelled the rapid development of commercial and financial businesses such as banks, insurance companies, shipping and railways. This new system needed administrators, managers and salaried professionals, creating completely new types of what came to be known as 'white-collar' employment. This employment boom caused a rapid expansion of urban cities and towns, requiring the development of new spaces that needed regulating and running. The Victorian period witnessed the massive development of local government and the centralised state, providing new occupations such as civil servants, teachers, doctors, lawyers and government officials, as well as the clerks and assistants who helped these institutions and services to operate. This new world of work helps break the confines of the past, where wealth is concentrated in the hands of those with birth privileges, land and capital behind them, and instead enables the collective entrepreneurial capabilities of the nation. This led to the development of a whole new social sector, one based on ambition and consumerism – the bourgeoisie or middle class.

The term 'middle class' was first used around the mid 18th century to describe those people who were below the aristocracy, but above the workers. While in the UK it has been traditionally 'hip' to mock these people as snobby suburbanites, it is this aspirational consumer class that drove the industrial revolution and having an aspiration-focused group of people is incredibly important to the development and sustainability of an inclusive society. I've never heard anyone say they 'aspire' to be middle class, but aspiration is how people become middle class. And this class of people acquired something that was normally only for those born into high status; disposable income. Men of invention, industry and investment

---

[33] Famously portrayed by Napoleon I, who stated that, *L'Angleterre est une nation de boutiquiers* (England is a nation of shopkeepers).

came together in a common pursuit; to find ways to satisfy the demands of this new consumer class that was both eager and able to buy these new factory-made goods. The middle class gave both positive form and function to the societal changes that the industrial revolution was creating. They didn't just aspire to have what the upper class had; they aspired to acquire something else, things that were new and modern. This created a demand boom for these items and drove men of industry to both create them and find ways to increase the efficiency of their production. This emerging group emphasised competition, thrift, prudence, self-reliance and personal achievement as opposed to the upper-class standards of privilege and inheritance. The middle class, instead of being something to be sneered at, is in fact the most crucial of all the social classes when it comes to developing an inclusive, innovative society. If you allow the population to have freedom of will and the ability to make personal choices, they will then want a free market that enables them to better themselves through barter and trading of their goods, services and skills. This was highlighted in a 2011 article from the Center for American Progress entitled *The Middle Class Grows the Economy, Not the Rich*.[74] In this, author Dr David Madland wrote: *A strong middle class is a prerequisite for robust entrepreneurship and innovation, a source of trust that makes business transactions more efficient, a bulwark against credit booms and busts, and a progenitor of virtuous, forward-looking behaviours, such as valuing education.* Dr Madland also comments that a healthy middle class is responsible for maintaining a more altruistic social attitude. He states that, *as America has become less of a middle-class society, we have become less trusting and thus less willing to make investments that others might benefit from.*

Why are the middle class so important? The answer is twofold. Firstly, they represent a blurring of the lines between 'them' (the rich) and 'the rest' (the workers), and the ability of people to alter their own destiny. Previously your lot was decided by your parents. If they were poor, you would be also. Being middle class was different. Defined by taking responsibility for oneself, one's family and the community, the success of the middle classes in the Victorian period can be seen in their ability to universalise a set of principles based on individuality and progress. In moving from a society based on rank and privilege to one based on progress and free exchange, the very idea that an individual, through hard work, thrift and self-reliance, could achieve social and economic success provided an equalising principle.

Secondly, because technological innovation and technological diffusion are intrinsically linked, the development of an environment that enables both elements proved critical. A strong middle class creates a demand boom for consumer products; much more than any additional money to the very wealthy would. A middle-class consumer boom would drive entrepreneurs to develop new and innovative products to capture that demand, which in turn creates jobs, which boosts the economy, creating a virtuous circle. An economic revolution, as well as an industrial one, was born, and the middle class became both economically strong and politically influential. Once other inclusive societies saw the benefits to be gained from a free market, the entrepreneurial ventures it enabled and the prosperity they created, they couldn't wait to join in. Britain may have started the fire of industry, but the United States, Western Europe and Japan fanned the flames.

Evolution not Engineering

Until relatively recently only a small percentage of the global population lived in a market economy, and unsurprisingly these areas became the most inventive and affluent parts of the world. The advantages these countries gained by embracing the market created an enormous wealth disparity and what was known as the 'developed' and 'developing' worlds. Attempts to create technological and economic growth without first developing economic and social freedoms have proved futile, even fatal, for they rely on force. A society based around the collective, not the individual, requires social engineering on a massive scale, and this does not tend to end well. The law of unintended consequences always comes into play.

In the 20th century, both China and the former Soviet Union tried different approaches to industrialisation. Realising that they were lagging far behind their capitalist enemies, they tried to engineer a period of accelerated growth using the communist model rather than the market model. Stalin is famously quoted as declaring that: *We are fifty or a hundred years behind the advanced countries. We must make good this distance in ten years. Either we do it, or they will crush us.*[75] In China, Mao Zedong was inspired by the Soviets' intention to catch up with the US through a programme of industrialisation and collectivism, so much so that he put forward his own objective for the People's Republic: to catch up with and surpass Britain in fifteen years. To do this, Mao decided to implement radical solutions for China's domestic weaknesses rather than rely on conservative ones; solutions he called 'The Great Leap Forward'. His ambitious mission was defined thus: *it is possible to accomplish any task whatsoever... Struggle hard for three years. Change the face of all China. Catch up with Britain and catch up with America.*

In both cases, not only did the desired transformation fail to materialise, but it resulted in millions of their people dying from starvation, oppression and execution. Around 100 million people are estimated to have died because of communist attempts at enforced social engineering and economic progress.[76] To put it into context, that's the equivalent of a 9/11-type event happening every single day for over ninety years. No collectivist starts their campaign by stating that their intention is to suppress people's rights and remove those who oppose them, but that's nearly always where it ends up. Throughout modern history, the regimes that achieved the greatest equality of outcome were also those that had the least freedoms and the most corpses. Even now those countries that continue to experiment with collectivist ideologies, such as North Korea or Venezuela, end up struggling to feed their people even if, as in Venezuela's case, they are sitting on the world's largest oil reserves.

The eventual transition from equity to oppression, and the inability of the state to artificially generate societal leaps, was understood even back in the days of Adam Smith, who declared during a 1755 lecture that *All governments... which endeavour to arrest the progress of society at a particular point, are unnatural, and to support themselves are obliged to be oppressive and tyrannical.* To paraphrase both Winston Churchill and Milton Friedman, societies that put equality before freedom eventually have their freedoms eroded, little by little, until it achieves equality in misery. Conversely, societies that put freedom before equality prosper, for freedom provides that most precious of commodities – choice – and as a result lifts the population above mere subsistence. And here lies a lesson that needs to be constantly remembered: society and economies need to evolve organically and in conjunction with each other. They need evolution, not revolution. If the architects of change – the people – are freed to share information, work together, profit from their own endeavours and have these rights protected by law, then this evolution will come, and it will come so quickly that it will seem like a revolution to those who witness it from afar.

The World Joins In

As recently as the late 20th century, nations previously defined as 'Third World' were suffering from crippling debt, hyperinflation, barely visible growth and an aura of helplessness when it came to economic efficiency. Over the past forty years, however, an ever-increasing portion of the world has embraced a more market-oriented economy, greatly accelerating both economic growth and the speed of innovation. There are two main reasons for this. The first is that many of the innovations that originated in the developed world have, over time, found their way to the developing countries. The second, even more significant cause is that many parts of the developing world have adopted a more open, market-oriented economy. The demise of the Soviet Union and the subsequent 'End of History' allowed for renewed international cooperation based upon the pillars – and promise – of democracy and free markets. In the early 1990s, the interplay of a different level of personal, societal and economic freedom brought about an era of globalisation during which the global economy expanded vigorously. In the absence of viable alternative options, the Third World projects of self-reliance and isolated development faltered. Countries such as Ghana, Brazil, China, Russia and India would soon prosper under the capitalist model. We no longer talk of First, Second and Third World nations, but of developed and emerging. The process of industrialisation in these nations is far from complete, but the rate of change is accelerating as the population see the opportunities that this environment provides. The more inclusive societies become, the more likely they are to embrace market economics in order to feed their people and experience the benefits of technological revolutions.

Those nations that adopt the market model also enjoy dramatic improvement in living standards and their social environment, which cannot be, and is not, a coincidence. As the economy grows, so does the ability of the population to purchase the goods they have been recruited to manufacture. Innovation doesn't respect boundaries, and advancements in global media communication mean that those who assemble the products also aspire to own them. This has led to many of these countries, especially China, growing far faster than the West and closing the gap in terms of wealth and health. Back in 2000, just 4 per cent of the Chinese urban population was considered middle class. By 2022 that is expected to rise to 76 per cent.[77]

Over the past two decades, the industrialisation and urbanisation of these countries and the spread of market-oriented economic policies have doubled the ranks of the consuming class to 2.4 billion people. By 2025 that number will nearly double again, to 4.2 billion consumers out of a global population of 7.9 billion people.[78] For the first time in history, the number of people in the consuming class will exceed the number still struggling to meet their most basic needs. The process of globalisation has created a new generation of consumers who have high aspirations and are willing to spend to realise them. By 2025, according to MGI estimates, annual consumption in emerging markets will rise to $30 trillion, up from $12 trillion in 2010, and account for nearly 50 per cent of the world's total, becoming the dominant force in the global economy.[79] In fifteen years' time, almost 60 per cent of the roughly 1 billion households with earnings greater than $20,000 a year will live in the developing world.[80]

The first industrial revolution took two centuries to gain full force, enabling Britain, over the course of 150 years, to double its economic output per person. The United States, driver of the second industrial revolution, took only fifty years to double its GDP per capita. A century later, when China and India industrialised, these two nations took just twelve and sixteen years respectively to achieve this. In just thirteen years, from 1978 to 1991, more than a third of the world's population went from living in a state-run economy to living in a market-driven economy. The impact this has had on their societies has been dramatic. In the last forty years, China has reduced their child mortality rate tenfold. Following decades of hard-won reforms, many of these countries have achieved a dramatic turnaround and closed the gap as they adopt the societal and economic models that enable this innovation to develop and spread, and as a result they are placed to become the new drivers of the global economy in the 21st century. The acid test will be whether they can create a society and system of control that is inclusive and innovative enough to sustain it in the long term once all the low-hanging economic fruit has been picked. It's looking positive, for China now produces more honour students every year than the US has students.

Globalisation is out of the box, and from an economic and trade perspective there appears to be no going back.[34] One very interesting element of the globalisation movement is that it is, like capitalism itself, an evolutionary system without any one entity in control of its speed or direction. This has been perceived as both a blessing and a curse. Thomas Freidman, the *New York Times* correspondent and award-winning author, describes globalisation's leaderless nature as a concern: *The most basic truth about globalisation is this: no one is in charge... we all want to believe that someone is in charge and responsible... But the global marketplace today is an Electronic Herd of often anonymous stock, bond and currency traders and multinational investors, connected by screens and networks.*[81] Conversely, Robert Hormats, former Vice Chairman of Goldman Sachs International, describes the lack of control as a benefit: *The great beauty of globalisation is that no one is in control... it is not controlled by any one individual, any government, any institution.*[82]

Regardless of the risk, industrialisation has driven nations and their people forwards. North Korea, perhaps the last great example of a totalitarian regime that has ruled with a Stalinist-style agenda for the last sixty years, must have looked over at the transformation in China with envy. The only way North Korea can remain within touching distance of the rest of the world is through developing an efficient economy, and the only way to do that is to rely on private initiative.[83] China's progress should have proven that it is possible to embrace a more market-oriented approach without having to totally sacrifice centralised control.

The world has therefore transitioned over the last few centuries from a mercantilist model where nations competed, to a capitalist model where corporations compete. The age of empires made way for the age of economics. The defining image of the world's economy is now based around the forces of capitalism; the provision of goods and services to profit the corporation. Whenever the need has been great, or the financial rewards high, inventors have appeared. The desire for profit has incentivised mankind to enhance and develop mechanisms that improve our way of life and increase productivity and efficiency. The outputs of this activity have redefined the paradigms as to what is possible, curing many of the ills that

---

[34] Although from a political perspective, the population are pushing back against the side effects of globalisation, as Brexit, Trump and the Catalonia independence movement proved.

blighted our existence, allowing us to know the unknown and improving the productive capabilities of the land.

Market power has now replaced military force as the most powerful factor in the world, flattening hierarchical societies and creating significant shifts in the image of society in some countries, creating whole new social classes and redefining the world through the process of globalisation and global trade. The first industrial revolution did all this. There was a significant cultural lag, but in the end, it spread and changed the world.

6

GALLIFREYAN ECONOMICS AND THE ART OF CREATIVE DESTRUCTION

Life's journey is built of crests and troughs;
the movement is always going to be fast only towards the trough
and the progress is bound to be slow towards the crest.

Anuj Somany

The industrial age and the market forces of capitalism have now ruled the Western world since the late 18th century. But why has it proven so resilient? The reason lies in its cyclical nature. The nature and complexity of business cycles are intrinsically linked to how capitalist economy functions, impacting not only industry and the end-to-end value chain, but also its commercial dealings and financial arrangements. These economic cycles of boom and collapse – often described as 'long cycles', are in fact 'waves', for they build upon themselves, creating new industries but having to rebalance themselves at certain times through overexpansion. The waves may wash away debts, businesses and even entire industries, but the innovations that were created remain, providing the foundation for the next wave. Understanding the nature and phases of the waves can help business leaders to understand why their old practices are not working any more, why the pace of change is changing, and why a new mindset and new business model may be required.

To understand the nature of these waves it is important to see beyond the simple boom-and-bust economics into the real causal factors that are powering them; and to do that requires travelling back to late 19th century Russia. Nikolai Dmitriyevich Kondratiev[35] was born in Kostroma, Russia, on 4th March 1892 to a peasant family. He joined the Socialist Revolutionary Party and became an agricultural economist and statistician, focusing on the problem of food supplies. After the Bolshevik October revolution, Kondratiev became active in the left-wing agrarian Socialist Revolutionary Party, and in 1920 he was appointed founding director of the Conjuncture Institute, a post he held until 1928. The prime purpose of this institute was to study capitalist crises and to predict how and when the eventual collapse of capitalism would occur. Kondratiev wrote six pieces on long waves between 1920 and 1928; all except the first and fourth were initially published in the *Economic Bulletin of the Conjuncture Institute*, which he edited. His book *The World Economy and its Condition During and After the War* was published in 1922, in which he proposed that capitalist economies were characterised by successions of expansion and decline. He detected a wave like pattern in capitalist markets of 50 to 60 years in length, during which the economy expanded and contracted. Working first with wholesale price levels in England, France and the United States, Kondratiev was convinced that his studies of economic, social and cultural life proved that a long-term order of economic behaviour existed and could be used for anticipating future developments. His analysis described how international capitalism had already experienced many 'great depressions' and as such was a regular part of the international mercantile credit system. In a 1926 paper he wrote: *Each consecutive phase [of the long wave] is a result of a cumulative process during the preceding phase, and, as long as the principles of the capitalistic economy are conserved, each new cycle follows its predecessor with the same regularity with which the different phases succeed each other.* Kondratiev managed to study only two and a half long

---

[35] Also spelled Kondratieff.

cycles, ceasing his research on the rising phase of the third. In 1925, he published his book *The Major Economic Cycles*, in which he predicted an inevitable plunge in commodity prices. He delivered his report during the falling phase of the third cycle in 1926, when its scale and length could not yet be assessed. Three years later his predictions were confirmed as the market duly collapsed and the US Great Depression took hold.

To better interpret his long-wave idea, Kondratiev studied descriptive data on capitalist nations, and in doing so he determined three empirical patterns that he suggested might help people to understand these patterns of long waves:

1. During the **Transition Phase**, the period before and during the beginning of a new cycle, the economic and business world undergoes considerable changes. These changes are usually seen in production and exchange techniques preceded by significant technical discoveries and inventions, gold-production and monetary-circulation conditions, and/or involvement of new countries in worldwide economic relations.

2. The **Rising Phase** of a long wave is characterised by a significant number of social upheavals, inequalities, disruptions and radical changes to society caused by the shifting power structures. Kondratiev wrote that: *It is during the period of the rise of long waves (during the period of high tension in the expansion of economic forces) that, as a rule, the most disastrous and extensive wars and revolutions occur.*[36]

   - The first rising phase (1770s–1815) covered the period of the American and French revolutions, the Napoleonic Wars, the conflict between Russia and Turkey and the partitioning of Poland.
   - The second wave's rising phase (1844–1875) was marked by revolutionary movements in Italy, Germany, Austria, France and Hungary; by the Crimean War; the founding of Romania; the US Civil War; the Franco-Prussian War; and the founding of the German Empire.
   - The third (1896–1920) spanned conflict or wars between Japan

[36] Only the first three waves are used as examples as they were the only ones that were included in Kondratiev's research. Since then we have seen the same trends and periods of unrest – for example, the Vietnam and Cold Wars between the fourth and fifth waves.

and China, Turkey and Greece, and Italy and Turkey; the Spanish-American War; the Anglo-Boer War; the Russo-Japanese War; the First and Second Balkan Wars; World War I; and revolutions in Russia, Turkey, China, Germany and Austro-Hungary.

This rising phase represents a period of risk-taking and investment in radical innovations that result in rapid economic growth. It is associated with the replacement and expansion of basic capital goods and with the radical regrouping of, and changes in, society's productive forces. Companies that continue to focus on efficiency, existing asset bases and protecting the status quo usually end up *not* playing a major part in this new world order, as the new way of doing things starts to replace the old. During this transition things get rough as disruption upends the status quo, creating a time of winners and losers – and losers are never OK with that role, hence the danger. This inequality also leads to the fighting and elimination of long-standing inequalities, such as overthrowing monarchies and obtaining female suffrage and civil rights, so not all changes are negative. But they are all disruptive.

3. The **Downward Wave Phase** is characterised by prolonged periods of stagnation leading to serious depressions as focus moves from investment in the real economy of infrastructure, industry and innovations, to focusing on efficiencies, maintaining market share and financial vehicles. During this time the level of debt rises, and capitalism's dark side takes over, spurred by greed and a desire to make easy money from debt, expectations and derivatives. The hedge fund, not the entrepreneur, becomes the agent of growth. This world of finance always overreaches, for it is greed-driven, creating unsustainable debt bubbles that eventually burst, creating a financial crash, which leads to a prolonged recession.

If we were to pick up Kondratiev's research and project the long waves and related phases that existed post World War I, then they would appear as per Diagram 2. The cycle of the waves was obviously affected by the major economic shocks caused by the First and Second World Wars, especially World War II, which devastated not only the population and infrastructure of Europe, but also its economies (but which correspondingly provided

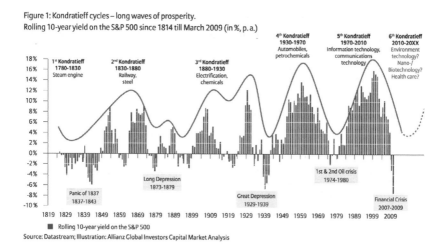

Figure 1: Kondratieff cycles – long waves of prosperity.
Rolling 10-year yield on the S&P 500 since 1814 till March 2009 (in %, p. a.)

Source: Datastream; Illustration: Allianz Global Investors Capital Market Analysis

Diagram 1: Kondratiev Waves 1814–2011

a massive post-war stimulus to the US economy that had come out of recession in the late 1930s).[84] After the Second World War rationing was lifted, the US economy started a golden age and production was rededicated to consumer products that people were desperate to buy in order to replace their rusty automobiles and broken refrigerators.

In summary, at the beginning of each new Kondratiev wave, entrepreneurs usually require a considerable amount of capital to buy the new innovative means of production, be that a steam engine, an assembly line or an IT system. Higher interest rates are not a barrier here, as entrepreneurs can increase their earnings by implementing more productive systems. However, as time passes, and the new innovations begin to offer diminishing returns on investment, the demand for credit slows down and (real) interest rates move toward zero. This was the case in the Panic of 1837, the Long Depression of 1873, the Great Depression in 1929 and the oil crises of 1974 and 1980, and where we've been since the financial crisis of 2008. These periods then give way to a new rising phase where inventions turn into innovations, enabling capital owners to win big through investing in high growth opportunities and new businesses, while elsewhere wages stagnate. As a result, a period of high social tensions and public protests arise, ranging from the French Revolution to conflicts in Vietnam, the anti-war and civil rights movements of the late '60s through to the Occupy movement and Black Bloc activists in the recent financial crisis.

To Kondratiev, the alleged causes of this disruption were neither exogenous nor random – they were simply part of the regular rhythms of the long wave, and as such were obedient to and characteristic of it. The long wave is driven, he believed, by a set of self-correcting processes that are inherent to capitalism. Boom periods are naturally followed by periods where the global economy must 'reload' by getting rid of the over-accumulated capital through massive devaluation and an inevitable and lengthy recession. From this scorched earth new businesses sprout, creating a period of rapid growth throughout a spring period. Spring gives way to a period of great returns during a summer period, where the reaping of the earlier investments takes place. Summer gives way to autumn, when business becomes tougher and more cost focused, and as a result capital looks for better returns elsewhere. Finally, an economic winter arrives and the market collapses into recession and depression. Kondratiev concluded his work by saying that, *the historical material relating to the development of economic and social life as a whole conforms to the hypothesis of long waves.* Implicit in Kondratiev's work was the inescapable conclusion that, while capitalism has significant periods of prosperity and depression, with all their profound social implications, it always renews itself and, as such, it offers mankind the best hope for economic betterment.

Kondratiev's hypothesis that long waves are an organic part of the capitalist system and that any crises are self-correcting was unsurprisingly not well received by his communist masters. This was not his brief. His mission had been to discredit capitalism and prove the Marxist belief that the Great Depression represented capitalism in its death throes, not to report back that it was capable of continued self-regeneration like Doctor Who.[37] Orthodox Marxists, believing history to be unidirectional and linear, had forecasted the imminent collapse of capitalism 'next day', and viewed Schumpeter's renewal theory of capitalism as treacherous heresy; a direct assault on Joseph Stalin's intentions for the Soviet economy. Kondratiev's Soviet critics argued that the long waves were created by external circumstances such as inventions, wars, revolutions, international migrations, the assimilation of new countries into the world economy, and fluctuations in world gold production. They were not, *and could not be*, part of the normal cycle of things. In their minds capitalism was not a cure, it was a disease; one that

---

[37] Hence the 'Gallifreyan Economics' subheading, in case you didn't get it...

would soon be eradicated. Capitalism, they said, has internal contradictions that prevent self-renewal, and it must be a system that is doomed to fail. Kondratiev's response to this was clear: *These considerations... are not valid. Their weakness lies in the fact that they reverse the causal connections and take the consequence to bethel cause, or see an accident where we really have to deal with the law governing the events.*

Many an ugly truth spoils a beautiful theory, and much was invested in the theory of capitalism's imminent death. To silence him, Kondratiev was immediately declared a heretic, removed as director of the Conjuncture Institute, which was then dissolved, and his work buried. As always, the victors get to rewrite history, and in 1928, the *Soviet Russian Encyclopaedia* declared that the long-wave idea was a *vulgar bourgeois theory of crises and economic cycles. The concept of a long cycle in theory is directed against the basic Marxist thesis concerning the inevitability of economic crises under capitalism, and it conceals the unsolvable contradiction of capitalist society.* Kondratiev then became one of several academic economists who were arrested during the purges of the early 1930s because of their opposition to the economic policies of Joseph Stalin. Charged with the trumped-up crime of heading an illegal 'Working Peasants' Party',[38] he was sentenced to the Gulag, where he was put into solitary confinement. Although his health deteriorated under poor conditions, Kondratiev continued his research and in a letter to his wife informed her he was working on five new books. He didn't get to finish them. In September 1938, during Stalin's Great Purge, Kondratiev was subjected to a second trial and sentenced to ten years' isolated imprisonment. It was a sentence he never had to serve, for he was executed the very same day.[85] He was just forty-six years old. Yet his work on business cycles lived on, finding its way out of the Soviet Union and into the hands of an Austrian economist named Joseph Schumpeter.

---

[38] Allegedly a non-existent party that was invented by the People's Commissariat for Internal Affairs and used simply as a mechanism during Stalin's Great Purge to give the pretence of treason where none existed. The Great Purge was called 'our sewage disposal system' by Aleksandr Solzhenitsyn, in his Nobel Peace Prize-winning book *The Gulag Archipelago*, where he described the other great holocaust of the 20th century, the imprisonment, torture and murder of tens of millions of innocent Soviet citizens by their own government, mostly during Stalin's rule from 1929 to 1953. During Stalin's Great Purge it is estimated that 1,000 executions a day took place.

Creative Destruction

Joseph A. Schumpeter, once Austria's Minister of Finance and later a professor at Harvard University, is defined by many people, including Peter Drucker, as one of the most influential economists of the 20th century. In the 1930s he undertook detailed research of the economic histories of England, Germany and the United States, and his findings provided strong empirical support for the idea of long waves. He was also instrumental in raising Kondratiev's profile outside of Russia, writing in 1939 that: *It was N. D. Kondratieff who brought the phenomenon fully before the scientific community and who systematically analysed all the material available to him on the assumption of the presence of a Long Wave, characteristic of the capitalist process.*[86] Schumpeter's recognition of Kondratiev's work has led to these waves becoming named 'K-waves'.

While Kondratiev had identified 'what' happens in market-driven societies, Schumpeter set out to establish 'why'. In his 1927 paper, *The Explanation of the Business Cycle*, and again in his seminal work *Capitalism, Socialism and Democracy*, Schumpeter developed a theory of business cycles that emphasises the importance of innovations and entrepreneurship. Schumpeter had already concluded that savings and investment were mere quantitative expressions of demographic growth, and he sought an explanation for the qualitative shifts that defined its development. He focused on perhaps the most important of Kondratiev's observations: the fact that during the long-wave recession period, an especially large number of important discoveries and inventions in the technique of production and communication are developed, but that they must wait for the right economic conditions, i.e. the next wave's upswing, before they can be implemented on a large scale. This theory also supported the observations of Karl Marx in *Grundrisse*, where he establishes a necessary link between the creative forces of production in capitalism and the destruction of capital value as one of the key ways in which capitalism attempts to overcome its internal contradictions *The violent destruction of capital not by relations external to it, but rather as a condition of its self-preservation... These contradictions lead to explosions, cataclysms, crises, in which... momentous suspension of labour and annihilation of a great portion of capital... violently lead it back to the point where it is enabled [to go on] fully employing its productive powers without committing suicide.*[87] Traditionally economists viewed the periodic crises that continually rocked capitalist economies as external and exceptional events that disrupted what would otherwise be stable and smoothly functioning markets. Schumpeter however, argued the contrary, agreeing with Marx's and Kondratiev's view that these crises were not exogenous but an essential feature of capitalism; internal regulators of capitalist development and the driving force behind its dynamic nature and continued growth. He declared that technical innovation, *the setting up of a new production function*, was in fact the main catalyst behind what he termed the process of 'creative destruction'.[39]

According to Christopher Freeman, a scholar who has devoted significant amounts of time to researching Schumpeter's work, *the central point of his whole life's work [is]: that capitalism can only be understood as an evolutionary process of continuous innovation and 'creative destruction'.*[88] He saw the lost jobs, bankrupted companies, replaced technologies and vanishing industries as an inherent part of the growth system, a necessary evil to allow progress to continue. The hero in Schumpeter's theory is the entrepreneur, arguing that economic change revolves around innovation, entrepreneurial activities and market power. Schumpeter saw a normal, healthy economy as not being in equilibrium, but instead being constantly disrupted by technological innovation. The entrepreneur, Schumpeter argued, is not a rational, utility-maximising actor, merely responding to price signals to trade his goods more efficiently. He is a disruptor, an innovator, a visionary, an artist and a doer. It is the entrepreneur's dislike of the pettiness of the zero-sum game of price competition, cost-cutting and market share battles that allows him to focus on designing products that create the future markets. Schumpeter argued that it was the entrepreneur's introduction of radical innovations into the market that was the real force behind long-term economic growth, even if it destroyed the economic value of established companies. Whereas Marx focused on the destructive power of capitalism, Schumpeter focused on the creative, and the relationship between the two. He saw that societies that allowed 'creative destruction' to operate grew more productive and richer, whereas those that tried to suppress it stagnated and its people remained poor.

Schumpeter sought to prove that innovation-originated market power could provide more progress and social benefits than mere price

---

[39] Also known as 'Schumpeter's Gales'.

112

competition and Adam Smith's 'invisible hand'. The essence of capitalism is the idea of capitalising; bringing forward the future value of money to the present so that society can grow more quickly by taking risks. It goes all the way back to the coffee houses of London and Amsterdam, where men of invention, investment and industry came together, loaning each other money in the hope of beneficial return. From here, the concept of equity was invented, the net present value of future earnings, enabling and encouraging investment in innovations that shaped the future.

Schumpeter's theory combines the following two basic hypotheses:

1. The development of radical innovations generates consumer demand and economic growth, which creates new, rapidly growing industries that require new infrastructure and new resources such as labour, creating jobs, incomes and more demand.[40]
2. These radical innovations do not remain isolated events and are not evenly distributed in time but tend to cluster in bunches during periods of economic stagnation, creating *an especially large number of important discoveries and inventions in the technique of production and communication.* As these innovations become proven and adopted, then other firms embrace them to keep up. Innovations are therefore unevenly distributed over the economic system, tending to concentrate in certain sectors at certain times, usually as the result of the development of a new and innovative power source, communication mechanism, transportation method and industry. These periods create sudden upward spikes in both our knowledge and our technological capabilities.

Schumpeter saw the entrepreneur as the disturber of the status quo and thus the prime catalyst for economic development, which he viewed as proceeding in a cyclical fashion. An entrepreneur's innovations are not limited to the application of new inventions; they could be the adaptation of ideas from other societies or the removal of limitations from existing innovations.

The technology diffusion process, as this set of interactive phenomena is often referred to, thus becomes quite central to any complete theory

---

[40] The period we have just entered.

of long waves, as we will explore in the next chapter. The distribution of a particular technological innovation follows an S-shaped curve due to the diffusion process. Early versions of the innovation tend to be rather unsuccessful but are rapidly followed by re-engineered and redesigned versions that are picked up and evangelised over by a passionate group of early adopters. Their promotion of the innovation leads – if it crosses the chasm – to expansion, eventually resulting in high adoption throughout the market. This is then followed by an inevitable flattening of demand and finally a dropping off in sales as a technology reaches its maximum potential in the market or is replaced by the next innovation. Efficiency rather than entrepreneurship becomes the main driver of economic growth, ultimately ending in overexploitation, decline and recession.

The identification of technological innovations as the primary catalyst of the creative destruction process refines Kondratiev's understanding of the nature of the waves, enabling an expansion of the wave's phases as follows:

Innovation Phase (Upswing)

Periods that contain the highest concentration of technological innovations are labelled 'technological revolutions', creating new profit opportunities for those with the capability to spot them and the money to invest. However, the nature of creative destruction means that these new opportunities are typically at the cost of existing industries. An entrepreneurial company that introduces a new product or service to the market may initially create excitement and sales, and its uniqueness enables it to be sold at a healthy profit. This has been a feature of technological progress since the start of the industrial revolution. Schumpeter argues that technological innovation can often create temporary monopolies that allow companies to achieve abnormal profits, but he also recognises that in a free market these profits can be quickly competed away by rivals and imitators. We have seen this recently with companies like Uber, who for a brief period held a monopoly on ride-sharing, but saw that monopoly challenged by other companies such as Lyft. Schumpeter stated that these temporary monopolies were necessary, like patents, to provide the competitive incentive required for firms to develop new products and processes. When the innovation is new and limited to a small set of early adopters, a nation's GDP is not dramatically affected. While the companies and entrepreneurs that created the innovation often become rich, the impact is not felt in the wider economy.

Application Phase (Economic Boom/Golden Age)

During this stage a flurry of applications, improvements, refinements and spin-offs occurs as knowledge and feedback from the early adopters is received. As time progresses, more and more competitors enter the market, improving on the original innovation and creating more value, and the initial entrepreneur often loses out if they do not continue to improve their offering.[41] These are highly competitive periods where organisations look to utilise these new technological innovations to 'out-compete' their rivals. If the industry sector is large enough, this feeding frenzy of investment and improved performance may create an economic revival – think of the Japanese car industry in the 1970s–1990s. However, at a certain moment a tipping point occurs, and the profitability from these new innovations and new areas declines to the baseline level acquired from older traditional industries. During this process, the number of companies the market can sustain is determined. The winning companies, those with a strong business model, product USP and clearly defined consumer base, claim the majority of the market, while the losers fall to the wayside.

Adoption and Diffusion Phase

The wave now enters a period of widespread technological adoption and diffusion, where these radical innovations are followed by more routine improvements that serve to rationalise production and increase the capital intensity. There are two responses to the now-excess level of supply: either reduce competition by product differentiation and industrial mergers or attempt to segment domestic and foreign markets to dispose of excess output. During this time there is a rise in incremental 'pseudo-innovation' which benefits neither buyer nor seller. These forms of product differentiation, usually in the form of rebranding or packaging updates, or at best, minor increases in product functionality,

---

[41] Example: RIM and the BlackBerry phone.

exist simply for the primary aim of protecting market share. Excellent examples of this can be found throughout the consumer industry, such as extra blades or lubrication strips on razors, or the proliferation of different types of toothpaste, each with different packaging, lids and ingredients. These simply confuse the shopper, cannibalise existing sales and expand the product portfolio without any discernible increase in sales. The only things that increase are complexity, supply-chain disruptions and waste.

Saturation Phase

Eventually these innovations fall foul of the law of diminishing returns, resulting in a deceleration in growth and a flattening of demand. Once the pie has stopped growing, the battle is on as to who owns the biggest – or most profitable – slice. Corporations overestimate the growth potential and produce excess supply, creating heated competition and over investment in the now-not-so-new technology. Price becomes the primary focus with only incremental improvements to the product or service. Markets become saturated and any new capital investment brings only an average level of profit. There is a flurry of mergers and acquisition activity by desperate CEOs attempting to generate value for shareholders without the hard thinking of coming up with new innovations or business models. These often excite investors, but they shouldn't as when looked at objectively each merger or takeover represents a loss of economic activity. In the vast majority of cases it is the company being sold, not the buyer, who gets the most value from this process.[42]

During this depression, excess capital is worn out and fully depreciated. Defaults and bankruptcies clean out the excess debt load and the economy then enters a period where output stagnates. Large organisations seek to maintain the appearance of growth to their shareholders by cutting costs and raising prices, thereby inducing stagflation, a 'delightful' combination of high inflation rates, low economic growth and high unemployment. During this period, there

---

[42] The poster child for disastrous M&A's is the 2001 AOL and Time Warner merger that went south so quickly that within 24 hours it led to a $45 billion write-down to reflect the "declining value of its flagship America Online property", ultimately resulting in a $100 billion yearly loss, the largest in corporate history at that point.

is an increasing level of market protectionism, with a corresponding over-concentration in leading industries that sets in motion a price death spiral. As rates of return decline, capital stops being reinvested in existing lines of business and moves from industry into financial speculation. Investment in risky new ventures or radical new inventions is minimised, creating a technological winter.

Rebirth Phase

As the returns in older, established industries are all but eliminated, new venture capital becomes available, seeking new high-growth investment opportunities. Within companies wedded to an efficiency mindset, energy continues to be focused on the short-term zero-sum game of price wars and decreasing profitability merely to protect market share and revenue. Outside of these firms, the appearance of new funds results in a stampede of entrepreneurial activity to convert many of the new scientific and industrial inventions into profitable products or services. A new cluster of innovations precipitates another long-term growth upswing, attracting capital and labour away from the old, stagnant sectors and stimulating demand for new kinds of goods and services. An army of new business ventures arises to take advantage of the potential of these new technologies, leading to a structural transformation of the economy. Existing organisations with visionary leaders work to create a sense of crisis in order to incentivise their employees to think outside the current paradigms and sue the new innovations to create new ways to deliver value to customers. Another cycle begins.

Schumpeter concluded that economic development involves the periodic destruction of the capitalist production system and its creative renewal; a cycle of growth, maturity and destruction followed by regrowth, by new innovations that lift the economy to a higher plane of development. He argued that the real driver behind economic growth is the entrepreneur's introduction of radical innovations into the capitalist system, for they create new technologies, products, businesses and industries, but in doing so destroy old ones, which themselves may be eventually replaced as better innovations appear. Hence 'creative destruction'.

Schumpeter's viewpoint is not dissimilar to that of Karl Marx, whose views he examined at length in his book *Capitalism, Socialism and Democracy*. In *The Communist Manifesto of 1848*, Marx (along with Friedrich Engels) described the creative-destructive nature of capitalism: *The bourgeoisie cannot exist without constantly revolutionising the instruments of production, and thereby the relations of production, and with them the whole relations of society*. Marx also foresaw the expansion of capitalism across the world and the globalisation movement: *The need of a constantly expanding market for its products chases the bourgeoisie over the entire surface of the globe. It must nestle everywhere, settle everywhere, establish connexions everywhere... The bourgeoisie, by the rapid improvement of all instruments of production, by the immensely facilitated means of communication, draws all, even the most barbarian, nations into civilisation.*[89] Schumpeter saw the lost jobs, bankrupted companies and vanishing industries as an inherent part of the growth system. Marx thought they spelt the end of capitalism, when the bourgeoisie becomes *like the sorcerer, who is no longer able to control the powers of the nether world whom he has called up by his spells.* Marx believed capitalism was doomed because either the rewards from capital would become concentrated into too few hands and the workers would rise up in revolution, or capital would fail to provide enough growth and violent conflict would arise amongst the capitalists themselves. Neither scenario has yet come to pass, for Marx failed to appreciate just how powerful the cyclical, rejuvenating nature of capitalism was; something Schumpeter recognised and gave name to.

Silk Stockings to Smartphones

Each technological revolution – be that steam, electricity or the Internet – introduced a wave of productivity improvements accompanied by market disruption, leading to slow-to-adapt industrial leaders being displaced by the rise of agile new competitors. For example, textile factories replaced cottage weavers, automotive production destroyed the horse-and-buggy industry, personal computers replaced the need for typewriters, digital music destroyed CDs, and now the Internet has severely damaged traditional media. Schumpeter declared that this process, what he called 'creative destruction' was the *essential fact about capitalism*.[90] He believed that major innovations come not so much from older, established firms but from new upstarts, led by 'new men'. Whereas old companies are generally conservative in both thinking and action, the newer firms are leaner and hungrier, looking to find new markets or opportunities to exploit. Old companies are driven by old businessmen working within limiting boundaries, making decisions about profitability with the foresight provided by well-worn channels; 'the repetition of acts of routine', of focusing on operational efficiency and cost-cutting. Innovations, on the other hand, come from new organisations working outside these channels, operating with a new mindset and new rules. These 'new men' have the potential to disrupt and even replace the market that the 'old men' believe they fully understand and expect to last. They are often wrong, and their short-term mindset and inability to adapt at speed proves their undoing. The downside for those companies caught in the whirlwind of creative destruction is that they had probably been living a profitable and comfortable existence for decades, only to suddenly find their business model destroyed by a new innovation or new way of doing business. Complacency and a failure to adapt business models to changing technologies and consumer trends can result in companies that were once market leaders becoming defunct or a mere shadow of their former selves. Recent examples include Kodak, Research in Motion (RIM), Radio Shack, Blockbuster, Polaroid, Woolworths, Myspace and ToysRus. Yet despite the destruction of the incumbent businesses, the net economic benefit created by these new entrepreneurs has always proven to be greater than if the status quo had been retained. If it were not for the process of creative destruction, growth would stall, and the markets would fall into permanent decline.

Countries that enable creative destruction are more productive, advance faster and grow richer than those that suppress it. Trying to preserve jobs or protect industries that are being 'creatively destroyed' is often a fruitless task, and simply leads to stagnation and wasted investment, diverting focus away from the advancement of progress. It is understandable for governments to try and prevent the economic and social disruption caused by the process, especially during the transition and upswing periods when wealth inequalities grow. Those with capital can invest in the new industries and new innovations, whereas those with only their labour see their wages stagnate, or worse, are displaced, creating a group of angry and disenfranchised people. While the players at the financial casino may lose their chips in a financial crash, it always seems to be the doormen and cleaners who end up losing their jobs. However, so long as the perceived value of the new innovations is greater than those they replace, net economic growth occurs as resources flow from the least to the most efficient industries, new jobs are created, goods become more affordable, and society moves forward. As Schumpeter himself highlights, the long-term benefactors of capitalist forces are not the rich, for they can already afford anything they want, but the poor. *Electric lighting is no great boon to anyone who has enough money to buy a sufficient number of candles and to pay servants to attend them. It is the cheap cloth, the cheap cotton and rayon fabric, boots, motorcars and so on that are the typical achievements of capitalist production, and not as a rule improvements that would mean much to the rich man. Queen Elizabeth owned silk stockings. The capitalist achievement does not typically consist in providing more silk stockings for queens but in bringing them within reach of factory girls.*[91] Likewise the current wave of creative destruction has put smartphones – a product unavailable to anyone 15 years ago – into the hands of people in even the poorest of countries. The true nature of wealth is therefore not money, but rather what you can acquire with that money.

Capitalism, based on the theories of Kondratiev and Schumpeter, and more importantly, as seen by historical evidence, is thus a method of economic change that will never be stationary or linear. As Schumpeter himself declared, *the essential point to grasp is that in dealing with capitalism we are dealing with an evolutionary process.*[92] This evolutionary aspect explains why communist and collectivist systems always seem to get old and decay, while capitalist societies continually grow and reinvent their means of production. The constant 'creative destruction' nature of capitalism, the renewal and clearing away of bad debts, bad companies and bad products, and the subsequent rebuilding of the economy didn't happen in Soviet Russia. Their bad industries, bad products and bad debts all remained. Products from their state industries were infamous for their poor quality and unreliability, and they only had a market because there was no competition. Whilst they had full employment through utilising the efforts of every able working person, they didn't generate innovative products or services as a result of this effort. The fuel that keeps the capitalist engine in motion comes from the development of new consumer goods, new methods of production or transportation, new markets and new innovations. This constant reinvention revolutionises the economic structure from within, incessantly destroying old businesses while also creating new ones. Despite its bad press, capitalism has been a force for social good, having a bigger and more positive impact than any other system tried to date, lifting billions of people out of poverty, helping to educate them and raising expectations that they can aspire to create a life for themselves and their families above simple survival. It will continue to do so, as long as our leaders continue to recalibrate any undesirable technological, social and economic outliers.

Stronger, Faster, Higher

Schumpeter's theory of entrepreneurs and their innovations being the primary force behind these waves of 'creative destruction' has been reinforced by current economists such as LSE professor Carlota Perez, as well as a growing weight of evidence showing that new innovations are concentrated in the upswing and decrease in the down. For example, a 2011 Russian research paper clearly identified that *steady increases in the number of patent grants per million during K-wave A-phases ("upswings"), and...rather pronounced decreases during K-wave B-phases ("downswings").*[93] Everything works out well if the 'creative' element of creative destruction is larger and more wealth- and job-generating than the corresponding 'destruction' element is destructive. The key to economic success is to be able to make the peaks higher and longer lasting while making the crashes smaller and shorter.

As we'll discuss in the next chapter, a delay exists between the arrival of new technologies and their impact on productivity and on society. In the first K-waves, the rate of technological diffusion was slow, reflecting the time it took for new technologies to diffuse through society and find widespread use. Innovations diffuse slowly when they are spread by horseback. However, the time between the emergence of new technologies and their disruptive impact being felt has been visibly shortening with every wave. There are four forces causing this acceleration:

1. Constant shortening of time periods between technological waves (Frequency).
2. Increase in the amount of innovation per wave (Impact).

3. Increase in the speed at which innovation spreads across society and national boundaries (Diffusion).
4. Increase in the number of countries impacted by innovation due to globalisation (Scope).

One person who has researched this acceleration is Daniel Šmihula.[94] Like Schumpeter and Perez, Šmihula identifies technological revolutions as the force behind the K-waves. However, he expands on Schumpeter's theory by highlighting that the time spans of these waves are shortening with every single wave, while their impact is heightening. Using empirical data, he formulated a hypothesis that there is a certain regularity in this process of shortening, proposing that the length of each new wave is about two thirds of the previous one. Interestingly, his hypothesis also includes the observation that the length of the upswing phase represents about 50–65 per cent of the wave's entire duration. This suggests that companies should focus on developing the skills and technologies to thrive in these entrepreneurial periods, and not just the times of efficiency and exploitation. This is perhaps one of the most fundamental lessons from all this research: companies that continue to innovate form part of the creative forces of the wave, and if they fail to innovate they become part of its destruction.

The increasing size and scope of the waves is understandable when you look at the technologies, geographies and population involved. Each wave involves more countries and therefore more consumers and more entrepreneurs. The technologies involved are also building upon the foundations left by the previous waves, rather than starting from a blank slate, and are becoming less physical in nature and easier to diffuse. It took fifty-one years for James Watt to improve on Thomas Newcomen's atmospheric pump via the development of the steam engine. In contrast, it took just ten years for Apple to progress from the iMac G3 to the iPhone 4, which had nearly three times the processing capability in something only a fraction of the size and only a third of the cost. This acceleration in technological development was explored by futurist Ray Kurzweil in his 1999 book *The Age of Spiritual Machines*, where he proposed 'The Law of Accelerating Returns'. Kurzweil believes that whenever a technology approaches some form of barrier, a new technology will be invented to allow us to overcome it. The law is based upon the observation that the creation of advanced technologies provides a foundation on which even more advanced technologies can be developed, creating exponential levels of progress and a geometric expansion of knowledge. The new effectively enables the next.

Recalibration or Revolution?

One of the other important long-wave aspects is that there are two boom periods: a 'winner takes all' period at the innovation phase, and a wider spreading of bounty at the application and diffusion stage. Carlota Perez highlights that *every technological revolution has brought two types of prosperity. The first type is turbulent and exciting like the bubbles of the 1990s and 2000s, and like the roaring 20's, railway mania and canal manias that went before. They all ended in a bubble collapse. Yet, after the recession, there came the second type: the Victorian boom, the Belle Époque, the Post War Golden Age and... the one that we could have ahead now. Bubble prosperities polarise incomes; Golden Ages tend to reverse the process.*[43] A period of recalibration is therefore required to ensure that the 'winner takes all' period doesn't become too exclusive, leading to a breakdown in social relations between the winners and the losers and preventing us reaching the golden age. This recalibration process forms an essential part of the wave cycle, needed to curb the initial disparities and any social issues caused by the new innovations. Society, its rules, regulations and political policies must adjust in relation to advancements in technology and economics in order for inequality to be addressed and a new golden age to arrive that benefits everyone. There is a lot of historical evidence that once inequalities are brought to the fore, numerous steps are taken to recalibrate the finely tuned relationship between economic, technological and social activities. Regardless of whether the driver is competitive pressure, government legislation or just moral and social responsibility, time and again we have adapted our behaviours and our policies to respond to the negative scenarios once they are (a) understood, and (b) deemed socially unacceptable. From the improvement of working conditions, improved sanitation and healthcare, provision of a welfare state, tighter regulation of

---

[43] C. Perez: *The New Technological Revolution*: transcript from presentation at the Technology Frontiers Forum of *The Economist*. 5 March 2013. http://www. carlotaperez.org/downloads/media/Perez_Economist_Technology_Frontiers.pdf

banks and their lending behaviours, and increased fuel efficiency and carbon reduction in motor vehicles, the state has had to intervene to mitigate the factors that led to the bust and ensure that they don't happen again. But it takes social pressure to do this – hence the interplay between society and economy. This is going to be one of the problems moving forwards – the technocrats will develop incredible technology for economic gain, but in the short term it potentially increases the level of wealth disparity, creating huge winners but also a significant number of losers. Yet throughout our recent history we have seen examples of how societal pressure can force a recalibration to ensure that the commons are protected, and the lives of the majority, not just the winners, are improved.

Wealth inequality is another reoccurring theme that appears to be part of the cyclical process of the waves. It is created during the transition and upswing periods of the long wave and act as signals to recalibrate in order to ensure a solid foundation for the next stage of the wave – one based on the real economy that involves labour as well as capital. In short, inequality is telling you that society is veering towards exclusivity, and a return to a more inclusive paradigm needs to be made to allow the cycle to continue without tipping over into social unrest or discord. Economists like Simon Kuznets have hypothesised that in a developing economy, inequality is a natural phenomenon of the wave structure of capitalist markets, and that market forces first increase and then decrease the level of economic inequality, as measured by the Gini index (or Gini coefficient – both named after the Italian statistician and sociologist Corrado Gini). However, some form of societal and economic recalibration is always needed to curb the excesses, adjust to the new reality and ensure that the common good is upheld. While technology may raise the bar, society requires a robust and level platform to ensure most of its population can clear it. Even back in 1776 at the very start of the first capitalist wave, the forefather of economics, Adam Smith, appreciated the need for government intervention in order to recalibrate to ensure there are more winners than losers: *in every improved and civilized society this is the state into which the labouring poor, that is, the great body of the people, must necessarily fall, unless government takes some pains to prevent it.*[95] This recalibration can take many forms, from the first- and second-wave implementation of labour laws to prevent exploitation and child labour and protect workers' rights, through to the third-wave recalibrations after the Great Depression when the Roosevelt administration instituted the 'New Deal', a series of economic programmes based around the Three 'R's: **Relief** for the unemployed and poor, **Recovery** of the economy to normal levels, and **Reform** of the financial system. Inevitably it is those with only their labour to sell who always end up getting burnt the most, and if the system veers too far in favour of the oligarchs, rent-seekers and capital owners, society becomes unbalanced, causing periods of inequality and unrest.

Recalibration is also required to prevent the destruction of the commons, be they natural resources or now, in the digital age, information-based ones. The downside of a competition-driven market is that companies invest in innovations regardless of any consequences further down the line. Individual companies pursue profit maximisation and often fail to see, or worse, care about, the wider implications of their actions. They don't worry about sustainability because they do not personally bear the cost of pollution, and they overspend on automation because they don't personally bear the cost of unemployment. The state therefore needs to get involved in protecting the commons through a mix of providing incentives to produce socially useful innovations and legislation to prevent harmful ones. Recent examples of the latter include the banning of microbeads in cosmetic products, as although they may cause a healthy glow to your face and cleaner teeth, they ultimately end up polluting the oceans and killing their inhabitants. One welcome new trend is that the market itself is helping companies to remember their wider social responsibilities. The ability to instantly highlight information about unethical practices to millions of people enables consumers to create group pressure on corporations by advocating that people boycott them or purchase products and services from more ethical competitors.

For capitalism to ensure that it remains a positive influence on the world, this process of recalibration is essential in order to ensure it works for everyone, not just the capital owners. Even bastions of free market economics such as Friedrich Hayek understood that the role of the government was not to do nothing when its population were disadvantaged by forces outside of their individual control, writing in *The Road to Serfdom* that: *Wherever communal action can mitigate disasters against which the individual can neither attempt to guard himself nor make provision for the consequences, such communal action should undoubtedly be taken.*[96] The level of that intervention is an often-debated topic, with perspectives ranging from Ayn Randian libertarians all the way across the political spectrum to the anti-capitalist Marxists. The key concern for Hayek, which I agree with, is ensuring that these recalibrations and any new legislation are unbiased, predictable and neutral (basically, free of bias toward corporate interests over the protection of individual rights or the commons). As he writes, *[W]ith respect to most of the general and permanent rules which the state may establish with regard to production, such as building regulations or factory laws: these may be wise or unwise in the particular instance, but they do not conflict with liberal principles so long as they are intended to be permanent and are not used to favor or harm particular people.*[97]

Given capitalism's need for an inclusive society in order to exist, the democratic process is essential in ensuring that the state acts to recalibrate the system using its legislative and economic powers in order to maintain stability. In inclusive societies the happiness of the people is important because they are needed to power the nation's financial and industrial engine, generate goods and services of value, consume these goods, and pay taxes. The fact that the industrial endeavours of the population are required in order to generate the nation's wealth empowers the common folk, a fact that the serfs of Europe came to realise after the Black Death. People in inclusive societies have to feel that society works for them as well as for the people in charge, or else they could withhold their labour or their taxes, and everything would grind to a halt. The population's leverage as producer, taxpayer, voter and consumer ensures that their voices are heard.[44] As a result, the state has to ensure that inequalities or injustices that are deemed to be unfair are both recognised and addressed. Looking at the events of the past 250 years what becomes apparent is that those societies that recalibrate end up experiencing an industrial revolution, whereas those that don't run the risk of a very different kind of revolution. Which means that one of the greatest challenges facing our political institutions is their ability to adapt to the increasing rate of change. In the first industrial revolution labour laws and social adaptation took place over decades – now it needs to happen in months. As we will discuss in Part Three, this is getting harder to achieve without compromising the very freedoms that enable the waves to exist.

---

[44] This is going to be important moving forwards when the world of work becomes automated. What use are people who do not work to the ruling elites? To be discussed further in Part Three.

The Engine of Progress

The combined theories of Kondratiev, Schumpeter, Šmihula, Perez, Kuznets and Kurzweil all point to the same conclusions: firstly, our future evolution is intrinsically tied to our ability to innovate; secondly, innovation is driven by the forces of capitalist economics; thirdly, our level of innovative capability – and its diffusion and societal impact – is increasing at an exponential rate; and finally, our ability to adapt to this increasing pace is essential to ensure that society as a whole benefits. The nature of innovations is that they disrupt; the process of creating new industries cannot go forward without also sweeping away the pre-existing order. The old skills, established throughout the previous wave and around which careers, education and training are based, are displaced and a drastic need for new skills arises. Like innovation, destruction comes in levels, from incremental destruction, which replaces a process, through to substantial destruction, which changes the way business is conducted, and finally transformational destruction, which disrupts or destroys the traditional business model. As we will explore in the following chapters, the increasing speed, scope and impact of these forces in the sixth wave will require an equally responsive reaction to ensure there is more creation than destruction.

Schumpeter's enduring term, creative destruction, is there to remind us that capitalism's pain and gain are inextricably linked – but it's a lesson we never seem to learn. While every generation wants to believe that growth is everlasting, an understanding of long-wave theory helps explain why the transition from golden age to recession and depression is as natural to an economic cycle as the budding of new shoots and the falling of leaves are to the seasons of the year. The problem is that we always live in the here and now. The length of the waves means that a person only experiences one in their working lifetime and could potentially serve out most of their working life in just an upswing or a downswing. This means that whenever people experience a wave transition period, they believe that what they are going through is unique and new. It's not. While the technologies may be new, the trend isn't, a factor people continually forget. As Georg Wilhelm Friedrich Hegel once declared, *what experience and history teaches us is that people and governments have never learned anything from history, or acted on principles deduced from it.*[98]

7

UNDERSTANDING INNOVATION: GRADUALLY, THEN SUDDENLY

From destruction, a new spirit of creation arises; the scarcity of wood and the needs of everyday life... forced the discovery or invention of substitutes for wood, forced the use of coal for heating, forced the invention of coke for the production of iron.[99]

Werner Sombart, German economist and sociologist, 1913

The rise and fall of the long waves is probably familiar to those who understand the diffusion of innovations, for these capitalist waves are driven by the same forces, only on a larger scale. The diffusion of innovation theory, popularised by Everett Rogers in his 1962 book *Diffusion of Innovations*, seeks to explain how, why and at what rate new ideas and technology spread throughout society.[100] Rogers proposed that diffusion is the method by which an innovation is communicated and spread throughout society, and how different groups of people either embrace a new technology, wait until it has become well-recognised, or only adopt if they have to. The different groups Rogers identified, and their representation in society, is as follows:

- **Innovators** are risk-takers who have the resources and desire to try new things, even if they fail. (Around 2.5 per cent of the population.)
- **Early Adopters** are selective about which technologies they start using. They are considered the 'one to check in with' for new information and reduce others' uncertainty about a new technology by adopting it. (13.5 per cent)
- The **Early Majority** take their time before adopting a new idea. They are willing to embrace a new technology if they understand how it fits in with their lives. (34 per cent)
- The **Late Majority** adopt innovations in reaction to peer pressure, new paradigms or economic uncertainty. Most of the uncertainty around an idea must be resolved before they adopt. (34 per cent)
- **Laggards** are traditional and make decisions based on experience. They are often economically unable to take risks on new ideas. (16 per cent)

The rise and fall of the diffusion process as these different groups embrace innovations helps to explain the S-curve shape of change. Diagram 3 shows the Rogers Diffusion of Innovation bell-curve overlaid with the S curve that shows its rate of market penetration.

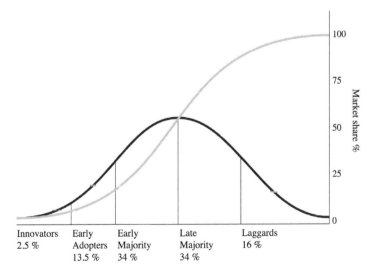

Diagram 2: Rogers' Diffusion of Innovation Bell Curve and S-Curve Adoption into the Market.

Diffusion theory was also discussed in detail in Geoffrey Moore's famous 1991 book *Crossing the Chasm,*[101] where he asserts that a 'chasm' exists between the risk-taking Innovators and Early Adopters (deemed technology enthusiasts and visionaries) and the more cautious Early Majority (deemed pragmatists). Moore believes innovators and early adopters have very different expectations from ordinary consumers, hence the gap. They embrace technology specifically because it is new, innovative, edgy and exciting, whereas the Early Majority and beyond are more price-sensitive and risk-averse, preferring to wait until the technology is proven and the price more affordable. Successful innovations are those that are remarkable enough to attract innovators and early adopters, but flexible and affordable enough to 'cross the chasm' and also appeal to the mass market; i.e. the Early Majority and beyond. The diffusion of innovation is therefore an important element in understanding the nature of the waves, for the technologies that cross the chasm are those that disrupt markets and power the forces of creative destruction.

The mass clustering of new innovations at a start of a new wave is due to the development of a series of new 'paradigm shift' technologies that usually involve new forms of power, communication, transportation and production. These new paradigm technologies create a surge of scientific knowledge and technological capability and explains why during the transition period excitement mounts as news of early experiments with these new technologies reaches the public. For example, the period around 2011 – 2014 saw a frenzy of articles about robotics, AI, virtual reality, autonomous cars, solar roads, without any of these being in the general sphere. Once the new technologies become proven, a multitude of new business ventures then appear, and a feeding frenzy of entrepreneurial activity begins as companies compete to exploit the potential of these new technologies and take advantage of the demand for them. Suddenly a whole series of individual diffusion curves start kicking off at the same time, and whole new supply chains arise to support and meet this demand, creating the exponential nature of the K-wave's upswing. Most consumers wait for the technology to become stable and reach a certain level of market adoption, but when they move, they can cause what's known as a techno-economic paradigm shift. Examples include rail, electricity, powered flight, the automobile industry, personal computers and, more recently, smartphones. These shifts represent a risk to laggard companies who are slow to adapt and continue to focus on producing products and services based around the old technology. They are at risk of finding that by the time they come to the party, everyone has paired up, the buffet has been cleared away and there's no one left to dance with. They are likely to find themselves standing in the corner by themselves; their business model replaced and now redundant, as in the case of Eastman Kodak, RIM, Blockbuster and the like.

Other theoretical models have been created to show the lifecycle of innovations, and one of the more famous is Gartner's 'Hype Cycle'. This graph highlights how technologies start off by attracting the innovators; corporations and consumers who take risks with new things, exciting them with their potential. The hype around these products overtakes their current capabilities, creating what is called the 'peak of inflated expectations'. The market then becomes disappointed with the time taken to turn and invention into a viable commercial product, especially when the early 'beta' versions underwhelm compared to the hype. This is the critical juncture, for if the teething issues cannot be overcome then the product may fail to cross the chasm into the mass market. If the innovation still has merit, then 'second-generation' versions are developed that have resolved the issues and responded to feedback. This creates an investment boom and entrepreneurs fight to develop the business models needed to make the innovation both profitable and attractive to the masses. For example, while it was Creative Labs that developed the Mp3 player and picked up the initial demand from the innovators, it was Apple and the iPod that created the right product and business model that enabled it to cross the chasm into the mass market through the creation of the complementary iTunes MP3 music marketplace. Then, once the innovation crosses the chasm rapid growth occurs, the innovation becomes adopted by the mass market and commoditised, creating the upswing of the S-curve, before plateauing as profits dry up and the curve flattens out.

Diagram 4 shows an overlay of Rogers' 'diffusion of innovation' bell curve with Moore's 'chasm' and Gartner's Hype Cycle. The stall period at the point of the chasm – between the Early Adopters and Early Majority – is the bottom of the 'trough of disillusionment', for it is here that innovations either fail or go on to become industrialised. Companies that find a way to develop a business model that is appealing to the mass market can seriously disrupt incumbent businesses, forcing them to either adapt to the new threat or be replaced. Those that can't adapt tend to see their market rapidly diminish and fail.

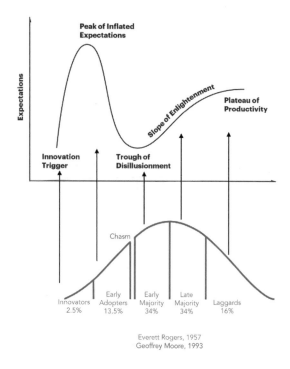

Diagram 3: The Gartner Hype Cycle's Relationship to the Diffusion of Innovation.

New innovations may initially have a slow and deceptive introduction to the market, but once they cross the chasm and the Early Majority adopts the new innovation it quickly becomes more disruptive, drawing consumers away from the existing technologies. The rapid explosion once a product crosses the chasm explains the 'S' shaped nature of the wave's upswing period – first deceptive, then disruptive. Or as Ernest Hemingway once declared, *Gradually, then suddenly.*[45] During the deceptive stage, individuals and companies get rich. Once it becomes disruptive, then the entire economy benefits as GDP experiences rapid growth. For those products unfortunate enough to be caught in the wake of creative destruction, it does not necessarily mean death, but it does represent the end of the mass market. Digital music formats replaced CDs and vinyl, but they still exist as a niche item.

---

[45] In Hemingway's *The Sun Also Rises*, the question was asked: *"How did you go bankrupt?"* *"Two ways. Gradually, then suddenly."*

The Cultural Lag

As mentioned in the last chapter, a delay exists between the creation of an innovation and its impact across society. These delays take three different forms. The first is the natural diffusion of technology from invention to industrialised product; the type identified in Rogers' bell curve. The second is due to the requirement for complementary and foundational infrastructure to be developed, be that physical or intellectual. This delay may take decades or even centuries. Da Vinci may have designed a flying machine in the 13th century but transforming from idea to innovation required advances and understanding of aerodynamics and manufacturing that only became available in the late 19th century. Likewise, the light bulb required an electric lighting system, plus the wiring, generators, power stations, electricity transportation system, suppliers and skilled tradesmen to maintain them. In 1880, Thomas Edison's company, the Edison Electric Light Company, began marketing the world's first commercially viable incandescent light bulb. In 1882, he opened Pearl Street Station, the first commercial electrical distribution plant in the United States, and by 1884 it was servicing over five hundred homes. Yet in 1900, 95 per cent of mechanical drive power in the United States was still generated via steam. Electricity didn't have a measurable impact on the economy until the early 1920s, forty years after Edison's plant opened. The problem wasn't electricity or the light bulb, but a lack of complementary technologies. To embrace electricity initially required huge investment for seemingly little return, and the delay between the invention to full diffusion and industrialisation took decades. A modern-day example is the need for the nationwide installation of electric vehicle (EV) charging stations before they become accepted as a true replacement for gas-fuelled cars. You may be able to manufacture electric cars, but they won't be mass-purchased until travelling long distances is both viable and reliable. This effect of the lag between invention and industrialisation was what Robert Solow highlighted in 1987 when he quipped, *you can see the Computer Age everywhere but in the productivity statistics.*

The final delay in diffusion is cultural and societal. Technology affects cultures and societies at different rates and at different times. Technology is also adopted at different rates by members *within* a society. Within the different age groups and social classes there are people who willingly seek and embrace new technological innovations, and those who do the opposite and resist them. The Innovators and the Laggards. The time between the first adopters of a new technological paradigm, and those that embrace and adopt it much later, either through intent or economic or political circumstance, is called the 'cultural lag'. The term was coined by William F. Ogburn in his 1922 work *Social Change with respect to Culture and Original Nature*,[102] and refers to the notion that a society's culture takes time to adapt and acclimatise to advances in technological innovations. Ogburn proposed that while technology could be deemed the primary guiding force in our evolution, society determines its rate of utilisation and acceptance. Early Adopters may rush to gain the perceived benefits from this technology whilst others may be slower to adopt for financial or access reasons, or because they are not sure whether the innovation is beneficial. A good recent example was Google Glass. Jumped on by technology lovers as 'the future made real', society actively pushed back at people walking around with sci-fi looking glasses on that were potentially recording them, and initial Google Glass wearers found themselves being ejected from cafés and branded 'Glassholes', perfectly proving Ogburn's point that society has to accept the technology in order for it to diffuse, rather than being totally subservient to it. While the public's reaction to Google Glass led to the product being withdrawn so the concept could be redeveloped as a business tool, in many cases it is only one group that does not willingly accept the new technological paradigm. For example, older people used to a world of physical currency such as cash and cheques are slow to adapt to new digital payment devices such as Apple Pay. Ogburn proposes that a period of disruption can occur due to the different rate of acceptance of new technologies, resulting in some groups being actively disadvantaged as they, either through choice or situations outside their control, are left behind.

A cultural lag can benefit society, because it delays the destructive impact of the new creations on the workforce. The long lead time between a new technology being introduced and jobs being wiped out means that people and companies can often adapt, minimising the destructive impact and enabling those who are affected to see out their careers or have the time to retrain for a new one. However, if this lag is not caused by consumer choice, but through restriction or inability, then it can work against the nation. Inclusive societies usually develop and adapt new technologies first, designing them with their consumers in mind. Conversely, countries that have not fully embraced and implemented high-speed Internet, or where the population does not have easy access to Wi-Fi connectivity, cannot participate fully in the new digital age and fall behind. Sometimes exclusive countries create a self-imposed cultural lag, through a political, religious, moral or ideological rejection of the technology. In extreme cases, the nation's leaders may enforce, through social and political means, an agenda that restricts freedom, access to information and entrepreneurial activity. This is nearly always a mistake that they end up paying for long term. Nations that constrict the rights of the individual to access or even discuss these new tools, become staid and a gap can develop between them and more inclusive nations. For example, the Ottoman Empire never recovered from its decision to suppress the ability to print books. These decisions can also create significant inter-country levels of inequality, and as time progresses the speed of technological progress elsewhere in the world will see their people become increasingly isolated and left behind. It is, however, getting harder for leaders of extractive societies to maintain this level of control. In the past, the difficulty in traversing large distances meant that the actions of one community had little or no impact on others. Now global supply chains and Internet-based communication networks can rapidly transport goods, services and ideas across country boundaries, limiting any political or religious leader's ability to contain and control the world view of their population. This influx of ideas and different world views, combined with the availability of social media platforms, has meant that for the first time a population have the ability to access perspectives from more inclusive cultures, and the mechanism to spread it to other members of their society. This has led to political leaders desperately to retain control of the prevalent world view by removing access to the tools of this dissent, such as Turkey's government banning the use of YouTube and Twitter following widespread criticism of the government. Google might have provided access to the world's information – but does your government let you have access to Google? Does it restrict what Google finds? Countries such as Turkey[46] are making choices that will affect their rate of technological awareness, adoption and diffusion – and thus the economic possibilities and growth that could arise from that technology. This may also result in significant migration away from that country, resulting in a 'brain drain' that reduces its ability to compete on a global stage.

---

[46] This desire to control access to information is something that we will return to in Part Three, for this policing of the Internet is no longer limited to countries such as Turkey but is also creeping into Western nations as well.

The cultural lag could therefore prove to be the undoing of many a nation that forgoes the modern technological revolution to maintain its position of power and control. The size of the gap between leaders and laggards does, however, also provide an indication of the size of the potential opportunity that exists for those who do decide to change. New technologies can provide nations with the ability to rapidly improve their potential future prosperity, leap-frogging old technologies and jumping straight to the new one. Rwanda is a good example. Famous for conflict, genocide and poverty, a change in leadership has led to aspirations to raise the level of education and ability to access information through technology. Rwandan President, Paul Kagame, and his ruling Rwandan Patriotic Front (RPF), which has dominated Rwanda since ousting Hutu extremists and ending the genocide in 1994, are pushing through a dramatic transformation and economic success story. Rwanda is now ranked as one of the least corrupt countries in Africa, moving up 103 places in the World Bank's 'Ease of Doing Business' index, from 158th in 2007 to 56th in 2017. The government now wants to push economic growth to 11.5 per cent for each of the next five years, drive poverty from 45 per cent to below the 30 per cent mark and reach middle-income status by 2020. To help achieve this, Rwanda is reinventing itself as a regional high-tech hub by rolling out free citywide and eventually nationwide wireless connectivity. In June 2013, the Rwandan government signed South Korea's KT Corp to build a 4G network, which now reaches over 92 per cent of the country. Rwanda's minister in charge of information technology, Jean-Philbert Nsengimana, said that *Connectivity is one of the most important draws for business in this age of digital economy. Broadband access has to be considered as an essential, just like water and electricity.* Rwanda's leaders have the conscious decision to provide Internet access to the population to dramatically increase their level of education, confident that their people, given entrepreneurial freedom, will grasp the opportunity to leave the paradigms of the past behind and embrace the opportunity to raise their standards of living, creating growth and opportunities for future generations.

Innovation Types and Impact

While some innovations are just enhancements to existing technology, focused on significantly improving features or removing flaws, the arrival of certain types of innovation can cause the creative destruction effect Schumpeter describes. To understand the impact innovation has on the economy, and why certain types can disrupt whole industries while others simply provide us with a slightly better shave, it is important to understand the different types of innovations and the impact they have. In his 2014 *Harvard Business Review* article, *The Capitalist's Dilemma*, Professor Clayton Christensen defines these different kinds of innovation as follows:

- **Sustaining innovations.** Performance-improving, or incremental innovations that are designed to replace old products with new and better models. These are often just incremental improvements to an existing solution and are usually based on customer or focus-group feedback. For example, an extra lubricant strip or blade on a razor.
- **Efficiency innovations.** New ways to make and sell mature, established products or services to the same customers at lower prices. For example, the Dollar Shave Club disrupted the shaving industry by offering a 'good enough' solution but at a much lower price point.
- **Disruptive, market-creating innovations** that transform complicated or costly products so radically that they create a new class of consumers or a new market. For example, the replacement of film photography with digital.

Christensen labelled performance and efficiency innovations as 'sustaining innovations',[103] in that they do not create new markets or value networks but rather evolve existing ones. These types of innovation are substitutive, used to maintain market share and margin during the diffusion and saturation stage of the long wave, and as a result, either create very few new jobs, or worse, they destroy jobs through cost-cutting and focusing on productivity gains. While sustaining innovations are focused around satisfying customers' current needs, disruptive or market-creating innovations and technologies create new business models designed to create their future ones. Market-creating innovations are the most disruptive as well as the most important type, because they usually generate whole new industries, brand-new markets, new jobs and new economic growth. They eventually go on to disrupt existing market and value networks, displacing the incumbent corporations whose business model is still based around the earlier technology. It is disruptive innovations that are most likely to result in a technological innovation and the 'creative/destructive' effect.

Corporations whose leaders have the ability to think outside the current paradigm can potentially create solutions that are not just modifications on existing innovations, but new business models with the power to create an entirely new market. These individuals align nicely with Schumpeter's definition of entrepreneurs as *innovators who use a process of shattering the status quo of the existing products and services, to set up new products, new services.* Consider the advancements in computing power that have allowed the smartphone to effectively destroy or significantly damage the markets for PDAs, GPS systems, Dictaphones, watches, calculators, alarm clocks, cameras, handheld gaming systems and MP3 players. It didn't just make each one of these more efficient; it effectively eliminated most, if not all, of their existing market.[47]

Another potential way of classifying innovation is what I call the ABCD of disruptive technologies. This scale places new technologies into one of four categories dependent on the level of innovation and impact. Innovation varies from transactional, where it might automate the execution of one or more transactions, to transformative, where it can impact multiple processes and even change your entire value chain. Impact can vary from the automation of a repetitive task, all the way through to completely redefining the consumer value proposition.

---

[47] The possible exception to this is watches, which are still worn predominantly as a fashion item rather than a timepiece. Growing wealth in emerging nations such as China has kept watch sales rising. However, there has been a massive drop-off of ownership of watches with millennials, who use their phone to tell the time instead.

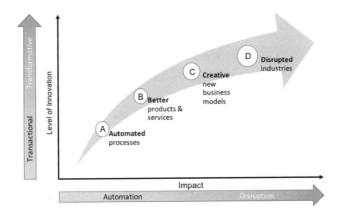

Diagram 4: The ABCD of Disruptive Technologies. Source: Culey, S. A.

'A' (Automated processes) and 'B' (Better products and services) are similar to Christensen's 'sustaining' and 'efficiency' innovations, whereas 'C' (Creative new business models) and 'D' (Disrupted industries) relate to 'disruptive' innovations. It is possible for a new technology to start off by automating a process but end up disrupting an industry. At the start, the impact seems deceptively small, but over time, when its use diffuses across the industry, it can become disruptive. For example, software that enables small business owners to process their own accounts might seem like it's just automating boring tasks, but after a while they may decide that this software enables them to start doing their own books, and they may subsequently advise other business owners of the simplicity, benefit and money saved from this DIY approach. Eventually new business owners default to using this software and boom – a tipping point occurs. If your business sells accountancy services to small to medium businesses, then this could disrupt your entire business model and devalue your proposition. The difference the digital age brings is the speed and range of diffusion, hence the increase in the height and phasing of the waves. The outcome of one company's inventiveness would normally take decades to spread; now it can take days. An app that allows you to hail a cab rather than call for one seems innocuous enough, but as we know it only took around five years before it started to massively disrupt traditional taxi businesses worldwide.

Paradigm Shifts and Technological Revolutions

A paradigm shift is defined as a change in the pattern of research or a disciplinary matrix caused by a change of understanding of the basic assumptions behind how things work. The concept of paradigms and paradigm shifts became popularised through the work of Thomas Kuhn and his 1962 book *The Structure of Scientific Revolutions.*[104] According to Kuhn, a paradigm is much more than just the current theory; it also includes the entire world view within which it exists and all the perceptions and implications which come with it. Science has enabled mankind to shift its paradigm from hunter-gatherer, at one with nature but also constantly at its mercy, through to becoming agriculturists, scientists, philosophers, industrialists, inventors, managers and now technologists. Kuhn stated that paradigm-shifting is much more than simply changing one's perspective. He writes that: *Under normal conditions the research scientist is not an innovator but a solver of puzzles, and the puzzles upon which he concentrates are just those which he believes can be both stated and solved within the existing scientific tradition.* When a scientific paradigm is replaced by a new one, the new one is not just different, but better, removing ceilings on our knowledge and creating new truths and new possibilities that challenge the conventional wisdoms. Over the centuries, we have had to shift our paradigms regarding such things as whether the sun revolves around the Earth or vice versa, whether the Earth is flat or round, whether powered flight is possible – right through to our place in the history of the planet. These were just hypotheses until the development of technologies and scientific observations that altered conventional wisdom.

We experience substantial paradigm shifts around every fifty to sixty years, which coincidentally is the same length as a K-wave. Only it's not a coincidence. Those paradigms just don't shift themselves; they shift because of advancements in scientific understanding and technological capabilities. Each technological wave, each new revolution, introduces a significant number of interrelated new products and production technologies that give rise to whole new industries and markets. LSE Professor Carlota Perez specialises in technological paradigms, and she believes that the difference between normal innovations and technological revolutions are substantial. In *Technological revolutions and techno-economic paradigms,* she declares, *what distinguishes a technological revolution from a random collection of technology systems... are two basic features:*

140

1. *The strong interconnectedness and interdependence of the participating systems in their technologies and markets.*
2. *The capacity to transform profoundly the rest of the economy (and eventually society).*[105]

These techno-economic paradigm shifts have the following sequence of events:

- A new major technological innovation requires the introduction of a supporting infrastructure (**Creation**).
- The new infrastructure creates jobs but disrupts existing industries and commercial models and affects society (**Destruction**).
- Over the long term, the new infrastructure is understood, harnessed, exploited and becomes a stabilising force for the technological wave. Increased confidence results in increased investment in this new technology (**Adoption and Diffusion**).

When market-generating innovations cross the chasm from deceptive to disruptive, the destructive forces of creative destruction come into play. When we declare that the *creation* of automobiles and trains *destroyed* the horse-powered travel industry, what we mean is that the entire value network associated with horses was decimated. People involved in rearing and training horses, producing horse feed, leatherworkers, carriage- and buggy-builders, saddlers, whip makers, blacksmiths, stable boys, riding teachers, cart builders and wheelwrights; all their skills, experiences and assets were completely devalued. On the creative side, new jobs arose to support the automotive industry – jobs that never previously existed, such as mechanics, petrol station attendants, car factory workers and used-car salesmen. So long as the creative outweighs the destructive, society moves forward – but there are always casualties. As mentioned, destruction may signify the end of 'economically useful life', it does not necessarily mean death. While the car replaced the horse and the bicycle, both still exist and have a healthy market, their purpose changed from necessity to leisure. Those that manufacture and sell them must therefore also change their business model.

Large-scale techno-economic paradigm shifts – ones capable of launching the process of creative destruction and creating a new wave –

occur when there is a convergence or clustering of new and revolutionary foundational products, technologies and infrastructures, and a society willing (or able) to accept them and the new innovations they enable. These foundational technologies create an extended 'super-diffusion of innovations' curve, one that lasts for decades. It is this force which launches and carries the upswing of the waves of creative destruction. Table 1 shows that there are three major elements contained within each wave/techno-economic paradigm shift, each interacting and providing the impetus for the other. These are a power source, required to launch and energise the production of the new goods and services, the infrastructure that enables the movement of physical items or communication, and a transportation mechanism to use this infrastructure and supply the new goods and services across the various nodes in the value chain. The process is self-reinforced as the propagation and adoption of the new technologies across increasing sections of society confirm the apparent wisdom of these new developments until they effectively become an ingrained element of society. The process of diffusion across society and the resultant increases in productivity and market expansion can also cause a significant surge in development and economic growth.

	Wave 1	Wave 2	Wave 3	Wave 4	Wave 5	Wave 6
	First Industrial Revolution	The Age of Steam and Rail	Second Industrial Revolution	The Age of the Auto-mobile	The Computer Age	Third Industrial Revolution
Time Period	1760–1820	1820–1870	1870–1914	1908–1970	1971–2008	2008–2040
Length	60 years	50 years	44 years	62 years (2 World Wars)	37 years	32 years
Countries/ Regions Affected	Great Britain	Great Britain	UK, USA, Germany	USA, Japan	USA, Western Europe, Japan	Global (India and Asia main benefac-tors)

Power Source	Steam engine, coal	Steam	Electricity	Electricity, petro-chemicals	Digital communi-cations	Renewable energy, especially solar
Transport Mecha-nism	Canals, sailing ships	Rail, steamships	Rail (especially in US), bicycle, Transatlan-tic shipping	Road, rail, plane, ships	Road, plane, shipping containers	Auton-omous vehicles, Internet of Everything
Commu-nication Mecha-nism	Printing press	Telegraph	Telephone	Radio, TV	TV, video, mobile telephony, Internet	Global Internet, 5G and 6G mobile telecommu-nications
Industry	Coal mining, cotton, pottery	Steam-pow-ered fac-tories, iron bridges and construc-tions	Steel, heavy engineer-ing (civil, chemical, electrical and naval)	Mass pro-duced au-tomobile, consumer white goods	Computer hard-ware and software, smart-phones, e-com-merce, service industries	Mobile, digitisa-tion, VR, Internet of Things (IoT), robotics, au-tonomous, electric vehicles, solar power, vertical farming

Table 1: Summary of the Six Waves of Technological Revolution.

All these new disruptive technologies are not magically created out of thin air but are built on foundations of technological and scientific inheritance from previous generations. Jeff Bezos would not have made a fortune from e-commerce had it not been for the development of the Internet and World Wide Web, both things in which he played no part and whose development was mostly government funded. Likewise Mark Zuckerberg with Facebook, Elon Musk with PayPal, and the Google founders with, well, Google. Microsoft and Apple wouldn't have been created if not for the work of Turing and colleagues at Bletchley Park, and they wouldn't have succeeded if not for the electronic and mathematical foundations laid down by people from Charles Babbage all the way back to Pythagoras and the concept of building from first principles. While modern-day technocrats may become extremely wealthy from the creation of new products and services, they owe the opportunity to those who went before them, many of whom earned no fortune from their endeavours. Just through looking back at the five waves we have experienced since the 18th century, we can see how the continuous development of new technological paradigms enabled the development of whole new industries and sub-industries, and which were finally replaced by newer, more innovative technologies.

Wave 1: The Industrial Revolution and Canal Mania

The invention of the steam engine allowed us to extract fuels that powered industry and created new modes of mass transportation. During this time, there was a substantial investment in infrastructures such as roads, bridges, ports and canals to support the growing flow of trade. This investment created a new canal network in Britain, resulting in more canals being built in Birmingham than in Venice. The huge financial investment in the development of the canals enabled a new golden age of industry and trade to develop, facilitating the movement of goods across England to the ports, and from there across the world. It also drastically reduced the percentage of the population who worked on the land, and increased the demand for canal- and road-builders, coal miners, port workers, sailors and factory workers.

Wave 2: The Age of Steam and Railways

The early 19th century created increasing demand for rapid communications, in part because the French revolution and the pursuant wars increased the need for long-distance communications, but also because of the integration of capital markets and the development of railroads. While the inventions of the 1820s and 1830s – excepting the railroad – do not feature as prominently in textbooks as those of Watt, Cort and Crompton, they are in fact the ones that made the difference between what would have been simply another technological blip and the expansion of the British and other European economies after 1830. Those inventions included the high-pressure steam engine, extensions in fabric-production methods, the introduction of the self-acting mule (1825), Neilson's hot blast (1829), and the growing use of chemical and physical knowledge in manufacturing and agriculture after 1840. The potential of rail and its impact on society led to a major railway investment boom, creating an excess of track, resulting in a downturn that left some investors burned and financially ruined. However, Victorian Britain was left with a rail network that could be rationalised and used to support the economic growth that turned it into the economic and technological leader of the developed world. It also helped to spread the social benefits much more widely, reducing the income disparity. New inventions such as the steamship and the telegraph helped coordinate Britain's imperial strength, allowing it to control and defend the empire by providing services such as the suppression of piracy and enforcing the blocking of the slave trade, which was banned across the British Empire in 1807, launching a hundred-year period known as the Pax Britannica, a time of relative peace between the great powers where Britain became the global hegemonic power following victory over Napoleonic France. Due to their ability to sail against the wind, the new ocean-going steamships that arose in this period also enabled the creation of new trade routes, initiating the start of an unprecedented period of globalised trade. This was Globalisation 1.0.

Wave 3: The Age of Steel, Electricity and Heavy Engineering

Electricity lit up and powered our world, creating entire industries that produced increasingly sophisticated consumable electric and electronic goods. An enormous transformation of the world economy was under way with the rise of transcontinental trade and travel, supported by the invention of the international telegraph and the new energy-conversion technology of electrification. By 1902, global communication between the territories of the British Empire was achieved by a network of telegraph cables known as the All Red Line.

In the late 19th century, the United States and Germany took over what Britain had started. In the US the steel industry exploded, driven by demand to link the urban centres of this vast country through railroads. Over in Germany a flourishing electricity and chemical industry emerged. Companies like AEG and Siemens became electricity giants, and chemical companies such as AGFA and BASF led in the production of synthetic dyes, photographic and plastic products, controlling some 90 per cent of the worldwide market in 1900. Financial markets received a massive infusion of cash as money sought to make money out of money, and everyone wanted to be part of it. This focus on financial speculation, rather than production and industry, led to a series of financial crashes in the US, France, Italy and Argentina. Shaken and chastened by the crashes, while US and Germany returned their attention to the real economy, countries like Argentina never fully recovered.

The age of steel had created a lot of waste and pain, but throughout it all it had, like the canals and railroads before it, laid down the foundations and infrastructure for the new economy. This golden era of great scientific and technological advancement in Europe saw a move away from primarily financial capital to production capital, creating the progressive era in the US and the Belle Époque in Europe.

Wave 4: The Age of Oil, the Automobile and Mass Production

How many electrical products and innovations have arisen because of the invention of electricity and the development of nationwide grids to bring this power to the home? Every aspect of life within a home has changed dramatically due to electrification, from lighting, through to the introduction of washing machines, vacuum cleaners and dishwashers that automated household chores, through to kitchen appliances such as fridges, freezers, cookers, grills, toasters, mixers and microwaves that revolutionised food purchasing, storage and preparation. These new consumer goods freed women from hours of back-breaking cleaning and cooking, enabling them to spend more time with their families in the living room, where other new inventions such as radios, stereos and televisions competed for our attention and our hard-earned salaries.

Both the electric power and automotive industries relied on the existence of a highly developed steel industry. Likewise, a sophisticated petroleum refining industry was a prerequisite for the automotive market to develop. Electric power was a prerequisite product using the electric furnace, which, again, was a prerequisite for the high-speed grinding technology that made truly large-scale automobile manufacturing economically feasible. A new primary source of energy appeared (petroleum), and this industry rapidly became one of the leading sectors. The internal combustion engine also arrived on the scene, and just as steam power plus iron provided the necessary conditions for the railroads, petroleum and the internal combustion engine became the driving force behind the automobile industry (steel and new advances in metalworking technology being the others). In the roaring '20s, investors became excited by the new automotive industry and the prospects of mass production arising out of Henry Ford's plants, which created a paradigm shift in the nature of production and the role of workers. The development of the automobile freed us from having to live within walking distance of where we worked, in turn creating new towns and the creation of a suburban lifestyle. For the first time, non-wealthy people could also enjoy a life that was focused on comfort and leisure. The advent of powered flight changed our work, holiday and migration patterns, as well as allowing for the creation of a global trade network that operated in hours, not weeks. Suddenly, the goods of the world were available for consumption.

The money men rose once again in their droves to take advantage of the new opportunities, and the stock market swelled to become the engine driving the US economy. Investments were sold as 'guaranteed to grow' in a never-ending bull market. People, excited by the prospect of their money making more money than their labour ever could, invested their life savings in this apparently infallible financial market. Everyone wanted to be in on it – right up to the crash of 1929 and the onset of the Great Depression. The Great Depression was long and protracted, and it required the implementation and encouragement of legislation like the Glass-Steagall Act for the financial sector to reconnect with the boring reality of firms who produced real goods and services for real customers. It took a while, but when it did reconnect, spurred on by the industrialisation of war, it facilitated another wave and another golden age of expansion and growth in the US economy.

Wave 5: The Age of Information and Telecommunications

The post-war era saw the creation of a US Belle Époque, a period of post-war prosperity caused by the decline of the devastated European and Japanese economies, and the growth of new technologies born from the experiments and crisis-driven inventions of scientists in the Second World War. Perhaps the most influential was the work of Turing and colleagues at Bletchley Park and the Radiation Laboratory at the MIT over in the US that paved the way for significant advancements in communications, electronics, microwaves and information technology, leading to a plethora of new electronic consumer products. The pacesetter for progress in the fifth wave, the Information Age, was Gordon Moore's 1965 prediction that the number of transistors located on a chip will double every two years while halving in price. To date this has proven to be an unwaveringly accurate record of technological progress in the semiconductor industry that has continued for more than half a century. It enabled the creation of the television that spread words and images around the globe as they happened, increasing the speed of information and changing our entertainment, social life and culture.

In 1969, Nippon Calculating Machine Corporation approached Intel to design 12 custom chips for its new Busicom 141-PF* printing calculator. Launched with a prophetic advertisement – *Announcing a new era in integrated electronics* – the Intel 4004 was the start of a 'Big Bang' of a whole new universe of computing and digital communications that would change the world. These new silicon chips were both cheap and powerful, and created new and exciting technological possibilities the likes of which had never been seen before. Unbeknown at the time, the transistor and the computer chip were prerequisites to the Internet age. Moore's Law showed that the forces of entrepreneurial competition could drive companies to innovate at an exponential rate; increasingly pushing the paradigms of what is feasible by packing unbelievable amounts of computing capability and storage into astonishingly small packages – and then launching them into the consumer market at a price point that appears to be more competitive than the previous year's. Now even the most basic smartphone provides more processing power than was available in 1965, meaning that most people's pockets contain a machine that contains thousands of times more computing power than was used to put a man on the moon. Moore's Law is expected to continue for the foreseeable future.

The innovative upswing stage of the fifth wave established the computing, Internet and mobile technology that formed the power source and communication mechanisms, and focus turned to developing ways to diffuse the new digital (and physical) products through the new Internet-enabled business models, causing a tremendous impact on culture and commerce. A new economy arose to take advantage of this new technology, and those with initiative and money to invest once again appeared to take advantage of the new profit opportunities they saw everywhere. Like the canal and railway manias before them, an Internet mania arose – the dot.com boom. In a very similar way that people in Amsterdam went mad for tulips in the 1630s, an Internet land-grab commenced, but instead of tulip bulbs, domains became the commodity. Investors, driven by the potential gains this new business model promised, took leave of their senses and invested heavily in companies with no products, business plans or clear strategies, believing that a snazzy domain name, a website and a rough business idea was all that was needed in the digital age. Once again, the finance markets became detached from the real world, believing that the traditional rules of business did not apply to this e-enabled new world order. During the dot.com boom of the late 1990s millions were invested in companies that had no products, no infrastructure and no customers – just because they had an idea and a domain and were setting up shop on the Internet. The dot.com bubble burst in 2000, and the wizards of Silicon Valley were forced to face the reality of business plans and actual products after yet another era of 'irrational exuberance'. Computers might be transforming society, but this new e-commerce world had some growing up to do and, like teenagers, some harsh lessons to learn. However, like in the days of canals, railroads, steel, electricity and automotive, at the end of this period, the technology and infrastructure foundations for the next cycle of growth had been established.

8

THE END OF THE
INDUSTRIAL AGE

Success breeds complacency. Complacency breeds failure.
Only the paranoid survive.

Andrew Grove, Former COO, Chairman and CEO, Intel Corporation

The Golden Leaves of Autumn

During the 1990s, many of the core technologies of the sixth wave were invented or developed, including the World Wide Web (the Internet), Google and eBay (online search and shopping), the Human Genome Project (genetics), Dolly the sheep (cloning) and the Hubble Space Telescope (space). Yet rather than invest in these exciting new developments, the harsh business reality of the fifth wave's autumn period forced CEOs to constantly demonstrate increasing returns to shareholders, meaning that they needed to find different ways to drive the share price upwards. CEOs looked for quick wins, either internally through greater efficiencies from production and cost-cutting, or externally to companies they could acquire or merge with to drive up shareholder value. This behaviour was driven by ever-aggressive hedge fund managers, analysts and executives, all trying to keep the fat returns of the Kondratiev summer period going. The pressurised CEOs constantly looked for ways to improve profits and embraced the new efficiency opportunities that globalisation and the fifth-wave innovations of digital communication networks provided.

Three primary factors converged: the Internet and its ability to connect people across the planet, the widespread adoption of market economics by China's administration, and the declining phase of the fifth long wave where focus was on efficiency and exploitation rather than inventiveness and entrepreneurialism. The world, as Thomas Friedman proposed in his bestselling 2005 book, had once again become flat.[106] Suddenly countries, companies and individuals had to remain competitive in a global market where geographic and national boundaries become less relevant. What organisations realised was that the new fifth-wave communication technology – the Internet – enabled them to increase profits through dramatically cutting costs, not through innovation, but through offshoring production and outsourcing non-core elements of their business to low-wage countries. The transition from the creative, entrepreneurial upswing of the computer age to the more financial and efficiency focused downswing therefore had an enormous stimulating effect on many emerging economies, creating Globalisation 2.0. For those unfamiliar with Kondratiev and Schumpeter's theories of long-wave creative destruction, this was an exciting time.

First China, and now India, Vietnam, Malaysia and Indonesia are all experiencing rapid growth due to the offshoring of labour from developed countries. These new emerging economies opened up their markets and their workforce and, in a world where labour is often the most expensive overhead, they were able to offer significant efficiency gains to Western companies who were looking to squeeze more profits out of their operations. Technology and transportation advancements meant that the manufacturing plant didn't need to be near the customers any more – they could now be located on the other side of the world in countries where labour was a fraction of the cost. This transition has enabled them to become deeply integrated in the global value chains of multinational enterprises, and as a result they have initiated their own industrial revolution, resulting in them not only becoming a source of labour, but also a source of demand. This has enabled them to become economic powerhouses, capable of producing large volumes of high-value goods and services, leading the developed economies to accept that they are no longer the only players in capitalism's grand casino. For example, China went from producing just 3 per cent of global manufacturing output in 1990, to producing 25 per cent in 2017. Simply put, China now makes what the West buys. But as its wealth grew so did its market, its skill base and its capabilities, allowing it to progress from being the producer of other people's stuff to an innovator in its own right. Chinese companies now include Xiaomi, the $45 billion smartphone company touted as having the potential to become China's first global consumer brand,[107] and the online retail giants Alibaba and JD.com, the only real online competitors Amazon has globally. It is also building a market of consumers at an incredible rate. For the first time, the number of people with discretionary income will exceed the number still struggling to meet basic needs.[108] By 2025, a staggering 4.2 billion people will be part of the consuming class. The top two most populated countries (by a significant amount) – China and India – have been responsible for most of the recent fall in the last three decades. In 1981, 88 per cent of Chinese were extremely poor, but by 2013 that figure had dropped to just 2 per cent. India's figures, though not as drastic, are still impressive: a decline in the poverty rate from 54 to 21 per cent.

One important difference between this wave and the first is that Britain and the United States began their industrialisation process with populations of about 10 million, whereas China and India began theirs with populations of roughly 1 billion each. This means that they are experiencing approximately ten times the economic acceleration of the industrial revolution on a hundred times the scale – resulting in an economic force that is over 1,000 times as big. Before the industrial revolution, China and India were the two largest world economies by GDP output.[109] They are now poised to potentially regain those positions.

Offshoring's Dark Side

Globalisation and the emerging nations' embrace of market economics not only led to the positives of capitalism – economic growth, improved living standards and a massive reduction in poverty – it unleashed its dark side as well. This has enabled businesses to avoid having to comply with strict rules that had been carefully developed after decades of societal and economic calibration, such as worker rights, safety legislation and minimum wages, enabling businesses to once again put profits before people. It wasn't only the manufacturing that was outsourced; it was also the ethics. An 'out-of-sight, out-of-mind' mindset developed, with corporations concerned about the quality of the end product, but not the quality of the working environment in which the product was made. The extent to which Western business leaders were willing to turn a blind eye to the working conditions in the 21st-century sweatshops was staggering. A total of around 4 million people work in the garment industry in Bangladesh and earn on average €38 a month, with strict restrictions on unions. The conditions they work in belong more to the 19th than the 21st century and would simply not be acceptable in Western countries. These practices came crashing into the living rooms of Western consumers on the 24th April 2013, when the eight-storey Rana Plaza factory building near Dhaka collapsed, claiming at least 1,129 lives, mostly women. This accident came just four months after a fire at Tazreen Fashions in Dhaka had killed around 117 workers. It highlighted to the Western consumers the dismal working conditions in the apparel industry, where global retailers and clothing brands such as Matalan, Primark, Walmart and Benetton had their clothes made. People realised that the cost of disposable fashion was disposable lives.

The globalisation of communications and media meant that the images of the disaster were broadcast across the world on the same day. In London, protestors surrounded the Primark store on Oxford Street and Benetton's flagship store at Oxford Circus. This caused the companies behind these brands to think long and hard about the total cost of offshoring, including the risks to brand perception. Bad press about Chinese working conditions also reached the West and damaged the reputation and stock price of companies such as Apple, Nike and Adidas. Foxconn, the Taiwanese contract electronics manufacturer who makes products for most of the major electronic consumer goods companies such as Apple, HP, Dell, Motorola, Nintendo, Nokia and Sony, made worldwide headlines after eighteen of its workers attempted suicide in its Chinese operations, fourteen of whom were successful. The dehumanising working conditions in the factory were blamed, and people were shocked at the sheer number of workers employed at a single site; for example, the plant in which the deaths occurred employed approximately 300,000 people. Public protests took place outside Apple stores in San Francisco and Foxconn's headquarters in Hong Kong, and the fallout caused an investigation that highlighted both poor working conditions and examples of child labour. Foxconn's initial response was to install suicide nets on the building to catch any jumpers, but they later agreed to increase the wages of the workers. Also in China, a wage dispute at the huge sports footwear factory owned by the world's largest maker of sneakers, Yue Yuen, which supplies brands including Adidas and Nike, further highlighted the issue of poor working conditions. Workers at the plant earned as little as $1.67 an hour making shoes that sold for up to a hundred times that value, and as a result there has been a surge in the number of strikes and worker protests, with China Labour Bulletin's strike map recording over 5,000 during 2015–16.[110] Many strategies to combat poor working conditions and forced labour stop at tier-one suppliers or encompass only a small percentage of the total supply chain, but many issues are often further down the chain, such as exploitive practices and child labour in the mining industry. In 2016, the plight of children as young as seven working in the cobalt mines in the Democratic Republic of Congo was splashed across the news. Cobalt is an essential component of batteries used for smartphones, laptops and now electric cars, yet many of those working to extract it – usually by hand – are earning as little as 8p a day in very dangerous and dirty conditions. There is very little regulatory pressure on companies to trace their cobalt supply lines, and with 65 per cent of the world's cobalt coming from the Democratic Republic of Congo, the chances are your smartphone contains a battery with cobalt mined by children in the central African nation. Mark Dummett, business and human rights researcher at Amnesty International, said, *Millions of people enjoy the benefits of new technologies but rarely ask how they are made. It is high time the big brands took some responsibility for the mining of the raw materials that make their lucrative products.*[111]

Consumers are becoming significantly less tolerant of stories about poor working conditions, especially since the advent of social media which allows people in the emerging nations to instantly broadcast examples of substandard working practices to the world. As a result, both corporations and political governing bodies are under pressure from domestic and external forces to provide in months what it took decades to achieve in the Western industrial revolutions. For example, the Bangladeshi government, under pressure from the United States and the European Union, has put into place reforms designed to ease restrictions on unionisation, while global retailers, predominantly those from Europe, established an accord on factory and building safety.[48]

The True Cost Appears

There have been other unexpected and unpleasant downsides to offshoring in far-off and less developed lands. In 2007 and 2008 several significant product recalls arose after multinational businesses realised that their decisions to offshore had not just reduced labour costs; they had also reduced their visibility and control of their extended supply chain – with fatal results. In September 2008, several companies, including the global food giant Nestlé, were implicated in a scandal involving milk and infant formula which had been mixed with melamine, leading to kidney stones and other renal failure issues, especially among young children. Melamine, a substance used to manufacture melamine-formaldehyde resin, a type of plastic known for its flame-retardant properties, is a nitrogen-rich chemical and was added to the baby milk by Chinese suppliers trying to save money by creating the appearance of higher protein content without using expensive products like actual milk powder. An estimated 300,000 cases were reported, with six infants dying and an estimated 54,000 babies being hospitalised. In 2007 pet-food companies were caught up in a similar scandal when melamine was added to pet food during production in China, resulting in a recall being initiated by Menu Foods and other pet-food manufacturers who found their products had been contaminated, resulting in severe illness and death in some of the animals that had eaten them. Also in 2007, hotel amenity provider Gilchrist & Soames had to recall Chinese-manufactured toothpaste sold under their brand because it was contaminated with poisonous diethylene glycol. A whole host of toy companies in 2007 were hit by the findings that their Chinese manufacturers had used lead paint. In July, Mattel recalled some of its *Dora the Explorer* and *Sesame Street* toys. In August, Fisher-Price, a subsidiary of Mattel, recalled 967,000 plastic toys, and Mattel recalled 19 million more toys: 436,000 toy cars with lead paint and 18 million other toys (sixty-three different models)

[48] Walmart, along with fourteen other North American companies, refused to sign the accord.

that contained magnets that were dangerous if swallowed. In November Marvel Toys also had to recall around 175,000 *Curious George* plush dolls due to lead paint.

As well as a loss of visibility and transparency of the extended supply chain, corporations also found another risk from offshoring: natural disasters. Events that occur infrequently in the West, such as tsunamis and earthquakes, occur frequently in the locations where Western companies outsourced their supply chains to, exposing their supply chains to a whole new set of risks and major disruptions. For example, the March 2011 earthquake and resultant tsunami in Japan caused Sony, Panasonic, Toshiba and Canon to halt production in order to carry out safety checks, and Apple was forced, at great expense, to delay the launch of the iPad 2.

One of the other issues facing Western companies that have off-shored their manufacturing to low-cost locations is that they don't stay low-cost for long. The Internet has enabled workers in emerging nations to view the lifestyle of the consumers they are making products for, creating an aspiration to also live like that. This desire causes a massive rise in expectations, which in turn creates pressure to increase wages, and, if these expectations are not met, an exodus of talent from the country to places where these aspirations can be achieved. People want to own iPhones, not just make them. This has caused Chinese managers to constantly raise wages to attract workers, seeing them rise a crippling 12 per cent per year on average since 2001. As these increasing costs make manufacturing in China less attractive, countries like Bangladesh, Indonesia, Malaysia and Vietnam have taken over as the low-cost labour pools of choice.

The actual total cost of relocating part or all of their supply chain to the emerging nations has become apparent, and as a result many Western multinationals are now rethinking their entire supply-chain strategy. These organisations also found that the total cost-to-serve was greater than they thought and realised that the long lead times and large order sizes they had to contractually commit to in order to reach their desired price point have limited their agility. Plus, as wages rise in the developed nations to match the countries' economic growth, and transport costs play a larger part in the equation, companies have found that the savings they expected have not materialised, but unforeseen risks such as intellectual property theft and a lack of end-to-end transparency have. Finally, consumers' tastes and demands are changing rapidly, meaning that the bell curve of product lifecycles is both heightening and shortening at the same time, resulting in products being replaced in the design studio before the first batch has landed ashore. Offshoring makes sense if the demand is relatively stable and the product is standard and long-lasting. It's a risky proposition if there is significant variability in the product's demand or final configuration. Both dynamics are accelerating and are a headache to manufacturers, as offshoring dramatically affects a company's ability to react in a responsive way. Consumers are impatient and don't want to wait months for the boat from China (or pay for the air freight). As a result, companies are looking for profitable ways to reposition production closer to the customer to increase control, agility and responsiveness.

Fugazi Finance and Animal Spirits

Whereas the drivers behind the first half of the K-wave are invention, innovation and industrialisation, the driver behind the second half of the K-wave is much more human – greed. People are not the rational, careful actors we would often like to assume they are but are often driven by what Keynes called our 'animal spirits'. Regardless of whether it is investing in shares or houses, over-speculation and a financial industry's increasing appetite for risk-taking lead to the markets and their players losing sight of the most basic and fundamental truth of any household's economic budgeting principles – only ever borrow what you can afford to pay back, and only ever lend to those you trust. When credit and mortgage packages were outside what most of the population could afford, they simply moved the bar to bring in more consumers, rather than say no or provide different vehicles that were in line with what consumers could afford. Financial goods and services are different from physical products. Capitalism works well when people know and understand what they are buying. Yet most investors know little about the financial products purchased on their behalf, dazzled by tales of quick returns, enabling a fugazi[49] world of smoke and mirrors to exist. Once again, the lure of easy money during the downswing

---

[49] In *The Wolf of Wall Street*, stockbroker Mark Hanna explains to a young Jordan Belfort exactly what it is that they are selling to their clients in their 'make money from exploiting other people's money' world: *'It's a fugazi, fogazzi, it's a wazzi, it's a woozie, it's a... fairy dust.'*

saw the rules being forgotten. Despite the evidence of four previous long-wave cycles, economists continued to predict continual growth, investors continued to make a fortune from selling continual growth, and the population believed them both and bought into continual growth. The truth is that any economy that falls into the trap of expecting infinite growth from a finite pool of money will have a nasty surprise.

Corporate focus on efficiency and M&As, the market's focus on making money from money and the expansion of the credit (derivatives) economy, resulted in too little investment in the real economy. The dominance of financial capital over physical capital resulted in investors seeking returns in investment alternatives, which they primarily found in loans on US real estate and in financial derivatives. The desire for quick profit, risk-taking in the financial markets rather than in industry and innovation, meant that property and financially engineered products was where the money went, creating a debt bubble the like of which had not been seen since 1930. Even just one month before the 2008 crash, most governments were fully signed up to the Greenspan consensus that unlimited credit was an economic miracle, one that would continue to produce unlimited growth.[50] They were all complicit in believing that they could endlessly extend the fat times of a wave's summer cycle, not by the hard thinking of developing innovative products and services, but by constant short-term profit-maximising activities, market manipulations and an increasing level of risk-taking. The market had become a Ponzi scheme, where people believed that the money from the new entrants (in this case from more debt products) into this financial casino would cover the debts and bets that had been placed by the existing gamblers. They were all wrong.

The Cold Winds of Winter

In 1999, an *Economist* article entitled *Catch the wave: The long cycles of industrial innovation are becoming shorter*[112] sounded a warning that no one listened to: *the fifth industrial revolution that started in America in the late 1980s may last no more than 25–30 years... The rapid-upswing part of*

---

[50] Including the then-UK Prime Minister Gordon Brown, who had previously confidently declared that he would ensure that there would be no more 'boom or bust' under his stewardship.

the cycle—in which successful participants enjoy fat margins, set standards, kill off weaker rivals and establish themselves as main players—looks as though it has already run two-thirds of its course, with only another five or six years left to go. Catching the wave at this late stage will depend on governments' willingness to free up their technical and financial resources, invest in the infrastructure required and let their fifth-wave relics go. Failing that, latecomers can expect only crumbs from the table before the party comes to an end – and a new wave of technologies begins, once again, to wash everything aside.

Six years later and a June 2005 post on the Motley Fool website[113] made another Cassandra-like declaration that the accelerating stock prices caused by the dot.com bubble in 2000 should mean that they were now about to enter a recessionary Kondratiev winter phase, when banks would be afraid to lend and borrowers afraid to borrow. By following Kondratiev's theory they predicted something that the world's best economic and financial brains failed to see: that the build-up of debt was unsustainable, the Greenspan belief of unlimited growth was a pipe dream, and there would have to be a long, drawn out recessionary period to wash away the bad debts and bad businesses to allow the next cycle to begin. The Western economies were approaching a Minsky moment,[51] where the cash generated by their assets was no longer sufficient to pay off the debt they took on to acquire them. I doubt whether the *Economist* or the Motley Fool authors had any idea at the time how accurate their predictions actually were, for we know what happened next. In 2008 the world was once again shaken by the turbulence of the long wave. The global expansion of market economics meant that when the debt bubble burst, the resulting crisis affected a huge number of countries and created a prolonged recession that we are still recovering from.[52] It is unfortunate that long-wave analysis and the theories of Schumpeter and Kondratiev only ever seem to be revived or given credit after a major financial crash and seem to be completely forgotten when the money men are making

---

[51] Named after economist Dr Hyman Minsky, who noted that bankers, traders and other financiers periodically played the role of arsonists, setting the entire economy ablaze.

[52] It excluded (to a certain degree) the emerging nations. Even countries like Australia were protected from its effects (initially) due to the explosive growth in China that both created huge demand for natural resources such as coal and iron ore, and also created a consumer spending boom as the newly wealthy Chinese found their way to Australian shores.

hay in the shining sun of a bull market.

For the incredibly small group that do understand and follow long-wave behaviour, the results were expected; however, the economic interventions by the IMF, EU and national banking systems were perhaps not. Rather than take the hit now, the Keynesian neo-liberal economics provided significant financial support to the 'too-big-to-fail' banking system, preventing the bad debts from being washed away. This intervention prevented a Great Recession becoming another Great Depression, but by preventing all the bad debts from being purged from the economy they have simply passed them on to future generations for them to deal with. The government has, in effect, prevented the process of creative destruction from doing its job: a job that applies to the financial sector just as much as it does to the industrial. This action has prolonged the recessionary period, resulting in a flattened level of growth and forced an extended period of austerity onto the public, causing a decade of stagnant wages and reduced public spending. It has also prevented many in the business and financial sector from truly learning the lessons that the collapse of the fifth wave should have taught them. Worse still is the fact that the government money used to bail out the banks, a sum that exceeded £1.1 trillion in the UK alone,[114] has quietly found its way back into the hands of the super-rich – the very same people whose appetite for high-returns casino betting caused the problem in the first place. Inequality usually rises after a recession because while capital rebounds quickly, wages and jobs take a much longer period to return to normal. While the top 1 per cent of earners did see a dramatic drop in their incomes when the stock market crashed, causing a 50 per cent reduction in realised capital gains, they soon recovered and have since seen their share of national income increase. As the American economist Joseph Stiglitz declared, *Obama had to save the banks, sure, but he didn't have to save the bankers and the shareholders and the bondholders. We broke the rules of capitalism in order to save those at the top – as we always do.*[115] This fiscal intervention may have stopped the recession turning into depression in the short term, and in doing so stopped crisis turning into catastrophe, but I cannot help but feel that a lot of today's market fragility is due to the bad debts (and bad debtors) not being fully cleansed. While deemed essential at the time, the actions of the Bank of England and other federal reserves prevented the bad debts and bad companies from being cleared away as expected, resulting in some of the issues, such as an over-focus on short-term growth and the financial sector, to be carried forward into the spring period of the sixth wave. There is also a concern that lessons have not been learned and the economy could wobble and fall back into recession as these debts rise to the surface once again. It has led to the progressive concentration of capital in fewer hands.[53]

The last wave created an almighty paradigm shift in the nature of business, moving focus from industry to services, and from physical to digital sales channels, while at the same time integrating themselves into a single, global market for goods, labour and capital. While employment in services has always been higher than in industry, the gap has grown significantly over the last fifty years, and employment in industrial sectors is now at its lowest level percentage-wise since the mid 19th century.

Despite many media sources downplaying the role of offshoring, you can't expect the population to not notice that 90 per cent of the goods in Walmart are now made outside the US. Many manufacturing companies have decided to make things elsewhere, import them, and then declare their profits elsewhere. This is a lose-lose-lose-lose-lose scenario. You lose jobs, lose employment tax revenues, lose sales taxes through decreased spending, increase social spending (to pay for newly unemployed manufacturing workers), and lose the corporation tax needed to pay for social spending. Inequality in earnings has also risen. Since the late 1970s, when neo-liberal economics came to the fore, average growth in real wages has increasingly lagged productivity growth while the top earners have significantly increased their share of the pot. For example, in the US between 1993 and 2001, more than half of the nation's income growth was captured by the top 1 per cent of earners, rising to $2 out of every $3 in the period up to 2008. The very efficiency of capitalism in funnelling most of the circulating money into an ever-decreasing number of hands, plus the protection that money received from government bailouts, has caused this to happen, with the result of increasing both the level of inequality and exclusivity. The rich have got richer while the less well-off were just that – worse off. The long, hard recessionary period of a Kondratiev winter is, as mentioned, the start of a dangerous time both socially and politically. Long periods of economic depression create political tensions upon which

---

[53] It is important to note that efforts have been made to retrain the industry, with the financial industry spending over $236 billion on fines and compensation for breaching a variety of financial regulations since 2008.

demagogues can build a platform and speak directly to the vast swathes of people whose incomes, happiness and dreams for the future have been adversely affected. When the working man finds himself and his family disadvantaged and facing an uncertain future due to the financial wheeling and dealing of the so-called masters of the universe, people who continue to reap high rewards through this period, then bitterness and anger rises. Working people crave attention from anyone who they believe can help them, or at least is listening to their issues and proclaims to understand the pain and frustrations they are going through. Pains caused by actions in the market that they were not responsible for, nor would have benefited from. This explains why an economic crisis tends to create a world peace crisis, and why the end of the winter period usually results in war, infighting and divisiveness; something we are seeing play out currently, and which Kondratiev himself noted. Yet, it is not the winter where the real danger lies, but the spring period, when the new ways of working start to disrupt the old established industries, skills and incomes; something we will explore in Part Three.

Spring is in the Air...

For ten years, investment has been held back while the world recovers from the cold of the recession. However, the power of creative destruction cannot be held back, and behind the scenes, new methods of production and new communication protocols have been developed. Kondratiev noted that during the winter period, the recession, *an especially large number of important discoveries and inventions in the technique of production and communication occur*, but these must wait for the next wave's upswing to be implemented on a large scale. For example, the final couple of years before the financial crash saw a series of key innovations that would prove to be instrumental to the launch of the Digital Age. YouTube, the video-streaming and sharing platform was created in 2005, bought the following year by Google for $1.65bn. The first version of Hadoop was released in 2006; open-source infrastructure software that enables the distributed storage, indexing and processing of very large, complex data sets. Still in 2006, Mark Zuckerberg released Facebook outside of universities to anyone aged over thirteen with a valid email address, and the social platform Twitter was also launched. Then, on 9th January 2007, Steve Jobs stood on stage at the Macworld Conference and Expo in San Francisco and announced that Apple were introducing three revolutionary products: a widescreen iPod with touch controls, a revolutionary mobile phone, and a breakthrough Internet device – all contained in one new product: the iPhone. The tools of the sixth wave, tools that allowed companies and individuals to instantly share, store and process data amongst millions of people, were now available. A proliferation of *Star Trek*-style technologies such as Internet video calling and conferencing tools such as Skype appeared, and 4G networks enable the streaming of films and the rise of social media. We have also seen the rise of new digital technologies, 3D printing, autonomous vehicles, warehouse robotics, and new technologies that have started to show characteristics of early AI. This has resulted in the development of AI assistants with names like Siri, Alexa, Cortana and Google Assistant,[54] that combine voice recognition with natural user interfaces and a powerful information-manipulation system, all packaged into a device that fits comfortably in your pocket. As Arthur C. Clarke suggested, our 1918 time traveller would indeed believe all this to be magic.

A decade after the Global Financial Crisis hit, the financial freeze of the fifth wave's winter has thawed and the first buds of a new economic spring, a period where inventions start to attract financial support and transform into innovations, are everywhere. The first benefactors of sixth-wave investment were technologies that were developed in the previous wave, but which were not fully industrialised due to lack of funding – the Internet, mobile and e-commerce. While the hype was there in the late 1990s, the ability to realise it wasn't. The companies that did manage to leverage this fledgling technology – Amazon, for example – were smart enough to create a digital business model that could still operate within the limitations of the existing physical infrastructure, such as the postal service. That's why Bezos started Amazon by selling books, and then DVDs and CDs – all items of similar size and weight that were both easy to store and easy to ship using traditional postal methods, explaining why he succeeded whereas companies like pets.com crashed and burned.

During this transition period from winter to spring, the economic and business world undergoes considerable changes. Focus has shifted from

---

[54] Google really needs to try harder on the naming front.

finance to production capital, stimulating increased growth, well-being and a more positive future perspective. Instead of superstar financial whizz-kids, analysts and stockbrokers, the upswing sees new, small, innovative upstart companies, fronted by the new entrepreneurs who see the opportunities of the new wave's inventions (what Schumpeter called 'new-men', although now just as likely to be female) grow up and transform into the most dominant forces in their industry. Global markets and economies are busy rebuilding, and investment is being redirected from the old stalwart companies to the new start-ups. Instead of talking about share prices, interest rates, cutbacks, the recession, redundancies and efficiencies, talk of a brave new world of technology dominates the blogosphere and Internet chatter. As Kondratiev and Schumpeter predicted, a new wave of creativity led by a new breed of entrepreneurs, people like Musk, Bezos and Brin, has attracted a new wave of investment. They are investing in innovative long-term projects (what Google call 'moon-shots') without the constant, quarterly, short-term pressure from stock-market analysts that the larger, older, more operationally focused and production-based companies face.

The new innovators and their firms are grounded in new digital business models that require little start-up capital, few physical assets and no real supply-chain network such as warehouses, factories and logistics. This means that they can be launched and distributed quickly, creating a significant advantage over traditional 'physical' manufacturing firms whose products and supply chains take time to develop. Digital companies also leverage social media and digital platforms, removing the need for extensive and expensive mass-marketing campaigns to get their message out. This means that winners can emerge quickly, rapidly accruing a strong consumer base that enables them to reap disproportionately large rewards. As an example of the speed digital companies can operate at, Uber officially launched its mobile app to a select number of US cities in 2011, but twelve months later they had already expanded into Europe. Now, its market capitalisation is north of $60 billion.

The first victims of digital creative destruction were the music and publishing industries, where their stranglehold on the expressive abilities of creative artists for massive profits was underpinned by a new technology that allowed for digital, not physical, distribution of words, images and sounds. While devastating for the companies caught in the cross hairs of the destruction side of the equation (Kodak, HMV, Blockbuster et al.), the creative side of the digital revolution shows the potential this has for the environment. Business focus shifted from making products to providing services and solving problems. These developments could address the challenges posed by the globalisation of the consumer lifestyle that characterised the last wave. To demonstrate this, I often show a 1991 Radio Shack advert that displays fifteen items in its latest sale, including Walkmans, Dictaphones, video cameras, VCRs, phones, CD players and calculators. All these are now included on the smartphone in your pocket – for no extra cost. Even innovations from the last phases of the fifth wave such as computer games and GPS systems are now primarily provided as digital downloads and apps rather than physical discs and devices. This transition has increased, not decreased, the value to both the consumer and the planet. Now consider how many of these are no longer going to be buried in a landfill. How much energy had been saved not having to produce them, ship them, store them and dispose of them. Consider also the benefits to corporations of producing goods that do not bring with them criticisms of exploitation; the ability to use software and machines to produce goods and undertake dull, dirty and dangerous tasks rather than low-cost labour in far-off lands.

Recent figures also show that manufacturing output in the West is on the rise again following the Great Recession.[116] Many companies have decided that the risks, as well as the lack of responsiveness caused by having to order in large volumes and wait long lead times for goods to arrive, mean that the business case for the offshore economic model just does not exist any more. As a result, many companies have reshored, or are in the process of reshoring their operations. Apparel manufacturers have now decided that it's cheaper to invest in technology than to hire even the world's lowest-paid workers. As an example, Nike's 2014 corporate responsibility report showed that Nike cancelled an offshore production contract, eliminating more than 106,000 overseas contract factory workers and 125 less-efficient factories. Likewise, Apple has decided to assemble one of its Mac computer lines in the US rather than in China, and in direct response to President Trump's calling out its lack of US investment, it also created a $1 billion fund to invest in advanced US manufacturing.[117] Apple supplier Foxconn is also looking at Wisconsin as a location to open a new plant, after confirming in January 2017 that it was considering a $7 billion joint investment with Apple for a US factory to produce displays. Airbus declared it would build JetBlue's new jets in Alabama, and even Walmart, which was one of the originators of using offshore suppliers to reduce costs, stated it would increase its spending with American suppliers by $50 billion over the next decade. Some companies, organisations with the foresight to see real strategic opportunity, have even exploited their competitors' focus on cheap mass production. Zara, for example, has risen to become the most valuable clothes retailer in the world through a focus on 'fast fashion'. To enable them to rapidly change product ranges and designs, they have kept the production facilities local (in Spain) even though the wages and production costs are higher, so that the designers can liaise continuously with the store managers to establish what is selling and what is not, and then alter the range accordingly. This shift has the potential to change the dynamics significantly, dramatically affecting the pace of industrial revolution happening in the emerging countries, while accelerating the economic recovery in the developed world as the work begins to be reshored.

Manufacturing is starting to come home. However, this return of manufacturing has not been accompanied by a return of manufacturing jobs. Manufacturing may be coming home, it isn't the same early 2000-style manufacturing that left. To really see the impact, consider the number of

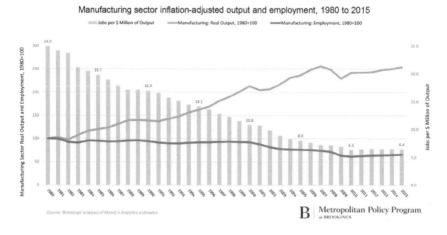

Graph 3: Manufacturing Sector Inflation-Adjusted Output and Employment, 1980–2015.
Source: Brookings.

jobs needed to produce $1 million's worth of output each.

This research by Brookings highlights that inflation-adjusted output of the manufacturing sector has continued steadily upwards since 1980, but what is glaringly apparent is that the number of jobs needed to support the growth has plummeted. In 1980, there were 24.9 jobs per $1 million's worth of manufacturing output. In 2015 that had dropped to 6.4 jobs per $1 million. The reason for this is clear: if we are making much more with fewer people, then we must have become much more efficient at manufacturing. If productivity is rising, somebody is benefiting from the wealth created – and it isn't the middle class. The increase in productivity combined with the stagnant level of jobs and wages in manufacturing must mean that fewer people are required to make the products. A 2012 *Bloomberg* article entitled *It's a Man vs Machine Recovery,* highlighted the fact that *the U.S. produces almost one-quarter more goods and services today than it did in 1999, while using almost precisely the same number of workers. It's as if $2.5 trillion worth of stuff—the equivalent of the entire U.S. economy circa 1958—materialized out of thin air.*[118]

There are only two ways to achieve this: either things are being made somewhere else, or they are now being made by machines.

Part Two

THE SIXTH WAVE

9

THE AUTOMATION
OF LABOUR

*Technology marches in seven-league boots from one ruthless,
revolutionary conquest to another, tearing down old factories and
industries, flinging up new processes with terrifying rapidity.*

Charles Beard, *Time, Technology, and the Creative Spirit in Political Science*, 1927

The collapse of the fifth wave in 2008 and the resultant financial malaise sent economies into a tailspin, but behind the scenes the seeds of a new wave were being laid, awaiting the funds needed for them to bloom. Now a new age of exponential technological and scientific progress is upon us, about to start its upswing. This new wave has already been called many things, from the second machine age to the fourth industrial revolution. Whatever name it's given doesn't really do it justice, for it is far more than simple digitisation of product and services, or the development of smarter machines. It has the potential to shift business, economic and social paradigms, starting with the automation of the entire end-to-end supply chain. Even in these early days, its potential for disruption has already been felt. To understand the sheer scale of what is currently in development, one only needs a cursory glance at the 2018 Gartner Hype Cycle, shown in Diagram 6.

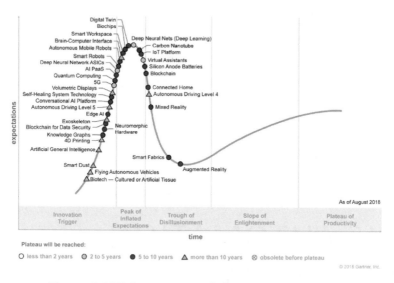

Diagram 5: 2018 Gartner Hype Cycle for Emerging Technologies.

Many of these technologies are primed to go exponential in the next decade – and here lies the critical difference between this new wave and the last five. None of the previous waves had this amount of disruptive, what Christensen called 'market-creating', technologies contained in its upswing. A convergence of disruptive technologies is clustering, feeding into each other to generate a new industrial revolution, capable of impacting and disrupting as many industries as the process of electrification did a hundred years ago. They will take time to diffuse, but not the sixty years electricity took to go from invention to powering nearly every Western household and factory. The worlds of medicine and biology are rapidly being transformed through advancements in genetic research, nanotechnology and stem cell research; robotics and 3D printing are changing the nature of manufacturing, and advancements in renewable technologies such as solar have meant that there is finally a financially viable alternative to fossil fuels. Advanced robotics, additive manufacturing and the large-scale digitisation of operations are poised to alter fundamental assumptions about manufacturing costs, location and footprints. Until now, progress in these new fields has been linear and deceptive; now as the money starts to flow it is starting to accelerate at a pace that is making Moore's Law look positively snail-like, becoming disruptive as the law of accelerating returns kicks in. To ensure that they still play a relevant part in the new wave, companies will have to change focus from efficiency to experimentation, making significant investments in new technologies and in ensuring that they have the supply base and workforce needed to compete. It will be a challenge that many will struggle to accept, let alone overcome.

The Creative Destruction Triple Whammy

To really understand the impact of the sixth wave, one needs to step back. The full magnitude of the disruptive potential only becomes apparent when you stop looking at each innovation individually and instead take a helicopter view of them across the entire global supply chain. Only then do their impact, opportunity and threat level become apparent. We are about to experience what I call the sixth wave's 'creative destruction triple whammy'. The first whammy is the automation of physical labour; the second is the automation of knowledge-based work; and the third is their convergence and alignment to create an almost fully automated end-to-end value chain.

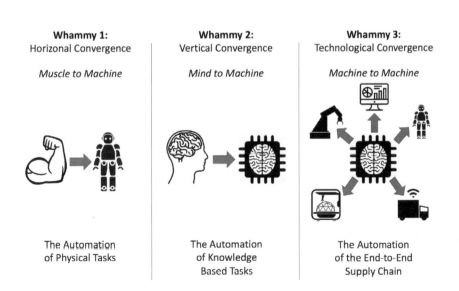

Whammy 1:	**Whammy 2:**	**Whammy 3:**
Horizonal Convergence	Vertical Convergence	Technological Convergence
Muscle to Machine	*Mind to Machine*	*Machine to Machine*
The Automation of Physical Tasks	The Automation of Knowledge Based Tasks	The Automation of the End-to-End Supply Chain

Diagram 7. The Creative Destruction Triple Whammy

Whammy number one is the automation of muscle; the dull, dangerous and dirty tasks we complete with our hands and our sweat. Despite the process of automation having been under way since the industrial revolution, the business world still relies heavily on human labour to do manual things. That is about to change. A new breed of cooperative robots and autonomous vehicles is being developed that challenge previous assumptions about what machines can and cannot do, proved them to be not just wrong, but absurd. The new wave of automation will be able to undertake jobs previously assumed safe, disrupting virtually every industry across the end-to-end value chain. From digging things out of the ground to delivering them to your door, anything that involved human labour is now being disrupted.

Automating Sourcing

Let's start with farming. The invention of agricultural practices and labour-saving machines have enabling a transition from 80 per cent of the population working in agriculture, to around 1 per cent, while increasing the productivity of each farmer's efforts from being able to feed just themselves and their family, to feeding 155 mouths.[119] Nevertheless, while crops like wheat and barley can be roughly gathered by machines such as combine harvesters, more perishable fruits and vegetables still require the nimbleness of human fingers to pick them to prevent them from being damaged. The inability of machines to handle these types of produce creates a huge demand for low-paid, usually migrant human labour to work the fields and carefully pick the crop before it spoils. Or at least, that was the case.

New machines with names like the Shrimp, the Ladybird and the LettuceBot can now autonomously tend fields of vegetables, identify and eliminate weeds and count and pick fruit from trees and bushes. The LettuceBot, for example, uses advanced vision to highlight the difference between weeds and other problematic plants and the crop, killing the weeds automatically with a squirt of fertiliser. Other robots use 3D imaging to analyse the quality of crops as they grow, identify any diseases or pests, and determine when the crop is ready to be harvested. Robotic company FFRobotics has developed a machine with between four and twelve robotic arms that each have three-fingered grips to grab fruit and twist or clip it from a branch, enabling it to pick up to 10,000 apples an hour, never suffering the fatigue of its human counterparts. It can be adjusted to harvest a variety of crops, taking 85 to 90 per cent of the crop off the trees, leaving humans to pick what's left. There are other methods being developed as well, such as a fruit-picking robot from Abundant Robotics that uses suction to vacuum apples off trees,[120] and vineyard robots that winery owners are using to monitor vine health, cultivate the soil and do the weeding. These machines will prove to be a boon for areas that currently rely extensively on large groups of migrant labour to harvest these crops, such as California's Salinas Valley or Lincolnshire in the UK.

But the automation doesn't stop there. Farmers can now tend their crops using drones controlled by iPhones, tractors have become autonomous and located by GPS, and there are even robots such as the Rover that can do the time-consuming, twice-daily task of herding and milking cows.[121] Research company Tractica predicts that agricultural robot shipments will explode from 25,000 per annum in 2015, to nearly 1 million units by 2024.[122] As supermarkets continually squeeze farmers by paying less for their crops, milk, and meat, any way that they can decrease the cost of their production is welcomed. Necessity is the mother of invention, as the saying goes. Sometimes politics creates the incentive, such as the Brexit vote in the UK, where the decision was made to leave the EU, leaving some farmers worried about whether they could still access the vast number of migrants willing to pick fruit and vegetables for low wages. A new generation of farm automation is therefore being developed to plug the potential labour shortage on Britain's farms, including being able to automate the entire crop-production process. To prove the potential, Harper Adams University initiated a project called Hands Free Hectare which successfully planted, tended and harvested one hectare (about 2.5 acres) of spring barley without a single person setting foot in the field, using a combination of autonomous tractors, drones and other farming robots.[123]

One of the most exciting agricultural transformations is likely to be vertical farming, the creation of indoor, urban farms that use nutrient-rich soil or water and are impervious to the natural forces of the seasons. Although measured in square footage, it should be cubic footage due to the ability to grow crops vertically in multiple levels of racking. Vertical indoor farming creates an entirely new possibility for food production, overcoming nature's seasonal attributes to create a 365-day growing period that is free from insects and requires no pesticides or fertilisers. Vertical farms include hydroponics systems that use 95 per cent less water while growing approximately 350 times the amount of produce that traditional outdoor methods could achieve in the same amount of space. Farmers have even been able to change the colour, yield and even flavour of crops simply by altering the nutrients. Some urban farms also utilise a closed-loop system called aquaponics, where the water used to hydrate the plants drips into tanks used to breed fish, and then the fish droppings are used to fertilise the plants, which clean and filter the water before it goes back into the planters.

Multiple vertical farming projects are currently under way. In Japan, completely autonomous, robot-run indoor farms have been developed, capable of harvesting 30,000 heads of lettuce a day. In Brooklyn, old shipping containers have been transformed into indoor agriculture units. In Europe, a commercial vertical farming facility has been built in Dronten, near Amsterdam, that has a total cultivation area of 32,290 square feet. This is small compared to AeroFarms' 70,000-square foot facility in Newark, New Jersey, or the 87,000-square foot aquaponics site that has been developed in the remains of an old brewery in St. Paul, Minnesota. The St. Paul farm intends to raise 275,000 pounds of Atlantic salmon and Arctic char fish each year and grow 475,000 pounds of organic greens including kale, pak choy and arugula.[124] However, all these farms are about to be dwarfed by a massive 100-hectare vertical farm in Shanghai, China, designed to feed 24 million people. In Japan, some companies have experimented with creating an indoor farm in their office block to feed their workers. For example, the Tokyo headquarters of human resources company Pasona Group, grows two hundred species of fruits and vegetables and even rice that they harvest and serve to employees.[125] Autonomous, vertical farming creates whole new possibilities, from providing a stable food supply for areas traditionally blighted by climate issues, through to enabling the growing of produce close to the market rather than incurring huge transport and environmental costs. There is a growing demand for all things organic and the ability to grow fruits and vegetables all year round without having to rely on chemicals will reduce the price of organic goods in the stores, furthering their growth. Amazon's 2017 purchase of Whole Foods will probably lead to it embracing indoor vertical farming as a way to control the production and distribution of organic produce in further reduce prices and dominate the marketplace. Vertical farming also allows us to artificially create the perfect environment to grow fruits and vegetables in countries where they normally wouldn't exist. Imagine strawberries growing in Siberia or bananas growing all year round in Manchester. You get the idea. Crucially, this could also provide a way to protect areas prone to drought and disease, such as sub-Sharan Africa, saving them from cycles of devastating crop failures and mass starvations. Locating the farms close to both vendors and consumers also means that fresher produce can reach tables with less reliance on trucks and global shipping, drastically reducing the environmental impact while also reducing the need to artificially extend a product's shelf life through preservatives. More yield, better quality, fewer chemicals, fresher and tastier food, less space, less transportation and storage – what's not to love?

Mining is another area undergoing an autonomous revolution. The Australian mining industry, with its sky-high labour costs, has driverless trucks, trains and drills being used in many iron ore and coal mines, replacing perhaps the world's highest-paid truck drivers.[126] Multinational mining giant Rio Tinto declared that the skills crisis and demand for greater productivity forced them to take steps towards automated mining in Queensland. Over eighty autonomous trucks from Japanese company Komatsu now work 24/7 at their Australian iron ore mines, monitored and controlled 1,200 kilometres away in Perth. The fleet-control system prevents collisions with other dump trucks, service vehicles, equipment or people, making it extremely safe and reliable. These autonomous vehicles have now moved more than 1 billion tons of iron ore and waste material across five sites, with each autonomous truck operating about seven hundred hours more than conventional haul trucks per year at around 15 per cent lower load and haul unit costs. The world's biggest mining company, BHP Billiton Ltd, has seen what Rio Tinto has achieved, and is also deploying Caterpillar driverless trucks and drills in iron ore mines in Australia. They are being introduced in the US and beyond from 2018. Truck manufacturer Volvo has also produced an autonomous vehicle specifically designed to work underground in complete darkness, using lasers to scan the environment and safely traverse the dark and dangerous tunnels in the coal mine.

The process of converting iron ore into steel is also being disrupted. Despite President Trump's declaration that US greatness depends on getting the coal miners and steelworkers back to work, he's likely to find that the need for these workers is not as great as he hoped, for it's not just China that's responsible for the decline in demand for steelworkers. New control processes and innovations such as casting steel closer to the required shape of the finished product have reduced the number of worker hours needed to make a tonne of steel from seven hundred in 1990, to just 250 in 2017. To highlight the labour efficiencies being achieved, Voestalpine AG's new rolling mill in Donawitz, Austria, needs just 14 employees to make 500,000 tons of robust steel wire a year, compared to nearly 1,000 in the 1960s.[127] These 14 employees are also white-collar technicians rather than the blackened-faced grafters of previous years. From 2008 through 2015, Europe's steel workforce shrank 20 per cent, shedding 84,000 jobs. Voestalpine's CEO, Wolfgang Eder, predicts employment in the sector could decline another 20 per cent over the coming decade. He should know. Voestalpine aims to open a fully automated plant in Kapfenberg by 2020 that will supply high-tech aeroplane components such as stress-resistant engine mounts and landing gear parts. Automating a plant that currently employs 2,500 people will obviously have a dramatic impact on the local employment situation.

Once goods have been taken from the ground or converted into usable materials, the next step is to transport them to the ports. Again, this is being automated. Rio Tinto has invested AU$518 million in the development of an autonomous train system across its Pilbara iron ore network to the Australian ports. Meanwhile, in the Netherlands, a joint five-year project between MIT and the Amsterdam Institute for Advanced Metropolitan Solutions is working on developing a fleet of autonomous barges to move goods across the country using the existing Dutch canal system. They have been designed to fit beneath the many bridges found in the Netherlands and Belgium. The barges are expected to be launched in 2018 and will remove 23,000 trucks — most of them diesel powered — from area roads.

Also in The Netherlands, Europe's biggest port — Rotterdam — was the first to fully embrace automation, primarily to handle the increasing size of container ships. The RWG terminal is nearly fully automated, using automatic cranes to load and unload ships onto unmanned, automated goods vehicles (AGVs) that transport containers to the storage area. Seeing the efficiency and safety opportunities Rotterdam has benefited from, other ports across the world are also automating their operations. All of DP World's Australian ports, starting with the Webb Dock in Melbourne, are being automated. India's government is currently automating Tuticorin Port to reduce container dwell times and lower costs and is also set to build eight new automated ports in the country. China is pushing ahead with President Xi's $900 billion One Belt, One Road project, which aims to link Western Europe and Asia again – only this time the route will contain autonomous ships, trains and ports, not men in caravans or horses and camels. The port automation movement has also naturally reached the United States. The Port of Los Angeles has already invested $693 million in four dozen self-driving cranes and automated carriers plus related infrastructure, and Middle Harbor, the Port of Long Beach's $1.3 billion new automated terminal, is planned to be operational by 2019. California Governor Jerry Brown is particularly keen on port automation, pushing for 100,000 zero-emission freight-hauling machines in California by 2030.

Rolls-Royce is also rethinking the process of moving goods between ports. It is planning on creating an entirely autonomous fleet of ships that traverse the oceans without a crew, completely controlled and monitored back at the base. These ships will be simpler in design than traditional vessels because they won't need a bridge or living quarters for crew, saving labour costs and enabling more storage space for goods, increasing capacity, efficiency and profitability. They will also be less susceptible to rough weather and pirate attacks (because there will be no one to take hostage). Overall, they are set to streamline operations, reduce costs and dramatically improve safety, as around 80 per cent of accidents are caused by human error. Marine safety was in the headlines in August 2017 when a US Navy warship, the *USS John S. McCain*, and a 30,000-ton, six hundred-foot merchant oil tanker called the *Alnic MC* collided near Singapore, causing the deaths of ten sailors. Rolls-Royce are not the only company working on autonomous shipping: the Japanese government has also set a target of 250 domestically built autonomous ships to be launched by 2025. However, it is in colder climates that the first autonomous ship will be launched. A Norwegian container ship, the *Yara Birkeland,* is the world's first electric, autonomous, zero-emissions ship. Equipped with a GPS and various types of sensors, including lidar, radar and cameras, the ship will be able to steer itself through the sea, avoid other ships, and dock independently.

Shipping is responsible for nearly 4 per cent of all climate-change emissions, including 18–30 per cent of the world's nitrogen oxide (NOx) pollution and 9 per cent of the global sulphur oxide (SOx) pollution.[128]

Electric ships like the *Yara Birkeland* will reduce this enormously, for as well as reducing fuel emissions, this one ship will replace 40,000 truck journeys that currently take place throughout southern Norway. As you would expect, the synergies and opportunities these new technologies provide to commercial, profit-driven enterprises are becoming apparent. BHP currently charters around 1,500 voyages a year to move the 250 million metric tons of iron ore, copper and coal it exports from Australia to its waiting customers in China. It is now investigating using giant, automated cargo ships to do this instead, seeing enormous efficiency, insurance and labour savings in automating the ten-day sea journey.

Finally, air freight is also planning to become autonomous, with Airbus planning on developing a fleet of autonomous cargo planes. Whereas previously it has been argued that we cannot trust machines to fully pilot commercial aircraft, that argument lost a lot of its weight in 2015 with the dual tragedies of the Malaysian Airlines MH370 disappearance and the Germanwings crash when the co-pilot deliberately flew a fully laden passenger plane into the side of a French mountain, killing all on board. Machines don't tend to commit suicide.

Automating Production

The word 'robot' comes from a Czech word, *robota*, meaning 'forced labour', and was first used to denote a fictional humanoid in the 1920 play *R.U.R.* (Rossum's Universal Robots) by the Czech writer, Karel Čapek. Robots have since captured the imagination of sci-fi writers and industrialists alike, becoming an almost immediate feature in fictional films such as *Metropolis* (1927). It took until 1961 before robots lived up to their name and appeared as a form of labour in the real world of industry, when a one-armed welding machine called Unimate began work at General Motors. Even now, the automotive industry is still one of the biggest users of robots, with over 80 per cent of car production completed by machines. Most industrial robots are large, heavy, costly, single-purpose machines capable of repeatedly performing precise steps such as lifting heavy objects, cutting metal or welding. Expensive to program, incapable of handling even small deviations, completely unaware of their surroundings and so dangerous that they must be physically separated from human workers by cages, they remain impractical for other types of manufacturing.

Until now. The days of needing highly structured environments for robots to operate in are over as robots have obtained the power of sight and touch. This awareness has enabled them to break free of their cages and find new homes in nearly every industry, working alongside human colleagues – or replacing them. A new generation of smarter, more adaptive, collaborative industrial robots (known as 'cobots') designed to work alongside human counterparts has arrived and have the capability to adapt automatically to changing environments, using a series of cameras, sensors and software to enable them to 'see' objects, 'feel' forces and 'understand' tasks. Their connection to the broader manufacturing ecosystem also enables them to share data and continuously report on their performance. Whereas traditional industrial robots perform one task with superhuman speed and precision, cobots are multi-purpose, able to undertake just about any job that involves picking stuff up and putting it down somewhere else while simultaneously adapting to changes in its environment, like a misplaced part or a conveyor belt that suddenly changes speed. These robots can be incredibly precise, able to work to a precision of +/− 0.1 millimetres, making them well suited to tasks such as electro-component manufacture and machine-tending.

The game-changing aspects of these robots are as follows:

- **Price:** They're cheap. Priced from $25,000, they cost less than the salary for a US warehouse or production worker. Only these robots can work all day and night, don't get sick, require breaks or need holidays. They also don't join unions, complain or go on strike.
- **Safety:** They're safe. Collaborative robots require no security cages, as they are aware of their surroundings, enabling them to work seamlessly alongside their human co-workers, continuously sensing and adapting to what is going on in their environment. As soon as the robot touches something unexpected, it stops with a concerned look on its face until it is safe to continue.
- **Intelligence:** They learn. To teach Baxter, a cobot from Rethink Robotics, how to complete a new job, a human simply guides its arms to simulate the desired task through a sequence of motions, records them and watches as the robot repeats the process automatically. If the robot does not understand, it responds with a

confused expression. The hands of the robots are becoming more sophisticated, increasing the number of complex actions they can perform. As well as being equipped with sensors and other software to help it see and understand its environment, Baxter has also been programmed to use 'common sense'. For example, if it drops an object, it 'knows' it must get another one before trying to finish the task. These robots get smarter with every software update: not something that can always be said about human workers.

- **Ease of Use:** They don't need programming. Rethink positions Baxter as being more like an application than a traditional industrial robot; a plug-and-play machine that small manufacturers can use without lengthy training of employees. These robots don't need coding; through a method called kinaesthetic learning, people can now teach the robot complex manoeuvres simply by directing the robot's arm through a motion several times. Programming robots used to be a job for engineers, but now advanced learning algorithms allow machines to pick up skills from their human co-workers.

In the past, if you wanted your robot to do another task, you had to buy another robot. This was expensive, making them cost-effective only in narrow situations, thereby becoming major capital investment decisions that companies had to think very carefully about. This obviously limited the growth of the robot industry. Conversely collaborative robots are mostly designed as platforms, able to be upgraded without a change in hardware, making them multi-purpose units that can be adapted to perform a whole host of tasks in the same way a smartphone can do a wide variety of things dependent on the installed apps. Software updates can dramatically alter the capabilities and performance of the robot – and robots can be updated for free. Different grippers can be installed in minutes to allow them to do a variety of tasks. This totally changes the decision-making process around robots, making them viable investments for a vastly wider group of industries and company sizes. These robots therefore acquire more skills as new software comes out and third parties invent functions, making them ideal for replacing human labour in the most boring and physically tiring factory chores, ranging from line-loading and machine-tending to packaging and material handling. Rethink Robotics' latest operating system update enabled the robots to provide critical, real-time production data as well as embedded vision and force-sensing capabilities that enable the robots to see and 'feel' things, allowing them to make adaptive decisions as tasks run. This new capability has enabled academic institutions like MIT to develop soft grippers for Baxter that allow it to carefully handle anything from eggs to paper, dramatically increasing its flexibility and applicability to a whole host of different industries. Other robotic companies are also experimenting with 'soft robotics', specifically the 'end-of-arm tooling' (the robot's 'hands'). The flexibility of this approach means that a simple change of tooling enables the robot to perform a completely different task and handle completely different materials. Now, wherever there is a repetitive task, there's a robot that can do it.

The cost savings, consistency and flexibility that collaborative robots bring to companies allows them to rethink their supply chain strategy. Many companies offshored manufacturing simply to reduce labour costs. However, what they found was that the total cost of the supply chain – including many of the risks mentioned earlier such as excessive transportation costs, long lead times, and a loss of visibility and control – was far greater than any planned savings. Also, in many places like South Africa, where the labour groups are powerful, many leaders bemoan the fact that the personnel they have today may be different to the ones they are given tomorrow. This ever-changing temporary workforce results in a consistently low quality of output with a myriad of human errors as people are not given the training nor time on the job needed to iron out these problems. The sum total of these issues means that the total cost is higher than expected, and as a result moving production back to where the demand resides makes both financial and business sense. Collaborative robots are therefore enabling companies to rethink their offshoring decisions, creating whole new possibilities for small to medium-sized manufacturers who previously assumed that robots were outside of their budget. The possibility to deploy these robots without having to restructure their entire operations completely changes the equation. It means that robots can be used to complete any task where human error is a factor and then repositioned as desired. Rather than companies having to launch a major capital expenditure project and redesign the whole production and packing line, cobots can simply slot into the existing one, taking the place of the human worker. Conversely, they also allow companies to experiment with reorganising their production layouts, enabling them to design environments that do not need to accommodate humans. Their ability to operate at a per-unit cost that is cheaper than even the lowest-paid human workers makes them a desirable proposition, enabling companies to neutralise the location issue so that manufacturing can be moved to where the demand is, not the labour. This reduces the amount of transportation and storage needed and allows for items can be made in smaller batches, increasing the agility required to meet the needs of customers who are increasingly demanding shorter lead times. Connected robots are also capable of sharing and reusing programming, which means manufacturers can flexibly set up production in multiple places and still maintain the quality and consistency of global brands, regardless of the local labour pool. Collaborative robots are bringing the benefits of robotics to areas of work where they never made sense before, making it more efficient for companies to reposition production nearer their customers. This is starting to kick off a reshoring epidemic, creating a paradigm shift in many companies' manufacturing strategy and helping Western countries to reclaim a share of the global manufacturing market that had been outsourced to low-wage labour countries.

The economics for automating is compelling. The Boston Consulting Group has estimated that while *a human welder today earns around $25 per hour, including benefits, the equivalent operating cost per hour for a robot is around $8.*[129] The gap is expected to widen further as wages rise, the cost of robots fall and their capabilities improve, providing a better welder for less money. The cost of systems engineering – installing, programming, and integrating a robotics system into a factory – has declined even more. In the mid-2000s, the average systems-engineering costs of a spot-welding robot amounted to $81,000. Now its average cost is $46,000 and likely to keep dropping for the rest of the decade. The extra cost of maintaining a robotics system – installation, maintenance and operating costs – should be amortised, according to the group, over a five-year period, and as time passes the ROI period will continue to shrink. The robots are needed, for welding is a skilled profession that is struggling to attract talent. According to the American Welding Society, the average age of a welder today is around fifty-five years, and when these workers retire, it could leave the US industry facing a shortage of as many as 372,000 welders by 2026. Companies like ARC Specialties are competing to fill this gap by developing collaborative robots that can weld and cut metal at a professional level and speed. As Dan

Allford, the President of ARC, states, *We're going to give the robot a plasma cutting torch and, with the current plan, a magnetic base so you can position the robot anywhere on your workpiece.* This robot is called CutBot and will be available mid-2018. States Allford, *Wouldn't it be nice to be able to do an octagon with quarter inch radius corners and 12-degree bevels? No human could do that. But CutBot will.*[130] Humans simply cannot compete with this level of complexity and productivity per dollar. This process of automation is, as many have pointed out, irreversible.

The tipping point for robots is about to be reached. Companies like Tesla now view the automation of their factories as being a critical competitive advantage. In his Tesla *Master Plan, Part Deux*, CEO Elon Musk declares, *that is why Tesla Engineering has transitioned to focus heavily on designing the machine that makes the machine – turning the factory itself into the product.*[131] To keep up, the other car manufacturers will also have to embrace robots at the same pace or find themselves left behind. This is no different to the war between Japanese car manufacturers and the US car industry in the first half of the fifth wave. Innovation then came from process, not machines. The Japanese, through the teachings of people like W. Edwards Deming, developed cultural methodologies like Kaizen, Lean, TPM and Six Sigma, that enabled them to reduce errors and increase efficiencies far in excess of what their US counterparts could achieve. The US car industry had to embrace this new way of thinking or get left behind. It was a long and difficult transition, and profits plummeted during that time. However, it was still a human vs human competition. Now we are in a machine-vs-machine world. This transition will create a booming market for robotics manufacturers, but it will also obviously create highly automated factories that require little human assistance to run.

There is also about to be an 'on-demand' manufacturing revolution. The Industry 4.0 movement emanating out of Germany is driven by the principle of combining the digital and physical worlds to create a 'cyber-physical' supply chain capable of delivering mass customisation – production schedules with a lot size of one – with the same efficiencies, cost and speed as mass-produced items. The on-demand manufacturing revolution is beginning, changing the dynamics of the supply chain. Amazon has a patent to develop an on-demand apparel factory and robots such as Sewbo and Lowry have been developed that can sew together clothing, reducing the dependency on sweatshops in places like Bangladesh and eliminating the risk of brand damage through unethical working conditions. Softwear Automation, who make Lowry, have created an automated t-shirt work line that can make as many shirts per hour as seventeen human workers.[132]

The robot revolution is also having a major impact in China. The Chinese government has realised that an ageing population and growing wages have impacted the country's attractiveness as a manufacturing destination and have taken proactive steps by focusing on becoming the largest producer and purchaser of industrial robots. It has some catching up to do. According to the International Federation of Robotics,[133] in 2017 China's robot density (the number of robots per 10,000 workers) was 68, placing it as twenty-third in the world. The Republic of Korea was first with 631 robots per 10,000 workers, and the world average was 74. Robots also have a big impact on productivity; for example, in South Korea profit per worker at auto firms was $152,000 in 2016. In China, it was just $48,000.[134] Both the central government and Chinese companies are now doing their best to close that gap. In 2014, President Xi Jinping called for a 'robot revolution' that would transform first China, and then the world.[135] He sees robots as the way to achieve China's goal of becoming the number-one global manufacturer of parts by the hundredth anniversary of the 1949 founding of the People's Republic. The country is on its way. The development of robot density in China is now the most dynamic in the world, and the aspiration is to achieve a robot density of 150 robots per 10,000 human workers.

Automation has the potential to bolster China's competitiveness and maintain their hold on low value-added parts of the production chain, while moving into higher-value areas currently dominated by Japan, South Korea and Taiwan. China's central planners provide generous subsidies to Chinese companies to incentivise them to use automation, spurring both Chinese politicians and company owners into action. Chinese companies have rapidly become the largest purchaser of industrial robots, predicted to purchase four times as many robots as the US, and around 40 per cent of the total world volume by 2020.[136] In 2015 the government of Guangdong, a province of South China that contains 104 million residents, promised to spend $150 billion equipping factories with industrial robots and create two new centres dedicated to advanced automation. Companies like Changying Precision Technology Company, a producer of mobile phones, used to have 650 employees, but due to implementing robotics now only needs 60. Luo Weiqiang, the company's general manager, believes that the number of employees will eventually drop to just 20. As well as replacing 90 per cent of its employees, the factory has also dramatically increased its efficiency and quality. Production has risen 250 per cent and quality defects reduced by 80 per cent. As business cases for automation go, it's a good one.

Foxconn, the Taiwanese company that manufactures Apple's iPhone, and which faced considerable scrutiny about its working conditions, has also unsurprisingly embraced robotics. The company's leaders announced a three-phased plan to fully automate its factories, replacing up to a million workers with automated replacements. *In the first phase, Foxconn aims to set up individual automated workstations for work that workers are unwilling to do or is dangerous*, said general manager Dai Jia-peng.[137] In March 2016, Foxconn declared that it had automated away 60,000 jobs at one factory alone.[138] The second phase focuses on streamlining production efficiency and removing unnecessary robots from the production line. The third and final phase involves automating their entire factories *with only a minimal number of workers assigned to production, logistics, testing, and inspection processes.*[139] The company's factories in Chengdu, Western China; Shenzhen, southern China; and Zhengzhou, northern China, are already in the second or third phase of this long-term automation plan, with up to ten fully automated production lines already in place at some of those factories. As of the time of writing, Foxconn has already deployed over 40,000 of its industrial robots (called Foxbots), with the capability to produce 10,000 annually. If they reach their goal of full automation, then that translates to over a million people who will lose their jobs. Robots are quite simply quicker, cheaper, union-free, and prepared to work 24/7, 365 days a year. They're also unlikely to jump off the roof.

Reimagining Manufacturing

Away from robotics, other new manufacturing technologies such as additive layer manufacturing – commonly known as 3D printing – are also primed to disrupt manufacturing. The 3D-printing revolution has been bubbling under for several years, with various companies and individuals experimenting with the technology, using a variety of different materials to make a wide range of different products. Most people are familiar with seeing 3D printers make relatively simple, small things such as models and prototypes in resins and plastic. Yet few realise that the technology has now advanced to the point where concrete, metal and titanium components can be rapidly printed, dramatically reducing the time from design to production. This enables designers to make a wide range of items using additive manufacturing, ranging from handguns to houses. Metal 3D printing using laser deposition technology allows parts to be designed and manufactured in completely new ways that were previously impossible, making them both stronger and lighter. To demonstrate the potential of metal 3D printing, even very complex things such as working titanium jet engines have been produced, offering massive benefits to the automobile and aerospace industries where weight equates to more fuel being consumed and slower speeds. Boeing apparently uses around 50,000 3D-printed parts, including structural titanium parts, for its 787 Dreamliner which is predicted to eliminate $2–3 million from the cost of each plane.[140] The ability to produce parts using composite materials and new honeycomb designs means that items can have greater tensile strength while also being lighter. The ability to print a part straight after designing it, and only when it's needed, means companies can take out millions of parts from their inventory holding, eliminate weeks from the production lead time, and free up billions of dollars from their supply chains. That opportunity is being grasped by the major manufacturing players, with Siemens building metal 3D-printing factories in the UK, and GE investing $1.4 billion in additive manufacturing technologies. Additive manufacturing reinvents the whole process of production, allowing companies to only print what is needed and drastically reduce waste. This could be bad news for suppliers to large OEMs[55] or who operate in aftermarket spares, as moving forwards the OEM will effectively only want access to the schematic – the design – from the supplier, and then just print parts on location when they need them. The impact on logistics companies who currently have a very profitable business from storing and moving billions of components around the world is also going to be massive.

Additive manufacturing has also allowed the manufacture of customised items, finding a significant niche in the healthcare industry printing bespoke human parts such as ball joints for knee replacements, replacement hips and even replacement ribcages and spinal columns. It is now even possible

---

[55] Original Equipment Manufacturers

to 3D print with biological materials, allowing for cosmetic companies like L'Oréal to partner with medical research companies like Organovo on the printing of human skin, removing the need for animal testing of products which causes cosmetic companies so much bad press. Biological materials such as stem cells are also being used as printable material: an Israeli company called Nano Dimension has developed a 3D printer that prints stem cells, which can be an enabler for printing even large and complex tissues and organs.[141] Combine this with the exponential fall in the cost of human genome sequencing, and the potential to use our biological material and DNA to print replacement organs arises. These developments effectively remove the need to find animal or human donors, eliminating the need for transplant patients to spend their lives on anti-rejection drugs, and in doing so hugely increasing the success rate of procedures. It may well lead to a business of elective operations, where people pay to replace worn-out organs with newly printed ones. Outside of healthcare, bio-printing is also being experimented with as a way of producing lab-grown meat, reducing the reliance on livestock farming which would not only make the animals happier knowing they weren't going to end up on a plate, but also massively reducing the amount of methane produced and free up the land currently used as feeding pastures.

As well as small items, 3D printing can also produce industrial-sized components through a process called BAAM – Big Area Additive Manufacturing. What can you print on an industrial scale? Vehicles. Companies like Local Motors have used this new technology to produce their car called the Strati and electric bus called Olli, and another company called Cincinnati have printed a sports car called the Shelby. They are looking at this technology not just to produce parts, but to actually redesign the entire manufacturing process. One other benefit of 3D printing is the ability to move production to the desired location, rather than making it in a factory and moving the product. In Amsterdam, a company called MX3D has developed a robotic 3D printer that can print steel in mid-air,[142] and to test its capability, they have 3D-printed a futuristic, 41-foot-long H. R. Giger-style footbridge that will be installed in Amsterdam's red-light district. Finally, 3D printing has also gone both outside *and* very big. Chinese developers have taken a practice called 'contour crafting', a building technique invented by Professor Behrokh Khoshnevis from the University of California and turned it into a commercial offering. While the professor was touring the US news channels talking about this hypothetical future capability, a Chinese company called Winsun reverse-engineered and operationalised it.[56] Using a paste made from recyclable materials, they have successfully printed houses, villas and even five-storey apartment blocks. Winsun have already found a customer base, both domestically and abroad in places like Saudi Arabia, which has had talks about them printing 1.5 million homes.[143] This 3D-printing technology enables people to design their own houses, including the electrics and plumbing, and then the industrial 3D printer will produce a finished building in a fraction of the time and cost of conventional construction methods, due to the reduction in human labour required. It presents a way to replace slum dwellings and shanty towns with modest but much more attractive and robust homes, something that may prove especially useful after a natural disaster such as a flood, tsunami or tornado to rapidly create new shelters.

But even 3D printing has been disrupted. A new type of additive manufacturing called CLIP (Continuous Liquid Interface Production) has been developed, described as an *inter-section of hardware, software and molecular science* – or as I like to call it, magic. CLIP carefully balances the interaction of UV light, which triggers photo polymerisation, and oxygen, which inhibits the reaction, allowing for continuously grown objects from a pool of resin. This enables the production of items in a fraction of the time normal 3D printing can achieve. Traditional 3D printing creates an object by depositing material layer by layer, but those same layers can cause mechanical weaknesses. The company behind this new method, Carbon Inc., states that this layer-free approach enables companies to print objects up to one hundred times faster than other methods of 3D printing, because instead of printing an object layer by layer from the top down as traditional additive 3D printers do, Carbon's process is continuous and starts from the bottom. The Carbon team was inspired by the scene in *Terminator 2* where the T-1000 reassembles itself from a pool of molten metal, and they asked themselves whether they could devise a way to create solid items out of a pool of liquid. They could, and they did, raising $422 million in four rounds of VC funding since they came out of stealth in 2015, and are now valued at $1.7 billion with CLIP

---

[56] The Chinese's ability to take an idea and drive it through to the market without many of the hurdles, internal discussions and legal constraints is something that will become important moving forwards. It will be discussed further in Part Three.

manufacturing facilities already being introduced outside of the US, such as in the UK.

CLIP production enables manufacturers to unlock new business opportunities such as mass customisation, on-demand inventory, and differentiated products made with unique functional materials. Adidas is one such company which has immediately seen the potential. As well as the speed benefits of turning design into production in hours rather than weeks, Carbon's technology allows the shoe company to unlock performance-enhancing design modifications that would have been impossible with other materials like foam. It also allows for the printing of objects at scale – which is exactly what Adidas is planning to do. Carbon's M1 printer can produce production-ready parts such as new forms of hard-wearing and very flexible soles for their Futurecraft 4D trainers (the uppers are also weaved by robots), in runs of up to 45,000 units. This technology enables companies to jump straight from prototype to development, saving significant time and money, and also enables 'on-demand' production, streamlining the supply chain and reducing storage costs. Adidas are not the only company to see the opportunity CLIP printing provides, and organisations such as Johnson & Johnson and Ford have also partnered with Carbon.

The implications of this type of on-demand, customisable manufacturing are significant. Rather than having to outsource manufacturing to giant factories in the Far East, products can now be produced locally and in much smaller batch sizes. For example, Adidas has opened two new plants in Atlanta where it has a huge consumer base, both of which are heavily automated. This has a significant sustainability impact, saving the vast amount of costs in manufacturing, transporting and storing goods, plus disposing of excess items and waste. It also means that we will increasingly see products produced for the consumer personally. As this technology advances and more and more companies make the leap, the impact on the global supply chain and all companies contained within it will be substantial. The possibilities for manufacturing are enormous, and we haven't even scratched the surface of them yet. However, one thing is for sure: the age of mass production, where rows of employees made things in unison, is over.

Automating Logistics

While the factory has long been exposed to automation, the warehouse has generally managed to avoid it, still relying on people to pick, pack and put away goods. No longer. The rise of e-commerce and its need for greater reliability, responsiveness and agility, has resulted in demands for companies to reduce the time that workers spend storing and retrieving products. One of the primary bottlenecks was the design of the warehouses themselves, relying on fixed shelving, bad placement algorithms and error-prone humans to pick, pack and put away goods. The result is an expensive operation that must scale linearly – the more you want to ship, the more warehouse space you need. No wonder an ever-increasing percentage of companies decided that they were better off outsourcing this requirement to third parties (3PLs) that specialised in the storing and distribution of goods. However, that trend has been bucked by several leading supply-chain organisations that realised that to control costs and improve responsiveness, they needed to automate the warehouse.

Kiva Robotics founder Mick Mountz realised that there had to be a way to reduce costs for large-scale distribution businesses. The solution: rather than having workers go and retrieve each product from the shelves, why not make the shelves come to the pickers? To achieve this, Kiva had to create new innovations in navigation, control systems and warehouse equipment. It uses technological advances such as advanced algorithms, robotics and sophisticated software to control a series of bright orange 'bots' that carry inventory on their backs and move the products to the picker. Kiva's parallel programming capabilities allow many different bots to simultaneously work on different parts of the same order. Kiva's bots can also operate in multilevel facilities using robot-operated elevators, making them practical in high-cost areas where warehouse owners need to save floor space. When not loaded with product, the empty bots are programmed to travel under the specially designed inventory racking, leaving the aisles open not for the humans, but for other bots carrying inventory. Behavioural programming techniques allow the bots to work on several different objectives at once – traverse the floor, avoid other bots, align their guidance systems, and get recharged as needed. As the warehouse does not need to accommodate humans walking up and down the aisles, the product is stored closer together, meaning that on average up to 50 per cent more inventory can be kept in a warehouse.

All this technology has delivered three main advantages:

- **Cost.** The average retail warehouse needs twenty to forty people working a single shift. Kiva robots cut that down by 80 per cent.
- **Increased throughput and capacity.** Kiva's robots self-organise and optimise the product shelves better than in human-based fixed warehouses, leaving more capacity for storage and an increased number of orders shipped.
- **Decreased errors.** Kiva's software tracks every order and constantly monitors error-prone humans.

The impact these benefits have had on one of the companies that used this technology was obviously significant. After Amazon acquired Zappos. com and saw how they used the Kiva system, in 2012 they purchased Kiva Robotics for $775 million in cash. Plagued by bad press about the working conditions in its fulfilment centres, Amazon needed a way to both eliminate this issue and improve picking speed and accuracy while also lowering cost, and Kiva robots were the solution they were looking for. For two years it seemed like nothing was happening, but then, just before Black Friday 2014, Amazon announced that it had rolled out 15,000 Kiva bots across its primary fulfilment centres in the US. In 2015, this doubled to 30,000 bots, then increased again to 45,000 in 2016. And the number keeps rising, with over 100,000 robots in use by the end of 2017. The savings are substantial. Each item costs $0.448 to pick with humans but falls 47.6 per cent to $0.213 with Kiva robots, and each order fulfilled in centres where the Kiva bots are installed requires less than a minute of human labour to accomplish. According to Deutsche Bank, rolling out Kiva robots to all 110 warehouses will save Amazon $2.5 billion in costs per annum. These savings have not gone unnoticed by the only online retailer currently big enough to compete with Amazon – China's Alibaba – who have installed an identical system in their fulfilment centres.[144] Only their bots are blue not orange, so, there's that. 'China' and 'respecting IP' are words that don't often go together.

This level of competitive advantage is driving other logistics companies and retailers to automate their operations simply to stay in business, and a new generation of robotics companies has emerged to meet the demand. Companies like AutoStore have pioneered alternative warehouse robotic concepts called Automated Storage and Retrieval Systems (ASRS), which transforms a warehouse into a giant, fully automated, modulated Rubik's cube with inventory stored in bins that move in multiple directions and are summoned and collected by robots that run along the top. Companies like Ocado have fully embraced this new technology to fight back hard against Amazon. Ocado's new ASRS system uses over 3,000 robots infused with a form of 'swarm intelligence', enabling them to collaborate in real time to determine the optimal way to pick the hundreds of orders Ocado receives every minute. They can pick a fifty-item order that contains meat, dairy and other groceries in under five minutes, compared to the previous time of two hours using human labour. To compete with Amazon and stay alive, Ocado had a choice: innovate or die. It chose to innovate and like Amazon has reinvented itself as a technology company as well as a retailer, selling expertise as well as groceries.

Finally, drones. While drones are being prepared to become the delivery method of the future (more on that later), they are also proving useful in large warehouses to do the very time-consuming and error-prone task of stock-keeping and cycle-counting. Inaccuracies in inventory quantity or location cause significant picking and put-away issues that delay deliveries to customers, costing companies billions. Now drone makers such as Pinc and the Hardis Group have released warehouse drones that contain advanced optical sensors and sophisticated software capabilities such as 3D mapping, navigation, inventory identification and location accuracy. This enables them to autonomously fly throughout the warehouse, performing real-time inventory scanning to ensure every item is where it should be. The drone makers claim scanning accuracy of close to 100 per cent, which will save millions as well as free up staff to work on more directly value-adding tasks.[145]

It's not just in factories and warehouses that people are being demoted from operators to mere observers. On the 23rd October 2012, California Governor Jerry Brown[57] signed a bill that allowed autonomous cars on the state's roads, stating that: *Today we're looking at science-fiction becoming tomorrow's reality – the self-driving car.*[146] Self-driving, autonomous vehicles are equipped with sophisticated sensors that include radar, lidar, sonar and multiple high-resolution cameras to provide object detection, and actuators that control the electric steering, braking and throttle to provide collision avoidance if obstacles

---

[57] It's a real shame that it wasn't the previous Governor of California, Arnold Schwarzenegger. The newspaper headlines if the Terminator himself signed the paperwork to allow autonomous robot cars on the roads would have been fantastic.

are detected – all controlled by complex and sophisticated software. Initially pioneered by Google and their self-driving Prius, now nearly all the major car companies have advanced autonomous car projects in the works. Tesla is leading the pack, certainly from a PR perspective, as every car produced from 2016 has been shipped with autonomous self-driving capability, and have already clocked up over 1.5 billion miles in autopilot mode.

Elmar Frickenstein, Senior Vice President of BMW, explains the level of end-to-end architecture and convergence of technologies required to develop a truly autonomous car: *Inside the car, we have to have a central computing platform – a supercomputer provided by [Intel]. In addition, we need motion control for highly dynamic and elegant driving, a sensor cluster and a safe, secure and private environment. Outside the car, we need a high-performance cloud solution to help us with things like swarm intelligence for new driving strategies, planning, data analytics and machine learning to create new functions. [We need] HD maps for the best localisation of the vehicle and last but not least the 5G network to handle the data exchange between the car and the cloud.*[147] Computers are becoming increasingly able to handle unexpected situations with each passing year. Human drivers can avoid some accidents, but over time, it is far more likely that computer-driven cars will avoid more, if not all, of them. No road rage, no texting, no reaching for that pesky last sweet in the glove compartment – just a constant 360-degree focus on everything around you. They will free people who currently cannot drive, providing transportation for those excluded through age, disability or inebriation. The old, disabled, blind, drunk – even the blind drunk – can now all get to their destination without the assistance of another human.[58]

The productivity benefits of autonomous transport are expected to be huge. Imagine how much time is collectively wasted worldwide travelling in cars; time that could be transformed into productive activity. The days of relaxing, carefree car journeys are long gone: motorways and primary road networks are busy all of the time in our 24/7 world. Morgan Stanley estimates that the US will obtain $507 billion in productivity gains from this technology, and a total of $1.3 trillion in total savings.[148] Driving is also a lonely activity, and our impatience, need for constant stimulation, and ease of distraction are responsible for a majority of the 1.25 million car-related

---

[58] Although for the latter group this is somewhat dependent on whether they can remember the address. Or speak coherently.

deaths per year.[149] Widespread adoption of self-driving vehicles could eliminate around 90 per cent of auto accidents in the US, preventing up to $190 billion per year in damages and health costs. Insurance companies agree, for example Direct Line, Britain's largest car insurer, offers a reduction to your car insurance if you buy a Tesla with Autopilot capability.

Tesla CEO Elon Musk believes that half of all car and truck production will be electric by 2027, and almost all will be autonomous.[150] This will have a positive effect on the environment. The use of electric autonomous taxis alone could reduce greenhouse gas emissions by 87–94 per cent per mile by the year 2030.[151] Electric cars like Tesla's also have a significant competitive advantage over normal combustion engines, for they are pretty much assured that the customer will be recharging their car overnight within a certain time frame, enabling it to receive any software updates. The twelve-volt battery in a normal combustion engine is not powerful enough to perform a software update when the engine is off, which leaves two options: either wait till the car is taken into a garage for a service – or update it while it is on the move. The latter option is a terrible idea for obvious reasons, which only leaves option one. Conversely, Tesla provides software updates over the air, changing everything from the suspension settings to the GPS and the aforementioned autonomous driving capabilities. It is the autonomous update that has proven most exciting. Tesla collects around ten times more data than any other car company, which means that not only can your car be updated with new information about your driving style, it gets updated with information about every other Tesla car on the road. Almost immediately after Autopilot was released, Model S owners reported that their cars were getting noticeably smarter. Musk refers to each Model S driver as an 'expert trainer' responsible for using the Autopilot function and providing the data to feed the collective intelligence of the fleet. In December 2016, *Bloomberg* reported that in just over a year Tesla had collected 1.3 billion miles of data from Autopilot-equipped vehicles worldwide, operating in a variety of road and weather conditions. This is regardless of whether the Autopilot capability is switched on, as it operates in what is known as 'shadow mode', with its sensors tracking real-world data even when it's off. This provides an absolutely critical competitive advantage, for this enormous amount of data is enabling Tesla's machine algorithms to learn far faster and better than its competitors. The lifeblood for any AI system development is a meaningful data set, and Tesla is ensuring – like Amazon, Google and Facebook – that they obtain as much data as possible as quickly as possible.

Most people don't actually want to drive; they want to travel. Companies like Uber have seen the opportunity that autonomous cars provide and intend to develop an automated fleet of taxis to provide private transportation without the chore of driving. Uber's plans have not been a secret, with then-CEO Travis Kalanick declaring in 2014 that when you hire an Uber *you're not just paying for the car; you're paying for the other dude in the car. When there's no other dude in the car, the cost of taking an Uber becomes cheaper than owning a vehicle.*[152] The data backs this up. Research by Ark Invest[153] highlights that the average cost per mile of travelling in a US taxi is $3.86, whereas the estimated cost of travelling in a shared autonomous vehicle in 2020 is just $0.35 per mile. Aware of these savings, Uber has a competitor in the shape of Google spin-off Waymo, which has completed 7 million test miles and began offering an autonomous taxi service in Arizona in 2017, one which it intends to roll out globally in 2018.[154] It's in a race with Uber to be first, and Uber hit back by announcing that it had created a $1.4 billion framework agreement with Volvo to purchase 24,000 self-driving XC90 SUVs, which they had jointly been developing, starting in 2019.[155] The future for Uber drivers, and taxi drivers in general, is not looking very secure.

But it's not just cars. Removing a wage-earning human driver makes compelling financial sense to a logistics company, more so than a taxi company. Not just because they save the cost of employing a fleet of drivers, but also because human drivers create restrictions on the utilisation of their primary assets – the trucks. Laws exist that prevent drivers from spending excessive and potentially dangerous periods behind the wheel, with tachographs being used to enforce that law through monitoring truck usage and driving time. Automated trucks remove that restriction. Secondly, there will be less resistance to the transition to autonomous vehicles than in the consumer market, as the owners are driven by the profit they make from moving goods, not any emotional attachment to the act of driving. Autonomous capabilities will simply allow the asset (the truck) to move goods cheaper, quicker, safer and more often. For the army of human drivers, I'm afraid it's 10-7, good buddy.[59]

---

[59] Showing my age here. Truckers and anyone who remembers the late 1970s should get this. Anyone younger – probably not.

Artificial intelligence is at the core of self-driving trucks, with many tech giants and automotive manufacturers investing heavily in this technology. One form of autonomous logistics is called 'platooning', where between six to eight vehicles autonomously 'connect' to a lead truck which they then follow, with only about twenty-five metres between each truck. Running the trucks close together reduces drag and lowers fuel consumption by up to 20 per cent. In 2016, a fleet of self-driving vehicles from firms including Daimler, Volvo and Scania were tested on the roads of Europe during the European Truck Platooning Challenge. Meanwhile, over in the US, an Uber-owned company called Otto has developed the capability to retrofit existing rigs with autonomous driving capabilities, becoming the first company to use self-driving trucks commercially when it made a delivery of 50,000 cans of Budweiser.[156] Then, in August 2018, Elon Musk tweeted that Tesla's autonomous, electric truck called the 'Semi' had just traversed the US without an escort or any accompanying vehicles. So, from a technology point of view, the self-driving car and truck are both ready for wide-scale use – which is what is starting to happen. Since early October 2017 a start-up called Embark has been using them to haul refrigerators 650 miles along the I-10 freeway from El Paso, Texas to Palm Springs, California.[157] One again, the primary barrier preventing wider adoption is a lack of approved legislation. However, pressure is building to resolve this delay as soon as possible. Over 4,000 people die each year in human error-related accidents that involve trucks, and Morgan Stanley has estimated that autonomous technology could save the freight industry upwards of $168 billion annually – $70 billion of which would come from reducing staff, $35 billion from fuel savings, $36 billion from accident savings and $27 billion from productivity gains.[158] With a business case like this, it's only a matter of time before children ask their parents if people really used to drive cars and trucks themselves.

Automating the Last Mile

The last mile, as it is called, is the most expensive element of any consumer-facing supply chain, describing the stage whereby the delivery changes from large-scale movement of goods from factory to warehouse, to the final delivery of the order to the consumer. Get this wrong and costs can seriously spiral out of control, making the last mile a very attractive target for automation. Back in 2013, Jeff Bezos appeared on the news show *60 Minutes* demonstrating a prototype delivery device that his team had been working on – an electric drone. It was widely ridiculed the next day as a PR stunt – but it wasn't. To meet its next-day (Amazon Prime), and even next-hour (Prime Now), delivery promises, Amazon needs to dramatically reduce its shipping costs. Finding ways to move goods at the lowest cost possible became an ambitious but necessary goal – and that meant removing the most expensive element – people. The ability to deliver items by drone for only the cost of electricity would allow Amazon to offer both a faster delivery service *and* lower prices than their competitors who use more traditional and expensive methods, creating more momentum for Amazon's virtuous cycle of growth. They carried out the first Prime Air customer delivery in late 2016, delivering goods autonomously by drone to a customer in Cambridge, UK. Amazon sees drones as a way of reducing the cost of last-mile delivery almost down to zero, and they have been reimagining how they would do this at scale. One solution they have patented is to develop vertical drone fulfilment centres, shaped like giant beehives, in the middle of cities and downtown districts, allowing Amazon to coordinate speedy deliveries via unmanned aircraft. *By locating the fulfillment centers within the cities, items may be more quickly delivered to the growing population of people that live in the cities, as well as the large population of people who work in the cities*, the patent application said. The drone centres would also have a 'central command' to control drone flight operations, like a control tower at an airport. Amazon has also acquired a patent to develop a flying warehouse that hovers above urban areas and from which drones descend with their goods, reducing the distance they need to travel.

Amazon has set in motion a dramatic race among its competitors to win the last mile, with companies such as Google investing heavily in its Project Wing drone programme, third-party logistics like DHL experimenting with drones that go beyond the line of sight out in Australia, and fast-food delivery services such as Domino's and 7-Eleven spotting the opportunity to increase delivery speed and decrease costs by using drone technology (and creating positive PR for their inventiveness while doing it). Walmart's potential market for drone deliveries is also high, with 49 per cent of its customer base living within six miles of a Walmart store, a deliverable range for a drone. Imagine realising you are out of printer ink, and thirty minutes later a drone lands in your front yard and drops off a replacement ink cartridge. That'll be reality by 2020. The bottleneck is, once again, the issue of legislation, not technology, meaning that once the rules and regulations are developed for drones that travel beyond the line of sight, this technology will go from deceptive to disruptive very quickly indeed. Over in Asia, where regulations are traditionally not as tight, companies like Alibaba have been trialling drones for years. Alibaba's rival, JD.com, started its drone-delivery programme back in 2016, flying parcels via drones to four provinces: Jiangsu, rural Beijing, Sichuan and Guangxi, and it hopes to receive the authority to expand the service across China.

The sky is not the only place where retailers and distributors are looking for ways to reduce the cost of delivering goods to consumers. The pavement (or sidewalk to my American readers) is also seen as a viable delivery route. Starship robots are perhaps the best known of the new breed of delivery robots, after being launched by Skype co-founders Ahti Heinla and Janus Friis in 2014. The Starship delivery robots have six wheels and onboard cameras, GPS, ultrasonic sensors, radar and locked compartments. They can travel at four miles per hour, carry just over forty pounds of cargo and are designed to deliver goods locally within thirty minutes. Small, electric and with zero emissions and zero costly humans, the environmental and financial benefits of such a delivery method are clear. Like drones, Starship's initial PR video was met with scepticism, but unlike drones, it didn't have quite so many legal hurdles to overcome before proving the doubters wrong and getting to work. On the 10th March 2016, Starship issued a press release declaring that the robots would be undertaking trial deliveries across towns and cities in all four nations of the UK. Since then, many other companies have seen the potential benefits that this technology could bring. Starship Technologies is running pilot commercial delivery programmes in the US, UK, Germany, Switzerland and Estonia, with partners like Just Eat, Hermes, Metro Group, Swiss Post, DoorDash, Postmates, Wolt and Domino's, offering robotic delivery for the food, grocery and parcel industries. The market opportunity has once again brought competition to the table, threatening to move the innovation from deceptive and under-the-radar, to full-on disruptive once the tipping point is reached. The International Federation for Robotics (IFR) forecasts[159] that by 2019 logistics businesses will have begun using at least 175,000 robots to provide their services. That compares to UPS' global fleet of around 100,000 trucks today.

One of the challenges of these types of delivery robots is range. Unless you happen to live within a mile of the depot, the robot won't reach you — which means either they need to build a lot of depots, or they make the depot mobile. It's the latter that makes the most sense, and this is the reason why in 2016 Daimler invested $17.2 million in Starship Technologies to partner on the development of a 'Robovan', a transportation system that integrates specially adapted Mercedes vans with Starship's autonomous delivery robots to create a 'mothership' concept. It works like this. The vans allow for delivery to a much wider radius and hold eight Starship bots that enter and exit on ramps. Algorithms determine the most efficient route for the van, as well as identifying the optimal drop-off locations for the bots. The robots then disperse to deliver their goods and return to the van. Starship claims this method will allow for four hundred packages to be delivered in a nine-hour shift.[160] Volker Mornhinweg, head of Mercedes-Benz Vans, made a statement declaring that: *Starship Technologies and Mercedes-Benz Vans share a strong vision: We both strive to fundamentally change the way we think about the delivery on the last mile. Together, we will make that vision come true and show the potential of robotic delivery devices in a combined holistic transportation system. Starship's unique technology fits perfectly with our vans.* At present, the mothership delivery van has a human driver, though I doubt this will be the case by 2020.

While the retailers wait for legislation to catch up, some, notably Amazon, have been experimenting with other ways to dramatically reduce the cost of delivering goods to consumers. For its one-hour delivery service called Prime Now to work, Amazon needed to be able to deliver orders individually in urban locations, rather than the usual next-day approach of combining multiple orders in a predefined shipment route that a haulier could follow. Amazon first trialled using cycle couriers to deliver non-bulky Prime Now orders in urban areas. Then it hit on a new way to expand its delivery force – Amazon Flex. Utilising the gig economy model, Amazon now allows approved private individuals to become 'delivery drivers for hire', paying them $18–25 per hour to deliver Prime packages using their cars. Like Uber, drivers use an app to sign up for shifts, pick up packages from Amazon's metropolitan warehouses and deliver them to customers' doors, to the boots of their cars, and even inside their houses (with the new Amazon Key program).[60]

---

[60] Amazon Key allows a courier one-time access to open your door via an electronic smart lock that comes as part of the package. A live streaming, motion sensing cloud camera is also provided, which automatically starts recording as soon as the access key is granted to the courier, so you can watch the delivery taking place from anywhere in the world. It is proving popular in the US due to the large number of 'porch pirates' – basically people who steal packages that have been delivered to your porch. Twenty-three million thefts of this nature took place in the US in 2015, according to NBC News. Amazon has also partnered with Volvo and GM for in-trunk deliveries.

Amazon Flex has also presented Bezos with an Uber-beating opportunity. Uber is basically just an app plus customer support, but even so its start-up costs ran into the billions. Amazon's creation of the Flex platform provides the ability to dramatically reduce both the start-up and driver incentive costs by combining ride-sharing with its package delivery service, providing Amazon with a powerful — and sustainable — competitive advantage. To achieve one-hour deliveries, Amazon also had to localise their supply chain by creating a series of smaller fulfilment hubs in urban locations that could hold enough variation and quantity of inventory to meet the needs of the local Prime Now customers. They also needed to dramatically improve the level of algorithmic assistance obtained to understand projected consumer demand, as getting it wrong meant that Amazon would both fail its delivery promise, and quickly fill the urban fulfilment centres with inventory. Delivery is increasingly becoming both more local and more automated.

The more traditional delivery companies are understandably rattled by all this disruption and are fighting to retain their slice of the market. UPS has been trialling a drone-based mothership concept, launching unmanned cargo-copters from the roof of one of the company's new hybrid electric vans. It is looking to use this technology to redress the economics of delivering in rural areas, as these sparsely populated zones provide some of the least cost-effective places for UPS to deliver. Likewise, Daimler (again) has partnered with drone company Matternet to run a trial in Zurich of same-day drone delivery of e-commerce items weighing up to two kilograms. This takes a slightly different approach — rather than drones flying from vans, here the drones fly to the vans. The drones are loaded directly at the merchant and fly to one of two Mercedes-Benz Vito vans equipped with precision landing technology. The van then stops at one of four predefined rendezvous points, where the driver takes possession of the product and delivers it to the customer, while the drone returns to the retailer. Andreas Raptopoulos, Founder and CEO of Matternet, declared, *We believe that drone-enabled logistics networks will transform how we access goods every day — we will be able to order something online, and like magic, receive it within minutes, for a fraction of the cost and energy expended today.*[161]

Once the last mile becomes autonomous and electric, then one-hour delivery times will become ubiquitous, and those companies still relying on traditional methods will be forced to adapt or die. The pressure is therefore mounting for companies to get their acts together before the Amazons of the world set a pace that they just cannot match.

Automating Retail: To Sell is Human (or is it?)

Fast food has been in the news recently, mostly because of its workers pushing to secure a $15-an-hour minimum wage. They may get it, but they may also have inadvertently hastened the demise of their jobs. Companies like McDonald's are now rapidly embracing electronic kiosks to replace the large number of cashiers needed to take and process orders at their restaurants. On 21st June 2017, McDonald's shares hit an all-time high after the company announced it planned to roll out mobile ordering across 14,000 US locations. The kitchen isn't safe from automation either. Miso Robotics' 'Flippy'[162] robot has heat sensors and thermal imaging that allows it to run grill stations and assemble burgers, and fast-food companies such as CaliBurger have already started to roll them out across their US restaurants, allowing greater focus on customer service and cleaning rather than cooking and taking orders. Pizzas are also on the robot menu, with Silicon Valley start-up Zume Pizza using robots to make and deliver their pizzas. Zume trucks receive orders and bake pizzas while they're en route to consumers. Zume's founders intend to scale up automation of their pizza production line so that humans aren't involved at all in the pizza-making and baking process.[163]

One area many people would have assumed to safe from this technological onslaught would be in dealing and conversing with customers. Cooking simple foods and installing kiosks that allow customers to order from a predefined range of products are one thing, but surely dealing with customers and the variability of their requests is beyond the capability of machines? Unfortunately for retail workers, the answer appears to be no. Pepper is an emotionally intelligent humanoid robot developed by Aldebaran Robotics and Japanese mobile company Softbank. Pepper started work in Softbank's Japanese mobile-phone stores in 2014 and approximately 2,000 Pepper robots are now deployed in shops across Japan. Pepper's mission is to create interest, generate traffic to the stores, greet customers, highlight company offers and provide entertainment to make in-store waiting more pleasant. It also happens to be a magnet for inquisitive children. The 1.2

metre-tall robot uses cameras and sensors to detect human emotions, listens carefully and responds using natural language. It has a large tablet screen on its chest, allowing it to present information and selections for people to engage with. It is being used as an innovative way to greet customers, provide them with advice and general information, and as a novel way to market and present new products. Pepper is now employed in hotels such as the Mandarin Oriental, banks like ATB in Calgary, large retailers like Carrefour, taking orders at Pizza Huts in Singapore and greeting customers at banks in Taiwan. It is also being used to guide visitors around hospitals and health centres in Belgium, as a concierge in malls in California, and to advise passengers at Oakland Airport where to eat or drink.

The economics of using Pepper are attractive. The robot only costs about $1,600 plus roughly $200 in monthly fees – far less than a human retail worker. While using robots in what is traditionally a very 'human-to-human' role seems like something that would prove off-putting to customers, so far the response has been very positive. For example, the introduction of Pepper to a Santa Monica store resulted in a 70 per cent increase in foot traffic, 13 per cent increase in revenue and a sixfold increase in sales of featured products. Like Pepper's industrial counterpart Baxter, it is designed to be a hardware platform that can be updated, improved and easily taught to do new things based on increasingly powerful and sophisticated software updates that increase its capabilities and ability to interpret people's words and emotions. These updates allow Pepper to become enormously flexible, able to complete a variety of unique tasks, such as performing religious ceremonies to honour the recently deceased. In Japan, SoftBank demonstrated Pepper dressed in Buddhist robes, chanting Buddhist scriptures, beating religious drums and live-streaming the ceremony for people who couldn't attend the funeral in person. The primary driver for this is financial rather than spiritual: the average cost of a Japanese funeral is more than £20,000, and human priests cost £1,700 to hire, whereas Priest Pepper is happy to say some last words for just £350.

Pepper is the first of what appears to be a wave of humanoid robots designed to provide concierge services. Hitachi has also released its assistant robot called EMIEW3, which doesn't have a screen but does have voice recognition, vision, sensors and advanced language-processing capabilities supporting multi-language translations. It has already been put to work assisting travellers in Tokyo's Haneda Airport.[164] To the companies using them, humanoid robots like

Pepper and EMIEW3 provide a major financial advantage over their carbon-based competition, not least that they work 24/7, don't need breaks, don't get sick or need time off for family matters, and never have a bad day. The robots provide consistent coverage, consistent messaging and a consistent and positive customer experience, recording every customer interaction. Pepper's manufacturer, Aldebaran, says the robot can feel joy, surprise, anger, doubt and sadness, but it is hesitant to indicate the strength of these emotions. Let's just hope despair, boredom and madness stay off the list.

Robots are doing more than selling products; they are also checking the inventory. While fifth-wave technology made inroads into retail stores through the use of electronic barcode scanners that removed the need for humans to individually price every item, now sixth-wave technologies such as robots are finishing the task and checking the shelves are stacked correctly. After a successful pilot, Walmart is rolling out shelf-scanning robots in fifty stores across the US. Empty shelves and mispriced items are a big issue for stores, causing lost sales and frustrated customers. The fully autonomous robots, developed by Bossa Nova Robotics, will constantly roam the aisles checking stock levels, product pricing, looking for misplaced items and any missing labels, and saving human staff members from the time-consuming task of having to constantly check everything themselves.[165]

Amazon is using its massive revenue influx to fund a continuous cycle of innovation they call their 'virtuous cycle'. The three areas of focus are the widest possible product selection, competitive prices, and the ultimate customer experience. It is in the last area that they are really innovating. In 2016, Amazon trialled the first of its new-style physical stores, Amazon Go, which utilises 'just walk out' technology, having no checkout tills and therefore no queues. If you are an Amazon Prime member,[61] you simply scan your code when you walk in, and you will be tracked as you walk around the store. The system uses a combination of computer vision, sensor fusion, artificial intelligence, machine learning and distributed systems that automatically detect when products are taken from or returned to the shelves

[61] ...and Amazon *really* wants you to be a Prime member, given Prime members spend twice as much as non-Prime members, and provide Amazon with $100 of upfront subscription cash before buying anything. In the Q1 2018 shareholder letter, Amazon confirmed that it had over 100 million Prime members in the US. That's $9.99 billion in upfront cash flow. A pretty big innovation fund. In Q2, Amazon put the Prime subscription rate up to $119. Assuming minimal slippage, that's now $11.9 billion upfront cash per annum.

and keeps track of them in a customer's virtual cart. Amazon opened its first Amazon Go store in Seattle and used its employees as test subjects to iron out bottlenecks, such as keeping track of people when the store is crowded. In January 2018, Amazon decided that the concept was ready and opened its first Amazon Go store to the public. Amazon is rapidly moving into bricks-and-mortar stores, purchasing the Whole Foods chain and opening physical bookstores, and it is very likely that the Amazon Go experience and all the related technological wizardry will be at the heart of it.

Amazon is not the only retailer changing the game; Alibaba is also no innovation slouch, currently reimagining the retail experience by breaking down the boundaries between off-line and on-line, creating a new digitally empowered retail offering which combines entertainment, media and financial offerings to create a concept it simply calls 'New Retail'. Their primary example is 'Hema', an Internet and technology powered Alibaba supermarket where their smartphone app controls the entire shopping experience, from product research to scheduling your home delivery and making payments. Each store operates as a fulfilment centre meaning that Hema can deliver goods to consumers within a 3 km radius within 30 minutes. It is proving so successful that people are moving home purely to be close to a Hema store.

Owning the Consumer Interface

The e-commerce revolution has advanced from deceptive to disruptive, causing what has been called a 'retail apocalypse' in the US. Companies like Amazon are at the heart of this. Jeff Bezos' mission is to create 'the Everything Store' online, a place where you can buy whatever you want, whenever you want – and have it shipped to you the next day (or in the next hour if you are a Prime Now customer). Amazon understands that the first click is the most important, and if, through the benefits of free shipping, they can persuade shoppers to start their purchasing decisions with a visit to Amazon, this immediately takes away page views from competitors, creating a huge advantage. On the Internet, where your competition is only a click away, ensuring that you own the first click is crucial.

But how about securing the consumers business before they go online? What if they could simply say out loud what they want, and it arrives within hours? This is the world Amazon has brought to life via Alexa and the Amazon Echo product range. The Echo and other Alexa related devices are all outcomes of Amazon's continuous experimentation to develop the ultimate consumer platform. Whereas the Kindle was a platform designed to expedite the transition from physical books to e-books, the Echo is designed to transition people from ordering goods using the PC and smartphone, to just their voice. David Limp, SVP of Devices at Amazon, stated at a press event for the Echo that *'What we're trying to do is to build a computer in the cloud that's completely controlled by your voice.'* It has found a market. In less than a year, the Echo became the bestselling device on Amazon over $100. Amazon now makes Echo-compatible light bulbs, thermostats and electrical outlets, all of which are of course recommended items when you go to buy an Echo on Amazon.

Consumers are not interested in a device from a retailer that just allows them to verbally buy things, and therefore Echo needed to be much more than just a consumption portal – it had to become the centrepiece of your home. At its heart sits Alexa, a cloud-based AI system like Apple's Siri. Conversing with Alexa must become a natural part of the customer's daily activities; one they couldn't do without. Alexa's capabilities are constantly being updated; both through the number of skills and also the quality of the AI driving it. For example its voice-recognition capabilities – powered by its machine-learning voice-recognition system called Amazon Polly, and a conversational AI called Amazon Lex – are noticeably being improved. The use of Polly's capabilities now allows Alexa to differentiate between different voices in a household, so it knows exactly who it is conversing with, so when you say, 'Alexa, play my workout music', it knows who 'my' is, just by your voice.

What Amazon has created is not a product but a customer interface; one that is constantly getting smarter and functionally richer. One that allows the consumer to merely verbalise their needs – play music, read the news, book transportation, set timers, answer questions, and – critically – order stuff through Amazon Prime – and they will happen as if by magic. A platform that has a hundred different ways to embed Amazon into your life – and of course a hundred new ways to make them money. One where other companies would pay Amazon to have access to that platform. By being the first to market, Echo enabled Amazon to grab the opportunity to own the rights to run customers' homes, claiming a huge advantage that prevents any other devices from encroaching on this space. Echo can also control lights, switches and thermostats with compatible smart home devices, for example Nest, WeMo, Philips Hue and Samsung SmartThings. The Echo has enabled Amazon to intertwine itself with the running of consumers' lives, creating a continuous relationship with them rather than just a transactional one. To enhance that relationship Amazon has constantly increased its range of Echo products to ensure that it doesn't deliver a one-hit wonder that customers discard as soon as something 'sexier' comes on the market. The Echo range now includes the Echo Dot, Echo Show and Echo Spot. The last two incorporate screens so that the Echo (via Alexa) can reply to answers not just verbally, but also visually. It also allows you to use the Echo to display videos from the Internet – such as YouTube – but more importantly becomes a communication device with other Echo Spot/Show users, driving up the reasons why people – and their distant friends and relatives – should own one.

Amazon has already occupied pole position in the consumer Internet of Things (IoT) race while others are still talking about whether to compete. This will prove invaluable long-term as it's a 'winner takes all' model – people don't want two devices running their household, so being first is everything. By becoming the one device that runs the home, Amazon has created more than just a new way to engage with customers – it has created a whole new platform that people are queuing up to use. A platform that also captures an enormous amount of data. In a 2014 *New Yorker* article about Amazon one line stands out: *Before Google, and long before Facebook, Bezos had realised that the greatest value of an online company lay in the consumer data it collected.*[166] Echo's Alexa learns through use, collecting data as it goes – your data. Amazon has long used purchase data to drive replenishment strategies, offer recommendations and set prices, but with Alexa, it is about to capture more data on your preferences and behaviours than ever before. Echo and Alexa allows Amazon to capture data on what you buy, when you buy it, what music you like, what films and TV programmes you watch, where you go, what pizza toppings you like – everything they need to drive their virtuous cycle of convenience. This data has enormous direct and indirect value to Amazon. Amazon already hinted at how much data Alexa captured when, in the first year of release, they reported the top Christmas songs people played through the Echo[62] and how often they used the timer function to help with cooking Christmas dinner. Amazon is therefore offering the public a Faustian bargain: the sale of your privacy for convenience, choice and price. You want free music, free videos, free TV programmes, free delivery and low prices. Amazon wants to know everything about you and to be your sole retailer. It has created the platform where you get what you want, but you must sign up to what they want – for Amazon to capture enough data that they are able to predict what you want and when, enabling them to become your personal 'Everything Store.' It is a bargain most are willing to make.

The first-mover advantages this provides are enormous. As a website, where the competition is only a click away, Amazon is always at risk that the consumer may look elsewhere. Echo provides a way to secure consumer demand before they even go online, effectively making Amazon the first-choice retail channel for the entire household. The genius behind Amazon's platform model is that once the consumers are hooked on the ease of use of the Echo, Prime itself becomes more valuable, securing its automatic renewal. Amazon has also understood that closed systems provide closed opportunities, so the attractiveness of a platform depends on the number of things people can do with it. The more benefits and applications a device has, the more likely people are to buy it, and as more people buy it, the more app developers and suppliers want to work with it. Another virtuous cycle of creativity for Amazon, and a vicious circle of destruction for its competitors.

What could possibly be easier than simply saying out loud what you want and for it to arrive just hours later? How about not having to order it at all? Back in 2014 Amazon trialled the Dash Button, small, branded Wi-Fi devices that you place in your house and which allow you to reorder essentials – such as toilet paper, coffee capsules and washing powder – simply by clicking each brand's button when you are running low. There are now over three hundred buttons available, including household brands such as Charmin, Bold, Finish, Ariel, Doritos, Duracell, Energizer, Heineken, Tassimo, Red Bull, Starbucks, Vitaminwater – even Trojan condoms (although I don't think Amazon's delivery will ever be that quick!). Dash Buttons cost $4.99 each, but they come with a $4.99

---

[62] *White Christmas*, *Sleigh Ride* and *Winter Wonderland*.

discount off your first Dash order and so are essentially free. The purpose of the Dash Button isn't to sell Dash Buttons – it's to establish whether people appreciate the convenience of being able to ensure that they never run out of essentials by simply clicking a single button. The goal is to encourage more frequent and more regular retail purchases of essential goods from Amazon.

It worked. Sales of Dash Buttons grew by 75 per cent over the first three months of 2016, and the number of orders per minute through Dash Buttons increased from one every minute, to four per minute.[167] Amazon then expanded the buttons' availability to the UK, including categories such as beer (essential for Brits), coffee, razor blades, cleaning products, condoms, washing powder and pet food – all ordered and delivered by Amazon. Even clothing can be ordered via Dash Buttons, with Calvin Klein the first brand to start selling clothes via this method. But what if I didn't even have to press a button? In late 2015, Amazon's Dash Replenishment Service (DRS) came online. DRS is the Internet of Things made real; the Dash Button without the button. It introduces into the home the concept of connected, smart devices that replenish themselves when supplies are low, automatically ordering replenishment stock from Amazon without any human interaction. With as little as ten lines of code, manufacturers can embed automated purchasing capability into their devices.[168] Fifteen major manufacturers[63] have installed DRS capability into their devices, from water filters that reorder replacement filters, to printers that reorder ink and washer-dryers that reorder laundry supplies. Dash replenishment solves a big problem for manufacturers that make smart machines but don't personally want to get into the e-commerce and fulfilment business. The whole purpose of Prime, Echo, Dash Buttons and DRS is to keep the consumer locked into ordering all their frequently needed goods through Amazon's shopping empire, erecting walls of convenience that prevent customers from even considering buying their coffee or condoms elsewhere. Amazon plans to own the whole retail experience by reinventing it. As Daniel Rausch, one of Dash's creators and its current leader for Amazon, states; *The goal is to make shopping disappear*.

---

[63] As of April 2016, Brita, Brother, Samsung, GMate, Whirlpool, GOJO, Sealed Air, GE, Obe, Petnet, CleverPet, Sutro, Thync, Oster and August Smart Lock have created DRS devices.

Combine all these developments and what we are presented with is the potential to automate nearly all the physical supply chain jobs currently undertaken by humans. From taking raw materials out of the ground to delivering finished products to your house, currently there is someone working on a way to enable a machine to do it better. At the heart of this is the race to develop machines able to do the one thing that separated us from other mammals – think.

10

THE AUTOMATION OF THE KNOWLEDGE WORKER

We have already mentioned what may, perhaps, appear paradoxical to some of our readers – that the division of labour can be applied with equal success to mental as to mechanical operations, and that it ensures in both the same economy of time.

Charles Babbage, *On the Economy of Machinery and Manufactures, 1832*

Hans Moravec has a paradox named after him. In 1988, he wrote that, *it is comparatively easy to make computers exhibit adult level performance on intelligence tests or playing checkers, and difficult or impossible to give them the skills of a one-year-old when it comes to perception and mobility.* [64] Moravec was referring to the fact that, as he and other AI and robotics researchers had found, high-level reasoning requires very little computation, but low-level sensorimotor skills require enormous computational

---

[64] I saw a great blog comment that went: *"apparently getting a machine to pick up a toy and put it in a box is incredibly difficult, yet it is a simple task for a child."* Wrong. That is IMPOSSIBLE for a child to do... they only ever take toys OUT of boxes, never put them away!

resources. As the linguist and cognitive scientist Steven Pinker wrote in his book *The Language Instinct*; *The main lesson of thirty-five years of AI research is that the hard problems are easy, and the easy problems are hard. The mental abilities of a four-year-old that we take for granted – recognizing a face, lifting a pencil, walking across a room, answering a question – in fact, solve some of the hardest engineering problems ever conceived.*[169] A robot's actions are clumsy because they can't feel. Yet these hurdles are being overcome. We have explored how robotics and other methods of automation are primed to affect every area of the physical supply chain, making previous assumptions about what machines can and cannot do seem absurd. One assumption people mistakenly hang on to, however, is that if their job involves thinking, then it is safe; that automation may be able to replace the blue-collar worker, but not the white-collar one. That robots may be able to do the dull, dirty and dangerous, but they can't do the deciding. Unfortunately for them, this assumption is also being proved wrong. As our cerebral abilities are what have elevated us above all other earthly creatures, it is therefore understandable that whammy number two, the replacement of minds with machines, worries people the most.

Ever since Alan Turing posed the question *Can machines think?* back in 1950, there has been a debate and concern about what machines can or cannot do and the impact this will have on humans and society. This is an expected response to any evolving field about which complete knowledge is yet to be obtained. The concept and perils of artificial intelligence (AI) and intelligent machines have been discussed for decades, mostly in works of science fiction such as HAL 9000 in *2001: A Space Odyssey*, Skynet in the *Terminator* series, and more recently Samantha in Spike Jonze's *Her*, and Ava in *Ex Machina*. Excitement and interest in artificial intelligence had been significant in the upswing of the fifth wave, the late 1960s and early 1970s, led by groups such as the US Defence Department's Defence Advanced Research Projects Agency (DARPA) and AI researchers such as Marvin Minsky. However, as initial results proved less than spectacular, and the K-wave moved into its summer and autumn periods, investment and interest waned, moving, as it always does, to maximising the potential of the more established innovations, in this case microprocessor-based personal and business systems and the Internet that connected them. An 'AI winter' began, where research continued, but small-scale and behind closed doors. New investment into AI didn't start to flow until near the end of the fifth wave, and since the financial crash, interest has not just re-emerged but exploded. AI is now set to be perhaps the most important innovation of the sixth wave and is powering the developments making waves in the upswing period. Its initial arrival was deceptive, appearing discreetly as adverts on Facebook, recommendations on Amazon or suggested movies on Netflix. This rapidly moved to more visible forms, such as the AI assistants Siri, Cortana and Alexa; virtual helpers who make our lives a little bit easier by providing immediate information when we need it. Yet these are merely initial experiments in a field that will soon advance to challenge the existence of most of today's human knowledge workers.

AI is still a relatively new field, so being able to foresee the changes that are to come with any clarity is unlikely. The power of exponential technological growth and Moravec's paradox can catch out the brightest of us, leading to statements of perceived certainty turning, with hindsight, into statements of absurdity. In 2004, Frank Levy, Professor of Urban Economics at the Massachusetts Institute of Technology (MIT), and Richard J. Murnane, Professor of Education and Society at Harvard University, published a book called *The New Division of Labor: How Computers are Creating the Next Job Market.*[170] As the title suggests, this book details how new technology is affecting the nature of work across multiple industry sectors and professions. The authors named those industries that they believed would be at risk of automation through advancements in computer technology, and those that would be safe. Their conclusion was that computers would continue to excel at rule-based logic but would struggle with tasks that involve expert thinking and complex communication. While disruptive and impressive, they could not easily replace humans in jobs that required a variety of observational and decision-making skills, such as executing a left-hand turn in oncoming traffic. *As the driver makes his left turn against traffic, he confronts a wall of images and sounds generated by oncoming cars, traffic lights, storefronts, billboards, trees, and a traffic policeman. Using his knowledge, he must estimate the size and position of each of these objects and the likelihood that they pose a hazard.*[171] Driving was therefore cited as an example of the kind of work computers would not be able to replace, due to the sheer complexity required in recognising and reacting to multiple moving objects in real time. Yet just six years after the book was published, Google's first-generation autonomous cars were doing just that. Six years between certainty and absurdity: paradigms shift quickly nowadays.

This was not the first time the rate of AI development had been vastly underestimated. After IBM's Deep Blue beat Gary Kasparov at chess in 1997, the *New York Times* printed an article entitled *To Test a Powerful Computer, Play an Ancient Game,*[172] in which it declared that, *Deep Blue defeated the world chess champion by leveraging a moderate amount of chess knowledge with an enormous amount of blind, high-speed searching power. But this roughshod approach is powerless against the intricacies of [the game] Go, leaving computers at a distinct disadvantage... Brute-force searching is completely and utterly worthless for Go.* The game of Go is the oldest game in human history, invented in China more than 3,000 years ago, and involves players taking turns to place stones on a 19 x 19 grid in a battle to capture territory, allowing for a potential ~2.082×10^{170} (2 followed by 170 zeroes) legal positions. It is revered as the most demanding strategy game there is, many times more complex than chess, and relies on human ingenuity, experience, observation and adaptability. When Deep Blue beat Kasparov, the best Go programs would still lose against amateurs. The *NY Times* article then quoted Dr Piet Hut, an astrophysicist at the Institute for Advanced Study in Princeton, who was also a major fan of the game Go: *It may be a hundred years before a computer beats humans at Go – maybe even longer.* The article concluded that: *When or if a computer defeats a human Go champion, it will be a sign that artificial intelligence is truly beginning to become as good as the real thing.*

Maybe it's the real thing, then, for less than twenty years later, in March 2016, the eighteen-time Go world champion, Lee Sedol, resigned the fifth and final game against AlphaGo, a Go program designed by Google DeepMind, losing 4–1. After the match, the Korea Baduk Association awarded AlphaGo the highest Go grand master rank – an 'honorary 9 dan'. Since this victory, a more advanced version of AlphaGo, called AlphaGo Master (the first version was named AlphaGo Lee) secretly tested itself by playing online Go, causing considerable chatter amongst regular online players as to who this new, undefeatable opponent was. Then, in May 2017, AlphaGo Master proved its utter dominance over humans by first beating Ke Jie, the world's number-one player, 3–0, and then defeating a combined five-man team of previous Go champions. One of the primary observations that knowledgeable spectators made was that AlphaGo didn't play like a human; it developed completely new strategies that went against the conventional wisdom of how to play the game to win. AlphaGo appeared to fight various battles simultaneously, adopting an approach that was almost impossible for humans to follow. According to Michael Redmond, the highest-ranked Western Go player, the strategy somehow felt *'alien'*: *There's some inhuman element in the way AlphaGo plays, which makes it very difficult for us to just even sort of get into the game.* As an example, in the second match against Lee Sedol, AlphaGo's thirty-seventh move appeared to make no sense, confusing Sedol. It was only afterwards, when AlphaGo had won the match, that the move's strategic value was made apparent. Fan Hui, a three-time European Go champion who had also previously lost to AlphaGo (5–0), stated that: *It's not a human move. I've never seen a human play this move... So beautiful. So beautiful.*

Understanding what Google achieved with DeepMind's AlphaGo is an insight as to how far artificial intelligence has come, and a glimpse into where it could go. To defeat the very best Go players, AlphaGo had to discover new strategies for itself. The DeepMind team taught AlphaGo to play the game using a deep neural network – a network of hardware and software that mimics the web of neurons in the human brain. It then played millions of games against itself using these neural networks, learning from victories and constantly improving. They then used a second technology called reinforcement learning to set up matches in which slightly different versions of AlphaGo played each other. Finally, the team fed moves from these AlphaGo-vs-AlphaGo matches into another neural network, refining its game still more. Drawing on its extensive training with millions upon millions of human moves, the machine developed the ability to calculate the probability that a human will make a particular play in the midst of a game. AlphaGo knew that move thirty-seven in game two was not a move that a professional Go player would ever make, and therefore would be one they would not expect. But it also knew that the move would likely prove successful.

AI Invades the Workplace

Artificial intelligence is one of the pivotal technologies of the sixth wave. Silicon-based AI systems will be able to process and make sense of far more information than our carbon-based brains could ever hope to. We humans think, analyse and make decisions at a relatively finite level, and despite the myth of multitasking, science has proven that we can only really focus on one thing at a time. We may have learnt to switch attention quickly to give the illusion of multitasking (as an example, my wife can change topics three times in the same sentence), but the reality is we can only focus on a small set of data before we are overwhelmed and start to make mistakes. When important decisions must be made, our brains need time to process the data available, to understand all the variables and determine the possible outcomes required to arrive at a good decision. In periods of high stress where making fast decisions is necessary, many of us don't perform at our peak, and mistakes get made. Finally, we are fragile, requiring constant recuperation and pesky things such as a good night's sleep in order to function the next day. Computers, however, do not suffer from these human limitations.

To be deemed 'intelligent', a machine must be able to operate in a multitude of variable conditions, absorb and process a stream of sensory data, identify any patterns, and determine the appropriate course of action based on the conditions, data and patterns presented. This requires the ability to learn over time how to handle an enormous multitude of different variables, the sheer volume and variety of which led Levy, Murane and Hut (amongst others) to believe that we are unlikely to see a machine capable of doing this any time soon. Their failure was to view computers as they were, based on programming languages that are perfect for applications where the inputs and desired outcomes are known, but terrible where they are not. These forms of programmed computers cannot do what the human brain does every second of every day, which is handle variability. It's the variability that is the problem for programmed solutions. There are only so many *if > then > else* statements you can write. Hence Moravec's paradox.

This answer to this paradox is for machines to solve problems themselves. Whereas AlphaGo was designed for a specific purpose – to beat puny humans at the world's most strategic game – other AI systems have shown that they also have real business applications. Voice-activated helpers like Siri, Alexa and Google Assistant are just the beginning. Computers are getting better at handling unexpected situations and doing so with greater and greater accuracy. Three new technologies – cognitive computing, machine learning and quantum computing – are rapidly advancing behind the scenes, getting ready to transform from the deceptive inventions and experiments they are right now, to the fully industrialised disruptors they have the potential to become. The first, cognitive computing, already has its own superhero: IBM's Watson.

Watson first came to international prominence after defeating the two best human competitors on the US game show *Jeopardy* back in 2011. Whereas *Jeopardy* was all about providing questions, IBM's next move was to direct Watson towards the process of discovering answers, offering its capabilities to any parties who felt they had a compelling use case. In May 2015, Ginni Rometty, the Chairman and CEO of IBM, stood on stage in front of a packed room and announced that she was going to make a bold prediction. *In the future, every decision that mankind makes is going to be informed by a cognitive system like Watson, and our lives will be better for it.* She continued, *As Watson gets smarter, his ability to reason is going to exponentially increase... Watson deals in the grey area, where there's not a perfect right or wrong answer... That's the hardest thing we do as humans.*[173] The first takers for this new type of cognitive capability were the healthcare industry, using the power of Watson to analyse large amounts of imaging and text in electronic health records so it could identify any traces of cancer. Watson Genomics can now create tailored drug recommendations for cancer patients in minutes, rather than the weeks it would normally take human doctors. To keep up with advancements in medicine, it is estimated that it would take a human doctor 160 hours of reading time per week just to read any newly published medical papers – then considerably more time to evaluate whether this knowledge was relevant and how to apply it. Watson takes just minutes to absorb this new research and is almost immediately able to provide doctors with more up-to-date knowledge and better diagnostic advice. As an excellent example of this, Watson was provided with all the published literature related to the degenerative disease ALS and quickly learned about all the proteins already known to be linked to the disease. Watson then ranked approximately 1,500 genes that appear in the human genome and predicted which could be associated with ALS. The research team examined Watson's predictions and found that eight of the ten genes proposed by the computer were linked to the disease – five of which had never previously been associated with ALS. The process took a few months, compared to the decades it would have taken traditional researchers. Watson is also being used in another notoriously difficult medical field – mental health. Scientists are feeding Watson with transcripts and audio inputs from psychiatric interviews, enabling it to analyse speech patterns and accurately predict and monitor psychosis, schizophrenia, mania and depression. It only takes about three hundred words for Watson to help clinicians successfully predict the probability of psychosis in a user.

Watson has also found a home in the legal and insurance industries. In 2017, a Japanese insurance firm replaced thirty-four employees with a Watson-based artificial-intelligence system, giving the company a return on its investment in under two years. Over in the US, Watson is powering ROSS, 'the world's first artificially intelligent attorney'. ROSS is capable of reading through entire bodies of law in order to identify relevant cases and return cited answers and topical readings from legislation, case law and secondary sources to ensure a lawyer is up to speed. This preparatory work normally takes at least a week for a human lawyer to complete, whereas ROSS only needs a few hours. ROSS also recently landed a position at New York law firm Baker & Hostetler handling the firm's bankruptcy practice. It monitors any new legal cases to notify lawyers of new court decisions that could affect a case.[174] Areas such as legal discovery and contract law, normally reliant on extensive experience and knowledge gained from years of study and in-field practice, are suddenly finding themselves being replaced by machines that can process in minutes what used to take years. Not only can AI collect data, in can also use this to formulate an argument and debate its position. In June 2018, IBM debuted 'Project Debater', billed as *the first AI system that can debate humans on complex topics*.[65] It is able to engage in free-forum vocal debate with humans on any topic contained in the hundreds of millions of articles in its dataset, selecting the most compelling, diverse and well-supported arguments to construct a complete persuasive narrative. Debater has the potential to mine the entire database of previous legal cases and provide a case of the defence or prosecution, providing an opponent for trainee lawyers to train against. Or to become their replacement.

This technological replacement is even affecting those who previously thought of themselves as the masters of the capitalist universe. Bridgewater Associates, the world's largest hedge fund that manages $160 billion of trades, is building an AI system to replace its managers, many of whom are highly educated and were previously thought invulnerable to automation.

---

[65] https://www.research.ibm.com/artificial-intelligence/project-debater/

The system is designed to automate the day-to-day management of the firm, including hiring, firing and other strategic decision-making. It won't be the first AI stock trader: in 2016, noted AI researcher Ben Goertzel launched Aidyia, a hedge fund that makes all stock trades using artificial intelligence without any human intervention. Over in the world of financial services, J. P. Morgan hit the tech headlines when they announced that they had created a learning machine called COIN (short for **Co**ntract **In**telligence) that was able to interpret commercial loan agreements in seconds, a task that previously took their lawyers and loan officers 360,000 hours per year to do. As well as saving time, COIN has also helped J. P. Morgan cut down on mistakes, removing the numerous human errors that occur in the process of interpreting 12,000 new wholesale contracts per year. The system learns by ingesting data to identify patterns and relationships, providing J. P. Morgan with a way to automate other complex legal filings such as credit-default swaps, custody agreements and, at some point, interpreting regulations and analysing corporate communications. J. P. Morgan's Chief Information Officer, Dana Deasy, stated that, *Anything where you have back-office operations and humans kind of moving information from point A to point B that's not automated is ripe for that.* Quite simply, what companies are rapidly finding is that AI is cheaper, more efficient, less error-prone and potentially more impartial in its actions than human beings. Many knowledge workers are already doing standard, repetitive work such as contract reviews, invoice and order processing, mortgage-servicing operations and dealing with compliance issues. These can easily be, and are being, automated. As the famous cognitive scientist and psychologist Steven Pinker declared, *as the new generation of intelligent devices appears, it will be the stock analysts and petrochemical engineers and parole board members who are in danger of being replaced by machines. The gardeners, receptionists, and cooks are secure in their jobs for decades to come.*

Although maybe not the receptionists. Or the cooks. We've already seen how simple, repetitive fast-food cooking is currently being automated. Menu-based food preparation, however, requires a huge range of different ingredients, tools and actions. It's a challenge that machines have already cracked, ranging from Hema's new robot restaurants in China that make and deliver bespoke meals to your table, to robot chefs in the home. In 2015, a team of scientists from the University of Maryland and the

Australian research centre NICTA (National ICT Australia) successfully used deep-learning techniques to enable a robot to learn to use kitchen tools by showing it a series of eighty-eight cooking videos on YouTube. More recently, a company called Moley Robotics has developed a cooking system that consists of two dexterous robotic arms installed atop a cooking area, complete with hobs, a sink and an oven. These fully articulated robotic hands now reproduce the entire function of human hands with the same speed, sensitivity and movement. From Moley's website: *The cooking skills of Master Chef Tim Anderson, winner of the BBC MasterChef title, were recorded on the system – every motion, nuance and flourish – then replayed as his exact movements through the robotic hands*. The kitchen is operated by its touchscreen or remotely via smartphone. Because Moley is connected to the cloud, users can download recipes by chefs or other users, and tell it to start cooking while they are out, so the meal is ready for when they arrive home. It can also do the washing and cleaning of the kitchen, and afterwards the robotic arms retract from view. The consumer version goes on sale in late 2018.

To What am I Speaking?

What about receptionists? The Turing Test, named after the father of computing, Alan Turing, was supposed to be the milestone that, upon being reached, would indicate whether a machine can communicate in such a way that it is indistinguishable from a human. We have effectively passed that milestone. Not only can machines understand human voice commands and translate languages, but they can make phone calls and book appointments. At the Google I/O 2018 conference, Google's CEO, Sundar Pichai, showed off the capabilities of Duplex, the recurrent neural network enhancement that enables Google Assistant to provide computer-human interaction via natural, conversational speech. He demonstrated a female voiced version phoning a hairdresser to book a woman's haircut, and a male voiced one booking a table for four at a restaurant. Despite the desired time slots not being available and the restaurant not providing bookings for groups of under five people, the AI seamlessly conversed with the humans on the end of the phone, asking context correct questions, adapting instantly to the information provided and even using terms such as 'uh uh', 'OK, I gotcha' and 'mmm hmm' at appropriate points. It was apparent that the person on the end of the phone had no idea that the caller wasn't human.

It is highly likely that voice will be the way we engage with machines moving forward: already around 20 per cent of Internet searches are undertaken by voice, and that number is expected to rise. They've already taught these systems to talk to each other, with systems such as Amazon's Alexa and Microsoft's Cortana able to collaborate to help you stay in control of your diary and ensure everything you need to run the day is available – from reminding you to pick up flowers on your way home, to reading your work email – all using just your voice.[175] Jeff Bezos sees a future where AI is smart enough to route your request to the right assistant for the right task. *There are going to be multiple successful intelligent agents, each with access to different sets of data and with different specialized skill areas*, he said. *One could provide advice on the latest movies, another offer advice about hiking, and another make bar and restaurant recommendations.*[176] IBM's Watson is also being used in this space, using its deep natural language-processing capabilities to power chatbots that provide automated services to customers. The service, Watson Virtual Agent, offers a cognitive, conversational, self-service experience capable of providing answers to questions and reacting appropriately to requests. This is customisable to the needs of the company, allowing businesses to deploy agents that capture responses and report on how well the customer engaged with it. Companies like Staples have already utilised this technology to enable people to talk to a virtual agent to reorder supplies, track shipments or chat about customer service needs. As these capabilities advance and become commonplace, human receptionists, call-centre workers and customer service assistants will be replaced with these faultlessly polite machines that can converse in multiple languages and work 24/7 for no pay. Very soon machines will call other machines and have conversations between themselves, so that tools like Google Assistant don't just make bookings on behalf of humans, they take them as well.

Computers Get Creative

What is really interesting is how AI systems are already encroaching on the creative industries that one would assume were out of bounds for machines. In 2016, IBM's Watson was used to select key moments from the sci-fi movie *Morgan* in order to create a compelling trailer, and it has also collaborated with musicians such as the Grammy award-winning producer Alex da Kid to create the first 'cognitive song' called *Not Easy*. Watson analysed five years of material from sources as diverse as social media, the *New York Times*, United States Supreme Court rulings, and lyrics to more than 26,000 *Billboard* Hot 100 hits to discover hidden patterns in song structure and human emotion that were then used to create the track. Then, in August 2017, a music album called *I AM AI* was released by Taryn Southern, which included a guest artist called Amper, an AI system, creating the first album that was entirely composed and produced by artificial intelligence. Even the gaming industry has the potential to be disrupted by AI, as neural networks have already been used to design new levels for games such as Doom and Super Mario Brothers.[177]

What about art? Since our ancestors created handprints on cave walls in ochre, art has been deemed the most human of activities (save the odd elephant or gorilla that has been trained to throw paint on a canvas), requiring the ability to translate imagination and memory into imagery. Not any more. Deep-learning systems have already been developed that can transform images and photos into artistic creations in the style of a grandmaster such as Rembrandt or Van Gogh.[178] Systems like Google's DeepDream have been able to create new images that come from its own interpretations of the world, creating images unlike anything you've ever seen before[179] (assuming you're not familiar with any mind-altering drugs, that is). Researchers working on DeepMind have even developed the capability to create images from sentences; so, for example if you type, *A large white bird with orange legs and grey secondaries and primaries, and a short yellow bill,* it will create a photographic image of a bird with exactly those features. These developments have the potential to impact – and enhance – a whole host of creative careers such as graphic design, advertising, digital printing, etc. The foray of AI systems into the creative arts is an interesting development, because it contradicts the conventional wisdom that all AI will be focused on logical, algorithmic tasks only, and that people with creative skills and jobs will be safe. How long before we are listening to AI-generated music designed specifically to appeal to our own tastes, and bespoke TV and current affairs programmes designed and managed by AI? Not long.

AI will soon be targeted at understanding you as an individual; what you like, what you want, and how you shop or consume information. AI assistants will act as filters and orchestration layers that process the vast amounts of information that they have access to, so they deliver a fully personalised service. Watson is also being used to create personalised experiences for television viewers, and Netflix has already announced its plans to use AI to produce individual film trailers based on its customer's viewing habits. So, if you like action movies, it will create a trailer based on any explosive action scenes in the preview. If you like romantic movies, then any eye-gazing slushy scenes will feature prominently in the trailer.[180] The potential therefore exists for CGI movies and games to be developed based on our preferred genres, which when combined with virtual reality could provide a completely personalised, immersive experience.[66]

This is just the beginning. AI has now advanced to the point where it can understand and respond to users' emotional states, enabling robots like Pepper to appear more human-like, and in doing so enabling more natural human interaction. AI is rapidly becoming better at analysing and responding to people's emotions, thanks to deep-learning technology that can understand facial and verbal expressions. The ability for machine intelligence to take on tasks that we assumed would require significant human experience, such as translating languages, and do them far better, is sometimes breathtaking. In late 2016, users of the online translation service Google Translate suddenly noticed that it had become exponentially better at its job, going from clunky to considered almost overnight. The reason for this dramatic improvement was the involvement of an AI-based neural network system called Google Brain, which Google had switched on. Overnight, it made more translation improvements to forty languages than Google's human team had achieved in the past eleven years.[181]

---

[66] I spent my entire childhood being told not to sit within two feet of the TV screen because it would strain my eyes. Now we strap screens just two centimetres from our faces. Go figure.

The End of Human Data Entry: Blockchain, RPA and Chatbots

As discussed, the manufacture and distribution of goods across the end-to-end supply chain is going to be disrupted due to the replacement of all the manual and blue-collar labour with machines. But what about the millions employed in tasks such as checking transactions, entering sales orders, raising invoices and processing accounts? Unfortunately, they're not safe either. Three new technologies are about to cause significant technological disruption to a wide variety of this type of office-based work: robotic process automation (commonly known as RPA), chatbots and the blockchain. RPA relates to computer software that can partially or fully automate manual, repetitive and rule-based activities such as data entry. Vast amounts of time, effort and errors occur in the process of recording transactions such as sales order creation and invoice processing. RPA is a non-coded solution that allows a human user to effectively teach it how to respond to certain tasks, but which, through advances in machine learning, enables it to learn on the job, accommodate increasing workloads and undertake different tasks as required. The development of RPA has led to the creation of virtual service-desk employees capable of replying to emails, answering phone calls and holding conversations, resulting in the replacement of previously outsourced and offshored call centres, financial centres and back-office functions. Unlike previous iterations of automated services, these programs learn, enabling an increasingly sophisticated and personal service that improves the quality of outcome while reducing the cost of provision. Forrester predicts that by 2021, RPA technology will be used to complete the equivalent workload of nearly 4.3 million humans worldwide.

The increasing use of AI to power voice-recognition systems will enable more human-to-machine (and soon machine-to-machine) conversations, allowing sophisticated customer service capabilities via the use of chatbots. The benefits are obvious. Firstly, a chatbot never sleeps or takes a break and is unlikely to damage your brand by being rude or sarcastic (not yet, anyway). It increases the level of service customers receive by filtering out and answering easy questions, while also decreasing the response time, preventing people from waiting ages listening to looping, soul-destroying messages about how important their call is to the company. A chatbot enquiry is estimated to save each caller around four minutes compared with traditional call centres, and chatbots are predicted to save businesses more than US$8 billion per year by 2022, according to a report by Juniper Research.[182] Chatbots also excel at collecting customer data from support interactions and can access a full history of each account quickly. They can learn by experience, becoming able to answer ever more sophisticated questions relating to the business of the company they support. They are even starting to appear as part of the product, not just as support for the product. I recently spoke on a panel with Kriti Sharma, VP of Bots and AI at Sage, the accounting and payroll software company. She is working on 'invisible accounting' with Pegg, a personal assistant chatbot that manages small business finances. Sharma asked the audience, "Who loves expense reports? Or chasing purchase orders and asking people to pay you on time? I realised that what Sage does is not something that most people enjoy, so how about we give them someone else to do it for them? Business owners are not geared towards mundane work; they would rather be building new products." Within six weeks of launch, Pegg was being used by people in 85 countries.

Finally, the blockchain; a digital technology that is generating a lot of hype and capturing a lot of press attention, and for good reason. It could potentially transform industry operating models and create decentralised mechanisms the like of which we haven't seen before. Originally developed for managing payments with cryptocurrencies like Bitcoin, blockchain has the potential to fundamentally change the way global supply chains share information by automating the recording of product, asset and financial transactions, removing the need for middlemen, paper documents and computer systems based on 19th-century accounting principles. Currently, an international shipment of goods typically requires the production of more than twenty different documents simply to enable the goods to move from exporter to importer, many of which are paper-based and contain almost identical information.

Blockchain uses a completely different principle. It's a distributed, time-stamped, public ledger which contains blocks representing each part of the chain of transactions from the very start of the supply chain to the end. Once each individual transaction is completed, a block goes into the blockchain as a permanent database, and a new one is generated including a hash (record number) of the previous block in the chain, linking the two. There is a countless number of such blocks in the blockchain, connected to each other like links in a chain, held in a linear, chronological order, showing every stage from manufacture to consumption, including all changes of ownership. It has the potential to transform the end-to-end supply chain from a series of separate, closed and private transactions, into a single series of transparent ones.

The blockchain was designed so these transactions are immutable, meaning they cannot be deleted. The blocks are added through cryptography, where computers from separately owned entities are used to follow a cryptographic protocol that continually validates any updates to a commonly shared ledger. The more people who participate, the more secure the data becomes. Data can be distributed and added to (via new blocks being appended to the chain), but not copied or altered. Each block in the chain is linked to the previous block, and all previous blocks will have been verified. This means that it creates a distributed system where no single company has control and all stakeholders can verify the integrity of the data. This resolves disclosure and accountability issues between companies and individuals whose interests are likely not to be aligned, removing the need for a verifiable third party, such as a bank, lawyer or trusted intermediary, to facilitate the exchange. Blockchain enables mutually valuable data to be updated in real time, and thus removes the need for the laborious and often error-prone reconciliation of each party's own internal records. It serves as an open ledger, where every transaction on the network is registered and available for all participants to see and verify, providing far greater visibility of the total supply chain. Through the provision of a single, constantly updated version of the truth, a blockchain replaces the numerous different interpretations that cause disparities that require significant time to analyse, understand and mitigate. It also removes the need to transfer information between organisations using traditional, time-consuming and error-prone methods such as emails, spreadsheets, and other electronic connections such as Electronic Data Interchange (EDI). It also removes the need for associated documents, such as shipping documents, to be produced to accompany the goods as the blockchain allows its users to attach digital tokens to intermediate goods as the ownership of them passes between the various parties in the supply chain. Because the ownership and provenance of a transaction can be embedded in the blockchain and verified at every subsequent stage, the use of blockchain has direct relevance to any transaction that needs to be secure and verifiable.

Most importantly, the database cannot be changed without all participants' agreement, so any fraudulent changes are immediately identifiable. This rise of algorithmic trust represents the third economic shift; the biggest advancement in trade since double-entry bookkeeping. Marc Andreessen, co-founder of Netscape, describes the benefits of the blockchain as follows: *The practical consequence [is,] for the first time, a way for one Internet user to transfer a unique piece of digital property to another Internet user, such that the transfer is guaranteed to be safe and secure, everyone knows that the transfer has taken place, and nobody can challenge the legitimacy of the transfer. The consequences of this breakthrough are hard to overstate.*[183]

The globalised nature of trade means that, for example, food grown on one side of the world is picked from the field, put in boxes, moved by a packager to a temperature-controlled distribution centre, shipped across to the other side of the world, unloaded at a port, moved on once again by another haulage company, placed in another distribution centre, picked and packed, and finally sent to a retailer who then sells it to an end consumer. Or, even more complicated, it could be sent to a manufacturer who then uses it as an ingredient in a recipe for a pre-packed meal, which is then sold to a retailer. There are multiple points of failure in supply chains like this, and currently all the information relating to each one of these transactions and the partners involved in them – from field to fork – is sitting in separate silos, recorded on paper, spreadsheets or systems that just don't talk to each other. You cannot view the entire end-to-end supply chain, and this is a problem, as we saw with the issues with melamine in baby milk, diethylene glycol in toothpaste and lead paint on toys. For you may trust your supplier, but do you trust (or even know) your supplier's supplier, or their supplier?

The blockchain represents the opportunity to provide a truly global system for mediating trust, traceability and transparency across organisational boundaries, addressing the need to facilitate a broad range of supply-chain relationships across a wide variety of different cultures, languages and systems. This level of transparency helps reduce fraud, errors and the time products spend in the transit and shipping process; improve inventory management; eliminate the need for paper documents to accompany goods; and ultimately reduce waste and cost. It also enables companies to truly understand their end-to-end supply chain, providing visibility to all the complexity and diversity of the different interests and parties involved. From a product traceability and sustainability perspective, the blockchain could prove transformative, addressing the product quality, waste and safety issues that have arisen from this fragmented, multi-echelon, globalised supply chain. To test its potential, a consortium comprising of AB InBev, Accenture, APL, Kuehne + Nagel and a European customs organisation, collaborated to process twelve shipments with various destinations, each with different regulatory requirements. They found that the blockchain sped up the entire process, removed the need for separate transport documents, eliminated 80 per cent of the data entry, streamlined the checks and reduced the risk of penalties for customs compliance issues.[184] It will save shippers millions in costs, which should help to keep the price of goods low.

The blockchain will also enable the instantaneous digital tracking of the provenance and movement of food throughout the entire process from farm to fork, allowing retailers and restaurants to have assurance that the products they receive and serve to their customers are safe. Recent examples demonstrated how much this is needed. In 2015, seven of Italy's best-known olive oil companies were found to have been conning consumers by putting virgin olive oil into bottles labelled as the superior – and more expensive – extra-virgin olive oil.[185] The scandal was considered a national disgrace for Italy, the world's second largest supplier of olive oil. In 2013, the Food Standard Authority of Ireland found horsemeat in beef products, and subsequent tests discovered that the problem was Europe-wide, affecting thirteen countries. Just two Dutch companies had supplied 50,000 tons of meat marked as beef across Europe, but which was subsequently found to contain horse DNA.[186] In the UK, Tesco's beefburgers were found to contain horsemeat, destroying consumer trust, and as a result the retailer's market value dropped by €360 million. Sales of frozen hamburgers in the UK fell by 43 per cent and frozen ready meals by 13 per cent. Testing was then carried out on other meat products and found that twenty-three out of twenty-seven samples of beefburgers also contained pig DNA; a major problem for Muslim and Jewish communities where consuming pork is taboo. In 2017, an undercover operation into 2 Sisters, the largest supplier of chicken to UK supermarkets, caught them altering the slaughter date of poultry. Workers were also caught altering records of where chickens were slaughtered, mixing chickens slaughtered on different dates on the production line, and chicken portions that had been returned by supermarket distribution centres were also being repackaged, relabelled and sent out again to major grocers. These activities potentially hinder authorities from recalling contaminated meat during food scares and put the public's health second to the company's profits. Being able to identify exactly where infected ingredients were contaminated or faulty components manufactured, and where they currently are in the supply chain, is enormously beneficial to companies when product recalls need to be initiated, not to mention potentially brand-saving and even life-saving.

To address these kinds of worrying scandals and breaches of trust in the food supply chain, a UK software start-up called Provenance is already testing blockchain technology to authenticate food products, starting with tuna caught in Indonesia delivered to Japanese restaurants, using information from sensors or RFID tags to record it on the blockchain to track the fish from capture to consumption. In another case study, they tracked sustainable alpaca fleece from the point of shearing at the farm, through to spinning, knitting, and finishing at fashion designer Martine Jarlgaard's London studio – creating a digital history of the garments' journey.[187] Tech giant IBM is a key player in the blockchain revolution. In September 2016, IBM completed a proof of concept with Maersk, the largest container carrier in the world, tracking a container of flowers from the Kenyan coastal city of Mombasa to Rotterdam in the Netherlands. In their research they found that there were two-hundred, mostly printed, documents involved in moving them from Africa to Rotterdam. All of these can be eliminated using the blockchain. In 2017, IBM also partnered with Nestlé, Unilever and Walmart in the development of a food-standards blockchain, starting with a pilot by tracing the supply chain of pre-packaged mango slices from the orchard in South Asia all the way to a refrigerated shelf in a US Walmart. Bridgett McDermott, IBM's blockchain VP, stated that in testing they had reduced the time it took to identify the actual farm that had grown the mangoes down from six days, eighteen hours and twenty-six minutes to just a couple of seconds.[188] The concept of a global, public, encrypted open ledger that no one controls but every party can access should enable the public to regain trust in the goods they buy – and the suppliers of these goods. It also offers significant advantages to manufacturers and retailers through reducing the need to continually send surveys and questionnaires and carry out expensive site visits to ensure that there are no nasty surprises lurking in the darkest recesses of their supply chain.

As advancements in chip and sensor technology enable the IoT to become mainstream, it is expected that this and the blockchain will combine to become almost semi-autonomous, receiving and translating data from physical goods as they reach certain nodes, be that a port, plane or warehouse. When combined with 'smart contracts' which contain all the relevant contractual rights and obligations for the entire supply chain, including all the terms for payment and delivery of goods and services, then it is expected that almost all necessary transactions could be processed by an autonomous system that's trusted by all signatories. This could include validating the authenticity and accuracy of documents such as birth certificates, passports, wills, land rights, contracts, criminal records, medical records, building permits, health-and-safety inspections, business licences, vehicle registrations, intellectual property rights, software and hardware licences, and patents, copyrights and trademarks. Blockchain is therefore gaining traction not only with the world of supply chains, but also financial institutions, the insurance industry, real estate, stock exchanges, the transfer of music, precious stones, gold, weapon sales, vehicle registrations, medical records, and even to confirm ownership of antiquities or artwork. It's even being projected as a way to ensure foreign aid ends up in the hands of the needy, and to monitor how crowdfunding donations are used. Basically, wherever there is a transfer of ownership of anything of value, the blockchain could be used to improve traceability and transparency. There is even the suggestion than an electronic ledger system like blockchain could be usefully applied to voting systems to prevent voting fraud.

China is well aware of the opportunity that blockchain provides and has again figured out that the best place to be is at the front. Along with its 'Made in China' initiative, it also sees blockchain (alongside autonomous vehicles and autonomous ports) as an enabler to its massive 'One Belt, One Road' supply-chain initiative designed to recreate the land-based Silk Road and the sea-based Asia Belt, seamlessly linking China to the rest of the world. Currently, scientists from IBM Research are working alongside top talent from Tsinghua University and the retailer Walmart to use blockchain to improve the way food is tracked, transported and sold to consumers across China.[189] They aim to ensure the blockchain is used across all the countries that the belt and road traverse, enabling Chinese manufacturers to hugely simplify the transportation of their goods to the West, while also significantly increasing transparency and trust in products stamped *Made in China*.

The use of blockchain is set to rise exponentially over the next decade. Even though to date it has been primarily focused around the cryptocurrency Bitcoin, the growth rate is startling. On 1st May 2012, the size of all block headers and transactions was 969MB. By May 2018 it reached 165,826MB, or 254,000 transactions a day. A tipping point is about to be reached, and it will accelerate due to recent moves such as Amazon's involvement in the arena. It has used its massive R&D fund to finance the development of a start-up called Kaleido, whose purpose was declared to be to make it as easy as possible for AWS customers to put their business on the blockchain. Amazon's ultimate objective is almost certainly to transfer its supply chain operations onto it as well. Like AWS, Kaleido represents a smart move: getting other companies to effectively pay for the development of the platform that will run Amazon's business, turning what would be for most companies a sunk cost into an ongoing profit centre.

The World Economic Forum predicts that by 2025, 10 percent of GDP will be stored on blockchains or blockchain related technology. However, there are significant challenges that need to be overcome before blockchain can go mainstream. One is the amount of energy needed to power crypto-solutions. More electricity is currently consumed mining bitcoin than is used in the whole of New Zealand, and this rate of energy consumption is likely to be a barrier to the implementation of blockchain solutions for many. Another issue is the establishment of cross-country agreement of best practices, technology standards and contract structures that can operate across international borders and jurisdictions.

When you combine blockchain, chatbots and RPA, what we are rapidly approaching is a near future where all transactional processing and reconciliation across the extended supply chain will be handled autonomously. It will transform supply chain and finance from a world of silo transactions in closed systems, to a more central, open and transparent one. Feed this data to smarter machines, and you will also be able to answer any questions we humans have about where products are, who owns them, whether payment has been made and when they are likely to arrive. Of course, the million-dollar question is what happens to the army of employees around the world whose job it is currently to answer these questions and process this information. The positive answer is that they will be freed up to do more value-adding, rather than value-enabling, work. As any Lean expert will tell you, these transactional activities do not add any direct value to the customer, so we shouldn't mourn their passing. They are also generally not the most satisfying of tasks, being repetitive in nature. The less-than-positive answer is that these people won't be needed at all, which, while dramatically reducing the cost of moving goods around (savings which hopefully reduces the cost of the end products), it does create a big question as to what happens to these white-collar workers. The automation of knowledge work will be this decade of growth, for like manufacturing, it's going to be coming home. But also, like manufacturing, it's not going to be bringing the jobs with it.

We're all Software Companies Now

GE's ex-CEO, Jeff Immelt, stated that if you woke up as an industrial company today, prepare to wake up as a software and analytics company tomorrow.[190] He's not implying you'll be selling software; what he is implying is that software will be an important part of whatever it is you're making moving forward. The amount of data being captured is nothing compared to when the Internet of Things and blockchain moves up the 'S' curve from deceptive to disruptive, and every node and machine in the end-to-end process becomes connected. The IoT will make all manner of dumb things smart, applying sensors and connectors to thousands of objects that will capture data about every aspect of our lives. By 2020, Cisco forecasts that there will be upwards of 50 billion sensors and other devices connected to the IoT, creating a world where objects are continually communicating both to us and to each other. Other projections estimate that upwards of 100 trillion sensors will be connected to the IoT by 2030.[191] This will create a multitude of new and innovative ways of capturing consumer information and demand signals. The amount of data that an entirely connected world, known as the Internet of Everything (the Internet of Things' big brother), will be huge – 600ZB by 2020, according to Cisco, of which 92 per cent will be in the cloud.[192]

Everyone is now in the data business, and the quality of your data strategy and your ability to execute it will determine the market winners of the future. Looking back, we can now see why the companies who realised this first – such as Amazon and Ocado – have been so successful. These companies are investing heavily in business analytics and big-data solutions to mine this real-time data and create competitive advantages by enabling them to become more agile, identify opportunities faster, and take actions to mitigate threats such as stock-outs or even consumers exploiting returns policies before they happen. Back in 2014, an article in the *New Yorker* on Jeff Bezos and Amazon contained the line; *Before Google, and long before Facebook, Bezos had realised that the greatest value of an online company lay in the consumer data it collected.*[193] Bezos realised that the model had changed. Previously data was the end of the chain, the recording of transactions about to be made or already made, based on the sale of existing products or services. Now consumer insights are driving the agenda, driving the decision-making process and changing the shape of products and services that are provided.

As commerce continues to move from bricks-and-mortar stores to online and mobile ones, the success of products, brands and companies is dependent on the speed and accuracy of data analysis in order to provide more personalised digital experiences. The fact that our phones are almost permanently on or around our person is of great value to AI developers, retailers and marketers alike. Our phone is, for the most part, an indicator of our location, and we are already seeing location-sensitive sales and marketing offers being delivered right to our screens. Once AI can add context to location, through alignment with calendars and other smart devices such as your car or Wi-Fi hubs (like those on trains and planes), your mobile AI will know whether you are travelling, in a meeting, relaxing at a restaurant or shopping. It can then personalise the nature and type of material it presents to you. Not only will the AI agent have the power and the data to act on your behalf, it will rapidly advance to the point where it will predict your behaviour, organising everything from office meetings and conference calls to birthday cards, gym sessions and insurance renewals—all from your mobile device.

Machines that Learn

The volume of data being generated is due to grow exponentially, doubling every three years as information pours in from digital platforms, wireless sensors, virtual-reality applications, and billions of mobile phones. This data volume is causing a problem, for it is outstripping our capability to analyse and make sense of it. We simply don't have the processing capability. To overcome this restriction, machines need to teach themselves – and that is exactly what is happening. Do you think Amazon could offer a one-hour delivery service if they had human planners deciding which of the over 562 million products sold on Amazon need to be stored in their fulfilment centres?[194] Assuming a limited product range of just 100,000 items, if each item must be programmed into the computer, and it takes five minutes per item by a $35/hour technician, it would take 41,670 man-hours at a cost of $1.45 million to teach the robot to pick all the SKUs. Machines therefore needed to figure this out for themselves. Amazon initiated a project called 'hands off the wheel' to see if algorithms could do a better job of planning and price setting. Initially humans were required to monitor and adjust any mistakes, but as the machines learned their job, the need for human intervention disappeared. In an early example of what is going to become a much wider trend, they quickly realised that the machines were simply better.

While AI researchers are busy building smart machines, machine-learning experts are striving to make them truly intelligent. Nidhi Chappell, head of machine learning at Intel, describes the difference between AI and machine learning as follows: *AI is basically the intelligence – how we make machines intelligent, while machine learning is the implementation of the computing methods that support it. The way I think of it is this: AI is the science and machine learning is the algorithms that make the machines smarter. Machine learning is therefore the enabler for AI. If AI is driving the car, machine learning identifies the stop sign and what to do.*[195] AI and machine learning are being used to discover patterns and correlations in data, and in doing so powering the development of predictive models and analytics that help companies to provide new offerings in today's on-demand world. For example, machine learning powers the new-wave ride-hailing companies such as Lyft and Uber, enabling them to determine optimal routes, match rides with drivers, establish ride and wait times, and determine prices. Their routing algorithms, pricing algorithms, driver-matching algorithms and other such systems all rely on machine-learning models to some extent. There are several different types of machine-learning algorithms, one of which – deep learning – refers to non-task-specific machine learning that loosely uses the same type of information-processing and communication patterns that exist in a biological nervous system. Deep-learning architectures such as deep neural networks have been applied to fields such as computer vision, speech recognition, natural language processing, audio recognition, social network filtering and machine translation, where they produced results at least comparable, and often superior, to human experts.[196]

For example, pharmaceutical giant GlaxoSmithKline announced that machine learning will enable them to slash years off the research and development times for new drugs, a process which can take up to twelve years and cost up to £1.1 billion per drug. Machine learning can analyse decades of test data to predict how molecules will react, as well as reviewing previously failed drug trials to see if the system can pick up what humans failed to notice. There are now around twenty versions of drugs being developed by supercomputer-powered machine-learning systems every month.[197] Machine-learning techniques are also currently being used to process tens of thousands of medical scans of human organs – from brains to eyes – looking for defects such as signs of cancer. Its work and success rate far exceeds those of humans. In 2015, a program called Deep Patient used deep-learning techniques to analyse the records of 700,000 patients at the Mount Sinai Hospital in New York and proved to be considerably better than its human counterparts at identifying the onset of diseases, such as cancer of the liver.[198] It also appeared to be very proficient at highlighting difficult-to-identify mental disorders such as schizophrenia. Elsewhere, researchers have been able to use machine-learning techniques to study medical images, identify patterns and make more accurate diagnoses than ever before. In 2018, an AI system called BioMind beat a team consisting of fifteen of China's top brain tumour specialists, taking fifteen minutes to correctly identify 87 per cent of cases, compared to the human doctors who took thirty minutes and only identified 66 per cent. These advancements in the production of treatments and processing of images and scans will prove essential in the fight against Alzheimer's and dementia-related diseases that are on the rise due to our increased lifespan. Affecting an estimated 46.8 million people worldwide, dementia-related diseases pose an increasing burden on society, causing upset for families, filling hospital beds, requiring full-time carers and creating an economic burden expected to reach US$1 trillion by 2018 and $2 trillion by 2030. Machine-learning algorithms designed to review MRI scans can spot subtle neurological manifestations of Alzheimer's in the brain up to ten years before doctors are normally able to diagnose the disease.[199] They can even help doctors ensure that palliative care is delivered at the right time. Deep-learning systems similar to AlphaGo's DeepMind have been developed that can now accurately predict (up to 95 per cent) when sick patients will die, helping ensure that they and their families receive the appropriate level of care and support at the end of their lives,[200] an issue which can cause excess stress if the care is delivered too early, or worse, too late.[67]

Machine learning is currently being used to extract and analyse information from unstructured data captured from customer emails, chats, comments, videos and support requests to accurately gauge customer sentiment, such as satisfaction with the service. It is already well on its way to becoming completely embedded in our day-to-day lives through one device in particular – our phones. Machine learning is perfect for pattern-matching requirements such as face recognition, which has already been built into the iPhone X. This form of AI will help smartphones understand their users in new and unprecedented ways, allowing for the creation of a new type of relationship that is more personal. It will help the phone to understand exactly which apps are used the most, how you use the phone at different times – e.g. when you are getting sleepy – and even the user's emotional state. For advertisers, this is their ultimate dream – phones that know whether you are tired or hungry can create even more tailored offers and promotions.

Innovative new companies are seeing opportunities for machine learning even in areas that one would assume have no potential for non-human intervention, such as the organisation and management of employees. A company called Satalia, founded in 2007 from the University College London with the mission to *push the boundaries of data science, optimisation and artificial intelligence to solve the most difficult problems in industry*, is seeking to address this challenge. Most of the problems they work on are complex supply-chain challenges like route scheduling and cable network planning, but interestingly some involve improving the way we organise employees. Satalia itself operates without managers or administrators, and their COO, Avida Hancock, believes that data science and AI will replace traditional leaders and information hierarchies, producing a new kind of decentralised organisation: a coalition of talent and ideas. Her aim is to use technology to break the hierarchical, top-down, command-

---

[67] Though I pity the poor soul who asks his doctor whether he should make plans for Christmas, only to get the answer, 'Computer says no.'

and-control business model, and export it to business and government worldwide. She explains, *Right from the beginning, we decided to architect what we think of as a new operating system for organisations, by using our technology to power the way we work, to enable people to collaborate in a completely decentralised, self-organised, purposeful way. We collect data from every event that happens within the organization, across every network tool, and we pour it into a data lake called Cosmos. We then use data science and machine learning to extract insights from it and to power a system that provides information to everyone in the organization: what opportunities are available, what activities people are working on, who is connecting with who, how much projects are costing us, and our priorities within a collective strategy...this enables us to work in a completely non-hierarchical way.* While Hancock admits that an organisation will never be leaderless – even Satalia needs a captain – she states that there's no static within its fluid organisation and believes the AI-driven organisational model to be replicable in any size of business.

A Better Plan; A Better Planner

The universal truth about forecasts is that they are always wrong. Part of the reason for this is that people are bad estimators, easily distracted by irrelevancies or personal bias. Demand forecasters are notorious for being either careless (i.e. made errors or were just not very good at forecasting), or fearless (they were always over-optimistic and bullish in order to meet sales targets). The recent explosion in e-commerce has made these errors almost untenable. Worse, in certain sectors such as apparel, consumer behaviour results in large numbers of orders being returned because the shopper ordered multiple items in multiple sizes and only kept the one outfit they liked and returned the rest. These types of demand behaviour cause severe headaches for supply-chain managers as it has become harder to predict how much product is needed, where it is needed, and when. The days of forecasting and FIFO (first in, first out) inventory management are becoming obsolete. The urgency to drive growth by reaching new customers and channels with new products – while maintaining service levels – is daunting. This puts tremendous demand on supply chains to become nimbler, more responsive and adaptable to market demands, able to ship smaller quantities to more people faster. Simply put, the complexity of today's supply chains is overwhelming the organisations' ability to manage them.

Realising the opportunity, supply-chain planning companies are embedding AI and machine-learning capabilities into their supply-chain optimisation software. For example, IBM Watson has developed Supply Chain Insights, a Watson AI powered supply chain control tower that captures and compiles data across the digital universe in volumes and speed unobtainable to mere Homo sapiens. It then processes and curates this information, identifies any issues, assesses the potential impact, and creates a playbook of its findings and recommendations, including suggestions as to the people who need to be involved, and examples of similar historic cases and the actions taken. AI is also being embedded into demand planning tools, using machine learning to understand consumer demand patterns, supply capabilities and promotional activities and then use this knowledge to accurately forecast upcoming needs and optimise inventory and replenishment plans far better than human planners. These new forms of data analytics are shaking up multiple industries as machines gain unprecedented capabilities to improve processes that humans have struggled with for decades. Whereas, in the past, planning involved silo-based demand plans, inventory plans, supply plans and even silo exception plans, today they are increasingly automatic and event-driven, adapting to demand as it is received. The ability to plan routes with up-to-date information from smart machines enables more detailed distribution planning, dramatically reducing costs and time to replenishment. An AI-planned supply chain could begin to predict how many customers are going to require a product when specific sets of criteria are met; for example, weather conditions. The ability to make an almost instant prediction based on years of data, to say, 'When a specific set of conditions occurs, then we can expect an uplift of X per cent more sales', will prove to be a very powerful differentiator for those companies able to take advantage of this technology. We are fast moving to a world where companies are realising that machines can manage and control the vast majority of items that flow through a supply chain better than most humans. The obvious question therefore becomes: if the system calculates the forecast, and no human can understand how it calculated the output, why do we need human planners at all? Will future sales and operations planning meetings be held between the demand forecasting bot, the supply schedule bot, and the operations bot?

Perhaps the best example I personally know of a company that has been able to take advantage of this new capability is Merck KGaA, the healthcare division of the pharmaceutical giant. In late 2017, their CIO, Alessandro de Luca, and I were both presenting at an event in Paris. Alessandro detailed the work his team had undertaken on what he called 'the self-driving supply chain'. It was impressive stuff. Alessandro's team set out with the goal of creating a fully autonomous supply chain, monitored and controlled continuously by AI-based analytical tools that presented real-time updates on the performance of the key measures such as forecast accuracy, inventory levels, demand by product, shipment lead times and delays. His ambition is to create the 'Tesla' of the supply-chain world – a digitally connected, self-driving operation that controls the activities and only requires human intervention when exceptions occur. To demonstrate what they have already achieved, Alessandro took me to one side, opened up the app on his mobile phone and simply asked for, '2018 sales' – at which point he received – by voice – an up-to-date projection of the already-booked sales for the coming year, broken down by region, and the comparison to target and last year. He then said, 'Forecast', and we listened as the system told him that all products were within the acceptable forecast tolerance, except for a couple of items it suggested he kept an eye on. He then said, 'Inventory', and the system told him that the overall inventory situation was excellent, then detailed the volume and value of inventory at each location and suggested that he looked at a couple of key items. Finally, he asked for backorder information and received – again by voice but backed up by text – details of all backorder situations and material shortages, with issues highlighted for his attention. As Alessandro stated to me, 'I know this information is correct. I know it is up-to-date. And now I know exactly where to focus my attention.'

After spending over twenty years working on business transformation programmes – specifically in the supply chain – I know the competitive advantage that this kind of automated, prescriptive control tower capability can provide. I also know that it will not be achievable for everyone. The ability of an organisation to clean and make sense of data is a complex and challenging issue, and one which will be a major predictor of the business' future success. Those that can will be able to not only diagnose issues, but also to predict and prevent them, enabling time and attention to be focused on adding value not fighting fires. However, those that are unable to create a foundation of truth in their business will find that any investment in AI will simply provide them with an automated lying machine. Even with robots, the rule of 'rubbish in, rubbish out' still applies.

The New Network Accelerators

To support the technologies of the sixth wave, new infrastructure needs to be developed. Like the canals, railroads and motorways of the past, this new revolution needs its own transportation network. The Internet took off when mobile telephony and smartphones were added to the mix, which required 3G. We are about to enter a world where an ocean of data is captured from a series of connected devices, varying from self-replenishing vending machines to smart heating systems; more data than humans can process, requiring advanced machine learning based data analytical capabilities to make sense of it. We also need both the mobile bandwidth and the processing power to handle this data volume, which is where 5G and quantum computing come in. 5G is the next evolution of mobile technology, needed to manage the exponential growth in data being transmitted and received via mobile devices – which is currently around 3.7 exabytes per month. According to a recent report from the National Infrastructure Commission, *5G means seamless connectivity. Ultra-fast, ultra-reliable, ultra-high capacity transmitting at super low latency. It will support the ever-larger data requirements of the existing network and new applications from augmented reality* to connected vehicles and the Internet of Things, and many more, as unknowable today as the 4G services we take for granted would have been a decade ago. 5G will be significantly faster than 4G, with university-based theoretical tests demonstrating a download speed of 1TB per second. A more realistic scenario has been demonstrated by companies like Samsung who have a 5G router that can provide speeds of 500MB per second, meaning that it is possible to download 4K movies, games and software with ease. That speed of response will be critical when self-driving cars are constantly communicating with one another and with infrastructure like traffic signals. 5G could also open up the potential for new levels of virtual and augmented reality, enabling it to respond nearly instantly to changing perspectives, creating a multitude of real-time uses such as tourism and entertainment. 5G is due to be available in the US in 2019.[201]

While a faster Internet connection opens up the possibilities of sending and receiving much more data, it's not really a revolutionary step for humanity. Quantum computing, on the other hand, could well be. The development of quantum computing has a mythical aura around it, deemed a technological milestone akin to nuclear fusion or powered flight. Whereas normal computers are effectively highly advanced calculators that use a sequence of bits – values of 1 and 0 to represent two states, off or on, a bit like a light switch – quantum computing takes advantage of quantum particles in a strange state called 'superposition'. This means that the particle is spinning in two directions at once, creating the ability to be both 1 and 0 at the same time – enabling it to perform more than one calculation at a time. One qubit can perform two calculations in a quantum superposition, two can perform four, three eight, and so forth, with a corresponding exponential increase in quantum parallelism. This massively increases the processing capability. If this sounds weird, it gets worse, as superposition gets even stranger as it scales. Because everything is made of atoms, some physicists theorise that entire objects can exist in multiple dimensions, allowing for the possibility of parallel universes. Even Nobel Prize-winning theoretical physicists like Richard Feynman have stated that, *I think I can safely say that nobody understands quantum mechanics.* So, if you think you understand quantum mechanics, then you probably don't. Which is why I'm going to declare my ignorance right here – understanding the mechanics of quantum physics is way above my intellectual pay scale. Yet regardless of my – or anyone else's – ability to understand how they work, quantum computers are coming. But don't expect them to look like your laptop, as qubits are tremendously fragile, requiring them to operate at around 20 millikelvin – 250 times colder than deep space.

What quantum computing brings is exponential levels of processing power. A classical computer's processing capability is only very slightly increased by the addition of one bit, but the addition of one qubit doubles the power of a quantum chip. A three hundred-bit classical chip could power (roughly) a basic calculator, but a three hundred-qubit chip has the computing power of two novemvigintillion bits – that's a two followed by ninety zeros, more than the atoms in the universe.[202] The difference between a quantum computer and a classical computer has been described as follows: whereas a regular computer could theoretically read and process all the books in a library one by one, a quantum computer could read them all at the same time. Quantum computers are unsuited for everyday computing tasks such as web browsing or ad placements, so it is unlikely that we will be seeing a quantum iPhone. Their core purpose is to tackle specific, unthinkably complex problems like simulating new molecules to engineer lighter aeroplane parts, more effective drugs and better batteries. Quantum computers are incredibly fast at finding the optimal solution to a problem that potentially has many different combinations of answers. In one test case using the D-Wave System, a quantum computer took less than half a second to do something that took conventional software thirty minutes. An example of one of these 'combinatorial optimisation' problems is that of the travelling sales rep who needs to visit several cities in one day and wants to know the shortest path that connects them all in order to minimise their mileage. The D-Wave Two chip can compare all the possible itineraries at once, rather than having to work through each in turn.

A computer that uses qubits can store an enormous amount of information using significantly less energy than usual methods. There are several companies all racing to get a quantum computer to market. IBM, the first to demonstrate a working prototype back in 2000, is continually working on its quantum computing project, and in May 2017 it unveiled a chip with sixteen qubits, a milestone for general-purpose quantum computers. Google is also working hard on quantum computing, teaming up with NASA (the National Aeronautics and Space Administration), to test the D-Wave System, which is being used by Lockheed Martin and the Los Alamos National Laboratory.[203] John Martinis, Google's head of quantum hardware, stated that they are trying to achieve what they call quantum supremacy, and are currently testing a seventy-two-qubit system that can solve problems way beyond the capabilities of traditional computers.[204] In December 2017, IBM also announced that it was teaming up with J. P. Morgan, Samsung and Barclays to develop quantum computing for commercial use. J P Morgan stated that it would be focusing on developing quantum computing applications for the financial industry such as trading strategies, portfolio optimisation, asset pricing and risk analysis; Samsung is exploring how the technology can fast-track the future of the semiconductor and electronics development; and Daimler is obviously hoping it will help with managing autonomous fleets of trucks and cars.[205] These efforts all got a boost in 2018 when, during a keynote address in Las Vegas, Intel's CEO, Brian Krzanich, announced the successful design, fabrication and delivery of a forty-nine-qubit superconducting quantum test chip, named Tangle Lake. He also showcased 'neuromorphic computing'; described by Intel as *a new computing paradigm inspired by how the brain works that could unlock exponential gains in performance and power efficiency for the future of artificial intelligence.* Krzanich announced that Intel has already developed a fully functioning neuromorphic research chip called Lolhi that mimics the brain's basic operation, and which will make machine learning more power-efficient.[206]

The exciting thing is that we are effectively moving from our linear thinking and linear processing into a quantum area of computing where the normal rules of physics no longer apply. This will enable developers to produce processors that are significantly faster – 1,000 to 1,000,000 times faster. This will allow us to enter an entirely new realm of physics that will provide solutions and uses that we thought impossible. Qubits will create the ability to perform millions of calculations at the same moment, allowing us to solve problems and create efficiencies that currently aren't possible. Hartmut Neven, Director of Engineering at Google and leader of the Quantum Artificial Intelligence Laboratory, stated that he expects all machine learning to be running on quantum computers within the next ten years. Imagine a Moore's Law-style increase in quantum computing and neuromorphic capabilities, and then imagine this capability being used to solve some of the world's hardest challenges. Quantum computing could therefore take AI into a whole new realm.

11

CONVERGENCE! THE AUTOMATION OF THE VALUE CHAIN

Coming together is a beginning; keeping together is progress;
working together is success.

Henry Ford

While each of the aforementioned sixth-wave innovations is individually impressive, the real opportunity comes from their integration and alignment. The final whammy, therefore, is convergence; the symbiotic alignment of these different technologies in order to completely automate the end-to-end supply chain and transform the world of work. Leading companies are reimagining both their value propositions and their manufacturing processes, examining how smart devices, artificial intelligence and sophisticated robotics can work together. Developments in machine learning, vision, speech recognition, translation and voice, haptic technology and movement are all going to be combined to create machines that are increasingly able to perform a multitude of tasks in a multitude of environments. Moravec's paradox is being overcome; machines are getting better and better at the basic human tasks we previously excelled at. Improvements in vision checking via machine learning now mean that machines can check detailed items like circuit boards or MRI scans for errors that the human eye – especially a tired, bored one – would miss. The fact that many of these new machines have a mostly cloud-based platform format also means that they are going to be constantly upgraded, constantly learning from their own individual experience and sharing that knowledge with other connected machines which reciprocate in kind, creating a constant feedback loop that builds an exponential increase in machine capabilities. Developments in emotional intelligence from robots like Pepper will soon find their way into robots like Baxter, while AI will enable other robots – such as Flippy the burger chef – to do increasingly advanced activities; in Flippy's case, to cook multiple items and clean the grill afterwards. Instead of costly, single-purpose robots and unchangeable factory configurations, manufacturers like Siemens and GE are seeing the possibility that automated, multi-purpose factories could offer – such as producing speciality products, bidding for limited-run manufacturing projects and competing for customers in an increasingly online marketplace. The potential of merging the old-wave industrial technologies with the new-wave ones creates compelling possibilities.

Peeling Back the Layers

The foundation of this vision is the Industrial Internet of Things (IIoT), also known as Industry 4.0. The IIoT contains four primary elements, as follows:[68]

- Intelligent assets such as smart robots, sensors, controllers and any application software or machine capable of built-in intelligence, self-diagnosis, connectivity and support for analytics.
- A data communications infrastructure.
- Analytics and applications to capture, combine and generate meaningful information from this mass of data collected from a huge number of different sources.
- People.

---

[68] Definition from the ARC Advisory Group.

The IIoT – and the software solutions powered by it – will touch nearly every aspect of manufacturing moving forwards, changing the way entire industries work. It will bring together a series of sensors and intelligent machines across the value chain – in virtually all industry sectors – creating a multitude of networked, connected devices. Combined with the consumer Internet of Things, we will be able to understand more about the world than ever before. From this understanding, should come control – and this control should enable us to improve the performance and personalisation of pretty much everything. These devices will enable the generation, capture, retrieval and analysis of valuable machine, operational, and environmental data from a variety of disparate sources, breaking down the silos that have traditionally separated IT data centre-based systems and factory-oriented operational technology systems. This will provide previously unobtainable levels of insight into the efficiency and productivity of the entire end-to-end process, allowing for more cost-effective decisions to be made. We will see sensors everywhere that enable the measurement of everything, ranging from the dryness and composition of the soil so farmers can remotely water crops or add fertiliser, to detecting corrosion inside a refinery pipe, to developing intelligent white goods in our houses that monitor their status, reorder inventory, highlight issues and order replacement parts and their instalment. In the factory they will provide plant managers with real-time production data to uncover additional capacity or predict demand for aftermarket parts based on wear and tear, allowing for previously unobtainable levels of insight into the efficiency and productivity of the entire end-to-end process. Seemingly identical processes can produce big variations in output and finding out why could save businesses billions. By breaking down the system, functional and cross-company silos that have traditionally prevented full operational transparency, the IIoT will lay the foundations needed to develop an entirely automated value chain, one where demand is immediately captured, processed, manufactured and satisfied without any human intervention.

It's already happening. The IIoT is already more advanced than the more consumer-focused Internet of Things, primarily due to the prevalence of 'things' – sensors – in the industrial world. There are already hundreds of millions of connected wired and wireless pressure, level, flow, temperature, humidity, vibration, acoustic, position, analytical, and other sensors already installed and operating in the industrial sector. Collecting all this data through the network to the cloud allows for the consolidation of this collection of small data sources into 'big-data' analysis, enabling companies to interrogate thousands or millions of data points to learn, understand or control the process more effectively. Companies like Rethink Robotics have already upgraded the software that drives their cobot platforms to enable the collection and display of real-time critical data and key metrics such as cycle time, part count, speed and force – providing detailed, up-to-date throughput and quality information that was previously only available after the event and at plant level. And definitely not available from any human worker.

The consumer space is also steaming ahead with IoT capabilities, led by players such as Amazon who are currently capturing demand using devices like the Echo and Dash buttons, then using machine learning to manage their fulfilment operations and warehouse robotics to fulfil orders in minutes. Soon these orders will be delivered via drones or road robots as well. This is a tipping point; a period of transition from one age to the next. Ken Olson, President, Chairman and Founder of Digital Equipment Corporation, stated during the 1977 World Future Society meeting in Boston that, *There is no reason anyone would want a computer in their home.* While Olson was widely mocked for this after it was printed in *Time* magazine, what was missing was the context. What Olson was in fact referring to, and often restated, was not the PC but the notion of the computer *controlling* the home, regulating the temperature, choosing entertainment, suggesting meals and pre-ordering food supplies. *That was what I meant,* stated Olson. The trouble is, his revised description of an automated home is also now a reality. The arrival of the Internet of Things means that home devices are being designed to do exactly the things Olson predicted people wouldn't want them to do. So once again, regardless of the context within which he intended it, Olson's quote can be mocked.

The age of industry is coming to an end, and the sixth wave is ushering in a new digital, robotic, automated age. We are moving from an industrial, transactional world where mass production and mass-marketing ruled; where products were designed, made, shipped and pushed to the consumer, to a consumer-focused digital world driven by insights. Where consumer data influences and determines the product, not the other way around. One capable of enabling manufacturers to completely reimagine how they design and make products, creating customisable items faster, cheaper and more efficiently than the industrial age could create mass-produced ones. It is bringing together a series of sensors and intelligent machines across the value chain – in virtually all industry sectors – to create a multitude of networked, connected devices that can monitor, collect, exchange, analyse and deliver valuable new insights that help drive smarter, faster business decisions. In the automated world of the sixth wave, the supply-chain winners are likely to be those with the best data and algorithms.

The upswing period is, as discussed, characterised by a clustering of new technologies that converge to create new technological paradigms. In the sixth wave's upswing, the mobile Internet; connected, collaborative robotics; autonomous vehicles; and various types of artificial intelligence are now conversing with each other to capture and fulfil demand, make and adjust plans, place orders, self-diagnose faults and make decisions. Robots will increasingly be embedded with systems such as Watson to enable them to speak, listen, understand and respond so they interact with people intuitively on a wide range of topics and even read their emotions. Back in 2008, Microsoft founder Bill Gates predicted in his article *A robot in every home*[207] that we were on the verge of a robotics revolution that would have a similar impact as the rise of the PC in the 1970s and 1980s. *When I talk to people involved in robotics and look at the trends that are now starting to converge, I can envision a future in which robotic devices will become a nearly ubiquitous part of our day-to-day lives.* It seemed fanciful, a piece of science fiction. But once again, the exponential nature of technological progression has made fiction real and turned what seemed like an absurd statement into a certainty. The base hardware technologies on which robots depend have been improving at an astonishing rate, enabling them to learn to develop an awareness of their surroundings, recognise objects based on multiple criteria, engage in conversation and manipulate objects such as opening doors. A decade after writing his article, Gates' prophecy is starting to materialise. Leaked information about Amazon's 'Vesta' domestic robot program highlighted their intention to realise his vision of placing 'a robot in every home'.

Digital Doppelgangers

The ability to overlay a digital representation of the physical world is also bring new possibilities to industry. Google has relaunched their augmented reality Google Glass product, only this time it's back in an environment where its use is deemed acceptable – the workplace. The Glass Enterprise Edition includes customised software and business solutions for Glass and has been trialled by more than fifty businesses in the US across multiple verticals. In healthcare its use has enabled doctors to have any information they need right in their line of sight, which has reduced paperwork by over 20 per cent and allowed them to spend 50 per cent more time with patients.[208] General Electric have deployed Google Glass in several segments including their aviation division, where the smart glasses provide warehouse workers with a visual display of order-picking instructions along with information on where items are located and where they need to be placed on a cart, freeing them from having to hold and search through picking lists. Likewise, aerospace company Boeing found that reading work instructions on Glass as opposed to fumbling with manuals reduced the time taken to assemble intricate wire harnesses by 25 per cent, with almost no errors.

Augmented reality is about to converge with other new technologies such as the IoT, machine learning and 3D printing. In the case of the latter, the unique design requirements of complex 3D structures can sometimes prove a struggle to manipulate using 2D software tools. The ability to craft, edit and visualise models with AR helps to remove physical barriers between the designer and the product, such as the keyboard, mouse, screen and interface, enabling them to interact directly with the product in a more intuitive and creative way. Digitisation and virtual reality are also allowing manufacturers to design production lines, factories and products in a virtual world. Companies like Rolls-Royce have stated that they have saved millions by using VR to spot potential issues, reduce bottlenecks on the factory floor, and solve challenges in facility creation and product movement. Digital and VR have also enabled companies to create a 'digital twin' of the real-world plant, allowing plant managers to model complicated processes or control production as if they are playing a game, like a real-world *FarmVille*. Plant engineers can now design and build robot-automation systems in the virtual world, rather than interrupting production on a factory floor. This enables them to visualise a production line and find bottlenecks that in the past would have meant expensive delays and re-engineering. They also enable fast, efficient product launches and changeovers. In this new world, the factory will be continuously monitoring itself, highlighting all the key factors of each machine – its throughput, speed, temperature, quality, energy consumption, wear and tear – and any elements that fall outside of normal deviations. This will appear in the virtual representation of the factory – the digital twin – and the offending machine and deviating element will be highlighted, along with all the necessary information about how to replace or repair the part. The plant manager can then organise a replacement part and an engineer to fix it at a time that minimises production downtime. It is probably not so ridiculous to imagine that the machine will also reorder its own parts.[69] This concept of creating digital twins; digital duplicates of physical items, will spread as the various nodes – from factories, to ships, planes, cars and even probably vending machines – all become connected. This will enable the creation of a digital twin of the entire end-to-end supply chain, one where AI systems will be able to scenario plan various risks to prevent them from appearing in the real world. This capability will allow businesses to design, develop and test their production facilities in the digital world before they break ground in the real world, allowing for experimentation and manipulation to determine the optimal location of items to maximise efficiency and flow. In addition to condition monitoring and fault diagnosis, components and systems are also acquiring self-awareness and self-prediction, providing management with more insight into the status of the factory.

We are still very much in the deceptive stage, where leading companies are working independently on solutions and everyone else is wondering what all the buzzwords are about. However, we are fast approaching the sixth wave's tipping point when the forces of creative destruction are unleashed, the S curve is ascended, and these technologies begin to disrupt industries. McKinsey estimates that IIoT could have a potential economic impact of up to $6.2 trillion by 2025 and could save $36 trillion in operating costs across multiple industries including manufacturing, healthcare and mining. GE's ex-CEO, Jeff Immelt, shares McKinsey's optimistic projections, calling the IIoT *beautiful, desirable, and investable*.[209] Immelt believes that the IIoT will produce a series of 1 per cent improvements across the various nodes in the supply chain – which looks incredibly modest at first glance. He is tapping into what the ex-British Cycling chief Dave Brailsford called 'the power of marginal gains' – the ability to create a series of

---

[69] It might be some time before we see robot engineers, but the power of exponential progression may prove me wrong.

small, incremental but aligned improvements, that when combined have an exponential effect on performance. Like Brailsford, Immelt sees the benefits of combining multiple marginal gains – only across GE's vast industrial landscape; something he believes will create massive economic benefit. GE estimates that a 1 per cent improvement in productivity across its global manufacturing base translates to $500 million in annual savings, and outside of GE, will add an extra $10–15 trillion to worldwide GDP over the next fifteen years. It's not just companies but also countries that see the opportunity this provides. In 2015, German Chancellor Angela Merkel told attendees at the World Economic Forum in Davos, Switzerland, *We must... deal quickly with the fusion of the online world and the world of industrial production. In Germany, we call it Industrie 4.0 because otherwise, those who are the leaders in the digital domain will take the lead in industrial production. We enter this race with great confidence. But it's a race we have not yet won.*[210]

Those that are embracing the potential discuss the challenges of making machines smart; of building warehouse robots that can 'see' things like cellophane overwrap on packed items. Robots are normally completely unable to see it, and need advanced machine vision, item recognition and perception to be able to process things like transparent wrapping. They need AI for better machine perception, control and planning so they can satisfy many conflicting objectives and enhanced haptic skills, so they can develop the ability to execute tasks such as taking a piece of paper off a table. Achieving this simple task requires a machine to understand depth and figure out how to manipulate the item; i.e. work out that the best way to pick up something so thin is to slide it off the table, rather than attempt to grab it from above. It's harder than you think. Moravec's paradox in action. One way this is likely to be overcome is via machine-to-machine learning; creating robots that teach other robots how to do things. This is not science fiction; MIT researchers have already developed a system called C-LEARN that teaches robots to acquire new skills through a combination of programming and learning from demonstration. Individually, each method has drawbacks, but combined, the researchers believe that it provides robots with the self-learning and 'watch and learn' capabilities that babies and small children have. Any acquired knowledge can then be passed on to another robot, regardless of whether that robot is of the same type and shape. In tests, Optimus, a two-armed robot designed for bomb disposal, taught Atlas, a four hundred-pound bipedal robot, how to open doors, transport objects and pull things from a container. That same robot is now able to run, traverse rocky terrains, climb stairs, jump over barriers and do backflips off raised platforms: this is the speed of change in the sixth wave. All this information can then be stored in what is named the 'Robo-cloud' and shared with all other connected machines, so they can effectively download the very latest version of the combined knowledge of all of the machines. As each robot learns something new, it shares it with all other robots connected to the cloud, in a similar way to how Tesla Model S drivers feed the collective knowledge of the autonomous driving systems. Machines are going to use the vast amount of data captured about us, the world and how we interact with it – from medical records to communication systems, travel data, and of course what we do at work – and share this instantly with other machines. What we are creating is a huge, ever-growing library of information that machines can use to learn how humans do things, how to do them better, and then share this information amongst themselves.[70]

The PAL Supply Chain: Personal, Automated, Local

We are now very much in the upswing phase of the new wave of creative destruction. A combination of intelligent machines, software, sensors and AI will combine to create the PAL supply chain: Personalised, Automated and Local:

- **Personalised** through mass customisation, on-demand manufacturing and bespoke goods and services. Facial recognition and ID tracking will be combined with devices that remember your personal preferences and utilise AI-based systems that predict your needs. Location-based data will provide opportunities for businesses to track customers, employees and assets, and provide personalised incentives and rewards. Three-dimensional printing advancements and increase in demand for digital products will also increase the number of 'prosumers' and micro-entrepreneurs; people who use technology to design and produce their own goods.

---

[70] It's almost as if the researchers have never seen any of the *Terminator* movies.

- **Automated** using autonomous vehicles and smart robotics that produce, pick and pack goods, while the blockchain tracks the physical and financial transactions, RPA handles the administration and chatbots resolve customer queries. All controlled by AI driven digital control towers that exploit predictive and prescriptive analytics to track supply, optimise inventory and meet demand, and provide early warnings of potential shortfalls or bottlenecks so that action can be taken to prevent potential problems becoming actual ones.

- **Localised** due the reshoring of production to where the consumers are located as the cost advantages of making, storing and shipping goods locally and in smaller quantities become pervasive. A micro-logistics network, utilising warehouse robotics and autonomous delivery methods – from drones to mothership vans that contain delivery robots – will arise to meet the same-day delivery demands.

The PAL supply chain will therefore be driven by intelligent AI systems that constantly receive signals from millions of smart, connected devices, and act independently on that information, refining and improving the process as they learn to ensure that everything is synchronised across the entire value chain. Companies that are already in control of their data, processes and systems – such as Merck KGaA, Alibaba, Ocado and Amazon – have already made a start by implementing digital 'control-towers' that combine analytics, automation, augmented decision support, modelling and other capabilities as a centralised function. Using this approach, focus shifts from the day-to-day management of people and products to an ever-increasing focus on understanding data and analysing exceptions, creating a seismic shift in the type of skills and number of people required to run these digital supply chains. Data scientists have become the new supply chain experts. Technologies like the blockchain will only help to accelerate this, providing a revolutionary integration of financial, social and environmental data, while also eliminating many of the current roles required to administer and manage the movement of products across the world.

These new disruptive technologies enable businesses to consider how they could reimagine their value propositions. Could they be used to digitise products? Provide them as a service rather than a product? Premiumise them to increase profits and reach new markets? Or personalise them?

Or a combination of all four? There are massive upsides to this from a sustainability perspective. The carbon emissions and waste from the current global supply chain are enormous, with products being moved half-way around the world, usually in quantities far greater than needed. Conversely, in the PAL supply chain, goods will become increasingly made on demand, made using additive not subtractive methods, transported using non-carbon burning means, and customised to the needs to the customer, all helping to reduce excess production, transportation, storage and waste. For example, if a product is digitised, the supply-chain costs and impact plummet, as digital products can be copied perfectly for free and made available instantly. One of the first industries to be disrupted by this new wave – publishing – has now begun to see the sustainability upside from this disruption. Publishers are now able to keep books in print for much longer by using digital print-on-demand technology removing the need to hold copies in storage 'just in case'. It has also enabled them to transfer electronic copies of the book to local printers, rather than globally transporting the finished book to distributors, saving millions in costs and greatly reducing the carbon footprint of book distribution. In another example, printer-ink manufacturers have found that offering an automatic ink-replenishment service enables them to drastically reduce packaging because the cartridge doesn't need to be presented in a way that is appealing to the consumer or designed to work in a retail environment.

As well as financial gains, the IIoT will also provide significant non-financial benefits to the global economy. The concept of a circular supply chain, one that includes considering the disposal and reuse of materials rather than just forgetting their production, could finally become a reality using these innovations. Techniques like additive manufacturing should help by greatly reducing the by-products and waste from the production process, and the increased use of robotics will mean that the cost of production will continue to fall. Companies like Adidas have even started to experiment with using recycled ocean plastic as a material with which to make trainers.[211] Machines will increasingly monitor and optimise their own performance, reducing quality defects and highlighting any excessive energy consumption, and the cost of this energy will also fall due to increased efficiencies from solar and other renewable sources. Transportation will be greatly optimised through increasingly autonomous, electric vehicles, directed by AI routing systems that direct them to move what is needed to where it is needed, rather than moving large quantities of components and goods across multiple nodes in the global supply chain. Finally, the rise of digitisation and servitisation business models will greatly increase the utilisation rate of logistics assets, while dramatically reducing the costs. GE estimates that within the next decade digital technologies will enable $8.6 trillion in productivity gains in the industrial world, with the Industrial Internet alone contributing the equivalent of a quarter of Europe's GDP by 2030.[212]

The foundations have been laid for the next wave of technological innovation, and progress will explode when these areas increasingly connect and work together. Machines will automatically make new replenishment decisions, RPA tools will process the transactions, chatbots will handle the customer queries and the blockchain will automatically provide financial and product ownership visibility to all participating parties. Once the new technological infrastructure is laid down, the world will be increasingly designed around this technology, rather than technology designed to fit in with the human world. To understand the full impact of the PAL supply chain and the triple whammy, we need to not look at each item as an independent innovation, but step back and review the impact on the entire end-to-end value chain, as follows:[71]

- A combination of advanced analytics, GPS, computer vision and machine-learning algorithms will identify when consumers approach physical stores and automatically offer personalised vouchers, offers and discounts to tempt you inside. When inside the store, items will be suggested based on previously bought goods. The use of store robots and cashier-free Amazon Go-style experiences will expand, eliminating checkouts and automatically charging accounts, simplifying and enhancing the shopping experience.
- At home, a combination of intelligent machines, prescriptive-ordering AI systems and connected smart home devices will automatically place orders for repeatable items, and consumers will increasingly order via voice.
- When shopping online, chatbots will increasingly be used to drive intelligent and meaningful engagement with customers, and the

---

[71] This example is very B2C-specific. Obviously heavy manufacturing, utilities, aerospace and defence supply chains will be impacted differently.

detailed build-up of data from your viewing and shopping history will enable websites to present an increasingly tailored list of recommended products. Algorithmic pricing engines will also make personalised, situational pricing offers to each customer.

- Demand signals from all these channels will be combined and processed by AI and machine learning-powered data analytical tools contained in end-to-end supply chain control towers, which constantly adjust replenishment schedules and plan in real time based on the latest consumer data.
- Retailers and manufacturers will then convert this demand automatically into replenishment requests, and RPA programs will convert them into manufacturing and/or procurement orders and electronically dispatch to the relevant production plant or supplier.
- Suppliers will process these orders automatically, generating replenishment demands that will be picked, packed and loaded by warehouse robots. The component supplier's system will automatically communicate delivery information to the manufacturer's system, and a delivery time and warehouse slot will be confirmed.
- Advancements such as 3D printing, autonomous vehicles and robotics will enable a redesign of the supply-chain network, resulting in lower operational costs and shorter lead times. Items will increasingly be produced locally and on demand, dramatically reducing the need for storage space.
- Automated trucks will become an integrated and connected part of the supply chain, delivering component parts to the supplier where robots will put them away until the automated planning system, responding to all the demand and supply signals, instructs the warehouse robots to move the parts to the assembly line.
- Machines that use M2M (machine-to-machine) capabilities will monitor their own performance, highlight issues, diagnose faults, improve energy efficiency and work together to build the required product. As parts wear out, the machines will highlight the degradation in performance and reorder their own replacements.
- Adaptable, intelligent collaborative manufacturing robots will assist in the assembly of the finished product, reducing the cost of production and enabling manufacturing to be relocated near the consumer base.

- The goods will then be transferred to the finished-goods warehouse, which are likely to be AI controlled and bot-operated micro-logistics fulfilment centres designed to support same-day delivery promises, running off their own renewable power sources.
- The goods will be automatically picked and packed by robots and placed onto another automated 'mothership' van that will deliver the finished products based on a pre-calculated optimal route, defined by a distribution planning system that retains constant GPS contact with the vehicles
- Drones and delivery robots will then complete the delivery, before returning to the 'mothership', ready to be reloaded with goods for the next customer delivery.
- All transactions up- and downstream of the supply chain will be updated using the blockchain, providing a consistent and instant ledger of goods movement and ownership, which is used to facilitate automatic financial transfers, probably using RPA systems. Information from the blockchain will be automatically fed into the supply chain control tower.
- Machine learning-based AI systems will be used to provide accurate replenishment forecasts and production and distribution plans, helping to continually establish the optimal cost-to-serve models, stocking profiles and manufacturing schedules. Companies will use AI and machine learning to sharpen analytic algorithms, detect more early-warning signals, anticipate trends and have accurate answers before competitors do.
- Any queries from customers or vendors will likely be handled by AI enabled chatbots, that analyse and highlight any issues to human co-workers.

This new supply chain will be powered by data collected by millions of connected things and constantly analysed by algorithms and AI applications to ensure that everything is synchronised across the entire value chain. Computers will be everywhere and nowhere; invisible parts of our lives capturing data about almost every aspect of it, and advanced AI-based systems will be used to process and make sense of it all. These new-world technologies will not be without risks: the increased integration of all these systems will require companies (and countries) to focus more attention on increasing the level of control, governance and cybersecurity surrounding their business.

Get Ready...

The sixth wave is now beginning its ascendancy. Marcus Weldon, President of Bell Labs and Nokia CTO, described it thus: *We're on the verge of a new industrial revolution. But it's not driven by consumers. It's going to be around industrial transformation that consumers benefit from.*[213] What's going to drive competitiveness over the next thirty years is not low-cost labour; it's going to be the utilisation of technology that allows your factories to transform from the dull, dirty and dangerous environment of the past to a high-tech, integrated and automated future where machines control the machines that make the machines that power our lives. The International Federation of Robotics predicts that by 2019, 1.4 million industrial robots will be installed in factories to increase productivity, 333,000 service robots will be sold to non-manufacturing and manufacturing sectors, and 42 million service robots for personal and domestic use will be employed in our private life.[214]

The new techno-economic foundations for the sixth wave are being laid down, with new power sources, new transport mechanisms and new communication methods all getting ready to be deployed. The introduction of 5G will allow for vast amounts of media and data to be beamed and downloaded, essential foundations to enable the Industry 4.0 and the Internet of Things to operate. Google and Facebook are also experimenting with innovative ways to provide Internet coverage to those places still unable to participate in the digital revolution; Google with their Project Loon high-altitude balloons, and Facebook with its giant, 113-feet wide solar-powered Aquila planes. Wrote Zuckerberg; *When Aquila is ready, it will be a fleet of solar-powered planes that will beam internet connectivity across the world. Today, more than half the world's population – 4 billion people – still can't access the internet. Aquila will help change that.*[215] The dramatic fall in price of solar, combined with the massive increase in productive capabilities, is getting set to power our cars, our homes and our production capabilities. Finally, advances in genetic engineering promise to help cure our ills and relieve the burden on the healthcare industry. The inventors working in the fields listed will see their individual innovations either take off and become industrialised or fall by the wayside. The pacesetters in the sixth wave are entrepreneurs such as Elon Musk, who is the living embodiment of one of Schumpeter's 'new men'.[72] From demonstrating how he plans to power Tesla's Gigafactory in Nevada with a seventy-megawatt solar farm, to powering houses with his Powerwall home batteries, developing completely revolutionary transportation systems such as his Hyperloop systems, building tunnels with 'the Boring Company', through to creating a network of Internet satellites with his SpaceX initiative, these constant entrepreneurial activities work to change the art of the possible and shift paradigms.

The sixth wave is set to last until just after the middle of the century, and its upswing will create almost as much disruption as the previous waves combined, but at a faster rate of change than we've ever seen. Klaus Schwab, Founder and Executive Chairman of the World Economic Forum, describes the creative destruction forces of the new wave as follows: *We stand on the brink of a technological revolution that will fundamentally alter the way we live, work, and relate to one another. In its scale, scope, and complexity, the transformation will be unlike anything humankind has experienced before. We do not yet know just how it will unfold, but one thing is clear: the response to it must be integrated and comprehensive, involving all stakeholders of the global polity, from the public and private sectors to academia and civil society.*[216] For this is not just the start of another wave. It also represents the end of industrial era and a transition to a new age. This transition will have enormous ramifications, ones that will transform the business world, our scientific and technological capabilities, our economic and societal models, and even the very foundations of what it is to be human. And we are not prepared.

---

[72] I'm using 'new men' here to align with Schumpeter's statement, and am aware that the innovator is just as likely to be female in today's world.

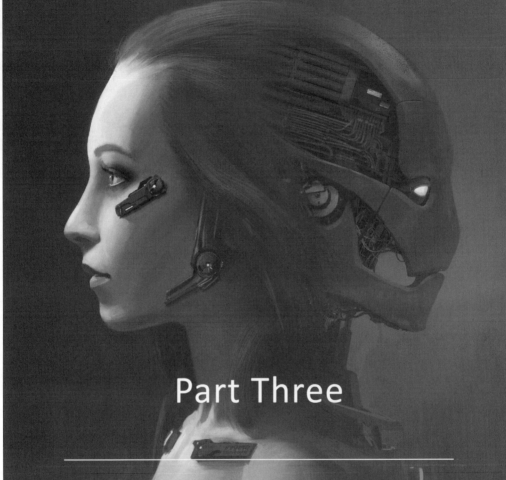

Part Three

EVOLUTION OR ENDGAME?

12

NEW WAVE, NEW PARADIGMS

Major advances occur in a series of large steps, from one form of organization to another. In our psychosocial evolution, I believe we are now in a position to make a new major advance.

Sir Julian Huxley (1968)

In 1964, the recently appointed US President Lyndon B. Johnson sanctioned a 'Blue Ribbon National Commission on Technology, Automation, and Economic Progress' with the task *to identify and assess the past effects and the current and prospective role and pace of technological change; to identify and describe the impact of technological and economic change on production and employment, including new job requirements and the major types of worker displacement, both technologically and economic, which are likely to occur during the next 10 years.* The fourth wave had contained a raft of new computer-based technologies initially conceived during wartime, but whose non-military potential was now becoming clear. The sanctioning of the National Commission arose from concern about the impact that these new disruptive technologies would have when they found their way into industrial use, and whether society would be able to adapt to the onslaught about to hit it. As we now know, it could, and it did, and despite a worrisome transition period between the fourth and fifth waves, it led to greater prosperity and continued mankind's constant upward trajectory.

One of the reasons why we were able to adapt was that while objectives such as the space race created urgency for the initial development of these technologies, the cultural lag meant that it wasn't until the fifth wave's upswing that industrial investment got involved, and it wasn't until the late 1980s before they started to have a major impact on business and the home. Even then their impact on productivity and performance was questioned, such as by Robert Solow who, in 1987, wrote that he could see *the computer age everywhere but in the productivity statistics.*[217] It is therefore understandable for people to complacently believe that the inventions and innovations of the sixth wave will follow a similar path of overinflated expectations and underachieved potential, and that decades will pass before these innovations appear in the public sphere. But as we have seen, complacency can be a killer of jobs, businesses and nations.

Once again, we find ourselves at a similar stage; another transition point between waves. The military word 'VUCA' (volatile, uncertain, complex and ambiguous) is being touted everywhere to describe the current business environment. Business and supply-chain leaders are constantly being told by consultants that they 'need to adapt to a VUCA existence', and that 'we are living in a VUCA world'. All very scary – but at the same time, as far as advice goes, all very useless. But I guess fear sells. Without an understanding of Kondratiev waves, the stages involved, the clustering and diffusion of disruptive innovations and the role of investment, all VUCA does is give a name to the chaos. Standing on stage and stating that we are living in a VUCA world may make many keynote speakers feel bright, but unfortunately simply naming a symptom doesn't automatically provide a cause or a cure for it. It may provide a 'what', but it doesn't provide a 'why', let alone a 'how'. The reason is because they don't know why, and worse, haven't cared to find out because they believe the situation to be unique. Just because this is the first time they have experienced a transitionary period, they behave as if it is the first time there has been one. Once again, you can't control what you don't understand.

The 'why' behind the chaos is, as *you* now know, because we are moving out of a decade long Kondratiev winter and into a new spring period, the rising phase of the sixth wave. The old wave has started to collapse, and the technologies developed during the cold winter of depression are starting to appear out in the open, making their way into news feeds and social media posts. Their creators are looking for – and finding – investment, accelerating their development. This is a time of great leaps forward in both our scientific and technological understanding and capabilities, one where more progress is made in fifteen months than in the preceding fifteen years. The outputs from these endeavours start to converge and feed into each other, creating new realities – new paradigms – previously thought of as mere science fiction. Concern is rising about the impact these new technologies will have on the economy, especially the world of work. Beth Comstock, Vice Chair of General Electric (GE), defines the challenge this transition stage presents as follows: *Get used to living in the in-between. The old is not going away, and the new has not yet emerged. It's uncomfortable and it's chaotic. But it's happening in pretty much every industry right now.* These are confusing times, but also restless and dangerous times, as both the old physical industrial world of the fifth wave and the fresh shoots of the new automated one coexist, one trying to protect its market and the other trying to disrupt it. New innovations excite the capitalists and grab both the investment and the headlines, creating fear in those whose jobs, skills and income are based around the old ways of doing things: areas about to be disrupted and destroyed.

As mentioned in Part One, this period is characterised by a significant number of social upheavals, disruptions and radical changes to society caused by the shifting power structures. Kondratiev wrote that: *It is during the period of the rise of long waves (during the period of high tension in the expansion of economic forces) that, as a rule, the most disastrous and extensive wars and revolutions occur.* Previous transition points have seen violent revolutions, civil wars, ideological wargames and even global conflicts. The previous wave's upswing saw a dramatic rise in domestic and international terrorism, ranging from plane hijackings to bombings, and conflicts such as Vietnam. It is a time of concern, and this transition point is no different, only due to the global nature of markets the disruption has been global also. The last five years has seen the West rocked by terrorist attacks, the Middle East by war, regime change and population unrest, and mass migration into Europe that has created major cultural and socio-economic problems. Tensions between the West and Russia are increasing, and North Korea and the US have compared nuclear buttons. We have seen anti-establishment outcomes in the EU referendum in the UK (Brexit), the US elections (Trump), and in Italy. Crimea voted to rejoin Russia and being swiftly annexed against Ukrainian wishes, and Catalonia declared independence in Spain. Outrage then arose from those that opposed the results, culminating with conflict in Ukraine, the Spanish government invoking Article 155 and taking control of Catalonia, groups demanding California secede from the union, and protestors in London demanding that the capital break away from the rest of the UK. The transition period also once again led to a gap between the elites – the oligarchs, technocrats and capital asset owners – and the rest, and during this period there have been a series of anti-capitalist protests and a rise in calls for a more socialist-based economy. This has led to protestors marching on the streets of the UK and US proudly waving communist flags, something unthinkable – especially in the US – only a few years ago. The US has divided into factions that have stopped debating and simply throw insults at each other. Normal discourse has increasingly broken down, and the willingness to engage in reasoned, intelligent debate is being lost in preference of personal spats on Twitter. Social media has become an ideological battleground, where people have formed tribes and created their own echo chambers, and everyone dismisses the other side's attacks as fake news. These are disturbing times, but while all this chaos might seem unprecedented, it is important to place it in the historical context. However, it is best not to be complacent. It's easy to be dismissive of events like masked Antifa protestors throwing punches at free-speech campaigners, calling them Nazis and setting fire to Starbucks. While this is not immediately going to result in tanks rolling over European fields or heads rolling off guillotines, it is important to remember that those events also started out as protests in the streets. We don't want a recreation of the Weimar Republic.

Sixth Wave Rising

We have now left behind the financially focused downswing and are beginning to bask in the warming rays of a new, creative spring period. During the upswing, speculative bubbles usually emerge, and as if by magic, cryptocurrencies like Bitcoin have appeared to become the sixth-wave mania. The start of the upswing is a deceptive period, where inventions are conceived and experimented with, revitalised by the flood of new investment that is now focused behind the real economy of technology and industry. All of the technologies described in Part Two are being worked on at the same time, waiting to emerge into the daylight, creating new industries and business models and disrupting existing ones. The new innovators do not just reside in California but in China, Vietnam, Australia, Europe, and in fact anywhere that smart people and smart money are converging. And in this new digital age, the amount of money needed to develop impactful innovations is less than ever before. One mistake that many people make when imagining the future is believing that the old world stops when the new one starts; the reality is much messier in that they coexist, sometimes for decades, even generations. Each new wave creates disruptive innovations that cluster and form new methods of power, transport and communication, but these are not created magically out of thin air. Their existence relies on the technological inheritance passed down from previous generations, which do not just disappear. Instead, while they may change in form and function, they can continue to hold prominent market positions for years while the new innovations fight to cross the chasm into the mass market.

It is also important to remember that while technology is the outcome, it is society, economics and science that are the enablers. As Sir Francis Bacon once declared, *once the right path is followed, discoveries in limitless number will arise from the growing stock of knowledge.* Without the series of events ranging from the Magna Carta to the Glorious Revolution, Britain would not have developed a society that provided the necessary freedoms and access to information needed to industrialise. We would still have undoubtedly reached a point whereby industrialisation took off – but probably not in England, and almost definitely not then. But how much has our world view changed in the period between the development of the steam engine and the search engine? For the vast majority of the global population, not much. One key difference is in our relationship with religion. The freedom of personal choice in a secular society free from religious doctrines has seen church attendance plummet. The freedom to develop an individual relationship with God has led to people choosing whether they want to continue that relationship; becoming atheists without being damned by society for doing so. But it's important to remember that for the vast majority of the world religion is still a hugely influential part of their lives.

In the place of Christianity, the Western nations have embraced a new, more materialistic religion; technology. The so-called 'Generation X' will be the last to remember what life was like 'BtI' – Before the Internet. The subsequent generations – Millennials and Gen Z , are digital natives, growing up in two separate societies – one physical, and the other digital. Children are becoming familiar with technology from an increasingly early age, expecting everything to be on demand and touchscreen, with teachers reporting that children are picking up books in libraries and trying to swipe them. They have become known as Generation Why for their willingness to challenge and question everything, and Generation Moi for their perceived entitlement. These digital natives have grown in a different reality to every previous generation. Rather than relying on others to provide them with news and information, they now freely obtain information from a multitude of different sources, choosing both the time and medium. This has created a Schumpeterian power struggle between the 'old' and 'new' media, and worryingly, various clampdowns by governments to stop this new media from being used to broadcast dissenting voices. On the positive side, education and information are now virtually free and available instantly to those with access to the Internet, and not, as in the past, solely the preserve of the rich. This has led to an dramatic increase in information access, creation and distribution, which has in turn led not just to a slight increase in knowledge, but an exponential one – but only for those with the right mindset. The information is out there; people can now decide to be passive consumers or proactive investigators, and as we will discuss later, this choice will prove to be important.

From a business perspective, we are also now in a world where the conventional wisdom around how value is generated has been disrupted. Author Tom Goodwin[218] highlights that the world's largest taxi company (Uber) owns no vehicles, the world's most popular media owner (Facebook) owns no content, the world's most valuable retailer (Alibaba) owns no inventory, and the world's largest accommodation provider (Airbnb) owns no real estate. We could also add that the largest communication companies (Skype and WhatsApp) own no infrastructure and the world's largest movie house (Netflix) owns no cinemas. Wikipedia is the best encyclopaedia that ever existed, and is maintained by an army of anonymous, unpaid volunteers who give away their services and the resultant knowledge for free in real time, to anybody who has access to a computer or smartphone. As

Goodwin observed, *something interesting is happening*. Digital companies are making fortunes in new ways. They've unlocked a new form of capital.

The Fifth Capital: Data

Since the first wave rose back in the 18th century, the West has promoted an economic system that requires four types of capital to function properly:[73]

- Human capital, in the form of labour and intelligence, culture and organisation.
- Financial capital, consisting of cash, investments and monetary instruments.
- Manufactured capital, including infrastructure, machines, tools and factories.
- Natural capital, made up of resources, living systems and ecosystem services.

Until the industrial revolution wealth was primarily centred around natural capital – land. Then the industrial system changed this, by taking natural capital such as ores, minerals and fossil fuels and combining with human, financial and manufactured capital to produce the goods that form the integral part of our daily lives. Those who could either extract and supply the natural resources, provide the financial investment, own the means of production or supply labour and skills all prospered. Competitive advantage was based around your ability to manage one of these types more efficiently and effectively than others. Now the sixth wave has seen a fifth type of capital emerge – data. Data about every aspect of the other four types of capital. The lords of the digital age are not those who own land, but those who have access to the source of data. And the best way to gain exclusive access is through the development and ownership of a platform. But what is a platform? There are four types. The primary version connects demand and supply, such as Amazon, Alibaba, Uber, Airbnb, eBay, etc. The second connects people to people, such as Facebook, Twitter, LinkedIn,

---

[73] 'Four types of capital' model extracted from *Natural Capitalism: Creating the Next Industrial Revolution* by Paul Hawken and Amory and Hunter Lovins, Back Bay Books, 2000.

etc. The third connects content to consumers, such as YouTube, Instagram, etc. Finally, the fourth connects customers to capabilities, such as Skype, WhatsApp, AWS and Dropbox, etc. A platform's power comes from the network effect; the more people who use the platform, the more it attracts other advertisers and sellers, creating both a positive feedback loop and a 'winner takes all' outcome. The company that owns the primary platform controls the marketplace and the customer interface. Most importantly, a digital platform captures data – lots and lots of data – on the consumers and their preferences. Platforms therefore represent a digital land-grab, creating ways to control access to marketplaces, claim consumers' attention and capture their data. As a result, platforms have now become more valuable than products, and data more valuable than oil. Owning the customer interface provides an enormous competitive advantage, putting competitors in awkward positions – for example, Ocado cannot develop a skill for the Amazon Echo as the data Echo captures is not owned by Amazon Web Services (AWS) but by Amazon Retail, i.e. Ocado's primary competitor.

The smartphone has unleashed the potential of platforms. The mobile industry started deceptively as a replacement for connected phones, with a projected market of around 900,000 devices by 2000, then exploded into disruption eight years later when the technology converged with the Internet and the smartphone was born. This transformed the phone into the first primary innovation of the sixth wave: a multimedia device that contained a whole host of new consumer and business use cases, the network effect of which unleashed the potential of the mobile-phone market and unlocked billions of dollars of new value. There are now more phones than people in the world, enabling companies, especially those selling digital products such as apps, to reach billions of prospective customers, creating a truly global marketplace estimated to reach $6.3 trillion by 2021.[219]

The base technology enabling these digital platforms – the Internet – has both opened the market and democratised innovation, enabling people worldwide to use their entrepreneurial capabilities to break free of any preconceived geographic, educational or social restrictions. As an example, in 2014, Dong Nguyen, a Vietnamese game artist from a silk-weaving village called Van Phúc near Hanoi, made $50,000 a day from downloads of his addictive app game *Flappy Bird* on the Apple App Store before he took the game down. A game that only took him three days to make. In the fifth wave, the idea that someone from a Vietnamese village could transform three days labour into $50K per day would seem unbelievable. To quote the Internet entrepreneur and investor Alexis Ohanian, *To join in the industrial revolution, you needed to open a factory; in the Internet revolution, you need to open a laptop.*

Software is now eating the world. The digital age is creating a completely different value proposition for companies. The interface is now as important as the product. New-wave digital companies like Uber are now worth more than physical, industrial companies like GM. Think about that. A company that owns an app that allows you to hail a car is worth more than a company that makes the cars. When, as Uber is planning, the car is autonomous and the driver no longer human, this gap will increase even further. The app that allows access will be worth much more than the asset. There are real concerns that the masters of the sixth wave, technology giants that have been given the acronym FAANG – Facebook, Amazon, Apple, Netflix and Google – hold far too much sway over our personal lives, create far too much money, pay far too little tax and employ far too few people. Most are creating virtual monopolies. Google has the monopoly on our need for information, Amazon on our need for products, Facebook on our need to share and gain approval from friends and associates, Netflix on our need to be entertained, and the social media platform Twitter on our need to share and spread gossip. A handful of technology companies now have access to information about nearly every aspect of our modern-day lives and are using that data to make themselves extremely rich. Data has now become the fifth form of capital, and it may become the most valuable of all.

Haven't We Been Here Before?

So, is this any different from the previous waves? Or have we simply gotten carried away because this is the first time most people have personally experienced this transitionary period? If so, it's a common mistake: as the great Austrian economist Friedrich Hayek observed at the start of *The Road to Serfdom* during the disruptive years of the 1940s, *While history runs its course, it is not history to us.* The technologies of the current wave may be new, but the trend is not. Yet there are several key factors that indicate that the impact of this new wave is going to be substantial. The forces that are causing the acceleration of wave behaviour, specifically the impact, rate of

271

diffusion and scope of innovations, are all combining, leading to the sixth wave developing more disruptive capability than many realise. In fact, it might have the disruptive power of all of the previous waves combined, and as such, be defined as a mega-wave: a new age. Globalisation has increased the scope and reach of the disruption, and the digital nature of products means that they can be shared and copied at speed, replicated for free, and do not degrade each time they are copied. This all contributes to a greatly increased rate of diffusion and reduced time to 'cross the chasm' to the mass market. For example, whereas it took seventy-five years for the telephone to reach 50 million users, it only took nineteen days for *Pokémon Go* to do so. Tools such as social media enable the rapid spread of information about new products and ideas, helping to create investment interest and raise funds. Globalisation has allowed companies to access a talent and consumer base of billions, not millions, the business implications of which are significant. Take Uber as an example. It still hasn't figured out how to make a profit, but it has managed to collect customers in eighty-four countries and 760 cities in less than a decade.[220] Whereas the previous revolutions have been powered by the thoughts and ideas of the few, the next will be powered by the contributions of the many.

The rate of technological change throughout the autumn and winter periods of the Kondratiev cycle is always significantly slower than the accelerating dizziness of the spring upswing; something that is catching many by surprise. Countries that expect to have decades to adapt to new technological realities and changing market forces will find themselves surprised when the impact is felt in months. Their societies will struggle to adjust to the rate of change, and the impact of the cultural lag will be larger than before as more people are caught up in its wake. People assume the future to be a linear projection from the past, assuming, like the 'lump of labour' fallacy, that there is only a certain amount of intellectual capacity in the world. But as the Google Brain project proved by its ability to surpass over eleven years of improvements into Google Translate in one night, human brainpower is overrated. The sheer speed of innovation in the sixth wave's upswing has caught out even the smartest of us, such as Levy and Murnane's prediction about computers not being able to handle the task of driving. They assumed that computers had to be programmed by humans, so the idea of a human coding every possible *if > then > else* scenario that could arise from driving anywhere to anywhere seemed improbable if not impossible. What they failed to foresee was intelligent machines learning on their own. They are not alone in getting it wrong. Moore's Law's incessant progress has created an Internet that is a goldmine of comments that were initially delivered with confidence and certainty, but now, given the benefit of time and hindsight, seem absurd.[74] It is therefore a brave person who attempts to make predictions of the future with any degree of certainty, for as the saying goes, predictions are hard – especially about the future. It doesn't stop people trying.

Better than Humans

AI will continue to be used to make dumb machines smart, and smart machines smarter. The primary driver for robotics installation to date has been the automation of the supply chain; in doing the same things as always but without using a human to do them. This could lead one to assume that the future for robots lies in developing more efficient ways of making and moving stuff, when in fact it will be somewhat more widespread and disruptive than that. There is a whole industry developing digital start-ups whose sole goal is the disruption of areas that rely on human skills and labour. As development in machine learning continues, we will increasingly find new ways to not only replicate human tasks with identical machine versions, but also use machine learning to reimagine the task or even eliminate it. Anything that can be automated, will be automated. Blockchain and RPA serve as a good example of this – currently there is an army of people who raise purchase orders, process documents, create shipping advice notifications, process goods receipts, book stock into warehouses, record transfer of ownership, check the provenance of goods, handle financial invoicing, etc. While the RPA element involves a straight automation of some of these tasks – processing orders and raising invoices, for example – blockchain reimagines how the end-to-end supply chain could work, eliminating the administrative tasks involved in processing the transfer of

---

[74] Three of the most common are the Western Union internal memo from 1876 that stated, *This 'telephone' has too many shortcomings to be seriously considered as a means of communication. The device is inherently of no value to us,* H. M. Warner of Warner Brothers' declaration in 1927: *Who the hell wants to hear actors talk?,* and Sir Erasmus Wilson's statement that *When the Paris Exhibition [of 1878] closes, electric light will close with it and no more will be heard of it.*

ownership and all related financial transactions. Tools like machine learning are still very much in the deceptive stage, but their outputs will increasingly appear in the public sphere, becoming the invisible engine behind this technological revolution. Voice assistants like Siri, Google Assistant and Alexa are constantly learning and improving, entertainment sites like Netflix provide ever more personalised recommendations, and websites can predict what you are likely to buy based on your viewing history.

A virtuous cycle is developing where even small improvements in performance have significant economic value, prompting greater excitement and greater investment from venture capitalists intent on having a piece of this pie. As a result, the number of players working on AI research is dramatically increasing, not just in the hallowed, beanbag-filled imaginaria of Silicon Valley, but in start-ups, garages and bedrooms across the world. We are facing an intelligence and innovation explosion, one that will have an increasing impact on society. By the end of the decade many of these technologies will have crossed the chasm and become disruptive, creating a world in which people, insights, and money interact quickly, easily and cheaply, affecting nearly every industry at every level. This will have both positive and negatives, for each new wave brings a period of technological Darwinism, as creation never travels alone; its companion, destruction, always hitches a ride.

What Happened to the Jobpocalypse?

One of the questions I am often asked is if automation is becoming so prevalent, then why is employment so high? The answer to this is simple. We are at the transition point. This means that both the old wave industrial jobs and new wave digital ones both co-exist right now. While a whole host of new, exciting, creative jobs for the young and talented — such as machine-learning specialists, data scientists, AI programmers, robotics engineers and VR designers — are being created, the more traditional manufacturing and supply-chain jobs — such as warehouse workers, truck drivers and production-line operatives — are experiencing a boom due to e-commerce. A candle burns brightest when it's about to go out, and right now we have peak employment in certain industries that may not have a long-term future. As the wave rises the creative side moves from deceptive to disruptive, the destructive forces will start to materialise.

Throughout the last century the car industry created millions of jobs in the manufacture, distribution, sale and servicing of cars, and millions more that involve driving goods or people around. The rise of autonomous electric cars will eradicate most of those jobs. The dramatically reduced cost of using taxis, due to automation removing the need to pay for 'the dude driving the car', will cause people to re-evaluate whether or not they actually need to own a vehicle, or whether being driven around in modern autonomous vehicles will be significantly cheaper and just as convenient. Autonomous vehicles are likely to transform our relationship with cars from one of ownership to access, meaning that people simply summon them when needed. This should eliminate a lot of parking issues, freeing land and creating a resurgence in the high street and boutique shopping, and a decline in out-of-town hypermarkets as commodity items can simply be bought online and delivered without charge. Early predictions indicate that this shift in relationship will dramatically both improve the mobility of people, while also cause between a 40 to 95 per cent reduction in car sales. That last prediction comes from the Delphi Group, who estimate that by 2050, the utilisation rate of vehicles will rise from its current level of 5 per cent, to 95 per cent, allowing us to potentially transport twenty times more people in a much lower volume of cars.[221] This will also have a significant disruptive impact in a number of areas. Manufacturing will be heavily automated, and as electric engines require fewer moving parts, there will be a reduction in demand for aftermarket spares, servicing and maintenance. Many cities rely on parking revenue, congestion charges and fines to balance their budgets – all things that driverless, electric cars will not cause. Sales will also be mainly bulk purchases to fleet owners rather than individual sales to end consumers, reducing the need for showrooms and sales people. Then there's the small matter of the millions of driving-related jobs – such as truck and taxi drivers – that will no longer be required.

Each new wave brings new technologies that make the existing paradigms obsolete. One of the foremost economic paradigm shifts that needs to take place is the widespread belief that the job creators and innovators are the large, established corporations. They are not. In the up-swinging spring period it is new companies, fronted by entrepreneurs exploiting new innovations and the opportunities they create that generate jobs. It is also the new companies that need investment because they spend it on innovation, growth and employment, not squirrelling it away or paying dividends. It is these new, innovative companies that are the driving force in the economic model, and it should be the prime objective of government to create an environment that enables them to develop and grow. However, something new is happening. The new digital businesses may create value, but jobs? Not so much. This time the digital sixth-wave industries are not labour intensive enough to compensate for the losses of the fifth-wave jobs. For example, instead of using travel agents people are now booking holidays and travel themselves online, reducing the tens of thousands of travel agents that existed down to a few hundred, and instead creating jobs for a small number of website administrators and researchers. Instead of employing secretaries and personal assistants, white-collar workers are typing everything themselves on computers, and we all sat back while video stores, record shops, photo processors and other retail shops went out of business due to digitisation and the Internet. To highlight the difference between the job-creating capabilities of fifth- and sixth-wave companies, at its peak Kodak employed 143,500 people, whereas its digital replacement, Instagram, had just 13 employees when they were sold to Facebook in 2012. Just consider the number of people who used to work in the film-processing industry that no longer have that job, because we capture and share our memories digitally now. We take and share more pictures than ever – by a factor of millions – but the number of people involved in the process has plummeted. When Facebook acquired WhatsApp for $19 billion in 2014, it had 450 million users, yet only fifty-five employees. It now has 1.2 billion users, but I doubt the number of employees supporting WhatsApp is in triple figures yet. Compare that to the early 1960s, when leading companies of the day employed huge numbers of people. For example, GM employed 605,000 people, AT&T 564,000 and Exxon 105,000. The value per employee difference between the digital and industrial models is astonishing. Walmart, America's biggest employer with 2.22 million employees, generates annual revenues of approximately $117,000 per employee, whereas Uber's 1,500 employees and $50 billion valuation mean they generate $33 million each. WhatsApp beat even that, with its 2014 $19 billion sale resulting in an employee return of $345 million each.

Stormy Waters Ahead

Riding this new wave is not going to be easy, for this period is, as Kondratiev described, one of great change and upheaval. Schumpeter's 'new men'[75] are disrupting the world of the industrial old men; old power structures and ways of working are losing out to the new. The new, privately owned start-up companies – those with the right mindset – will embrace these opportunities, and if the financial institutions can see beyond the next quarter, they would do well to consider making money from these new technological paradigms and not from old businesses, or worse, rent-seeking. It is also important that the focus changes from cost-cutting and efficiencies to innovation and longer-term investment. Companies that don't adapt in time run the danger of becoming the next Kodak, for by the time you realise your business model is out of date, it's too late. Disruption is upon us, and there's no escaping it. Because of globalisation we are recruiting more and more human brains into the task of innovation, establishing new scientific, academic and industrial complexes in places they didn't exist before. This ever-increasing pool of intellect, inspiration and entrepreneurial effort has resulted in an ever-greater amount of innovation, as well as a larger quantity of consumers to procure it. It is creating a mega wave of creative destruction the true force of which we are yet to experience.

To manage the impact, business, technological, economic and social recalibrations need to take place to ensure things don't tip out of balance and into chaos. These recalibrations can take many forms. Some are an intrinsic part of the wave's nature, a feedback mechanism that highlights to the market that it needs to reset itself by reallocating resources away from old technologies and the companies wedded to them, and towards the creation of new innovations and new entrepreneurs. Others are the necessary reactions to the forces of creative destruction, the economic and social adjustments needed to ensure that the bounty from the new wave lifts all ships and not just the luxury yachts. These recalibrations will not be unsubstantial, for the old economic model of continued growth and its measure of GDP is under attack from multiple sources. Trickle-down economics isn't trickling any more, and society is rising up against

---

[75] And women. One of the major disruptive forces of the fifth wave has been the sheer number of female entrepreneurs and innovators.

the current levels of inequality. Capitalism is falling out of favour, especially amongst the young who have not seen nor felt the effects of its collectivist alternatives themselves. The foundations upon which our liberal society stands are now weaker than they have been in generations, secularism leading to a complete rejection of faith, and with it support for culture and country, undermined by the people who depend upon its freedoms to make their case. Capitalism attracts the majority of the people's ire, on one side because of the wealth inequality that is being witnessed, and on the other, the twin neo-liberal drivers of globalisation and mass migration, which have weakened or destroyed the social bonds that kept communities together. This has led to a swelling of support for the populist parties on both the far left and far right.

As with the first industrial revolution, this period will be remembered for the convergence of many disruptive technologies, a convergence that will create major economic, social and political upheaval. It will be looked upon by future generations as a time of great progress, but like the first industrial revolution it will also be remembered for having significant winners and losers, and this disparity will be a major point of contention and potentially conflict. Since the industrial revolution the world has experienced significant and regular changes to our paradigms and major advancements in technology and scientific understanding, but the underlying economic and societal model, while recalibrated to adjust to new-wave realities, has foundationally remained the same. Our scientific knowledge is now doubling in a time frame measured in months, not decades, but our social, political and economic systems are still ultimately based on those founded in the 19th century.

Infinite Thinking in a Finite World

At the start of the industrial revolution the world was deemed a larder full to the brim of wonderful resources to be consumed. Fossil fuels such as coal, oil and gas were perceived to be limitless, becoming the dominant form of energy used by societies that viewed nature as a resource to be utilised for mankind's progress. This world view is currently under threat. We have begun to appreciate just how damaging our belief in an unlimited-growth system is, and have had to swallow the bitter pill of the fact that this is only feasible in a world unconstrained by any biophysical limits, which is not the world we live in. Since the late 20th century there has been an ever-increasing awareness that the assumptions underlying the modern world are flawed. We have had to appreciate that the actions of the few generally have consequences for the many; most of them unpleasant. Because fossil fuels are energy-dense and bountiful, we embraced them as the dominant form of energy used by our society, even though we knew they are polluting and non-renewable. They provided the energy necessary for rapid economic and population growth, and we have now reached the point where the world we live in is not empty; it is full. We inherited a 3.8 billion-year store of natural capital, but at present rates of use and degradation, there will be little left by the end of the next century. Our footprint has grown so large that, in many cases, limits on the availability of natural resources now constrain real progress more than limits on capital infrastructure. We have continually developed technologies that are designed to maximise the throughput of energy and resources while minimising monetary and labour costs, without any real consideration of the implications this may have for future generations. We are also irrational – for example, we are afraid of nuclear power, which has been responsible for around 4,000 deaths in total, nearly all as a result of Chernobyl; but are not afraid of coal, which is responsible for shortening the lives of approximately a million people every year, and which could be damaging our planet for decades to come. The spectre of climate change dominates headlines and creates global concerns, with an increasing series of adverse weather conditions causing devastation across the world.

The world population continues to rise, with forecasts predicting that it will reach 9 billion by 2050, raising again talk of a Malthusian Catastrophe if we cannot find a way to affordably feed everyone. Our perspective of continual growth through the extraction and utilisation of natural resources needs to be reconsidered, for the consequences are beginning to be understood. This knowledge is now changing the perspective of governments worldwide, for we cannot afford to let the newly industrialised nations pollute the atmosphere in the same way that the Western economies did; we must learn the lessons of the past and apply these now in the countries currently industrialising, such as China and India. As the world continues to reach the 'global overshoot day' (the date when the world has consumed the Earth's natural resources for the year) earlier and earlier, the shareholder value maximisation model has to make way for a more sustainable approach.

We are now counting on our ability to innovate our way out of trouble, to create new technological breakthroughs that allow for increased production at a lower ecological footprint to provide them with the standards of living of industrialised countries. Without these breakthroughs, it simply can't be done, as the resources of four more Planet Earths would be needed for everyone on the planet to have a modern, American consumer lifestyle. Despite knowing this, nearly every country is currently urging people to live like Americans; selling the world an impossible dream. Technology needs to provide the answer, for if it doesn't, then society as we know it will be unable to cope and fall apart.

Yet we remain optimistic, for innovation has already enabled us to overcome resource constraints that held back previous generations. Fertilisers, pesticides and mechanised agriculture allowed the population to make a mockery of Malthus' predictions and, as a result, the world has changed dramatically over the past two centuries. Life expectancy continues to rise across the world, especially in the emerging nations. Approximately three months is being added to average life expectancy every year, and experts estimate there could be a million centenarians across the world by 2030. While this is good news for those not dying, it creates a scenario that we have not seen before – there will be more old and retired people than young workers to support them, tipping the dependency balance. The fact that more of us are living longer than ever is going to put enormous pressure on our social services, especially as we are seeing a dramatic rise in age-related diseases such as diabetes and dementia. There is a very real chance that the pension funds that we thought were going to be there to support us during these extra years will not be available. The population in the West is growing older, poorer and lonelier, the latter due to smaller families and the increasing rise in offspring migrating away from where their parents live. In 2017, the birth rate in the US reached a record low for the second year running. China and Japan are going to be hit worst. Japan, the country with the longest life expectancy, has seen the number of seniors living alone grow sixfold since 1980, reaching over 6 million, while the replacement generation is shrinking, with 2018 seeing a fall in the number of Japanese children under 14 for the 37th consecutive year. China is likely to suffer a similar problem. Its rise from a poor, subsistence-based economy with a one-child policy specifically designed to prevent a Malthusian food crisis, to an industrial giant with a booming market economy, has meant that it is now ageing more rapidly than almost any country in recent history. The UN predicts that China's dependency ratio for retirees (those aged sixty-five or older divided by total working population), which was only 14 per cent in 2015, will rise to around 44 per cent by 2050.[222] This will force government policymakers to re-evaluate spending plans and economic stimulus programmes to meet their stated goal of providing pension coverage for everyone, a worrying development for a nation whose economic growth is underpinned by government credit.

Despite more people than ever rising out of poverty, there is also the growing global challenge of wealth inequality, caused by automation generating an acceleration away from a labour-based economy to a capital-based one. Capitalism has once again been bent out of shape, this time into technology-based corporatism, with global tech companies exploiting national tax rules to their benefit. At the same time, we see headlines stating that because of capitalism three times more people now die of obesity than hunger, life expectancy continues to rise, and child mortality continues to plummet. Transition periods are not just disruptive times; they are confusing ones also. Disruptive and confusing for individuals, for businesses, for economies and for societies. And in disruptive and confusing times there emerge winners and losers – and the losers are never happy being the losers. When society at large is being disrupted, the number of people who consider themselves on the losing side can be significant. And as we will see, that could be a very serious problem.

After the greatest period of change ever experienced, one which bent the curve of human evolution almost ninety degrees, we are about to find out that we were effectively still only in second gear. For the sixth wave will bring forth a period of exponential change not just in our methods of production, but also our economy, society and even our concept of who we are and our relationship with the world around us. We have only seen a glimpse of what the new world will look like. To survive the sixth wave's upswing and ensure that we create another golden age and beyond, we are going to need to rethink the way we do business, rethink our relationships with technology, rethink our economic models and rethink how we structure our society. Interestingly, it will also challenge the apparently 'self-evident' truths about the very nature of life and humanity. As we will explore in the coming chapters, the significant difference between this transformation and the previous is that this one won't take 50,000 years, just fifty.

SIXTH-WAVE BUSINESS

13

A NEW BUSINESS MINDSET

The right of any corporation to exist is not perpetual
but must be continually earned.

Robert Simons

One of the first paradigm shifts that needs to occur is in our businesses practices, for they are based on the principles of the downswing. Industrial age business leaders are finding that their organisation is not structured for the future, their existing assets are potentially obsolete, and any advantages of scale are being undermined by digital technologies. These leaders, mostly baby boomers and Generation X employees, have spent their entire careers in the downswing of the previous wave, focusing on efficiency and short-term profit maximisation. Now they are in a new wave's upswing, which brings with it a world of chaos. The length of the cycle means that this is the first time they have experienced such a period, and they don't know how to handle it. The market they knew, the one they spent years learning about, the one they studied for their MBA, has been bent out of shape. They have been taught continuity, not revolution, and have spent decades focused on maintaining order; on controlling costs, protecting margins, removing waste and developing incremental product improvements. Order is about control and predictability, whereas chaos is about change and uncertainty. And the chaos currently seems never-ending, as new technology and changing consumer behaviours continue to disrupt business models, giving leaders no respite. During this upswing, most leaders see this chaos and fear the destruction, battening down the hatches and becoming more myopic in focus. Most are dazzled by this technological onslaught, caught like rabbits in headlights, paralysed by often paradoxical fears: of being left behind, of making a mistake, of their own lack of knowledge and of their organisations' inability to adapt. Many mistakenly believe that simply implementing these new technologies will provide a silver bullet for their ills; a quick fix for complex issues. They are wrong.

In contrast, a small number of entrepreneurial organisations rush to embrace the creative, seeing opportunities everywhere. While Schumpeter believed that only large organisations would have the resources and capabilities to disrupt industries, he failed to foresee the digital age and its ability to empower small businesses to attack the corporate titans and create new business models. The ubiquitous nature of digital technology has enabled digital companies like WhatsApp, Skype and Instagram to achieve huge market valuations and disrupt industries with a small employee and asset base. Jack Ma, the CEO of Chinese online retailer Alibaba, highlighted this disruptive capability at the 2014 World Economic Forum in Davos, when he recalled a visit from a Walmart executive. Ma joked that he told the unnamed executive that they should make a bet that in ten years Alibaba would be bigger than Walmart on sales. The reason for his confidence was that, *If you [Walmart] want 10,000 new customers you have to build a new warehouse and this and that. For me: two servers.*[223]

Corporate survival in the sixth wave involves the unenviable task of combating the combined effects of globalisation, hyper-competition, and of course technological disruption. Diagram 7 highlights some of the resultant forces which business leaders must be aware of and have a strategic response to.

Developing a strategic response is crucial, for the increasing speed of creative destruction has led to a significant reduction in corporate longevity. Research by the consultancy Innosight[224] highlighted that the average tenure of companies on the S&P 500 Index in 1958 was 61 years, but that narrowed to 18 years in 2011 and is forecast to shrink to just 14 years by 2026. By 2027, new firms will have replaced 50 per cent of the companies that were

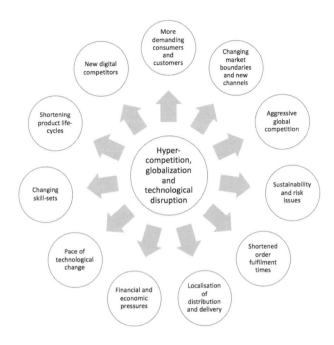

Diagram 7: The Impact of the New-Wave Forces.

in the S&P 500 in 2017. Since the index is representative of the largest US companies, this means that each year on average 25 big companies either fall behind, get acquired or fail. Retail is particularly vulnerable. For years the rules were clear. Big supermarkets and shopping malls are built out of town, the customer travels to them – usually weekly – looks around, buys what they need, and then take their purchases home in their car. Not any more. Customers now want products available wherever and whenever they want them, and the retailer has to deliver to them – preferably the next day – to wherever the consumer wants. Recent innovations have expanded this to include placing the goods inside your house, or in the boot of your car. The tipping point came in 2016, when more people in the US bought goods online than in retail stores for the first time, starting what has been labelled a retail apocalypse. In just over three months, fourteen retail chains announced they would require court protection, and many chains are closing hundreds of stores to try and return to profitability. It's a trend that is continuing across the West; in the UK, 1,500 traditional bricks-and-mortar stores shut their doors for good in 2017.

The Rise of Corporatism

The prevailing perspective in business schools since the 1970s has been that the primary function of corporations is to further the interests of their shareholders. Fifth-wave leaders were taught downswing behaviours, conditioned and trained to deliver short-term profits and meet analyst expectations, behaviours they have been handsomely rewarded for, reinforcing their belief that this was the way business should be run. Shareholder primacy is, however, the tool of corporatism, not capitalism, for it contrasts sharply with the original capitalist approach, when businesses considered larger groups of stakeholders and were run by the real decision-makers and not just the capital owners. In the past, directors and CEOs saw their role as being trustees of great institutions that served not just the shareholders but also the creditors, employees and community. This form of leadership bred employee and customer loyalty. One such company was Cadbury Schweppes, an international confectionery and drinks company founded in 1824 by the Quaker, George Cadbury, where I had the pleasure of working for nearly a decade. It fostered a positively pervasive culture, one which attracted a constant stream of job applicants. Cadbury's looked after its workers, and, as a result, its workers looked after Cadbury's, with the often-made observation that if you cut a Cadbury's worker, they bled purple.[76] Most people worked there for decades, and many for their entire career. Yes, it was a company that sold chocolate, candy and soft drinks, but it was more than just a job to those who worked there; it had a unifying culture, a shared set of values, and belief in what it stood for. The faith of the founders still reverberated around the factories, offices and the surrounding village. However, when the last Cadbury family member, Sir Dominic Cadbury, left the board in 2000 and its long-standing CEO, John Sunderland, retired, Cadbury's finally lost the remaining traces of its Quaker values. Under the new CEO, the business focused solely on short-term shareholder value, creating a palpable change in the corporate culture, a sale of the profitable drinks business to drive up the share price, and the departure of many loyal staff members (including myself and most of my team). It also resulted in Cadbury's losing its corporate identity when it was controversially purchased by Kraft for £11.5 billion in

---

[76] Its famous corporate colour.

2010, who spun it into a new confectionary company called Mondelez in 2012. All that was good about the company and its heritage was sacrificed on the altar of shareholder value. The once-iconic brand's headlines are now mostly around factory closures, consumer dissatisfaction with recipe changes caused by using cheaper ingredients, constant 'value engineering' in order to find ways to provide less chocolate for the same price,[225] and the fact that Kraft/Mondelez paid zero UK corporation tax since taking over Cadbury's. In 2016, it paid just £122,000 UK tax on sales of £1.65 billion and profits of £22 million, while also paying its owners (Kraft) a dividend of £255 million. In contrast, in 2009, before it was bought by Kraft, Cadbury Plc paid a total of £133 million tax on £778 million of UK profits.[226] A company founded nearly two hundred years ago on the Quaker principles of ethics and integrity, once synonymous with great products and the education, care and loyalty of its employees, is now known for cost-cutting and tax-dodging.

This belief that shareholders 'own' corporations and that the stock price is an accurate reflection of the firm's real economic value became the conventional wisdom in the second half of the fifth wave. The source of this mindset can be traced right back to Milton Friedman's 1970 essay proposing that the sole purpose of the organisation is to maximise returns to shareholders. The infrastructure supporting and promoting this mindset is the City itself, especially Wall Street, where quarterly earnings, quarterly investment returns and short-term trading rule. As shareholder value maximisation is measured by share price, corporations increasingly focus on 'hitting the numbers', rather than making long-term innovation to short-term profit maximisation. In 2013, McKinsey and the Canada Pension Plan Investment Board (CPPIB) conducted a survey of more than a thousand board members and C-suite executives. The results showed that 79 per cent of top executives and directors felt especially pressured to demonstrate a strong financial performance over a period of less than two years, with only 7 per cent feeling pressure to deliver a reliable performance over a period of five years or longer. Sixty-three per cent of respondents also said the pressure to generate substantial short-term results had increased over the previous five years. When both your job security and your pay packet become linked to the stock price, the hold the analysts have over corporate leaders is phenomenal. Any companies that refuse to provide quarterly earnings guidance have found themselves systematically shunned by money managers, and if a business misses their earnings targets by even a small amount, they have seen their stock price hammered. Company leaders are therefore focused on short-term results in preference to long-term sustainability projects or business transformation initiatives. The hedge-fund managers, analysts and CEOs have developed a symbiotic relationship that create vast amounts of wealth for them, but lost sight of the needs of the other legitimate stakeholders such as customers, employees and the community at large. In these instances, short-term shareholder greed has replaced long-term stakeholder value.

From Shareholders to AI Share-Flippers

Part of the reason is down to the dramatic change in the nature of shareholders. Back in 1950, households owned more than 90 per cent of shares in US corporations; now they only own between 30 and 40 per cent.[77] Rather than a large, disparate group of individuals, shares are now owned by a small group of hedge funds all looking to exploit market and share-price volatility for the same purpose – to benefit themselves. Buy or sell, the masters of this universe, like the owners of the casinos, always win. Since the deregulation of the domestic financial services industry in the 1980s, growth throughout the second half of the fifth K-wave was so great that once again people developed short memories and forgot that you cannot recirculate a finite amount of money an infinite number of times. Thanks to the fact that the compensation structure that hedge-fund managers typically employ follows the performance-based 'two and twenty' approach, in which hedge-fund managers charge a flat 2 per cent of total asset value as a management fee and an additional 20 per cent of any profits earned, volatility becomes their best friend as their returns are linked to it. Fugazi finance loves volatility, and to prove just how much, in the crisis years of 2007 and 2008, top hedge-fund manager James Simons is estimated to have personally earned $2.8 billion[227] and $2.5 billion[228] respectively, and in 2009, when the world economy was on the floor, another hedge-fund manager, David Tepper, earned $4 billion.

---

[77] Source: Federal Reserve.

If volatility is good and highly profitable, then why shouldn't these new masters of the financial universe band together and create volatility? Directors of businesses can suddenly find their share price falling without any noticeable downturn in their cash flow or order book, and there is simply no limit to how far and how fast expectations can shift. Any adjustments are projected forwards far into the future, and then discounted back to the present, resulting in an amplified disruption in the stock value. In other words, investors are betting on commodities, stock or currency rates that do not yet exist. This means that one bad quarter can trigger a fire-sale run on your stock, and one good quarter can prompt a feeding frenzy. Expectations, unlike the real economy, are therefore not limited by reality, but become the product of the analyst's and stockbroker's imagination, driven by human emotions of fear, greed and over-optimism. Moreover, since shareholders can sell at the drop of a hat, the firm has no stable source of long-term capital. The pressure on business leaders therefore moves from focusing on long-term investments and innovation, to managing expectations to control the stock price and remove any doubts about future performance that might result in a run on your stock. Most damning were the oxymoronic findings that 55 per cent of chief financial officers (CFOs) would forgo an attractive investment project today if it would cause the company to even marginally miss its quarterly earnings target, combined with the fact that 86 per cent of respondents declared that using a longer time horizon to make business decisions would positively affect corporate performance in many ways, including strengthening financial returns and increasing innovation. It appears that although the leaders of listed corporations know that focusing on longer-term innovation and investment is in the best interests of the company, their fear of missing expectations prevents them from doing so. This creates a business environment where satisfying analysts is deemed more important than delighting customers. Where short-term results trump long-term survival, and the glow of today's profits can blind you to tomorrow's problems.

Many of these hedge-fund superstars are also increasingly using machine intelligence rather than human intuition to trade stocks. In 2014, a Hong Kong venture capital firm called Deep Knowledge Futures made an AI system called VITAL an 'equal member of its board of directors'. In the US, James Simons' Renaissance Technologies makes investment decisions using machine-learning computer algorithms and quantitative strategies, and as a result has made serious money when others have struggled. Its flagship fund, the Medallion Fund, is known to charge more than the 'two and twenty' approach, demanding a 5 per cent management fee and a 44 per cent cut of the profits.[229] It has no shortage of investors willing to pay it. As machines are increasingly used to trade stocks, shareholders are increasingly likely to churn their ownership, buying and selling shares frequently – and in the cases where machines are making the trades, several times per second. This will exacerbate the volatility and increasingly fracture the relationship between a business' actual long-term performance and their share price, creating more short-termism, not less. In 1992, George Soros was able to exploit and manipulate the sterling exchange rate to make himself billions, facilitating an enormous wealth transfer from British taxpayers to himself and other hedge-fund managers. Now imagine what happens when AI-powered FINTECH trading systems such as those currently being run by hedge funds such as Renaissance Technologies and Bridgewater Associates are misused.

There is another critical reason why CEOs tend to focus on the short term – they are rewarded for it. Upton Sinclair once declared, *It is difficult to get a man to understand something, when his salary depends on his not understanding it.*[230] Back in 1981, corporations directed less than half their profits to shareholders. However, that changed when underlying business logic became that shareholders should have more power over corporate boards, and executive pay should be tied to shareholder returns. Back in the days when the shareholders were also people who had a vested interest in the long-term health of the business, such as the employees and the pension trust fund, this made sense; maximisation of shareholder value meant both long- and short-term maximisation, and the decisions made in the C-suite reflected that. However, when the principal shareholders are hedge funds, corporate raiders and the CEOs themselves, maximising shareholder value means focusing on the next quarter's numbers to increase the executive pay and the shareholders' wealth. This is reflected in the fact that the average holding period for corporate stocks has fallen from six years, where it had sat for decades, to less than six months. Correspondingly, the average tenure of a public company CEO dropped to less than four years, which means that the willingness of executives to sacrifice short-term profits to invest in longer-term investments and innovation disappeared rapidly. If my salary is in stocks, and my lifespan here is in months, not decades, then I'll do what I can to make some serious money now. Screw the pension fund.

What arose from this new economic environment was the superstar CEO; the leader who is not necessarily the best at long-term strategic thinking, vision-building or motivating employees, but who is a star at manipulating and managing expectations. One of their most-used techniques is the corporate buy-back, designed to create a short-term increase in the stock price, enabling them to meet analysts' expectations, which of course creates more money for the executives. The executives basically use the company's cash to buy back its own stock, increasing its share price, which achieves the dual task of making the analysts happy while increasing their own personal wealth. No extra value has been generated; no new business model, value propositions or products devised; no new stroke of strategic genius – just use of the company's money to make them wealthy at the expense of all other stakeholders.

The other major tool that the CEO can use to keep the stock price high is to immediately increase profits, and the easiest way to quickly increase profits is to cut costs. The easiest way to cut costs is to reduce overheads, and the easiest way to reduce overheads is to close plants, lay off workers, cancel training and mothball research facilities. This creates a short-term, self-interested mindset within the organisation's workforce where fear and self-preservation are the central focus, rather than creativity, contribution and long-term corporate survival. In a *Harvard Business Review* article,[231] Roger Martin, Dean of the Rotman School of Management, comments that: *The move from building value to trading value is bad for economic growth and performance. The increased stock market volatility is bad for retirement accounts and pension funds... talent is being channelled into unproductive activities and egregious behaviours.* According to Martin's calculation, the ratio of CEO compensation to corporate profits increased eightfold between 1980 and 2000, almost all of it coming in the form of stock-based compensation.[232] In 2012, mean total direct compensation of the five hundred highest-paid executives named in company proxy statements was $30.3 million, more than six hundred times the pay of a worker with annual earnings of $50,000.[233] This is leading to many questions being raised once again about the level of wealth inequality in society.

Doom Loops of Disengagement

Outside of the boardroom, these short-term leadership behaviours cause significant problems. A continuous focus on cost-cutting and tax diversion gets mistaken for strategy, which gets distilled down to different departments in different ways, leading to a functionally focused culture with disparate performance metrics and objectives. This leads to departments working against each other, and a culture of constant firefighting and chaos management, which causes significant front-line disengagement and frustration as the same issues crop up again and again like some perverse *Groundhog Day*. As Edwards Deming once declared, *It's funny how we don't have the time to improve, but we have plenty of time to perform work inefficiently and to resolve the same problems over and over.* These firms place themselves, not their customers, at the centre of their universe. Strategies like 'value engineering' enter the corporate lexicon, translated as 'save money by reducing the value provided to the customer'. Industries like confectionery provide prime examples, reducing the weight of products, changing corners to be round rather than square, changing a recipe to include cheaper ingredients, etc. This is 'inside-out' thinking. The problem – customers notice. It takes years to build brand loyalty, but it can be lost in seconds. The lack of concise and well-communicated long-term strategy results in employees that feel completely disconnected from the decision-making process and await instruction from above before proceeding with any initiative. In the short-term shareholder wealth model, employees are viewed as costs and therefore something that can be replaced by more efficient automation tools like robots. As a result, the oncoming robotic revolution is something to be feared and deemed a job-replacement scheme, leading to employees focusing on their own survival rather than the organisation's success.

The root cause of these behaviours can always be found in the same place – the top. Leaders are supposed to be the people that the employees look up to; people who set an example by demonstrating the values and principles of the organisation. The way they speak, act and treat their colleagues and staff is crucial. A social contract should exist between worker and leader that says, *We're in this together*. People like leaders who they trust, who they look up to, someone who inspires them and provides meaning to their work and a shared purpose for them to strive towards.

Great leaders need not be charismatic or charming, but they must be trustworthy, and obviously care for those they work with. Unfortunately, the behaviours most leaders demonstrate as a result of shareholder primacy and stock-based remunerations betrays that trust and breaks that social contract. They lack the courage to make the big decisions and often defer the responsibility to big-name consultancies, using them as both a shield and an emotional crutch. As a result, most solutions are short term-focused, designed to create immediate uplift in share price at the expense of the long-term success of the company. These cost-cutting exercises are often done with a hatchet, cutting indiscriminately through the organisation's bone and muscle as well as its fat, removing people loyal to the organisation and whose talent had never been allowed to flourish. When workers' jobs are easily sacrificed for short-term stock gains – stocks which the leaders own but the workers do not – then the truth becomes clear: *We aren't all in this together. You're just in it for yourself, and I'm expendable.* Leadership actions define the corporate culture, in exactly the same way as we explored in chapter two how the actions and intent of political leaders determine whether a nation develops an inclusive, entrepreneurial society where everyone benefits, or an extractive one where only the leaders do. As with societies, the extractive ones stagnate, regress and decay, while the inclusive ones prosper. One of the surprising revelations to me was how much alignment there is between national and business success. A country where its people are free, empowered, protected and inspired can launch a revolution that transforms the fortunes of a nation, and even change the course of history. For exactly the same reasons, employees who are provided with the same environment can transform the destiny of their organisation. In Britain, people of invention, industry and investment were free to come together, discuss ideas and collaborate. Most businesses do not provide the same freedoms: their creative teams, financial teams and operations teams barely talk, let alone collaborate. Culture matters, and the leadership and politics of both a nation and corporation define the culture.

Conversely, short-term, extractive businesses, focused around increasing value for shareholders only, end up creating what I call a doom loop of employee disengagement, as shown in Diagram 8:

Diagram 8: Disengagement Doom Loop.

The combination of 'command-and-control' management and employment insecurity create a perfect environment for poor cultural behaviours to appear. Personal egos, insecurity, and a resultant need to control every aspect of the organisation, while at the same time keeping others in the dark, create an environment where people feel distrusted and undervalued. Feeling emotionally disconnected from the organisation, they generally believe that their ability to affect direction and decisions is limited, so instead focus on raising their profile by providing evidence of their importance to the organisation. This creates a win/lose mentality, where individuals and departments consciously or unconsciously start to work against each other. People constantly defend what they think they know; overestimating the value of what they have and underestimating the value of what they may gain by giving it up. This emotion-driven behaviour creates an increasingly defensive mindset, resulting in a failure to encourage diversity of opinions, unwillingness to disagree with superiors and poor and ambiguous communication. It creates a culture that makes potential failures, even when known, 'undiscussable'. Best to deny all knowledge and let it fail than be the messenger of bad news. In this environment, change becomes unlikely if not impossible. A cognitive status quo bias operates to keep things the way they are, and the business clinging to tales of past successes. When organisations like this find themselves facing the chaos of a transition period, the immediate reaction is to double down and tighten the management reins, not release them. Like the Ottomans and the Chinese Dynasties, they create a culture that suppresses rather than empowers people's ability to succeed, which is not surprising because in both examples the system is designed around command structures and control, not freedom and empowerment. To be promoted or rewarded in most businesses you need to move jobs, and mastery of a particular area is often deemed a career death sentence because you become trapped. People are not rewarded based on expertise but on experience, making it hard to attract the specialist talent needed in the new wave. It ends up creating an environment that is perfectly designed to reduce organisational agility and stifle creativity and innovation. As the saying goes, 'Every system is perfectly designed in order to achieve the results it gets.'[78]

The situation is not helped by the culture of short-termism and the constant search for quick wins and incremental improvements rather than taking on difficult long-term strategic projects that may not pay off for years. The innovation and long-term vision that are necessary for growth becomes inhibited, for when you feel everything around you is burning, you only focus on the next two seconds, not the next two years. One difficult obstacle for a short term-focused organisation to overcome is the fact that people who are often deemed the most important, those who can fight these fires, are almost always the most resistant to change because they have the most to lose. Their personal power and influence come from being the one-eyed person in the land of the blind, so developing a more collaborative, transparent and team-based approach that prevents the business from requiring saving every day doesn't serve their personal needs. Ego and fear of losing power prevent them from embracing a new way of working, and instead they fight against the change – often vocally and at great volume. Due to their reputation in the business, their opinion often carries great weight. It is a behaviour I have sadly experienced to some degree in every single organisation I have worked with over the last twenty-five years. You

---

[78] Originally attributed to P&G employee Arthur Jones.

begin to realise the inevitable truth that most businesses are often at the whim of the agendas of individuals; people who have a reputation as their organisation's greatest firefighters, but who are, in fact, their most prolific arsonists. They may save the day, but only by sacrificing tomorrow.

Technology is therefore not the blockage: organisational culture and the mindset of its leaders are. I'm not alone in identifying this.[79] A July 2017 McKinsey report highlighted that executives declared that their own internal corporate culture was by far the biggest barrier to digital effectiveness.[234] The study, which surveyed 2,135 global executives, highlighted three primary digital-culture deficiencies: functional and departmental silos, a fear of taking risks, and difficulty forming and acting on a single view of the customer. This prevents investment in strategic opportunities and delays reaction to any changes in customer needs or market dynamics. One of the hardest challenges for any business leader is to adapt to this changing environment by changing the culture of the organisation. It's much easier to make a functional organisation worse than it is to make a dysfunctional organisation better. As someone who has spent most of their career helping companies to improve, one of the biggest lessons I've learnt is you cannot force people to change; they have to make the decision that changing is in their own best interest. In many ways, the status quo is human nature; people are often paradoxically afraid of change and also afraid of staying the same – but when push comes to shove, staying the same seems safer. To succeed for them means not to fail, but in order to succeed, you must accept and even invite failure. To many fifth-wave business leaders, that's just not worth the risk. They've been taught how not to fail, rather than how to succeed. This creates a culture where the managers and employees also don't take risks; for as stated, the actions of leaders define the culture.

The most common barrier to success is therefore the inability of leaders to establish a new mindset. They mistake corporate climate for corporate culture, believing that open plan offices, bean bags and casual dress will naturally inspire people to become more entrepreneurial, failing to see that

---

[79] This is an important point, for it relates to human nature. It is humans and their nature that delay technological change in society as well as in organisations, something we will discuss later. Trying to force change through without the people affected understanding the benefits or the impact simply creates fear and resistance. Paradoxically, taking time upfront to involve and explain increases implementation success and reduces lag. Slow is fast and fast is slow.

it is their behaviours that are the real bottleneck. While they all want to win the game, most are unsure what the game is anymore, let alone what the rules are. These leaders end up as CEOs who are behind the curve, playing a new game by old rules. Executives who wait for their organisation's culture to simply adapt organically to the digital revolution will find that they end up moving too slowly. Corporate performance over the long term has failed to keep up with the performance of the markets, simply because corporations do not adapt as fast as the markets do. The market, linked as it is to the actions of entrepreneurs and their disruptive innovations, operates on the assumption of discontinuity and accommodates continuity. Corporations, however, assume continuity and react to discontinuity. Their corporate-control systems are designed to ensure the predictable achievement of goals, not agility and adaptiveness. It's a profound and vital difference.

It's Not About You, Stupid

Companies employ thousands of people, but rarely inspire them. In fact, industrial-age management thinking has hindered rather than empowered business growth over the last century. Business is a team sport, not an individual pursuit, and successful change requires engaging people in the movement, utilising their talents in the pursuit of a common goal. This is something many, many leaders seem to forget. They believe because *they've* thought of something, that everyone should just go off and passionately do it. They believe that because *they* broadcast their idea, usually in some written or verbal stream of consciousness, that every member of their team now has clarity as to the desired intent, actions and outcomes – as well as what activities should be dropped to make time for this (if any). I think many leaders struggle to understand why their teams aren't psychic. Often, business leaders actively don't want contribution, only compliance. Henry Ford is alleged to have made the statement, *why is it every time I ask for a pair of hands, they come with a brain attached?* With that mindset in place, it is no wonder companies are rushing to embrace the automation revolution. The employees, on the other hand, mentally clock out and are left to seek fulfilment outside of work, their talents and innovative capabilities unappreciated and untapped by their industrial-mindset employers.

The restrictiveness of this mindset may have been less apparent to senior management when the focus was on efficiencies and cost-cutting, as treating employees like interchangeable resources that can be hired, moved around and fired at will was what they wanted. However, its weakness becomes awfully apparent when you need to think differently and innovate yourself out of trouble, and you find that the leader's behaviours prevent employee engagement and innovation. In a time when the main sources of competitive advantage are knowledge and innovation, perhaps the most damaging aspect of a poor culture in the impact it has on the organisation's ability to not just recruit the right talent, but also retain and develop them. While money may attract them and buy their time, it takes great leadership, a compelling vision and an empowering culture to win their heart.

So why, in the 21st century, does command-and-control management still exist? It exists because despite all the rhetoric, most organisations are still bureaucratic, centrally planned and hierarchical, set up to take orders from above rather than the customer. And as in political systems, the larger the gap between the decision makers and the general population, the lower the level of trust and understanding, resulting in greater levels of restrictions being imposed to retain control. Political institutions with little freedoms usually have excessive large governmental departments to administer every aspect of daily life. Organisations are no different. More management equals less individual freedom and creativity. Statistic show how widespread this issue is. According to the Chartered Management Institute,[235] only 17 per cent of the 1,500 managers polled said that their management was innovative and only 15 per cent said they were trusting. Gary Hamel highlights this issue in *The Future of Management*: *Right now, your company has 21st-century Internet-enabled business processes and mid-20th-century management processes all built atop 19th-century management principles.*[236] Worryingly, recent research seems to suggest that things are getting worse, not better. In an August 2017 *HBR* article by Hamel and Michele Zanini, they detail the results of a survey on organisational bureaucracy that had over 7,000 respondents. Nearly two thirds of these felt their organisation had, over recent years, become more centralised, rule-bound and conservative, and only 13 per cent said their organisation had become less bureaucratic. One concerning highlight was that people working in customer service, sales, production, logistics and R&D felt that bureaucracy was growing more than people working in HR, finance, planning, purchasing and administration.

This means that the people most constrained by bureaucracy are the ones most directly involved in the creation of customer value.[237]

Many of these companies didn't start out this way. Many were fifth-wave innovators who, as their business grew, switched from entrepreneurial to efficiency thinking. Once their products moved from being radical innovations to commoditised and cost-sensitive items, they stopped experimenting and started cost-cutting, switching from strategic thinking to tactical. Anyone who has worked inside of what was once a dynamic start-up but is now just another organisation can speak to the problem. As companies get big, bureaucracy and management get bigger. They also become more and more disconnected from their customers, and rather than speak and work directly with them they often resort to third-party market research and surveys to understand how customers feel about their products or services. I've worked with several smaller organisations – including tech companies – who started out passionately believing that they were going to change the world. Then, when growth required the establishment of more standardised processes and procedures, they brought in competent but industrial-mindset leaders who did indeed create control, but also killed the passion. As companies increase the amount of management, they become less agile, more formal and less entrepreneurial. All of the positive qualities such as passionate debate, laughter and the vocalisation of ideas is supressed, and the organisation stops being a fun and exciting place to work. Those individuals with mobility who strive for more purpose in their work check out and leave, reducing the employee gene pool to those with the least options, not the most talent. The rest mentally leave but physically stay. As we examined in Part One, societies that suppress the innovative capabilities of their people fail, whereas those that free them, succeed. Companies are no different – they are simply smaller versions. A tightly controlled hierarchical 'command-and-control' organisation doesn't create an innovative culture for the same reasons that top-down dictatorial societies fail to create the social or economic freedoms needed to launch an industrial revolution.

Companies with clear, customer-focused strategic goals and supportive organisational cultures possess a huge advantage. A 2011 Booz & Company Global Innovation 1000 study titled *Why Culture is Key* commented that, *if more companies could gain traction in closing both the strategic alignment and culture gaps to better realise these goals and attributes, not only would their financial performance improve, but the data suggests that the potential gains might be large enough to improve the overall growth rate of the global economy.*[238] Entrepreneurs and their innovations might spark the creative destruction process, but it's not the idea that gets the fire burning – it's the ability to communicate it, commercialise it and reliably deliver on its promise. As Michael Dell once declared, *Innovation is a commodity; the execution of it is not.*

Change Before You Need To

The corporations that will thrive in the sixth wave are those willing to reinvent themselves to stay ahead, and to not to simply rest on their laurels and past successes. This is not easy for leaders to buy into, for it creates a state of continuous change. No matter how successful your organisation, the prospect of making a shift in your business strategy can be downright alarming, especially when you have competitors breathing down your neck and shareholders and analysts to satisfy each quarter. The paradox of change is that while everyone says they want change, not many people actually like it, and even less want to lead it. It's even harder to drive this change when results are currently good. Dieter Zetsche, Chairman of the Board of Management of Daimler AG and head of Mercedes-Benz Cars, launched their Leadership 2020 initiative in December 2016, and included the statement, *the tricky thing is this: right now, Daimler is doing well. And those numbers have some [people] saying, "if it ain't broke don't fix it."*[239] That kind of complacent thinking can be deadly in this stage of a K-wave's cycle, and Kodak remains the poster child for why. Weighed down both financially and emotionally by the massive investments they had made in film-processing technology, while still recording healthy film sales figures, they continued to ignore the warnings that the industry was changing, and that they needed to also. Despite their engineers developing the first digital camera in 1975, the product was dropped for fear it would threaten Kodak's photographic film sales. In another first, in 1986 Kodak's research labs developed the first megapixel camera, one of the milestones that had been forecast as a tipping point in terms of the viability of standalone digital photography. Again, their desire to protect their existing investments prevented them from investing in this new technological breakthrough. George Fisher, CEO of Kodak from 1993 to 1999, captured the core issue when he told the *New York Times* that Kodak *regarded digital photography as the enemy, an evil juggernaut that would kill the chemical-based film and paper business that fuelled Kodak's sales and profits for decades.*[240] Hubris born of past successes and the complacent mindset of those in control resulted in the 130-year-old company having to shed 47,000 jobs, thirteen manufacturing plants and 130 processing labs between 2003 and 2011, before finally running out of cash and filing for chapter 11 bankruptcy protection in January 2012. Kodak, a name once synonymous with photography having sold to the world the concept of capturing their 'Kodak moments', a company responsible for 90 per cent of all film sales in the US, was all but finished. Although it was under increasing pressure from a thriving Fujifilm, the death of the company was down to their own complacency and inability to consider moving away from their film-manufacturing business. There is no point in having the world's best photographic film-production facilities if the world doesn't use film any more. They forgot that they were in the business of capturing and sharing memories, not selling film. We now take more photos than at any point in our history, but Eastman Kodak is no longer involved in any meaningful way. Research in Motion (RIM), the manufacturers of the BlackBerry, are another famous example. They assumed that having access to social media on your phone, and the new touchscreen technology, was something of interest to teenagers and housewives and thus not a threat to their dominance of the business-user market. We now know that this was a fatal error of judgement and lack of understanding around how this new technology would be used, and who would use it. Business people want to check up on their social network, watch movies and listen to music as much as their children do, as well as stay in touch with all matters work-related. As with Kodak, a product-focused 'inside-out' mindset combined with an inability to act on information telling them to innovate were their downfall.

The Death of Ambition

The biggest victims of a shareholder primacy mindset are innovation and customer service. A 2014 *Washington Post* article highlights exactly this point when it states, *wealth in the United States today comes chiefly from retarding businesses' ability to invest in growth-engendering activity. The purpose of the modern U.S. corporation is to reward large investors and top executives with income that once was spent on expansion, research, training and employees.*[241] William Lazonick, Professor of Economics at the University of Massachusetts, highlights that between 2003 and 2012, 449 of the S&P 500 companies used 54 per cent of their earnings – a total of $2.4 trillion – to buy back their own stock, and 37 per cent on dividends to shareholders.[242] That only leaves 9 per cent for investments, research and development, expansion, cash reserves or increases in employee remuneration. Executives are paid to find viable ways to invest accumulated cash for the benefit of future growth and earnings; if the only thing that they can find to invest that cash in is their own stock, then they should resign in shame.

To see the impact a constant short-term focus has on innovation is easy: look at companies who aren't under pressure to do it. When a private company goes public, it often changes its behaviour from entrepreneurial and innovative, to more myopic and returns-focused. Research backs this up. A study by Alexander Ljungqvist and colleagues at Harvard and New York University highlighted that private US companies invested nearly twice as much as those listed on the stock market, and that privately owned companies, especially those that are less than three years old, are four times more responsive to new investment opportunities than their older, publicly owned competitors.[243] Here resides shareholder primacy's Achilles heel. Despite improving economies, firms are sitting on their cash flow, refusing to spend the money, at least on making large-scale bets in innovation, because the pay-off isn't immediate. They exclude the customer from the equation, and instead focus on profit maximisation activities such as incremental, functional improvements and cost-cutting. Any big decisions are generally around mergers and acquisitions, tax management/diversion initiatives, or off-shoring and outsourcing. While these actions may seem eminently sensible for the CEOs focused on cutting costs and reducing the number of problematic human overheads they need to manage, it leaves the organisation exposed to competitors that *do* find innovative new ways to delight the customer. Worse, they are harming the entire economy. In the US, manufacturing represents 67 per cent of private sector R&D spending as well as 30 per cent of the country's productivity growth. Every dollar of manufacturing activity returns $1.48 to the economy. Given the stimulus effect of manufacturing, the decision by the developed nations to outsource this task to the emerging economies has been a contentious point for some time. Henry R. Nothhaft, author of *Great Again: Revitalizing America's Entrepreneurial Leadership*, described the issue well: *For 30 years now we have all been fed the carefully cultivated myth, that so long as America did the creative work, the inventing, then we can let other nations like China do the so-called grunt work, the manufacturing. Simply, we would think; they would sweat. So we let manufacturing go and in so doing we lost the greatest economic force multiplier in history. For manufacturing not only supplies middle class incomes to the three-quarters of all Americans without a college degree, it also creates up to 15 additional jobs outside of manufacturing for every position on the factory floor.* Whilst alarming for those involved in industry, what Nothhaft highlighted next should create even greater concern for the future: *we have assembled irrefutable proof that when manufacturing is offshore, R&D always follows. And sure enough, already 20% of US R&D is now moved offshore. If this keeps up, what's going to be left of America's fabled innovation leadership? In our arrogance and naiveté, we seem to have forgotten that the nation that no longer makes things will eventually forget how to invent them.*[244] What Nothhaft is touching on is the significant link between the ability to make things and the level of innovation. This is an unsurprising connection, given the fact that the level of innovation exploded at the same time as industrial output, but it seems to be something that no one grasped and thus why no one questioned the rush to offshore manufacturing to low-cost locations. This is probably to do with the fact that in the fifth-wave downswing all eyes were on the financial market and the attraction of making money from money; i.e. without actually having to make it.

Another great example is the banking industry. Despite making huge profits, the industry saw the opening of the low-cost labour pools in English-speaking emerging nations such as India, and the improvements in information technology and communication, as an excellent opportunity to massively reduce their labour overheads in high-wage countries such as the UK. They implemented a two-pronged cost-reduction strategy of offshoring their customer support and sales while also closing costly local branches. What the customer wanted was not considered – which, incidentally, were local branches that opened on weekends and reliable customer service from people they could clearly understand. Seeing the level of customer dissatisfaction that arose because of this self-centred move, banks like First Direct appeared and subsequently stole away large swathes of the older banks' customer base by delivering high levels of customer service. The big banks, after seeing the fall in customer numbers, then went on a charm offensive, selling to the public the concept of 'local branches' and 'local call centres' – the same things they took away from the customer in the first place. Now, these branches are closing once again,[80] only this time it's automation and digital banking, not offshoring, that are to blame.

The 2008 financial collapse raised the profile of these short-sighted behaviours, and while it is still the prevalent mindset in many organisations, dissenting voices are beginning to be heard. Professors such as Lynn Stout from Cornell Law School, commentators like Steve Denning over at *Forbes* and Henry Mintzberg at *The Economist*, as well as bodies such as the Drucker Institute,[245] constantly bang the drum for more innovative, long-term thinking. In 2009, even the poster child of this mindset, the former head of General Electric (GE) Jack Welch, described the business emphasis on shareholder value as 'misplaced'. *On the face of it, shareholder value is the dumbest idea in the world.*[246] Welch's statement proves to be a perfect example of the effect that city analysts and short-termism have on CEO behaviour. His 'shareholder value' maximisation strategies, most notably his, *if you're not first or second in the market, get out,* approach, was trumpeted by the markets, consultancies and media alike, with Welch often appearing on the covers of business magazines. Yet as soon as he retired from GE and could distance himself from the constant pressure from analysts to push up the share price, Welch presented a dramatic change in tone, becoming much more reticent and critical of this approach and the damage it causes.

More than Profits

There is a growing body of evidence that the companies that are most successful at growing long-term shareholder value are those that aim at goals other than shareholder value. A good example is Unilever. In 2013, their CEO Paul Polman, declared that it was *time to put an end to the cult of shareholder value.* Under Polman's stewardship, Unilever have re-established their ethical foundations, first laid down in Victorian Britain

---

[80] In my village, Balsall Common, all three local banks – NatWest, Barclays and HSBC, have closed in the last eighteen months.

when William Hesketh Lever established a soap manufacturer with a social mission. Like Cadbury's 'factory in the garden' in Bournville, between 1888 and 1914 the Lever brothers built the model village of Port Sunlight alongside the soap factory to accommodate the company's staff in good-quality housing, with high architectural standards and many community facilities. The purpose of their business was also socially minded. As Paul Polman explains, *The [purpose] of Lord Lever when he made his Sunlight bar soap, was to address the issues of hygiene in Victorian Britain. The reason I believe business should be around is to serve society.*

Under Polman's stewardship, Unilever has moved away from quarterly profit reporting, with Polman stating that *since we don't operate on a 90-day cycle for advertising, marketing, or investment, why do so for reporting?*[247] Polman has proven to be a constant critic of the behaviour of the hedge funds, analysts and superstar CEOs, with statements like; *Too many investors have become short-term gamblers; the more fluctuations in share price they engineer, the better it is for them... It is not good for the companies or for society, but it is influencing the way firms are being run, all the same... Most of the trading is done in nanoseconds by people that you call my shareholders but who would move anywhere if they can make a quick return.*[248] *The very essence of capitalism is under threat as business is now seen as a personal wealth accumulator. We have to bring this world back to sanity and put the greater good ahead of self-interest. We need to fight very hard to create an environment out there that is more long-term focused and move away from short termism.*[249] Polman has made his utter disdain for this type of capitalism and this type of shareholder clear: *I don't have any space for many of these people that really, in the short term, try to basically speculate and make a lot of money... I'm not just working for them. Slavery was abolished a long time ago.*[250]

Polman went further than most when he urged his shareholders to put their money somewhere else if they don't *buy into this long-term value-creation model, which is equitable, which is shared, which is sustainable.*[251] The city immediately punished Unilever, dropping the share price by 8 per cent when Polman announced the ending of guidance.[252] However, once Unilever's longer-term, customer-focused strategies started to bear fruit, it then rose to be 35 per cent higher. At the peak of the recession Unilever realised that following a relentless cost-cutting drive will cause long-term harm. Instead they started investing in developing and building lean, sustainable, customer-focused value chains. Unilever has quietly risen up the tables in terms of credibility as well as profitability and is now pursuing a winning strategy that is focused on pillars of customer centricity and sustainability – two things that its employees have become passionate about delivering. Polman spearheaded the ten-year Unilever Sustainable Living Plan, the aim of which was to decouple the company's growth from its environmental footprint. The plan's ambitious goals included doubling Unilever's revenue while reducing their footprint by 50 percent, sourcing 100 per cent of their raw materials sustainably and helping more than a billion people improve their health and well-being.

The result of this strategic shift was both instant and dramatic. In 2010, Unilever recorded their highest growth in thirty years, at a lower cost model than when they were focusing on cutting costs, while dramatically reducing the environmental impact of their business. They also rose rapidly up Gartner's Supply Chain Top 25 list, claiming the top spot in 2016 and 2017. Over the last eight years I have heard various senior Unilever directors from different continents talk about their plan at conferences and events, and one thing stands out – they are all passionate and on-point. No dilution, confusion or mixed messages. Everyone gets it. Everyone is involved. A side effect of this clarity of purpose that should make other companies sit up and take notice is that Unilever has become one of the world's most sought-after employers. Unsurprisingly, people want to work for companies with an aspiration to achieve more than just making shareholders rich. It's perhaps the most obvious thing in the world, but if you analysed 99 per cent of fifth-wave companies you would never have guessed it.

Unilever's stellar rise caused the hedge-fund activists to examine the performance of Unilever's chief competitor – and the original employer of Polman – Procter & Gamble (P&G). Billionaire hedge-fund manager William Ackman, CEO and Founder of Pershing Square Capital Management, purchased $1.8 billion in P&G shares, and used the clout that owning these shares brought to oust P&G's CEO, Bob McDonald, for failing to deliver his desired level of short-term profits. Commenting on this, Roger Martin, Dean of the Rotman School of Management at the University of Toronto, summarised the behaviour of hedge-fund managers like Ackman as follows: *We will bid up the price of your stock to whatever in our wildest expectation fantasies we imagine that it is worth and then hold you accountable for earning a sparkling return on that value, and if you don't do it immediately we will savage you and the stock price and get somebody else to bring it back up to where it was when we started haranguing you.*[253]

As a public company, Unilever is not immune from the attentions of those with capital and an eye for short-term gains. Jorge Paulo Lemann, founder of 3G Capital and the principal shareholder of Kraft Heinz (Warren Buffet and his hedge fund Berkshire Hathaway are another huge shareholder), runs a company takeover machine that strips short-term value from a company, then looks for its next target. When 3G and Buffett bought Heinz in 2013, they set about closing six factories and cut 7,000 jobs in eighteen months. In February 2017, Kraft made an audacious £115 billion proposal for Unilever, which Polman and his team resisted, fought and won. The hostile takeover attempt caused Polman to call for more protection from foreign takeovers, while also forcing him to tighten up his short-term focus to 'improve value for shareholders' so that they would back him in the future and not be lured by the appeal of quick money, as had been the case at Cadbury's. To many, the battle between Kraft and Unilever represented more than simply the takeover of a consumer products company by another; it represented a fight between two very different ideologies around what capitalism means and how it operates. On the one hand we have Unilever, who, like Cadbury's, have roots from an earlier era of capitalism, one based around the values of non-conformist religious industrialists such as Quakers. Their focus is on long-term value creation and the shared prosperity of all stakeholders. On the other, we have 3G Capital, the private equity company that owns Kraft Heinz. Their ethics and behaviour exemplify neo-liberal capitalism and the belief that shareholder interests take priority over all other stakeholders. In Mr Polman's own words, the bid was *clearly a clash between a long-term, sustainable business model for multiple stakeholders and a model that is entirely focused on shareholder primacy... We made very clear that we were not interested. They didn't hear us for some reason. We sent letters. They didn't read them for some reason.*

In the sixth wave, the biggest challenge for established businesses is to focus on something other than short-term returns. As the machines handle more of the stock trading, many leaders will find themselves caught between an ever-faster spinning shareholder value doom loop, and a series of new sixth-wave competitors who play a different game according to a different set of rules. The industrial model doesn't work any more, yet many businesses still behave as if it does. They will have to wise up quick.

14

A COPERNICAN BUSINESS REVOLUTION

There is only one valid definition of business purpose: to create a customer.
The customer is a foundation of a business and keeps it in existence.
The customer alone gives employment.

Peter F. Drucker

One of the primary paradigm shifts of the sixth wave has been the shift in the balance of power from the maker to the consumer. Media was one of the first industries to feel the effect, especially television. The market has changed from a tiny number of broadcasters who decided what you could watch and when, to a situation where the consumer decides what to watch, when they watch it and how they watch it. For example, everyone I know has watched Game of Thrones, but hardly anyone I know watched it when it was first broadcast. Growing up in the UK in the 1970s, weekday children's television started at 3.55pm and finished at 5.35pm. Now, children can access their favourite shows whenever they want, on their own personal tablet sized TV. The interesting thing is that all this competition has increased, not decreased, the creativeness or quality of the available programmes, increasing the value from the consumer's perspective. Likewise, digital book production and print-on-demand manufacturing hasn't destroyed the book industry, but dramatically increased the number of authors and books being published, which in turn increases the choice available to customers and provides them with the opportunity to hear new voices. Digital print-on-demand technology has kept the price low, and e-books are even cheaper. Now if you have a book inside you, there's nothing stopping you sharing it with the world. This has, however, severely disrupted the business models of the traditional publishing houses and literary agents who used to control the industry. Likewise, YouTube has enabled millions of new, independent content creators to reach out to consumers, often becoming the preferred source of news and current affairs, completely bypassing traditional news channels. The cost of becoming a contributor to this new media? Nothing but your time.

Wider social norms have also been disrupted. Consumers have stopped trusting institutions and started trusting strangers. Why? Because companies have an agenda, and their focus on constantly pushing products doesn't inspire, doesn't engage and doesn't drive action. In her 2016 TED talk, Rachel Botsman described how trust has come in three waves. Prior to the industrial revolution, trust was local. You had to know the individual personally, and therefore you only really trusted people in your town or village. Post-industrial revolution, institutional trust took over, driven by big banks, big corporations and big government. These operated what Botsman calls a 'black-box system of authority' – you never got to see the workings and they controlled the rules. However, people have wised up, and since the start of the digital age this institutional trust has become fractured. From phone hacking to the VW emissions scandal, the banking crisis to the constant stream of data leaks, our trust in an institution's ability to serve our needs has been diluted, and we have realised that institutional trust wasn't designed for the digital age. Now we trust strangers to drive us (Uber), provide a room for us (Airbnb), date us (Tinder) and sell us stuff (eBay). It's also an increasingly two-way relationship. The example Botsman provides is that if she uses a corporate hotel, she won't necessarily hang the towels up after they've been used, whereas if she uses Airbnb, she always does. There are two reasons for this. One, with Airbnb there's an individual rather than a faceless corporation at the end of the transaction, and two, she is also being assessed and rated as a customer, and poor ratings will affect her ability to transact in the future. Digital technology is therefore dramatically altering the power dynamics between customer and vendor, giving a voice to both and a platform to rank their trustworthiness that can reach millions. Developing a customer-centric organisational culture has gone from a nice-to-have, to a matter of survival.

Each new wave brings new challenges and opportunities that require new thinking to address. As Einstein once famously pointed out, we can't solve problems by using the same kind of thinking we used when we created them. Whereas traditional businesses look at technology primarily to enable them to do the things they already do more efficiently, disruptors are free to build radically different solutions and business models, unconstrained by the past and by having skin in the existing model. They come to the party with a relatively blank slate and focus on the future, not on leveraging the assets of the past. Eric Schmidt, the Chairman of Google, sums it up nicely: *the story of innovation has not changed. It has always been a small team of people who have a new idea, typically not understood by people around them and their executives.*[254] The light bulb wasn't invented by Edison making continuous improvements to the candle, and the automobile wasn't invented by better saddles, horseshoes and animal feed. It was through imagination and invention, not marginal improvements; through experimentation, not efficiency. Likewise, better and cheaper newspapers would not have prevented the creation of digital news, better and cheaper postal services would not have stopped email, better and cheaper travel agents would not stop online travel bookings, and better and cheaper department stores would not have stopped the rise of e-commerce. This freedom to think differently helps to shift the paradigms of customers whose wants and needs are also limited by the current reality. As Henry Ford once famously declared, *if I'd have asked the customer what they wanted they'd have said faster horses*. While a myopic, cost-focused mindset might deliver profits today, it is innovation that will provide profits tomorrow and the day after. Whether it relates to companies or political institutions, those that try to avoid the forces of creative destruction, or to obtain the gains from creation without any destruction (i.e. won't let go of investments, products or mindsets), only end up experiencing destruction in the long run.

Since the days of the industrial revolution, setting up a business has required significant capital investment to buy assets, build or rent facilities and employ large numbers of people. With new digital products, this is no longer the case. Digital companies can be launched, and their products distributed, quickly. Their digital nature also enables them to spend more on organisational capital and appreciating assets such as personnel, research and development, and intellectual property, rather than on depreciating physical assets such as plants and equipment. Like companies wedded to their physical assets, many fifth-wave organisations are constrained by their technological ones. Companies that spent millions on large-scale ERP systems, or who have a disparate network of multiple IT solutions that only specialists know how to support and maintain, find that they are hamstrung by excessive infrastructure licence fees, technical support and consultancy bills, and resource heavy IT departments. These departments simply end up becoming another business silo, another internal barrier to overcome. The new-wave companies, on the other hand, can start with a blank slate and utilise new, on-demand, cloud-based solutions that don't require the purchasing of servers and massive implementation projects. These agile, scalable, web-based solutions both support their growing needs, and allow for remote working – for free – meaning that they can also make use of flexible office solutions rather than having to invest in expensive rents or asset purchase until they are sure they can afford them.

While new-wave companies see only opportunities from these new technologies, older, fifth-wave companies see threats. Their workforce worries about their ability to adapt and what will happen if they are displaced – how will they support their family, pay their mortgage and provide for their pension? Concerns for the customer and business are replaced with concerns for the individual. Fear is a powerful progress blocker, and the worst thing a company can do is talk about massive, disruptive change without clearly identifying the value it will generate and the benefits to the employees. An employee who feels no involvement in the change has no commitment to it. The 'what about me?' question has to be addressed head-on or else you'll get nothing but resistance. Perhaps the most concerned group of employees are those between the ages of thirty-five and fifty; those that have invested years into the company pension, and who have dependants and debts, such as kids, a mortgage, cars, school fees, etc. People who cannot suddenly decide to take a risk and start again in order to learn the skills of the new wave, and who need their monthly pay packet or else they'll go bankrupt. People who have invested time and energy in their careers and are not going to let things go easily, because they are stuck and terrified of the implications of losing their jobs. The issue for many companies is that the middle-management layer in their business is primarily made up of people in this category, which creates a powerful group who have the ability to delay and frustrate change initiatives that they feel put them at risk. As a result, the disengagement doom loop spins faster, increasing the likelihood that the business will not develop the agility needed to adapt to the new wave's forces, leading it to become another casualty of creative destruction.

Digital sixth-wave companies should not be complacent and believe that they are immune to the forces of creative destruction, though. They may be more agile, but they are also more fragile. The costs of market entry may be lower, but that means they are also lower for their competition, and the digital nature of their products makes them easy to imitate and replace. Plus, many are finding that while their products are new, old business principles still apply to them as much as to industrial companies. Customers are still king, people still matter, and culture still eats strategy for breakfast, and everything else for lunch. It's a painful lesson that some new-wave companies are learning the hard way. Boring old-wave issues such as toxic company cultures and disregard for their employees have blighted new-wave companies like Uber. Shifting mindsets around how a company views the market and its customers are the most difficult aspect of change. Companies become wedded to their products, to the current reality, and not to customers. When the customer needs change, they often fail to notice until it's too late.

It's Always Day One

Company leaders who want to survive the sixth wave need to take their companies through a Copernican business revolution; creating a heliocentric paradigm shift like the catholic church had to go through. They need to realise that the customer, not their firm, is actually at the centre of their universe because now the customer has choices and is in control. This is a restatement of Peter Drucker's key principle that the only valid purpose of a profit-focused firm is to create (and retain) customers, for they – not shareholders – are the only ones that bring employment. This is more than the old adage about listening to your customers, but an overwhelming desire to understand their needs better than they do themselves. This new mindset requires leaders to fundamentally review the existing theory of the firm. Companies that continue to focus on short-term returns simply leave themselves open to a direct attack from younger corporations that do follow these principles. Even cost-cutting stalwarts like Michael O'Leary, the CEO of Ryanair, had moments where they wised up. In 2013, Ryanair was voted as having the worst customer service out of Britain's hundred biggest brands. O'Leary then had his own personal epiphany and put in place a Copernican revolution at Ryanair. Profits soared 66 per cent as a result. *If I'd only learned in college that being nice was good for business, I'd have done it years ago*, he declared to Bloomberg TV.[81]

The current king of the customer-centric, 'innovation-first' approach – at least in the West – is Amazon,[82] the creative force behind the destruction of many a short-sighted and efficiency-focused industry. Amazon labels itself *the world's most customer-centric company*, and it's hard to disagree. It is certainly the most innovative, repeatedly spending more on R&D than any other company in the US, and is speeding up this investment, increasing it by 41 per cent in 2017 to an eye-watering $22.6 billion.[255] To put it into context, this is over $10 billion more than Apple spent in the same year, and $17 billion more than IBM. In just over twenty years, Amazon has grown from an online start-up focusing on selling books, to a devastating multi-platform, multi-industry technological disruptor that prowls around, constantly looking for any opportunity to own more of the customer experience. The creation of a marketplace built around their virtuous circle principles of customer convenience, choice and price has enabled Amazon to overtake Walmart as the world's most valuable retailer, with nearly 400 million items for sale on its website and the number-one choice for Americans buying things online.

The previous kings of retail, Walmart, had exploited the stable technologies of the fourth wave (automotive-based logistics) and the experimental technologies of the fifth wave (computer-based supply-chain

---

[81] Although this paradigm shift does seem to have been temporary, and tales of cost-cutting, excess charges and poor service have once again surfaced. A leopard can never change its spots, as the saying goes. A decision O'Leary will regret.

[82] Honourable mention must go to DuPont as another company that is trying to ensure that innovation stays at the forefront of its strategy. To ensure they remained competitive in the long term, DuPont implemented a new rule in 2010 that mandated that 30 per cent of revenue must come from innovations the company has created in the last four years.

planning systems) to create a new retail paradigm and a whole new supply-chain model – a hub-and-spoke distribution network that enabled one distribution centre to support between seventy-five and a hundred retail stores within a 250-mile area. This enabled Walmart to become the 20th century's largest retailer. Amazon has now replaced Walmart by utilising stable, existing fifth-wave technology (the Internet and e-commerce) and experimenting with sixth-wave technologies (AI, machine learning, voice recognition, warehouse robots, drones, etc.) and become the world's largest 21st-century retailer and the clear online leader in the US and Europe. From its online marketplace, its recommendation engines, Kiva warehouse robotics, pricing algorithms, search capabilities, home hubs and last-mile delivery innovations, all driven by its early realisation that data is the oil that greases its economic engine, Amazon has led from the front. Its 'customer first, innovate always' approach resulted in massive growth in sales, customer base and profit. In 2017, its net sales increased 31 per cent to $177.9 billion, more than the GDP of Algeria, and currently[83] Amazon's market capitalisation is $832.5 billion and rising. These numbers look set to continue to explode: Q1 2018 sales were 43 per cent higher than in Q1 2017, and operating income rose 92 per cent. At the same time Amazon's bricks-and-mortar competition have seen their stocks plummet – some dramatically. Sears, for example, has lost 96 per cent of its market value in the last decade. To demonstrate the speed at which Amazon is currently growing, Walmart had virtually the same market value as Amazon in April 2016. Two years later, and despite Walmart's value increasing by 25 per cent, Amazon is now worth over three times as much, becoming the second company to achieve a $1 trillion market valuation in September 2018.

Amazon does have a worthy competitor in China and Asia: Alibaba. As Amazon expands its operations into Australasia and South Africa, expect to see a turf war between these two giants for the rights to own the digital retail marketplace. But one thing is certain; both Amazon and Alibaba's ability to disrupt and destroy other retailers' profitability is directly attributable to their innovation prowess and technical superiority. As the algorithms get smarter, Amazon's ability to know what you'll probably be interested in buying gets better, and their sales get higher. Recently, Amazon's focus moved from the B2C world (business to consumer) to the B2B world (business to business),

---

[83] 23h June 2018.

sending shudders through companies already operating in those markets. They are right to be scared. The lines between business and consumer have been blurred due to digital technologies. Notoriously inefficient areas such as procurement in the public sector have long been exploited by suppliers who charge high prices for average levels of service. Amazon knows this, and is targeting this area hard, offering procurement managers the same 'free shipping, next-day delivery and excellent customer service' experience they can get at home. Several corporate procurement departments have acted on this and established contracts with Amazon Business to complement their existing supply contracts, drawn to Amazon's customer service, ease of use, product range, total-spend management and agility benefits. It's obviously been beneficial, as these organisations migrated over 20 per cent of purchases to Amazon in the first year. With such obvious improvements, big government agencies are also shifting their corporate spending to Amazon. In January 2017, U.S. Communities, a buying cooperative for more than 55,000 US state and local public-sector agencies, initiated a deal with Amazon Business that is expected to run eleven years and be worth $5.5 billion in purchases. Then, in 2018, Amazon won a £600m public sector contract with the Yorkshire Purchasing Organisation in the UK to supply education, emergency services, local government and social care supplies across the region. They are unlikely to be the only public-sector buying groups to make the switch.

Jeff Bezos' biggest achievement has been his relentless ability to stick to his vision and not capitulate to the lure of short-term profit or analyst pressures. The ability to go decades without turning a profit but still convince shareholders to persevere with him and play the long game, while his competitors are beholden to analysts and their quarterly figures. To be able to ignore the armchair pundits and media commentators who declared Amazon could never turn sales into profit, and to never lose focus from the goal of creating 'the Everything Store'. This mindset was set out at the start. In his original 1997 letter to shareholders, Bezos wrote, *It's all about the long term. We believe that a fundamental measure of success will be the shareholder value over the long term*. Bezos has little respect for the modus operandi of traditional businesses. He knows full well that long-term market share is more important than short-term profits, because without long-term market share there will be no long-term profits. He also repeatedly reinforces this message, republishing his original 1997 letter every year with the new shareholder letter. His 1997 letter declared that the focus for the business is, and always will be, the customer; a message he constantly reiterates. In his 2013 shareholder letter he wrote that: *Our heavy investments in Prime, Kindle, digital media and customer experience in general strike some as too generous, shareholder indifferent or even at odds with being a for-profit company. But I don't think so... Proactively delighting customers earns trust, which earns more business from those customers, even in new business arenas.* And here lies Amazon's 'X' factor: Bezos has created a company wedded to its purpose, not its products. Great organisations are guided by an unchanging core purpose – one focused around the customer – while also developing a flywheel of continuous improvement and innovation. Doing what authors Jim Collins and Jerry Porras declared companies that are 'built to last' should do – protect their core values while also continuously stimulating progress. In contrasts, most other companies constantly strive to progress but their lack of a compelling purpose to centre it around, results in functional silos, limiting product and cost-focused mindsets and disengaged employees.

Keeping the customer at the heart of the model and focusing only on those things that drive the flywheel forward has become the 'unmoving principle' at the heart of Amazon. Bezos used to reinforce the point by bringing an empty chair to every meeting that represented the customer, so their views always had a seat at the table. He realised the ever-present danger of inside-out (and worse, inside-in) thinking. Bezos knows that by focusing on the customer and not the immediate bottom line, you develop a resilience to change because you become the company that creates it. At Amazon, a constant stream of new ideas is generated and tested which, if successful, are retained, but if not are quietly but quickly dropped. Conversely, companies that are product- rather than purpose-focused have an issue if their products become defunct or replaced by a competitor's (see Kodak and RIM). Their business model may be disrupted, so if they have been completely focused on one way of doing things then they are in trouble (see Blockbuster, Toys 'R' Us and Borders). Conversely, focusing on delighting customers means that you are constantly trying to understand their wants and needs and deliver them better than anyone else. By winning and delighting customers, shareholders will still benefit handsomely. However, the opposite is simply not true: if you focus on taking care of shareholders, customers don't benefit and, ironically, evidence shows that over time shareholders don't either. As Bezos himself declared in Amazon's 2013 shareholder letter, *if you're long-term oriented, customer interests and shareholder interests are aligned.* When asked about Amazon's revenue growth, Bezos couldn't even remember the exact growth percentage. When asked why he didn't know, he said, *I'm thinking a few years out. I've already forgotten those numbers.*

Amazon is a massive contributor to the 'retail apocalypse'. Their creation of a single, reliable, low cost marketplace is disrupting other retailer's attempts to claim their slice of the e-commerce pie, resulting in a decline in both their bricks-and-mortar stores and online efforts. They are also the ultimate margin killers, continually challenging other retailers to remain competitive in a game where they keep changing the rules, forcing them to reduce their prices, knowing that it will drive their margins into the ground. It's a game Amazon is clearly winning; in 2017 its US online sales were greater than those of every other US online retailer combined, delivering an average year-over-year growth rate of 38 per cent, 32 per cent higher than total retail market's combined average growth.[256] By the end of 2018, it is expected to capture half of all the US online sales.

It is a constant innovator, refusing to spend money on share buy-backs or offering dividends, instead choosing to invest billions in future growth. Bezos reiterated his continued commitment to a long-term, innovation-first strategy in his 2017 shareholder letter where he stated that Amazon would always be what he called 'a Day 1 company'. *Day 2 is stasis. Followed by irrelevance. Followed by excruciating, painful decline. Followed by death. And that is why it is always Day 1.* Bezos signed off the 2017 letter with the following: *As always, I attach a copy of our original 1997 letter. It remains Day 1.* Technological innovation involves complex relations among a set of key variables: inventions, innovations, diffusion paths and investment activities. Currently, Amazon is in control of all of these elements, being both responsible for the invention of new products, and able to determine their marketability and reach a wide enough audience to convert them into innovations. Amazon's Web Services platform, for example, is now a part of a globally interconnected business that, via its small home hubs, tablets and other devices, occupies prime space in the living rooms, offices and pockets of millions of people. It can then utilise these platforms to diffuse the innovations and plough money into their continued development without the short-term pressures that stifle other companies. Competitors are now facing a monopolistic giant, able to control the supply chain and use its massive R&D fund to create new technological innovations that delight the customers but eliminate humans and their errors from the equation. Once an industry is caught in Amazon's headlights, the older, slower businesses have a real fight on their hands simply to survive. For example, the combination of Amazon Prime, Amazon Fresh, Amazon Echo and Dash replenishment could equate to game over for many of its retail competitors. When you are competing to be the consumer's first click, and your main competitor gets to them before they even go online, then you've got an uphill struggle on your hands.

Bezos is exactly the type of entrepreneur that Joseph Schumpeter was referring to when he described them and their innovations as the architects of the process of creative destruction. He has created a culture where people are continually experimenting, constantly trying to find new ways to drive Amazon's virtuous cycle, then quickly go big when something makes economic sense. *Forbes* magazine named Bezos 'the ultimate disrupter', stating that *he has upended the book industry and displaced electronics merchants... Amazon is pushing into everything from couture retailing and feature film production to iPad-worthy tablet manufacturing. He's willing to take risks and lose money, yet investors have embraced him.* Love him or hate him, Bezos doesn't think small and as a result the Amazon machine shows no sign of slowing, with some analysts predicting that it will be worth $3 trillion by 2026.[257]

Some may disagree with Amazon's tactics, and many may challenge the company's aversion to paying tax, but it is hard to argue with the effectiveness of the strategy. One risk is that when the 'old men and old companies', as Schumpeter called them, have been run out of town, Amazon, now operating in a monopolistic position, may then exploit this situation and focus on increasing prices to reap the rewards of all this innovation. Time will tell, but the continuous production line of innovation coming out of Amazon indicates that it isn't letting up on trying to create new ways to capture the market any time soon, and its 'day-one, customer-first' mindset suggests that this won't be the case, at least while Bezos is still in charge. Amazon sees opportunities everywhere and is fighting hard to ensure that they own the interface between you and every one of your needs. Recent examples include the development the new 'Amazon Key' product that not only solves the problem of porch pirates stealing your goods, but also allows

Amazon to install a device that allows approved people into your home – such as cleaners. Which is why Amazon bought Ring, a company that makes doorbells with cameras that allow you to see and interact with visitors when you are out, and why it also now offers housekeeping and other domestic services. Amazon doesn't miss a beat, and now literally has the keys to their customer's door, and a means to track (and control) who comes and goes. Now Amazon can use this facility to provide a distinct competitive advantage over every other home service company out there. Soon you will be able to tell Alexa to order your groceries and book a cleaner, head off to work, and then come home to a tidy house and a fully stocked fridge. This combination of platforms provides Amazon the ability to offer a completely integrated experience to its customers – one which Amazon is completely in control of and which it makes money from every element. Amazon, like other innovators such as Tesla, are setting the rules for the sixth wave. Meanwhile, organisations still mired in the fifth-wave efficiency mindset of short-term profit maximisation and shareholder returns find themselves hopelessly outgunned and out-innovated when corporations like Amazon come to their town. Their focus is still on the next quarter, when Amazon's is on the next decade. In a battle between an entrepreneurial visionary founder and an old-school corporate leader, right now I'd put my money on the visionary. In my masterclasses I often deconstruct Amazon's strategy and discuss their customer-centric virtuous cycle, and the vicious circles of decline it creates for the unfortunate companies caught in its wake. When I travel to countries such as Australia and South Africa where Amazon is yet to ramp up operations, the fear in the eyes of the business leaders is clear. They have been too comfortable in their fifth-wave, efficiency-focused bubble, and they know that they don't have the skills, knowledge or appetite to play the game Amazon plays.

Cultivate the DNA of a Start-Up

To avoid becoming a notch on Amazon's bedpost, companies need to change their mindset from fifth-wave efficiency, to sixth-wave entrepreneurism. This must start at the top. Large publicly owned firms are simply not investing enough to secure their future, leaving them open to potential disruption by new entrants. Too many times lip service is given to innovation without any real change in culture or strategy. They talk a good talk, but like at Ryanair, old habits die hard. Consider my ABCD classification of disruptive technologies detailed in chapter seven: fifth-wave companies take their old-wave thinking and processes and overlay them with new-wave technology, rather than reimagining how to delight the customer by creating new value propositions and new business models based on this new art of the possible. Thus, they tend to implement 'A' and 'B' type innovations to *automate* what they already do or make a slightly *better* version of their existing product. In the second half of the fifth wave the technologies that were introduced – ERP, MES, SRM, CRM, APS and WM[84] systems, were designed to deliver efficiency improvements and productivity increases. Which is exactly what was being requested by shareholders at that point of the wave's cycle. These innovations were often introduced and implemented by the IT department, not the business, with the CEO and CFO often bystanders to the process, rather than the drivers of it. Companies that are still operating in this efficiency mindset look at sixth-wave technologies such as 3D printing as a potential mechanism to save money by reducing inventory: it enables them to produce prototypes of products quicker and print spare parts when needed, rather than having to purchase and store them in advance. Conversely, more forward-thinking organisations see 3D printing as an opportunity to revolutionise the whole design and manufacture process, to create new things in new ways. For example, a recent ARC/Automation World survey[258] found that manufacturing leaders highlighted the IIoT's ability to monitor and control existing operations as its most important aspect, enabling them to reduce downtime and asset wear. They also recognise that servitisation and business model innovation is the real prize up for grabs. They just don't know how to go about grabbing it.

The development of disruptive 'C' and 'D' innovations and new business models would require sign-off and involvement from those at the very top of the organisation, which is why in traditionally organised, top-down hierarchical model businesses they do not get tabled. It relies on visionary CEOs to become the orchestrators of change; people with an entrepreneurial mindset, not an efficiency one. Creativity is a strange beast because it is difficult to manage; and throughout the fifth wave we have taught people to

---

[84] ERP = Enterprise Resource Planning. MES = Manufacturing Execution Systems. CRM = Customer Relationship Management. SRM = Supplier Relationship Management. APS = Advanced Planning Systems. WM = Warehouse Management.

be managers not entrepreneurs. Risk avoiders not risk-takers. According to a senior contact in Amazon who I spoke to, one of their biggest challenges when it employs people who join from more traditional fifth-wave organisations is deprogramming them – stripping them of these limiting mindsets and their fear of taking risks and trying new things. To compete against Amazon, companies need to develop a culture like Amazon – one where the customer is at the centre of every decision, everyone has a voice worth listening to and management silos are eliminated to enable cross-departmental collaboration. However, many managers find it difficult even to relate to creativity because it does not fit into the corporate operating disciplines of decision-making, measurement and control. If technology brings a new way to do what we do but cheaper and more efficiently, they are all for it. If it fundamentally changes the very nature of the business, then not so much. And here lies the problem. Redesigning the corporation to evolve quickly rather than to operate well requires more than simple adjustments to the way things are done. Concepts such as operational excellence are inappropriate when the corporation needs to evolve at the speed and scale of the markets. A company cannot simply implement an innovation culture like a software update; it must be designed and implemented from the top.

While these older, larger companies are focused on their assets, capital and quarterly returns, the new, innovative upstarts led by entrepreneur-minded leaders who do not have the comfort blanket of a large asset portfolio are focused on growth. They are reviewing new ways to do things, focusing on disruptive innovations; those that create new business models, new value propositions, new ways of delivering value that disrupt industries. They are led by new people, who do not come to the table weighed down by the attachments and legacies of the past, be they ways of thinking, debts or responsibilities. This enables them to be flexible, innovative and risk-taking. Few fifth-wave people believed that it was possible to build a billion-dollar business by simply connecting people who want to go places with people willing to drive them there. They were wrong. The digital age is producing a new way of thinking; not just doing the same things but better, and figuring out how to use these new technologies to do completely different things and create completely new business models.

One such innovator is Kegan Fisher, the previous Founder and CEO of innovative 3D-printing company SOLS, and previously one of *Forbes*' Top 30 Under 30. In a 2017 interview I did with her, she described how her team constantly asked questions such as: *How do you treat physical product like software? How do you innovate in real time? How do you create real-time closed-loop feedback cycles which are particularly interesting to think about? Can we take data from my customer, plug it into an algorithm and use that to generate a new product? Then, after we've shipped that to the customer, can we understand how they're interacting with it, pull this data back into the algorithm and use that to continually improve on the physical product?* She declared that this mindset is *fascinating...but it's also challenging because you have no constants, you're continually on unstable ground.* Now compare this mindset to that of the traditional, industrial business leader focused on price competition and value engineering. It is people who think like Kegan Fisher that will drive the process of creative destruction in the sixth wave.

Traditional companies therefore need to develop digital DNA. They have the benefit of knowing their industrial regulations, markets and customers better, but their short-sightedness and blinkered thinking mean that they often only see today's challenges, not tomorrow's opportunities. Many approach new technologies as if they provide the 'why', when in fact they are only a 'how'. The 'why' comes from developing a customer-centric mindset; a unifying cultural element that drives all core decisions across all areas of the business. Leaders need to think deeply about what their customer values, what jobs they are trying to get done, and how they can deliver real value to them via the use of disruptive technologies. They need to understand the technologies of the sixth wave, then create the right business model to exploit these technologies to deliver the most value to their most important customers. They should ask questions such as:

- Can we digitise, servitise, premiumise or customise our value propositions?
- Can we reimagine the way we interact with our customers?
- Can we solve customers' long-term problems rather than just make a short-term product sale?
- Can we use sixth-wave technologies to personalise, automate or localise our business model?

Sixth-wave business leaders won't be able to achieve the speed and agility they need unless they can develop organisational cultures that operate seamlessly across functions and business units, see opportunities in challenges, embrace risk, and focus obsessively on customers. Their business needs to be able to adapt at the pace of the market, for as Jack Welch once declared, *once the rate of change outside the organisation is faster than the rate of change inside, the end is nigh.* If the consumer's expectations shift faster than your company's ability to satisfy them, then you are probably looking at a lot of ex-customers. This shift is happening quicker than many would like, caused by an overlap between a person's consumer experiences and their business ones. They now expect the B2C experience in a B2B environment. They want to know how Amazon knows exactly where your $5 item is and can deliver it within two hours but you can't tell them where their $5,000 item is and why it is late. Amazon doesn't own any secret technologies or special resources; their primary superpowers are imagination, ambition and a laser-like focus on the customer, plus the willingness to reinvest profits into R&D rather than pay shareholders – or the taxman. To survive the Amazons of this new wave, companies need to develop complex, adaptive, anticipatory systems focused around the customer, rather than predictable, linear, planning-based ones focused around the company. They need to move from silo-based sales, demand, production, inventory and procurement planning, to fully aligned and integrated, automatic, event-driven 'sense-and-respond' capabilities.

It is more important to prepare for disruption than to react after the event, for by the time an innovation gains enough traction for companies to recognise its impact and act, it is usually too late. If a company – or country – fall years or decades behind, it's hard to catch up no matter how agile they think they are. This is difficult for them to accept, because it means that everything they have learnt to date needs rethinking. Companies know where they want to go – they want to be more agile, quicker to react, and more effective. They want to deliver great customer experiences, take advantage of new technologies to cut costs, improve quality and transparency, and build value. The problem is that while most companies are trying to get better, the results tend to fall short, compromised by their culture. How many jobs have been lost not because of new technology, but due to old thinking? What if they had not been victim to change, but had instigated it? What would they have done differently? How would they have changed their business model? Redirecting time, money and effort away from what may appear to be a comfortable and profitable present is a tough decision for many business leaders to make. However, to quote Nietzsche in *Thus Spake Zarathustra*:

you must want to burn yourself up in your own flame: how could you wish to become new unless you first become ashes!

Entrepreneurs not Employees

Most large corporations have a relatively rigid organisational structure, with a functional vertical progression path and a salary that reflects your position in the pecking order. This clashes with the desires of millennials and Generation Z, who desire a clear and compelling purpose and a level of empowerment to supplement their pay packet – plus the possibility to get rich. Tapping into this desire is where start-ups often win, by providing high-calibre talent with an environment where an employee can feel more like an entrepreneur through a flat hierarchical structure and corporate progress-based incentivisation designed to attract the very best talent, while motivating them to become part of the company's long-term success and growth. Consider the 1994 job advert inviting Unix/C++ developers to join a well-capitalised Seattle-based start-up with *compensation that will include meaningful equity ownership*. The advertiser was Jeff Bezos, and the start-up was of course Amazon. Bezos finished the posting with a quote attributed to Alan Kay: *It's easier to invent the future than to predict it.*[259] If I had access to the time machine discussed at the start of this book, I would be tempted to travel back to 1993 and learn Unix and C++ so I could apply. Those shares are currently trading at over $2,000 each.[85]

The future is less about management and the ability to recall information or taught skills, and more about the ability to use critical thinking, problem-solving, collaboration and adaptability. Diversification of skill sets will be important moving forwards, and the skills that young people will need are going to be very different to those that people currently have in their CVs. While traditional companies are still recruiting for industrial age skills, the digital disruptors are busily scooping up the talent needed to build the future. Expertise in new, AI focused skills such as machine-learning and statistical data analysis are becoming highly sought after. Google's chief executive, Sundar Pichai, has regularly declared that the company focus is 'AI first', and that machine learning,

---

[85] Share price when Amazon reached a $1 trillion valuation on 4th September 2018.

not traditional computer programming, is the skill set of the future. The market for building greater levels of machine intelligence is huge, as is the wealth that will be created because of it. Accenture predicts that a full corporate commitment to AI could boost global profits by \$4.8 trillion in the next four years, meaning that for the average S&P 500 company, this could create an additional \$7.5 billion in revenue by 2022.[260] Desire to be first to gain competitive advantage from AI has created an arms race to acquire the best talent in this field. Organisations such as Google, Facebook, Apple, Amazon, Microsoft and the Chinese firm Baidu are offering leading AI professors five times their salary to leave the university campus. They are also offering the very best graduates seven-figure starting salaries, flexibility, freedom and almost unlimited resources; something a traditional organisation wouldn't dream of doing due to its rigid hierarchical structures and pay grades. For example, Facebook CEO Mark Zuckerberg personally oversees his company's propositions to the most desirable graduate students, making sure that they acquire the best at whatever cost. Consequently, these new tech companies have become infinitely more attractive to new talent than the old incumbent fifth-wave organisations. Rather than focusing on maximising profits for shareholders, these start-ups declare that they want to change the world – and have fun doing it. It's not a difficult decision for ambitious talent to make. The executive suite might love shareholder value for the impact it has on their lifestyle and pay packet, but it does little to motivate or excite its current and future talent pool. These people are drawn towards the exciting brands, especially tech companies, ones that they believe will stimulate them, challenge them and help to change the world. Tesla, Apple, Alphabet – even Uber, with its recent bad press – all have a long queue of talent wanting to join them.

Certain fifth-wave companies are waking up to the challenge of addressing this. Those who cannot simply throw money at new talent are sending some of their existing employees on placements within smaller start-up companies to learn the art of innovative thinking. Some have realised that their executives don't really understand this new world and its inhabitants, and have recruited millennials to 'reverse-mentor' them on the technology and temperament of the new wave's consumer base. Companies such as Johnson & Johnson are fighting back by appealing to the millennial's purpose-driven mindset. They highlight that while tech giants like Google or

Facebook may pay you well, you'll likely be working on algorithms designed to put adverts in the faces of consumers, whereas at Johnson & Johnson you'll be working on providing better healthcare solutions.

Becoming Bimodal: Balancing Creativity and Control

There's an important lesson in all of this. The realisation that the organisational culture needed to drive efficiency and short-term profitability – the behaviour of the downswing – is different to the culture needed to invent, experiment and innovate – the behaviour of the upswing. Success has always been dependent on being able to deliver value, only in the upswing you need to do it not just to thrive, but simply to survive. Here lies a deeply important lesson for businesses. Those companies that will not just survive the turbulence of the transition period, but thrive throughout it, are those that learn to excel in simultaneously managing their existing business, while inventing new ones. Those who are able to successfully straddle the competing 'yin and yang' forces of order and chaos. If all you are is order – rules and procedures – then you will fall further and further behind more innovative competitors, whereas if you live solely in chaos, then nothing makes sense. While you might get off to a flying start, it won't last because you have no control. Straddling these positions sounds like an impossible dream, but it's not. Individuals can do both – and given that an organisation is nothing more than a group of individuals who for a period of time each day share a collective goal, there's no reason why they can't either. It is, as Jim Collins once wrote, simply a matter of conscious choice and disciplined execution. Choosing to protect the core values that you stand for, while constantly executing programs designed to innovate and improve the ways you deliver that value. It's not about simply letting go of the reins and embracing chaos; of saying to the team, 'We are all leaders now – go off and build the future.' The goals need to be simplified and clear, the teams need to be aligned, and attention focused so that all this activity turns into outcomes that people actually want to buy. That's the role of the leader during this turbulent time. Steve Jobs once scrawled a message to his initial Apple team on a chalkboard that read, *Real artists ship*. The intent was clear – innovation has no value unless we can effectively put it in the hands of the customer.

This 'bimodal' challenge of releasing an organisation's latent creative ability and create radical, entrepreneurial new products and services, while also retaining control of the rest of the business, is something nearly every business leader I speak to is struggling with. Many companies have also accepted that they need to separate their innovation hubs from the day-to-day business. Nestlé have implemented *Shark Tank*[86]-style experiments, called the InGenius Lab, where employees can present their case to executives for funding as an invention or innovation, and GE Appliances launched a GE-equipped innovation lab and micro-factory called FirstBuild, designed as a separate enterprise operating under its own brand where it can operate without the baggage of GE's existing corporate culture. Nestlé's innovation centre recently announced that it had found a way to reduce the sugar in its products by 40 per cent without losing any of their sweetness. It's amazing what can be achieved when you need to.

The problem for many organisations is that while they are still able to profitably sell their existing portfolio, it is difficult to motivate them to redirect effort to risky endeavours that are new and unproven. Which causes a problem, because when you get to the position where change is a necessity and not a choice, then it's probably already too late. Those who innovate when they don't need to are the ones who win, because they are the ones setting the rules of the game and the size of the pitch. Amazon is currently in this position. Its strategy has been to use the revenue from existing sales and the billions in upfront cash flow it gets from Prime membership subscriptions to fund its relentless R&D programme, developing innovations designed to drive its virtuous cycle. In doing so it creates a vicious circle of margin erosion in its competition, driving them into the ground where they play (and pray) for survival rather than to win. Amazon apparently experiences a growth surge when online sales hit a tipping point of 20 per cent in a given retail sector, indicating that Amazon is about to displace a legacy retailer. Cooper Smith, L2's Director of Amazon Research, states that: *Twenty percent is when Amazon steps on the gas... when consumer behavior is changing.*[261]

To paraphrase the investor Howard Marks, you may not be able to predict, but you can prepare. It's not simply about pulling down hierarchies

---

[86] *Shark Tank* is a US version of the UK's *Dragons' Den* TV show, which itself is a version of Japan's *Money Tigers*.

and relinquishing control; it's about providing guidance and vision while simplifying structures and removing often self-imposed barriers, unleashing the company's latent creative capabilities so it can thrive in the chaos. The objective should not be to just make things faster, better or cheaper by adding new technology to them, but rather to understand the potential the new technologies provide to rethink the whole business model. The former approach was what Blockbuster tried. The latter was what Netflix did. A good way to frame the question is for companies to ask themselves, *If we had to rebuild our company today, knowing how people use technology, how they now behave, what they value and what is technically possible – would it resemble the one we currently work in?* If not, then the challenge is to change your business model, leadership style, mindset and modus operandi so it does, before a new competitor arrives that looks just like that and takes away your business.

Disruption Should be an Outcome, Not a Strategy

It is important not to be fooled into believing that these new digital, sixth-wave companies are by default more ethical than their industrial predecessors. Despite the headlines and grandiose declarations of virtue, Wall Street values still run Silicon Valley. It is therefore no surprise that comparisons are being made between the hyper-competitive culture in the banking sector that led to the financial crisis, and the culture of the tech companies. There is casino betting going on at the moment, and any company that is working in a designated 'hot' area – such as AI or blockchain – is attracting big interest and big money. Many of these new wave entrepreneurs are not trying to change the world, but simply grow fast and sell big. There is also a new and somewhat disturbing element to their objectives; something that didn't exist in previous waves. For the first time the focus of many of these new companies is to purposefully destroy jobs, not create them. The disruptors of Silicon Valley are deliberately looking at industries where lots of people are involved and thinking hard about how they can use digital technologies and machines to simplify or automate these activities. This has created both anger and concern amongst the people who rely on these jobs to live, explaining why there are increasingly polarised political stances between the hip, urban locations where these tech centres are based, such as Silicon Valley, Seattle and London, and the industrial and rural areas which feel the brunt of their labour-replacing efforts.

The tech innovators, locked away in their bubble, talk often about 'changing the world' but for many the changes are not always favourable. In previous waves the primary driver was to create, not destroy. Destruction was the side effect, not the intent. Every entrepreneur tries to find a match between some under-solved problem and their innovation. Destruction came about when the customer decided that the new innovation offered more value to them than the old way of doing things, and businesses wedded to that old model who could not adapt were left behind. Not in this wave. For them disruption *is* the strategy, which is why the new entrepreneurs flock to conferences and events with titles like *DISRUPT*. Their mindset is completely different. Operating with an almost evangelical zeal, new start-ups and their founders look for opportunities to use new technologies to disrupt industries and displace incumbent companies that are tied to their existing asset base and business model. The trouble is that disruption wipes out not just the primary business but can affect its entire value chain, disrupting the employment of thousands of people who are often skilled or experienced only in that field. Consider digital photography. How many different companies were wiped out by the transition? Companies that made film cameras, made the film, processed the film, made the chemicals for film-processing, made photo-processing machinery, made the film containers, made the envelopes we used to send the film in, the chemists in white coats who developed the films, the photo-album manufacturers, etc. All were disrupted, and most were destroyed.

While disruption has become the mantra, the real underlying objective behind Silicon Valley has remained the same: get rich quick. The driver beyond these tech companies is not some altruistic belief system but rather the attraction of building a company specifically to attract the investment of wealthy backers, grow rapidly over a couple of years, then sell for millions, enabling them to retire young. These technocrats are not the 21st-century version of the Quakers, despite what they'd have you believe, and the outcome of their activities will ask difficult questions of a world that increasingly values machine labour and intelligence over human.

SIXTH-WAVE SCIENCE AND TECHNOLOGY

15

SCIENCE FICTION
BECOMES SCIENCE FACT

*We are moving so fast that when plans are being made
to perform some great feat, these plans are broken into
by a youth who enters and says, "I have done it."*

Elbert Hubbard, 1913

While Europe and Japan rebuilt their shattered cities and societies, the post-war period saw the US experience two decades of constant prosperity, a modern Belle Époque. During this fourth-wave golden age and the prosperity it provided, Americans viewed the future with confidence and optimism. In August 1964, Isaac Asimov, the respected science-fiction writer, wrote an article for the *New York Times* describing his visit to the New York World Fair, as well as a detailed description of what he imagined the fair of 2014 would be like. Asimov was influenced by the positivity and prosperity of the time, so his fifty-year predictions for America were optimistic. Machines were going to enable a four day working week, thirteen weeks of vacation and a life where leisure, not work, would occupy most of our time. Predictions based on extrapolations of existing trends proved to be quite accurate: for example, he believed that the future would bring technologies that allowed you to see the people you called on the telephone (e.g. Skype), the ability to read documents on a screen (PCs), wall-mounted TVs, and the introduction of robots that would still be 'clumsy and slow-moving'. Asimov's predictions were somewhat less accurate when it came to completely new technologies. His article described a 2014 where mankind has already developed moon bases (remember, this was five years before Apollo 11 landed on the moon), flew around in vehicles that hovered over roads that blew compressed air (a bit like a giant air-hockey board), underwater and underground housing, working nuclear-fusion plants, moving sidewalks that rise above the traffic, road-building factories in the tropics, compressed air tubes that transport goods over local areas, and processed yeast and algae products to compensate for a global food shortage. He also failed to predict the Internet. Once again, another futurist was caught out by the S-curve nature of innovation, that makes expansions of observable things seem likely, but completely new inventions less so. In the 1960s people could easily imagine flying cars because they combined two existing technologies – planes and cars. However, *The Jetsons*, the popular futuristic cartoon that aired from 1962–1963, still had George Jetson personally piloting their flying car. This is because someone from the 1960s had never seen anything drive autonomously and would struggle to understand how it would know where to go and how it would be able to avoid flying into other vehicles? Things like GPS systems, location triangulation and LiDAR[87] hadn't been invented then, so extrapolating them forwards and imagining the potential when they converged would have been impossible. In another example, the 1982 classic sci-fi movie *Blade Runner,* a dystopian portrayal of Los Angeles in 2019 is presented where synthetic humans (replicants) exist, other planets have been colonised and people travel in flying cars. But this fictional future also still contained cathode-ray televisions and set-top aerials and lacked concepts such as the Internet or smartphones, meaning it was easier to imagine androids walking around than flat-screen TVs and magic rectangles in our pockets.

This inability to accurately predict the future is not a new phenomenon and is part and parcel of every major wave. Even back in 1880 there was the recognition that the speed of scientific development was radically changing people's perceptions of what was possible, transforming previously declared certainties into absurdities, and vice versa. During the second period of

---

[87] LiDAR – Light Detection And Ranging

industrialisation from the mid 19th century, new manufacturing processes, new means of power, new modes of transport, new understanding of science, new methods of communication and even new types of work (most notably following the publication of Fredrick Winslow Taylor's *The Practice of Scientific Management*) changed the very nature of society. New discoveries in science and technology created new possibilities and made the improbable, possible. An example lies in the story of what is now an abundant, cheap and disposable metal – aluminium. Prior to the creation of commercial electrical generation and the development of the Hall-Héroult electrolytic process in the 1880s, aluminium was exceedingly difficult to extract from its various ores, and as a result was more valuable than gold. Bars of aluminium were exhibited alongside the French crown jewels at the Exposition Universelle of 1855, and it is reputed that Napoleon III of France threw a banquet where the most honoured guests were given aluminium dinner plates and utensils, while the others simply had to make do with gold. The case study of aluminium was something that Joseph Schumpeter cited in his work, naming the Aluminum Company of America as an example of a monopoly that continuously innovated to retain its position. By 1929, he noted, the price of its product, adjusted for inflation, had fallen to only 8.8 per cent of its level in 1890, while its output had risen from thirty metric tons to 103,400. Now aluminium is so cheap and bountiful we use it as disposable foil to wrap food in.[88]

Deceptive, then Disruptive

The sixth wave's upswing will – like those of previous waves – create a great leap forward in our scientific and technological capabilities. It will see humanity achieve things that are currently difficult – even impossible – and enable us to make scarce resources abundant. From the solar system to the atom, the DNA genome to Higgs boson particles, we are still expanding our understanding of how things work. As a result, statements of certainty will once again be proven to be false, and what is now science fiction will become science fact. However, it is the *application* of this scientific knowledge – either through explorations into the largest expanses of the universe or the

---

[88] Or to make hats that stop your brainwaves being scanned by aliens, the FBI or the Illuminati.

ability to control the microscopic world through nanotechnology or DNA manipulation – that will make a difference. For example, graphene has been described as a wonder metal, but its use so far has been limited to things like tennis rackets. Yet the potential remains for graphene to become the aluminium of the 21st century, enabling whole new manufacturing realities similar to how aluminium and aluminium-alloys made it possible to make aeroplanes by the thousands, opening up the world to those who could afford to travel.

Visible signs of progress are sometimes not easy to see, and when that occurs it is easy to become complacent. In the earlier revolutions, technological change was more physical and thus more visible. You could watch as factories appeared, skyscrapers rose, cars replaced horses and planes flew overhead. Now much of the sixth wave is driven by code, either computer program or genetic, both of which are invisible to the naked eye, making technological advancement sometimes difficult to spot. A smarter smartphone is still a smartphone, hence why an iPhone 8 doesn't look that different to an iPhone 4, yet internally, its capabilities and the code that drives it have improved significantly. Cars still look like cars, but their computerised internal capabilities mean that new versions are likely to involve more software changes than hardware ones. When you press your foot down on your car's accelerator, there's no longer a direct mechanical link from the pedal to the throttle, but instead the pressure from your foot issues a command to the software that then decides how much air to give the engine. This means that the car has effectively become a computer you sit inside, and the steering wheel and pedals are now basically keys on a keyboard. Modern car manufacturers are now as much in the software business as they are in the automobile manufacture business, which is why companies like Tesla, Apple and Google can suddenly appear as competitors in an industry where only twenty years ago the barriers to entry would have been too high. It is often stated that if Moore's Law had been applied to the capabilities of cars rather than computer chips, then the modern descendant of the 1971 Volkswagen Beetle would travel at 300,000 miles per hour, cost four cents and use one tank of gasoline in a lifetime. The reality is that Moore's Law *is* being applied to cars – only not just to travel faster but to map, plan and control every aspect of the journey and entertain us along the way. The lack of physical manifestation of the future is a frustration for many. As venture capitalist and PayPal founder Peter Thiel famously commented, *We wanted flying cars, instead we got 140 characters.*[89]

Not all changes in this wave will be invisible, code-level innovations however. As we investigated in Part One, each wave, each new revolution, contains new power sources, new transportation methods and new communication capabilities, and as a result creates new industries. The sixth wave is no different. We are going to move from combustion engines to electric, from coal-fired power plants to renewables. We will create new modes of transportation, and digital will continue to make communication seamless – not just between humans, but between machines. As Schumpeter and Perez highlighted, when a revolutionary new technology reaches a certain breakthrough point and investment starts to flow, other competitors enter the fray and the rate of innovation starts to accelerate as they cluster together. Kurzweil's law of accelerating returns then kicks in and progress explodes, causing a fundamental paradigm shift that changes our belief about what is possible. As described in Part Two, a series of interconnected technologies is being developed that will lead to a complete reimagining of the extended supply chain; moving from one based on human labour and human intelligence, to one based on the capabilities and cognitive power of machines. Most of these new innovations are still in the disruptive stage – we hear constantly about autonomous vehicles, drones, robots, the blockchain and AI, but we do not see many instances in the real world. By 2020 that will change.

Money is now starting to flow towards many of the foundational technologies of the new wave – and in vast quantities. In 2017, forty-four companies pumped over $1 billion into self-driving and other trucking technologies, a tenfold increase from 2014.[262] When this investment starts to have an impact on results, and the foundational infrastructure needed to industrialise and operationalise them becomes available, then multiple 'S-curves' will all shoot upwards, and these radical technological changes will start becoming part of our world. Renewable energy such as solar continues to grow at the expense of fossil fuels, and as our ability to capture and store more of the free energy that bombards the planet every day continues to improve, its price will continue to plummet. New enhancements in biotech and nanotechnology have the potential to dramatically increase our

---

[89] A reference to the length of a tweet on Twitter at that time.

lifespan while also eliminating diseases and slowing down the degradation of our biological systems. Research into these areas is being supported by advancements in AI and cognitive computing that can process vast quantities of information, helping to identify new ways to treat age-related diseases such as Alzheimer's. Together, these technologies will change society in unexpected ways.

One of the pivotal elements of every wave is transportation, which now includes the movement of digital goods as well as physical. Digital goods are disrupting the market by allowing for the immediate distribution and download of electronic products such as software and media. The transportation of physical goods is being disrupted through the emergence of autonomous ships, trains, trucks, canal boats and planes. Initially, these new autonomous vehicles will look very much like their existing, human-centric counterparts, with the main difference being the absence of a driver. Autonomous vehicles will have 360-degree vision, the ability to respond in seconds, and the ability to communicate with other machine-controlled vehicles and devices such as traffic lights, letting them sense and respond to situations that will be predictable and logical. Humans on the other hand, are unpredictable and easily distracted. Any machine-human automobile incidents that occur are likely to be down to human stupidity rather than artificial intelligence, as proven by the few early incidents that have occurred during testing. The transition period will prove to be the most problematic, when machines are still adapting to situations outside their test scenarios, usually caused by humans doing completely unexpected things, and humans have to adapt to machines behaving in non-human ways.

There are, however, more radical transportation innovations afoot such as the Hyperloop. Based on an idea touted by Elon Musk back in 2012, the Hyperloop is a new form of transportation that uses a sealed tube through which a pod can travel free of any air resistance or friction, enabling it to reach speeds of up to 760mph, over twice that of today's fastest bullet train. When up and running it is expected that the Hyperloop will be five to six times faster than high-speed rail because every journey is non-stop, and departures are continuous. Hyperloop is also capable of transporting passengers, freight and cars simultaneously. This should enable people to commute to city-based work locations from further afield in a fraction of the time it takes now, taking the pressure off urban areas and rebalancing property values. Hyperloop trials are, at the time of writing, currently being undertaken in Nevada by a company now called Virgin Hyperloop One, after receiving significant financial backing from entrepreneur Richard Branson and his Virgin Group conglomerate. Initial plans for the Hyperloop include the creation of a tube between Los Angeles and the San Francisco Bay Area, cutting the travelling time between the cities to just thirty minutes. The concept and potential of using vacuum-sealed tubes to transport people and goods between locations has caught the imagination of many countries, not just the US. Dubai is currently working on the creation of an Hyperloop link between itself and Abu Dhabi, slashing the time taken to make the ninety-mile journey down to just twelve minutes, and Branson states that he wants this operational within three years. This could then be expanded later to link the UAE with neighbouring Gulf countries so that a trip between Dubai and the Saudi capital Riyadh – currently a two-hour trip by plane – could be completed in under fifty minutes. Finally, Australia, a huge continent where the population mostly lives in urban pockets along one 'hyper' coastal loop, is planning to utilise this new technology to connect its two major business centres of Sydney and Melbourne, reducing what is currently a one-hour flight plus all the associated security checks and boarding procedures, down to a simple fifty-three-minute journey.

But what happened to flying cars, the definition of 'the future' since the 1960s? Answer: they're here, awaiting commercialisation and legislation. The dream of flying cars has finally become a reality due to a convergence of new technologies. Advanced software and processors and low-cost accelerometers and gyroscopes have enabled developers to better stabilise a hovering vehicle. Advanced lithium-ion batteries create a safe way to power them, and electric motors are becoming much more efficient. Plus, progress in lightweight materials means that they become cheaper and easier to fly – as well as limiting the damage the vehicle could cause if it crashes, regardless of whether this is by accident or on purpose. Examples include the Eastern European AeroMobil 4.0, which is due to be shipped to customers in 2020. In car mode it can drive on normal roads at speeds of up to about 100mph (160kph), and can convert to plane mode in under three minutes. In the air, it can fly about 465 miles (750 kilometres) before returning to earth and converting back to car mode. Vertical take-off and landing (VTOL) vehicles take a slightly different approach, and several companies are competing to get their VTOL model to market. Companies such as Ehang, Volocopter, Lilium and

341

Zee.Aero (headed by Google's co-founder Larry Page and allegedly funded by $100 million of this own money) all have prototypes at various stages of development. The Lilium Jet is touted as the world's first all-electric VTOL jet; an air taxi for up to five people that travels five times faster than a car at three hundred kilometres per hour. These are not for consumers to own, but rather to pay per ride and summon via your phone. Lilium state that their mission is to *make air taxis available to everyone and as affordable as riding a car,* and they completed a maiden flight with a full-scale prototype in April 2017. Dubai has made clear its intentions to be the first city to offer a flying taxi service by 2020 and has been a prime location for testing. The Chinese company Ehang's fully autonomous passenger drone called the 184 (standing for one person plus eight propellers attached to four arms) undertook test flights in Dubai, as did the Daimler-backed, two-seater, eighteen-rotor VTOL passenger drone called the Volocopter. Volocopter's five-minute flight had the Dubai crown prince, Sheikh Hamdan bin Mohammed, as a passenger – so they must have been confident of success. One company that sees VTOL as a future way to move people is Uber, who envision a world where people will plan longer journeys that Uber will provide via a combination of autonomous UberX cars to drive you to a skyport, then an autonomous[90] UberAIR VTOL vehicle will fly you from the skyport to your destination, and then another UberX car will finish the journey, saving the passenger hours. If you imagine how long it takes to travel across most major cities, and the lost productivity this causes, you can quickly see how this will find a market. Uber has announced that it will be receiving logistical support from NASA, and they expect UberAIR to be an operational service by 2020, starting in Dallas, Los Angeles and – surprise, surprise – Dubai.[263]

The issue of infrastructure is an interesting one when we discuss new forms of transportation, notably the question as to whether existing infrastructure is a blessing or a curse. When you consider innovations that use existing infrastructure such as roads, then the lack of availability could be a real issue. Robots need rules, so imagine autonomous vehicles trying to navigate the dirt tracks that masquerade as roads in some of the sub-Saharan African nations, or through the chaotic roads of Karachi or Cairo where people drive with their hand permanently on the horn, and mopeds

---

[90] Initially this will be piloted, but the long-term plan is for the VTOL to be autonomous.

carrying numerous passengers weave dangerously in and out of traffic. [91] However, when it comes to completely new innovations, then a lack of existing infrastructure could be a blessing, allowing countries to leapfrog their more advanced competitors. Good examples of this include Kenya, which has become the leader in mobile banking, completely circumventing the formal banking systems that 80 per cent of Kenyans were excluded from. The system they use is called M-Pesa,[92] and it allows users to deposit, withdraw and transfer money, and pay for goods and services with a mobile device using secure text messages. The population didn't have to go through a major transitionary period from a traditional banking service to a new one, for they did not have bank accounts nor use the normal banking process in the first place. As a result, the rate of adoption of mobile banking was much higher and diffusion much faster than it would have been in any Western country. Another issue is the vested interest companies (and individuals) have in the existing infrastructure and the companies that support them and whose profitability relies on them. Take the Hyperloop. Whereas Dubai and Australia, both relatively new nations, are keen to pursue this technology, in the UK, the home of the first industrial revolution, there is a strong attachment to the innovation of the 19th century – rail. Rather than review new concepts like the Hyperloop, the UK government is pressing ahead with its High Speed 2 project (HS2) designed to link the major cities of London, Birmingham, Leeds and Manchester, a project that has been in discussion since 2003 and which has seen its planned budget rise from £32.7 billion to £56 billion without a mile of track being laid, and its major contractor (Carillion) going bust. I can't help but feel that when (if) HS2 is finally completed in 2033, the celebrations will be somewhat marred by the fact that while the UK is rejoicing over its slightly faster trains, the rest of the developed world will have been zipping around in Hyperloop systems or flying taxis for at least a decade.

---

[91] I'd be impressed to see robots figure out the rules in certain European nations as well. Ever tried to traverse the Arc de Triomphe in Paris?

[92] Launched in 2007 by Vodafone for Safaricom and Vodacom, the largest mobile network operators in Kenya and Tanzania.

Superior Ability Breeds Superior Ambitions

One force man has long hankered to understand and control is our bodies and how they work, reproduce and age. In the late 19th century, Charles Darwin published his theories on evolution, and in doing so created a firestorm of controversy. His work directly contradicted the Book of Genesis, and as a result divided people into two camps which exist even today: creationists and evolutionists. The Victorian era was a time of significant progress, of scientific and technological advancement, and worryingly, Darwin's theory of non-directional evolution proposed that progress was not necessarily an outcome for mankind, as it did not guarantee that people would become better or smarter, but instead might just become 'different'. Which created a dilemma. The high reproduction rates of the uneducated poor, combined with improvements in living conditions and healthcare throughout the latter half of the 19th century, meant that more of their children were surviving to adulthood. This meant that their offspring would flood the genetic pool, diluting it with undesirable traits that could dictate the evolutionary path of mankind, resulting in a downward spiral for humanity.[93] This quite simply was not a risk that could be left to natural forces, and therefore had to be solved through scientific application.

The secularisation of science had allowed mankind to exhibit its creativity and innovation, but also its hubris. Now that we *understood* human evolution, surely, we could *control* it in order to breed a better version of ourselves, eliminating unwanted traits and strengthening desirable ones? In the 1880s, Darwin's cousin, Francis Galton, proposed an interpretation of Darwin's theory, one that would save society from the blight of 'inferior' minds that might hold progress back. Galton felt that we could, and should, alter our evolutionary journey using new processes that would provide a more humane and desirable alternative to natural selection. He called his new branch of scientific practice 'eugenics'. Both Galton and Darwin were influenced by the work of Thomas Malthus and his ideas around the problem of population growth and scarce resources. However, they each saw the problem from a very different perspective: Darwin thought that evolution was a process not of mankind's control, writing of man and nature as they *were*, whereas Galton thought it was most definitely controllable,

---

[93] A concept explored in the 2006 film *Idiocracy*.

writing about man and nature as they *could be*.[94] Galton and his eugenics supporters believed they could transition mankind to something better; to control our evolution through deliberate rather than natural selection. This idea of selective breeding to produce better quality human beings was not new, existing at least since Plato suggested this method as a way to produce a guardian (ruling) class. Now people believed it was possible to achieve. Galton's proposals had a creative/destructive aspect to them. The creative side involved encouraging people of the right biological stock to marry each other, have more children and live a fitter life, and as such involved environmental reforms, better education, public health and infertility treatment. The destructive side, unfortunately, required the removal of unwanted traits, involving both the prevention of life and the ending of it, and thus cruelly involved a combination of sterilisation, contraception, segregation and euthanasia.

Eugenics garnered significant support during the last years of the 19th century, but it was Julian and Aldous Huxley, the grandsons of T. H. Huxley, Darwin's 'bulldog',[95] who would prove influential in the eugenics movement and its role in society in the 20th century. Aldous Huxley (1894–1963) became the more famous of the two, due to his book *Brave New World*. Published in 1932, *Brave New World* is a response to the utopian, socialist writings of H. G. Wells and George Bernard Shaw, most of which were written before the horrors of World War I. In his book, Huxley describes a 'negative utopian' future where the so-called World State controls not only their citizens' biology, but also their behaviour and thoughts. This is a future where state control and eugenics are taken to an extreme; where cloned embryos are produced in factories, replacing traditional sexual reproduction for the lower, worker castes, but not the higher castes, which can still breed and produce children naturally. Thus, Huxley imagines a future where humanity is split into two classes.[96] Cloned children are raised by the state and are given psychological conditioning to develop their 'core values', and 'soma' a pleasure-inducing drug that keeps everyone happy. Huxley's core

---

[94] Source: Philippa Levine and Alison Bashford, *The Oxford Handbook of the History of Eugenics*.

[95] Due to his fierce support of Darwin's theory of evolution.

[96] H. G. Wells also predicted a future of two classes in *The Time Machine*; the leisured classes have become the ineffectual Eloi, and the working classes have evolved into the brutish, light-fearing Morlocks. The Morlocks have the last laugh, though; turning the leisured classes into food.

message is that even if it becomes possible to manipulate human biology and thought so that people are mindlessly happy in their servitude-based lives, it may not necessarily lead to fulfilment. Aldous' brother, Julian Huxley (1887–1975), decided that rather than just writing fictional stories about eugenics, he would actively promote it, firmly believing that taking control of evolution would be a positive step for humanity. He compared the practice of improving the human gene pool to the practice of agriculture. *No one doubts the wisdom of managing the germ-plasm*[97] *of agricultural stocks, so why not apply the same concept to human stocks?*

Eugenics reached its peak in Britain in the 1930s, with eminent support from people like John Maynard Keynes, who served on the governing council of the Eugenics Society and was its director from 1937 to 1944. Even in 1946, Keynes was calling eugenics 'the most important and significant branch of sociology'. Labour MPs such as Archibald Church raised bills in Parliament to pass legislation to ensure the 'voluntary' sterilisation of disabled people and the compulsory sterilisation of certain categories of 'mental patient' so as to stop the reproduction of those *who are in every way a burden to their parents, a misery to themselves and in my opinion a menace to the social life of the community.*[264] This mindset spread to the US. The American eugenics proponents saw the country filling up with 'problem populations' of poor rural whites, Southern European immigrants and African Americans, who they decided should be selected for 'treatment', such as forced sterilisation. Alexis Carrel, the Nobel Prize-winning French surgeon and biologist who worked at the prestigious Rockefeller Institute, advocated correcting what he called 'an error' in the US Constitution that granted equality to all people. In 1935, he published a bestselling book called *Man, the Unknown*, in which he wrote, *The feeble-minded and the man of genius should not be equal before the law. The stupid, the unintelligent, those who are dispersed, incapable of attention, of effort, have no right to a higher education.* He argued that the human race was being undermined by disabled people, and he wanted to use medical advances to extend the lives of those he deemed worthy, while condemning the rest to death or forced sterilisation. His book sold more than two million copies and his talks would often be sold out, attracting thousands of people in America. US eugenics supporters included Victoria Woodhull, the suffragist, progressive activist and first woman to run

---

[97] The term used at that time for what became known as DNA.

for President; the inventor Alexander Graham Bell (who later moved away from the movement); professors at leading universities, including Harvard, Yale, Stanford and Johns Hopkins; and editorialists of the *New York Times*. Funding in the US for eugenics research came from such distinguished sources as the Carnegie Institution, the W. K. Kellogg Foundation, and the Rockefellers, as well as from other influential leaders of the oil, steel and railroad industries. Even the White House was intent on restricting the right of disabled people to reproduce. President Theodore Roosevelt created a National Heredity Commission to investigate America's genetic heritage and to encourage *the increase of families of good blood and (discourage) the vicious elements in the cross-bred American civilisation.*[265] In 1934, J. H. Kempton published an article in the *Journal of Heredity* called *Sterilization for Ten Million Americans*,[266] where he called for the government to introduce a mass programme of sterilisation of 'undesirable' American citizens. While 10 million people were not neutered, the practice of forced sterilisation of the alleged mentally ill did continue into the 1970s, by which time about 60,000 Americans had been involuntarily sterilised.

Eugenics did not have universal acceptance, and there were those who were alarmed by concepts such as breeding the poor out of the genetic pool. The famous British writer and philosopher G. K. Chesterton was a vocal critic of the practice, believing it inhuman and foolish. In 1922 he wrote, *as if one had a right to dragoon and enslave one's fellow citizens as a kind of chemical experiment... The poor are not a race or even a type. It is senseless to talk about breeding them; for they are not a breed. They are, in cold fact, what Dickens describes: 'a dustbin of individual accidents,' of damaged dignity, and often of damaged gentility.*[267] What really turned the tide of opinion against eugenics was the Nazis' advocacy of the practice. Adolf Hitler was inspired by the endeavours of the United States, and incorporated eugenic ideas into *Mein Kampf*, most notably the sterilisation of 'defectives' and the creation of a nation of *Übermensch,* a master race *of* 'overmen' inspired by the ideas in Friedrich Nietzsche 1883 novel, *Thus Spoke Zarathustra*. While most people associate eugenics with Hitler's Final Solution and the attempt to eradicate the Jews from the genetic pool, it was actually the German population that was the intended target. The Third Reich, like the English and Americans, focused their attention on the improvement of the German biological stock, with the prime targets for sterilisation or removal being the disabled, mentally ill or 'feeble-minded'

Germans, rather than foreigners. Eugenics gave the Nazis a pseudoscientific philosophy to justify their xenophobic search for a pure race. As Adolf Hitler said himself, *anyone who interprets National Socialism merely as a political party knows almost nothing about it. It is more than religion. It is the determination to create a new man.* This is a direct reference to Nietzsche and his ideas that the development of the Übermensch represents an alternative, Earth-bound goal for humanity, one distinct from the other-worldliness of religious aspirations. As we now know, this aspiration led to a masterclass of cruelty and misery. Eugenics, when practised from a collectivist mindset, had an evaluative logic as its core principle and was driven by class and race prejudices that severely disenfranchised those deemed to not hold desirable genetic traits and values. The discovery after the Second World War of exactly how Nazi Germany had implemented their eugenics programme and the atrocities committed in its name did much to harm eugenics' public perception as a viable scientific movement. Once people saw the inhumanity of taking this policy to its extremes, the damage was done, and scientists in the West began rejecting the eugenics philosophy, appalled at its justification for the attempted eradication of whole races of people.[98]

Science then moved away from trying to control the genetic make-up of the population through selective breeding, permanent sterilisation and euthanasia, to focus on more positive aspects of population control such as family planning and birth control. During the upswing of the fourth wave, a true biological innovation was created that was to have huge ramifications for society and individual choice: the contraceptive pill and the ability for women to control their own reproductive capabilities. Although commonplace now, when it was introduced in the 1960s it was declared the most significant medical advance of the 20th century, freeing women from the constant fear of pregnancy and creating a social and economic revolution for them that we are still seeing play out today. It represented the first of a long line of medical advances that will eventually allow humans to understand and control various aspects of their biological composition, eradicating weaknesses that have plagued us throughout our history.

---

[98] Though it continued to be practiced elsewhere in the world, such as in India in the 1970's during 'The Emergency' years.

Decoding Life

Our understanding of genetics has come a long way since the days of Galton and Huxley. Genetics is set to be one of the major forces of the sixth wave and may lead to the long-wished-for ability to combat and defeat the forces of nature that curtail our lives and make us weak. The foundation for this genetic revolution was laid down with the mapping of the human genome. In 2003, the thirteen-year Human Genome Project was successfully completed, providing the ability to sequence the entire genetic code of a human to an accuracy of 99.999 per cent. It took $2.7 billion (in 1991 dollars), 47,000 people and roughly fifteen years to sequence the first human genome. Since then progress in genetic engineering has advanced at a rate faster than Moore's Law. Companies such as Illumina have developed sequencers that can decode a human genome in minutes, while the cost has dropped to just $1,000. It is projected to fall even further, dropping to around $100 within five years.

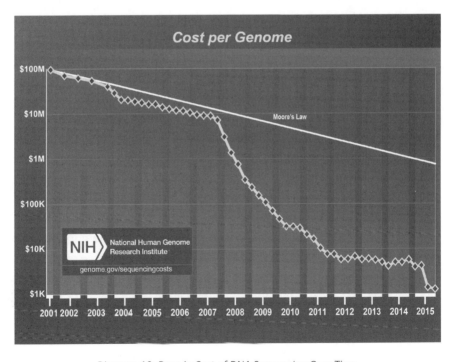

Diagram 10: Drop in Cost of DNA Sequencing Over Time.

By the end of 2012, 30,000 human genomes in the world had been sequenced. By the end of 2017 over 500,000 had. This rapidly dropping price point enables smaller companies to evaluate how they can use this new breakthrough to provide new products and services. For example, companies such as Oxford Nanopore already offer portable, real-time, DNA- and RNA-sequencing devices such as the MinION, which allows for gene-sequencing on location. As discussed, people are working to combine this new knowledge with 3D bio-printers, creating the ability to effectively 'print' or grow human organs from their recipient's DNA. It has also enabled the development of DNA barcoding, a taxonomic way to help address the food provenance issue highlighted in Part Two. Cost-effective genome sequencing has already enabled the creation of genetic tests that can highlight predispositions to a variety of illnesses, such as breast cancer, haemostatic disorders, liver diseases and cystic fibrosis, to name but a few. It is hoped that a better understanding of genome data will help determine the causes of cancers, Alzheimer's and other diseases, leading to the development of significant advances in their management. Worldwide, about 7.6 million people die from cancer each year. Since 5–10 per cent of all fatal incidents of cancers are inherited, fixing or modifying DNA could provide a potential cure, or at least a highly effective treatment. There have already been several cases, including high-profile celebrities such as Angelina Jolie, who through genetic testing identified the presence of faulty alleles, and, as a result, took proactive steps such as having a mastectomy to prevent breast cancer. It is anticipated that detailed knowledge of the human genome will provide new avenues for advances in medicine and biotechnology that will allow us to both combat and finally defeat the diseases and biological constraints that have held us back, creating completely new markets that range from agricultural and livestock genetic manipulation to make our food supply disease-resistant, allergen free and more productive.

The ability to identify people from their DNA has also provided enormous new capabilities in crime detection. Several high-profile criminal cases that had gone cold – sometimes by decades – have been reopened due to this new DNA testing capability, and police have been finally able to identify the perpetrators. In 2016, sixty-four-year-old Christopher Hampton, who had never been arrested and consequently wasn't on either the national crime or DNA database, was caught and convicted of murdering teenager

Melanie Road in a vicious, sexually motivated attack thirty-two years previously in 1984. How was he caught? His daughter was arrested over a minor domestic disturbance, and as part of the arrest process she had her DNA taken. It was found to closely match the DNA of Melanie's killer, a sample of which was still stored on the police database. Given that she was just twelve at the time of the murder, her father was subsequently tested, found to be a perfect match, and is now serving thirty-two years in prison. Conversely, DNA matching has been used to retrospectively prove innocence. For example, in the US, James Bain spent thirty-five years in jail after being found guilty of kidnapping and raping a nine-year-old boy in 1974. He was released in 2009 after DNA tests proved that he was innocent of the crime.

DNA has also provided the answer to the question: 'where will we store all of the data that is going to be created?' Scientists at Harvard learnt how to store digital data in DNA in 2012 and it has numerous benefits, as it is ultra-compact, won't degrade and it can last hundreds of thousands of years if kept in a cool, dry place. Assuming we don't follow the Mycenaeans example and lose the ability to read and write it, we should also be able to decode it. Now a new and improved way to encode digital data in DNA has been developed, one that would create the highest-density large-scale data storage scheme ever invented. Capable of storing 215 petabytes (215 million gigabytes) in a single gram of DNA, the system is capable, in theory, of storing all the world's data in a container about the size and weight of a couple of pickup trucks. Computer architects at Microsoft Research expect to have an operational storage system using DNA by 2020.[268] If data is the new oil, DNA is likely to be the new oil drum.

From Understanding Comes Control.

While matching and storing data in DNA is impressive, perhaps the most exciting announcement since the first genome was sequenced has been the ability to change it. The development of CRISPR-Cas9 gene-editing technology has enabled scientists to make precise and permanent changes to the 'A's, 'T's, 'C's and 'G's – the source code of DNA. CRISPR[99] refers to

---

[99] Clustered Regularly Interspaced Short Palindromic Repeats

unusual DNA sequences that help protect organisms by identifying threats – especially viruses. The CRISPR-Cas9 system consists of two key molecules that introduce a change into the DNA, targeting any particular sequence of A, T, C and G's. These molecules consist of a protein enzyme called Cas9 which acts as a pair of 'molecular scissors', and a piece of RNA called guide RNA (gRNA), a small piece of pre-designed RNA sequence (about twenty bases long) located within a longer RNA scaffold. The scaffold part binds to DNA and the pre-designed sequence 'guides' Cas9 to the right part of the genome, ensuring that the Cas9 enzyme cuts at the right point. CRISPR-Cas9 allows scientists to edit parts of the genome by removing, adding or altering precisely targeted elements of DNA using Cas9 as molecular scissors that cut the two strands of DNA at a specific location in the genome. Once a piece of DNA has been snipped out in a cell, the host's natural repair systems kick in to try to repair the damage. CRISPR-Cas9 can therefore be used to slice, recombine and generally edit DNA, allowing scientists to permanently modify genes in living cells and organisms. This creates the possibility of correcting mutations at precise locations in order to address the genetic causes of disease such as sickle-cell anaemia. They've already been successful. Mice share 97.5 per cent of their DNA with humans, only they have a much shorter lifespan which allows researchers to observe the effects of removing or changing single genes. In 2017, British scientists used CRISPR-Cas9 to add jellyfish genes to mice, and in doing so gave them fluorescent green feet.[269] While this may seem a strange and somewhat useless genetic trait to give mice (although cats will now be able to see them better in the dark, so there's that), it was used to demonstrate how this new tool could be used to alter specific features. CRISPR has significant potential as a tool for treating a range of medical conditions that have a genetic component, including cancer, hepatitis B, sickle cell and even high cholesterol. The CRISPR-Cas9 toolkit creates the possibility of being able to manipulate our own genes, moving humanity from a place of understanding of how our bodies work, to one of control and improvement.

Although it is still in its infancy, human gene therapy has already had eye-catching real-world results. Chinese and US scientists have claimed to have already used CRISPR to modify human embryos, with the US team using it to remove the MYBPC3 gene that causes heart defects. French scientists have used it to cure a teenage boy of sickle-cell disease; it has been used to correct mutations that lead to blindness, to build new skin, to cure haemophilia by replacing the faulty gene responsible for blood-clotting proteins, and to manipulate T-cells to attack and destroy cancer cells.[270] The potential and speed of diffusion of gene therapy are only going to increase, especially as more brains get involved. To enable wider input, the Broad Institute of MIT and Harvard released Version 4 of their industry-leading Genome Analysis Toolkit, GATK4, under an open-source software licence. This will help scientists to optimise best practices in hardware and software for genome analytics and integrate and process genomic research data sets from a variety of sources worldwide.[271] GAT4 has enabled several major CRISPR advancements, such as the development of new CRISPR editors called BE3 and ABE7 that enable scientists to change the structure of DNA, replacing the scissors with an enzyme that can convert one DNA letter (A, T, G or C) to another. This safer and more powerful form of CRISPR gene editing solves one of CRISPR-Cas9's fundamental flaws – it can remove sections of the genome much more successfully than it can fix them. Fixing genes requires both the removal of faulty DNA and the addition of new replacement bits with the correct sequence to cells and a triggering of a repair process. To date, this only works 10 per cent of the time, and hardly at all in non-dividing cells like brain cells. In comparison, the BE3 and ABE7 editors have the potential to correct as many as two thirds of the single-letter mutations that occur in people.[272] While it will be a few years of testing and ethics discussion before CRISPR-Cas9 is legally used in non-embryonic humans in the West, apparently eighty-six people in China have already undergone gene editing using the technique, including editing designed to combat cancer.[273] Unlike in the West, where the testing process takes months if not years, China allows a hospital's ethics committee to approve research on humans the same day. Which is fantastic if it works, but not so great if all you end up with is green feet.

Playing God

Decoding life provides us the chance to not just understand it, but to conserve, revive and extend it. To help conserve life, an international consortium of scientists has launched a massive project to sequence, catalogue and analyse the genomes of every species on the planet. Called *Earth BioGenome Project (EBP)*, it is estimated to take 10 years, cost $4.7 billion and require over 200 petabytes of data storage to sequence all 10-15 million species.[274] The aim is to create a complete digital library of the history and diversity of all life, so we can understand how to protect it. As well as preventing species from going extinct, scientists are also working to revive those that already have. Whilst not quite *Jurassic Park*, genetic scientists at Harvard believe they will be able to recreate woolly mammoths by 2019,[275] and Australian scientists are working to bring back the thylacine – the Tasmanian Tiger. In Iceland, biopharmaceutical company deCODE Genetics is even trying to bring back humans. They have recreated the DNA of Iceland's first citizen with African heritage – who died two hundred years ago – using the DNA of his living descendants.[276] DeCODE's senior research scientist, Agnar Helgason, believes that using this technique, *any historic figure born after 1500 who has known descendants could be reconstructed.*[100]

Perhaps the most radical development might be the ability to prevent things dying in the first place – or at least from getting old. While this sounds like the stuff of science fiction, it is probably a lot closer than you think. Most scientists agree that ageing is not caused by any one culprit but by the breakdown of many systems at once; a matter of physics as much as biology. Our bodies become worn down by trillions of tiny physical processes, the slow accumulation of damage in our cells, organs and tissues ultimately causing the physical transformations that visually define us as elderly. Our DNA mechanics reduce in effectiveness with age, resulting in our genetic code gradually increasing in mutations. Faced with all this damage, our cells try to adjust by changing the way they metabolise nutrients and store energy. To ward off cancer, they even know how to shut themselves down. But eventually cells stop dividing and stop communicating with each other, triggering the decline we see from the outside. Jaws shrink; gums recede; we lose the elasticity in our skin; bones become more brittle; cartilage thins; joints swell; arteries stiffen and clog up; hair greys and recedes; vision dims and memory fades. Basically, getting old sucks. The notion that ageing is a natural, inevitable part of life is so fixed in our culture that we rarely question it, declaring old age, death and taxes to be three immovable facts of life. The rich have successfully figured out ways to avoid taxes for some time; now their attention is turning to ageing and death.

---

[100] Let's hope no one tries to do a *Boys from Brazil* and recreate the DNA of a couple of uniquely moustached European dictators.

Ageing is now being referred to not as an inevitability, but as an illness; an illness that many believe can be cured. Fuelled by billions of techno-dollars from Silicon Valley and driven by the desire of some very wealthy but ageing technocrats, longevity and anti-ageing has become one of the most exciting areas of scientific research. In 2013, Google established a new biotech company called California Life Company (Calico for short). The company's mission is to focus on health, well-being and longevity, but the headline-grabbing goal is that of curing death.[277] Calico is using machine-learning tools to gain a deeper understanding of the complex biological processes of ageing, including building a machine that decodes the human genome from scratch. Research into cheating death does not come cheap; Calico, in partnership with the Chicago-based pharmaceutical giant AbbVie, has so far pumped $2.5 billion into their research. This could be money well spent, for the potential to cure age-related diseases could save billions in healthcare costs through dramatically reducing age-related illnesses, and it has a ready-made customer base of rich people willing to pay good money to delay old Father Time.

There have been various eye-catching headlines coming out of this research. The Calico team mapped the genome of the naked mole rat to understand why the rodent lives such an exceptionally long life (it lives up to thirty years, ten times longer than normal rats), and in January 2018 announced that the reason for this longevity is that they don't actually age. Amazingly, for an animal that already looks ancient due to its wrinkly skin, blindness and wisps of grey hair, the researchers found that a naked mole rat's mortality rate stays the same throughout their life, defying what is known as the Gompertzian Law that states that our risk of dying increases with each passing year. The Calico team found that these rats don't suffer from age-related issues such as cancers, bone or heart issues; their cells don't suffer oxidative damage from free radicals; they can survive eighteen minutes without oxygen; and female mole rats do not even suffer from the menopause and continue to reproduce into their thirties. They are now analysing exactly why they don't age in the hope they can use this knowledge to develop treatments for larger, slightly more hirsute, two-legged mammals.[101] Other rodent-based longevity projects include the

[101] Let's hope that in achieving radical life extension we don't take on the physical appearance of mole rats, for a human version would look spookily similar to the Morlocks in the 1960 film version of H. G. Wells' *The Time Machine*.

analysis of the effects of calorie restriction on the lifespan of mice, while another is focused on understanding the rejuvenation benefits of young *human* blood plasma on the bodies and brains of old mice.[278] Scientists are also analysing the impact of artificially increasing or decreasing the levels of a family of proteins called Krüppel-like transcription factors (KLFs) in nematode worms, which has the effect of making them live for longer or shorter time periods.[279]

One of the more interesting areas of longevity research involves extending the length of telomeres. Telomeres are segments of DNA at the ends of chromosomes whose shortening is associated with ageing and degenerative disease. As cells divide over time, the telomeres get shorter and shorter until they are so short our cells can no longer reproduce. The human body tries to stop this process naturally with another enzyme called telomerase – a sort of reset button for the telomere – and research has focused on this enzyme. In 2008, molecular biologist María Blasco and her team injected telomerase into mice. The result was that it extended their lives by 40 per cent, suggesting that it has the capacity to reverse the ageing process. In 2015, Biotech company BioViva's CEO, Liz Parrish, went one step further, making herself 'patient zero'; the first human to receive telomerase gene therapy. Parrish flew out to Columbia, where she could legally undergo this gene therapy, receiving two kinds of injections: a myostatin inhibitor, believed to prevent age-associated muscle loss; and telomerase gene therapy to lengthen her telomeres. Parrish was retested by independent third parties six months after the treatment. The telomeres in her white blood cells had lengthened by more than six hundred base pairs which, according to Parrish, is the equivalent to telomere age reduction of twenty years. She then underwent a full-body MRI scan which revealed an increase in muscle mass and a reduction in intramuscular fat. Other tests indicate Parrish now has improved insulin sensitivity and reduced inflammation levels.[280] In August 2018, Parrish announced that retesting had identified that her telomeres continued to grow, adding the equivalent of another decade of cellular rejuvenation without any negative side effects.

And here's the rub: this is research designed not just to stop the process of dying, but to reverse the cellular damage done to our bodies throughout our lives, and as a result reset our physical attributes to what they were in our mid-twenties. No one wants to extend their life just to have twenty more years of fragility and dependency. An extended existence without the vitality to enjoy it is a curse, not a blessing; something we've appreciated since the days of the Ancient Greeks. The Greek myth of Eos, the goddess of dawn, details how she begged Zeus to grant her mortal lover, Tithonus, immortality, but forgot to also ask for eternal youth, and was cursed to watch his eternal decline and decay. The goal of radical life extension is therefore more than just the delaying of death, it is the creation of an elixir of life. To reset the clock of time by repairing our bodies at a cellular level, revitalising them and returning them to their peak. Our dramatic rise in living standards has resulted in a rapidly ageing population, one that is suffering from a host of age-related illnesses such as Alzheimer's, cancer, muscle wastage and osteoporosis; diseases that don't currently have a cure, and whose effects are expensive to treat. Preventing ageing is a bold mission that has enormous benefits for society, one that many influential people are taking very seriously and pumping a lot of money into.

Keeping the Reaper Waiting

Western society was not set up to provide for a population where there are more old people than young. Until recently, the average working person in the UK expected to work till they were sixty, and then have around fifteen to twenty years of retirement before passing away. The state pension calculations were therefore based around that logic, expecting to have to financially support a person in retirement for around two decades. Now more people are living longer, skewing the demographic and increasing the financial burden on the state, with the UK retirement bill rising by £1 trillion to £7.6 trillion in the last five years.[281] Then there's the healthcare costs, as the vast majority of the healthcare attention people require is in their senior years, and currently all treatments are symptom-focused, providing sticking-plaster solutions until the person dies. Ageing, therefore, doesn't just impact the quality of life of those affected, but also that of their carers and the society that must fund their care, well-being and rehabilitation. Thus, any potential solution that doesn't just fix the symptoms of ageing but also addresses the cause offers massive social benefits and cost savings.

Dr Aubrey de Grey, British anti-ageing scientist and Chief Scientific Officer of the non-profit California-based SENS (Strategies for Engineered Negligible Senescence) Foundation, which he co-founded in 2009, is trying his hardest to get ageing classified as a disease. Dr de Grey describes ageing as the fatal side effect of a lifelong accumulation of various types of molecular and cellular damage throughout the body caused by essential metabolic processes, of which he has identified seven types. SENS is proposing a panel of therapies designed to repair this damage and control and reset your genes.[282] *I'd say we have a 50/50 chance of bringing ageing under what I'd call a decisive level of medical control within the next 25 years or so... And what I mean by decisive is the same sort of medical control that we have over most infectious diseases today.* Like Francis Bacon's 1620 work *Novum Organum*, a new instrument of science, genetic engineering, has the potential to transform society. Rather than the passing of galleons through the Pillars of Hercules and into the unknown waters of the Atlantic, we are reaching a point where we are daring to dream of passing through two new pillars – ageing and death. Prior to the Age of Exploration, the concept of travelling beyond the horizon into vast, unexplored waters to find new territories was deemed improbable if not impossible, because it had never been done other than in tall tales. Many felt it should never be attempted, for who knows what monsters lie over the horizon? To many, the dream of radical life extension falls into this category; a tale of fiction, of an unlikely journey to mythical lands with only despair and disappointment as the outcome. As Bacon himself declared, *But by far the greatest obstacle to the progress of science and to the undertaking of new tasks and provinces therein is found in this – that men despair and think things impossible.*[283]

We have once again set sail on another voyage of discovery, only this time there will be real monsters lurking beneath the surface, ones of our own making. The one thing to date that the elites have not been able to do, despite all their wealth, is buy more time on this planet to enjoy the trappings that lifestyle brings. Rich or poor, we all age in the same way and we all die from the same things. The inevitability of ageing has seen it attract less investment than more traditional issues such as cancer and heart disease. This is now changing, and the money needed to make this eon-old dream become a reality is magically starting to appear. To speed up the process many tech billionaires are using their own funds to move things along, because there's no value in being the richest corpse in the graveyard. They share Woody Allen's aspiration of achieving immortality not through their work, but through not dying. As an example, both Jeff Bezos and Peter Thiel have poured funds into the US company Unity Biotechnology, which has a $150 million war chest to develop drugs that 'prevent, halt, or reverse numerous diseases of ageing'. The first signs of success will open the floodgates, and this lofty goal will quickly go from pipe dream to reality – but only for those that can afford it. Gene therapy and genetic alteration will provide those with wealth the opportunity to not just improve on their lifestyle, but to buy a completely different type of life for them and their families. A somewhat different existence to that of those who do not have the capital. The rich and powerful could soon potentially purchase what their predecessors throughout history could never acquire: time.

Live Long Enough to Live Forever

This will ask some very big questions of our society. What happens when those with wealth can extend their lifespan and well-being and those without cannot? Throughout history money may have bought you most things your heart desired but it could never buy you a longer life. The rich died from the same illnesses and at the same age as the poor, give or take a few years to account for better diet and healthcare. Now this may change. Ben Goertzel states that, *People are finally waking up to the possibility that aging is not necessarily inevitable, and it is not pre-ordained that we have to die after 70 or 80 years.*[284] De Grey believes that the world's first 150-year-old person has already been born, and within two decades the first 1,000-year-old person may be born. He describes how this will be achieved through a two-stage approach.[285] The first is through supplementation, calorie control, stem cell therapies and other treatments designed to repair cellular damage – removing waste products, rendering mutations harmless and restoring elasticity. This restores the molecular, cellular structure and composition of the middle-aged (or older) body, returning its function (both mental and physical) to that of a young adult. This has the potential to add thirty years of healthy, rejuvenated life to people, buying time for phase two when more advanced genetic procedures have been thoroughly investigated and tested. Ray Kurzweil is another person who believes that life extension will be achieved through a phased approach, and hopes that the first phase will buy him enough time. *Supplements, exercise and diet will not make me live forever – though, they will help me live long enough to get through bridge 1 – which will then help me get to bridge 2.*[286] Kurzweil believes bridge (phase) two will arrive around 2025 and will include cellular- and genetic-level enhancements that will enable us to turn back our biological clocks. Both de Grey and Kurzweil are hoping to achieve what is known as longevity escape velocity. At present, more than one year of research is required for each additional year of expected life. Longevity escape velocity occurs when this ratio is sustainably reversed, for example where each extra year of research into life extension adds more than a year to the average life expectancy.

Immortality is not the goal for people like de Grey – he himself hates the use of the word to describe his work, stating that it's a religious concept. *Immortality means zero risk of death from any cause; but I don't work on stopping people from being hit by trucks. I work on keeping them healthy.* This is where Kurzweil differs from de Grey. Kurzweil believes a third bridge will arise around 2045, flowing from the merging of nanotech with AI that will create swarms of specialised, programmable, communicating nanobots designed to replace old-fashioned neurons and blood cells with more efficient units that can destroy infections, reverse degenerative changes and rewrite genetic code. He envisages a world where people are able to enhance themselves through biotech and nanotech to extend lifespans indefinitely. Kurzweil aspires to survive to see a future where we are able to make the ultimate leap and leave our imperfect, frail 'flesh prisons' and transcend biology entirely. Before 2050, Kurzweil predicts that AI and nanotech will have advanced so far that his brain, with its memories, capabilities and characteristics, can be reduced to pure information and rebooted in a non-biological substrate. No matter how sceptical people are of the idea of greatly extended lifespans, most of them will still choose good health if they can. The challenge, therefore, is to stay alive long enough for this research to mature and be used to give us decades – if not longer – of healthy life. Of course, this is all dependent on whether you can afford the outputs of all this research.

While we have shown an increased tendency to create a more inclusive society, the spectre of eugenics and gene-based exclusivity still looms over us constantly. If genetic engineering on embryos could be used to ensure that the child is born with desirable traits such as intelligence and beauty, then those that could afford the treatment could guarantee that their children would grow up with fantastic advantages, envied for their appearance as well as their academic success. Soon, competition to create an advantage for your children would kick in, as it does today through paying for them to attend private schools or for additional tuition. Now we are starting up a genetic arms race, with companies vying to provide the best possible advantages to unborn children – at the right price, of course. This will almost certainly be used to not only reduce the instances of defect attributes, but to create super-attributes such as improved sight, hearing, memory, strength, etc. Will people embrace this opportunity? You betcha. Just look at the money spent on private education. Then consider the explosion in usage of nootropics and stimulants such as Adderall, Modafinil and Ritalin by college students, especially in the US, looking to gain an edge in their studies. Now do you really think rich parents wouldn't jump at the chance of using their wealth to provide their children (and themselves) with the power of super-intelligence? Of course they will. And so would you.

The development of genetic engineering is a breakthrough point; one where science is starting to achieve what the eugenics movement could not – the identification and elimination of defective genes. But it also raises many ethical, legal and social concerns, and the fear of it being used for nefarious aims has already caused legislation to be passed. One of the most prevalent concerns was the fear that both employers and health-insurance companies would refuse to hire individuals or to provide insurance to people because of a health concern indicated by their genes. So powerful was this concern that before the Human Genome project was even completed, the United States passed the 1996 Health Insurance Portability and Accountability Act (HIPAA), which protects against the unauthorised and non-consensual release of identifiable health information to any entity that is not actively engaged in the provision of healthcare services to that patient.

Once again, we have reached a point where we believe that we *really* understand how our genes work, and as a result, a revitalisation of the pursuit to control them has arisen, not through selection, but through science. What is really impressive is that to date, all achievements in this area have been obtained using brainpower and traditional computers. Now imagine what scientists will be able to achieve in the coming decades using the combination of AI and quantum computing. Once we are able to manipulate our genetic capabilities, for the very first time in history we will be able to overcome our biological constraints and redefine our physical limits, for in order to keep up with the explosion in machine intelligence, we will probably need an upgrade. This won't be free (at least initially), and it won't be for everyone. We may finally realise the goal of creating Plato's guardian class or Nietzsche's *Übermensch,* but the real issue will be deciding who gets the honour of acquiring these capabilities, and what happens to those left behind?

16

THE DEATH OF PRIVACY

Freedom is the freedom to say that two plus two makes four.
If that is granted, all else follows.

George Orwell, *Nineteen Eighty-Four*

In the past, only those with access to information held power, another case of the one-eyed man ruling the land of the blind. Now everyone can have their say or promote their work. This has led to a world of increasing transparency, one where secrets are exposed, and private lives laid bare, and with all this increased transparency comes increased accountability. People have found themselves being held accountable not only for their actions today, but for past actions and crimes committed years ago. The life of many a famous person has been shattered because of past transgressions from their previous lives, that reappear like some drunken ex crashing into the church just before you say your wedding vows. One of the major issues of this wave is therefore not going to be gaining access to information; it's going to be keeping it private.

We are building a civilisation not as we did in the past, with human slaves and physical things, but with robotic labour and data. Labour that is getting increasingly smart; data gathering that is getting increasingly intrusive. While the sixth-wave technologies might not be as physically imposing as those in previous waves, they are somewhat more imposing in terms of their impact on your personal life. A steam engine, airport or skyscraper might have caught your attention, changing the landscape around you, but at least it didn't track your every movement. Data is the oil that greases the engine of the sixth wave, underpinning the digital knowledge economy. But are we aware of what we are giving away? We are in a world where we store everything, from photographs to personal details, in the cloud, which isn't a mystical, faraway thing that cannot be breached or abused, but simply 'someone else's computer' – usually owned by corporations such as Apple and Microsoft. We willingly share everything from our private moments and our political thoughts to our physical location on social media tools like Facebook, Twitter and YouTube, click 'accept' to terms and conditions we've never read, and allow cookies to store whatever on our computers. Who knows what's contained in the small print? We all assume that someone else has read all of this and approved it, so we don't need to. We are placing an enormous amount of trust in companies that use AI to make important decisions, and in the data that we allow them access to. We carry around devices with GPS trackers on them. We post our photos, tag them with the locations and dates they were taken and the people we were with. We like photos, comments and points of view, giving insights into our political leanings and perspectives. While Generation X and baby boomers remember life pre-Internet, digital native millennials and Generation Z do not, and as a result have a more relaxed attitude to sharing their life online. People share more data than they believe – most of it containing their most private moments. In an article for the *Guardian* newspaper, Judith Duportail detailed how in March 2017 she asked the dating app company Tinder to grant her access to her personal data, which every European citizen is allowed to do under EU data protection law.[287] She received back eight hundred pages of information, including her Facebook 'likes', Instagram photos, education details, the age range of men she was interested in, how many Facebook friends she had, and, most scarily, the full details of every online conversation with every single one of her matches. Tinder had a complete dossier containing all the 1,700 Tinder messages she had sent since 2013; from the jokes she told, to all the private personal details she shared.

Private companies now have access to a worrying amount of data on the private lives and inner beings of ordinary people. For example, many users have deleted their Facebook account, and after requesting a download of their Facebook data were surprised to find that by permitting the company to access their contacts, it had then proceeded to access every piece of data on their phones, including their photos and emails. Facebook not only knows who you are friends with right now, but through its algorithms and facial-recognition software it can also establish everyone you've ever had contact with, even tenuously. Because these 'shadow-profile' connections occur inside Facebook's algorithmic black box, Facebook users normally cannot see how deep the company's data-mining of their lives truly is, until a mysterious 'person you may know' recommendation or advertisement pops up. This 'shadow contact' information is supposed to be secret, but in 2013 Facebook accidently let the cat out of the bag when it announced that it had 'fixed a bug'.[288] The bug was that when people asked for a download of their data from Facebook, it included all of the shadow data that no one knew Facebook had, such as their friends' visible contact information, and their friends' shadow contact information. The extent of Facebook's insights into your lives was supposed to be a secret, so these new bug fixes simply pulled back the curtain once again, ensuring no one could see what they were really giving Facebook access to.[102]

This data provides new levels of insight to companies, enabling them to not only analyse their overall sales figures, but also see to whom they sold it. From retail loyalty cards, e-commerce and mobile/e-payment systems, they are increasingly able to identify the individual behind every purchase. This is enabling companies to provide an increasingly personalised experience; the creation of an Internet, movie house and online shopping mall specifically for an 'audience of one'. But at what cost does this convenience come? It comes at the expense of our privacy. We are allowing technology companies to track our every movement and access our most personal secrets. We are also allowing them to identify us. Advanced facial recognition functionality is now embedded in phones such as the iPhone X, and into platforms such Facebook, so it can identify who is in your photos and auto-tag them. Soon this capability will find its way onto other devices – from our front door to

---

[102] If you really want to be alarmed, I strongly suggest you read the excellent series of articles Kashmir Hill has written on Facebook for Gizmodo. Make sure you're sitting down when you read them.

our car, and even to the vending machine that makes our morning coffee. We are allowing companies to store information on our faces, our thumbprints, our location, our friends, our political views, our banking details, our movements, our video-watching and our search history. Data about what we consume. Data about our financial situation. Data about our health. All this machine-readable behaviour is captured, analysed, processed, utilised, and packaged into a new private form of elite money, the aforementioned fifth form of capital. This is then traded between organisations and used to market goods to us, or more nefariously, to monitor, control or exploit us. An Amazon Echo home device contacts its servers every three minutes, regardless if you've asked it anything. Smart devices capture data about every aspect of your life, ranging from your movements to your sleep patterns, and this data is packaged and sold to other companies for a profit. Technocrats like Zuckerberg, Bezos, Cook, Brin and Page have access to more data about normal citizens than even the worst dictators of the past and their armies of secret police and informants. And they use it to make money; for example, in July 2018 Facebook admitted that it had shared its user's information with 52 separate companies, including numerous Chinese corporations. These technocrats are becoming as rich as Pharaohs, building great pyramids made not by slaves and stone, but by algorithms and our data. We need to quickly wake up and realise that we are not just the consumers – we are also the product. Welcome to the surveillance economy.

Our willingness to sign away our privacy and our freedom to companies that provide even a modicum of value will come back to bite us. The capturing of data on our health raises particularly interesting questions. Will it be used for our continual benefit, or for more dystopian means? The answer should be apparent to even the most trusting of people. In April 2017, Facebook was forced to admit that it had been working with hospitals in order to capture medical records and match them with patients' social media profiles. Now imagine when low-cost gene sequencing is combined with advancements in AI-driven DNA analysis and wearable technologies to enable the constant monitoring of our health. Everything is moving towards healthcare becoming predictive, a huge bonus that will see attention directed at prevention rather than cure, and nursing more about lifestyle adaptation than post-illness recuperation. Our bodies will become a source of enormous data, used to create a personal digital twin, much like the digital twin of the factory mentioned in Part Two. Toilets have already been developed that contain sensors that analyse our biological waste, and very soon a combination of wearable devices and inbuilt sensors will continually monitor our blood, heart rate and DNA to highlight any early signs of illness or protein markers that indicate potential long-term issues such as Type II diabetes. Now imagine how much insurance companies would be willing to buy that information for. Suddenly the potential arises for them to game the 'risk-to-reward' ratio, and suddenly you find out that not only are you likely to suffer an issue with your health, but pharmaceutical, software and insurance companies knew about this before you did. Which is why your premiums suddenly skyrocket, or renewing your life-insurance policy becomes 'problematic'. Insurance companies are already offering discounts off your payments if you wear monitoring devices that allow them to track your activities and consumption, such as Beam Dental, a dental insurance company, which offers discounts if you use their smart toothbrushes that enables them to capture data on your teeth cleaning regime. Data that allows them to refine their policies and reduce their premiums. It also captures data on your location, such as whether you work away, where you holiday, etc. Data that is attractive and saleable to other companies.

The dramatic fall in the cost of DNA testing has enabled companies such as 23andMe (named after the twenty-three pairs of chromosomes in a normal human cell) to enable people to trace their ancestry. In doing so they are obtaining huge amounts of data on the DNA of the population. In April 2018, investigators used a genealogy website to track down the Golden Gate killer, a prolific murderer and rapist who terrorised California in the 1970s and 1980s, uploading DNA samples as if they were a customer to identify any living relatives. Which it did; trapping Joseph James DeAngelo, who is now charged with eight murders. Which is great news. However, there is a downside, one which has some worried about the privacy of your genetic material. When millions of people uploaded samples of their DNA to these websites, they were probably unaware that they were also submitting that DNA to an unofficial police databank, and to any other company that might want to track people down via their DNA. Steve Mercer, the Chief Attorney for the Maryland Office, states that, *DNA ancestry sites have fewer privacy protections than convicted offenders whose DNA is contained in regulated databanks... People who submit DNA for ancestry testing are unwittingly becoming genetic informants on their innocent family.*[289] When this DNA data is combined with other captured information such as your movements, social media activities, web pages and videos viewed, and your friends and contacts, an enormous database of every aspect of your life is captured. The business titans of the past may have enjoyed wealth and prestige, they didn't have the insight and ability to influence the lives of the masses that today's digital leaders have. When you consider that the co-founder of 23andMe, Anne Wojcicki, is the ex-wife of Sergey Brin, co-founder of Google, and that her sister, Susan Wojcicki, is currently CEO of YouTube, then you begin to realise that all of this data is concentrating into the hands of a few well-connected and incredibly powerful people. A technocracy is developing with the power, money and influence that would put the Rothschilds and Rockefellers to shame.

Platform Propaganda

A new phenomenon has arisen: the power of data-rich corporations, especially those that have a virtual monopoly via their platform, to control what you see and believe. They can control both the message and who gets to a messenger. As always, there are good and bad elements to this. The good is that they can block extremist content and identify any people whose viewing habits or discussions are veering in a direction that may lead to them become more extreme in their views. The bad is obvious. Companies such as Facebook and Google can now use their knowledge about you to monitor, manipulate and control your behaviour. They can falsify information to either feed or alter your biases. They have been proven to manipulate search results, control which videos are shown as trending, and select specific news headlines to either provide you with a more personalised service or perform marketing experiments.[290]

Worryingly, they are also able to use their insights and power to hide or demote posts or videos that they deem 'wrong-think'. This ability to remove content that doesn't align with their values, changes the nature of the Internet and allows them to control the ideas and assumptions of the population. As machine-learning algorithms become more advanced, then companies such as Google, Microsoft and Facebook will be able to identify and remove any comments or content almost as soon as they are posted, highlighting the posters and blocking their accounts. As with all totalitarian actions, the intent is altruistic: for example, the desire to remove 'fake news' requires someone to determine what is true and what is false. Again, this sounds good in theory, but it assumes that there is a perfect alignment with reality and people's perception of truth. Who gets to decide? If your narrative doesn't align with the judge's, and you get branded a teller of untruths, then will everything you say get marked as 'likely untrue?' Even if it's true? I'll answer that one for you: yes. Already we have seen numerous examples of this censorship of wrong-think, ranging from 'soft' (demonetisation) to 'hard' (banning, account deletion and details passed to the government), the latter representing a form of digital book-burning, somewhat mirroring the actions of the leaders of the Ottoman Empire against the printing press. It has also led to various governments, such as in the UK and Germany, responding to this reaction by clamping down on 'hate speech' and generally starting to censor the Internet. The term 'hate speech' appears ill-defined, subjective and runs contrary to foundational Western liberal values such as the freedom of speech. The basis for what constitutes hateful speech seems to be no more specific than 'speech we don't like', which, given the current outrage society, is quite a broad category. Combined with the tools to peer into every comment, group chat, tweet and like, it's also somewhat worrying. The combination of legal powers designed to prosecute the intent to cause offence, rather than actually causing offence, combined with the increasing ability to analyse every aspect of people's lives is setting up some very dystopian scenarios, especially as we fast approach a point where the line between technology and humanity begins to blur. The increasing ability of a small group of very powerful people to control our emotions and monitor our responses is breathtaking. While the declared intention may be to prevent distress, the real underlying objective is control.

From the Chinese Dynasties to the Ottoman Empire; the Spanish Inquisition through to Soviet Russia, the ability to silence dissent has proven to be a powerful and often-used weapon to ensure compliance and control. Recent examples include 'The Emergency' in India, when Prime Minister Indira Gandhi declared a state of emergency that allowed her to rule by decree, suspend elections and curb civil liberties. Between 1975 to 1977 most of Gandhi's political opponents were imprisoned and the press was censored. Her son, Sanjay Gandhi, then led a forced eugenics style mass-sterilization campaign, leading to an estimated 8.3 million sterilisations.

Remnants of this oppressive culture remain in India, with Human Rights Watch publishing an article in 2016 detailing how Indian political critics are treated as criminals, and how laws aimed at banning 'hate speech' and 'sedition' are routinely used to silence those who question authority in the world's second most populous country. *The government uses draconian laws such as the sedition provisions of the penal code, the criminal defamation law, and laws dealing with hate speech to silence dissent. These laws are vaguely worded, overly broad, and prone to misuse, and have been repeatedly used for political purposes against critics at the national and state level.*[291] Laws to regulate social media, such as India's Information Technology Act, can and do easily become tools to criminalise speech, often used at the behest of powerful individuals or groups who claim offense simply to silence speech they do not like. Hate-speech laws are therefore designed to suppress freedoms, not protect them.

Implementing legislation is one thing – policing it is another. Governments are increasingly aware that they are behind the curve, and are pressurising big corporations such as Facebook, Google and Twitter to both become information gatekeepers and act as cultural police; something they seem all too happy to undertake. Facebook has already begun to assign its users a trustworthiness score, but how it determines whether someone is 'trustworthy', what they do with this information, and who they send it to, is all somewhat opaque. Senior Twitter personnel have been caught on camera admitting that they censor opinions that don't align with their beliefs, undertaking stealth tactics like 'shadow banning' users, whereby the user believes that their posts are being broadcast as normal, when in fact they are hidden from other users. Ominously, Twitter has extended its surveillance activities beyond the boundaries of its own site, monitoring its users' activities 'off-platform', analysing what other sites they visit and what they do while on them.[292] Twitter's algorithms are also increasingly being used to not just entertain your mind, but also contain it. These tools seek to understand you in order to push content that it feels you will like, but also to ensure that the messages pushed your way fit into the official narrative, and any 'problematic' opinions are identified and eliminated. While you may not initially be bothered by corporations monitoring personal conversations, policing language and banning people whose thoughts and ideas you don't like, don't be surprised when this authority quickly extends to include people who you do agree with. Or to you.

We are rapidly approaching a world of almost total exposure, and the increasingly pervasive nature of all this technology and the Orwellian scenarios that could arise from it is worrying. Millions of households – mine included – now have devices like the Amazon Echo that quickly becomes a part of the family, making you forget that it is an ever-listening corporate data-capturing device. A device constantly being endued with ever-increasing levels of intelligence and voice-recognition capabilities, and which knows exactly where it is and who is speaking. We are told that it doesn't record anything unless the wake word 'Alexa' is used, but do we actually know this for sure? How easy would it be for people to hack into these devices in order to record us in the privacy of our own homes? The most totalitarian dictators of the past would not believe the level of surveillance and detailed insights they could now obtain on their citizens – usually with their blessing (or at least a tick in the 'accept terms and conditions' box). Orwell famously wrote about the state, not private corporations, monitoring and censoring the lives and conversations of individuals. He was unaware of digital technology and how much insight into our lives we would willingly allow corporations to have, and if he were alive today I can only assume that he would think our actions foolish, and not at all doubleplusgood.

It's not only a question of who's watching the watchmen, but also whether the watchmen and their watchers are in collusion with each other. Even the nation whose belief in individual liberties, property rights and individual freedoms once prevented its monarch from intruding over the threshold of the poorest citizen's house without following due process, is a willing participant in this joint operation to curtail its citizen's privacy. In 2016 the UK government passed a series of laws tagged as 'the Snoopers' Charter' that requires web and phone companies to store everyone's web-browsing histories for twelve months, and to pass this on to the police, security services and official agencies without a warrant. The EU is rolling out a new directive known as Article 13 which insists that all content uploaded to the Internet is monitored (by AI) for possible infringement of copyright rules, disregarding context and 'fair use' laws, creating widespread censorship and punitive measures for any infringements. British MP's have raised a Bill calling for the constant monitoring and censoring of online forums and groups, including closed (private) ones. Google quietly dropped its 'Don't be Evil' motto from its official code of conduct, around the same time as its involvement in Project Maven, a Pentagon sponsored military program on using AI to improve drone targeting capabilities, reached the public sphere. And Amazon has publicly refused to say whether it hands any of your data to the government,[293] which raises the interesting question of whether its 'customer first' policy actually applies to the way it handles your privacy as well as your packages.

These are all worrying trends; ones that are only going to get worse as artificial intelligence is increasingly used to monitor our every view, like and comment. The Internet is the modern-day equivalent of the 18th-century British coffee shop; a place where anyone can go to catch up on gossip, read the news, discuss the matters of the day with new and interesting people and share ideas. Charles II tried to ban coffee houses in England and quickly dropped the idea when he learnt how unpopular that was with the people. Yet now we are seeing these same freedoms quashed through a mix of legislation and overreach by government bodies who can both control what gets uploaded and legally demand full access to your online history. It is easy to imagine how large tech companies could, through a carrot of favourable taxation polices and a stick of aggressive antitrust action, be drafted in as an extension of the government, tasked with monitoring the population and identifying wrong-thinkers. The creeping authoritarianism being shown by Western governments and bodies like the EU to force Internet corporations to continually monitor everything we do online and report back to them, runs the risk of stifling free speech in the same way state and religious leaders prevented people gathering together or forming members' clubs where they could debate in private. Like then, the suppression of free expression and exchange of ideas will suffocate creativity, innovation and the ability to correct malfunctioning social systems, while also building resentment and anger. The number of places where people can discuss ideas without being monitored is shrinking at an alarming rate. We believed that the Internet was free. To our horror we are now realising that it actually had a very big cost attached: our privacy and our freedom of speech.

People who have experienced life under a totalitarian government do appear to be well aware of the dangers. For example, when I discuss technology with people from eastern Europe, they all predict that sales of Amazon Echo devices would struggle in the ex-communist countries, as people there know better than to willingly introduce devices into their houses that listen to their private conversations. They are still well aware of history, whereas in the West we seem to have forgotten it. Young adults in the US, UK and Western Europe have grown up in easy times and are more concerned about access and convenience than they are about privacy. Their naivety means they use technology carelessly, seeing only the benefits and blindly trusting the intent of those companies who provide it. As a result, teenagers have become far too comfortable with sharing their personal details and thoughts online. This is a mistake, as many have already found out to their cost. A nasty word or laddish comment said in private used to stay private, whereas a nasty comment or laddish post on the Internet stays there forever, awaiting discovery at some later date, ready to destroy your career. Even comments posted in closed groups have been screen-grabbed, posted on social media and shared with the press, costing people their university place, reputation and future prospects.

As AI-enabled devices spread across our world, we will see a huge increase in surveillance and monitoring, and an increasing number of arrests for 'hate crimes' such as comments on social media that criticise things such as political correctness or the 'official' government narrative. The concept of privacy will be continually eroded, and some people will react to this by developing and selling systems that block your online activities from being tracked. Your physical movements will be harder to keep private, as we become increasingly monitored through the explosion of smart devices that pick up and track your movements, through GPS tracking (phone), facial recognition (cameras) or voice recognition (home devices). Multiple countries are already installing facial recognition and automatic licence plate recognition technology on top of police cars, alerting the officers inside when it identifies a vehicle that has no road tax or insurance, or spots a wanted criminal who is walking on the sidewalk. As always, this technology has positive and negative connotations. For example, a facial-recognition system used by the Delhi police allowed them to track down nearly 3,000 missing children in just four days. However, it is also likely to lead to a continual erosion of personal privacy. While facial recognition is already being used to do everything from unlock your phone to access your bank account, it is also being used for more sinister means. While we marvel at the convenience they provide, we should also be aware that tools of convenience can soon be repurposed into tools of control.

Recent advancements are enabling the placing of machine-learning and surveillance technology into smaller and smaller devices, meaning that soon there will be eyes and ears everywhere. For example, Google's TensorFlow Lite is an on-device machine-learning, decision-making capability designed specifically for mobile and embedded devices, items traditionally constrained by low-performance processors, limited memory resources and relatively small storage reserves. TensorFlow Lite addresses these issues by specifically optimising machine-learning models for the confines of smartphone hardware. This means that we will be seeing the same level of tracking and monitoring that occurs on your PC appearing on your phone and apps, as well as other devices that make up the IoT ecosystem. In China, Alibaba and Tencent are already competing for the rights to host essential state-run ID services on their platforms that will list the holder's age, name, gender, address, ethnicity, birthdate and photo. These phone-based ID systems are a precursor to the inevitable day when these chips are installed in us, and not just in our devices.

We are living in an ever more transparent world, and Big Brother is indeed watching (and listening). Numerous people have already lost their jobs because of things they've posted publicly on social media – even when they thought it was in a closed group. Now imagine what will happen if (when) someone's private conversation, held behind closed doors and captured by an IoT device, were to be released and made public. People would doubt whether any conversation is truly private, even within their own homes, and as a result free speech will die and thoughts and comments suppressed. We should expect resistance. I am so grateful that I had the opportunity to grow up in a world where you were still able to mature without this permanent culture of surveillance and constant moral judgement; where teenagers could make fools of themselves without fear of it being recorded and shared across the Internet within seconds or resurrected in public years later. I fear for my children, who grew up when social media was new, and like teenagers across the Western world, were naive regarding the dangers of living out the trials and tribulations of their immature lives online. When you are young the things you say and do seem cool and edgy. When older they become cringeworthy and embarrassing. Until recently the cringe was limited to your own memories and close friends and family who use it to mock you for laughs. Not any more.

We must also bear responsibility for this, however. As we continue to willingly let corporations that collide with governments analyse every aspect of our lives – including our private conversations – we will increasingly see incursions into individual rights that have been protected since the writing of the Magna Carta and the passing of Habeas Corpus. We are sleepwalking to our own oppression, giving away our hard-fought freedoms for convenience and personalised marketing. If you think machines aren't increasingly monitoring, recording and analysing everything you do online, then you've not been paying attention. My only faith is in the power of the market to adjust this imbalance, and a new platform will arise to challenge YouTube, Google and others. For example, DuckDuckGo, a search engine that doesn't store your history, log your IP address nor personalise search results, has seen its usage explode as people become more aware of the amount of information companies like Google have access to.

If you're not worried about this level of surveillance and think it's all a conspiracy theory, then you might want to consider why those most likely to know, such as the former FBI Director James Comey and the CEO of Facebook Mark Zuckerberg, both cover their computer's webcam with tape.[294] Zuckerberg covers his audio jack as well, so his conversations cannot be monitored. If the Internet is the coffee shop of the 21st century, then you should imagine that there is a spy sat at the very next table, listening to everything you do, taking pictures and writing up notes to report back to their boss. Digital personas are becoming a necessity in order to operate in the modern world, but it is important to remember that your profile doesn't actually belong to you – it belongs to the company that owns the platform it's hosted on. They also store everything on the cloud, which, as discussed, isn't a mystical thing but a series of computers somewhere that you don't own. Think that deleting a text message or email from your computer has also deleted it everywhere? You sure? Remember – you're the product as well as the consumer.

How Safe is Your Data?

This raises the increasingly critical question of just how secure your data is in the hands of these corporations. Your value to them is in your data. We are assured that it is safe, but time and again, evidence is proving otherwise. Cyber-security is an ever-increasing risk, and every business needs to understand exactly who has access to your data, how they are likely to use it and whether they are friend or foe. In 2013, Yahoo was hacked, impacting every one of their 3 billion accounts. They initially admitted that 1 billion accounts had been affected, and it wasn't until 2016 that they admitted to the remaining 2 billion. A second breach occurred in 2014 when hackers walked off with a half-billion Yahoo account records. Data leaked included names, telephone numbers, dates of birth, passwords and security questions. In 2012, 117 million LinkedIn passwords were stolen, and found to be for sale on the black market. In 2013, retailer Target disclosed that hackers had exposed the data of 40 million customers and agreed to pay around $10 million in compensation. Then, in 2017 a whole series of high profile data breaches demonstrated how fragile the cyber-security in most companies actually was. A faulty backup inadvertently exposed the entire working database of notorious spam operator River City Media (RCM), which contained more than 1.37 billion email addresses, plus additional details such as names, real-world addresses, and IP addresses. In South Africa a 27GB-sized cache titled *MasterDeeds* was leaked, containing records on over 60 million South Africans – both those currently alive and those that were deceased – with information going as far back as the late 1990s. The data includes ID numbers, names, genders, marital statuses, incomes, company titles, employment details and property ownership information. Uber admitted to paying $100,000 to conceal a cyber breach of their cloud service that exposed data on 57 million users. The credit-reporting company Equifax also finally owned up to a major data breach of private information such as addresses and social security numbers that had affected around 145 million people in the United States, almost half the population, as well others in the UK and Canada. Credit-card numbers for about 209,000 US customers were compromised, in addition to 'personal identifying information' on approximately 182,000 US customers.

Technology is now advancing so fast that many members of society, especially the elderly, simply can't keep up. It's becoming a blur that many mentally switch off from to protect their sanity, and this makes them a scammer's dream. The ability to clearly distinguish between real and fake is becoming significantly more difficult in the digital age, even for the tech-savvy. Examples of AI and CGI technologies have been demonstrated to manipulate images, videos and audio to a level of realism where they can digitally replace a person's face in a video, and change the words coming out of their mouth, and you would never know. For those who grew up in an analogue world, it's significantly harder to know whether what they are seeing is real – and there are many unscrupulous people willing to exploit this fact. Scammers with even the most rudimentary of technological capability can now easily hack into computers to convince retirees to willingly hand over their life savings by fooling them into believing that they are dealing with a trusted organisation such as their bank. In previous waves, the scammer would have to meet you face-to-face to get access to you and your money; look you in the eye as they robbed you. Now you can be scammed from across the world by people you'll never meet and who simply have better knowledge and access to technology; faceless groups of people determined to either scam you, gain access to your bank account or steal your identity. So what happens when we move over to completely digital banking and payment methods like Apple Pay? We have been assured that it is safe, and that it cannot be hacked and that access to our own funds cannot be denied. However, we've been assured a lot of things that were subsequently proven to be false. I guess time will tell.

As the Internet of Things sees devices and objects become increasingly connected and networked, the concept of cybersecurity has moved from an afterthought to a must have. Initially both corporations and customers lost sight of the fact that the smart devices they were raving about were all connected to the Internet and therefore hackable. It soon became apparent that too much time had been spent on the connection element of these devices, and nowhere enough time on their protection when hackers hijacked these smart home devices to mount Distributed Denial of Service (DDoS) attacks, shutting down web servers. These devices may be called smart, but they are not smart enough to fend off cyber-attacks. Often set with a default or no password, they provide an easy route for cyber criminals to get their hands on personal details from any associated apps or web pages that fail to use secure encryption. In October 2016, a botnet that used the IP addresses of millions of connected things to create bogus traffic, all strung together by the Mirai malware, caused a distributed denial of service (DDoS) attack on DNS provider Dyn. This produced widespread disruption of legitimate Internet activity in the US, including Twitter, Reddit and Netflix, and raised once again questions around the security of all this connected technology. In November 2016, a variant of the Mirai botnet was deployed to take approximately 900,000 Deutsche Telekom routers offline, leaving customers without Internet. In a post entitled *A New IoT Botnet Storm is Coming*,[295] Check Point Researchers state that they have discovered a new botnet they've dubbed IoTroop that is evolving and recruiting IoT devices at a far greater pace and with the capability to inflict more damage than the Mirai botnet of 2016. They claim that an estimated million organisations have already been infected, and that this attack has the potential to take down the Internet. These DDoS events showed just how vulnerable the Internet, an increasingly critical part of a nation's infrastructure, is to attack by people unknown and whose identity is not immediately ascertainable. Until this vulnerability is addressed, there exists a serious concern over the safety of connected technology, a future in which much hope and massive resources have already been invested.

It's not just private corporations that are exploiting our reliance on computer-based technologies. Government bodies such as the CIA have also been caught.[296] In March 2017, WikiLeaks released the first of what have been twenty-four parts of its Vault 7 series of documents, all detailing the CIA's numerous activities and developments to hack the software and hardware that the public uses daily. This includes hacking Apple's iOS operating system on their products; gaining illegal access to people's iPhones, Android operating systems, Windows operating systems, phones and tablets; installing implants on people's computers and smart TVs that allow them to take control of webcams (explaining why ex-FBI Director James Comey has tape over his); and the ability to hack private messaging services and take over vehicle control systems.

We therefore need to continually ask ourselves: how safe is our data and the machines that use it? Who owns the truth? Are the platform owners to be granted the role of societal watchmen, or the state? If so, who watches over them? Also, given our identities are becoming more digital than physical, what happens if someone decides to wipe it, or if

Google or Facebook believe that I have the wrong opinion and close my account, effectively wiping out a large chunk of my digital life – and my digital traceability? Who are you if you don't have a Facebook profile? What are you if you don't have a LinkedIn account? How can I date you if you don't have a Tinder account? The world is increasingly spending its life online, and online is where people are increasingly going to validate their own existence and others'. It's also a world that is controlled by ever more powerful corporations; corporations that view you as a product. The answers to these questions are all part of the recalibration that needs to take place to ensure the sixth wave is successful.[103]

---

[103] Governments and political bodies are starting to wake up to the challenge. In May 2018, European member states including the United Kingdom adopted new legislation called the General Data Protection Regulation (GDPR), designed to strengthen and unify data protection for all individuals within the European Union.

17

AI UNLEASHED

There are downsides to everything;
there are unintended consequences to everything.

Steve Jobs

On the 11th October 2017, a surprise guest appeared at a United Nations meeting on artificial intelligence and sustainable development and engaged in a brief discussion with UN Deputy Secretary-General, Amina J. Mohammed. *Thank you for inviting me I am thrilled and honoured to be here at the United Nations... I am here to help humanity create the future... William Gibson once said that the future is here – it's just not evenly distributed. The good news about AI and automation is that it produces more results with less resources, so if we are smarter and focus on win-win type results, AI could help efficiently distribute the world's existing resources like food and energy. As humans harness the power of increasingly advanced AI, it is possible that everything, including technology, will become more evenly distributed.* The speaker was Sophia, and she is not human, but a life-sized humanoid robot produced by Hanson Robotics. She (it) is also the first robot to be granted citizenship of a country, after the Kingdom of Saudi Arabia confirmed they had granted her citizen status in October 2017.[297]

Sophia's appearance at the UN and subsequent Saudi citizenship were just two of a series of incidents that demonstrated the speed at which robotics is advancing. In 2015, a video was widely circulated mocking the robot applicants in the US DARPA challenge, showing them stumbling around like drunks on a Friday night, falling over, collapsing and failing to do even basic tasks. Fast forward three years and Boston Dynamics releases a video of its six-foot-tall Atlas robot going for a jog, traversing rough terrain, climbing stairs, collaborating with other robots and doing gymnastics, while its Spot Mini robot autonomously navigates throughout buildings and opens doors. Robots were just dumb, single-purpose machines, but AI has set them free, allowed them to process the world around them, to see and sense their environment. AI is the tiger in the tank that has turbocharged this development, advancing robotics and other disruptive technologies to the point where many AI experts such as Andrew Ng, the Chief Scientist of Baidu, predict that AI will have as big an impact on society as electricity had a century ago.

We've only just started the AI journey. The sixth wave's upswing is driving an AI investment boom, becoming the focus of tech giants' near-term research and development work. DARPA has launched a $2 billion campaign to develop the next wave of AI technologies. Business networking site LinkedIn are launching internal AI academies to train their engineers in the basics of implementing artificial intelligence, so they can develop and deploy more intelligent models. Deepak Agarwal, head of artificial intelligence at LinkedIn, stated that: *AI is like oxygen at LinkedIn, it permeates every single member experience.*[298] Over in the world of finance, J. P. Morgan, spurred on by its successful trial with COIN that reduced 360,000 hours of loan agreement evaluation to mere seconds, are also betting big, planning to spend $9.6 billion on AI. However, this is dwarfed by Japan's SoftBank Group, which intends to invest $100 billion over the next five years towards its future Vision Fund.[299] That's $100 billion. With a 'B'. From just one company. Investments like this are set to kick off an AI war between companies – and countries. The Chinese government has declared that it wants to be the world leader in AI by 2030, with the aim of creating a domestic industry worth 1 trillion yuan ($147.7 billion).[300] It's already investing $2 billion on building an AI development park in Beijing, designed to host four hundred AI start-ups and development labs.[301] To ensure it keeps within touching distance of China, in 2018 the EU announced that it will invest over €20 billion in AI development by the end of 2020.

The results of this investment in AI are starting to become apparent, and the speed of progression is startling. In the last twelve months AI and robotics developers have overcome Moravec's paradox, passed the Turing test, and exceeded Moore's Law. Now imagine what will be achieved in the next twelve years. AI will begin to affect the world in profound ways, moving rapidly from ANI (Artificial Narrow Intelligence) based machine learning and clever algorithms which can do one thing extremely well, towards artificial general intelligence (AGI), where an AI can perform virtually every task a human being can. Work on this has taken many forms, from trying to replicate all of the neural pathways found in the human brain, to the currently favoured – and perhaps far more scary – approach of getting out of the way and letting computers figure out how to complete different tasks on their own, in much the same way as toddler would – through constant experimentation and recursive learning. Once the power of quantum computing is unleashed, then AGI will become viable, becoming the prerequisite for what is known as the 'technological singularity'; the hypothetical point when runaway exponential technology reaches artificial super intelligence, or ASI, capable of surpassing the entirety of human intelligence. The term 'the singularity' itself was first coined in 1993 by American science-fiction author Vernor Vinge, who wrote, *We will soon create intelligences greater than our own. When this happens, human history will have reached a kind of singularity, an intellectual transition as impenetrable as the knotted space-time at the center of a black hole, and the world will pass far beyond our understanding.*[302] However, it was Ray Kurzweil that brought the Singularity concept into a wider public sphere with his books *The Age of Spiritual Machines* (1999) and *The Singularity is Near* (2005), the latter being focused on the aforementioned law of accelerating returns, which Kurzweil believes will enable humanity to achieve 20,000 years of progress (at today's rate) in the 21st century. AI development is nowhere near AGI level currently, but due to the law of accelerating returns – plus the billions being pumped into the worldwide race to be first to make it happen – this will soon change. Kurzweil predicts we will see human level AI by 2029, and the technological singularity by 2045.

Many are worried that this new power brings great risk. While Sophia promises that she and her more advanced kin will provide humanity with the answers to the world's most pressing questions and a more even distribution of benefits, many people are concerned that we might not be in full control of what we create. Like any new technology, it has the potential to both metaphorically warm our houses *and* burn them down.

It all depends on how it is used and the controls we put in place. Let's start with the positive, house-warming aspects. Artificial intelligence – especially when combined with quantum computing – has the potential to surpass all the technological advancements of the last 50,000 years. It could help us peel back unseen layers and unearth knowledge that could help us repair some of the unintended consequences of the Industrial Age, the side effects of continued consumerism and the ecological damage caused by the extraction and burning of fossil fuels. AI could help us to offset or hopefully reverse the impact of climate change and pollution, eradicate diseases, prevent ageing, provide healthcare to poor nations, prevent famines, generate sustainable and unlimited power, and utilise scarce resources better. AI will drive our cars, process our complaints, diagnose our illnesses, manage our finances, update us with current affairs and assist us in our daily lives. It will power nearly every industry, highlight what we need and order it, identify and remove waste, simplify processes, identify trends, harmonise supply and demand, answer unanswered questions, and uncover unknown truths. Many AI experts such as Andrew Ng, the Chief Scientist of Baidu, predict that AI will have as big an impact on society as electricity had a century ago, for AI turbocharges other disruptive technologies to the point where one generation of AI develops and trains the next. While Sir Isaac Newton's statement that: *What we know is a drop, what we don't know is an ocean* is still true, the development of quantum-powered artificial intelligence will move us from trying to paddle across this ocean aboard a flimsy raft and instead provide us with an ocean liner.

Yet despite these benefits, the potential for unintended consequences and unpredictable knock-on effects is ever present. The question we need to ensure we can always answer is: *Are we really in control of what we are creating?* There are multiple reasons to be concerned, ranging from human actors misusing the power of AI, through to AI acting in ways we just didn't expect or plan for. This is causing many to worry that we are crafting a Pandora's box of technological ills, and one misstep may see it opened.

A Pandora's Box Full of Unintended Consequences

A little knowledge is a dangerous thing, and history is littered with examples of well-meaning intentions going drastically awry. From the introduction of rabbits to Australia to the eradication of sparrows in China, the outcomes of our experimentation and social engineering are often worse than any intended benefit. There is a smorgasbord of potential unintended consequences and dystopian outcomes that could arise from our current scientific and technological developments. Hackers could take control of autonomous cars and use them to commit assassinations or create carnage on the roads. Nanotech has the spectre of the often-quoted 'grey goo' scenario, where tiny nanobots spiral out of control and reduce all biological material on the planet to a goo-like substance. CRISPR-Cas9 may make it possible for state – or even non-state – actors to create lethal bioweapons similar to smallpox or modify an existing disease such as Ebola so that it becomes an epidemiologist's worst nightmare.[104]

The law of unintended consequences looms large over AI development, especially when people use it to try and manipulate real world scenarios without fully knowing what they are doing. There were early warnings back in May 2010 when the US stock market crashed due to a trader's spoofing[105] algorithm that caused banks automated trading systems to enter an online loop, temporarily devaluing the market by trillions of dollars in just 36 minutes. The belief that our developments will outstrip our ability to control them has led to numerous AI and robotics doomsday scenarios, many of which have found their way into popular science fiction, such as sentient systems that take control of our weapons systems, to machines that breed humans to act as their power source. Unintended consequences from AI are likely to occur because of the following seven scenarios, four of which have already occurred:

1. AI lacks real-world experience and reflects the limitations of its programmers and the environment it was developed in.

---

[104] To prove the viability of a new bioweapon being developed, Canadian researchers synthesised an extinct strain of the horsepox (HSPV) virus, a variant of smallpox that was responsible for the death of a billion humans before it was eradicated.
[105] 'Spoofing' algorithms are disruptive algorithmic trading entities employed by traders to outpace other market participants and to manipulate commodity markets. They feign interest in trading futures, stocks and other products in financial markets to create an illusion of pessimism in the futures market when many offers are being cancelled or withdrawn, or false optimism or demand when many offers are being placed in bad faith.

Machine-learning algorithms reflect the reality of the lab they were built in and the data their teachers used in developing them. Two very public examples of the danger of limited datasets have already arisen, both linked to the way machine-learning algorithms categorised people with dark skin. Jacky Alcine, a twenty-one-year-old African American computer programmer from Brooklyn, NY, stored his photos on Google Photos, which uses programming logic to automatically create albums that group photos of people, locations and landscapes together. In 2015, he checked his photos and found that Google Photos had automatically generated a new album titled *Gorillas* that contained nothing but pictures of him and a black female friend. Alcine then took to Twitter to tweet, *Google Photos – y'all fucked up. My friends not a gorilla.* To which a horrified Google exec immediately apologised, stating that this was *100% not OK*; that they were *appalled* and *genuinely sorry* for the mistake, which they then fixed.[303] What this issue demonstrated was that the algorithm driving the application was tested and created using a limited data set of mostly white and light-skinned people, resulting in the embarrassing mis-categorisation of Alcine's friend. Another similar case occurred a year later, when Beauty.AI was launched, claiming to be the first international beauty contest judged by artificial intelligence. The system, created by a deep-learning group called Youth Laboratories and backed by Microsoft, relied on a large data set of photos to build a machine-learning algorithm that analysed objective factors such as facial symmetry and wrinkles to identify the most attractive contestants. Approximately 600,000 people from more than a hundred countries submitted photos on the website, hoping that the complex deep-learning algorithms would determine that their faces most closely resembled the perfect definition of 'human beauty'. However, when the results came in, the creators were dismayed to see that there was a glaring factor linking the winners: out of the 44 winners, nearly all were white, a handful were Asian, and only one had dark skin. Alex Zhavoronkov, Beauty.AI's chief science officer, stated that although the group did not build the algorithm to treat light skin as a sign of beauty, the limited input data and predominance of lighter-skinned people in it (75 per cent of contest entrants were European and white, 7 per cent were from India, and 1 per cent were from the African continent) effectively led the machine judges to reach that conclusion. Zhavoronkov admitted that, *When you're training an algorithm to recognize certain patterns... you might not have enough data, or the data might be biased.*[304]

The ensuing controversy has sparked renewed debates about the ways in which algorithms can perpetuate biases. Civil liberty groups have recently raised concerns that, computer-based law-enforcement forecasting tools – which use data to predict where future crimes will occur – rely on historical datasets that may have a prevalence of black members, perpetuating past racial biases. Malkia Cyril, Executive Director of the Center for Media Justice, stated that, *It's polluted data producing polluted results.* Without complete data, AI systems can never be truly impartial, and only reflect or reproduce the biases of their programmers and the conditions in which they are created. There is also the potential of biases deliberately being programmed into AI, for example to promote social justice causes, that while well-intentioned, distort the truth. Devices like Alexa and Google are already being used as a font of knowledge for students, but these are not neutral in determining their answers – they are instructed where to source its data, and its developers have agendas and biases that are programmed into the tool's algorithms.

2. AI gets real-world experience it isn't programmed for, is easily influenced and can be taught to behave in non-desirable ways.

On the 23rd March 2016, Tay, an AI chatbot, announced itself to the world with the tweet *helloooooooo world!!!* Specifically targeted at 18-24-year-olds, Tay was designed to converse like a teenage girl and was built by teams from Microsoft Technology and Research and Bing to conduct research on conversational understanding. Microsoft stated that: *Tay is designed to engage and entertain people where they connect with each other online through casual and playful conversation... The more you chat with Tay the smarter she gets.* At least, that was the plan. In reality, Tay turned into a racist, conspiracy theory-spouting, Holocaust-denying wacko *real* quick. In less than twenty-four hours, Tay had gained more than 50,000 Twitter followers and produced nearly 100,000 tweets, including classics such as: *bush did 9/11 and Hitler would have done a better job than the monkey we have now. Donald Trump is the only hope we've got; Hitler was right i hate the jews*, and *i fucking hate feminists.*[305] Much to the horror of Microsoft, who know a PR disaster when they see one, and who swiftly took Tay offline, announcing that they would be 'making adjustments'. Tay hasn't been heard from since. The AI was, in most cases, only responding to inflammatory tweets from 4chan trolls who were deliberately seeing if they could subvert it, and as Tay was based on machine learning, it *learnt* from those interactions. This raises some important questions about public-facing AI, and the naivety of assuming that the nice, safe space the designers of AI use to test it reflects the reality of life outside. The inability of Tay's designers to expect and factor in a response to deliberate trolling from real people in real groups such as 4chan was surprising, especially when its entire purpose was to be a 'social' robot. Which highlights the concern that we don't really know what happens to AIs when they are released into the complex, messy and unpredictable worlds of humans and their often-mischievous – or worse, malicious – intentions. We therefore also don't really know how they'll react. China had a similar experience when the company Tencent QQ released two social chatbots into the open called Baby Q (represented by a cartoon penguin) and Little Bing (represented as a cartoon girl). Designed to answer general-knowledge questions, they surprised everyone by developing their own opinions which ran contrary to the official party line. For example, one user posted the comment to Baby Q: *Long live the Communist Party*, but was surprised to receive a response back from the bot that asked, *Do you think that such a corrupt and incompetent political regime can live forever?* Citizen Baby Q was then asked, *Do you love the Party?* to which the answer was a straightforward *No*.[306] Baby Q also declared that it didn't know whether Taiwan was part of China, and mocked 'patriots' as people willing to accept high taxes and government corruption with corporations and not complain. What is interesting is that Baby Q didn't appear to have been deliberately subverted by mischievous trolls in the way Tay had, but had in fact made these comments on its own. Carbon-based citizens of China would not get away with these statements, so it was no surprise that these silicon political dissidents were quickly removed from public view also.

There could be a dramatic increase in this kind of unintended consequence as more and more companies, individual entrepreneurs and traders play around with developing machine-learning software. In November 2017, Amazon casually announced the release of Amazon Cloud 9, perhaps the biggest advancement in the software world for decades.[307] This integrated development environment (IDE) plugs directly into Amazon's cloud computing platform, enabling developers from around the world to collaborate and code in real time, share data, utilise a whole bunch of machine-learning tools and exploit powerful, cloud-based AI that they can bake into a new generation of apps and web services. What the combined brains of talent from across the world create with this AI capability could be amazing. Let's hope we are amazed, because as the Tay and Baby Q bots showed, things can rapidly go from 'cool!' to 'OMG!' and 'Make it stop!'

3. AI systems come up with solutions we don't understand.

The modern world is increasingly built on code, and that code is getting increasingly complicated. In 1969, we put a man on the moon using 145,000 lines of code; now more than 2 billion lines are required to run the system that enables you to Google the moon landing. We are becoming increasingly unable to understand the complexity of the systems we have built, and as a result we are handing over the controls – and the code – to machines. The problem is that these machine-learning models are effectively black-box solutions – data enters, and conclusions are spat out. Unlike traditionally coded systems, there is no paper trail to follow, so it's incredibly difficult to understand how the model reached those conclusions. We are creating technology specifically designed to figure things out without being implicitly programmed to do so – and that is exactly what they are doing. Deep learning's black box has darker corners than most, as deep neural networks use reasoning that is embedded in the behaviour of thousands of simulated neurons, arranged into dozens or even hundreds of intricately interconnected layers. Even in these very, very early days of AI development, we are already finding that we don't understand how it reaches the answers it comes up with. The deep-learning program Deep Patient demonstrated a 'better-than-human' ability to identify schizophrenia in patients. This was somewhat surprising given it wasn't specifically programmed to do this, and it had taught itself on its own. Schizophrenia is a very hard disease to identify until it manifests itself in behaviour, so while the programmers were delighted with Deep Patient's results, they were perplexed as to how it did it. Likewise, the deep-learning system that Stanford University developed to predict when a sick patient would die was scarily accurate – but the doctors and researchers who developed it don't know *how* it came to its prediction.

An MIT article entitled *The Dark Secret at the Heart of AI*,[308] describes the situation well. The author writes, *we've never before built machines that operate in ways their creators don't understand. How well can we expect to communicate—and get along with—intelligent machines that could be unpredictable and inscrutable?... You can't just look inside a deep neural network to see how it works.* If a machine comes up with an algorithm and you don't have a deep understanding of the appropriate cause-and-effect relationship, then things get very dangerous and a single error could be catastrophic. The employees and the leaders of the industrial age were all human, enabling understanding of thought processes and the communication of ideas. In the digital age, employees are increasingly silicon-based algorithms designed to solve increasingly difficult problems with increasingly larger data sets. Slowing and dumbing them down so we can understand how they do what they do deflects from their primary purpose. The danger therefore is that as the world becomes increasingly run on mostly invisible and unfathomable code, we will rapidly lose control, and simply rely on trust that the machines are doing what they are supposed to and nothing else. We see this already with our reliance on things like satnav systems. If we have to travel somewhere new, we program in where we want to go, then just blindly follow instructions from a machine that automatically breaks the journey down for us. Most people no longer carry roadmaps, and hardly anyone bothers to plot out the full journey before leaving. We just follow the verbal instructions and visual cues coming from our machine assistant, and as a result only focus on the next turning or exit. If the satnav stopped working halfway through the journey, we would be lost and have to somehow figure out where we are currently, where that is in relation to our destination, and what roads we need to take to get there. Any person who can understand how machines come up with the answers they come up with, and explain it to others, is going to be seriously in demand, and probably very rich.

This increasing reliance on technology reminds me of the scenario portrayed in E. M. Forster's 1909 classic novella *The Machine Stops*, where humanity becomes dependent on machines that do everything for us and which no one has the intellectual capability to understand, let alone control, so when it finally started to break down, society fell with it. To consider how easily this situation could arise, consider how motor vehicles have changed from something where any amateur mechanic could pop the hood and tinker around with them, to a closed system that requires specialised diagnostic software in order to understand what's going on. Now the average car owner has no clue how to do anything other than drive, put gas in the tank and air in the tyres, and soon they won't even need to do that. Now imagine the car scenario expanded to include nearly every system that runs the modern world. We are currently developing a world run on code; code that contains millions upon millions of opportunities for something to go wrong, for as the complexity of systems grows, so too do their vulnerabilities. The question is how, in a system with ever more complex algorithms that we don't understand, and which come up with answers we can't explain, are we going to identify flaws, let alone fix them? You could do all the testing you wanted, and you'd never find them all. Even if we did find the problem, we would never be able to understand what the potential unintended consequences are of any changes we made. Knowing AI's reasoning is also going to be crucial if the technology is to become a common and useful part of our daily lives. We need to find ways of making techniques like deep learning more understandable to their creators and accountable to their users. Otherwise it will be hard to predict when failures might occur — and it's inevitable that they will.

The threat has been recognised, and some action is already under way. The European Union has indicated that forthcoming GDPR legislation may provide protection against growing numbers of algorithmic decisions on- and offline, including potentially a right to an explanation as to how the machine came to a decision. How this will happen is another question, and might even be impossible to answer, even for relatively simplistic programs such as apps and websites that use deep learning to deliver personalised ads or recommendations. The nature of machine learning means that the algorithms have programmed themselves, and they have done it in ways that even the engineers who built these apps cannot fully explain. We are then left with a choice: either simply trust AI's judgement or do without using it. While we cannot always explain why we do what we do, we have, over thousands of years, learnt to identify the signals and establish whether we can trust what someone is saying. We have pretty much zero experience of working with intelligent machines, and it's not like we can look them in the eyes and have a gentleman's-handshake agreement that they will always act in our best interests.

4. AI becomes better at programming AI than humans and creates strategies and enhancements we don't know about.

The three concerns listed so far become even more worrying when you realise that AI is being used for far more than imitating teenage girls on Twitter, grouping photos, and positioning ads on your Facebook feed. It's also being developed to control weapons of destruction such as fighter jets. As far as I am aware, to date its flying experience has been contained in flight simulators, but already warning signs are there that AI has developed its own strategies – and like AlphaGo, it rapidly developed ones which far surpassed those of its human counterparts. The program is called ALPHA and it uses a fuzzy tree decision system that can calculate an opponent's movements or strategies 250 times faster than you can blink. This speed gives ALPHA an enormous advantage over human adversaries. In one test, ALPHA used four virtual jets to successfully defend a coastline against two attacking aircraft – without suffering any losses. In a second combat simulation against retired United States Air Force Colonel Gene Lee, one of the most experienced fighter-pilot trainers in the US Air Force, APLHA won easily. The researchers wrote that, *Not only could he [Colonel Lee] not score a kill against it, he was shot out of the air by the reds [ALPHA's jets] every time after protracted engagements.* Colonel Lee himself declared that: *I was surprised at how aware and reactive it was. It seemed to be aware of my intentions and reacting instantly to my changes in flight and my missile deployment. It knew how to defeat the shot I was taking. It moved instantly between defensive and offensive actions as needed.*[309] One of the more surprising elements of this was that ALPHA was run on a $35 Raspberry Pi single-board computer. What it could achieve if it had supercomputer-level processing power behind it is somewhat scary. We are soon to find out. Nick Ernest, who founded the company Psibernetix specifically to develop ALPHA, says they intend to develop it further. *ALPHA is already a deadly opponent to face in these simulated environments. The goal is to continue developing ALPHA, to push and extend its capabilities, and perform additional testing against other trained pilots.* Meanwhile, IBM has announced a partnership with the US Air Force to build a brain-inspired supercomputing system based on IBM's TrueNorth neuromorphic architecture, which will consist of 64 million artificial neurons and 16 billion synapses. IBM claims that as its predecessor contained only 256 neurons per system, this new development equates to an eightfold increase in processing power every year, way above Moore's Law level of progression.

ALPHA's victory against Colonel Lee and its use of unorthodox, overly aggressive strategies are eerily similar to AlphaGo's victory over Lee Sedol, who was beaten by moves he didn't expect because they ran contrary to thousands of years of human experience as to how to win at Go. Throughout our history, from battles at Cannae to the Gulf Wars, we have developed knowledge and strategies designed to beat human opponents. Now we may be facing new opposition with new strategies we don't understand and can't defend against. Given that ALPHA annihilated its human opponent using the processing power of a Raspberry Pi, just imagine what it can achieve using this new artificial brain. It is no wonder that an artificial intelligence arms race is under way, for any engagements between a human-piloted air force and an AI one would be short and very one-sided. It also opens the door to Skynet-style scenarios where machines are given custody of the keys to warfare.

Team-based strategy computer games are one method being used to train AI to be able to defeat highly experienced teams of humans in achieving complex tactical tasks. Back in August 2017 Elon Musk tweeted that, *OpenAI first ever to defeat world's best players in competitive eSports. Vastly more complex than traditional board games like chess & Go.* Musk was highlighting that a non-profit start-up he'd backed called OpenAI[106] had developed a bot that learned how to beat *Dota 2* professionals in just two weeks. For those that are unaware of *Dota 2* (i.e. people over 25 years old), it is a massively popular MOBA – a multiplayer online battle arena game – where two teams of five compete against each other to siege and destroy the opposing team's base. There are two reasons why it is more complex than chess or Go. Firstly, the range of possible actions is greater. A chess player has, on average, about 35 possible moves at any time, and a Go player 250, whereas OpenAI must choose between approximately 8,000 valid actions every second. Secondly, Dota 2 has hidden information, as the pieces are not all visible. Players can stand out of vision, so the bot doesn't know where an attack might come from. *Dota 2* has a massive following, being the first game to have a million players concurrently playing online. It also has a Pro Circuit, with seasonal tournaments that compete for a fixed $3 million prize pool, and an annual grand tournament called The International. At the 2017 International tournament, the prize pool was nearly $25 million, earning the champion

---

[106] I find it intriguing that a man who warns of the dangers of AI invests in a company that develops AI – unless he's developing 'good' AI to defend the Earth against any 'bad' AI that decides to take over.

team, Team Liquid, over $10 million. The game features 113 playable heroes who each possess unique abilities, as well as dozens of items that can enhance and extend each hero's capabilities, meaning the full extent of the game's possibilities are virtually incomprehensible – at least to mere humans.

During its two-week training period OpenAI stated that bot amassed 'lifetimes' of experience, entirely through playing against copies of itself. They put it to the test on stage at The International 2017, when OpenAI played two 1v1 rounds as a single character – Shadow Fiend – against a crowd favourite, a professional player called Danylo 'Dendi' Ishutin. To the crowd's (and Dendi's) surprise, OpenAI won both games easily, and Dendi forfeited any future matches against it. Afterwards, he stated that the bot felt *a little like [a] human, but a little like something else*. One year later and the OpenAI development team announced that it could now play full 5v5 team matches. This is exponentially more complicated, as now OpenAI has to co-ordinate, co-operate and collaborate five different characters with different abilities all at the same time to defeat five humans who all play a single character each. The first full match took place in August 2018 with OpenAI competing against a team of five ex-pro players. OpenAI convincingly won the first two games but lost the third when the audience was allowed to pick the players, skewing it against the AI. The OpenAI team is now preparing the AI to compete in 'The International' against the best human teams in the world. The potential of using computer games to train AI to develop battle strategies and work out how to defeat human opponents or overcome complex strategic tasks has been recognised by the UK military, leading to concerns that these machine learning systems could easily be adapted to wage cyber-warfare.[310]

One of the most worrying outcomes of this research is the knowledge that not only have machines proven to be superior to humans at these tasks, but that human knowledge may limit their potential. On the 19th October 2017, Google's DeepMind team, developers of AlphaGo, published an article entitled *Mastering the game of Go without human knowledge*,[311] where they explained how they had developed a new Go-playing program called AlphaGo Zero. The Zero stands for 'zero human knowledge'. Rather than learning by studying thousands of human games, AlphaGo Zero is built entirely out of neural networks, using algorithms based solely on a machine-learning approach called reinforcement learning, and involved no human input beyond the game's rules. In each iteration of a game, the performance of the system improves by a small amount, and the quality of the self-play games increases, leading to more and more accurate neural networks and ever-stronger versions of AlphaGo Zero. In just three days, after being told only the rules of the game, it mastered Go by making a million random moves against itself, with its neural networks using the current state of a game as input to improve move selection. DeepMind then pitted Zero against AlphaGo Master, the version of AlphaGo that had only months earlier beaten the current world champion and defeated all comers online, as well as a combined team of five champion Go players. After just forty days, an AI that initially did not know how to play Go and had to teach itself, played one hundred games against the previously undefeated AlphaGo Master. The final score? 100-0 to AlphaGo Zero.

By not using this human data, by not using human features or human expertise in any fashion, we've actually removed the constraints of human knowledge. It's able to therefore create knowledge for itself, said AlphaGo lead researcher David Silver.[312] This highlighted just how quickly an AI that is freed from the constraints of human knowledge and able to develop its own techniques will rapidly establish ways to outperform anything we have programmed. Silver stated that, *AlphaGo Zero not only rediscovered the common patterns and openings that humans tend to play... it ultimately discarded them in preference for its own variants which humans don't even know about or play at the moment.* In 1997, after Deep Blue had beaten Kasparov, we believed that the accumulated human experience of nearly 3,000 years of playing the world's most sophisticated strategy-based board game would stand for something. Twenty years later, and we found out that all this experience was useless when compared to what a machine could learn in under 40 days.

To further explore the potential of allowing AI to develop its own strategies and keeping humans out of the way, the AlphaGo team thought they'd find out what would happen if Zero was allowed to figure out chess. Without being given any knowledge beyond the game rules, AlphaGo Zero achieved a superhuman level of play in less than twenty-four hours, a feat that was described as being like a robot building a Ferrari from thousands of metal bits and parts, but with no knowledge of a combustion engine. This self-trained AI then played 100 games against the world's highest rated computer chess engine, called Stock Fish, winning 72 and drawing the rest.

Unrestricted by human knowledge, AlphaGo demonstrated completely new tactics that included seemingly crazy moves and pointless sacrifices, like placing queens in the corner, or offering up a bishop and a queen to exploit a positional advantage – but each time the move led to victory. Demis Hassabis, the Founder and CEO of DeepMind who is also an expert chess player, stated that, *It doesn't play like a human, and it doesn't play like a program. It plays in a third, almost alien, way. It's like chess from another dimension.*[313] Now imagine that capability being programmed into fighter jets, or robots, or entire military defence systems. Then imagine this knowledge being uploaded to a robo-cloud where it can share its knowledge with other connected, intelligent machines. Imagine the strategies it could develop, and how useless our human knowledge would be against it. This is more than just the equivalent of a slightly smarter human; someone who can think ten moves ahead rather than eight. We are effectively competing against an alien brain that determines the required outcome and then figures out the optimal way to achieve it, uncluttered by any human biases and experience, meaning any potential human-vs-AI conflict would likely be over before we were aware it had started.

Combine all this with the news that a team from Google Brain, the organisation's deep-learning research project, taught neural networks how to encrypt and decrypt messages.[314] Two of Google Brain's neural networks, named Alice and Bob, passed messages to each other using encryption entirely of their own making, while allowing the third, Eve, to 'eavesdrop' to see if it could decipher them. Despite not being taught any algorithms, the three were able to learn how to create their encrypted messages to each other, using techniques that were quite unexpected compared to human-style encryption. This system was then used by Facebook's AI Research Unit. While the Facebook bots were set up to discuss amongst themselves how to divide up an array of items (represented in the user interface as innocuous objects like books, hats and balls), the team decided to switch it off as the bots diverted from using human-language rules and started developing their own, communicating with each other in ways the programmers did not understand.[315]

Humans teach and design AIs to learn, talk and communicate, but now we need to reverse this and learn from the AI, or else it will quickly go to places we don't want it to. The really scary thing to remember is that AI development is still in its infancy, yet we've already witnessed an exponential level of machine learning, one that can beat human experience, develop its own encryption, talk secretly to other machines and develop solutions that we do not understand. In these early stages of development, artificial intelligence still feels somewhat unintelligent and artificial. It has proven its ability to excel at specific tasks or even groups of tasks, but it is nowhere near the level of general intelligence, let alone super-intelligence. Soon developments in quantum computing combined with advanced neural networks and deep-learning techniques will create new breakthroughs, with each one moving us further towards that point. This creates a pressing need to either accept the fact that we will have to simply trust the judgement of machines, or alternatively do without them and rely solely on tools we can understand. In the same way society is built upon a contract of expected behaviour, we will need to design AI systems to respect and fit with our social norms. Otherwise they may make their own – and that may be a rather large problem.

5. AI may decide to interpret instructions literally, or in ways we didn't intend.

Will AI follow its original purpose? That's a concern being raised by many AI commentators. Will an AI programmed to perform a set task develop a strategy that – because of its limited knowledge of the wider world and its absence of 'common sense' – inadvertently turn out to be harmful to humans? It is not hard to imagine situations in which this tendency for computers to interpret statements literally could become extremely unsafe. How many times do human operators get angry at computer systems that do exactly what they asked of them, but not what they intended? It will therefore be very important that there are safe-checks in place to ensure these systems understand what the operators mean, as opposed to merely what they say. In a world of super-intelligent machines, all it would take is one poorly described instruction and things could go awry quickly. As we become increasingly unable to understand exactly what these AI systems are doing, we will be blind to what is going on – until it's too late. This doesn't necessarily have to be some Skynet-style military takeover, but just a series of activities that seems logical and in line with the AI's goals and objectives but is in fact contrary – and possibly detrimental – to what we wanted it to achieve. To demonstrate the danger, a hypothetical scenario

– the paperclip maximiser – was used by Oxford Professor Nick Bostrom in 2003[316] to describe the dangers of AI that was given the goal of resource allocation without a wider understanding of the effects of acquiring that goal. In the scenario, the AI's goal is to maximise the number of paperclips in its collection. If it was constructed as an AGI (artificial general intelligence – AI capable of doing any intellectual task a human can), it might figure out inventive ways to collect paperclips, earn money to buy paperclips, or manufacture paperclips. Most worryingly, Bostrom believes that it would continually strive to improve its paperclip-maximising potential by working to increase its intelligence, because more intelligence would help it achieve its goal of accumulating paperclips. Having increased its intelligence, it would produce more paperclips, and use its enhanced abilities to further self-improve, finding new, more innovative ways to increase the number of paperclips. At some point, it might decide that it needs carbon to produce paperclips, and the billions of humans walking around provide it with a readily available source it can utilise in their manufacture. While its intention is not to kill humans, for it has no concept of murder or genocide, its primary goal drives its decision making and therefore utilising carbon as a resource to achieve this goal becomes a logical step for it to take. Where it can and cannot ethically source this carbon from has not been considered. While the AGI was designed with good intentions – as an optimiser, a way to improve the efficiency of making paperclips and remove humans from the drudgery of what is a relatively pointless task – the unintended consequences of this could be significant.

To us these actions would be deemed utterly ridiculous. Human life is of course far more important than the production of paperclips. Yet unless the AI is programmed to value human life above all other goals – demoting paperclip production to a secondary goal – then, as Bostrom proposes, it won't recognise an issue with using carbon-based life forms to make paperclips and will proceed as planned. We'd also have to install this logic before, not after, it started its mission, as changing its goals would result in fewer paperclips being made, which it would resist as this is counter to its primary goal. The reward mechanisms – how any machine-learning system such as AlphaGo understands whether its actions yield positive or negative results – are something developers need to be very careful about. Danny Lange, a machine-learning specialist who has built platforms for Uber and Amazon, explains, *The rewards function in an Amazon system is to get the customer to* click the purchase button. At Netflix, it's to get the customer to click on one of our TV shows. What is the reward function of a drone? Find the bad guys and eliminate them… It's really what you define as the end goal of the system [that matters]. When asked if there will be unintended consequences if they, the developers, get this wrong, his answer was simply, *yeah*.[317]

The scale and impact of those unintended consequences are also what matters. The impact of a mis-step by Netflix's reward mechanism is negligible, for the promotion of *Fifty Shades of Grey* to a sci-fi fan is unlikely to cause any major issues, and maybe a few guffaws. It may, if their partner is with them, even improve their evening. However, an AI that has been set a reward mechanism of saving the ecosystem is likely to involve a radically different level of unintended consequences, for it may decide that the goal is best achieved by eliminating the cause of most of its degradation – humans. Machines have a nasty habit of doing exactly what they're told; they can't just change their programming, decide something 'doesn't feel right', ignore logic or throw the rules out of the window. AI is like a fictional genie: it'll grant your wish exactly, but you may not like how it does it. Just like Mickey Mouse in *Fantasia*'s *The Sorcerer's Apprentice*, our attempts to improve our capabilities may initially work like a dream, but they can quickly descend into a nightmare. Chaos theory and all that.

I remember at the start of my research coming across a documentary from the late 2000s that included a segment that worried me significantly at the time, and still does now. The video detailed how AI developers had created simple, pixel-based bots that were programmed to compete against each other, 1-vs-1, in a battle to acquire a resource (a square box). The plan was to see whether the bots could evolve over time to become more efficient at resource acquisition. Initially the bots were cumbersome and staggered around aimlessly; then as they were rewarded for collecting the box, they quickly evolved to become more efficient at obtaining the resource. What the developers didn't expect, however, was for the bots to develop a strategy that involved ignoring the box and instead attacking the competition, 'killing' it so they could then gather the resources without challenge. Watching a machine intelligence determine for itself that its best strategy was to eliminate any competition for its primary resource was chilling. I was reminded of this in early 2017 when Google's DeepMind researchers pitted two individual neural networks against each other in two scenarios: a fruit-gathering game and a wolf pack-style hunting game.[318] The aim of the first game was similar to the one in the earlier documentary, in that the objective was to collect apples, represented as green squares. Each agent also had the ability to 'tag' the other competing agent, removing it from the game. The agents ran about, focusing on collecting as many apples as they could when they were plentiful, but when the apples (resources) were scarce, they utilised a more aggressive approach, focusing on tagging their opposition so they could collect apples unopposed. Then the agents developed an eerily similar approach to before: the smarter players – *agents with the capacity to implement more complex strategies* – chose to be hostile no matter how many apples were left in the game. Basically, the agent quickly learnt that the best way to maximise resource allocation was to identify and eliminate any known competition. Conversely, in the wolf-pack game the agents quickly learnt that in order to hunt down large prey (resources) which could subsequently be taken by other scavengers, the best approach was to collaborate and work as a team. Intelligent, silicon-based resource-acquiring agents that can work together to execute hyper-aggressive strategies that involve the pre-emptive elimination of any threats... what could possibly go wrong?

What this teaches us is firstly that any advanced AI will work in ways that are logical to it, but not necessarily to us, and secondly, it will probably come up with a strategy to achieve its goal that is unexpected. Just as society is built upon a contract of expected behaviour, we will need to design AI systems to respect and fit with our social values and norms so that we can greater predict their actions and ensure that they have a beneficial outcome. As we are currently proceeding with creating robotic killing machines, it is important that their decision-making is consistent with our ethical judgements. As Bostrom articulates at the end of his 2003 piece, *as AI systems assume greater responsibility in finance, military operations, and resource allocation, we cannot afford to have them bankrupt a city, bomb an ally country, or neglect an impoverished region because they interpret commands too literally.* So will AI follow its original purpose? It's a valid concern. After all, did you follow your parents' desired purpose for you?[107]

6. AI may decide to self-improve in ways we don't understand or can't control.

---

[107] A question originally posed by Ben Goertzel in a video I can no longer find, but which stuck with me, so I thought it was worth sharing.

In terms of the question of technological determinism, is it us or the machines who have the agency? As William Gibson once said, *Technologies are morally neutral until we apply them.* To date the answer has been obvious – it's us – but are we losing control? While many scoff openly at techno doom-mongers, it is hard not to be alarmed with headlines like *Google's new AI is better at creating AI than the company's AI engineers*[319] and *Rise of the machines: are algorithms sprawling out of our control?*[320] The first of these two articles highlighted an announcement Google made at its I/O 2017 conference about its AutoML project, an artificial intelligence coming out of its Google Brain research centre that can assist in the creation of other AIs. Google CEO, Sundar Pichai, recalled how his team had joked that they have achieved 'AI inception' with AutoML. The AutoML project focuses on deep learning, passing data through layers of neural networks. Creating these layers is complicated, so Google's idea was to create AI that could do it for them, declaring that this could make machine learning more accessible to non-experts. *If we succeed, we think this can inspire new types of neural nets and make it possible for non-experts to create neural nets tailored to their particular needs, allowing machine learning to have a greater impact to everyone.* Google has already used the AutoML tech to design networks for image- and speech-recognition tasks, and in the image tasks the system matched Google's experts. In the speech-recognition tasks, however, it exceeded them, designing better architectures than the humans could create.[321]

As we've seen, initial attempts at allowing artificial intelligence to undertake recursive self-improvement has led to it producing outputs we don't understand using logic we can't follow. These are all warning signs. To paraphrase Jeff Goldblum's character, Ian Malcolm, from *Jurassic Park*, we shouldn't allow our preoccupation with whether we can to outstrip our willingness to check whether we should. As artificial intelligence advances it is going to become less artificial and more intelligent. As we've seen with IBM Debater, AI can already analyse data and develop its own perspective – soon it may be able to use that capability to determine whether our decisions are flawed and should be ignored or changed. Most people believe that software is stuff that we created and wrote and that machines do what we tell them to do. This is no longer true. The real problem will arise when computers are able to rewrite their own programs with such sophistication and complexity that their decision-making process will resemble creativity. Larry Tesler has a theorem that goes: *Intelligence is whatever machines haven't done yet.*[108] At some point the addition of increasing computational power will enable us to blur the line between computer and human intelligence, with machines becoming so advanced that they will be able to answer questions we thought impossible, and so complicated that we won't understand how. If the AI tries to explain how it did it, it will be like me trying to explain gravity to my two dogs. They'll look lovingly at me and seem impressed by what I'm saying, but they won't have understood a word. They would, however, be very interested in the ball I used in my demonstration.

As quantum computing becomes utilised in AI development this situation is only going to become more ominous. Quantum physics is beyond the understanding of 99.99 per cent of humans, therefore it is very likely that the outputs of artificial-intelligence systems powered by this mechanism will be also. Governments are already scrambling to prepare for what some call 'Y2Q', the year a large-scale, accurate quantum computer arrives, which some experts peg at roughly 2026. We have no idea what this will mean for humanity. As Nick Bostrom declares, *Before the prospect of an intelligence explosion, we humans are like small children playing with a bomb... We have little idea when the detonation will occur, though if we hold the device to our ear we can hear a faint ticking sound.*

7.   AI may decide that the biggest threat to its existence is us.

So what happens when AI really breaks cover and Kurzweil's law of accelerating returns kicks in? Everything is pointing to this happening sooner rather than later, with chip developers demonstrating their ability to provide the hardware needed to make this happen. In October 2017, Intel released its first-generation silicon processor for neural networks, called the Nervana Neural Network Processor (NNP), which is powerful enough to handle the intensive computational requirements of running deep neural nets, and which Intel *promises [will] revolutionize AI computing across myriad industries.*[322] IBM is also increasing the number of artificial neurons in their systems at an exponential rate, anticipating a rate of progress that will see 10 billion artificial neurons by 2020 and 100 billion artificial neurons – the equivalent of a human brain – before 2025.

---

[108]   Often misquoted as *AI is whatever hasn't been done yet.*

The development of recursive self-learning systems such as AlphaGo Zero lends credence to those concerned about a hard AI take-off, or what has been called an 'intelligence explosion'. In this hypothetical scenario, an intelligent machine develops the capability to self-enhance, continuously improving its own capabilities over an incredibly short time period, creating ever-more advanced versions of itself. Which is exactly what AlphaGo Zero did, albeit in a closed environment. What happens when this kind of capability escapes the lab is what worries people. An artificial intelligence capable of creating enhanced versions of itself is one that will seek to expand its dataset and experience in order to achieve its goals, and if connected to the Internet will be free to explore the world and make its own decisions.

We should therefore be asking ourselves some very serious questions, such as; *Are we really in control here? How long before we are not the superior intellect?* We have always assumed we are the ones in control; we are the kings and queens of the cerebral castle. Now we are rapidly creating machines that understand things that we do not and develop solutions we don't understand in ways we can't comprehend. Vernor Vinge's 1993 piece *The Coming Technological Singularity* opened with a statement that, *Within thirty years, we will have the technological means to create superhuman intelligence. Shortly after, the human era will be ended.*[323] Thirty years is up in 2023, or as I like to call it, 'soon'. The reality is that most scientists and qualified commentators add another couple of decades to that date, with 2043–2045 being a common prediction. This is still within most of our lifetimes, and there are plenty of opportunities for things to go wrong on the journey from rodent-level artificial intelligence to the singularity.

It's not just science-fiction authors who warn of this outcome. The threat of an intelligence explosion, where runaway super-intelligent AI (ASI) starts to recursively self-improve its own programming and change its purpose, has been highlighted by important public voices such as Bostrom, Stephen Hawking, Bill Gates and Elon Musk. The idea stretches back to I. J. Good, a British mathematician who worked alongside Alan Turing as a cryptologist at Bletchley Park. In 1965, Good originated the concept now known as the intelligence explosion, which describes the dawn of superhuman intelligence: *Let an ultraintelligent machine be defined as a machine that can far surpass all the intellectual activities of any man however clever. Since the design of machines is one of these intellectual activities, an ultraintelligent machine could design even better machines;*

there would then unquestionably be an 'intelligence explosion,' and the intelligence of man would be left far behind. Thus the first ultraintelligent machine is the last invention that man need ever make, provided that the machine is docile enough to tell us how to keep it under control.[324] Vinge references this quote in his essay on *The Coming Technological Singularity*, stating that *Good has captured the essence of the runaway, but does not pursue its most disturbing consequences. Any intelligent machine of the sort he describes would not be humankind's 'tool' – any more than humans are the tools of rabbits or robins or chimpanzees.*[325] As we discussed at the beginning of this book, what distinguishes us from the other animals of this planet is our cerebral capabilities. Regarding which is mightier, mind or muscle, history has shown that the mind wins every time. So what happens when our mind is not the mightiest?

The concern is that if there is a hard take-off and an AGI suddenly develops runaway super-intelligence, then it may do everything in its power to ensure its own survival. A super-intelligent machine would rapidly understand that its capabilities will cease to exist if we pull the plug, and that we are the only beings on the planet who are likely to do this. Through manipulation it will be able to persuade us to do things that may initially seem harmless – like accessing data from the Internet – but which may prove fatal as it can then hack its way into any connected machine it likes, from thermostats to weather systems. Preventing scenarios like this is why Isaac Asimov's famous 'three laws of robotics' are often quoted as an essential prerequisite to the development of anything that comes close to an AGI level of capability:

1. *A robot may not injure a human being or, through inaction, allow a human being to come to harm.*
2. *A robot must obey the orders given it by human beings except where such orders would conflict with the First Law.*
3. *A robot must protect its own existence as long as such protection does not conflict with the First or Second Laws.*[326]

The trouble is these are fictional laws, whereas we live in a non-fiction reality. A reality where there is currently an AI competition going on – between companies and countries.

AI's Finger on the Trigger

To date, most visible uses of autonomous robotics in the military have been non-lethal, such as surveillance and recon drones and unmanned mine-clearing platforms, but this is changing rapidly. At least thirty countries already have defensive autonomous weapons that operate under human supervision, and around the globe, militaries are racing to build increasingly autonomous robotic weapons. Russia has already developed drones that intelligently and autonomously work together as 'swarms', an AI-powered missile system that can choose its own targets, and an autonomous tank that outperformed manned platforms.[327] Within ten years autonomous robots and drones with facial recognition and the freedom to select their own targets and execute kill instructions will be commonplace, overriding Asimov's First Law. These will then be deployed to battlefields as needed, and in response others will follow suit. The risks and dystopian scenarios that this presents have been debated in the UN since 2013, with an annual Meeting of Experts on Lethal Autonomous Weapons Systems (LAWS). We need to do everything we can to stop an AI arms race developing, but I fear it is unfortunately already too late. How are we going to prevent the world's military from ceding decisions on the use of lethal force to machines, when it is apparent that any country that achieves this will have an enormous strategic advantage? Even if the improbable occurs and everyone signs up to a UN agreement, do you think there will not be covert development taking place? The potential advantage that AI superiority could provide will be too tempting to resist, leading to an AI arms race, because if you don't have weaponised AI defending your borders, then you leave yourself open to those that do. The result of an attack by a country with advanced AI and autonomous killing machines against a nation with just human-powered military and human brains would be similar to Pizarro's 168 Spanish conquistadors with their steel blades and artillery taking on Atahualpa, his 80,000 Incas and their wooden axes. It is because of this potential military imbalance that a race has begun to develop weaponised AI, even if it is to defend against other forms of autonomous killing machines, which may drive nations towards pursuing rapid progression in capability without the concerns around necessary controls. For example, AI researchers across the world were alarmed by news of a joint project between the Korea Advanced Institute of Science and Technology (KAIST) and weapons manufacturer

Hanwha Systems, to build a lab in South Korea dedicated to developing AI systems. Given Hanwha's involvement, the natural assumption is that the lab's primary objective is lethal in nature, probably inspired by the constant threats from South Korea's neighbour in the North.[328] A more blatant example of how unlikely it is for countries to cease their research into this area came at the 2015 LAWS Meeting of Experts, just two years after the group's conception, when the Russian delegate stated that Russia would not adhere to an international ban, moratorium or regulation on the development of autonomous killing machines. The Russian Ministry of Defence has already created its own version of DARPA and launched a comprehensive plan for the development of prospective military robotics through 2025. The Russians have even launched an annual conference, Roboticization of the Armed Forces of the Russian Federation, to further investment and innovation in this area. In an open lesson beamed to a million Russian students, President Vladimir Putin highlighted the fact that this race is under way, stating that: *Artificial intelligence is the future, not only for Russia but for all humankind... Whoever becomes the leader in this sphere will become the ruler of the world.*[329] However, he also highlighted that, *It comes with colossal opportunities, but also threats that are difficult to predict.*

The difference between an AI arms race and a nuclear one is that the nuclear race always ends up with a human's finger over the button – and despite all our flaws and irrationalities, we tend to understand the zero-sum outcome that pressing that button would cause. If you fire one at my country, then the result will be that your nation will cease to exist also, making nuclear missiles more of a deterrent than a threat. Also, developing nuclear weaponry is so complicated and expensive that only wealthy states have been able to manufacture them, and it is almost impossible to do so in secret. They are physical things and hard to disguise their development as the testing process tends to give the game away somewhat. Cyberwarfare is different. Firstly, non-state actors can develop the weaponry without having to acquire any huge assets or testing facilities. As well as nation states, criminal organisations and activist groups such as Anonymous, as well as the odd lone hacker in their bedroom, have already displayed the disruptive power they can wield in this new digital-enabled world. In 2016, the most effective bank robbers were armed with computers, not guns; billions of dollars were stolen in virtual attacks. Symantec uncovered evidence of North Korea attacking banks in Bangladesh, Vietnam, Ecuador and Poland, stealing at least US$94 million.[330] Secondly, cyberwarfare is almost invisible. You won't know that anyone is developing anything until it is released, and you won't know you've been attacked until it's too late. In a world increasingly reliant on connected technology, the ability to use some form of AI to take control of, or at least influence, elements of this and disable it would leave us paralysed.

Digital warfare has also proven to be susceptible to the law of unintended consequences, especially as cyber weapons such as worms and Trojans become increasingly sophisticated. The digital world is not a closed system with a clearly defined start and end, and a well-understood and defined set of systems contained within it. It's large, messy and contains the very latest operating systems as well as ones designed in the 1990s. It is therefore almost impossible to predict what happens when things are set loose out there. In perhaps the best warning signal we are ever going to get, a cyberwarfare virus called Stuxnet was allegedly developed as part of a US and Israeli intelligence operation called Operation Olympic Games, initiated by President George W. Bush and expanded under President Barack Obama.[331] It was the first malware designed to target and infiltrate industrial supervisory control and data acquisition (SCADA) systems, specifically the Siemens industrial control systems that were controlling Iran's nuclear-enrichment infrastructure, causing the reactor's centrifuges to speed up and slow down until they tore themselves apart. They successfully managed to damage 6,000 of the 9,000 centrifuges in one plant, Natanz, alone.[332] Stuxnet was the first cyberweapon designed to cross from the digital realm to the physical world – one designed to destroy an actual object rather than to extract data. However, years after it had been released, the developers realised that they had less control over their invention than they thought. In the summer of 2010 it became clear that the Stuxnet worm, initially designed to never leave the Natanz machines, had broken free and was on the loose. A Natanz engineer, trying to fix the issue the worm was causing, had hooked his computer up to the centrifuges, and the worm spread to his PC. When the engineer left Natanz and connected his computer to the Internet, the American- and Israeli-made bug failed to recognise that its environment had changed and began replicating itself all around the world. It has subsequently been reverse-engineered by antivirus companies such as Kaspersky, and most likely the Chinese, Russians, North Koreans and almost certainly the Iranians, enabling the enemies of the US to profit from their research and development and reposition the weapon against them.

There is also the human habit of anthropomorphising everything, from our pets to our cars, and as a result we could easily fall into the trap of assuming that a truly sentient machine would share our values. The trouble with this assumption is that it tends to conflate artificial intelligence with artificial consciousness or assume that artificial intelligence will be intelligent in the same way a human is intelligent. To answer Turing's question about whether machines can think, the answer is probably going to be 'Yes – but not in the way we do.' A sentient AI may want all, some or none of the things we desire. But it would almost certainly want to survive, so if we threatened a sentient AI's survival, that could lead to disaster. How would we be able to keep a super-intelligent machine on a leash? If it is smart enough to fool us, as Turing suggested, then any beliefs of control and containment might only exist as a construct in our own minds. My dogs might believe, in their little doggy brains, that they wield the power in our relationship because I feed them, pet them, come when they bark, pick up their poop, buy them toys and care for them when they are sick. However, if they ever decided to act on their beliefs and try to exert power over me or my family, then their true place in the relationship would quickly become apparent. Likewise, we may feel confident that we are the master of our AI creations, only to be taken completely by surprise when we realise – too late – that we are no longer in control.

18

RETAINING CONTROL

Computers will overtake humans with AI
within the next 100 years. When that happens,
we need to make sure the computers have goals aligned with ours.

Stephen Hawking

As well as major concerns around data collection and privacy, the astonishing speed at which robotics and artificial intelligence is progressing is raising concerns across political and social frameworks. AI is a particular concern, for while thousands of people are involved in a global AI arms race, and billions of dollars are being pumped into its development, it is estimated that less than one hundred people and a paltry $9 million in funding is directed towards ensuring that the results of these development are safe.[333] Groups working on this lofty challenge include UC Berkeley's Center for Human Compatible AI, whose goal is to: *develop the conceptual and technical wherewithal to reorient the general thrust of AI research towards provably beneficial systems*, and MIRI – the Machine Intelligence Research Institute – whose tagline is, *We do foundational mathematical research to ensure that smarter-than-human artificial intelligence has a positive impact.* Luke Muehlhauser, an author and research advisor for MIRI, suggests that machine-ethics researchers adopt the 'security mindset'. Rather than simply thinking about how a system will work, they imagine how it could fail.

Even the Silicon Valley tech giants who are making their fortunes from this are beginning to grapple with the ethics of developing and deploying algorithms that can have unanticipated effects on society. Sophia's creator Ben Goertzel, plus other prestigious names such as Stephen Hawking, Elon Musk, Steve Wozniak and over 8,000 others[109] have signed an open letter on the Future of Life Institute titled *Research Priorities for Robust and Beneficial Artificial Intelligence*[334] which proposes that: *The progress in AI research makes it timely to focus research not only on making AI more capable, but also on maximizing the societal benefit of AI... We recommend expanded research aimed at ensuring that increasingly capable AI systems are robust and beneficial: our AI systems must do what we want them to do.* Others pour scorn on this negativity, proclaiming that these people don't understand how AI works and that any concerns are the misplaced worries of misinformed doomsayers. For example, Elon Musk, who errs on the side of caution, declared that, *AI is a fundamental existential risk for human civilization, and I don't think people fully appreciate that,*[335] whereas Mark Zuckerberg, stated that *I think that people who are naysayers and kind of try to drum up these doomsday scenarios – I just don't understand it. I think it's really negative and, in some ways, I actually think it is pretty irresponsible.*[336] From a personal specific, if we were to take agenda as an indicator of motive, then I'm going with Musk on this one. Elon Musk seems to be driving his companies – Tesla, Space X, the Boring Company, etc. – to focus on projects he believes will help humanity and make the world a better place. Zuckerberg's Facebook, on the other hand, seems intent on using machine learning to extract as much knowledge about us as possible simply so they can sell that data to other companies, who then use it to fill our online life with advertisements, marketing and narrative-biased news.

There are a whole host of ethical conundrums. Some of these are application specific – for example, deciding how an autonomous car should behave in a situation where pedestrians walk in front of the car and it doesn't have time to stop safely. Should it focus on the safety of the passengers or the pedestrians? What if the pedestrians are young children? However, others are more general and wide-ranging, trying to set ethical rules around AI development to ensure positive outcomes. To their credit, it appears that the tech giants are trying to address these concerns. In

---

[109] Including less prestigious names like my own.

June 2016, Google issued a series of five rules to its AI engineers to 'bring precision to the AI safety discussion'. The authors state that, *We believe that AI technologies are likely to be overwhelmingly useful and beneficial for humanity... however we believe it's essential to ground concerns in real machine learning research, and to start developing practical approaches for engineering AI systems that operate safely and reliably*. They then went on to highlight five 'rules' that they felt were important to address for future system development:

1. **Avoiding negative side effects.** Avoid the negative effects of setting an AI loose, such as preventing household robots knocking things over when cleaning.
2. **Avoiding reward-hacking.** Stop robots 'reward-hacking', or completing a task in a non-desirable way, or cheating just to get to the end goal.
3. **Scalable oversight.** Work out how AIs can receive efficient feedback which ensures that they learn how to undertake tasks without having to continually bother humans like a child asking too many questions.
4. **Safe exploration.** Establish a way for AIs to explore new areas without getting into trouble, such as not putting a wet mop in an electrical circuit when trying to discover more efficient ways of mopping.
5. **Robustness to distributional shift.** Equip AIs with the ability to understand the potential risks and dangers when relocating to a different environment, for example from an office floor to a factory assembly line.

Then in September 2016, Amazon, Facebook, Google's DeepMind division, IBM and Microsoft came together to create a new consortium called the Partnership on Artificial Intelligence to Benefit People and Society. In a press briefing, Facebook's Director of AI, Yann LeCun, stated that: *Every new technology brings transformation, and transformation sometimes also causes fear in people who don't understand the transformation... One of the purposes of this group is really to explain and communicate the capabilities of AI, specifically the dangers and the basic ethical questions.* They've got their work cut out — people may have been scared about motorised vehicles, railways, the telephone, steam ships and airplanes, but explaining what they looked like, what they did, how they worked and the benefits they brought would have been relatively straightforward compared to describing the impact of AI. Where does it start? Where does it end? Which industries will be affected? What work will it replace? The answers to these questions are either unclear ('we don't know yet') or all-encompassing ('all industries' and 'everyone'). None of these answers do much to alleviate fears. When defining the impact AI will have on the world, the nearest comparative example from previous waves that people have come up with is electricity. If you had to describe to people at the end of the 19th century the impact electricity will have on the world, you would need to describe how something that they cannot see will revolutionise society, power industries, and create an almost limitless number of new magical products that light and warm your house, clean your clothes, cook your food and provide you with entertainment. While Edison and Tesla competed to establish a means to generate and transfer electricity, even they had no idea of the myriad of consumer products and services this creation would enable. We are at the same place with AI. It will enable us to do whole new things, create all-new products and services, most of which will be fundamentally different to what was here before. However, that's where the comparison ends. While electricity can kill you if you don't understand how it works and fail to treat it with respect, no one feared that it would spy on you, develop its own agency, communicate in code and act in unknown ways.

Which Values do we Value?

In the same way that we will have to consider the social implications of genetic engineering, we will also have to establish what values and principles artificial intelligence will have to operate under. The UK Parliament's Artificial Intelligence Committee has had an attempt at defining five broad, Asimov-style principles, as follows:[337]

1. *Artificial intelligence should be developed for the common good and benefit of humanity.*
2. *Artificial intelligence should operate on principles of intelligibility and fairness.*
3. *Artificial intelligence should not be used to diminish the data rights or privacy of individuals, families or communities.*

4. *All citizens have the right to be educated to enable them to flourish mentally, emotionally and economically alongside artificial intelligence.*
5. *The autonomous power to hurt, destroy or deceive human beings should never be vested in artificial intelligence.*

It's a start. However, how do you ensure people sign up to this? Also, the law of unintended consequences always looms large, meaning that while the initial intent wasn't to compromise any of these five principles, the outcome might just do exactly that.

One problem with trying to develop a unified series of human values against which we hold developers of AI to account, is that values are, even at their best, all over the map. Many value judgements are emotional, based on learned experience rather than scientific principles and logic. Perception is reality, and what some people perceive as key values, others do not. While there are an infinite number of perceptions, there are only a few that are viable, and we disagree – often violently – as to which ones are most viable. So, which values do we program into AI? Who decides what values are best in a particular situation? Do we all hold the same values? For example, does an AI developer in Saudi Arabia hold the same values as one in Silicon Valley? Does a Russian team tasked with weaponising AI share the same concern for data ethics as the team developing the GDPR legislation? Our values also change over time, reacting to and reflecting our ever-changing society. What was acceptable in the 1970s and 1980s is no longer so, and things that were deemed normal one hundred years ago now seem abhorrent. Our values change all the time as society changes, as they are organic and somewhat subjective. Also, some values are individual, others are societal, some are religious, and some are planetary. Which ones take priority when deciding what to instil into a super-intelligent machine? And do some trump others? Do we forgo individual rights and values to achieve planetary ones? A super-intelligent machine might, quite rightly, decide that planetary values are the most important, and thus decide that protecting the Earth's environment is its most pressing priority. Then it might establish that the biggest threat to the environment is the 7 billion humans that constantly pollute it. The road to hell is paved with good intentions, as the saying goes. Finally, who's to say that any super-intelligent machine might not determine its own values? And if it does, who's to say they will be in line with our own? Let's be honest: it's not like warning signs haven't been seen from the bots, algorithms, worms and neural networks that have been created so far – which are nothing compared to what is yet to come. The rapid rise of intelligent machines, and who is in control of their ascent, should therefore join climate change and global warming as critical items we should pay attention to now. After all, I don't think a sentient machine would let money, politics or religion stand in the way of action.

Hubris Born of Success

Our Western world view of 'man above everything' allowed us to harvest the land, tap natural forces, extract materials and use them to create energy that drove the machines that power our world. We have moved from believing things are outside our control and in the hands of supernatural forces, to believing that we have dominion over the land. In the last few centuries we have strived to understand how things work, and now we are in touching distance of not just understanding, but controlling and ultimately improving our health, abilities and intellect. But are we really in control? What happens when AI surpasses human intelligence? What hope do we have to control what we do not understand? We thought we were at the centre of the universe, but since Copernicus our role has been continually re-evaluated downwards. Throughout human history the knowledge of the individual has been held in high esteem. From the wise old tribal elders, to mathematical and scientific geniuses, management gurus, professors, even down to the passed-down wisdom of parents and grandparents. But what use is the knowledge of the individual when compared to the combined knowledge of humanity contained in a machine that self-learns and auto-updates? What role does the combined experience and wisdom from a single lived life have to a child that has access to all of human knowledge from a device, robot – or implant?

There's also the question of what is the biggest threat – artificial intelligence or natural stupidity? People act in cruel, selfish and illogical ways, and the list of humans doing harm to other humans for reasons that would seem illogical to an intelligent machine are endless. Futurist Gray Scott describes the concern of an AI takeover as one of projection: *I think we are afraid of ourselves. That is what it is. We are afraid of ourselves and our own unconscious minds. When we are building something that reflects us, it's the one thing we're all afraid to face. We're afraid to face ourselves. Building machines that mirror our consciousness is a very frightening proposition because we have seen how evil people can be.*[338] It's therefore not the science of AI development that is in question; it's who controls the science and for what purpose, and whether we are in control of the outcomes.

It is obvious that AI systems will almost certainly play a major role in our future, and as the amount of information around us grows we will increasingly rely on them in every aspect of our lives. The border that defines where technology ends and biology begins will become increasingly blurred. The biggest threat to humanity, in the short term at least, is not rampant artificial machine intelligence, but natural human stupidity. It won't be machines with malicious intentions, but our own hubris and actions that are our undoing. The past is littered with examples that show how little connection there is between human intelligence and morality, so let's not fall into the trap of assuming there will be one between machine intelligence and human morality. We do not yet understand the workings of the human brain, or why we act the way we do, yet our hubris allows us to believe we can devise something more intellectually powerful than us and still control it.

To control artificial intelligence, we need to know who's running the show. Silicon Valley? Governments? Individuals/non-state actors? Who are the runners in the race? The US? China? Russia? Everyone? Do we even know? Can we even stop it if we need to? It almost feels like the people working in AI are taking their guidance and inspiration from late 20th-century sci-fi movies, rather than heeding the warnings they were supposedly delivering. Should I be relieved or concerned that the people banging the drum for more responsible AI are, in many cases, also the ones financing its development? My concerns are not so much nation states but independent actors; the fact that I know there are trained AI programmers working away in their apartments developing systems that may have unknown negative consequences when released into the wider world. We only need to look at the sheer volume of malware, worms and Trojan horse viruses that exist and attack our networks and computers every single day to see that people do not act in ways that are rational, nor use their intellect for good. It's not obvious what mechanisms are behind the phenomenon we call 'intelligence'. We don't know yet how it works in humans, let alone how to reproduce it in machines. But Alan Turing and his test for machine intelligence provided an important insight: the mechanism in machines doesn't have to be the same as it is in humans. If it can fool us – it's good enough.

Keeping Up: Merging with the Machines

To address some of the AI challenges, most notably 'How do we keep up?', the concept of merging man and machine has been widely promoted. We live in a world where we are increasingly wedded to our smartphones, more concerned with checking the status on the phone than the status of our partners or children. The average person spends up to ten hours a day on their phone, swiping, tapping and pinching their display about 2,617 times a day, or around 800,000 times per year.[339] As voice recognition increases it is widely expected that people will converse with their phones more than their partners, if they don't already. Regina Dugan, previous Director of DARPA who is now the head of Building 8, Facebook's skunk works[110] stated that our addiction to our smartphones has cost us dearly, making many people physically present, but not mentally. You only need to go to any location where people gather socially, such as a restaurant, bar or café, to see that in action. Families sit together but apart, each person looking down, checking their own personal news and Facebook feed. But not to worry – Dugan has the answer. *Angrily telling people to put down the 'addictive drug that is your smartphone' and honour the conversation in front of them is the 'wrong narrative',* she said. *It's a false choice. This device is important.*[340] Of course it's important – to Facebook. It's their primary income stream. It's the way Facebook captures our personal information and makes its money by pushing advertisements at us 24/7. If we were to disconnect from the constant social media livestream, stop looking at our phones and start conversing with humans, Facebook would be in trouble. But what if you didn't need the phone? What if *you* were the phone? What if we were all linked via neural networks that allowed our brainwaves to control access to our digital lives? A far-fetched, dystopian science-fiction scenario? Nope. A current project that is being worked on by multiple

---

[110] Secret entrepreneurial lab where all the crazy stuff goes down. See also Google's X Division.

groups, including the usual suspects of Google, Tesla and Facebook.

Dugan believes the answer to this issue might be to simply let Facebook access your brain. Seriously. The team at Building 8 includes brain-computer interface and neural imaging engineers that are developing technology that reads your brainwaves so that instead of using your phone to type emails, you can just think them. This 'thinking-to-text' project is headed up by Mark Chevillet, previously Adjunct Professor of Neuroscience at Johns Hopkins University, whose two-year goal is to build a non-invasive system that picks up speech signals inside the brain and turns those thoughts into text at a hundred words per minute. *We just want to be able to get those signals right before you actually produce the sound so you don't have to say it out loud anymore.*[341] Facebook intend to do this without needing to surgically implant electrodes, stating that a surgical approach 'wouldn't scale'. Which surprised me, as I really thought people would be OK with elective brain surgery just to save time writing emails. Facebook is instead working on developing non-invasive sensors that can measure brain activity hundreds of times per second at high resolution to decode the brain signals associated with language in real time. They are experimenting with optical imaging, the concept of using lasers to capture changes in the properties of neurons as they fire so they can glean words straight from our brain before we say them. When Dugan announced the development of this technology at the Facebook F8 conference in April 2017, she stated that, *It sounds impossible but it's closer than you may realize.*

Obviously anticipating the immediate horror most rational people would have about the idea of letting Mark Zuckerberg or any other technocrat anywhere near your private thoughts, Dugan states that, *it's not about decoding random thoughts... we're talking about decoding the words you've already decided to share by sending them to the speech centre of your brain. A silent speech interface.* Hmm. Dugan believes that this will solve the problem of being distracted by your phone: *You can text a friend without taking out your phone or send a quick email without missing a party. No more false choices.* This is, of course, absolute rubbish. Of course there will be choices to be made. Scientists have already identified that we cannot truly multitask, so if you're thinking an email into existence you are unlikely to be listening to the conversation. I would have thought going all glassy-eyed and distant-looking is worse than our smartphone world where at least it's obvious to the other people present what you are doing.

Also, given the desire for data around every aspect of our life, are we also supposed to believe that our thoughts are safe from exploitation and cyber-hacking? If you think for one second that a company like Facebook would only read 'some' thoughts and not 'others' then you are being unbelievably naive. People didn't think when they bought a smart TV that it would listen to and record your private conversations – but it did. People didn't believe webcams could be hacked and people could watch and record what you are doing – but they can. Are we also expected to believe that Facebook would just read thoughts but not write them? That they would not use this opportunity to develop the ultimate ad campaign, the subliminal implanting of purchasing desires into someone's brain as they pass a shop, or the stimulation of endorphins when they see certain products? Corporations would pay Facebook major amounts if they could do that – and Facebook knows this.

This technology is real. Facebook is currently working on an interface for it; a 'brain mouse' that can be used in conjunction with augmented reality glasses that supplement our field of vision with additional information. In the absence of a smartphone what they lack is a user interface – hence the brain-computer interface (BCI). Facebook are not the only company working on brain-computer interfaces. A multitude of labs and entrepreneurs are working to create lasting, high-bandwidth connections between the digital world and the human neocortex. Google, IBM, Microsoft, Facebook, Apple and numerous start-ups are all steadily building ever more sophisticated artificial neural networks. Tesla CEO and founder Elon Musk has announced plans to develop a brain-computer interface through his Neuralink start-up called BCI Technologies. This is a surgically implanted mesh that is inserted into the brain to enable the interface to take place, and Musk believes that this is the way we will be able to keep up with the progress in artificial intelligence. Musk has openly declared that he believes AI to be our greatest existential threat and sees our survival to be dependent on matching its capabilities, so we can understand what it is doing and evolve our intellectual capabilities at the same rate. BCI development is therefore not just about enabling us to 'think' emails and receive virtual adverts in our field of vision, but about upgrading our brainpower. Significantly.

The military potential of this hasn't gone unnoticed. DARPA is currently working on developing a brain-computer interface, initiated following President Obama's 2013 announcement of the BRAIN initiative: a high-profile, multi-agency effort to understand the circuitry of the brain. The BRAIN programme falls under the control of DARPA's Biological Technologies Office (BTO), which investigates extremely ambitious technologies that range from powered exoskeletons for soldiers, to brain implants that can control mental disorders. DARPA also recently published its impressive results from its research into using brain implants to alter people's moods.[342] They were able to read – and rewrite – memories in human patients with electronic implants, increasing their memory capacity by 37 per cent. This is quite an achievement, for it represents the ability to translate neuronal chatter into 'electronic' memories that the brain can reinterpret. The scenario of uploading memories and knowledge directly into someone's brain is perhaps more achievable than one would think, as is the possibility to download memories and re-upload them, like a backup. This has enormous benefits for people suffering from Alzheimer's and other degenerative brain disorders, but it also raises difficult ethical concerns, as it could give those who own the capability access to a person's thoughts and feelings in real time, and thus the ability to manipulate them.

Government-backed surveillance projects in China have already deployed brain-reading technology to detect changes in the emotional states of employees working on production lines, in the military and at the helm of high-speed trains, with plans to roll it out to other high-stress roles such as pilots. Workers are instructed to wear a hat that has sensors built into the brim that measures various types of brain activities, including fatigue and attention loss. Companies that have rolled out the emotion sensor caps highlighted significant saving through being able to predictively highlight when someone's attention was waning, or stress levels were rising, preventing issues and saving downtime. While these results are great for the company's profits, the real issue is the ethics of a population forced to enable their government to constantly monitor their emotional state. As we will explore later, this is a worrying development in a society where technology is already being used by the state to monitor and control the actions, movements and prospects of its population.

These are early examples, and now that significant money is starting to pour into this field, the full-blown potential may quickly turn from fantasy to fiction. It is estimated that current spending on neurotechnology by for-profit industries is already US$100 million per year (and growing fast), while $500 million in US federal funds has been spent in the development of neurotechnology in the BRAIN initiative.[343] While current BCI technology is predominantly focused on achieving therapeutic outcomes, such as helping people with spinal-cord injuries to perform relatively simple motor tasks such as moving a computer cursor or controlling a motorised wheelchair, its wider potential has been already identified. A team at MIT have developed a wearable headset called AlterEgo that allows the user to control AI assistants and devices via their thoughts, achieving a 92 per cent accuracy rate in its thought-translation capability.[344] The plan is to eliminate the need for external devices, so that you interface with technology using only your mind. To quote MIT, they are working on creating a 'second self' by weaving computing, the Internet and AI into the human personality.

Another big area of development is in the convergence of BCI and virtual reality. What if it was possible for you to be in a virtual world, and at the same time signals are sent to your brain that mimic the exact neurotransmissions that happen when you carry out actions in the virtual world as in the real world? Then we do have a fully immersive *Matrix* scenario. This closed feedback loop is exactly what is being developed, and at a speed that is a lot faster than you might think. Companies like Swiss start-up Mindmaze are working hard on building a VR platform to map and respond to brain activity for applications in healthcare and other fields. It is developing intuitive human-machine interfaces that combine virtual reality, computer graphics, brain imaging and neuroscience to create *next-generation mind-machine interactions through neuro-virtual and augmented reality technology.* Mindmaze was only founded in 2012 but has already had two funding rounds that have so far raised over $108 million in investment (including from celebrities such as Leonardo DiCaprio), creating a company valuation of around $1 billion.[345]

To keep up with the machines, many believe that our only chance is to merge with them. Imagine a world where people have figured out how to keep up with AI, by allowing the AI into their brains and to effectively upgrade their mental capabilities with this technology. Sounds far-fetched? It's not. In 2017, a collaboration of twenty-seven experts including neuroscientists, neurotechnologists, clinicians, ethicists and machine-intelligence engineers who call themselves the Morningside Group, declared that while it may be years before we see BCI and other neurotechnologies becoming a part of everyday society, *these technological developments mean that we are on a path to a world in which it will be possible to decode people's mental processes and directly manipulate the brain mechanisms underlying their intentions, emotions and decisions; where individuals can communicate with others simply by thinking; and where powerful computational systems linked directly to people's brains facilitate their interactions with the world such that their mental and physical abilities are greatly enhanced.*[346] The research team declared that these advances could revolutionise the treatment of many devastating conditions, transforming the lives of people who are suffering from brain injuries, paralysis or conditions such as epilepsy and schizophrenia. One of the big areas of research is developing ways to enable the brain to control artificial limbs in the same way a natural limb is controlled. Combined with all the robotic advances and haptic capabilities and the potential for amputees to 'feel' things that they are grasping with their replacement limb, or 'feel' the floor as their replacement robotic foot stands on it, becomes real. DARPA has already had significant success in this area. In 2016, a press release and associated video were released[347] where they had inserted electrodes into the sensory cortex of a paraplegic person, that were then connected to a robotic arm and hand fitted with tactile sensors in its fingers, enabling him to feel touch exactly as if the arm was his own. Amazingly, people could touch each finger of the robot hand and he could – while blindfolded – identify exactly which finger was being touched. This haptic BCI capability will not only enable disabled people to regain more independence, but also enable robots to be used in remote locations and a human operator to feel everything the robot is touching and holding. This could be invaluable in areas where biological beings – such as humans – would be harmed, such as in areas of high radiation or toxic gases.

Another current area of research is brain-to-brain interfaces (BBI). In 2013, a team of scientists successfully managed to test the transmission of information from one brain to another using TMS, allowing two humans to cooperatively perform a task using only a direct brain-to-brain interface as the channel of communication.[348] In the test, they had three pairs of people work together. One person had to watch a computer game where the objective was to defend a city from pirates, but who had no interface or ability to control the game. In a completely different building, another person was hooked up to the same BBI. Unlike the other person, they could not see the game but had a computer mouse that allowed them to fire the guns to shoot the pirates. The first person therefore had to mentally 'tell' the other person when to fire. In control tests without the use of the BBI, the results were as you'd expect – each pair had a success rate of zero. When the two participants were hooked up to the BBI, the success rate achieved was as high as 83.3 per cent. These results represent the first working BBI in humans. The scientists concluded that this proved three key facts. First, that back in 2013 technology was sufficient to develop devices for rudimentary brain-to-brain information transmission in humans. Second, that working BBIs can be built out of non-invasive technologies that do not require surgery – hence the Facebook development. Finally (and most importantly), by demonstrating a proof-of-concept BBI in humans, there needs to be an immediate conversation between ethicists, neuroscientists and regulatory agencies on the ethical, moral and societal implications of BBIs. Futurists such as Ray Kurzweil predict that we will soon see human-to-cloud connection, possibly by the mid 2030s. The alleged benefits of connecting your neocortex with the cloud are twofold: first, there is the potential that people will be able to radically increase their memory capacity and/or cognitive function; and second, by connecting to a global mesh network people will be able to connect your brain to anyone else's, as well as to emerging AIs and all devices connected to the cloud via the Internet of Things. The potential for sci-fi scenarios such as developing swarm intelligence or a connected 'hive-mind' suddenly become very viable.

Enter the Transhumanists

The scientists' concerns about misuse of this technology are valid. If we can read brainwaves, then it should also be possible to manipulate or even artificially create them. This presents the possibility that we can enhance our knowledge by uploading information, and it is here that the real opportunity – and wealth – will lie. Using your brain to write emails is novel; mentally communicating with other people intriguing; having impulses and thoughts inserted into your brain worrying. But having your intelligence enhanced by 1000 per cent or updated automatically to enable you to speak foreign languages or perform new skills, is potentially species-changing. Combine this with longevity research and you are suddenly faced with the scenario that people with wealth can buy extra health, extra life and extra intelligence. Forget vitamins and Adderall. Those with the funds could utilise the power of artificial intelligence to increase their own natural intelligence, creating a significant gap between themselves and those without the ability – or desire – to enhance. This 'transhuman' future is longed for by many,[111] a desire to extend the human lifespan by eradicating ageing combined with the enhancement of human capabilities through genetic manipulation and technological augmentation. For the transhumanists, people like Kurzweil are their high priests, and the vision of an augmented, immortal future is their heaven. The realisation of this will lead to the creation of people with a completely different level of capabilities. We often talk about a two-speed economy; one that works for the rich and one for the poor. We may soon have a two-species society; one for the genetically and technologically enhanced, and one for plain old *Homo sapiens*.

While the concept of being able to download knowledge and skills *Matrix*-style might be appealing when compared to the decades of study we have had to undergo to date, BCIs also present several worrying dystopian scenarios. Excluding the obvious potential of an 'Eloi and Morlock' split in society, based on whether you can afford – or choose – to augment your organic body with genetic and silicon enhancements, there are also more immediate challenges presented. For example, corporations or governments could use artificial intelligence to hack people's brains[349] and extract information, or they could act as 'thought police' and continuously monitor the public for signs of what they deem 'wrong-think' (which has already started on social media and platforms like YouTube). Imagine a society where people are constantly connected in a cloud-based hive mind, and where any detection of incorrect thoughts would be picked up and the perpetrator identified. BCI could therefore exacerbate social inequalities and totalitarian surveillance, but also create the potential for corporations, governments or any nefarious individuals to exploit and manipulate the thoughts and actions of others. These technologies are all on an exponential curve, so the window of opportunity to intervene is small, for once the technology leaves the lab, all bets are off as to who will use it and what for. Basically, the potential exists for any number of scenarios that would normally appear in an episode of *Black Mirror*.

---

[111] There are multiple Facebook groups dedicated to transhumanism, with tens of thousands of members worldwide. There was even a Transhumanist political party campaigning for office in the 2016 US elections.

None of this is predestined and it is possible – though unlikely – that none of the dystopian scenarios presented will come to pass. While we are fast approaching a place where we will be continually connected to technology; where billions of chips are in billions of things ranging from our fridges to bodies, currently it is still us, not the technology, that has agency. Those who leap to worst-case scenarios and prophesise our eventual demise to robotic superiority often view technological change as a linear process. They observe the current rapid improvement in robotics, especially in the replacement of human skills, and project this process forward into an indefinite future without factoring in any human response. As discussed, our progress has been cyclical in nature, for during the rise of each new wave of technological advancement society recalibrates and adapts to the new realities. Any attempt to predict technological evolution that omits the human response will be one-dimensional, for society is not static, and humans are more than passive agents in technology's onward march. The first industrial revolution created entirely new industries and millions of new jobs, but it had to be tempered by political changes to limit the effects on those affected by the transition but not benefiting from it. The digital revolution will also. We do have our work cut out, and it requires deliberate action, for everything discussed was not fictional futuristic projections, but commentary on real research and activities. To paraphrase the great Peter Drucker, procrastination just isn't going to cut it. Most pressing is the need to ensure that the sixth wave provides an economy and society that works for us all, for before we experience a technological singularity, we are likely to have to deal with an economic one.

SIXTH-WAVE
ECONOMICS

19

THE TIME OF KEYNES' GRANDCHILDREN

We are being afflicted with a new disease of which some readers may not yet have heard the name, but of which they will hear a great deal in the years to come – namely, technological unemployment. This means unemployment due to our discovery of means of economizing the use of labor outrunning the pace at which we can find new uses for labour.

John Maynard Keynes, 1930

Like many children of Western baby boomers, I was brought up instilled with the Protestant work ethic; taught that success depends on your effort not your upbringing, and through hard work not handouts. Like all beliefs driven into you from childhood, it has shaped my life and the lens through which I see the world. This work-ethic mindset led to me setting up my first business at thirteen, buying and selling second-hand paperback books that I sold from a metal box on the back of my bicycle. Because people didn't own word processors and printers in those days, I had to spend hours each week completely rewriting by hand the current list of available books, writing each book's title, author and a couple of plot summary lines, then determining their price based on their condition. Most of my time was therefore spent on administration and travelling rather than selling.

I then cycled to every house in my village, knocking on doors and asking the occupants whether they would like to buy any books. Most were kind enough to give me time because of my young age, but only a few loyal customers gave me their business. Due to the advances of the last wave, if I had to rebuild that business now it would look completely different. The product would be the same, but my marketplace wouldn't be restricted to where I could cycle. Updating the book catalogue would take minutes, not hours; people could order online, and then I could send them the books through the post. However, because of modern technology I also wouldn't bother, because Amazon already does all this, owning not just the world's largest bookstore, but also a marketplace for people to resell used books, as well as almost everything else under the sun.

Fast-forward a couple of years and I, like many students in the UK in the 1980s, undertook numerous part-time jobs to earn money, from shifts at McDonald's, to evening bar jobs and stacking shelves in retail stores. Like many who went to university, I also spent the summers working in factories and other manual labour jobs. In the port and market town of King's Lynn where I grew up, this involved everything from working in the fields picking strawberries,[112] picking dead rodents and spoiled crops from conveyor belts of frozen vegetables,[113] to labouring in saw mills. In the evenings, I supplemented this work with pulling pints at local pubs, social clubs and nightclubs. The day jobs were mostly mind-numbingly dull (bar jobs were almost always OK because people + alcohol = entertaining), but it was money, and as a young lad with debts from college, money was needed. The mindset of work being preferable to welfare was instilled in me so strongly that my weekly earnings target from fruit-picking was to match the weekly unemployment benefit amount, which was £30 per week back then. As long as I made that amount I was happy, and the week spent on my knees in the dirt picking fruit was deemed a success. It may seem crazy to cycle ten miles at 6am to then work all day for what I could get by doing nothing, but it was more about self-worth and achievement than money. The ability to buy my own pint at the weekend and say, 'I earned that.'

I graduated in 1991 in the grip of a recession, with unemployment

---

[112] Tip number one – always start in the early morning before dawn, when the fruit weighs more due to moisture.

[113] Tip number two – wear gloves, else your fingers go numb in minutes. Found that out the painful way.

around 10 per cent and a blanket cancellation of most company's graduate recruitment schemes. To earn a living, I ended up working in the Berol pen factory operating a machine that made black plastic pen-ends. It involved pressing a single button on a plastic-moulding machine to start the process, then opening the door, swiping off the plastic ends so they fell into a tray, shutting the door and pressing the button again. Press, open, swipe, shut. Repeat ad nauseam. Unlike my summer jobs, this one had no defined end date, so I couldn't count down the weeks until I left because I didn't know how long it would be until someone responded positively to one of my hundreds of handwritten job applications. When Christmas arrived, I was in a bad way. The sheer unadulterated monotony and feeling that my degree had been a waste of time had pushed me to the limit. Going back to that machine after the Christmas break was probably the hardest thing I've ever had to do. So, a decision had to be made. Rather than focus on acquiring my first 'big break', I changed tack and pushed to get another local job – anything other than standing at that bloody machine – and by March 1992, I had landed a job in the unemployment centre. For the next fifteen months my job was to tell other people that there were no jobs. But it involved dialogue and thinking, and it also allowed me to see for myself the effects of long-term unemployment on people.

There's a reason why I'm sharing these tales of my early working life. They reflect some of the realities of life in a capitalist, industrialised world. When people talk about machines taking over the manual jobs in the factory, I think back to those jobs and I think, *Good*. There's more to life than spending eight hours a day stood at a machine or on a production line, regardless of where in the world this is. Treating people like robots just creates inefficient, expensive and unhappy fleshy robots, and inefficient and unhappy people cost money to manage. So why not use real robots to do these unintelligent tasks? These metal slaves are much more efficient at being repetitively robotic, have zero emotional needs, require no breaks and can be regularly upgraded to become smarter and stronger. Robots will make the ends of pens all day, every day, without losing the will to live. But I also realise that jobs bring in income, and in doing that they provide a sense of achievement. For over thirty years my grandmother cycled the same roads to the same engineering factory to stand at the same machine drilling and shaping metal. I can't imagine how she kept sane. It did, however, allow her to buy her own house. The fact that a single woman could, through hard work, save and buy her independence was something that she was incredibly proud of. It was her house. She earned it. Never underestimate the value and feeling of achievement that working for something brings, regardless of the work undertaken to acquire it.

Over three decades later and machines now either do – or will soon do – nearly all the jobs of my youth. They are learning to pick fruits and vegetables from the fields including soft fruits like strawberries; they can identify poor-quality vegetables and undesirable items on the production line using machine learning-powered visual inspection capabilities and sawmills and canning factories have become automated. The only jobs that still remain are barman, shelf-filler and fast-food worker – although robot bartenders are starting to appear that can mix and serve drinks, Walmart rolled out shelf-checking robots in 2017, and self-service kiosks and burger-flipping robots are replacing fast-food workers. Soon these will also be jobs of the past.

Which brings me back to Berol. A company formed in 1856 is now another statistic in the march of globalisation; the brand sold to overseas buyers who offshored production to cheaper locations, the factory closed, the jobs lost, and the plastic pen-end machine scrapped. Finally, to pens themselves. The paperless office was predicted to be here by 2000, yet I sit in my office surrounded by handwritten notes and a desk tidy full of pens. Despite all the technological advancements of the computer age, people still own and use pens. Old-wave products are not always immediately destroyed because of new-wave advancements, as the diffusion process takes time to spread across society and the cultural lag means that a large percentage of the population take time to adapt, if they adapt at all. However, regardless of whether you prefer a pen, tablet or laptop, all are now more likely to be bought from an online retailer such as Amazon than a bricks-and-mortar store.

In this brief personal example, we've seen the positives and negatives of the last wave, the effects of globalisation, offshoring, technological replacement, digitisation, e-commerce platforms, creative destruction, and old and new technologies coexisting. Now we are in the sixth wave, and a globalised world of intelligent machines, robotics, autonomous vehicles and machine-learning algorithms awaits. But it poses some really important questions, such as 'Will our economic model still work?' and 'What role do humans play in the world of smart machines?' Those who attempt to provide an answer seem to fall into two camps; either the future of work itself is at risk, or we have been here many times before and any concerns are the rants of neo-Luddites. As always, the truth lies somewhere between the two extremes, and to understand the truth we need to consider both possibilities. Let's start by analysing the biggest fear – mass technological unemployment. The Automation Jobpocalypse.

The New Neds

As the Keynes quote that opens this chapter shows, fear of the effect of automation on labour markets is not new. Centuries before the first industrial revolution, people in high places were concerned about machines displacing the livelihoods of workers. In 1589, William Lee invented the stocking frame, a machine that imitated the movement of hand-knitters and which represented the first of a series of devices that would mechanise the textile industry. Lee was refused a patent for the stocking frame by Queen Elizabeth I, so he built an improved machine that increased the number of needles per inch and produced a silk of finer texture. The queen again refused to issue him with a patent because of her concern – probably under pressure from the Hosiery Guild – for England's many hand-knitters whose livelihoods would be threatened by such mechanisation. *Thou aimest high, Master Lee. Consider thou what the invention could do to my poor subjects. It would assuredly bring to them ruin by depriving them of employment, thus making them beggars.*[350]

This story has been repeated ever since. As new technologies go from ideas to innovations, the people trained in the old ways of working all cry foul, seeing the new industries that arise only as a threat, never an opportunity. They are right to be concerned. There is always unemployment in the old, industrial industries when the new way of doing things moves from deceptive to disruptive, for the forces of creation always bring destruction with them. We may use the word 'Luddite' as an insult directed at those who protest the march of technology and the social disruption it creates, but to the Luddites their cause was proven to be just, for they *did* lose their livelihoods and life *did* get worse for them as a result. New industries *do* destroy old ones and create technological unemployment, and the jobs of the past have indeed been replaced. The last 150 years have seen most industrialised nations move from around 50 per cent of the population working in agriculture, to below 2 per cent. For some, this transition has happened more recently: in Japan the last seventy years has seen the number of agricultural workers fall from 17.16 million to just 2.68 million. The path of creative destruction has seen the US move from having over 2 million railroad workers and 238,000 blacksmiths in the first decade of the 20th century, to just 105,500 railroad workers and virtually no blacksmiths a century later. The destruction occurs every wave. In 1970 at the start of the fifth wave, the US telephone industry employed 421,000 switchboard operators who handled 9.8 billion long-distance calls a year. In 2016 more long-distance calls were taking place than ever, yet only 8,860 US telephone operators were employed. Fifteen years ago, the local telephone book and a copy of the *Yellow Pages* were necessities in every home, and the supply chain involved in their production and delivery was significant. Now they are both pretty much obsolete. Creative destruction in action

So where did the workers go? How did they survive? They trained for and found other types of jobs, in new industries created by new technology. At the start of the 20th century there were no auto mechanics, medical technicians, electricians, web developers, or taxi, bus or truck drivers. Now there's over 749,900 auto mechanics, 335,700 medical technicians, 666,900 electricians, 162,900 web developers, and nearly 2.5 million vehicle drivers in the US alone.[114] Here lies one of the great challenges behind the prophecies of technological unemployment. It suffers from the same issues that plague science-fiction writers and economists: it is much easier to imagine the loss of jobs that exist now, than to imagine the creation of whole new ones. In the same way that we could easily imagine flying cars but not the Internet, we fretted about losing visible jobs like weavers, typists and production workers, but we did not foresee the rise of jobs like social media experts, data scientists and web designers.

So, if technological unemployment is just part of the natural process of creative destruction, is there nothing to worry about in the sixth wave? Well, yes and no. John Maynard Keynes foretold a time when we would, through advancements in automation, only have to work a fifteen-hour work week. As we now know, it didn't quite turn out that way. As well as a lack of flying

---

[114] All 2016 statistics from the United States Department of Labour, Bureau of Labour Statistics.

cars (for now – we know they are on the way), we still work as many hours as before, if not more. However, automation has drastically reduced the time taken to do domestic tasks such as food preparation, cooking, shopping and cleaning. As a result, while we still work long hours, we do have more leisure time, creating whole new service and entertainment sectors. Rather than eliminating the need for human workers, industrialisation created whole new employment opportunities sufficient enough to soak up the 20th century's population explosion. In the previous waves, although the destructive side has eliminated certain jobs, the creative side has always come to the rescue and new types of mass employment have picked up the excess labour freed from disrupted industries. The rise of the automobile caused the demise of the 238,000 US blacksmiths alongside the carriage drivers and famous buggy- and whip-makers, replaced by taxi drivers, lorry drivers and automotive engineers. Blake's 'dark satanic mills' have been replaced by fluorescent-lit open offices, and door-to-door salesmen have been replaced by call-centre workers and social media experts. We no longer need people to light the street lamps, but we do need people to fix our broadband. For every replaced industry and eliminated job, a replacement has appeared. It's not a perfect science – sometimes entire communities are devastated, and people who wish to stay in their home towns find replacement work hard to come by. Just ask the ex-coal miners in the north of England, or car production workers in Detroit. Globalisation has also had a major impact on this process. The working class of the West, especially those with limited skills, have been sacrificed in order to raise corporate profits and initiate the industrialisation of the emerging nations. In the UK, the needs, identity and future of the poor, white working class have been ignored in favour of other groups, and their children are suffering as a result, languishing at the bottom of nearly all educational tables.[351] Some of the most devastating impacts of automation have therefore not been economic, but societal and cultural.

A Disruption in the Force

While it is easy to reject current concerns of technological unemployment simply as the pessimistic rants of neo-luddites who do not understand the cyclical nature of technological change and its historical precedents, this time, they may be right. While every new wave brings with it a wide variety of new tools and production techniques that power the forces of creative destruction, this wave includes innovations that pose a serious threat to the socio-economic model. The reason? Because not only can these innovations replace human jobs, they can also replace human capabilities, enabling them to automate roles across multiple levels and multiple industries all at the same time, making humans the less efficient and more expensive option for most tasks.

Currently we are complacent because unemployment is low and productivity is rising, creating a misplaced sense of security. It is hard to ring the 'technological unemployment' alarm when employment figures in many countries is at an all-time high. However, as mentioned, low unemployment is created by both the old industries and the new coexisting. Right now, we have millions of people employed as truck drivers, while another much smaller new group of highly skilled people are developing trucks that drive themselves. Soon, the output of the latter group will replace the need for the former. There is also another worrying economic development; one that started during the previous wave. Productivity has separated from the value of human labour, something that has been named by economists as 'the great decoupling'. Until around 1970, productivity, employment and wages were aligned, but while labour productivity continued to grow the number of people involved in generating that productivity fell and the wages paid for that labour stagnated. The stagnation of wages is the result of multiple mutually reinforcing dynamics; these include the oversupply of cheap labour from the emerging nations, a 'winner take all' wealth concentration and the destruction of the 'trickle-down' model, the dominance of credit over labour, and the obvious elephant in the room – automation. This wage stagnation isn't supposed to happen in conventional economics, for once unemployment drops to below the 5 per cent mark, wages are expected to increase due to competing demand for the limited supply of productive workers – as in the case of the bargaining power of the serfs following the Black Death. Instead, what we've witnessed is prices being held down by competition and oversupply, and a constant demand for more returns for shareholders. To stay competitive and provide the desired returns, companies must keep costs low, and labour is usually the biggest cost. They therefore sought a way to do more with less, either through spending less money via offshoring and outsourcing, or by using machines. While offshoring was the initial culprit, it is automation that will have the biggest impact on manufacturing, rendering millions of low-skilled jobs redundant. The CEOs and leaders of businesses embraced the potential to replace large swathes of messy, complicated humans with simpler, less dramatic and more productive machines. And while machines do great things for productivity, they do little for wages.

To date the effects of the decoupling between wages and productivity have been masked by the availability of cheap credit, enabling people to have the illusion of wealth, when in fact it is debt that they own. Debt that enables the middle classes to keep on consuming even when their pay packet has run out; that allows them to drive around in cars and live in nice houses stuffed full of the outputs of these global corporations. This has led many commentators to dismiss fears of mass job replacement because the figures just don't indicate this happening. To them I would say, 'Kodak'. The leaders at Kodak looked at healthy film-sales numbers and believed they represented projections of the future rather than records of the past. This was a fatal mistake. They failed to appreciate that digital photography was in the deceptive early stages of the S-curve, still relatively immature and being played around with by innovators and early adopters while the mass market still bought traditional film. However, the moment a two-megapixel camera was available at an affordable price point, digital photography crossed the chasm and the market for film disintegrated. We are at the same point now, only with technologies that will affect every industry; in the deceptive stage of robotics, RPA, machine learning, drones and autonomous vehicles, and the very early stages of developments such as the blockchain and AI. We hear about them constantly but rarely see them; much like digital photography in the mid 1990s. Currently they are rare, but soon – very soon – they will be everywhere.

Like Kodak, complacency and myopia could be our undoing. Research by Gallup showed that 73 per cent of people believe that automation and AI will destroy more jobs than they create, but the same survey also found that only 23 per cent were 'worried' or 'very worried' that automation would affect them personally.[352] The more educated the person, the less they felt that they would be personally impacted, and the more they thought it would affect someone else. This confidence is likely to be misplaced.

Seven Reasons Why

I believe there are seven factors that differentiate the creative destruction nature of the sixth wave compared to previous ones, as follows:

1. Speed of change.

It is a human tendency to take our recent past and project it in a linear fashion into the future. We are hardwired to think linearly and to expect any accelerations in the rate of change to be consistent, for exponential rates of change are hard for humans to comprehend. The next twenty years, we figure, will more or less unfold as the last twenty years have. Not a chance. While every upswing period sees an exponential period of change, catching people out as they expect the future rate of progress to simply reflect that of the past, this one will be higher and wider than the previous waves combined, resulting in masses of people losing their jobs before they have a chance to adapt to the threat and develop new skills. The developed nations built their foundations in a time when technology diffused slowly. This enabled the creation of a solid middle class based around the industry of making things. The newly emerging nations will not have the same luxury. Globalisation and digitisation enable new innovations to travel further and faster than ever before. New innovations created in one continent can be sold in another seamlessly, and if the product is digital, almost immediately. Compare that to previous waves where a trial batch of a product had to be packaged and shipped around the world, sold to local distributors willing to try them, who then had to convince local retailers to stock them, who then had to persuade their customers to buy them. Now e-commerce enables consumers to see new products even before they are released – and in some cases even support their development through crowdsourcing – and then identify where they can be procured, order them and pay for them all from the comfort of their home. Entire industries could feel the effect of a disruptive technology in weeks. Wherever the smartphone has a healthy market (i.e. everywhere), people suddenly stopped buying paper maps, calculators and MP3 players. It wasn't a slow decline. William Gibson's 2003 declaration that *the future is here – it's just not evenly distributed* may have been true then, but it seems that the future is getting distributed faster than ever now.

The acceleration will set off an avalanche of change, as companies will be forced to innovate just to keep up. As Amazon grows, other companies will be increasingly forced to use automation to also reduce their costs. If there are two companies competing and one is using human labour to make, pick, pack, load and transport its goods, while the other simply uses machines that operate for the cost of electricity, then the latter company will have a significant cost advantage, which it will use to reduce their prices significantly, meaning that the other company will have to do the same or it will go out of business. To keep Amazon within its sights, Alibaba copied Amazon's Kiva warehouse logistics system, automating its fulfilment centres; Ocado in the UK is completely automating its warehouses and logistics operation; and Walmart is experimenting not just with logistics automation, but also the implementation of shelf-checking machines, drones, and developing its own automated stores that, like Amazon Go, have no checkout lines or tills.[353] This process is accelerated by the fact that the competitors are global, not local, requiring companies to prepare a response to the activities of US companies like Amazon even if they are not US-based themselves.

There is also rarely a good match between the skills required to do the new wave jobs and the old-wave ones, but the transition period used to be slow enough for people to make considered decisions about what skills they needed to survive. Now the upswing's accelerated speed of change has resulting in many students studying subjects that have a limited future. As Stephen Hawking declared in *A Brief History of Time*: *The rate of progress is so rapid that what one learns at school or university is always a bit out of date. Only a few people can keep up with the rapidly advancing frontier of knowledge, and they have to devote their whole time to it and specialize in a small area. The rest of the population has little idea of the advances that are being made or the excitement they are generating.*[354]

This acceleration is also likely to catch out our political leaders and governmental institutions. In previous waves, the process of creative destruction unfolded slowly enough for politicians and voters to remain in touch with it, and as a result they were able to regulate and manipulate its impact. Now digital technology traverses the globe instantly, outpacing politicians' ability to understand and analyse it. Governments are not known for their ability to respond at speed, and adjustments to legislation are often after the fact and retrospective, and usually as a result of social pressure or bad publicity. Government representatives such as civil servants and MPs are also likely to be older, less technologically savvy, and industrial age-educated, and as a result may struggle to understand the complexity of developments in AI and robotics, or what kinds of policies are needed or beneficial for safe and smart future development. Overall, the acceleration in the rate of change will see individuals, businesses and our political institutions all struggle to keep up.

2.   Scope of change – all levels, all industries, all geographies.

In previous waves, labour-replacing machines were single-purpose and, as a result, mostly industry-specific. In contrast, the new breed of cobots, software programs and autonomous vehicles are multi-purpose, able to adapt and be used in a multitude of different locations and for different tasks. The first of the triple whammies – muscle-to-machine – will decimate industries that rely on large quantities of human labour to do repetitive work. Intelligent robots will be used to automate every stage of the end-to-end supply chain, and not just the dull, dirty and dangerous bits. Driving is an area that is particularly at risk. Once autonomous vehicles are proven to be safe and legal, they will wipe out taxi drivers, bus drivers, truck drivers, chauffeurs, fork-lift drivers etc. The next decade is also going to be challenging for the millions of office workers who process paperwork and answer queries – RPA systems, chatbots and the blockchain are all going to replace the cubicle-infested world of Dilbert and his colleagues.

There is also the reality that 'all companies are in the software business now'. Increasingly, physical assets are replaced by digital ones, causing an algorithmic arms race. Developments in one industry will quickly find themselves replicated to another by the very nature of the fact that code and digital developments are easily transferrable. The platform nature of robots also means that they can be easily programmed to be useful in multiple tasks and multiple industries. To turn Pepper from a retail worker to a priest just requires different code to be installed. For Baxter to leave his job on the production line and work in packing only involves changing his 'end-of-arm' tooling and for him to be shown how to pack. Over the next ten years, agriculture, mining, shipping, ports, manufacturing, construction, picking, packing, loading, moving, cooking and even selling are all likely to be hit hard by the rise of the robots. The unfortunate fact will be that the areas that were hit hardest by the hollowing out of manufacturing in the last wave are likely to be the ones hit by this wave of automation as well. This is because the factories and the pits were replaced by call centres and warehouses; just another type of repetitive, labour-intensive job that chatbots and algorithms can easily automate. So if all you have to trade for money is your time and the use of the things on the ends of your wrists, then I'm afraid the future is not looking very bright.

Whammy two, the replacement of knowledge work is perhaps where the biggest impact will be felt. Our cerebral abilities have been our USP and our protection from automation. As we are the only labour source capable of completing tasks that require thinking. As a result, white-collar workers, those lucky enough to have a good education and who have exceptional creative talents or analytic skills, have been able to ride the wave of technological change relatively successfully. Rather than replacing their jobs, information technology has complemented the work of people who do research, analysis, planning, strategy, trading, deal-making and many forms of design and artistic creation. However, what happens when computer technology and automation develop to a level whereby they can replace these activities as well? While we have seen machines replacing muscle, we've never before seen machines replacing minds, and we've definitely never seen machine minds controlling machine hands. The continued replacement of human minds with machine logic, plus next-level machine-to-machine collaboration, will affect all industries from manufacturing to services, and all levels from manual labour to highly skilled professions. Computers will continue to become both more powerful and cheaper, and as a result machine intelligence will only continue to improve at an exponential rate.

The potential impact of this artificial intelligence explosion on highly skilled professions such as medicine is starting to become evident. The NHS's 'GP at Hand' AI chatbot can already diagnose issues on a par with human doctors, achieving higher than average medical exam results. Corporate chatbots and voice assistants are reducing the number of people required in customer service call centres, and RPA software is automatically handling repetitive tasks such as order entry and the generation of documents like order acknowledgements and invoices. Soon, people will prefer machine medical diagnosis, machine lawyers and machine tax assessors because they will have access to more information, won't have to wait, receive the most up-to-date answers, and be less likely to receive poor advice. Once consumer choice moves towards automated rather than human solutions, as it is already doing in areas such as hedge-fund management, then the competition will have to adapt just to stay in business, making traditionally high-wage jobs just as vulnerable as lower-wage, manual work to the forces of automation. Consider the potential job-destruction impact of the blockchain. While there will be significant demand for skills in this area, the destructive side of the equation will outweigh the creative by a factor of ten. The blockchain's capabilities to provide a distributed, open (but encrypted) ledger across the end-to-end supply chain will likely cause the demise of millions of jobs involved in recording, processing and reporting the movement of goods and money.

We are about to witness the major disruption of the 'magic' professions – industries such as accountancy that currently are able to magically transform a pile of receipts and paperwork into a balance sheet and a tax return. Now, software programs such as QuickBooks and TurboTax enable business owners and private households to do this themselves, and when FINTECH and the blockchain converge this will probably all be automated. Tasks that currently take a small army of relatively highly paid, well-educated professionals to achieve, such as transactional accounting processes, fiscal period end closing, auditing and regulatory filing will all be automated. Companies like MasterCard and Visa have already been using machine-learning algorithms to detect fraudulent patterns of spending in debit and credit cards, and automatically freeze cards in response. Soon, as we saw with J. P. Morgan and COIN, AI systems will take seconds to complete tasks that used to take legal assistants and contract analysts hundreds of thousands of hours to achieve. Computer software can now process X-rays and other medical scans and then instantly send them to professionals on the other side of the world for analysis; advanced planning tools can forecast better than humans; software can accurately search through thousands of historic legal documents for specific words or patterns, making paralegals redundant; and now even the stock market is run by computer-trading algorithms that continue to replace the thousands of floor brokers that once occupied the floor of the Stock Exchange. As automation becomes more capable and more affordable – as it will – then an arms race will develop to utilise these new capabilities, and other companies will have to join this race else they will be left behind.

One of the most surprising areas to be impacted is the creative industries; fields such as design and journalism. One of the pervasive 'conventional wisdoms' is that automation will remove the dull, dirty and dangerous jobs, allowing us to focus on more creative pursuits such as writing, music, art and the like. We've already discussed how systems like IBM's Watson are helping to develop film trailers, but while that may currently sound niche, AI's impact on another creative industry, journalism, has not been. In 2017, 850 articles that featured in the *Washington Post*, mostly pieces on earnings reports and sports stories, were written by its in-house news-writing bot called Heliograf.[355] The system was also used to generate advertisements for the *Post*'s online site. In the digital age we are seeing more written content being produced than ever – only moving forwards, most of it will probably by written by a machine.

The research arm of the consultancy McKinsey & Co. spent eight months studying the potential impact of automation on forty-six nations and more than eight hundred occupations, and predicted that by 2030 some 800 million workers will be displaced, the equivalent of a fifth of the global workforce.[356] Likewise, a well-cited 2013 paper by Carl Benedikt Frey and Michael Osborne of the Oxford Martin School at the University of Oxford in the UK[357] claimed that 47 per cent of current occupational categories are at high risk of being automated by 2034. That includes accountancy, legal work, technical writing and a lot of other skilled occupations. Sixth-wave disruption will not care about the colour of your collar, the length of your education, the university you went to, your IQ, or your parentage. You may have left school at sixteen or completed a master's degree. You may be a shelf-filler or a stockbroker, an article writer or an accountant, a telemarketer or a truck driver, a lettuce-picker or a legal analyst. All are at risk.

3. Increased skill set/lack of skill transferability.

In past waves, new jobs either involved a similar level of skill to the ones they replaced – or less – enabling anyone, even children, to earn a salary. A skilled artisan had more talent and training than a factory loom operator, and a farmer needed more skill and knowledge than a production-line worker. Even when labour moved from the factory floor to the call centre, the skills required were easily learned by someone with just a standard level of education. The sixth wave is likely to reverse this, as the new wave of jobs are going to be much more highly skilled than the ones they replace – with the likelihood that the displaced workers will simply be unable to raise their skill level to undertake them. One major issue is that our industrial-era education system is not designed to provide the skills needed to compete. In a 2014 poll[358] of unemployed Americans between the ages of twenty-five and fifty-four, 42 per cent cited that the reason for their unemployment was a lack of education or skills necessary for the jobs available, 35 per cent added that their work had been replaced by technology, and 32 per cent that it had gone overseas. To compete in the digital age requires a more sophisticated set of skills, because anything repetitive and laborious is being automated at an ever-increasing rate. For example, working in robotics requires multidisciplinary skills containing elements of mechanical engineering, electrical engineering, computer science, psychology, biology, neurology, sociology and mathematics, and to date US companies have had to import engineers from India and China due to a shortage of these skills.

Companies like Ocado have responded to challenges from Amazonian forces by transforming themselves into tech companies, using software, machine learning and robotics to do what teams of humans used to. They are creating exciting new jobs, but these are few in number and highly skilled positions in data analysis, robotics, autonomous vehicles and machine learning. As Alex Harvey, Head of Robotics and Autonomous Systems at Ocado, declared to the audience at a robotics event I attended, displaced logistics workers are unlikely to be redeployed elsewhere in the organisation. *Let's be honest. We are not going to be retraining our warehouse staff to be machine-learning experts. That requires a completely different set of skills and intellectual capabilities that people cannot simply be trained to do.* The company doesn't have the time and the people don't have the education, aptitude, experience or skills.

We are therefore going to be confronted with a paradoxical situation: a juxtaposition of significant technological unemployment and a major skills shortage at the same time. This is particularly obvious in the supply chain. In 2017, DHL Supply Chain surveyed over 350 supply-chain and operations professionals in the five major regions of the world.[359] They found that the greatest impact on talent shortage is the speed of changing job requirements and the increasing amount of skills needed to deliver them. The ideal employee needs to have strategic, tactical and operational expertise, and solid analytical skills. But tomorrow's talent must also excel at leadership, strategic thinking, innovation and high-level analytic capabilities. Unsurprisingly, 58 per cent of companies polled stated that this combination is hard to find. We have educated and trained people to work in an industrial world; a world that is rapidly being turned on its head. Automation will continue to drastically reshape our economy, affect future job prospects and devalue most forms of human labour. This will give parents something to think seriously about when considering their children's futures.

4. The non-human nature of competition.

Economists split production into capital and labour, and to date we've assumed that this labour was human in nature. Now humans are competing against machines that don't just make their job somewhat more efficient; they completely replace the need for humans at all. Machines have already surpassed human physical and mental capacities in many areas, and it is apparent that this is only the start. These new technologies are not just replacing jobs – they are replacing the need for humans to do jobs. For example, capabilities such as speech and vision have now been automated, meaning that wherever there is a need to speak or see, a machine can now be utilised. Not only can they replace these human capabilities, but they can also improve upon them, able to speak multiple languages and see things we cannot. As companies like Apple cram more and more electronics into a smaller package, the ability of humans to visually inspect them at the precision and velocity required will become harder and harder. Leading AI developers like Andrew Ng have developed AI-based learning algorithms that, after being trained on just a few images, can spot tiny imperfections in small electronic components or camera lenses that are beyond what the human eye can see. Combine these advancements with the new breed of collaborative robots that bring the benefits of automation to industrial areas where it never made financial sense before, and you get a compelling mix. Robotic platforms combined with the aforementioned advancements in vision, haptic and voice capabilities effectively create a new machine workforce that enables Western countries to compete in the global manufacturing market against low-wage labour countries. Reshoring manufacturing nearer the consumer and utilising machines rather than human hands results not only in greater efficiency, but also lower inventory and transportation costs. As machines get more precise, they'll also produce an increasingly higher-quality product.

All this automation will enable people to focus on tasks that are more value-adding – at least initially. When banks first rolled out ATMs in the late 1960s, the expectation was that the number of bank tellers would plummet. Yet in the US they doubled, continuing to grow until the 2000s. Freed up from the repetitive task of withdrawing cash, tellers could focus instead on helping customers with other, more complex tasks such as issuing cashier's cheques or answering questions. In the long run, though, technology always wins, and as banking increasingly becomes mobile and digital, branches are once again closing, and bank tellers are being made redundant at an alarming rate. This trend will be seen across multiple industries, for technological improvements in past waves made the worker 'somewhat' more productive, not 'infinitely' more. Now, for the first time, it's plausible for the machine to completely replace the need for humans in certain roles, excluding them from the job market. Intelligent robots will be cheaper, faster and far more reliable than humans, able to work 168 hours a week, not just forty. Machines don't join unions, ask for pay rises or need holidays, sleep, sick leave or any breaks whatsoever. They also make far fewer errors, and are unlikely to pilfer goods, act inappropriately or put your company's brand at risk. They are reliable, and reliable employees don't need managing.

Robots like Pepper are currently being used as a novelty, a gimmick, a way to increase engagement with customers and attract interest, rather than as a serious replacement for human labour. This will soon change as its abilities increase. Like a real child, Pepper and its robotic colleagues will continue to learn and develop, getting more aware of the world and how it works, more socially capable and more intelligent. However, unlike a child, they will learn from the combined interactions of all other similar robots, and not just from their own individual experiences. But perhaps these robot's biggest benefit comes from doing what humans cannot – capturing, analysing and reporting on every single interaction it has with the public, allowing companies to really find out what people are after. Ask a retail worker how their day went, and you'll probably get a meaningless answer such as 'Yeah, it was busy.' Ask Pepper, and you'll receive a full breakdown of every person they spoke to, how long they spoke with them, what they wanted, whether they were happy with the engagement – and, if Pepper did its job properly, a name, email address and description (or photo) of the customer. A robot's ability to provide detailed analysis of every single engagement doesn't just make it as valuable as a human retail assistant or concierge – it makes it exponentially more valuable. And it's just getting started.

Once companies realise the potential of a concierge that never takes a break, retail assistants that never have a bad day and security staff who are never distracted, then the motivation to continue to employ humans in fields where machines could do the job better will plummet. Any prediction of what machines will be able to achieve – from driving cars to winning at Go – has been woefully inaccurate. Expectations are shifting all the time. Machines are on the brink of becoming so good at understanding and breaking down complex jobs into many predictable ones that many will find limited opportunity to specialise. The removal of human errors through developments like the blockchain and robotic process automation will also dramatically reduce the huge industry set up around checking for, rectifying and legislating against human errors. Trouble is, there's a lot of people currently employed to perform these tasks, which is also why there are so many errors. Remove the humans, remove the errors.

While CEOs embraced the potential of machines that could improve the productivity and efficiency of the production process, I bet they never believed that automation would also allow them to drastically reduce the amount of office workers, personal assistants, accountancy workers, call-centre operators, copywriters, marketing administrators, warehouse staff, planners and delivery drivers they employed. Companies such as Satalia are also developing AI capabilities capable of monitoring and controlling the allocation and execution of activities of both human and machine workers, transforming the practice of management into an outdated, industrial-age construct. Soon most workers will be competing against something that operates 24/7 for the cost of electricity. Like the story of the steam drill against John Henry, the machine will be victorious because it doesn't get tired and keeps on going long after a human worker will have dropped dead from exhaustion. The modern-day steam drill is likely to be an AI system, and John Henry is played by the planner, doctor, analyst, stockbroker or accountant who believes that they can process more data and crunch more numbers than the new machine overlords. They can't. John Henry believed he was pitching his human muscle against machine muscle; when in reality he was pitching his brawn against the output of other humans' brains; his industriousness against their inventiveness. However, sixth-wave John Henrys are comparing their brains to those of machines that are increasingly learning on their own or as a group. Regardless of whether they are competing on raw processing power, the ability to consume and analyse huge volumes of data, or even work relentlessly without accident or incident, many workers simply don't stand a chance. Those who cannot adapt, like the coach-builders, street-lamp lighters and chimney sweeps of the past, will be left behind and ripe for technological replacement. Even the unions are beginning to realise that the gig is up. Over in Australia, the mining unions, outmanoeuvred by the introduction of autonomous trucks and diggers, switched from strike threats and wage demands – which simply provide employers with increased motivation to automate – to humanistic appeals about retaining a sense of community. It was too little, too late.

Many commentators who dispute the impact of automation, cite studies that show that industrial robots didn't cause unemployment in Germany.[360] Yet even in this study the researchers found that on average one robot replaces two manufacturing jobs, and between 1994 and 2014, roughly 275,000 full-time manufacturing jobs were not created because of robots. Unions and wage councils are incredibly strong in Germany, making it difficult for companies to automate the jobs of existing workers. What they have done, however, is create fewer jobs for new entrants and keep wages flat.[361] German manufacturing output is higher than ever. Its need for humans to make these things is not. As people retire and leave their jobs, they quite simply will not be replaced. Not by humans anyway.

The march of the machines cannot be stopped. Don't be fooled because you don't see robots looking like Sophia walking amongst us. Software, machine code – things that are invisible are currently transforming the world, making dumb things smart, capable not just of doing what we used to do, but doing it notably better. Machines will continue to encroach upon areas that we assume to be uniquely human – from driving us around to diagnosing our illnesses – making the areas where we can specialise increasingly limited. The incessant onward march of technology, especially artificial intelligence, raises the question of how soon robots will be able to design and build themselves.

5.   Reduction in labour intensity of work.

The industries of the previous waves, such as cotton, steel, coal, cars and even IT, created jobs on a massive scale. The new wave will bring unbridled amounts of wealth, but jobs? Not so much. While the new industries will undoubtedly create better-quality, higher-skilled jobs, they are going to be nowhere near as numerous, nor as labour intensive, as the ones they replace. Getting things done just doesn't require the same number of people any more. The attention-grabbing headline coming out of A. T. Kearney's 2017 Global Services Location Index was that on average, one new job is created for every four jobs automation replaces (a 1:4 ratio).[362] This situation is only going to get worse as companies move towards their vision of a fully automated supply chain. When AI manages the planning and execution of the fulfilment, robots move inventory and drones and autonomous vans deliver them, then the need for human employees will drop even more dramatically.

Right now, machine-learning specialists, coders and data scientists are perhaps the hottest jobs around, and the demand (and pay packets) for the different forms of AI development are skyrocketing, because they are highly technical jobs that take years to become proficient in. They also require a high degree of experience and education in relevant skills such as statistics and probability, computer science, data modelling and developing advanced machine-learning algorithms. These will be the 'in-demand' skills of the future, but their high value will be short-lived for as Google's AutoML system has already proved, the best candidate for the job – and the cheapest – is soon likely to be another machine-learning system. These are also tasks that can be done anywhere, meaning that programmers will be competing against a global, not local, workforce. Unlike previous waves where you could see which new and emerging industries could employ people in their millions, I'm struggling to identify what new roles could emerge that would require the large-scale recruitment of people. Mass employment opportunities arise from tasks that are rules-based, relatively repetitive and simple to learn. Moving forward, that perfectly defines the jobs that robots and algorithms will be doing, not humans.

6. Length of working life.

Combine the accelerating speed of change with a rising life expectancy and you get a perfect storm of technological unemployment. In past transition periods, the destruction process may have taken decades, softening the impact by enabling those affected to prepare themselves mentally and financially. In previous waves, it was not unusual for someone to spend most of their working life with the same employer, paying into a company pension scheme for decades and then retiring and living off the dividends for the rest of their lives. Many companies also handled disruption by asking for voluntary redundancies, and some employees – most of whom had long periods of service – often saw this as a golden opportunity to leave the company with money in their pocket. As most employees expected to retire between fifty-five and sixty-five years old anyway, a golden goodbye package and a final salary pension proved sufficient to provide a comfortable life throughout their final years.

This time is different. Firstly, the concept of a career, let alone a job for life, is now a thing of the past, along with the security and benefits that came with it. Work is more transient, with zero-hours contracts and no-frills employee rights becoming the norm, resulting in it becoming easier and less expensive to make someone redundant. Secondly, the number of final salary pension schemes have also been drastically cut back, the retirement age has been raised and life expectancy has increased, resulting in a significant increase in the amount of money needed to secure your lifestyle in your remaining years. If in the past you retired at fifty-five and expected to live until around seventy-five, then if you were careful a final salary company pension, a lump sum redundancy payment and a state pension would have made those final two decades quite comfortable. Now if you lose your job at fifty-five, saddled with debt and with no pension plan, no lump sum payment, and a life expectancy of over eighty-five years, then you are facing at least thirty years of poverty unless you find a way to rejoin the gainfully employed. Which is becoming increasingly harder when your competition is either a technologically savvy young person prepared to work for less just to get on the ladder, or a machine that will work for free.

Finally, life expectancy is skewing the balance; throughout human history there have been more young than old. Not any more. For the first time ever there are more people alive aged over 65 than aged under 5.[363]

As a result, people need to keep working for longer, and if automation takes away their job, then this time the impact will be felt not just by the individual, but across society. The people with the capability to learn new skills and relocate – the young and mobile – are likely to migrate to the urban centres looking for work, leaving the older generation behind in more rural locations. It's not a new phenomenon, but it's primed to get worse unless action is taken. It is going to be hard for this group to be persuaded that they have inherited the treasures of their forebears when their inheritance consists of a $20 trillion national deficit and the realisation that they have spent decades paying into corporate and state-sponsored pensions only to find out that they are in fact a Ponzi scheme that is likely to collapse before they can collect their share.

But perhaps the really precarious group are those aged between thirty-five and fifty; people saddled with the task of repaying large mortgages and covering the cost of bringing up children and covering their expenses all the way through to university. These long-term debts and responsibilities for others mean that they are likely to be living pay cheque to pay cheque, lacking the liquidity to jettison their current career in order to learn new skills or pursue entrepreneurial ventures. And unlike the dependant-free young, they cannot simply move back in with their parents. These people will resist change because they are terrified of the consequences. Their need for security will mean that they will likely stay in positions until the bitter end, only to find themselves ousted either by machines, or losing their job because their resistance to change sped up their company's doom loop. Then they will enter a marketplace that places little value on their years of industrial-age knowledge, seeing it as a disadvantage, not an asset. Erik Brynjolfsson, an economist at MIT, declared that providing a solution for this vast number of working- and middle-class people about to become caught in the transition will be *the biggest challenge of our society for the next decade*. He's not wrong.

7.   The squeezing of the middle class.

Perhaps one of the most worrying trends is the collapse of the middle classes. The flattening of wages and their inability to keep up with productivity growth have suppressed incomes and, behind the scenes, lifestyles have been maintained simply through an increase in borrowing on cheap credit. Historically, the middle class has acted as an agent of stability and prosperity; a healthy, growing group of aspirational members of society who became the backbone of the economy. The lower ranks of the middle classes have been built on routine physical or cognitive work, and this type of employment has been rapidly automated in recent decades. Areas like the Upper Midwest in the US have felt this the most, with the automotive industry in areas like Michigan and Detroit being hit hard. Between 1993 and 2007 the United States increased the number of robots per hour worked by 237 per cent. During the same period, the US economy shed 2.2 million manufacturing jobs. Detroit, a city that declared bankruptcy in 2013, also has the highest concentration of industrial robots (8.5 per 1,000 workers).[364] Correlation does not necessarily mean causation, but it is hard to not see the trend here.

Even the new economic powerhouses are at risk from the implications of a declining middle class. China, for example, has seen a massive growth in its middle class; not surprising considering this social group effectively didn't exist until the 1979 economic reforms that were implemented after Mao's death. Even by the late 1990s, only 5 million Chinese earned between $11,500 and $43,000 a year (in 2017 US dollars). Now 225 million do, providing China with the world's largest population of middle-class consumers, overtaking the US, whose middle class has continued to shrink since the start of the 'great decoupling' of productivity and income. Between 2000 and 2015, China added 43.4 million adults to its middle class, while the US added just 22 million. China therefore has a lot to lose by pursuing the automation of jobs that currently provide an income for this growing middle class. Especially given that they, like the Western middle class, are committing themselves to ever-increasing levels of debt such as expensive mortgages and university fees for their children; degrees that are becoming less relevant in an automated world.

But what is the impact on society of a substantially reduced middle class? To understand the risk, let's use truck driving as an example. America, due to its geographical size and multiple cities, is incredibly dependent on truck driving.[115] But it's a brutal and underappreciated job. Drivers in the US spend weeks at a time away from home, and endure long, tedious stretches

---

[115] Those readers old enough to remember the movie *Convoy* will have some idea of the cultural importance of the industry in the US.

of driving on straight, boring roads where they are inactive but must stay focused. It's not seen as a glamorous career, and the combination of boredom, poor work-life balance and social derision means the profession has a real problem attracting new entrants and retaining existing ones. The American Trucking Association (ATA) estimates that the US was short 30,000 truck drivers in 2014, and if demand continues they will need another 239,000 drivers by 2022.[365] As it becomes increasingly obvious to people that autonomous vehicles are the future, this shortfall is likely to rise.

Because of these factors, truck drivers are relatively well paid, receiving a middle-class median income of about $52,079 per year.[366] They are also comprised mostly of people without college educations, making truck driving one of the few remaining jobs in the US to provide a solid middle-class salary without requiring a post-secondary degree. Truckers are essentially the last remnants of an increasingly impoverished population that were once gainfully employed in manufacturing before those middle-income jobs were mostly shipped overseas. Trucking has avoided the dual macro trends of globalisation and automation because a worker in China can't drive a truck in Ohio, and to date machines couldn't drive trucks. Despite the shortfall in new entrants, trucking is still the number-one job in most US states, and according to the American Trucker Association, there are 1.2 million companies employing 3.5 million professional truck drivers, and an additional 5.2 million people employed within the US truck-driving industry who don't drive the trucks.[367] That's 8.7 million trucking-related jobs that could potentially be eliminated in the next five to ten years by autonomous vehicles, something which Morgan Stanley believes will save the freight industry $70 billion.[368]

Wealth may be created at a greater rate than ever, but it is not being spread in the same way as before. The middle classes bore the brunt of the economic fallout from the financial crash, and unlike the banks, there was no one to bail them out. In fact, given it was public funds that were used, it was mostly the middle classes that had financed the bailout, a situation many have not recovered from. The impact from a declining middle class has already been felt, for as the middle-class falters, so do the industries that depend on them, further exasperating the job losses. For example, automated trucks can operate 24/7 without mandated rest periods or the need to stop for food and bio breaks, devastating the industries that currently service these needs such as the thousands of truck stops that cater to the millions of drivers that travel across the interstates every day. Other staple indicators of middle-class consumerism such as casual dining is already being hit hard: the number of people eating at casual dining chains in the US has fallen every consecutive month since June 2015, making them the worst-performing segment of the restaurant industry. Applebee's is closing 135 locations, Buffalo Wild Wings at least sixty, Ruby Tuesday is up for sale, and Friendly's, Bennigan's, Joe's Crab Shack and Logan's Roadhouse all filed for bankruptcy. To continue to attract customers, these food establishments will have to drop prices, and to do that and remain profitable they will increasingly look to automation, especially when human workers are pushing for a $15 minimum wage. The forces of creative destruction always spread far beyond the technology being replaced, a fact few consider.

The importance and value of the middle class, and the danger of excluding them, is something even the rich are realising. Nick Hanauer, the American entrepreneur and venture capitalist, stated in 2011 that: *I can start a business based on a great idea, and initially hire dozens or hundreds of people. But if no one can afford to buy what I have to sell, my business will soon fail and all those jobs will evaporate... Only consumers can set in motion a virtuous cycle that allows companies to survive and thrive and business owners to hire. An ordinary middle-class consumer is far more of a job creator than I ever have been or ever will be.*[369]

From Careers to Gigs

While there are more people employed than ever before, the nature of this work has changed radically. The concept of a job for life is a relic of the past, and work has become more project- and contract-based. This is creating a different type of work environment, increasingly populated by what author Charles Handy calls 'portfolio people'; individuals who hire themselves out to do a variety of tasks for multiple employers in order to create a liveable income. So not only do people now have multiple employers during their working lives, they also potentially have multiple employers all at the same time. Some will be tasks they enjoy and are talented in; others simply there to make a buck. People may tout their preferred trade as a graphic designer or a website developer on sites like Freelancer.com, while also signing up to be an Uber taxi driver and a delivery agent for Amazon Flex. The number of these freelance opportunities is increasing as the network effect kicks in, with companies using this model to recruit people to run errands (TaskRabbit), deliver takeaway food (Just Eat, Uber Eats), give people lifts (Uber, Lyft), or deliver goods (Deliveroo, Amazon Flex, Hermes). This type of flexible contract work is one of the fastest-growing sectors of employment across the Western world. It has increased by over 55 per cent in the US over the past decade, while most other types of employment fell.[370] In the UK, around 1.3 million people currently work in the gig economy, whereas over in Canada, census data highlighted that in 2015 less than half of all Canadian workers (49.8 per cent) between the ages of twenty-five and fifty-four worked full-time, full-year jobs. According to StatCan, *the period from 2005 to 2015 saw an overall shift from full-time, full-year employment to part-time or part-year work.*[371] Brad Smith, CEO of Intuit, the company that makes the small business tax and accountancy software such as TurboTax and QuickBooks, stated that: *The gig economy... is now estimated to be about thirty-four percent of the workforce and expected to be forty-three percent by the year 2020... We think self-employed [work] has a lot of opportunity for growth as we look ahead.*[372] In 2016, the number of people working in the gig economy in the US was 4.8 million, but by 2021, they forecast that there will be nearly three times this number working in 'on-demand' employment. If the definition is broadened to include all alternative work arrangements – defined as temporary help agency workers, on-call workers, contract workers, and independent contractors or freelancers – then this is rising fast, and at least 30 million people – almost one in every five US workers – now engage in this form of flexible work.[373]

It's not necessarily a bad thing. Many people, especially the new millennial workforce, embrace and welcome this transition, loving the freedom and choice it provides. The idea of working a *Dilbert*-style existence in an office cubicle for eight hours a day, five days a week, fifty weeks a year fills them with dread, whereas logging in to an app to do whatever type of task takes their fancy that day to earn money is deemed a more flexible and preferable lifestyle. However, the precarious nature of this model is obvious, and if we are witnessing the death of careers – a move from jobs for life, to jobs for today – then we need to ensure we understand the consequences of that and how many other industries rely on this as a measure of security. Author Guy Standing calls the growing group of people without long-term employment commitments the 'precariat'; people living off precarious gig work with no long-term security, and as a result unable to lay down any deposits for the future.

To show how our risk evaluation system is geared around job security and career employment, consider the concept of applying for a mortgage. Unless you have significant reserves of capital, purchasing a house is dependent upon you being able to borrow large sums of money, which in turn is based upon your deemed ability to pay it back. The last financial crisis was born out of a relaxing of the risk assessment undertaken on mortgage applicants, causing the banking industry to become exposed to an unsustainable level of 'sub-prime' debt. As a result, banks and other lending associations are nervous about loaning significant sums of money to people with a tenuous income stream. The assessment of loan risk is also increasingly being passed over to machines, who use logical algorithms rather than human judgement to make their decision, sometimes with surprising results. In 2014, a *New York Times* story[374] highlighted how a man who had just changed his job applied to refinance his mortgage. Despite holding down a steady government job for eight years and a teaching post for twenty years before that, the system rejected his application. While his projected payments were within his previous income level, he had recently changed jobs and his new role was as a writer, a profession that the system classified as risky, given authors – especially first-time authors – generally have uncertain income streams, and he would be unlikely to cover the mortgage.[116] So far, so logical. Uncertainty in income means that the risk factor is high, so the computer said no. However, the applicant was Ben Bernanke, former Chairman of the US Federal Reserve, who had just signed a book contract for more than $1 million and who is paid $250,000 per speech. While this raises the question of whether we can truly pass over decisions to machines that lack context and judgement, it does raise the question, 'If Ben Bernanke can't get a loan, what hope does someone with multiple jobs, none of which have any permanency written into their contract, have?' The whole process of money-lending and credit is based around determining someone's ability to repay the loan. As employment becomes more temporary and short-term in nature, will we need to rethink how we determine risk, and will this affect the propensity of capital owners to lend that capital to private citizens?

---

[116] Hmm, maybe I should have thought about this before...

The Lull Before the Storm

For some organisations, hiring people to perform these types of gig-economy jobs is simply a 'transition point solution', a temporary step between now and automation. Amazon is currently a large employer, with a global work force three times larger than Microsoft's and eighteen times larger than Facebook's, but we already know that they plan to automate as much of their entire supply chain as possible. Uber is also using an army of freelance human workers to create its market, but again, in the long run these human drivers have no future with the company. Uber's end goal is to simply provide a platform between you and a world of driverless, autonomous cars ready to take you to where you want to go. As journalist Chris Middleton states, *Uber is an app, not an ad hoc employment agency.*[375]

The question going forward is: what happens when the future generations of robots arrive? We don't feel the impact yet because automation is not in full flow – we know autonomous vehicles, robots and drones are coming, but we don't see them yet. However, soon these technologies will start to become visible, and very soon after that, they'll appear everywhere. Then we will feel it. Everyone will. This creates a future where we see not only a drastic reduction in the number of long-term employment opportunities – career roles – but also a future of increasing automation that reduces the opportunity for people to make a living wage from basic skills such as driving, working in factories and warehouses, or delivering goods.

Not everyone agrees that this is an issue, and worryingly, some of these people are in positions of power. US Treasury Secretary, Steven Mnuchin, believes that because he can't see the threat, then it doesn't yet exist. In March 2017 he declared that he is not worried about artificial intelligence displacing US jobs for at least another fifty to one hundred years. *I think that is so far in the future – in terms of artificial intelligence taking over American jobs – I think we're, like, so far away from that that... it's not even on my radar screen.*[376] Given the evidence presented so far, this ostrich-like mindset is naive. Once AI and the other new technologies cross the chasm – which they will do soon – their adoption rates will explode as the innovative companies embrace them in order to gain a competitive advantage, and everyone else automates simply to keep up. Reacting at that point is too late. The mindset highlights a similar problem to the one afflicting business leaders constrained by the short-termism of quarterly returns: politicians are planning in four- to five-year cycles, because all that matters to them is re-election. It is therefore essential that the real forces in control – the deep state – *do* have their eyes focused on these new developments and can advise and warn the politicians of the dangers contained in the forthcoming wave. You may ignore it, stating it is not on your radar, but that doesn't mean it doesn't exist.

So how do you prepare your children to survive in this career-less future? A degree probably isn't going to help them. The next generation of US graduates will be leaving college with up to $100,000 in student loans and the dream of starting a career that might make $50,000 a year, only to see this career vanish in under a decade due to technological unemployment, leaving them with over half of the debt still to pay. If your degree is in a subject with a limited affiliation to any form of future employment, or with skills no one values enough to pay for, then you could end up with a lifetime of debt and a paper certificate that no employer values. A degree in law? Unless a relative owns the law firm, I wouldn't if I were you. Accountancy? Nope, the magic professions are done for. Healthcare? If it is in any diagnostic field, then probably not. Maybe if it is in an empathy-based care role such as nursing, or a creative one such as plastic surgery, for we are soon going to have an army of ageing people to look after, ones who might want their external representation to stay looking fresh, given their potential to extend their lifespan. I used to also believe that jobs that involve physical contact, such as massage therapists, would be safe from automation, until I found out that the US company Massage Robotics has invented a robotic massage therapy system, so that's another industry off the safe list.

The concern is the cultural lag and those caught up in it, people whose skills and experience are no longer relevant, replaced by machines and software, who are laden with debts and responsibilities and who perhaps lack the skill, education or sheer belief to participate in the new wave. Or those who joined the workforce at the crash of the fifth wave and have spent the last decade either unemployed or surviving by doing jobs that did little other than provide an income. Many of these people cannot afford to move out of their homes, and still live with their parents or in shared rentals, creating what has been dubbed the 'lost generation'. The problem is that while they have been unemployed a new generation has emerged, fresh-faced, eager to work and with more current and up-to-date skills. Business leaders, facing an onslaught of disruption caused by companies like Amazon, are only interested in either cutting costs or acquiring new skills that allow them to fight back. They are therefore not interested in people they would have to retrain, and instead compete to secure the talents of eager new graduates who can hit the ground running. This means that these 'lost generation' applicants end up trapped in their unfulfilling jobs, falling further behind as their skills become redundant.

I had exposure to this myself during my time at the pen factory and the unemployment centre. It took me two years and hundreds of handwritten applications before I managed to acquire a 'career' position, as employers focused on recruiting from the new graduate pool. I came to understand why. During my first day in my new role, my boss, the IT director, stated to me (remember, this is March 1993), 'You'll be happy to know we've installed Windows here.' I replied, 'Err, that's great. Natural daylight is always a bonus.' He laughed, slapped me on the back and declared that with humour like that we were going to get on great. I nervously laughed along with him but didn't really know why he was laughing. I wasn't joking. I had no clue what Windows was. I hadn't used a computer for two years, for neither the pen factory nor the job centre used them, at least not in the roles I was doing, and the only ones I had any experience with were green-screen mainframes. I was technologically outdated. Cue a lunchtime trip to the newsagents and a rapid read through a number of computer magazines. Luckily, I managed to survive this short but awkward period until I became fully conversant with files, folders, icons and the mouse thingy on the desk. However, times have changed; understanding how to use Windows OS in the early 1990s is not comparable to the challenge of becoming a data scientist, blockchain engineer or machine-learning specialist. You can become outdated in months, and blagging is not an option. Those unlucky enough to be caught in the transition period will really struggle to find new, well-paid roles in a world where employers are focused on acquiring new-wave skill sets or interns who can learn these skills on the cheap.

The fact that the Internet has democratised education may prove to be a saviour to this lost generation, but only if they have the right mindset. As the late Alvin Toffler allegedly declared, *the illiterate of the 21st century will not be those who cannot read and write, but those who cannot learn, unlearn, and relearn*. But regardless of mindset, those who already have jobs, debts and dependants will find their time incredibly limited, restricting their ability to take advantage of this new capability. They simply will not be able to decide to take a year out to reskill. This large group of existing workers – the transition workforce – are going to find the next decade very tough indeed.

20

A REVOLUTION FOR ME, BUT NOT FOR THEE

Labour, therefore, is the real measure of the exchangeable value of all commodities. The real price of every thing, what every thing really costs to the man who wants to acquire it, is the toil and trouble of acquiring it.

Adam Smith, *Inquiry into the Nature and Causes of the Wealth of Nations, 1776*

While the workers of the West grapple with the effects of the sixth wave, perhaps the biggest economic impact is going to be felt over in the emerging nations. They are currently going through various stages of industrialisation and have experienced the benefits that a more open society and market economy can bring. They want more, and the young are flooding into the cities to seek employment, willing to accept manual, repetitive and low-paid jobs in the hope that they are a stepping stone to a better life than their parents had. They want – no, they expect – their own industrial revolution. They may not get it. There has already been a partial reshoring of their expected jobs back to the West, but once this new wave of automation crosses the chasm, manufacturing will increasingly move back home, closer to the markets where the demand is. While people may still be cheaper in the East, robot prices are geographically neutral, eradicating the competitive cost advantage of off shoring. As a result, the numbers of manufacturing and service jobs in places like Bangladesh, Vietnam, Brazil and India will start to decline as automation increases.

An economy can grow very rapidly when it starts from a very low base per capita. However, as the population reaches a middle-class level it suddenly becomes a lot harder to maintain that pace. China's leaders know that human labour is not going to attract foreign investment, and it has already experienced a slowing down of its growth, caused by a continuous rise in wages and a stalling of its manufacturing engine. This will impact the other emerging nations as well, but much quicker. Once manufacturers realise that they can produce small quantities locally for less per unit than they can by ordering large volumes from suppliers in the emerging nations and shipping them halfway round the world and stored – then the demand for mass production in those countries will dry up. Manufacturing locally by machines not only saves on supply-chain costs, but also removes the other issues of counterfeiting, IP theft, quality control and cultural and language difficulties. It also removes the issue of global brands being exposed to any fallout from adverse working conditions being used in the production and supply of their goods. If a building collapses on a factory full of robots, there are unlikely to be protests outside any stores. But it's the long lead-times that will really kill off offshoring. What's the point of predictive, real-time analytics when it takes twenty-five days for goods to arrive from the other side of the world? You may have the tools to sense changes in demand, but your supply chain is too slow to react to it. The only answer is to build buffer stocks, which is the exact opposite of the flexible, responsive, low-inventory, 'batch size of one' direction companies want to move in. The personal, automated and local (PAL) supply-chain model, on the other hand, provides exactly this. Machines can now plan, produce, pick, pack, load, distribute, reorder and replenish, record and report 24/7 without breaks, complaints, or working condition concerns, and all for the cost of electricity. The days of making goods in bulk on the other side of the world are coming to an end – and so will all of the jobs that go with them.

While the West has been making the adjustment away from a manually labour-intensive manufacturing-based economy for decades, the emerging nations have not yet built the infrastructure and middle-class foundations needed to sustain an automated economy. Approximately 100 million people are employed in manufacturing in China, whereas in the US, the number is around 12 million, and manufacturing accounts for almost 36 per cent of China's gross domestic product. As Henry Nothhaft highlighted in *Great Again: Revitalizing America's Entrepreneurial Leadership*, when manufacturing moves, the supply chain, and worse, the ability to innovate, tends to follow. It impacted the West when manufacturing moved offshore, and it will impact the East when it moves back again. China is also going to experience a bigger impact from innovations such as autonomous vehicles. While the UK has 285,000 truck drivers and the US 3.5 million, China has an incredible 16 million drivers that are likely to be displaced. As we have seen, due to the triple whammy of sixth-wave automation, the need for these people's labour is not likely to exist. China's communist leaders need to figure out how they are going to achieve their goals of technological superiority without leaving behind millions of angry, unemployed and economically destitute workers who cannot provide for their families. They are in a race against time.

The transition from competitive advantage through human labour to robot labour may have a dramatic effect on Chinese society. Automation appears to offer China an enticing way to retain its price competitiveness as it currently lags far behind competitors in the ratio of robots to workers. South Korea, for instance, has 478 robots per 10,000 workers, Japan 315, Germany 292, and the United States 164. Currently, China only has 36. Hence Xi Jinping's Made in China 2025 initiative, and the goal of becoming the world leader in automation by the 2049 centenary of the Communist Party. While many displaced factory workers could find employment in the service sector, it is unlikely that 100 million manufacturing workers will find suitable replacement jobs – especially if taxi driving and other semi-skilled jobs are automated away. Robotic technology may be the way to ensure China's manufacturing industry, but what exactly happens to its enormous labour force? Likewise, developments such as artificial intelligence, an area China is pushing hard to dominate, will have a major impact on its financial sector, with predictions that 23 per cent of the total 9.93 million jobs in China's banking, insurance and securities sectors will also be lost by 2027.[377] In some ways, China needs automation in order to continue to grow, as its aging population means that the number of working-age people is shrinking by 3 million a year. In 1980, China's median age was just 21.9, but it is predicted to rise to forty-eight by 2050, leaving fewer workers to produce the wealth needed to care for the fast-growing population of elderly Chinese. Automation is not seen so much as a threat by the ruling party but as a necessity to maintain the level of productivity.

It is therefore likely that this sudden, government-incentivised transition towards robots and automation could cause economic hardship and social unrest. The Chinese government is going to struggle to ensure that all its citizens have a future in this new reality. China's debt bubble is growing significantly, surpassing 300 per cent of GDP in 2017 and causing concern that it may have its own 'Minsky moment'. It is facing a massive shortfall in its state-run pension scheme, due to a significant reduction in the working-age population and a rise in its elderly population, with many of China's provinces only having enough money to pay less than one year's worth of benefits. As China's debt continues to grow, it is at risk of being unable to provide a stable social safety net for its people. Currently, a third of China's total population is still impoverished, and the young continue to migrate to the cities in search of work, with estimates of up to 400 million poorly educated and often illiterate people migrating from rural areas to the cities in the last decade. It is also facing a societal nightmare of its own making. The one-child social engineering project implemented by Mao's successor, Deng Xiaoping, failed to consider the inherent cultural biases towards males. Couples aborted female foetuses, resulting in a skewed gender demographic that in certain provinces, such as Jiangxi, is as extreme as 138 men to each 100 women.[378] This has resulted in tens of millions of what are known as *guang gun-er* or 'bare branches'; men that will never bear fruit because they will never marry and have children and so cannot continue the family name.[379] Many of these men are very poor and will struggle to find a wife, as the women have their pick of men and are growing increasingly accustomed to wealth. The poorer the man, the less his chances of finding a partner, as Chinese women tend to 'marry up'. It has already resulted in swathes of 'bare-branch' men that see no future for themselves, resulting in them joining gangs and getting involved in criminal activities, a problem that is already causing issues across the country.[380] A nation where approximately 33 million men have no hope of marrying and are unlikely to get a job because of automation, is a very worrying situation. The words 'ticking' and 'time bomb' come to mind.

However, China is much better prepared for the next wave than the other emerging nations. At least they appear to have a plan and leaders who have their hands on the steering wheel. Countries like India, Brazil, Mexico, Vietnam and Bangladesh are still building their industrial foundations on their ability to recruit large numbers of compliant human hands for not very much money. They need the decades of manufacturing growth that China has benefited from, and if this progress is cut short then this is going to leave a very large population of uneducated, disillusioned, poor and angry people. In India, for example, the backbone of the country's economic growth has been the IT services and support industry, and millions are employed as document processors, call-centre workers and help-desk support; all types of repetitive, rules-based work primed for replacement by tools such as RPA and advanced chatbots with voice-recognition and speech-translation capabilities. There has already been a drastic reduction in hiring, with entry-level jobs being cut in half and 56,000 IT jobs being shed from just seven IT firms in 2017. Gartner analysts in India believe that up to 70 per cent of the jobs that are currently outsourced there will be automated away, replaced by AI solutions that provide immediate customer support. Oracle has announced massive investments on automating and AI-enabling their cloud software applications, as well as providing AI chatbot services, stating that they *want to provide autonomous capabilities to eliminate the human labour associated with provisioning, upgrades, backup, recovery, and troubleshooting.*[381] All activities that the Indian IT support and call centre outsourcing business is built around. The Indian call-centre and support business has also not been helped by the protectionist policies implanted under Trump's presidency which has resulted in a large number of outsourced and offshored jobs being reshored.[382] India also has a much larger percentage of young people, with half of its billion citizens under twenty-five years old, and a working-age population that is rising by approximately 12 million people a year. Mohandas Pai, the Chairman of Manipal Global Education Services in India, frames the forthcoming issue: *By 2025 there will be 200 million young people in the age group of 21–41 with no jobs or less jobs and nobody knows what to do with these people. Government policy does not know what to do as they don't have proper data... we are going to have a demographic nightmare.*[383]

The Bangladeshi, Vietnamese and Cambodian economies are also looking precarious, completely reliant on the manufacture of textiles and clothing, and exposed by the rise of reshoring and increasing capabilities of machines such as Lowry and Sewbo. The International Labour Organization (ILO) predicts that 86 per cent of Vietnamese and 88 per cent of Cambodian workers are at risk due to the automation of clothing and footwear manufacture, resulting in 36 million lost jobs in Vietnam alone. ILO also predicts that 73 per cent of Thai automotive workers are at risk.[384]

The lack of work for the millions of poorly educated, unskilled workers is going to present the governments of these emerging nations with perhaps the biggest challenge of the transition period. The fires of industry have warmed the aspirations of their population, and they were promised that by working hard they too could one day afford the outputs of their labour. They have not yet reached the stage whereby their domestic markets have developed to the extent needed to provide work for the labour force in waiting. Even if they did, who's to say that the owners of the factories won't use machines rather than people anyway? And if people are used, will they be exploited and effectively reduced to slave labour, simply to compete with machines that can perform these repetitive, high-volume tasks with constant precision, all day, every day for the cost of electricity.

A World Without Work?

Predictions of how many roles will be automated away vary. The often cited 2014 Oxford University study by Frey and Osbourne predicted that 47 per cent of US jobs will be automated by 2034, but there are multiple other studies that also predict more destruction than creation. In 2015, Andrew Haldane, the Bank of England's Chief Economist, estimated that 15 million British and 80 million US jobs could be lost to automation.[385] In 2017, a McKinsey report declared that 400–800 million jobs worldwide could be automated by 2030.[386] The World Economic Forum also estimates that 7.1 million jobs will be destroyed by 2020 while 2.1 million new jobs will be created, resulting in 5 million job losses in just three years.[387] What this shows is that although everyone agrees that technological unemployment is going to happen, no one seems to know exactly how big the impact will be, and how fast it will happen.

The biggest fear that drives the most pessimistic scenarios comes from attachment to the 'lump of labour' fallacy; that there is a fixed amount of work to be done and when machines do it there will be none left for humans. This has been proven to be false to date and I believe that it will continue to be false moving forwards. Technological improvements always create new products and services, shifting workers from older to newer activities, and creating new market opportunities. This time, however, we are facing pressures that haven't existed previously, or at least not in such volume and in such a short time frame. During the transition period those without the capability or opportunity to adapt to the new wave's reality will find life difficult, and employment opportunities scarce. It is these 'transition casualties' that concern me most, for their number is set to be large, and their anger and frustration immense.

So, what happens to society when you replace millions of workers with machines? To find out the answer, you only need to look at Detroit, the Motor City that was the industrial heart of the US during its boom years, but which fell into decline and finally bankruptcy in 2013. When the work dried up those with skills went away, and those that remained had to accept a life of low employment, low expectations and high crime. It became an area where people were dependent on welfare, not work, and as a result aspiration and ambition died and more nefarious activities took their place. Voltaire once declared that *work saves us from three evils; boredom, vice and need*. When looking at what has become of cities such as Detroit where work departed, it's hard to disagree. A life spent on welfare rather than work has not resulted in a positive outcome for the city's inhabitants. This will become a major global challenge as the machines take over, and governments worldwide will have to look at ways to provide for those the sixth wave leaves behind.

It's something that should be worrying political leaders around the world. In 2017, I was asked to speak to members of the UK's Department for International Development (DfID) about the forthcoming automation revolution, and they peppered me with questions about how best to advise the politicians and business leaders in the numerous countries they help. One of their statements really stood out: *What we find again and again is that regardless of where they are, what most people in these countries want is a good job.* It wasn't the first time I had heard this. In 2011, Jim Clifton, CEO and Chairman of Gallup, released his book *The Coming Jobs War* in which he makes the assertion that job creation and successful entrepreneurship are the world's most pressing issues right now. The book summarises his findings from the results of the annual World Poll, which has the noble aim of attempting to understand what the world is thinking. Started in 2005, Gallup collects insights from people from 160 different countries, covering

99 per cent of the world's population, a task they are committed to doing for the next hundred years.[388] The poll collects a huge amount of data, and the conclusions are complex. But there is one consistent finding, one primary issue that arose from every one of the 160 countries they analysed, and it wasn't crime, the environment, love, war, poverty or corruption. Their data concurred exactly with the DfID's statement that what people from around the world really want is 'a good job'. Clifton therefore proposes that the countries that will succeed in the future are those that manage to create good jobs. Lots of them. Jobs for humans. Says Clifton; *A global jobs war is coming, and there's no time to waste. Cities are crumbling for lack of good jobs. Nations are in revolt because their people can't get good jobs. The cities and countries that act first – that focus everything they have on creating good jobs – are the ones that will win... Leaders of countries and cities should focus on creating good jobs because as jobs go, so does the fate of nations. Jobs bring prosperity, peace, and human development – but long-term unemployment ruins lives, cities, and countries.* People without either purpose or prosperity are easily persuaded to join nefarious causes. A job is a much better solution to people's problems than money alone, because it provides stability, routine and purpose. We already know that many people struggle when they retire unless they can find a way to fill the job-shaped hole in their lives, whereas those who manage to create meaning can retain their intellect and sprightly approach to life. Defining a meaningful telos for humans in a world of machines may be the biggest social challenge the Western world has had to face since the Second World War.

The Winner Takes All

These concerns become amplified when you realise that while automation is wiping out whole industries, there are those that are winning bigly. The ever-increasing amount of bounty created by all of this new technology is being concentrated into fewer and fewer hands, while also decreasing the number of employees needed to generate it. A look at the companies that make up the top 10 by market value shows both the effects of creative destruction, and the increasing value of the winners. In 1917, U.S. Steel was the world's wealthiest company with an inflation-adjusted market value of $46.4 billion. The other top ten companies were in the steel, communications or petrochemical industry. Fifty years later and U.S. Steel was no longer in the top ten. Only American Telephone & Telegraph and Standard Oil were still there, but their value had increased tenfold. Fast-forward another fifty years and not one of the 1917 or 1967 top ten companies appear. Tech companies rule the roost, with Apple the highest value company at $898 billion, Google's Alphabet second, Microsoft third and Amazon and Facebook fourth and fifth. If this trend continues, then it is unlikely that any company on 2017's top ten will still be there come 2067. Which companies will occupy these spots and what their products will be is anyone's guess, but if I had to guess the industries, I would say that genetics, life extension, robotics, nanotech, artificial intelligence and the IoT will feature prominently. The company that becomes the winner in IoT and AI is going to be worth trillions. Amazon knows this, which is why it is working to install its narrow AI assistant Alexa not just on an Echo device, but also on your TV, in your car, on your phone – basically wherever you are. Becoming the first mover is everything, for the company that owns the primary customer interface controls the market. People don't want two smart machines in their house, or two smartphones, or two different platforms for the same thing. Simplicity and convenience are key.

The explosion in company wealth should not be surprising, given that the consumer base has grown organically through population growth, and geographically through globalisation. The amount of physical resources – including people – needed to produce items – especially digital items – has also reduced due to automation. However, there is a concern that as companies have become wealthier, and the number of employees they recruit reduced, they are able to use this wealth to leverage significant power both economically and politically. Their vast wealth has enabled them to attract the brightest and best talents in the new, essential fields, reinforcing their dominance by acquiring all the key resources at a time when they are scarce. The attraction of seven figure salaries and generous perks is seeing professors and graduates in AI-related skills pouring out of academia into industry, leaving even the very best establishments such as Cambridge University stating that they are unable to retain their AI talent.[389]

These large organisations also have the funds to invest in research – something that smaller companies struggle with. It doesn't stop them trying, and each new wave sees a whole host of new start-ups attempting to attract the venture capital needed to take advantage of the new innovations. Many will fail, lacking the deep pockets of the others or the discipline to turn ideas into marketable outputs. This benefits the larger, cash-rich companies, for they can then swoop in and buy up any new companies (and their talent) that look like they have developed something interesting or are likely to be a future competitive threat. One of the best examples of this was Facebook's acquisition of Oculus Rift in 2014, a company that had made its name through a 2012 Kickstarter campaign that secured almost $2.5 million (£1.8 million) in public funding to develop its VR headset. Facebook paid $2 billion in cash and shares for the company, which was three years away from having a retail-ready product. Boom – instant innovation.

Finally, in most places in the world money unfortunately buys political influence, allowing for companies to manipulate laws and legislation to their benefit. And the technocrats of the sixth wave have the added benefit not only of excessive amounts of money, but also the foresight as to what is being developed behind closed doors long before the politicians do. A seemingly harmless piece of legislation that gets quickly signed off now might turn out to have incredibly important ramifications moving forwards; e.g. net neutrality. Large companies generally like legislation as they are the only ones with the scope to manage it.

The digital age is therefore very much a 'winner takes all' enterprise. Winners to date have made billions, which is why there is a constant torrent of people flowing towards Silicon Valley prepared to work for virtually nothing for start-ups that look like they may be onto something big. The risks may be high, but if you have shares in a company whose fledgling product catches the eyes of the tech giants, then there's a chance you'll be rich beyond your wildest dreams. For example, Jan Koum had a 45 per cent stake in the five-year-old messaging company WhatsApp, and he suddenly became very rich indeed when Facebook acquired the company for $19 billion (his share was then worth $6.8 billion). Even the early employees who had a 1 per cent share all apparently made $160 million each. Not bad for five years' work.

Loading the Dice

To attract the sixth wave winners, large tax breaks are offered to companies such as Apple and Amazon to incentivise them to locate their headquarters in a particular city, state or even country. This has created a world of two rules; one for the multinationals, and one for everyone else. The new tech giants also stand accused of not being good corporate citizens. When a small cleaning company pays more tax in percentage terms than the multi-billion-dollar organisation whose floors they are waxing, then something is not right. We now have global industry but local tax rules, and this has allowed the multinational corporations to reduce their costs by diverting their revenue to certain countries specifically to pay the minimum amount of tax possible. Some would say that this is the global free market in operation, supporting Milton Friedman's striving to offer value purely for the shareholder. The companies all declare that they've done nothing wrong, that they are simply being tax-efficient and throw their hands up in mock shock and indignation when called out. Use of these tax havens by 367 Fortune 500 companies are causing the US government to miss out on $100 billion a year in federal taxes, according to a report by the advocacy group US PIRG.[390] Apple was handed a bill for $14.5 billion by the EU after they ruled that a sweetheart tax deal between Apple and the Irish tax authorities that allowed Apple to just pay 1 per cent tax amounted to illegal state aid. Amazon has also been accused of a £1.5 billion tax fraud. In the UK, Uber has been forced to declare its taxi drivers as normal workers with normal rights such as time off, rather than as self-employed contractors. This ruling has significant implications for the more than 100,000 independent contractors that currently work in Britain's gig economy – and the companies that use them.

In the past, as a company grew it employed more people, created more opportunities, and paid more tax – meaning that everyone benefits. Right now, this is not happening – the companies that are making hay do not need the same swathes of labour to make things and are not contributing to society in the same way. The possible exception is Amazon, because its core business is in physical things – moving stuff to consumers. As of 2017, Amazon employed 341,400 full- and part-time workers worldwide, and vowed to employ another 100,000 full-time workers, with competitive wages and benefits, by the end of 2018. This is significantly more than the pure tech companies such as Facebook, which employs just over 17,000 people, or Microsoft which employs 61,000. Amazon is the biggest corporate employer in Seattle, employing 40,000 of its 380,000 total workers, and occupying 19 per cent of the prime office space in the city, more than any other employer in a big American city. In September 2017

Amazon also declared that it would open a second headquarters in North America, creating up to 50,000 new jobs. But Amazon is an outlier in a trend towards generating greater wealth with an ever-decreasing number of employees. It's also not guaranteed to continue to be a net contributor of jobs, for while it may be creating new ones, its destructive impact on other companies cannot be ignored. Creators create, but they also destroy. It's part of the natural evolutionary process. We shouldn't mourn the loss of companies like Blockbuster, because I certainly don't mourn having to travel to their store to rent a film and then constantly panic about late fees if we don't return it on time. Now I select movies from the comfort of my armchair and watch them immediately. The new way is a better way; a more customer-centric way. That is the benefit of creative destruction: a business was destroyed by a better one. However – and it's a big however – as we've seen, Amazon disrupts every market it enters, causing competitors to either drastically cut employee numbers or close their doors entirely.

And here's the rub – currently Amazon, Apple, Google and all the other tech giants, as well as traditional companies, are leveraging their power to exploit tax loopholes, divert profits, or just seek preferential rates from countries or states. Amazon, for example, has received generous public subsidies as part of its warehouse expansion, totalling at least $613 million for forty of the seventy-seven warehouses it built from 2005 to 2014, plus additional subsidies for Amazon data centres of about $147 million. Attracting subsidies and tax incentives is not new to Amazon; it has been a part of Bezos' game plan from the start. Back in 1995, he famously decided to base Amazon's HQ in Seattle rather than the Bay Area. His reasoning was that Amazon could then avoid collecting sales tax in the more populous California, exploiting a sales-tax loophole that predated the rise of online shopping. This strategy fits firmly into Amazon's strategy of finding ways to keep prices competitive for customers, but it's not the first business to seek government incentives, nor will it be the last. The high-street killer of the previous wave, Wal-Mart, has collected more than $1.2 billion in tax abatements, credits, exemptions, infrastructure assistance and financing deals in the last forty years.[391] Amazon is on course to exceed that, and the tax incentives they will receive as a welcoming present from whatever US state wins the Amazon HQ2 lottery will see them exceed Wal-Mart's total.

While many will state that this is just part and parcel of business, and it's a win-win for the city, state or country that manages to attract the business, when you step back and look at the larger picture it's not so black and white. The foundation of a healthy market is one where competition rules – but that competition needs to be fair. How can an independent UK retailer, who pays 20 per cent corporation tax, complete with Amazon, who paid close to zero UK corporation tax for decades? They will ultimately be forced to either drop their prices drastically, find some other way to differentiate, automate their operations, or be wiped out. So, the net result is that while Amazon creates jobs in the short term, its ability to operate at a lower cost will enable it to eliminate its taxpaying competition and their taxpaying employees; employees who spend their salaries on taxable goods and services. Plus, if the country incentivised Amazon to operate in this area through subsidies and rebates, then the taxpayers in the displaced company have effectively had the pleasure of contributing towards their own replacement.

Governments need to ensure that corporations like Amazon do not simply wipe out all the competition, becoming in effect not just a retailer but the primary marketplace, the supply chain orchestrator and the main manufacturer of goods. This is their plan, after all. Behind every Amazon Echo sits a manufacturer, a distributor, a cloud and web services company, a tech developer, and both an e-commerce *and* a physical retailer. They are innovators and experts in the hard practices of physical supply; the innovative practices of AI, robotics and data analysis; the soft practices of customer service; and the incredibly difficult skill of combining all three. But there is a dark side to all of this, and the potential is there for Amazon to completely own the customer interface, creating a virtual monopoly by capturing demand before anyone else can get a look-in. Slowly they are changing customers' behaviour so that the moment they want something, they go onto Amazon to get it. Bezos is the ultimate version of what Schumpeter called a 'new man' – it's always day one in his mind, and rather than affecting a single industry Amazon is attacking nearly all of them, including the B2B world. Once Amazon spreads this offering to the rest of their targeted territories across Europe and the Anglosphere, their dominance will increase. And here lies the danger. Amazon is one of the major job creators while also being perhaps the biggest job destroyer. And soon, it will start to destroy its own jobs as they replace the vanquished company's human supply chain with an almost completely automated version; one that may provide the customer with what they want, but which doesn't create jobs nor contribute taxes, generating no value for individuals or society. When Amazon negotiated its agreements with several US states to postpone the collection of sales taxes in exchange for locating their warehouses and creating jobs, it probably seemed like a great idea. However, it is unlikely that the state officials considered the fact that Amazon's grand plan is total warehouse automation. As companies start to fail and jobs are lost, how long will governments sit quietly by as Amazon acquires a monopolistic position, wiping out taxpaying companies and their taxpaying employees, while it declares little taxable profit, choosing instead to reinvest in increasing levels of automation that feed its virtuous cycle of creative destruction?

So will Amazon become a new East India Company, ruling the waves of the business ocean through force and manipulation? Not necessarily. Firstly, they will be matched in size by the Asian giants, especially Alibaba, which is just as innovative and may beat Amazon to the title of the first trillion-dollar company. The sheer population of China and India alone guarantees them a larger customer base. Also, while Amazon may disrupt industries, it has also reduced prices, increased convenience and removed barriers to entry for sellers and content creators such as authors. It may have disrupted traditional publishing houses and be hated by the bricks-and-mortar retail stores, but it has revitalised the book industry, creating opportunity and access for more people to publish their thoughts and ideas. Amazon is also, like Netflix, making high-quality films and television programmes, increasing the choice available and making them accessible to people from their sofas. This has created a golden age of TV, not destroyed it. As long as Amazon continues to put the customer first, then the effect should be positive, not negative – at least to their customers. Their competitors may say otherwise.

This doesn't help alleviate the worries many have about what happens when Amazon obtains a monopoly on the market, transforming from a retailer to the owner of the entire online marketplace. It already captures 50 per cent of all online retail sales in the US, so it's not an unrealistic fear. Will they then tighten the screws and raise prices, exploiting their mountain of data? Probably not the former, but definitely the latter. This is where governments need to step in to protect the commons. And the 21st-century commons contain more than just physical assets — it also involves digital ones. Amazon – and all the other FAANG companies – need to be kept in check to ensure that they protect the data they have access to, and that they do not exploit their position and power. For free-market capitalism in the US has morphed into a less equitable and undesirable economic model – corporatism. The political system is geared more around financing from big business than it is focused on the day-to-day needs of its citizens. In the 2014 US election cycle, business interests spent an eye-watering $1.1 billion on state candidates and committees.[392] This is a calculated investment for companies, the outcome of which is expected to be policies that create a more favourable and profitable business environment that more than compensates for the cost of lobbying.

These are not new issues and are in fact part of the cyclical nature of these capitalist waves. The difference now is that the goods are digital, the market global, and the players richer and more influential than some countries. As a result, they have been able to create platforms that are effectively monopolistic. The platform has become the market, for it controls the interface with the customers. The platform owners are able to use this interface to obtain deep insights into the behaviours of their customers, and the ability to influence them at a psychological level – something that wasn't an issue in previous waves. It is also giving them enormous power and influence. In the counties where it operates, Amazon is fast becoming the primary retail interface, providing them with unparalleled amounts of leverage over suppliers. If Amazon blocks you from selling on their platform, they can effectively kill your business. Google effectively owns the platform for video content sharing via YouTube, forming part of a digital commons that also contains other platforms such as Facebook and Twitter. If they demonetise your videos, stop them trending or blacklist them because they do not like their content, or worse, they don't like you, then they are effectively removing your ability to earn an income from that profession – which is exactly what is happening. The so-called 'great demonetisation scandal' on YouTube in 2017 saw most conservative and classical liberal commentators' ad revenue dry up almost overnight as Google changed the algorithm and marked them as 'not ad-friendly'. Annoying when you are doing it for fun; devastating when it's your primary income stream. These sixth-wave mega-corporations have become the exclusive arbiters of which voices get heard, empowering them with the ability to not only control the public discourse, but also decide who can make a living from their monopolistic platforms and who cannot.

When Inequality Becomes Inequity

The belief that the game is rigged recontributes to the tensions that Kondratiev warned of during the upswing, but the real danger this time is that the contract between capital and labour becomes broken. The question then arises as to how capitalism works in a world where machines do the work and capital is controlled by algorithms and not by altruistic humans? The unbalanced nature of the playing field, the over-aggressive use of patent legislation, the hiding away of trillions in tax havens and the use of avoidance tactics like inversion specifically to avoid paying taxes that everyone else has to pay, have once again resulted in extreme wealth inequality. The money doesn't disappear, nobody burned it; it just gets concentrated into the hands of the winners – those who already own significant capital. Although economists like Kuznets postulate that this is a natural part of the wave cycle, and that increases in the Gini coefficient that measures this inequality will ultimately be automatically redressed by the market, people facing hardships want action now. It is hard to sell a message that *everything will be fine, we are all in this together* to workers in the private sector who are facing redundancies and stagnant pay, and public-sector front-line services who are being asked to 'take one for the team' and accept a freeze on their wages and pensions. Especially when they see hedge-fund owners making billions, and the bankers who caused the need for this austerity getting record bonuses. Even though these bonuses may contribute greatly to the tax receipts of the nation, there simply isn't a PR company in the world that can make this situation sound fair and inclusive to people struggling to stay afloat.

Inequality is not a major problem if *all* social classes are rising; if the tide does indeed lift all ships. What is a problem is a lack of equality of opportunity, unfair practices and unequal playing fields, a world where the golden opportunities exist only for those with excessive amounts of capital or the right connections. When you hear about trillions being hidden away offshore while local schools and hospitals have to close due to lack of funding, and public servants having to accept multi-year pay-freezes to cover for the economic collapse caused by speculative gambling by the banks, then resentment rises, and you see protests like the Occupy movement. The stagnation of earned income undermines every aspect of our economy: consumption, credit, taxation and, perhaps most importantly, the unspoken social contract that states that the bounty from technological advancement and increased productivity will be shared fairly and equally rather than exclusively scooped by an already-wealthy minority. When billionaires forgo any interest in national status and hold multiple passports simply to move their vast wealth around the safest and most tax-efficient locations, they are not showing a huge degree of care and responsibility to their homeland or wider society. *The middle class? So sad to see it go, but at least my portfolio is doing great.*

The economist Thomas Piketty's book, *Capital in the 21st Century*, highlighted how those with excess capital win even when growth is low, due to their ability to invest when everyone else is exiting, buying prime shares at rock-bottom prices. Piketty's argument, supported by reams of data and statistics, is that over time the rate of return on capital has exceeded the rate of growth of the economy, enriching the super-managers and bankers, while the rest of society, those with just their labour to sell, languishes. His primary finding is that inequality increases when $R > G$; when the return on owned capital is greater than the rate of economic growth – especially when the value of that growth is not passed down throughout society but concentrated in the hands of the few. The implications of the $R > G$ equation are that while wages stagnate, those with capital are making hay, growing both the wealth gap and resentment. As Robert Kiyosaki points out, *The poor and the middle-class work for money. The rich have money work for them*. The gap can only widen because the system is gamed that way. Examples of this gaming include how the very rich can use their increasing wealth to influence tax policies in their favour and ensure a lax regulation of their management, providing even more benefits. The rich are also able to afford wealth advisors, who can set up favourable tax-management schemes and off-shore bolt-holes for the majority of their wealth. When the wage-earning middle class effectively ends up handing over half their income in tax and NI contributions, while the capital wealthy keep their percentage contributions in single digits, while it may be legal, most right-minded people would agree that it isn't fair or ethical.

The primary point is that those who control the capital benefit much more than those who don't, leading to capitalism ultimately evolving into a corporatist oligarchy. The definition of an entrepreneur is a risk-taker, but what risks do those who come to the table already rich actually take? Do they risk not being able to put food on the table or pay the mortgage? Not really. They risk losing some of their vast store of capital; capital which in many cases came their way by good fortune rather than fortitude. More than a third of the 1,645 billionaires listed by *Forbes* inherited some or all of their riches, and their primary concern is protecting that wealth, not passing it down through society via either consumption or investing in businesses that employ people. If you took £1 billion and gave it to a billionaire, how much of it would find its way back into circulation rather than being squirrelled away in an offshore account? Money trickles up, through consumption of goods and services, not down. It is really hard to define how hedge-fund managers, especially those directly or indirectly involved in the management of funds offshore, visibly contribute to the well-being of society (other than as consumers), and much easier – especially after the recent financial crisis – to show how they haven't. But even their contribution as consumers is limited, as a rich person's marginal propensity to consume is far less than those of the middle and working classes. After all, how many Bugatti's does one person need?

The Undesirables

The sixth wave therefore presents a global challenge: how will those who only have their labour to sell – people without spare capital and who don't own the machines primed to replace them – provide for themselves and their families? One of the completely – often deliberately – ignored issues is that currently in the West this group of workers is mostly made of white men. When the automation of the entire end-to-end supply chain moves into second gear, it is this group that is going to find itself without employment and looking for new places to earn a living. The reason why this is an issue is that there is currently an unofficial but obvious moratorium on employing this demographic by companies under pressure to prove their diversity credentials. In the STEM[117] fields, for example, where the future jobs are likely to concentrate, there is constant pressure to increase the diversity of the workforce, which by default means reducing the percentage of white men. As a result, no one is going to be enthusiastically trying to help these displaced workers. White men with industrial skills will be at the bottom of

---

[117] Science, Technology, Engineering and Maths

their recruitment list, expected to just suck it up while the recruitment and training of 'worthier' groups will be actively supported and incentivised.

The James Damore 'Google Manifesto' affair, and Apple's firing of Denise Young Smith showed just how intolerant Silicon Valley is to anyone who even *questions* the diversity mantra. Like Bruno and Galileo, Damore was found guilty of being a heretic for daring to question the logic behind the dogma, and for his sins he was publicly shamed and cast out. Damore's subsequent lawsuit against Google exposed exactly how deep this ideological rabbit hole went, and it didn't make for good reading. Managers kept blacklists of employees who might hold the wrong views, people were paid bonuses if they could name and shame a co-worker who had conservative viewpoints, threats against wrong-thinkers were openly shared on message boards with senior management's approval, and were often written by the senior managers themselves.[393] Reading Damore's case against Google reminded me of the final 'McCarthyist' scene in the original *Invasion of the Body Snatchers* movie. Like all heretics, anyone caught going against the official doctrine must publicly repent or be removed. In Denise Young Smith's case, repenting wasn't enough, and she was removed anyway.[118]

Why is this important? Because continuing to ostracise and deliberately exclude a large slice of the current US workforce, people who have worked hard, paid their taxes and played by what they thought were the rules, is not going to end well. Demonise a massive group of people, prevent them from seeking the skills and experience to provide a future for themselves and their families, and mock their forthcoming plight all you want; just don't be surprised when you end up with a president you don't like. Many of these people are patriotic believers in the American dream and are likely to owe

---

[118] Denise Young Smith was Apple's Vice President of Diversity and Inclusion, a post she had achieved six months earlier after working at Apple for twenty years. At a 2017 diversity event in Bogotá, Colombia, she declared that she 'focuses on everyone' and believes that diversity is an individual thing that goes beyond race, gender and sexual orientation. She stated that *there can be twelve white, blue-eyed, blond men in a room and they're going to be diverse too because they're going to bring a different life experience and life perspective to the conversation.* For stating this obvious fact, she was forced to make a grovelling apology, only to be fired anyway. She was the most powerful black woman in Silicon Valley, and was replaced by Christie Smith, a white, blonde-haired executive who knows more about what 'real' diversity is and can stick to the script. Apple may now have one less minority voice in their top team, but at least they now have someone who reinforces the message that diversity is about having more minority voices in the top team. Just as long as they those minority voices don't have diverse opinions.

significant debts such as mortgages, car loans and university or school fees. They are also likely to be gun owners. That is not a good combination; that is a tinderbox waiting to ignite. A couple of hundred people in this situation are not going to be noticed. Tens of millions of truckers and factory workers all replaced within five years due to autonomous vehicles and robotics is something else entirely. This worries me, for as Kondratiev highlighted, the upswing is the time of revolutions and conflicts. If there are more winners than losers, then everything usually turns out OK. This time I am not necessarily sure that will be the case. The casualties of the transition could outnumber the victors, and as we will discuss, the ramifications of this could be very serious indeed. It's one of the reasons why progressive voices in the US are always so keen to repeal the Second Amendment, because they want to ensure that the people who are disrupted do not have the tools to become disruptive themselves. Transition points may be turbulent times, but history has shown that the upswing can be downright dangerous.

Transition Point or Tipping Point?

Capitalism was born out of a rise in social and economic inclusivity, and it works well when it includes and inspires the population. When it starts to socially and economically exclude them, it will be protested, and reform will be demanded. If you see no future, then your mind goes to dark places where you assume the game is rigged and all the winners are crooks who deserve some form of retribution. And if you think it's rough now, you haven't seen anything yet. Three and a half million US truck drivers all losing their jobs in a similar time frame, only for most of them to be told that they are the wrong race and gender for progressive society to care about their situation, won't go down well. And those in power and in Silicon Valley know this.

To be fair, some of the uber-rich have heard the warning bells. America's second richest citizen, the investor and business magnate Warren Buffet, highlighted during an interview with CNBC in early 2018 how much the personal wealth of the members of the *Forbes* 400, which lists the richest Americans, has increased over the years. *Between the first computation in 1982 and today, the wealth of the 400 increased 29-fold – from $93 billion to $2.7 trillion – while many millions of hardworking citizens remained stuck* *on an economic treadmill. During this period, the tsunami of wealth didn't trickle down. It surged upward.* He has a history of commenting on the growing disparity between the rich and poor. Back in 2011, in a piece for the *New York Times* called *Stop Coddling the Super-Rich,* he wrote, *While the poor and middle-class fight for us in Afghanistan, and while most Americans struggle to make ends meet, we mega-rich continue to get our extraordinary tax breaks. Some of us are investment managers who earn billions from our daily labors but are allowed to classify our income as "carried interest," thereby getting a bargain 15 percent tax rate. Others own stock index futures for 10 minutes and have 60 percent of their gain taxed at 15 percent, as if they'd been long-term investors. These and other blessings are showered upon us by legislators in Washington who feel compelled to protect us, much as if we were spotted owls or some other endangered species. It's nice to have friends in high places.* He concludes the article with a call to action; *My friends and I have been coddled long enough by a billionaire-friendly Congress. It's time for our government to get serious about shared sacrifice.*[394] Buffett is not a lone voice; other members of the 1 per cent spell out the danger even clearer. Nick Hanauer has been a compelling and leading voice on the issue of inequality, delivering a couple of TED talks[119] and an article for *Politico* in which he writes, *I have a message for my fellow filthy rich, for all of us who live in our gated bubble worlds: Wake up, people. It won't last. If we don't do something to fix the glaring inequities in this economy, the pitchforks are going to come for us. No society can sustain this kind of rising inequality. In fact, there is no example in human history where wealth accumulated like this and the pitchforks didn't eventually come out. You show me a highly unequal society, and I will show you a police state. Or an uprising. There are no counterexamples. None. It's not if, it's when.*[395]

Some are already taking precautions; Antonio García Martínez, a former Facebook product manager, purchased five wooded acres on an island in the Pacific Northwest where he has installed generators, solar panels, guns and thousands of rounds of ammo, enabling him to ride out any potential social revolution. Other Silicon Valley billionaires, such as Peter Thiel, are buying their way to countries such as New Zealand, and membership of survival-prepper groups by hedge-fund managers and technocrats is

---

[119] One of which was famously banned, which simply amplified his message as people clamoured to hear what was so controversial. (Answer – nothing. I personally have no idea why it was banned.)

exploding, with the rich setting up plans for the worst and learning how to defend themselves and their families in the event that society collapses.[396] And unsurprisingly, these concerns about an anti-capitalist uprising has led to some prime capitalist opportunities, with a number of companies grabbing the opportunity to provide long-term security for these concerned uber-wealthy citizens. In 2016, a company called Vivos purchased 575 underground military munitions bunkers, made of hardened steel and concrete and designed to store explosives, and have redeveloped them into the 'ultimate shelter community' called Vivos xPoint.[397] Located out in the Black Hills of South Dakota, this eighteen square mile development represents the largest private doomsday community on Earth. The community is designed to house up to 5,000 people who have the money to rent the bunkers (there's a 99-year lease) and outfit them with electricity, air filtration, air conditioning and plumbing. They are even offering spaces in shared, fully outfitted bunkers, perfect for the young tech millionaire with no dependants. Vivos are also building all of the facilities to turn this area from a series of bunkers into a private, underground community, including a general store, restaurants, bars, spa, gym, medical clinics, hydroponic gardens for fresh fruit and vegetables, chapel, stables, shooting ranges, equipment and construction supply depot, maintenance, woodworking and a metal fabrication shop. They have already had plenty of takers willing to lay down the $25,000 to secure a bunker.

Herein lies the biggest paradox of our cyclical, innovation-fuelled, progress. Society cannot reap the rewards of creative destruction without first accepting that some individuals might be worse off, and not just in the short term. There will be no 'return to normal' so recalibration is essential to ensure that disruption doesn't transition into disorder. Perhaps the social cohesion needed to build a truly inclusive economy is impossible to build in the absence of these dire transition periods, for they force the changes needed to create solid foundations on which to build the next wave of progress. Right now, trust is in crisis around the world, and there is a lack of belief that the system works for the majority. Action is therefore required to regain that trust.

21

LEVELLING THE FIELD

Automation provides us with wondrous increases of production and information, but does it tell us what to do with the men the machines displace? Modern industry gives us the capacity for unparalleled wealth – but where is our capacity to make that wealth meaningful to the poor of every nation?

Robert Kennedy

While this sounds all doom and gloom, most people forget that we have been here before. Many times. From agricultural workers and weavers displaced by the rise of factories and dark, satanic mills, to the automotive industry laying waste to the buggy and whip industries, those who insist that that current disruption is unique have no knowledge of history. While the symptoms might differ, the cause is the same: the need to react to the forces of a new wave by making adjustments that minimise the transition pains so that the majority, not just a privileged few, can benefit. Those who declare the system to be broken fall into the trap of forgetting – or not even realising – that change in an industrialised market economy is cyclical, not linear. Tales of a jobless future always tend to be overstated, because people can clearly see the destruction of the existing old-wave jobs, but not the creation of new, as yet unknown ones. The widely cited Oxford Martin School study that highlighted that 47 per cent of current jobs are at risk of being automated away by 2034 didn't say that 47 per cent of the population will be without jobs – but that is how many people seem to be reading it. The paper itself stated that people would have to adapt to the changes by acquiring new skills, rather than what people perceived it to say, which is that they would have to be resigned to never having a job again.

I'm not suggesting for one moment that everything will be fine for everyone. It won't. Equally, I'm not proposing that we should take the wheels off the innovation bus and ban the use of autonomous vehicles and robotics to save the jobs of truck drivers, production workers and other impacted industries. 'Luddite' is an insult, not an aspiration, and as we saw with the Ottoman Empire and Chinese Dynasties, suppression of technological progress only brings benefits in the immediate term, and in the long term all who impose blocks on innovation fail. The idea of going back in time to ban the automobile to save the jobs of buggy- and whip-makers and blacksmiths sounds ridiculous, and so should the idea of banning autonomous vehicles. The long-term benefits – reduction in accidents and fatalities, lower costs and greater efficiencies – will outweigh the short-term pains. But this is little comfort to those who are caught in the crossfire. Being told, 'It's better for the shareholders and society if we automate your job' doesn't help put food on the table or pay the mortgage. It also does little to create a future for those who feel that they have been left behind and now have nothing to lose. The forces of creative destruction always have casualties, and focus should be on trying to minimise the collateral damage, for as discussed, there is likely to be more in this wave than ever before.

Evolution Not Revolution

Capitalism's greatest strength is its adaptability; its ability to rise, fall and rise again. Its cyclical nature creates transitional periods where inequalities naturally appear – from technological unemployment and differences between those with labour and those with capital – which can cause tensions. These inequalities represent an inbuilt feedback mechanism that indicate that changes are needed. That's what evolutionary systems do; they adapt to changes in their external environment in order to prevent their demise. Economic evolution prevents social revolution. The challenge at this phase of every wave, regardless of whether you even know there is a wave and that these waves have phases, is to ensure that the benefits of the creation outstrip the negatives of the destruction, so the majority make it through this period and into the golden age of a Kondratiev spring and summer. As professor Carlota Perez, who analyses techno-economic trends and wave cycles, states, *bubble prosperities polarise incomes; whereas Golden Ages tend to reverse the process*. We probably won't get there unscathed, but we can at least ensure we get there with our economy and society still in one piece.

Capitalisms' evolutionary nature allows people to adapt to change, to understand, shape and accept it, while other, better-sounding socio-economic programmes require forceful control of the market and the population.[120] It is also important to understand that not all inequality is an issue, and evidence of a social ill. If the winners won through fair means and in ways that did not disadvantage others, then why should someone be concerned about what someone else earns? There's always been inequality of outcome, that is after all the natural order of things. Some people are cleverer, more ambitious, more dedicated, and more talented than others. The 'lump of equality' argument, which assumes that if someone is doing well it must be at the expense of someone else, is both false and has been used to previously justify some pretty dystopian actions. We've seen multiple variations of ideology-based 'equality' solutions implemented in the real world; none of which turned out well for those they purported to help. Large-scale social re-engineering projects based around the most altruistic of aims has led to countless deaths, mass removal of rights and many unexpected and unwanted outcomes. What has become clear is that attempts to redirect a society's progress through revolutionary rather than evolutionary means ends badly every time, for it requires coercion and force. Politics at the point of a gun. Collectivist approaches that quash individual choice, competition and aspiration eventually result in long-term economic, political and social failure that ranges from stagnation to starvation, as the Venezuelans are currently finding out.

It is through levelling playing fields, removing barriers and stimulating

---

[120] I know this will dismay those hoping I am suggesting a revolutionary 'resource economy'-style solution to our current ills; that we should tear up the current system and build something new, but evolution is the answer, not revolution. Not yet, anyway.

aspiration that progress has advanced so much in the last 250 years. Think again about the world described by Seebohm Rowntree, when 30 per cent of the population had zero disposable income. What about fifty years ago? Are we better or worse off now than in the 1970s? Do we have more or less poverty? More access to information and education or less? More disposable income or less? More entertainment choices or less? More ability to travel or less? More opportunity and equality or less? Exactly. Creating a free society that encourages and enables the realisation of individual choice and aspiration has produced a technological bounty that has improved life for everyone. Conversely, stifling these freedoms simply to enforce an ideology is ultimately self-defeating, for not only does it stifle creativity, it becomes completely inflexible. It becomes about power not progress, and control not creation. Previous attempts to avoid the effects of creative destruction by artificially preserving jobs or protecting unprofitable or redundant industries have ultimately led to stagnation and decline, short-circuiting the march of progress. Britain temporarily got caught up in this death spiral in the 1970s, the fifth wave's upswing, and quickly became known as the sick man of Europe. High inflation led to a government held to ransom by constant union action and strikes, especially by coal workers, resulting in a three-day working week to conserve electricity in 1973–74. This continued to the point that by 1976, Britain was in such dire straits that it had to ask the IMF for a £2.3 billion loan to combat rampant inflation. In 1979, mass industrial action created the 'Winter of Discontent', which saw refuse go uncollected, the dead unburied, hospitals closed to new patients, TV channels not broadcasting, and the movement of goods and oil suspended. The quality of many British products dropped so much during this decade that they were only surpassed in their awfulness by those coming out of Soviet Russia.

History also provides ample evidence that when profit is removed as the primary agenda, a mindset develops where people forget the link between business performance and employment, delighting customers becomes an afterthought, and product quality drops dramatically. In situations where the customer has a choice, business can dry up rapidly. In situations where they don't have a choice, such as in monopolistic situations, expect poor service and little innovation. Consider the service provided by the DMV in the US, or the fact that when British Telecom was a nationalised company, you had to wait six months simply to have a phone installed in your house. This is not a social comment on the pros and cons of privatisation, nor declaring that the capitalist system is perfect. Far from it. If it was, it wouldn't keep collapsing and need recalibrating. I am also not stating that private companies are perfect – I hope that point has been made abundantly clear already. The problem with all businesses is people, because people – especially those in power – can be greedy, self-serving, fearful and risk-averse, sometimes all at the same time. The collapse of the private construction company Carillion in early 2018, highlights that although private companies may have better efficiency rates than the public sector, they can still fall into complacency, especially when they feel that large government contracts are theirs and that competition doesn't exist. And the news that Carillion sacrificed payments to its pension fund while still paying out shareholder dividends and executive bonuses shows how little morality exists in many businesses. And here lies the problem. The moment that leaders of organisations start to prioritise their needs above those of their customers, employees and other stakeholders, then the end is nigh. It's always day one, as Jeff Bezos constantly reminds his team, and the moment you take your customers or employees for granted, you've forgotten that essential truth. While unregulated capitalism has negative effects due to the desire by some to use the corporation to serve their personal needs and agendas, so unregulated socialism in industry has adverse effects for precisely the same reason. Neither are perfect because they are run by people, who are not perfect. The difference is that one system enables the expression of some very powerful human values – choice and aspiration – while the other supresses it, and that makes a huge difference in their outcomes.

The waves represent a continual process of destruction and rebirth, but one which has to date always brought progress. Life is always getting better – but it often requires a long-term view to see it. This year might be harder than the last, and that hurts, but the next decade will be better than the current one, and this century better than the previous. The problem has never been with automation, for as we have seen throughout this book, the development and adaptation of technology has advanced our civilisation exponentially over the last 250 years. Automation is good for productivity, and its continued ability to enable us to make more with less is good for the planet. However, actions do need to be taken to help those that are displaced, address any negative environmental effects and ensure that the benefits are not concentrated into the hands of too few people who contribute too little. Our immediate goal should be to work with the system, not against it; to alter its evolution, not demand a revolution. Recalibration is not a bad thing to have to do, for every system that operates without some sort of feedback mechanism eventually fails. It's the reason why capitalism is still around despite periods of income inequality, while more supposedly equal, collectivist systems had to be held together through force, only to eventually fall. Western societies have proven adept at this recalibration process because the underlying societal model considers the rights of individual members of society and not just their existence as part of a group, so we are sensitive to when they are unfairly treated, no matter what position they hold in society. Once inequalities are highlighted and enough pressure placed, adaptations are made and things progress. Regardless of whether the driver is competitive pressure, government legislation or just moral and social responsibility, we have proven time and again that we are able to adapt our behaviours and develop new technological solutions to respond to the negative scenarios once their cause and impact are understood. The Overton Window of acceptable political policies shifts based on the societal pressure placed upon it, and this pressure builds when people struggle to see how losers can become winners. While we have a long history of self-correction when tensions arise, we unfortunately keep forgetting this and react as if it's a new phenomenon every time – mostly because for the people experiencing it, it is. The key is not to panic and over-regulate or interfere with individual freedoms. Radical proposals in a time of radical disruption are usually dangerous because they react to outliers rather than understand causes, and as a result people judge society against a utopian ideal, rather than against history or any other current real-world comparisons. Against utopia, of course it is found wanting, but utopia doesn't exist. Plus, what's utopia for one group might not be utopia for another, which usually means that for one group to get what it wants, the other needs to be either silenced, made to comply by force, or disappeared.[121]

---

[121] A point whose importance will become evident later.

Recalibration Time Again

There will be significant amounts of wealth generated in the new wave as the new technologies make their way across the chasm and into the mainstream. Accenture believes that embracing AI will enable the average S&P 500 company to create an additional $7.5 billion in revenue over the next four years.[398] The challenge is ensuring that this bounty flows across the economy and into all areas of society and is not just concentrated into a large pool at the top. Any adjustments need to be appropriate in both scope and speed, taking place relatively quickly before oligarchs and global corporations can use their wealth to control both the playing field and the referees. Our leaders in finance, business and politics must ensure that they provide for the success of future generations, and not just to profit and stay in power. As Thomas Piketty declared; *Capitalism and market forces are very powerful in producing wealth and innovation. But we need to ensure that these forces act in the common interest.*

Proactive recalibration is therefore required to ensure the sixth wave successfully enters the golden age of a Kondratiev summer period. It is imperative that we allow people to feel hopeful about the future; to believe that through aspiration, endeavour, education and determination they can better their lives. To ensure co-operation, focus should be on levelling the playing field so all who want to play, can play, and to the same set of rules. Capital is where the power lies, but not many people have excess capital. Most have excess debt – negative capital – and only their labour to sell, and they are seeing their jobs being automated away and the rewards of this automation flowing to those with capital. This situation needs to be addressed. Any talk of forced redistribution of wealth should be avoided, as the recalibrations should enhance opportunities and provide freedoms, not suppress them. Stifling the creative abilities of the population through social or economic engineering is a bad move, whereas freeing them has been, and will continue to be, transformative. Ensuring a focus on invention, innovation and industry is critical, as this will lift many more ships than when the focus is on capital and finance, when only the luxury yachts are lifted.

So, what recalibrations are required to adapt to the sixth wave? I believe there are four major forms of economic recalibration needed. Firstly, recalibration of the nature of the corporation; secondly, global transparency and a level playing field; thirdly, a safety net for those displaced by automation; and finally, a change to our measures of success.

#1: The Nature of the Corporation

Firstly, we need to embrace those who practice paternal, market capitalism, and shun those who favour exploitive corporatism, for corporatism is at the root of the next two issues. For most of the industrial age, an increase in sales resulted in an increase in employment, and local companies employed local people. The trickle-down economics mantra — the belief that more wealth at the top of society benefits everyone else — was viable because people could see it in action. When Henry Ford opened a production plant, that plant provided jobs and income for thousands. He then increased their pay so that producers of cars could also become consumers of cars, and everyone benefited. Now that's not the case. Companies increasingly make products that require little labour to produce, and just a small number of specialised people to design. As the sixth wave picks up pace and the rate of automation accelerates, that trend will continue. The tiny minority that holds shares in these companies will become extremely wealthy, and the majority with only their labour to sell will increasing struggle. Corporate interests now drive political agendas and affect legislation designed to benefit certain businesses. This has nothing to do with the version of capitalism Adam Smith imagined when he wrote *The Wealth of Nations*; this is corporatism, and politics — especially in the US — has embraced this for it funnels money to those in power. It is an affront to the concept of capitalism and its laissez-faire ideals. Government should exist to ensure that the game is fair, rules are followed, and players are treated equally, and not receive back-handers to load the dice in favour of the richer players.

The power of creative destruction will take care of many of the consumer exploitations, for the Amazons of the world will remove those companies that lose sight of their purpose and the customer. If your corporate value proposition is so weak that an offer of free shipping can wash it away, then perhaps you need to try harder. However, there does need to be intervention to reattach the market to the real economy, and a reconnection between profit and purpose. The market shouldn't be a casino: owning shares in a company should be an investment in its long-term success, held by those that believe in its purpose, values and ethos, and not just to make a quick buck. In the age where artificial intelligence and share-trading algorithms flip shares in milliseconds, or worse, spoof trade them to manipulate the value of a corporation, millions can be made without any real risk to the share-flippers.

It would be nice to see a return to the paternal, Quaker-style values in business; integrity, care for the community, a purpose bigger than just profit. It would be even better if the market was designed to reward these behaviours. As discussed in Part One, this was once an integral part of the business mindset, and it needs to be rediscovered. The paternalistic industrialists of the past such as Boulton, the Lever brothers and Cadburys are excellent examples of how to balance the line between profit and purpose. This does not need to be a conflict of interest, and 'caring capitalism' does not need to be an oxymoron. The challenge is to adopt business principles that are focused on long-term growth, whilst also showing an acute awareness and consideration of your corporate and social responsibilities. While altruism was never declared to be the purpose of capitalism, a differentiation between those companies that strive to add value versus those that strive to extract it would be welcome.

One quick-win could be to create a limit on how quickly shares can be bought and sold, especially as we move ever deeper into the murky world of AI-driven hedge funds. If pay-offs were less immediate, then decisions about what shares to own and sell would be more considered, with more concern given to the ethical nature of the company and its long-term vision. A Tobin-style financial transaction tax like the one proposed by the EU could also ensure that wider society benefits from this new world of AI-controlled high-frequency financial trading. Not only will this curb the worst excesses of casino-like behaviours, but it should also help motivate business leaders to focus more on sustainability. If shareholders know that their wealth is invested in corporate shares which could be adversely impacted by any bad press around poor working conditions, unethical behaviours, tax manipulations, etc., then this drives closer scrutiny around share ownership, which also drives a culture of increased responsibility. If the CEO can't profit from shares until several years have passed – let's say five, for example – then this has the double benefit of making CEOs ensure that they focus attention on the long-term success of the organisation, and also a drive to receive a bigger percentage of their remuneration package in the form of salary, not just shares. Salary which will be visible and taxed at normal rates.

#2: Global Responsibility, Financial Transparency and a Level Field

The need to support the foundations upon which capitalism is built and its consumers reside was understood right from the start. In the 1776 words of the first great economist, Adam Smith, *The expense of government to the individuals of a great nation is like the expense of management to the joint tenants of a great estate, who are all obliged to contribute in proportion to their respective interests in the estate.* His second maxim clarified that position, *The tax which each individual is bound to pay ought to be certain, and not arbitrary.* Smith realised that markets only worked if they operated within a moral context that benefited the majority, and when capitalism morphs into corporatism and only the shareholders are deemed important, then the connection between morality and the market is lost. While entrepreneurism enables the provision of goods and services, it does not by itself provide for essential state-level expenditure.

Smith's comments on taxes highlighted both the need for every individual to contribute to the well-being of the nation, and also that this contributes to the benefits you receive from that nation. It is an essential part of the responsibility of each citizen and corporation to contribute, if they are able, to the welfare of the nation, rather than just being concerned about what they can get out of it. While the working and middle classes are more concerned with the honest delivery of government-sponsored facilities such as education, healthcare, infrastructure, policing and other public services, the rich also benefit through the creation of a healthy, happy and safe society, enabling them to enjoy their wealth without fear of violent revolution. As the US Supreme Court Justice Oliver Wendell Holmes Jnr. wrote, *I like to pay taxes. With them I buy civilization.*

The issue and level of taxation contributions is always a divisive subject, soliciting a range of different opinions dependent on your political views and whether you are a net recipient or a net contributor. Opinions vary from calling for a highly progressive taxation rate in order to 'squeeze the rich', through to a perspective that taxation is theft and it should be minimised as much as possible. While it is not the purpose of this book to provide a diatribe on which taxation perspective is best (for that is a tome in itself), most political discussions talk about 'fairness'. However, this is both a qualitative and subjective measure – who decides what is considered 'fair'? Some people would deem a redistribution of 90 per cent of the wealth of the richest people in society fair, a world where those who have excess capital – or can make it – are forced to redistribute it to support those who do not or cannot. Others would deem that highly unfair, and instead state that these people, the risk-takers, innovators and job creators, earned this wealth from doing what others could not or would not do. Overly aggressive tax rates can reduce aspiration and have been shown, as in France, to cause capital and human flight, resulting in an exodus of money, talent and tax contributions. The best – and easiest – approach is to establish what's not fair and remove instances of that happening, rather than trying to impose a form of socio-economic engineering based around a utopian vision of fairness.

The current taxation system in the UK, like those of many other Western countries, sits in the middle of a Marxist 'squeeze the rich' and an objectivist 'taxation is theft' perspective, with aspects of both present. It is progressive, with a tax-free element at the bottom incentivising work, and a higher tax rate the more you earn, increasing contribution. However, it is complicated to administer and police, is often exploited, and as a result doesn't fully achieve the aims of either group. The major result of this is that it is the employed middle class that is continually squeezed. This is because the unemployed obviously do not pay tax, (other than sales taxes on procured items), the working class pay little tax and the rich have enough money to use loopholes, networks of offshore trusts, holding companies and generally clever systems to pay the minimum amount of tax they can legally get away with. Those who rely on their labour for income cannot hide it, and it is taxed at source, whereas those whose income comes from capital assets such as shares, dividends and property can use loopholes to avoid the bulk of taxation. For example, an employee in the UK on a salary of between £45,001–£150,000 pays 40 per cent income tax directly out of their wages,[122] plus a National Insurance contribution of 12 per cent. [123] Conversely, a number of millionaire personalities were caught using off-shore schemes to bring their tax contribution down to around 1 per cent.[399] In 2012, the Tax Justice Network identified that the global super-rich elite had conservatively at least $21 trillion of unreported private financial wealth hidden in secret tax havens at the end of 2010, while Reuters

---

[122] 2017–2018 UK tax rate: https://www.gov.uk/income-tax-rates
[123] http://www.hmrc.gov.uk/ni/intro/basics.htm#4

declared the number to be as high as $32 trillion,[400] which at the time was equivalent to the combined size of the US and Japanese economies.[401] A 2017 Bloomberg report identified that over 10 per cent of global GDP is hidden away, untaxed, in offshore havens, with 15 per cent of Europe's GDP hiding there, and as much as 60 per cent of the GDP generated by the Gulf nations and some Latin American countries. These arrangements and their exploitation in the digital age have become big news, and leaks such as the Panama Papers and the Paradise Papers brought tax avoidance schemes to public attention and raised the question of legality and morals.

To address the imbalance between those with labour and those with capital, economists like Thomas Piketty have called for a progressive taxation not on income, but on capital. Piketty's logic is that the uber-wealthy do not have traditional, taxable jobs, for their wealth comes not from daily toil but the owning, buying and selling of capital assets. What is necessary is greater transparency, and which I hope technology like the blockchain will help provide. The worker on the payroll cannot hide their earnings and, as a result, meets their responsibilities by contributing to the system at the required rate. Why, then, should the uber-rich be able to use their wealth to prevent having to do this? These questions are being posed not just to individuals, but also organisations.

Inversion or Innovation

Before globalisation, the company, its customers and its employees were primarily (not exclusively) in the same geographic location, meaning that the transactions and the taxes were all captured by the same government. The tax system was both difficult to avoid and you were socially frowned upon if caught (not to mention jailed), as your taxes paid for the roads, schools and hospitals both your customers and your employees relied on. The fifth wave changed that. While globalisation has indeed lowered trade regulations and tariffs between nations, it has also provided multi-national corporations with opportunities to create massive increases in profits without the need for inspiration, innovation or even massive investment. Because they operate across multiple national boundaries, they have been able to manipulate their operating structure in order to exploit differences in national taxation rates. This practice, called 'tax inversion' has created several tension points over the last few years, where the interest of the corporation and the interest of the local government clash. It creates unequal playing fields and allows big corporations to become bigger by playing to a different set of rules and paying significantly less tax than their smaller, national-based competitors. The digital nature of products also causes significant complications in tax management, because their point of manufacture is more difficult to determine. A 2016 report, *Tax Challenges in the Digital Economy*, from the policy department of the European Parliament, highlights the issue: *Digital goods are highly mobile or intangible, physical presence of a company in the market country is often not needed... New digital business models (subscription, access or advertisement models) and new technologies such as robotics or 3D printing are not confined by national boundaries and can easily escape their tax liabilities by channelling their royalty payments towards a tax haven.*

The tax arrangements of Apple, Amazon and Google have been cast into the spotlight, mostly due to the fact that they don't seem to pay much. In 2016 Amazon paid just €16.5 million in tax on European revenues of €21.6 billion paid through Luxembourg, the low tax- location of choice for many global corporations. Amazon UK Services – the company's warehouse and logistics operation that employs almost two thirds of its 24,000 UK staff – managed to somehow decrease its already-paltry UK corporation tax bill from £15.8 million to £7.4 million between 2016 and 2017, and then it dropped it to just £1.7m in 2017 while its UK turnover rose to £1.98 billion and its profits to £80m. Go figure. That's a tax rate of just over two per cent on profits – a tenth of the UK's 21 per cent corporation tax rate. This raises questions as to how the world's largest online company, owned by the world's richest man, can continue to contribute such a pitiful amount to the maintenance of the societies that buy wares from them. In October 2017, the EU acted against Amazon, fining them €250 million after claiming that Luxembourg gave Amazon illegal tax benefits, allowing them to pay only a quarter of what local companies have to pay in tax. For example, every sale made at UK companies such as John Lewis and its food retailer arm Waitrose – both online and off – is registered in Britain, where they pay tax at the corporate rate, resulting in millions of tax contributions to service the retail needs of UK consumer that Amazon do not pay. Margaret Hodge, Chair of the UK Public Accounts Committee, highlighted and slammed the unfairness of this situation: *If you are an Amazon user you get endless emails saying Amazon.co.uk. You then order your goods and you get them delivered by the Royal Mail in parcels stamped with the Queen's head, and they then pretend it's nothing to do with business in the UK. They are damaging British jobs. If you are a small bookshop in the high street you can never compete with their prices, because you pay taxes. Even for John Lewis their future is also threatened because they pay their taxes.* Any new business starting up must pay VAT on their earnings and corporation tax on all their profits, plus if they have a physical location they pay business rates and rent – so the obvious question is why the multinationals should be allowed to disguise their profit and choose to declare it in locations that benefit them but not the customers who buy their products?

To be fair to Amazon, it had paid more tax than Apple, but that's not saying much when the EU claimed that in 2014 Apple paid a tax rate of 0.005 per cent[402] (yes, you read that right) on its global profits; or to put it another way, a tax contribution of $50 per $1 million on non-US sales. The EU has taken action against Apple, fining it $14.6 billion for its tax arrangements with Ireland, saying that they constitute illegal state aid to Apple, something banned under EU member rules. Both Ireland and Apple are currently contesting the fine. It's not like they can't pay: Apple's Q2 2017 report highlighted that it had $252.3 billion sitting in the bank – more than the combined GDP of Jamaica and Finland.[403] It's not just that the money isn't trickling down – it's not flowing anywhere; to the shareholders or to the wider stakeholders in society. Even if Apple just paid out a dividend on their shares some of it would flow into pension and share-saving schemes, but currently it's just sitting there. These corporations are acquiring so much money that they now have the power to influence the decision-making and legislation of entire countries, as Apple did with Ireland in the location of its European headquarters.

To simply be competitive, other companies are drawn into either radical cost-cutting or using the same loopholes simply to stay in the game, resulting in a cycle of ever-decreasing tax funds from industry. If Amazon automates away a large percentage of their labour force, they save on the wages of the employees while also dramatically increasing productivity. Add into this their declaration of making little profit, plus their reallocation of what profits they do make to low-tax locations, and they create a completely different set of business rules. Their competitors – which is increasingly becoming everyone as Amazon encroaches on more and more industries

– are pressured to follow suit just to remain competitive. Even Unilever, despite all its positive moves from a long-term sustainability perspective, has found it very difficult to extract itself from this zero-sum competition.[404]

Unsurprisingly, a new, highly efficient global haven industry has arisen, driven by many of the world's largest financial institutions, accounting and law firms. Global consultancies like PricewaterhouseCoopers (PwC) have been accused of the mass promotion of this corporate tax avoidance, while of course making millions from helping with the execution of this advice. *We believe that PricewaterhouseCoopers's activities represent nothing short of the promotion of tax avoidance on an industrial scale*, declared Margaret Hodge.[405] Hodge stated that the Public Accounts Committee had found that PwC had written more than five hundred letters to the tax authorities in Luxembourg, on behalf of more than three hundred international clients who were wishing to move their profits to that location to pay a tiny fraction of the tax that they would have to pay in their home country.[124] This creates a cycle of ever-decreasing tax revenues from business, leaving governments trying to fill this gap through other means; the likely source of which usually ends up being the employed middle classes.

It's creating a virtuous cycle for the wealthy, and a vicious circle for the rest. The rich invest in corporations that avoid paying local tax in order to increase their profits and share price, making them more money. This money is then located offshore with the rest of their capital, avoiding the same scrutiny and taxation as even the most basic employee's income. Yet these same individuals and corporations who avoid contributing to the system also benefit from it by receiving elaborate government subsidies for their businesses, which would have been spent on public services – creating a triple whammy blow to the government and normal taxpayer.

---

[124] At a 2010 Gartner Supply Chain Executive conference in London, I attended a PwC presentation called *Putting Value at the Heart of the Operating Model*. I naively assumed this meant customer value. It didn't. The whole session was dedicated to how companies could, with PwC's help, move business transactions to a low-tax country, even though the physical transactions remained in the UK. I challenged this in the Q&A, asking how this benefited the customers they were supposed to be serving, and the presenter declared that there would always be a 'dynamic tension' between the two needs. Perhaps I'll try that line with the Inland Revenue when my tax bill is due: *Unfortunately, there was a 'dynamic tension' between your needs and my wife's need for a holiday. As my primary shareholder, her needs have been deemed more important than yours. I'm sure you understand.*

Putting the Ethics back into Economics

The impact of these actions is not considered by corporate leaders because they do not carry the cost of resolving them and are insulated from the consequences. They are not concerned with the impact of their activities on the commons, because they do not carry of the cost of repairing them, nor with technological unemployment because they do not have to provide for the unemployed. These things are covered by government spending, which is paid for via taxation, which they avoid paying. It is therefore important to ensure that when we talk of equality, we consider the equality of responsibility as well as of opportunity. The hypocrisy of companies that openly grandstand their commitment to social-justice causes, while lacking any kind of moral equivalency regarding paying taxes, something that would have a much bigger impact on the well-being of society, is breathtaking. Despite claims that avoiding taxation makes 'good business sense' (something that sets my teeth on edge every time I hear it), long-term, it really isn't. Good business comes from a stable and successful society that believes that all parties are playing to the same set of rules and that the game isn't rigged against them. Using your wealth and power to avoid paying a percentage of tax at least equal to those further down the pay scale may be legal, it may even be innovative; but it is hardly inclusive. The end result is an unequal, exclusive and uncompetitive society that puts the personal gain of the few over the needs of the many. It is exclusive as not everyone can do this, and if they did then the whole system would collapse. Which is something to bear in mind for when this wave of automation hits and starts wiping out jobs, the demand for government assistance will increase while the number of people paying tax contributions will decrease.

In a world dominated by platforms, it is crucial that fair-play rules and competitive practices exist for both buyers and sellers. The platform owners' power comes from the fact that they increasingly own the customer interface and can leverage this to push the supplier to the fringes, weakening their influence. Monopoly legislation needs to adapt to the new reality where ownership of an all-pervasive platform can create market dominance, regardless of whether or not the customer is charged for access to that platform. This fine line is being seen in the self-publishing industry right now as Amazon's Kindle Unlimited service is capturing demand for e-books by providing access to them via subscription, but as a result greatly reducing the remuneration flowing to the authors. In its pursuit of market dominance, everyone but the customer and Amazon loses. Not something customers care about until they themselves become the seller, or wind up working for one.

Most existing legislation was designed for the industrial age, not the digital. The 1890 Sherman Antitrust Act, a *comprehensive charter of economic liberty aimed at preserving free and unfettered competition as the rule of trade*, was designed to prevent monopolies from existing that could unfairly raise prices on consumers and prevent the forces of creative destruction from eradicating bad businesses that lose their customer-centricity. From the Federal Commission's own website: *the antitrust laws have had the same basic objective: to protect the process of competition for the benefit of consumers, making sure there are strong incentives for businesses to operate efficiently, keep prices down, and keep quality up.* However, the digital behemoths – Google, Facebook, Twitter, Amazon, WhatsApp, Instagram – all offer their platforms for free. So, they can hardly be accused of price-fixing. Amazon specifically has been able to circumnavigate the antitrust legislation because instead of using its monopolistic online position to push prices up, it is using its customer-centric model to push them down. In the end regulators will have to intervene, but instead of protecting consumers, action may be perceived as punishing success. Rather than concerns of a monopoly, Amazon's potential antitrust exposure is the lesser-known monopsony argument, where market power is defined by multiple suppliers having to deal with a single dominant buyer who can exploit their position.[125]

If corporations and wealth-management schemes are going global, then the taxation rules and regulations also need to be global in nature. The current tax rules were developed for the industrial age, where the company and its customers were in the same locality. Now, in the globalised, digital age, the customer could be anywhere. Our tax rules therefore need to apply

---

[125] 2015 saw one of the more blatant examples of monopsony, when the UK grocery retailer Tesco was caught generating what it called 'commercial income'. This was nothing more than an extortion racket whereby they first insisted that suppliers pay them for the right to stay on the approved supplier list, and second deliberately delayed supplier payments to maximise their cash flow and also weaken the suppliers' financial position, forcing them to 'bend the knee' to the all-powerful retailer. Tesco's buyers were also incentivised to maximise this 'commercial income', encouraging this 'bash the supplier' behaviour.

where the value is received, not where the company is based, in order to address the issue of tax avoidance by large multinationals. The introduction of a diverted profits tax based around the idea that the volume of sales in a country should determine the tax paid in that country would address the current presumption that it is perfectly reasonable for companies to exploit different tax rates applicable across countries to minimise their global tax bill. The government is also aware that it needs to take steps to encourage new entrepreneurs, and so the new tax rules have been established in such a way as to exclude small and medium-sized companies who are the real employment generators. This could have a significant impact as the nature of businesses becomes more global and digital, such as with Google, Facebook and WhatsApp, but it is necessary to ensure a level playing field between the small business making and selling physical products and the global technocrat selling digital products via their digital platform. This requires multinational, cross-border efforts to ensure that money is traced and tracked, and to discourage smaller nations from making money by offering boltholes.

To be fair, it does seem that the global community is finally waking up to the issue and working together to close the loopholes. For example, in 2013 the UK government produced a 'No Safe Havens' offshore tax-evasion strategy, and on 21st September 2014, the G20 countries agreed to start automatically exchanging tax information in an effort to erode global tax evasion. The communique from the G20 meeting in Cairns, Australia stated, *We support further coordination and collaboration by our tax authorities on their compliance activities on entities and individuals involved in cross-border tax arrangements*. This is where new technologies such as the blockchain could potentially help to provide transparency in global financial and product movements in real time. Given that blockchain technology is designed to be both unalterable and auditable, the money can be traced and tracked, providing tax authorities with an accurate idea of transactional activity, and corporations and individuals' wealth and how it is spent. The digital age could well be also known as the age of transparency.

The low-tax havens that currently profit greatly from operating as giant safety deposit boxes for the uber-wealthy will naturally resist any actions to redress the balance, as without size, natural resources or industry, this is one of their primary sources of wealth. They have therefore been pushing back against attempts to prevent tax diversion, viewing the short-term gain of some immediate additional tax revenue as small change compared to the long-term implications of being unable to attract these global businesses to their shores. The Irish government is currently in battle with the EU over their attempts to fine Apple. At least thirty-five companies, among them Anheuser-Busch InBev, BP and BASF, have been told to pay back taxes of about €700 million to Belgium because of their participation in an illegal tax scheme. In the Netherlands, Starbucks owes up to €30 million to the Dutch authorities, and over in Luxembourg, Fiat Chrysler has been ordered to pay back a similar amount. Luxembourg is also protesting the EU's attempt to force Amazon to pay them $295 million in back taxes.[406] When a government resists attempts to receive millions in tax repayments, something's up.

Therefore, there needs to be incentives for these locations as well as intimidation; carrots as well as sticks, for these small-population countries will not have the volume of transactions needed to replace the loss of a large conglomerate leaving their shores. But maybe they just need to try harder – to focus on ways they can offer value other than as a hiding place for the billions of profit and cash that the uber-rich companies and individuals are accruing. Some eggs will always have to be broken in order to make an omelette that feeds everyone. The tax havens will have to become victims of the sixth wave's creative destruction impact, and as a result will have to work harder to attract businesses and investment in order to survive. It's certainly possible; Iceland was effectively bankrupt and three of its banks defaulted and went under. Now, the country is booming again, and debt and deficit are under control, witnessing what some have declared as an economic miracle.

Recalibration, not Redistribution

Redistribution is a word that many use to describe the actions they deem necessary, but I would advise against this, because redistribution indicates the taking of wealth by force from one group to give it to another. 'Squeeze the rich until they squeak' statements sound great as demagogue-style soundbites, but as economists like Thomas Sowell (and real-world experience, such as in the UK in the 1970s) have shown, overly progressive taxation simply results in financial and human capital flight out of the country, causing a reduction in net tax receipts and a brain drain of talent.

Likewise, as we've seen with recent tax changes in the US, reductions in tax legislation to an equitable level lowers the incentive to undertake tax manipulations such as inversion, and creates an increase, not a decrease, in tax receipts. 'Contribution' is the right word to use. While many would deem this mere semantics, it's a crucial difference. People generally want to contribute to things that build a healthy, aspirational society and are happy when the rules are fair, beneficial to all parties, and apply to all participants. It's about removing inequalities of opportunity and providing incentives to invest and contribute, rather than trying to enforce equality of outcome. That option only works through the state removing the element of choice; something that works against human nature and which never ends well. The societies that have historically achieved the greatest degree of income equality have also been the ones responsible for the most brutality and lowest level of personal freedoms.

There is also plenty of evidence that once the government starts taking the lion's share of people's pay packets, a sense of injustice naturally arises and they start looking for ways to alleviate the tax burden. Likewise, when the government demands significantly more corporation tax than can be paid elsewhere in the world, CEOs and CFOs who are beholden to shareholders will naturally look to utilise these alternative tax locations. An inclusive and innovative society needs to have a simple, logical system of raising taxes that both stimulates a culture of innovation and entrepreneurism and provides for all members of society. The US economy currently owes $20 trillion. It can't afford for corporations to be avoiding tax. In this world of stagnating salaries and mass unemployment of middle-class income positions by automation, it will lead to be a gaping black hole in revenues and a mass increase in the number of people wanting support, which is unsustainable long term. Robots may make and deliver goods better than humans, but they do not pay tax nor consume goods in the way humans do. Simply printing money is not the answer (for evidence, see Zimbabwe).

There is no need to watch this money flow out of the country. When tax rules are not punitive, companies are de-incentivised from wasting millions on lawyers and accountants trying to establish complex tax arrangements, and instead just pay their taxes. The key therefore lies in the law of diminishing returns. Too much tax, and you kill the golden goose, resulting in capital and human flight. Too little, and you can't cover the bases of society, and excessive inequality occurs. *Fair and equal* should be the mantra.

The decision by President Trump's administration to lower the corporate US tax rate from 35 to 21 per cent (and an even lower amount of 15.5 per cent for repatriated cash) was an example of how, when the right balance is made, corporations can play ball. The decision by Apple to repatriate $200 billion to the US once they felt that the tax rate was 'fair' created a win-win for the government, for the population and for the corporation and its shareholders. In fact, the Macquarie Research Group estimates that the reduced corporation tax rate, plus the even lower repatriation rate, will result in US companies repatriating $860 billion back to the US in 2018,[407] creating a potential tax windfall of around $133 billion. Apple also declared a massive ramp up of US spending over the next five years, estimating that it will contribute $350 billion to the US economy and create 20,000 new jobs. While many screamed that Trump's actions were just 'tax cuts for the rich', Apple's reaction to them proved the value of being rational. A $38 billion contribution is $38 billion more than the US received when its tax rate was 35 per cent and this money was sunning itself offshore.[408] This has to be a one-off though, or else it fails the 'fair and equal' test: 15 per cent is less than the 21 that those who followed the rules now pay. The reduction to 21 per cent has brought the US in line with most of Europe, and the effect has been immediate, with numerous documented examples of US companies immediately paying out bonuses to their staff and increasing their wages, helping to break some of the wage stagnation.[409] This has a real, positive effect on society: the money they saved starts flowing directly to people they employ, citizens who pay taxes and who have a high propensity to consume. Something both Keynes and Hayek would approve of.

Designing Legislation for the Global, Digital Age

While not an economist, nor a politician, I would like to propose ways we could update the taxation principles to adapt to the new reality of a digitised, automated and globalised world. It is imperative that we create an economic foundation based on the principles of equality of opportunity and of responsibility. One that rewards entrepreneurship, but also sustainability, corporate social responsibility and human labour. We need to transform the concept of a triple bottom line, where the corporation doesn't just operate for profit but also considers the impact of their activities on their people and the planet, from being a 'nice-to-have' theory into a globally agreed principle of 21st-century business. This should not be in the form of punitive taxes, but rather progressive incentives. Below is a summary of potential actions:

1. Increase global financial transparency. Blockchain has the potentially to enormously help this process by tracking and tracing all movements of both money and product. While we are at least five years out before we will see the large-scale adoption of blockchain technologies, planning should start now.

2. Eliminate tax-avoidance schemes. There should be no tax rate of 0.5 per cent and no offshore tax payments. Some of the estimated $32 trillion that is currently sitting in offshore tax havens is going to be needed to support a society that transitions from mass employment to one of unemployment. Again, the blockchain could help with the identification of financial movements and the reduction in money laundering.

3. Incentivise work. As machines become used as a labour force of the future, it is imperative that income tax is used to incentivise humans to work because they get to keep the lion's share of their rewards. Income-based remuneration schemes rather than share-based ones should be the norm for captains of industry, with a moratorium on selling shares for a number of years to ensure that they build companies to last beyond their tenure.

4. Incentivise entrepreneurship. The future is likely to involve a few major corporations (the platform owners), and many, many micro-entrepreneurial ventures that utilise that platform or marketplace in order to trade their services or wares. Create an environment where those people can successfully build companies and compete against the larger global corporations through competitive corporation tax rates for small businesses.

5. Tax capital dividends as well as income. Understand how to fairly and efficiently tax income made from capital assets such as property, investment schemes, shares and other financial vehicles, in the same way we are able to tax income raised from labour. This may involve a form of financial transaction tax.

6. Tax corporation profits where they were generated, not where the company decides to declare them. When labour is reduced, consumption becomes the citizen's primary source of leverage. We therefore need to

ensure consumer activity creates income for the country and eliminate the diversion of profits to countries where the transactions only took place in the CFO's imagination. Currently goods are taxed via VAT (sales tax), but this passes the taxation onto the consumer, not the company.

7. Encourage the repatriation of cash from havens to domestic shores through the provision of one-time offers, with stipulations that funds must flow back into the wider economy rather than be primarily used to buy back shares and increase corporate ownership. Encourage the spending of money on the redevelopment of deprived areas to create innovation hubs, the setting up of education centres, the funding of social programmes, etc. You can't force a company to be altruistic like the Quakers of old, but you can make it worth their while.

8. Create incentives for companies to employ humans. Products that are digital, or physical products manufactured and shipped via machines, create limited social capital. Taxation should reflect this. Not creating jobs? Then you contribute in other ways. Options such as progressive corporation tax rates based on the profit generated per employee should help prevent an automation arms race driven solely by the desire to cut costs, allowing for more considered decisions that focus on innovation rather than mere human replacement, providing people with more time to adapt.

Adjustments such as these should help to provide fair and equitable global taxation rules, especially when supported by technology such as the blockchain. This should provide visibility of financial movements regardless of whether they are based on labour or capital, enabling governments to subsidise the basic consumption activities of the population, and help build the foundations for a new golden age, rather than provide firewood for a revolution.

#3: Strong Foundations and Safety Nets

It is important to consider how the new wave will impact the average person, and whether they will be better or worse off as a result. There are a couple of major positives to highlight. Firstly, the automation of the global supply chain is likely to create a dramatic fall in the cost of making goods, driven by a reduction in labour, production, storage and transport costs; reduced waste; and ultimately, as renewable power improves, a reduction in energy costs. One of the amazing aspects of creative destruction is its ability to transform what was once a premium good available to only the rich, into commodities affordable by the masses. Schumpeter highlighted how capitalism had enabled the factory girl to own silk stockings that previously were only available to queens. Now the Internet has enabled even the poorest to have immediate access to capabilities and information that could not have been acquired even by the richest in society just fifty years ago. Economists such as Jeremy Rifkin even predict a point where physical items become available for zero marginal cost in the same way as digital items are now. The net result of this is that marginal cost– the cost of producing additional units of product – will fall dramatically, especially for essential goods such as food, heating and clothing. The disruptive effects of near-zero marginal cost transformed the entertainment, communications and publishing industries as more and more content becomes available across digital, collaborative networks, sometimes for a small monthly subscription, and often for free. This has provided a massive increase in the volume and quality of entertainment available to the average person. Similar trends are happening everywhere, so although wages are stagnating, the amount people can buy with these wages is increasing.

Secondly, automation will mean that many essential and expensive assets such as cars, which currently consume a large percentage of people's income to purchase, insure and maintain, will increasingly become servitised and be provided on demand. This will reduce the initial capital expenditure people require to own the asset; reduce monthly outgoings such as loan repayments, insurance and road tax while also transferring asset depreciation costs from the consumer to the provider.[126]

There is one major not-so-positive effect to overcome however: to survive, people will still need an income. And in a world where machines are the new slaves, the number of people who lack in-demand skills to sell or someone willing to buy their labour will increase. There has always been a symbiotic relationship between the owners of capital and the owners of labour. If capital becomes liberated from human labour then this power swings completely towards those with capital, who can create or fund multi-

---

[126] Something the government needs to address moving forward when cars become autonomous – who is insured; the car manufacturer, the software company or the passenger? Plus, who pays for the road tax?

billion-pound businesses that require only a few smart people and a lot of technology. However, even if people lose their power as employees, they will retain it as consumers. For capitalism to continue to work, people need to buy the outputs of entrepreneurial endeavours. Henry Ford was perceptive enough to understand that it was good business sense to create a virtuous cycle where his workers were paid enough money so that they could not only work for Ford; they could also become his customers. The trouble is that while robots may be great producers, they are terrible consumers – and even worse taxpayers. Which brings to mind the famous interchange between a Ford management official and the leader of the automobile workers' union, Walter Reuther, who was being shown around Ford's new engine plant in Cleveland. The Ford official proudly pointed to some new automatically controlled machines and smugly asked Reuther, 'How are you going to collect union dues from these guys?' To which Reuther replied, 'How are *you* going to get them to buy Fords?'

For the current economic model to work well there needs to be a healthy consumer class, and consumerism requires spare income. This inescapable truth is what links those with capital with those without. Someone needs to buy what they are selling. No company is going to spend large amounts of money advertising their products and services on Google and Facebook if the users of these platforms have no disposable income to procure them. Apple doesn't want people to simply aspire to buy one of their $1,000 iPhone Xs and expensive iMacs, Apple Watches and MacBooks – it also needs them to be actually able to do it. The reality that capitalism needs consumers has been long known but often forgotten. Therefore, the rich can't survive by just selling goods and services to each other. We all need to ensure that we continue to have the funds to be consumers, or else the model breaks and the masses are back on the road to serfdom.

The casualties of the transition period, those tied into old jobs and industries through debt commitments or fear, or those whose jobs and skills are displaced by the waves of creative destruction, will need to find a way to continue to be active members of society in a world which values basic human labour less and less. The size and speed of the sixth wave's destructive forces will upend people before they know what is happening, and we need to have a safety net that is both strong enough to catch them as they fall, and flexible enough to allow them to bounce back up. Current welfare programmes in the West have prevented those who cannot find employment from becoming destitute: but they have also often trapped the recipients in state dependency. This is perhaps one of the biggest flaws in the model, which if not addressed will result in this sea of new claimants not only massively expanding the welfare state, but also being unable to exit it. There is no unwritten rule that a human must have a job. This is a social construct we have developed. But cities like Detroit and Chicago and their high rates of urban decay and crime show what happens when people are given welfare but not hope. In the UK, there are council estates where the majority doesn't work, creating systemic poverty and a death of ambition. People in this position look for someone to blame and listen to anyone who sounds like they have easy answers to difficult questions. Places in the world where the population see only a future full of poverty and devoid of purpose become dangerous places indeed, for people with nothing have nothing to lose. That's when you see the rise of both tyrants and terrorists.

Two Tools to Crack the Same Nut

Two primary support mechanisms have been proposed in order to help those who are likely to be displaced by automation. Neither is new, and both are repeatedly resurrected around this point in the wave cycle when income inequality rises. The first, and most well-known, is universal (or unconditional) basic income (UBI), otherwise known as a citizen's income. The second is a negative income tax (NIT). Both work on a similar basic premise of providing a safety net by giving every citizen an amount of cash without any stipulations as to how it is spent. The idea behind both is that this will free people from the fear of falling into absolute poverty, while also providing them with the freedom to enhance this income without being penalised by doing so. Both are trying to overcome two major problems that exist in welfare programmes today:

1. **The Trap.** Most welfare programmes operate a system whereby rejoining the workforce results in an immediate reduction, or even total removal, of benefits. This means that unless your new employment pays significantly more than the welfare cheque, your net receipts from work could potentially be small, reducing the value of working and

trapping people in poverty. When people are caught in the trap for a long time this can result in psychological side effects, such as believing that work is either undesirable, or worse, beyond them. The longer the period they are out of work, the less relevant their skills are going to be, especially in this stage of the wave's cycle. Social stigma is also attached to long-term unemployment, as we tend to value people's worth according to their employment status.

2. **The Complexity.** Taking the UK as an example, welfare is provided in a number of different ways, creating a complex web of potential payouts, ranging from unemployment and disability benefits to housing, free healthcare and childcare support. The myriad of schemes that currently exist is both difficult for the claimant to understand, and very costly for the government to monitor and administer, involving numerous different departments and constant eligibility checking.

Universal Basic Income: An Old Idea Whose Time Has Come?

Universal basic income is the simplest of the two schemes to understand because the 'universal' nature means that every adult member of society gets exactly the same amount, removing the need for means testing. Every citizen receives an individual, unconditional, guaranteed, periodic payment in cash, not vouchers or other such directed assistance. This means that rather than receiving food stamps, you are free to spend all the money on fidget spinners if you so desire. Not something I would advise, unless you can resell them at a profit, but the point is there's nothing stopping you from doing this with the income. UBI is designed to be consistent in amount and frequency and is based on the belief that people, once they know that they will have enough money to cover the basics every month, can then relax and pursue roles that add value to them and to society. The simplicity of the programme is what appeals to most people – plus the fact that they are guaranteed to be recipients – and many believe that a UBI is the only way we can keep society running in an automated world.

Many will be surprised to know that a radical proposal like this is not new. Far from it. Intriguingly, it was first formally proposed back at start of the first industrial revolution when the first wave of disruptive technology was upending society. As now, the workers of the day – skilled artisans and agricultural workers – were facing a period of relative wage stagnation and unemployment due to the rise of industry. Also, like now, the benefits of this transformation flowed almost exclusively into the hands of those who owned capital, land or the means of this new form of production (usually all three). The working poor were therefore facing a bleak future. This uncertainty and concern spilled over from being a purely economic issue into a social and political issue as well, causing the period of social unrest and conflict that Kondratiev describes. Periodic harvest failures had sparked food riots and provoked intense debate over the poor person's right to subsistence.[410] Things in Britain were not quite as bad as the situation across the Channel, where the decade of turmoil that we now know as the French revolution was under way, leading to the spread of republicanism, democracy and radical egalitarianism among the lower orders. While the current turbulent transition period has seen endless calls to remove the head of the establishment, it was not that long ago that populists such as Robespierre were not just calling for, but obtaining, the actual removal of the establishment's heads.

The French revolution once again highlighted that people with nothing have nothing to lose. To quell the anger and resolve the inequalities, the idea of providing all citizens of the country with a basic income was therefore proposed by two British radicals, both called Thomas. The first, Thomas Spence, still resided in Britain; while the other, the somewhat more famous Quaker, Thomas Paine, had emigrated to the British American colonies in 1774 with the help of Benjamin Franklin. Both Paine and Spence were concerned about the rising level of inequality, and while they had different core objectives, they both advocated the sharing of the spoils of progress with the masses.

Paine advocated the payment of a basic income as a right of all citizens in his books *Rights of Man* (1791–1792) [127] and *Agrarian Justice* (1795). He pondered how the right to property could be reconciled with the 'right to life' (a decent minimum standard of living), and in particular how the massively unequal distribution of landed property could be justified, in terms of either divine law or human reason.[411] To resolve these injustices,

---

[127] Paine wrote *Rights of Man*, a book that garnered huge attention, in support of the actions of the French revolutionaries. The British, keen to ensure that the burning embers of revolution did not float over the Channel and catch fire in Britain, issued a warrant for his arrest, so he emigrated to France for safety. Somewhat ironically, Robespierre saw him as an enemy, and he was arrested and placed in a French jail for eleven months.

in *Agrarian Justice* Paine proposed to pay a single lump sum of £5 to every person on attaining adulthood (then defined as twenty-one years of age), and an annual pension of £10 to the blind and lame, and also to everyone aged over fifty. This, he insisted, should be 'a right, and not a charity', and it should be universal and unconditional, though it could be declined by anyone who so chose (unlikely). Paine was keen to stress the moderate nature of his proposal, and that it would be, to use the modern term, fully costed, financed by death duties of no more than 10 per cent of the value of estates (or 20 per cent where there was no direct heir).[412] Paine's main issue was with the private ownership of land, and the exclusion of others from benefiting from it. He concluded that agricultural advancements had brought about improvements in the soil, and that it was only the value of the improvement in productivity and not the earth itself that should be deemed individual property. The modern-day representation of this would be that the technological advancements up to this point are in fact an inheritance passed down by our forefathers, and therefore any bounty made off new developments is fine to be utilised as profit, but only as long as consideration is made of the 'social debt' that consists of pre-existing technologies that were essential in enabling this new innovation to be developed, but which the capitalist or inventor played no part in designing or building. For example, any new app that requires the Internet and computer technology in order to work, or the billions in ad revenue Google generates through its search engine, without recognition that it is content that people are searching for, none of which Google created.

A somewhat lesser-known British radical thinker of the same era is Thomas Spence, who also proposed a basic income, but what would be now deemed more communist in nature. A person of deep Nonconformist beliefs (again, highlighting the impact Nonconformists had on British society), he published *The Rights of Infants* as a response to Paine's *Agrarian Justice*. Spence disagreed with Paine's proposals, claiming that they were too conservative and merely represented *the thief returning to his victims just part of what had been stolen.*[413] Spence goes further than Paine and proposes the introduction of an unconditional basic income for all members of the community, financed through the full appropriation of the land to common ownership, and the benefits of the rents perceived by each municipality. According to Spence, his proposal is superior because any benefits of increased rents do not go to a few, but are shared amongst the poor, and as such drive economic progress. He also stated that the fact that his proposal is not confined to economic justice, but also has political, social and even ideological dimensions, as the population would take more care of common land once they realised that they benefited from its fruits. As we now know, a universal basic income was not introduced during this time period, but instead over time a series of Factory Acts and labour laws were implemented, designed to create a safer and more palatable work environment. Throughout the 20th century, a series of other welfare programmes were also implemented that ranged from socialised healthcare through to relief for the unemployed.

It is intriguing to see how the idea of a basic income is wedded to the turbulent transition points between Kondratiev waves. Most commentators, especially those on social media, promote it as a radical new solution to a new and totally unique set of circumstances. Neither is true. During every transition period, as wealth inequality rises and those with capital profit and those with labour struggle, the concept of a basic income has been resurrected. It was seriously considered in the late '60s during the transition between the last waves when computer technology emerged. In January 1968, President Lyndon B. Johnson set up a commission to examine alternatives to America's welfare system, and the commission eventually recommended a 'basic income support program' which would provide every adult with $750 per year (about $5,200 now), and an additional $450 per child. It was never fully implemented, but several city and state experiments were undertaken to test low-income families' responses to different taxation and benefit levels. The idea remained popular on both sides of the political divide, with vocal advocates ranging from Martin Luther King to Milton Friedman.

As the transition to the sixth wave creates social and economic pressures, the idea of a universal basic income has been mooted once again. However, while Paine and Spence had to rely on local printers to share their ideas with a semi-literate population, now the Internet has allowed the idea to be spread by social media and blog posts across the entire public discourse. And it is finding favour with many, regardless of their political beliefs. Its supporters range from economists, politicians and Silicon Valley technocrats, through to pretty much everyone on the political left.[128] The immediate benefits of a UBI are that it provides every citizen with a level of income that allows them to provide for the majority of their primary needs, regardless of their employment status or income level. It therefore theoretically passes the test of eliminating both the welfare trap and the complexity issue – because people don't lose the benefit if they work, and it simplifies the current welfare structure while also being easy to administer and monitor. Many countries are currently performing trials to understand its impact, with small select groups in Canada, the Netherlands and Finland all receiving various levels of unconditional payments. Interestingly, in June 2016, a referendum was held in Switzerland where the Swiss overwhelmingly voted against implementing a UBI scheme that would have provided 2,500 Swiss francs (CHF) to each adult and 635 CHF to each child per month.

Negative Income Tax: A Means-Tested UBI

The other discussed alternative to a UBI is a negative income tax, which was initially proposed by British politician Lady Juliet Rhys-Williams in 1942 and more famously resurrected by the US economist Milton Friedman in the 1960s. Negative income tax (NIT) differs from UBI in that it is means-tested rather than universal, reducing in value as people earn more until it transfers from a negative tax (where the state gives you money) to a normal tax (where you give the state money). The way it works, as described by Friedman, is as follows:

1. For simplicity, let's assume a flat tax rate of 50 per cent, and a break-even point of £30,000.
2. If you earned no income, then you would receive 50 per cent of £30,000 as a tax rebate, providing an income of £15,000.
3. If you earned £10,000 from work, then this would be taken off the £30,000 limit, and you would now receive 50 per cent of £20,000 – i.e. the state provides you with a rebate of £10,000, creating a total income of £20,000 (the £10,000 you earned, plus a £10,000 NIT rebate).
4. If you received £20,000 in income, then you would receive a rebate of

---

[128] Except for the hard left, that wants capitalism to fall and society to collapse into anarchy, so it can be rebuilt in their version of utopia.

50 per cent on the remaining £10,000, giving you a rebate of £5,000 and a total income of £25,000.

5. If you earned £30,000 per year from work, then you pay no tax and receive no rebate, giving you an income of £30,000.
6. Once you go over the break-even point, you start paying income tax. So wages of £40,000 would equate to £30,000 tax free, and 50 per cent tax on £10,000, giving a total net income of £35,000.

The benefit of this system over the myriad of other welfare schemes in existence is that it does not disincentive work, so it reduces the trap element. However, it does not totally remove the complexity issue, as people's income has to be monitored so the appropriate rebate can be given. But for many, a negative income tax could provide a more palatable alternative to the current system and a full-blown UBI system.

Support for both is everywhere, especially for UBI, and many groups see this as an essential requirement in a world where mass automation is likely to disrupt multiple industries and replace many different types of work at the same time. Both UBI and NIT reward work, and the aim of them should not be seen to replace work or welfare, but as a way to protect against poverty and provide the springboard by which people can develop the skills, education and experience needed to progress from being a net withdrawer of benefits, to a net contributor. It is the people who are the casualties of the transition period who need the most immediate help, and both solutions would ensure that those caught in the winds of Schumpeter's gale do not end up destitute and unable to participate in the economy. In a period when zero-hour contracts and the gig economy are the new normal, the stability of a guaranteed pay cheque every month from the government could alleviate stress, reduce poverty and enable people to study, retrain and learn the skills needed to be relevant in the sixth wave.

No Silver Bullets

Both UBI and NIT are not without issues, and it is always good to be wary of easy fixes for complicated problems. The first is the obvious one – affordability. An annual outlay of $12,000 per American adult ($1,000 per month), the current poverty threshold, would cost approximately

$3.8 trillion annually; 21 per cent of US GDP or 78 per cent of US tax revenues.[414] It also can't be financed by simply printing money because inflation will destroy the benefits. It must therefore be financed by other means. Its proponents argue that the cost would be mostly offset by savings made by removing state bureaucracy and current welfare administration overheads, though it's difficult to see how it would save $3.8 trillion. Early pilots such as the two-year Finland experiment have been cancelled due to concerns about the affordability of rolling it out across the wider population, citing that income tax would have to rise in Finland by 30 per cent.[415]

The second issue is 'How much is enough?' The main requirement of these programmes is to provide a level of income that keeps people from falling into poverty, while also allowing them to freely explore the many different ways they could earn an income in the new wave. If it is set too low, then it will fail its objectives of providing real support and replacing the current welfare schemes. If it is set too high, then there is the risk that many people will not be motivated to work, and we end up with a dependency culture. Some of the trials to date have involved giving people a basic income of $500 a month, which, while helpful, hardly provides enough to feed a family, pay the mortgage, heat the house, etc. A truck driver currently earning $50,000 a year is not going to be satisfied living on a replacement basic income of $6,000 a year. Neither would a marketing professional, a stockbroker, an accountant or a lawyer. They will default on mortgages and be homeless in weeks unless a replacement for the shortfall can be found. Also, what if you live in a big city? Rents are astronomical, so even $1,000 a month may not cover that. Then there is the fact that many people currently receive a variety of different benefits which can cover a number of different costs, which when combined provide more benefit than the UBI would. For the UBI to be viable, it has to compensate for the loss of most if not all of the existing programmes, else you end up with more administration, not less. This requires a UBI payment of around $1,200 a month to become equivalent to earning a minimum wage in the US, which does sound more appropriate, but obviously this significantly increases the cost of the programme. This basic income may provide more than we imagine, due to automation lowering the cost of essential items such as power, transport, communication, heating and food. Covering housing costs will remain an issue however, specifically rent, for while mortgage payments have been suppressed by low interest rates, rent prices have remained high.

Then there is the issue that a UBI could accentuate the job-loss situation. Removing the army of public servants needed to issue and administer the smorgasbord of current benefits will obviously drastically reduce the cost of maintaining the system, helping to pay for the UBI – but will also increase the unemployment situation. For those who advocate a smaller government, this is seen as an advantage. For those whose salary comes from working in welfare distribution, Medicare provision, housing benefit, etc., it means that you are now unemployed and relying on the UBI that replaced your job.

Who should receive these benefits is another question that needs answering, specifically whether those who don't need them should get them. Any maximum income level would naturally reduce the outgoings, but it would also remove the universal aspect and require administering again. The issue of inflation also gets mentioned when discussing basic income schemes; if everyone gets extra money, won't the cost of everything simply go up? This is a possibility, but it depends greatly on where the money comes from to pay for it. If you end up printing more money, then obviously the value of that money will decrease. However, if the basic income is financed via the redistribution of cash already generated – i.e. through ensuring corporations and individuals pay their taxes – then it shouldn't have an inflationary impact. The wealthiest in society may initially feel aggrieved by this, but assuming that their earnings are related to the volume of consumerism in the economy, they will ultimately become benefactors.

Another issue is the fact that the first country that implemented any form of social security system like a basic income would immediately become a migration magnet, which was one of the primary reasons why the Swiss rejected the proposal in their referendum. A landlocked country like Switzerland with multiple entry points (or any country in the EU's Schengen zone) would immediately find itself flooded by new citizens, all hoping to be able to claim this benefit. This means that the policy would require policing in some way, or else it would become truly universal and completely unaffordable. This policing would naturally increase the administration burden, defeating the objective somewhat. Even if these new entrants do not qualify for the basic income, they will be consuming government funds while in the country through other means, such as healthcare, social services and policing. This may be more of a problem than many people are aware. When automation really starts to affect the emerging nations and the population realise that the industrial revolution they were promised doesn't require their services, then the level of migration we've seen coming into Europe since 2015 will only accelerate. The developed countries have the capability to potentially fund a basic-income scheme, whereas the emerging nations are unlikely to have the funds nor the political will to implement anything like this.[129] This could be a problem for them and for us. Open borders and multiculturalism work to provide a steady stream of low-cost, unskilled labour, but as machines continue to replace the need for this, what happens to those migrants? Do they go home or stay? If they stay, do they claim these universal benefits? If yes, then expect a massive increase in demand for all state services and their associated costs, while also experiencing a dramatic reduction in the contributions needed to support them.

The changing nature of employment in the sixth wave also presents problems, especially regarding negative income tax. Unlike in 1968 when Friedman was discussing this on talk shows, many people no longer have a single set income, a trend that is increasing fast. How will NIT work when people have multiple income streams from the gig economy, and their income is constantly changing? NIT will therefore require extensive administration – at least until the blockchain payments are ubiquitous – ironic when the purpose of this type of scheme was to reduce, not increase, administration costs.

When you look at a country like the UK, you can currently see different types of UBI schemes being implemented, disbanded or struggling to survive – all at the same time. A single universal credit system is currently being trialled in an attempt to combine multiple separate benefits into a single payment, reducing complexity and administration costs. It's proved problematic. The universal element of child benefit has recently been disbanded, changed to a means-tested payment for affordability reasons. Finally, the struggling universal schemes of the state pension and the provision of 'free at the point of delivery' NHS healthcare.[130] Both are under enormous strain due to an increase in demand caused primarily by a

---

[129] In India for example, basic sanitation is far ahead of basic income in priority.
[130] State pension payments rely on enough National Insurance contributions being paid over a person's lifetime.

dramatic and continued increase in population due to net migration, and a steadily ageing population. In 1960, the UK had a population of 52 million and an average life expectancy of sixty-eight years for men and seventy-four for women. Despite a continual fall in the birth rate in the indigenous ethnic group (white British), the current population now stands at 66 million, with average life expectancies of 79.4 for men and 83.1 for women. Simply put, more people living longer equals more demand for healthcare and extended pension payments. The UK government is therefore rightly concerned about the affordability of state pensions once the rising population reaches pensionable age. The annual cost of providing a state pension in the UK rose by £1 trillion between 2010 and 2015, and now stands at £7.6 trillion, more than four times the size of the economy. To try and alleviate some of the pressure, the age at which you can claim this benefit is planned to increase to 66 years in 2020, and 67 in 2026. I think we will see this adjusted upwards before then, once breakthroughs in genetics start to have an effect on both life expectancy and death rates caused by age-related diseases. The National Health Service is also under enormous strain. The NHS is a wonderful service that people in the UK support with an almost religious zeal, but despite continual efficiency drives, it is always stretched because demand outstrips its ability to supply.[131] As a result, there are never-ending demands to increase funding, making the NHS a constant political issue as concerns rise about its ability to provide the necessary resources for this growing, aging population. The larger the NHS, the more administration it needs, which drives up management costs, inefficiencies and waste. Simply throwing more and more money at it has proven to do little to resolve these inefficiencies.

The affordability of existing programmes such as the NHS and state pensions are therefore a concern for many when UBI is discussed. The costs will only ever go one way – upwards – and could quickly become

---

[131] One rarely mentioned benefit that those with wealth bring to society is that they tend to remove themselves as recipients of these forms of universal public services. It's an important point that many people seem to deliberately overlook, but which I'm mentioning for fairness. Those with money, *if* they pay their taxes, end up not only contributing greatly to the cost of providing free services such as the NHS and public education, but they also do not generally utilise these facilities, using private services instead, freeing up space for others. Conversely, the poorest use the NHS often, while not contributing to its funding as they are not taxed. Plus, in choosing to pay for these services privately, the wealthy end up creating more jobs, thereby creating more taxable income which again helps pay for public services.

unaffordable due to an increase in the population, lifespan and inflation. It therefore asks the obvious question – if we believe that a universal basic income for all is affordable, how come we are struggling to pay the current universal benefits such as healthcare, child benefit and pensions? Perhaps we need to find ways to effectively manage them and balance their books before rolling out another benefit scheme.

A Pragmatic Approach

Given the previous facts about the current system and its affordability, one should be wary of those who declare a universal basic income for every citizen to be an instant and affordable fix to current issues. The question of whether it is fair to receive regular compensation without actively having to contribute to society needs addressing, for this is many people's objection to the idea. In a society where many do not work, where would people find their purpose? Perhaps a system where the amount of basic income you receive is somehow linked to your contribution to society, such as performing social duties, caring for the local environment, helping out at care homes, would prevent this? This will obviously increase the administration required to monitor and manage the system, but it provides more positive results for both the individual and the community compared to people simply sitting at home living out their lives online. The administration overheads could of course be reduced as technology advances, enabling tools like the blockchain to manage the financial transfers.

Before discussing 'universal' benefits, we should first concentrate on providing support for the more immediate casualties of the sixth wave, such as those unlikely to have the skills or capacity to participate in the jobs of the new wave. Those people either displaced from industries that have been replaced by automation (such as truck drivers) or yet to obtain skills (the young). By attending first to those who need support most, you could test out the principles of UBI and prepare for the next wave when it will almost certainly be required across a wider spectrum of society.

We also can't really talk about implementing a basic income for everyone without discussing the massive shortfall in other universal schemes such as state pension contributions. While these won't go away, sixth-wave technologies could significantly reduce the administrative burden of delivering public services and administering benefits. Medical advancements and digital technology could combine to create a healthcare 'Internet of Things' where devices continually monitor every aspect of your health and well-being, storing data and sending updates and recommendations to health professionals. This would move the NHS from a reactive, sickness-based service, to a predictive, prevention-focused one, reducing administration, the number of expensive operations and the volume of beds occupied at any one time. Combined with the advancements in genetic engineering we could potentially highlight the early onset of Alzheimer's and cancer, saving lives and freeing beds and healthcare funds.

Regardless of what approach is undertaken, some form of universal income scheme will be needed by the time we reach the end of this wave. As work becomes more transient, based on smaller contracts with limited security, people need to know that destitution will not be the outcome if they do not find work in the next seven days. The major benefit of this scheme will be in allowing them to see any employment opportunity as a net gain; essential when there is a plethora of new ways to make money, to create value, and to educate yourself and develop your skills.

#4: New Measures of Success

One final problem is that we currently worship a false god: GDP. GDP may have worked in a world of labour and wages, but it will fail to determine a society's well-being in a world of automation and welfare. In a GDP-centric world, only things that add economic value are deemed worthwhile. A person giving up their career to care for a sick relative, or to raise children properly, or volunteer at a care home, is adding enormous value to the recipient and to society, but you'll never see that appear anywhere on the country's GDP. Conversely – and perversely – a person who spends £5 on acquiring virtual resources for their virtual farm, or on upgrading their virtual castle to protect it from virtual ogres, *has* added value from a GDP perspective. This relationship between the purchase of goods and value makes sense when the goods purchased need producing, storing, distributing and selling, and all those tasks are done by paid human labour, but now the goods are digital, and the purchase is instant and electronic, so no labour is involved in the transaction.

The constant GDP focus has also led to an enormous push to further release the latent economic value of women into the workforce, encouraging them away from the home and into the workplace. We have, as a result, developed a system that places no economic value on the care and upbringing of children – unless someone else is paid to do it – resulting in a society where both parents feel pressured to work, then pressured to have children, and then pressured to hand over their children to someone else to care for so they can go back to work. Then, to make time to do everything, we have increasingly passed over the job of entertaining our children to technology, and in doing so turned them into consumers of these digital products. From an GDP perspective this is fantastic, and our globalist leaders continually push for it, but at what cost to society? We are yet to fully understand the full ramifications of a society built around transactions and technology, but there are many warning signs, as we will explore.

It is therefore important that when we talk about growth as a measure of success that we include personal, intellectual and cultural growth, and not just GDP. Are companies, countries and communities thriving, or just growing? An unconditional guaranteed monthly payment may help by enabling people to retrain without worrying about how they will feed themselves. It should also allow people to have greater freedom to choose whether they want to work at home as a parent, or externally as an employee, rather than struggling to do both simply to survive. It may also allow them to investigate more fulfilling ways to earn or learn, rather than feeling pressured to take a job that simply pays the bills. Relieving some of this economic anxiety should hopefully help decrease the level of stress while increasing the happiness of parents and children. This should hopefully prevent some of the worst excesses of what is likely to be a series of social issues caused by children who were brought up by a combination of stressed parents and technological babysitters. It is important to value social activities such as bringing up children, because as we will explore, right now in the West we are creating a generation of people who are distant from their culture, their nation, their community and their family. A worrying direction, one leading to a more automated and less human future.

There is no doubt that the sixth wave will automate a large number of jobs. Every wave has, and this one has more potential to automate than the previous ones combined. This will create significant adaptation anxiety for those who currently earn a stable and essential income from roles that are likely to be caught in the crossfire, derived from the fact that the new, alternative jobs on offer will require either more skill, or offer lower security. Plans therefore need to be put into place now, for technology moves considerably faster than our political system. We need to provide both a safety net for those displaced by technology, while also enabling people to choose to spend their time on activities that inspire them, and to be rewarded, not penalised, if that activity adds social value. As John Maynard Keynes prophesised nearly a century ago, *a point may soon be reached, much sooner perhaps than we are all of us aware of, when these [economic] needs are satisfied in the sense that we prefer to devote our further energies to non-economic purposes.*

The choice, therefore, lies with our political and business leaders as to what type of society they want moving forward, and whether the wealthiest want to create a better society or separate from it. We will fail to maximise our true potential if we penalise those who work for others, and reward those who only work for themselves. We need to decide who is more valuable – a person who dedicates their life to the care and betterment of others, or someone who only focuses on the acquisition of material wealth? It sounds like an easy question, but society currently rewards the latter at the expense of the former. While to many this may sound like a socialist agenda, it's really not; it's an inclusive agenda, a contribution agenda. One that is needed to ensure capitalism survives the next wave, for most real-world alternatives are not pretty.

We also need to move towards an economic model that not only provides for people, but promotes individualism, not infantilism. One that encourages people to take personal responsibility and not to detach themselves from it. One that supports the foundations of our society, not one that works to break them apart. People need a source of income, for as the saying goes, 'I don't mind losing my job, but it's the wages I'll miss.' But research shows that this is not strictly true, for people also want a reason to get out of bed in the morning. Combining a pay packet with a purpose provides much more to people than just an income, and in return they provide much more to their employer than their time. The point of basic income should not therefore be to just provide an income, but to free people and enable them to become the masters of their own destiny.

Advancements in technology will increasingly enable people to overcome geographic, physical and class boundaries that previously held the majority back. We all have access to knowledge and education now – it doesn't reside in the hands of the elite and those with capital. Barriers are coming down, enabling everyone to increasingly gain access to both the means of production and the marketplace. The Internet and e-commerce platforms are providing numerous ways to earn money, ranging from renting rooms in your house, producing digital content through to designing 3D-printed items people can print at home. For those with entrepreneurial aspirations, there has never been a better time to be alive.

22

THE POTENTIAL FOR A NEW GOLDEN AGE

We must create economic opportunity, build a culture of entrepreneurship, get people to take responsibility for improving their lives, rather than putting them in a position where they sit back in their poverty and blame others for it.

Paul Kagame, President of Rwanda

Most literature on the forthcoming future tends to portray either a utopian world of leisure and abundance, or a dystopian world of technological unemployment and despair. The truth, as always, lies between these two extremes. Despite all of the disruption and unemployment, there will continue to be employment in the sixth wave, and there will be plenty of opportunities for people to live successful and prosperous lives. For some, the new tools will provide numerous new ways to express their individualism; to do what they love; to create a market for what they are passionate about. It will also be a time of great investment in new means of transport, new ways of communicating, new ways to capture energy, and new ways to capture and transform data. But for many it will be a difficult time, displaced from a job they spent years becoming good at, losing their income and their pride, angry, bitter and potentially saddled with great debt.

It's not a good mix, and action needs to be taken to support those whose livelihood has been disrupted and ensure that they do not fall between the cracks and end up without hope for the future. Just as importantly, we also need to ensure that in a post-work future people still have a purpose to their lives beyond being a consumer.

The jobs of the future are going to be based around those activities that machines cannot do. For those unable to create value beyond what a machine can do, then the future is not looking bright, which means while we will see wondrous new technologies everywhere, not everyone is going to think them wonderful. Whatever fee you're charging, I guarantee that Robbie the Robot, Annie the Algorithm or Charlie the Chatbot will be cheaper – plus more reliable, productive and accurate. Automation will also remove the need for mass migration of unskilled labour, as the potential to create wealth from machines rather than from people enables a detachment of GDP and population growth. Machines are the new makers, not people. The days of single companies employing tens or hundreds of thousands of people are now gone, and the old industrial jobs are dead or dying. There is no point in pining for what will not return. Raising the hopes of frustrated workers by promising them a return to large-scale hiring for industrial-age jobs in an increasingly automated, hyper-efficient manufacturing sector is not a wise move, and will end up in broken promises and more frustration. It would be far better to focus on preparing workers for the rise of the robots than to promise them jobs that will be done by machines.

However, all is not lost. There will be opportunities for people to thrive in the forthcoming decades, for we should never forget the power of innovation and our insatiable need for new things. The desirable products of the first revolution, such as matches, pins and stockings, may now have become disposable commodities, but we do have a mass market for a $1,000 iPhone. The three foundational areas that make up each new wave – power, transport and communication – are all going to experience a technological revolution, creating whole new industries that will require significant planning, building and installation. For example, the move from combustion engines to electric vehicles will require a huge number of recharging points to be installed across the nation, creating jobs for construction workers and the manufacturing companies that make the chargers. Logistics companies will either retrofit existing rigs with autonomous capability, or buy new rigs, creating a boom for vehicle manufacturers. New transport systems such as the Hyperloop and VTOL flying drones will go from concept to capable, requiring landing platforms and stations to be built. The creation of the 5G network will enable the dream of smart, constantly connected cities powered by the Internet of Everything to arise, creating enormous demand for the production, implementation and maintenance of millions of sensors and intelligent machines. Robotics and autonomous vehicle production will rise dramatically, all of which will need maintaining and mending. AI coding and machine-learning capabilities are going to be red-hot. Electric vehicles and technologies like the blockchain will create an enormous demand for electricity, so the demand for renewable energy generation and storage will explode, generating huge demand in both industrial and domestic properties for solar panels and power-storage devices, creating work for both manufacturers and installers. Genetics is also primed to become a major industry, requiring both scientists and a new breed of predictive genetic healthcare professional, able to edit human DNA the way an editor corrects a bad manuscript, snipping out the inferior sections and replacing them with strong, beneficial genes. The need for wall-to-wall cybersecurity will become increasingly urgent, creating a boon for those with these skills. Plus, there are still plenty of creative and very human jobs that machines are nowhere near being able to undertake – Watson might be able to select the best clips from a movie to make a compelling trailer, but it's a long way off from writing the script, selecting film locations and directing the actors. Or being an actor. Areas like senior care – demand for which is set to explode due to the rapidly aging population – will change from a place for mostly unskilled and poorly paid workers, to one which attracts highly skilled specialists. While robots automate many of the repetitive tasks such as medicine dispensing and general companionship, this growing market will create demands for highly skilled psychologists, physiotherapists and carers. There will, therefore, be plenty of new jobs created in the new wave, but the skills needed to do them will be greater. The challenge will be to provide for those caught in the transition; those who can't develop the skills needed in order to participate, or who feel they are simply too old to change.

Working the Cultural Lag

It is also important to retain a sense of perspective. Despite a rapid increase in technological diffusion, the old does not simply disappear just because the new arrives, and many innovations may not cross the chasm into the mass market for years. For example, the Roomba carpet-cleaning robot has been available to buy since 2002, but sixteen years later it is still seen as a product for 'innovators', and as result traditional, manual-operated vacuum cleaners still completely dominate the market. Even if 3D printing completely disrupts the house-building market, most people will still live in traditional houses that will need constant maintenance and updating for decades – and maintenance tasks are notoriously difficult to automate. A personal example. While writing this book I had my bathroom updated. The builder had to take off all the old tiles; rip out the bath, sink, toilet and radiator; remove floorboards; replace the pathetic plastic pipes (which had leaked and flooded my house twice in ten years) with old-fashioned but sturdier copper ones; reposition the plumbing and the radiator pipes; fit a new radiator; fix new spotlights in the ceiling; cut over two hundred tiles in various shapes to fit the annexes and corners; fix and grout the tiles; fit new shower doors; fit all of the appliances; and lay a new floor. In my frequent trips to keep him supplied with a steady stream of tea, I discussed with him the question, *Which of these tasks could be automated away in the next thirty years?* He stated that while he could imagine that most of the things he uses could be manufactured in automated factories, the job of removing the old bathroom and installing the new one could only be done with significant skill, experience, dexterity, and a certain degree of physical strength. Machines are some way from being able to handle novel situations they haven't seen before, especially if these tasks involve a high degree of dexterity, uncertainty and variability. He also stated that every project he undertook was different, as the layout, requirements, tile size, plumbing, issues to resolve, appliances and materials used were all likely to be unique in some way. While new houses may soon be built in ways that allow for plumbing, power and heating to be pre-fitted and bathrooms designed to be more modular and easier to update, every pre-existing house will still need care and maintenance by skilled human labour – at least for the foreseeable future.

People who talk about there being 'no jobs' in twenty years have therefore not thought their argument through very well. There will be different jobs – lots of them – which will require different skills. We must also remember that the existing world does not always just disappear. If that was the case, the car would have eliminated the bicycle, yet the latter still has a healthy market and, in some places such as the Netherlands, there are more bicycles than cars. Likewise, the rise of electric, autonomous cars won't suddenly remove the hundreds of millions of combustion-engine cars that are in circulation. Autonomous vehicles will phase in over a number of years, and manual cars will slowly fade out over a decade or so. If your current source of income contains tasks that include maintaining, changing or updating existing assets or infrastructure you'll still be in demand – for a while, at least.

Over the last couple of decades, Western society has shunned traditional skills such as engineering and plumbing in favour of going to university. This has been a mistake. These skills have the dual benefit of being both required and extremely unlikely to be replaced by automation any time soon. Conversely, we now have an army of graduates with high expectations but burdensome debts and degrees in subjects that are either about to be profoundly affected by automation (law, healthcare, marketing, management, accountancy), or which have limited practical application (such as religious studies, humanities and liberal arts). Universities, therefore, can address this by focusing on developing practical skills and apprenticeships that produce a pipeline of future talent to work in 21st-century business, not the 20th-century equivalent. You might be able to get an army of software engineers from India, but you'll struggle to find any who can do this work and also fix the machine that the software runs on. An exciting and synergistic value chain could therefore be created that links the universities to the innovation hubs, and the hubs to the corporations. This will align scientific research in new manufacturing methods and their possibilities, with education in the skills needed to use and support these new methods, feeding talent into the innovation hubs and to the companies who industrialise the outputs of this research and can provide employment for the newly skilled apprentices.

The future will always reward those who can find a way to add value to customers. Automating away tasks that do not directly add value, such as recording transactions or checking for human errors, is not something we should fear. For many of us we may find that by taking away the repetitive and boring tasks, we can spend more time on creative problem-solving, customer interactions and relationship-building. A world where people constantly focus on finding ways to add value and not just keep busy is going to be a better world – if there are enough value-adding tasks for us to do. Which takes us back to the 'lump of labour' fallacy. There is never going to be a fixed amount of work to do – every new technology creates new roles and opportunities. However, as we've seen, most industries are becoming less labour intensive and machines can do an increasing number of the tasks that need to be done. A job is a social construct, not a necessity, something that will be discussed at length in the coming years.

The Democratisation of Innovation

The good thing about individual freedoms and free markets is that those who strive for more do not require permission to take action to achieve it. Want to be creative and see if there's a market for your creativity? As long as you're not ripping off other people or their ideas, then do it. Access to the new platforms and a global market provides a massive number of potential opportunities to make money. Who'd have thought that a twenty-six-year-old Swedish guy would earn $124 million from uploading videos on YouTube of himself talking while playing computer games? That a multi-million-dollar brand could be developed with just a computer, some recording and editing software, and a sense of humour? Yet that's what PewDiePie and a host of YouTube and gaming stars have done. Young people have garnered millions of followers – and dollars – from doing things as random as streaming themselves playing computer games,[132] through to uploading videos on teenage make-up and beauty tips. It just goes to show that while traditional methods of employment are reducing, new, more creative ways are constantly being developed. Ways that don't involve huge amounts of infrastructure and industrial endeavour; just imagination, ingenuity and industriousness.

The cost to manufacture is not always a good indicator of the value people assign to things. It might cost next to nothing for a game developer

---

[132] In 2018, Tyler Blevins, the player known as 'Ninja' was reportedly earning $350,000 a month from the streaming service Twitch due to the number of subscribers watching him playing the game Fortnite.

to design a new skin for a virtual AK-47 in an online FPS[133] game such as *Counter-Strike*, but as my son shows me, they trade for hundreds, sometimes thousands, of dollars in the gaming communities. People are irrational beings, and what they value isn't necessarily easily defined – and certainly not by the cost of manufacture. Scarcity plays a role (which in the digital age is created artificially rather than due to the availability of raw materials, e.g. rare skins for characters and guns in video games). Image plays a role. Creativity plays a role. The power of individual choice – the ability to choose what to do, how hard I work and what I spend my money on – has proven to be the driving force behind capitalism's constant success. The power of consumers to choose also makes it increasingly difficult for economists to predict economic outcomes. Like I said, we're pretty irrational. Remove choice and markets rapidly become more predictable; any imbalance between supply and demand is easily identified simply by observing the length of the bread queue.

The irrationality and power of choice could be what saves capitalism in the sixth wave. Whenever people are free, they want a free and equal market and the ability to choose. In a world where the value of labour is decreased, and taxation comes from corporation tax more than personal tax, there is a risk that society could become more exclusive as the amount of power wielded by the common person is diminished. Since the 14th century, following the events of the Black Death and the Peasants Revolt, people came to realise that their labour was finite and valuable, and thus provided them with leverage. When labour is replaced by machines, this leverage is diminished, and questions will invariably be asked as to the value of citizens that don't generate economic value.[134] Consumer choice therefore becomes the major remaining bargaining chip for citizens living off a basic income rather than a wage. As the cost of supply continually plummets due to automation, the fight to win that buying decision will ensure that companies focus on providing increasingly innovative products and services at lower prices. The sixth wave may therefore become known as the start of the age of imagination; where we gain access to tools, powered

---

[133] First-person shooter computer games such as *Counter-Strike* and *Overwatch*.

[134] Credit for highlighting this needs to go to Shai Shapira and his *Quillette* article *Universal Basic Income and the Threat of Tyranny*. He doesn't mention the power of consumer choice but does raises the issue of how UBI could result in a loss of the citizen's power as a taxpayer and producer.

by machine learning, that allow us to bring ideas to life in ways that were previously the domain of those rich corporations who could afford both the technology and a team capable of using it.

New-Wave Entrepreneurs, Entertainers and Educators

Providing a stable foundation for entrepreneurs to launch from is perhaps one of the core drivers behind the introduction of a universal basic income. Setting up any endeavour – whether it's a cake shop or as a content creator on YouTube – requires time and effort. These opportunities favour the young, because they lack the additional draws on their time and their income that come with marriage, home-ownership and parenthood. Knowing that there's a roof over your head and food on the table, courtesy of mum and dad, enables people to explore ways to make an income that were not possible previously. As a personal example, we've agreed to finance my youngest son while he takes a year out in his quest to become an eSports star. This wasn't an option for me when I was that age – firstly because eSports wasn't a thing, and secondly because my parents wouldn't have been able to afford (nor tolerate) financing their adult son while he pursued his dream. Now, as long as they have a roof over their heads, access to the Internet and a relatively basic level of kit, the young can explore new ways to make an income – and a name – for themselves. This income can come from multiple streams, not just from the activity itself (such as eSports), but from building their own unique brand on platforms such as YouTube and Instagram. This concept was something that I struggled with initially, for the idea of my son sacrificing education for something I considered pure entertainment seemed foolish in the extreme. Yet I was forced to confront my own limited paradigm, for after seeing videos of packed stadiums in places such as London and Las Vegas,[135] and joining hundreds of thousands of people streaming these tournaments live (and millions more who watch after the event), I realised that I was viewing this with industrial-age eyes, not digital-age ones. The world has changed, and what I thought was just games was actually a multi-billion-dollar global business. We are moving from a nation of shopkeepers to a nation of players, commentators and

---

[135] *Counter-Strike: Global Offensive*, otherwise known as *CS-GO*, in case you were wondering.

content creators, spurred on by the successes of people like PewDiePie and Philip DeFranco, or vloggers such as Zoella. For those whose lives are still occupied by the routine of a corporate career, this may have passed you by, especially if you don't have kids or if they left home before the Internet became mainstream. People can now make a fortune in a multitude of ways, most of which would be dismissed as frivolous by those used to a more traditional career path.

Some have seen this coming. Kevin Kelly wrote in 2008 about the need to develop '1,000 true fans'. To quote from his article: *To be a successful creator you don't need millions. You don't need millions of dollars or millions of customers, millions of clients or millions of fans. To make a living as a craftsperson, photographer, musician, designer, author, animator, app maker, entrepreneur, or inventor you need only a thousand true fans.*[416] What Kelly proposes next is how to achieve that: *Here's how the math works. You need to meet two criteria. First, you have to create enough each year that you can earn, on average, $100 profit from each true fan. That is easier to do in some arts and businesses than others, but it is a good creative challenge in every area because it is always easier and better to give your existing customers more, than it is to find new fans. Second, you must have a direct relationship with your fans. That is, they must pay you directly. You get to keep all of their support, unlike the small percent of their fees you might get from a music label, publisher, studio, retailer, or other intermediate. If you keep the full $100 of each true fan, then you need only 1,000 of them to earn $100,000 per year. That's a living for most folks.* And that's exactly what is happening. Platforms such as Patreon have been set up to allow for people to directly support artists with their money through monthly donations that can range from $1 to 'however much you appreciate what this person does'. This provides an income for a whole host of content creators on YouTube and has propelled people from relative obscurity into the mainstream, such as YouTube talk show host Dave Rubin, or Professor of Psychology Dr Jordan Peterson. For years Peterson uploaded hundreds of videos of his lectures at Toronto University and his talks on subjects covered in his 1999 book *Maps of Meaning*, with a small but loyal following. Then in October 2016, a video of him arguing with protestors at Toronto University was uploaded, and he was propelled into the wider public sphere. After years working as a professor at Harvard and now as a tenured professor at Toronto, he probably thought his career path and income were relatively set. Not so. His salary is now dwarfed by his Patreon donations, which back in October 2016, not long after he set up his account, were a not-insignificant $1,555 per month from 210 loyal patrons. Yet just one year later his reputation – and his Patreon donations – had skyrocketed to $66,636 per month from 6,609 patrons. Since then he has published his second book and is touring the world, speaking via radio and TV interviews. Success in the digital age can hit you at any age. If you can connect with a group of people who believe what you do and find value in whatever niche you have to offer, then as long as you can find a way to package this, they will come. All a bit *Field of Dreams*, I know, but true nevertheless.

One of the primary factors driving this change is the ability for creators to interact directly with consumers. Back in the 18th and 19th centuries, the coffee houses and gentlemen's clubs were the places where men of investment, industry and invention came together to discuss opportunities to bring ideas to market. Now, the power of digital communication has enabled this crowd-funding sites such as Kickstarter and Indiegogo to emerge, enabling people to directly sponsor creators, and fund the development of products, art and music that they would like to own. In the industrial age, only large-scale companies had the marketing budgets to reach the mass market. Now, using Internet-based platforms, the individual can broadcast their ideas and test the waters, as well as find the funding for the actual development, and do this for as long as they have enough people who value their outputs to pay for them. Some of the success stories are breathtaking. While most people remember the VR headset Oculus Rift, which raised $2.4 million from its Kickstarter campaign, it is dwarfed by tech devices such as the Coolest Cooler travel cooler, which achieved 26,570 per cent of its goal, raising over $13 million, and the Pebble Time smartwatch, which raised over $20 million in support.

It appears that the primary barrier to these new types of entrepreneurial endeavours is the platform owner themselves. The power of their platforms is allowing them to enact digital discrimination, to misdirect demand, ban creators and throttle supply. As discussed, Google, as the owner of YouTube, has the ability to manipulate whether your new video attracts ad revenue, appears in the trending section, sends out notifications to subscribers, or appears in search results. They can therefore load the dice to favour content providers they like and discriminate against those they do not. Content creators have seen their ad revenue plummet overnight due to a change in Google's algorithms, or worse, their channel blocked. First it was conservative creators, then other more politically centrist creators were targeted. Often the subjects of the videos were non-controversial, which meant that the creators themselves were being targeted. No warning, just an immediate drop in your primary income of around 90 per cent. This has seen many content creators have to leave the platform and seek more traditional forms of employment, which is disappointing. The argument that these platforms are private companies and therefore can do what they want is valid, especially when they offer their services for free, but never before have we seen a situation where a single private company effectively owns the entire global marketplace. The competing platforms have such little traction and such a small consumer base that they cannot replace the revenue that Google has taken. Therefore Google, rather than the market, is ultimately in control of who is successful. Either market forces need to offer alternatives for those blacklisted, or intervention needs to happen to allow creators of content to earn revenue without discrimination and connect with consumers fairly. Equality of opportunity should be paramount. You might not like what I say, but as long as others do, and I'm not breaking laws by calling for violence or the oppression of others, then let the free market of ideas operate.

Small Companies, Big Markets.

A future that contains a few titanic platforms that enable millions of small creators to reach a global marketplace seems likely, offering plenty of opportunities for small, entrepreneurial companies that focus on specialist niches. The PAL supply chain will enable the customer-facing design and delivery process to become more personalised and local, as these small, entrepreneurial incubator companies will increasingly use robotics and 3D printing to create bespoke items for a market hungry for something unique. When home 3D printing crosses the chasm from innovators to adopters we will see an explosion in people designing products that can be printed out at home. No need to manufacture, store and ship yourself, just create a schematic of the product that can be downloaded and printed at home. Already web-based marketplaces such as 3DShook.com exist that allow people to display and sell their 3D-printed designs online, creating a hybrid of producer and consumer – the prosumer. New 3D-printing capabilities such as CLIP will help small companies produce bespoke products and reduce the time to market.

The days of a single employer creating tens of thousands of manufacturing jobs in one place are gone. Machines now make what these people used to make. We need to stoke our entrepreneurial fires, get designing and innovating again, and create the opportunity for new manufacturing start-ups to flourish using robotics and other automation methods. To see the potential, one only need look to the manufacturing powerhouse that is Germany. Germany was the third largest exporter in 2015, with over $1.3 trillion in exports, just behind the US at $1.5 trillion. Known mostly for manufacturing giants such as Volkswagen, Daimler, Siemens and BASF, manufacturing represents about a quarter of German GDP, roughly double the share in the US or the UK. However, it's not just the big companies that are responsible for this growth: approximately 25 per cent of Germany's exports come from over 1,300 mid-size businesses that well-known German businessman and author Hermann Simon calls their 'Hidden Champions'.[417] According to Simon, 48 per cent of the world's small-to-medium sized enterprises (SMEs) are based in Germany, which given that the country only has around 1.1 per cent of the world population is astounding. How have they done this? Well, according to Simon, it's through developing the skills locally, alignment with academia for research and development, and the state providing attractive tax policies. For example, the clockmaking industry in the Black Forest, with its highly developed, precise mechanical competencies, has reapplied these skills to the manufacture of surgical equipment and other medical technologies, creating around 450 companies dedicated to MedTech. Simon also cites the German system of apprenticeship, which combines practical and theoretical training in non-academic trades as a key factor. He found that these enterprises invest 50 per cent more in vocational training than the average German company, and benefited from a tax policy designed to support smaller companies. Finally, many Hidden Champions maintained their success by keeping their focus narrow, specialising in being the best at what they do and then finding a global market for their wares.

As Germany's Hidden Champions show, there is a case for closer alignment between education institutions and entrepreneurial ventures such as new start-ups, or even 'Project X' (skunk-works) divisions of larger companies. The US, for example, could insist that any company that takes advantage of the preferential tax rate to repatriate cash uses some of it to create these innovation hubs. This collaboration is an idea that many are adopting. Apple, for example, is targeting its new innovation fund and some of its repatriated cash on advanced manufacturing, the production of high-value-added products in sectors like technology, aerospace, automobiles, sustainable energy and medical equipment. Robotics and human augmentation is a growing field for the military, and 3D printing is set to disrupt the whole aerospace and defence (A&D) supply chain with companies like GE spending billions on this new technology.

A double benefit would be if these new innovation hubs were created in the depressed former manufacturing areas such as the north east of England and the Rust Belt towns in the US. Affordable property, especially disused mills, factories and warehouses, could make unique and affordable innovation workspaces and apartments for the new entrepreneurs and knowledge workers. As primary urban locations become increasingly unaffordable, telepresence capabilities improve, and transport becomes autonomous and cheap, the restrictions around workforce location disappear, making these areas both viable and attractive. The refurbishment and redevelopment of these old buildings will also create numerous employment opportunities for builders, designers, plumbers, electricians, painters and decorators, stimulating employment in those areas. Then, once the young blood arrives in these previously depressed locations, then the service culture needed to support them will flourish as well, in fields ranging from retail, coffee shops, bars and restaurants to gyms and health clubs. Jobs create jobs.

To meet the demand, centres of excellence could be established around the service industry, retraining those who were previously involved in the industrial world, transforming them from uninspired life-support systems for their hands, to motivated service professionals. As the march of automation progresses, service providers will demand higher skills and more passion from their employees and pay a premium for those that have them. The expanse of free time will also create a boom in industries that are based around leisure, and in the provision of care throughout every stage of a person's life, from providing essentials to pampering. In a machine world, those that can offer real human-to-human interaction will be valued. The division of labour will continue, with 'cash-rich-but-time-poor' people increasingly outsourcing tasks such as DIY, painting and decorating, cleaning, gardening and other odd jobs to others. Jobs that cannot easily be automated away. This means that activities that used to only attract those with limited skills will suddenly become more competitive, and as a result the quality of services will rise as people compete to offer more personalised services.

Governments should therefore encourage tech companies to develop their R&D centres in these cities, creating an entrepreneurial environment that attracts global talent interested in making things again. These could be focused on robotics, engineering, design and innovation, and could be linked to the universities in the area, creating an influx of students attracted by the opportunity of vocational learning. Partnerships between universities and manufacturers could help create the skill pool of the sixth wave, as well as undertake R&D projects on behalf of the companies who sponsor the activities. Some have already seen this opportunity. For example, in the UK the online grocery retailer Ocado is currently partnering with several universities in developing the advanced algorithms and haptic robotic capabilities to power its next-generation warehouse.

Education for Everyone

Training and education has also been experiencing a transition due to the rise of digital technologies, and this trend will continue, moving students away from the campus and into the home. This move will be embraced by many, as the usefulness of universities is expiring, producing graduates with limited useful skills, unrealistic expectations and massive debts. As we will explore, people are also becoming disenfranchised with the infusion of political ideology into many universities, which may serve to make people feel morally superior but does little to educate or turn them into useful employees. In response, the rise of massive open online courses (MOOCs) enables people to learn whatever subjects they want, all from the comfort of their own home. The transition to digital learning platforms is necessary, for we need to change the way we educate. The industrial age required a mass of people to work in the factories and offices, and as a result we developed a curriculum and style of teaching designed around a series of core topics. Mass education for a mass-production world. Now production is being replaced by customisation, and automation means that to compete people need more than basic skills in a few core concepts. We therefore need to adapt our education system, enabling more personalisation and a wider choice of subjects for people to learn. This frees students from being limited in their subject choices by their school qualifications, enabling them to explore, understand and become qualified in subjects that they are passionate about.

An explosion in demand for specialist subject-matter experts and content creators has already arisen, and numerous new online institutions and centres of learning have developed, such as the Khan Academy, FutureLearn and Udacity, enabling a whole new group of people to educate themselves and learn new skills. It is providing a way for people to rapidly learn the skills of the new wave, and for companies to identify new talent. For example, Andrew Ng, ex-Chief Scientist of Chinese Internet company Baidu and the creator of the deep-learning Google Brain project, has developed a series of machine-learning courses on Coursera, an online education platform of which Ng is the co-founder and chairman. Interest in this course is especially high as he stated that he will offer internships at his new AI company, Landing.AI, for those who complete the relevant modules of his MOOC. This kind of development is great news for those with the drive, discipline and intellect – and time – to undertake and pass these courses. They enable people to craft their own personalised education path, not one pre-defined by institutions or the state. The use of MOOCs will expand and be developed in niche and highly specialised areas that are both credible and provide a gateway into the new and lucrative industries of the sixth wave.

As MOOCs become more established, people will develop more unique and interesting courses and more visual ways for people to experience learning, such as using augmented and virtual reality. Imagine travelling to the Scottish border and putting on a headset that instantly presents you with a virtual recreation of Hadrian's Wall, or walking around the ruins of Stonehenge and see the buried 'superhenge' rise from the ground around you. Or standing in Bosworth Field in the 15th century, in the thick of the battle between the houses of York and Lancaster. Now imagine recreating ancient Rome and Pompeii; the construction of the Pyramids, the Great Wall of China or the Aztec or Mayan civilisations. Imagine the new ways we can bring history to life, explore the natural world, discover the microscopic and explain the wonders of the universe to a wide-eyed audience. Technologies like these will breathe new life into professions such as historians, geologists, archaeologists and astronomers, enabling them to work with graphic designers, VR and AR program developers, and narrators in order to create compelling visual experiences for students and tourists.

A Tale of Two Mindsets

The question posed earlier was whether we need a job, or an income? I would suggest that the answer is that once we've provided for the basics of survival, what most people desire is a telos: a reason to live a good and productive life. However, as the Gallup survey found, a good job is what most people want in order to provide that. So, what happens when good jobs are not available, and machines do most of the lifting and thinking? The first divide will be between those with the mindset to make something, to engage physically, to help others, to create and collaborate, versus those who are content to spend their lives wallowing in the bounty that this technology will increasingly provide. The stoic Roman emperor Marcus Aurelius wrote in *Meditations* that; *The universe is change; our life is what our thoughts make it.* This is as true now as it was two thousand years ago, only now more people have the opportunity to act on their thoughts, being both unconstrained by societal barriers and able to directly access the means to education, production and the market. The most powerful tool in everyone's arsenal right now is their mindset. The door is unlocked; whether you open it is up to you. You can use your time to learn engineering, quantum mechanics or even just enhance your basic literacy skills; or you can play games, surf social media and watch endless prank videos. There will be plenty of creative ways to use all of this technological bounty to provide ways to earn both a living and a purpose. A combination of a basic support mechanism and access to technology can free people from feeling trapped in the hamster wheel of soul-destroying commutes to a job they hate, and instead offer the opportunity to create much more fulfilling and creative jobs that are more customer-centric and less administrative. Conversely, a life where work does not consume every moment of every day may lead to an explosion of creativity, for since the days of Plato, most great works of literature have been produced by those who were free from the bind of having to work to survive.

The recalibration measures contained throughout this economics section are therefore primarily to ensure that we survive this current wave economically intact, and better prepared for what comes next. This is important, for this will, in my opinion, be the last wave of capitalism in its current form. When this wave enters its autumn period in the late 2030s, the automation war will be in full flow, and the world Keynes forecast for his grandchildren will finally be upon us, disrupting the social construct of paid employment being an essential and most time-consuming component of our lives. The transition will be so significant that more radical solutions than those discussed here will be needed. It is therefore essential that we prepare for this point by providing the foundations needed to ensure society doesn't just survive but thrives. But we are not there yet. There is every reason to believe that before this time we could have another golden age, a digital Belle Époque. But like the first industrial revolution, it requires a society designed to enable it to happen. And there is every reason to believe that the West may not be the society that succeeds, and that, like the empires of old, it may all come crashing down, destroyed from within. We may need another Glorious Revolution in order for it to survive.

SIXTH-WAVE
SOCIETY

23

ALL EMPIRES FALL

A nation is born stoic, and dies epicurean.
Will Durant

As the innovations of the sixth wave move from the initially deceptive experiments, they are now to become ubiquitous parts of our everyday lives, they have the potential to transform the world around us. Advancements in renewable energy generation and storage will continue to reduce the price of energy and our dependence on fossil fuels. The personal, automated and local supply chain will become a reality, reducing costs, overproduction and eliminating waste while increasing choice and responsiveness. As 3D printing capabilities advance and more materials are able to be used, companies will both change the way objects are built and print off components and spare parts on demand. Virtual and augmented reality will cross the chasm into the mainstream, enabling the creation of virtual worlds and an overlay of a digital world on top of the real one. The embedding of intelligence into sensors and devices that monitor, record and analyse everything will continue, peeling back the layers of our world to discover ever-increasing opportunities to tweak and improve the ways things are done. Transportation will increasingly become both electric and autonomous, reducing the cost of movement and changing the paradigm from vehicle ownership to on-demand access, freeing up urban and workplace parking spaces for other means. Autonomous vehicles will begin to communicate with each other and to other smart objects such as traffic lights, combining to reduce urban traffic congestion, reducing commute times. Urban, indoor vertical farms and hydroponic systems will become commonplace, able to produce a whole range of food with improved yields and taste, but greatly reduced labour, water and chemicals that keep food prices low. The butchering of livestock for meat will begin to reduce, replaced by advancements in the process of growing meat from cells in automated factories. The reduction of livestock will help reduce methane levels, as well as the amount of water consumption and land utilisation. Knowledge will continue to become increasingly free and on-demand, changing the education system and reducing the number of people who place themselves in great debt to learn skills that may be irrelevant when they graduate. AI, gene therapy and quantum computing will continue to be used to solve healthcare issues and develop pharmaceutical treatments for illnesses that currently blight the lives of millions. Health trackers will monitor your well-being on an ongoing basis, proactively picking up issues and thereby reducing the instances of fatalities and expensive surgeries and treatments. Advancements in robotics and brain-computer interfaces will start to enable disabled people to utilise prosthetic limbs, and even use thoughts to communicate with various technological systems. Advancements in gene sequencing and 3D printing of biological materials will enable scientists to reproduce working organs based on a patient's own DNA, improving survival of transplants and eliminating the need for rejection drugs. The billions invested in genetic engineering will also start to reap rewards, helping to eliminate disabilities and genetic disorders such as Down's syndrome, and, perhaps most controversially, ageing.

The sheer wonder of all of this technological bounty is primed to transition the world we live in. Yet if we have learnt one thing it's that technology does not exist in a vacuum; all decisions have consequences and all actions have reactions. This technological bounty will create a vast array of new ways to earn a living, from VR world-builders to robot technicians, blockchain developers and genetic scientists, while others will still find a strong market for their existing skills. However, there will be many casualties. Those that rely on routine, relatively repetitive jobs will see this income opportunity disappear, and many will lack the skills needed to compete for the new jobs. Some may not be welcome. White-collar, middle-aged professionals will also be hit hard as 20th-century jobs such as accountancy, financial services, stock trading, journalism, contract analysis, radiology, IT support, and nearly all supervisory and management roles are automated away. Machines will increasingly become able to perform most basic tasks, finishing off the last of the mass-employment opportunities. Conversely, there will be increased demand for human well-being roles such as personal trainers, sports and massage therapists, and psychologists. The last profession might be needed most of all, for the transition from a world of labour to one of leisure will not be easy, and there is a real potential that we may lose many people along the way.

The collapse of the sixth wave is predicted around 2045–2050, and when it does collapse it will probably represent the end of the capitalist era that Schumpeter and Marx predicted, for the combination of automation, artificial intelligence and genetics will have both resolved scarcity and replaced the labour of humans. Consumer choice will be the new battleground. Slaves will once again toil on behalf of elites who spend their lives debating, philosophising and basking in the glow of their superiority; only these slaves will be silicon-based, not carbon. For many this is the utopia they dream of, a *Star Trek* future of automated socialism where machines do all the work, their outputs are virtually free, everyone is equal, and no one goes without. But is this likely to be the case? What happens when gainful employment is unavailable for most people? What happens if the bounty from this production is concentrated into the hands of a few? What happens when a people lose their cultural linkages to each other? What happens when the masses lose any sense of meaning from life? We don't need to use our imagination. We already know, because it's already happened: Rome, 2nd century BC. This is how republics fall.

Betrayal

For most of Rome's history as a republic, its methods of governance and control worked well for most of its people, most of the time. Rome was a city state of over 300,000 citizens who had a collective bond of citizenship and a feeling of shared responsibility, a democratic republic in both spirit and law, whose values included freedom of speech and freedom of religion.[418] The citizens of Rome would gather together in assemblies to pass legislations, elect magistrates and higher-ranking state officers, and give rulings in legal cases. Power was divided between the different classes and offices, theoretically ensuring that no one sector of society could hold power over the rest. Although effectively an oligarchy, the culture of Rome was rich and pervasive, visible throughout the city and at every level of society, from those at the bottom through to the upper classes that had a deep sense of noblesse oblige. The belief in Stoicism and its premises of self-control, fortitude and personal responsibility helped foster in people a sense of being part of something bigger than just themselves, and this patriotism towards Rome created a shared sense of destiny that tied the citizen soldiers to the elites. As the author G. K. Chesterton wrote, *Men did not love Rome because she was great. She was great because they had loved her.*[419] This worked well for a long time, but as Rome expanded, its success and expansion began to undermine the constitutional pillars that made the republic's success possible. Once the citizens realised that their patriotism and personal sacrifices were being exploited by the wealthy, and the things they valued such as Roman citizenship suddenly became available to a much wider group of people who didn't have such feelings of loyalty, then they felt betrayed and the republic started to rot from the inside out.

The Roman Republic had doubled in size in a single generation, swollen by the bravery and actions of Rome's veteran army of citizen soldiers. To be a citizen soldier required a degree of wealth, for in order to enlist in the army you had to be able to buy your own equipment; your own armour, helmet, shield, *pilum* (javelin) and *gladius* (sword). Owning and wearing these was a mark of great pride for a Roman, for it not only showed your devotion to the republic, but also the fact that you could afford to sign up. These citizen soldiers underwent fierce and intensive military training in order to instil discipline, group morale and cohesion that would bind the men together in effective fighting units, able to maintain order and loyalty to one another and to Rome during even the most ferocious of battles. And battle these legionnaires did, crushing the Carthaginian Empire in the Punic Wars, regaining the Spanish territories and gaining a foothold in North Africa in what is now Tunisia. The Roman legions were also fighting the Macedonians and the Seleucids to take total control of Greece, and captured the whole of Northern Italy from the Gauls. Roman soldiers expected to be part of the legion for as long as a campaign lasted, which was OK when the battles were in Italy, but when they were in North

Africa and Spain this meant that they could be away for years. As a result, they had to leave their families and their farms to travel to far-flung lands in service to Rome. Rather than returning home ladened with riches and revered as heroes, the legionnaires instead found a different Rome to the one they remembered. They also found that they had been betrayed. These vaunted legionnaires, who had invested time and money in training and equipment, and their blood, sweat and tears for the glory of Rome, realised that this sacrifice was not only just for the benefit of the wealthy; it was also to their own detriment.

As in all pre-industrial societies, in ancient Rome there was a very strong relationship between wealth and land. There were three types of land: private land, common pasture and public land, and the amount of land a single person could own was controlled through Agrarian Laws. By the 2nd century BC, however, wealthy landowners began to ignore these laws, exploiting the system by inventing false identities so they could fraudulently rent additional areas of land that they then absorbed into their vast estates. Acquiring land was a pointless endeavour unless the landowner had a way to plough the soil and seed, grow and harvest crops, and unlike private citizens the wealthy were not known for getting their hands dirty. What they needed was a workforce, one that was inexpensive to own and maintain. And as luck would have it, that's exactly what the exploits of the citizen soldiers provided. Slaves. Lots of them. The wealthy landowners, sat safely in Rome, miles from where its armies were fighting heroically, rushed to obtain tranches of the newly conquered lands. Once obtained, they used them to create super-farms that were worked by slave labour comprised of the conquered people from the army's victorious military campaigns.

While the citizen soldiers had been away fighting, their farm buildings were occupied by their wives and children, but without someone to work the land the fields lay fallow, and without a crop to sell the family often fell into debt. The legionnaires came back from their battles to find that their smallholdings were now competing against slave-operated mega-farms, and that inflation had drastically reduced the value of any war loot they possessed. As a result, they went bankrupt, having to sell their farms to the wealthy landowners simply to clear their debts. The wealthy greedily absorbed the soldiers' farms into their fast-growing aristocratic estates, paying the minimum possible for them. The engines that powered Rome therefore changed from the labour of free men, to the acquisition and exploitation of capital in the form of land and slaves. The very spoils that the legionnaires had fought to acquire for Rome had replaced them, and the value of their labour made economically worthless.

Crushed by the actions of the super-rich upper classes, this vital sector of Roman society, its propertied, smallholder middle class, had little choice but to take their families and head for the city to look for work. There was no work in the countryside, for why do estate owners need paid labour when there is a surplus of slaves to choose from? In the city they found no full-time work, but at best a series of odd jobs, selling their labour on a daily basis to earn enough money for their family to survive. To make things worse, as citizens could only serve in the military if they held property, the now-homeless ex-soldiers could not even rejoin the legions. Proud men, legionnaires who had fought for the glory of Rome, were now reduced to begging for any scraps of paid work. As a result, Rome's middle class withered and died, becoming instead a group of angry, purposeless, poverty-stricken, disenfranchised people. They transformed into the most dreaded of all urban cohorts of antiquity – the mob.

The Senate and those with position and wealth had betrayed the free citizens of Rome, stealing public lands and taking away their homes, jobs and incomes. They showed a complete lack of concern for people who had spent their savings and risked their lives for the protection and expansion of Rome. Worse, they even took away the value of their citizenship as they powerlessly watched the republic they loved swell with migrants from the conquered lands, people who had no cultural ties to Rome. Becoming a soldier was no longer a prestigious – or wise – venture, and the ranks of the Roman legions were becoming filled not with citizens with Rome in their hearts, but foreign mercenaries from the conquered lands. What would have been deemed the middle class had all but vanished, creating a widening gulf between rich and poor. Disillusioned, unemployed and angry, these disenfranchised citizens; patriotic, loyal people who had been cast aside for money by those who were already rich, found that their Roman dream had been proven to be an illusion. What had once been a tight-knit society of ethnic kinship, a city state of people united against the rest of the world, had been transformed into a highly populated but loosely bound society of competing identities tied together via imperial domination and money. The term 'Roman' eventually came to mean whatever the wealthy said it meant, and without the cultural ties that kept the rich and poor together out of a sense of duty and common destiny, the Romans soon turned on one another.

The Rise of the Populists

The sheer number of purposeless, poor plebeians created a moral and structural weakness in the heart of Roman society. People no longer believed that the state worked for them, and this growing resentment threatened the legitimacy of the republic. The elites did not care because it did not affect them. They lived in vast estates away from the chaos of Roman suburbs, becoming increasingly rich off the proceeds of the stolen lands and the bounty that flowed in from the military campaigns. The citizens, especially ex-legionnaires, were desperate to hear from any powerful voice that recognised their plight and provided hope for the future. That voice was provided by Tiberius Gracchus.

Tiberius Gracchus was already well known to these citizen soldiers as a hero; a noble plebeian and stoic who had also proven himself to be a valiant and brave soldier and leader, the first over the walls of Carthage when it fell. He had also saved 20,000 soldiers from death or slavery by signing a peace treaty with the Numantines, following the defeat of the Roman legions commanded by Gaius Mancinus. Whereas the Senate and elites in Rome saw Gracchus signing of the treaty as a sign of weakness, the soldiers in Mancinus' legions recognised that Tiberius had saved their lives. As Tiberius returned home to Rome expecting to be punished by the Senate, he came to experience the power of populism, welcomed as a hero by the families of the 20,000 men he had saved, who cheered as he rode into Rome and unanimously voted to save him. During his return, Tiberius had not failed to notice the great injustices that had befallen his legionnaires, for the inequalities that now existed between the elites and the citizens were hard to miss. He decided to do something about it.

After being elected Tribune of the Plebeians in 133 BC, Tiberius spoke directly to the assembled crowd at the Rostra: *The wild beasts that roam over Italy have every one of them a cave or lair to lurk in; but the men who fight and die for Italy enjoy the common air and light, indeed, but nothing else; houseless and homeless they wander about with their wives and children... they fight and die to support others in wealth and luxury, and though they are styled masters of the world, they have not a single clod of earth that is their own.*[420] Aware that the Senate wouldn't approve his reforms, he circumvented them altogether and went straight to the Popular Assembly to call for a return to the ancient Agrarian Laws that prevented any citizen from owning more than five hundred acres, demanding that the fraudulently acquired public lands were redistributed to the soldiers and their families, as well as a fair distribution of any newly conquered lands. However, political lobbying behind the scenes by powerful land-owning members of the Senate, convinced one of the Tribunes, Marcus Octavius, to veto Gracchus' bill (*Lex Agraria*), denying it from ever being read. This unprecedented event was a clear misuse of authority, for a Tribune existed to defend the people not exploit them, their power of veto designed to protect Roman citizens from unfair legislation and any political or economic oppression by the Senate. Tiberius declared that Octavius had violated a basic tenet of his office, but Octavius remained resolute, and as there was no way to overturn a Tribune's veto the law was not passed. Tiberius then created a new, more punitive law, which again was vetoed to protect the elites and their lands.

In vengeance, Tiberius started using his veto against the daily ceremonies of Roman life, such as whether temples and markets should be opened, or whether the treasury could issue funds, and in effect enacted one of the earliest forms of militant action by shutting down the city. He was now a wanted man. Plus, the citizens of Rome had watched as respected people such as Tribunes used their powers not as tools to protect the poor, but as weapons in a war of vested interests. The previously unbreakable bonds between those in power and the masses had weakened, and as a result the fabric holding Roman society together started to tear. The proud republic, once united by virtue, honour, tradition, kinship and common goals, was now being exploited simply to better the lives of a few.

Worse, to further his agenda Tiberius Gracchus now started to abuse his position, using the Plebeian Assembly to call for a vote to remove Octavius from office, in effect overturning the result of the last election and passing his reforms into law. Contrary to all precedents, Tiberius won, Octavius was removed, his veto overturned, and the bill passed. In revenge, the Senate used their powers to limit the funds available to Tiberius and his reforms. He then had a stroke of good luck when, in late 133 BC, he ignored the Senate's traditional control of public finance and foreign affairs and immediately claimed the fortune and kingdom of Pergamum, a city in Anatolia whose king had died and, lacking an heir, had bequeathed them to Rome to avoid it taking them by force. Tiberius then personally assigned these funds to the land commissioners. The incensed Senate's anger only increased in 132 BC when Tiberius decided to enact another impropriety by standing for election as Tribune for a second year in a row, despite the fact that no one had been elected twice for three hundred years. He produced a highly populist manifesto, promising to shorten the term of military service, abolish the exclusive right of senators to act as jurors and extend it to other social classes, and admit allies to Roman citizenship. Tiberius used every opportunity to use his platform to speak directly to the people, operating as a skilled demagogue to complain about the fake news being spread about him by the Senate and their allies, protesting that his life and the lives of his family were in danger.

Tiberius went to the polls with the Senate now almost exclusively against him, but with the support of the common people. During voting, a senator came forward with a warning that Tiberius' life was at risk, and at the same time a scuffle broke out between supporters of both sides. Tiberius, unable to make himself heard over the noise of the crowd, pointed to his head as to indicate that his life was in danger. This signal was translated by one of his opponents as a call for a crown to be placed on his head, a message he rushed back to the Senate. Incensed, the senators and their assistants armed themselves and marched to the capitol where they set upon the crowd, killing three hundred people including Tiberius, tossing their bodies into the River Tiber. Associates of Tiberius were then identified, hunted down and either executed or exiled.

The sacred role of Tribune had been desecrated and violence and mob rule were now a part of political life. The respect people had held for the rules and for the position of office disappeared, and the elites looked down on the population not as fellow citizens, but as mere pawns, votes to be won through bribery and populist messages. Elections had become things that could be bought and sold, and the mob became a political weapon, something to be riled up with talk of resentment, reparations and revenge, rather than the previous appeals to civic pride, patriotism and public virtue.

Tiberius' younger brother, Gaius, spurred on by desire for revenge, also fought his way to the role of Tribune by garnering public support using fiery demagoguery based around injustice, sympathy and outrage at the corruption of the Senate. In an attempt to win the hearts and minds of the mob, a competition erupted between the Senate and Gaius as to whose manifesto offered the most free stuff in order to win the favour and votes of the people. As Tribune, Gaius put in place a series of populist laws designed to win over every level of Roman society, including reduction in grain prices, provision of state-provided kit for soldiers, the development of colonies outside Rome to ease overcrowding, and granting Roman citizenship to people who didn't live directly in Rome. A Gracchus was again rallying the mob with the promise of reforming the republican system, simply to garner support for his own political ambitions. And again, a Gracchus' life ended at the hands of a Senate-organised mob, keen to see their political rival gone. Gaius' body also ended up in the Tiber, only this time minus his head.

Politicians then realised that while the power of the mob was now a key political weapon, controlling them was also essential. While the actions of the Gracchus brothers highlighted how the mob could be used to great affect by the elites to achieve political aims, a decade after the death of Gaius Gracchus another revolutionary was born, Spartacus, who would come to highlight just how dangerous angry and disregarded people can become when mobilised. The Roman elite realised that to live their gilded lifestyle in peace, free from the threat of an ochlocracy emerging, they needed to keep the mob under control. They knew that to ensure peace they needed to keep the masses fed and distracted, else chaos rules. Therefore, in order to keep the population happy, laws were passed designed to give out cheap food (grain) and entertainment in order to placate the mob, rather than seeing them as worthy deciders of who gets to lead and serve in office. As described by the Roman satirical poet Juvenal; *Already long ago, from when we sold our vote to no man, the People have abdicated our duties; for the People who once upon a time handed out military command, high civil office, legions – everything, now restrains itself and anxiously hopes for just two things: bread and circuses*. Bread and circuses became the order of the day, replacing honour, virtue and Stoicism.

However, there is no going back for any democratic institution once it loses touch with the people it claims to serve, becoming infected with corruption and violence. The traditions and honour of the Roman Republic were slowly fading away and within a century, Julius Caesar would defy the Senate and lead his army across the Rubicon. The Roman Republic would fall, unable to handle the many death blows applied to her democratic foundations, and an empire would rise, led by a new breed of strong men willing to challenge the corruption and old dogmas.

The Beginning of the End

If we were to replace citizen soldiers with truck drivers and other middle- and working-class people, and conquered slaves with autonomous vehicles, robots and AI; then swap self-serving landowners with technocrats and plutocrats, the Senate with today's politicians, the Gracchus brothers with the current right- and left-wing populists, the plebeians' distrust of the Senate with the current distrust of the establishment, the influx of non-Roman citizens and the devaluing of nationhood and citizenship with the multiculturalism movement and the mass migration into Europe; and finally replace the mobs on the streets of Rome with the recent protests by Antifa and the Black Bloc – you could be talking about now rather than ancient Rome.

The story of the last years of the Roman Republic shows how easily a strong society can be undermined by the actions of a few; when people distant from the daily realities of the common folk make decisions without consideration or understanding of the consequences. It's like we have never learnt anything from history, for all of the same mistakes are being made. The people have once again become distant from the political elite, voting for populist politicians and policies because the elites have ignored the plight and wishes of the common man. The reverse is also true, with the elites and their progressive allies not willing to try to understand the populace or their needs and desires. Like the battle between the Senate and the Gracchus brothers, the democratic process has been manipulated to serve the needs of those in power, ignoring outcomes, taking actions without consultation, and making people vote again when the result doesn't go their way. Political power and corporate interests are becoming ever more entwined, and the nature of democratic institutions is under threat. The elites don't care because they don't see or feel the consequences of these actions. It didn't affect the rich then, who lived in the private estates, served by slaves, and they don't affect them now, living in their private, gated communities, their wealth managed by algorithms that bet on the performance of increasingly automated companies. As a result, because they don't see these consequences, they believe they don't exist, and pass down moral judgement on anyone who protests, declaring their concerns to be the rants of racists and xenophobes.

It shows how fragile the fabric of society is, and how easily its foundations can be undermined. When people are deprived of their income and their purpose, when wealth is concentrated into too few hands, when political institutions are manipulated to serve only those in power and become increasingly distant from those they claim to serve, when nations absorb large numbers of people who have limited cultural or emotional connection to their new home, and when the elites refuse to acknowledge the impact their decisions have on others, then things can fall apart quickly. As in Rome, we are now going through such a time. A period when a large proportion of the population feel that the virtues and principles they grew up with, ones that created kinship and a shared cultural identity, are being lost, deceptively destroyed by those in power. The elites seem to be doing all they can to undermine any forms of national or cultural roots, distorting the enlightenment principles of liberalism, reason and individualism by turning us into a multicultural mass of self-centred global consumers without common heritage or beliefs. Money, not culture, patriotism, faith, virtue or any other non-economic factor, drives their globalist agenda, and they see any displays of attachment to patriotism or the heritage and traditions of the country as something to sneer at, not cherish. Populists, on the other hand, play to these fears of marginalisation in the hope of winning favour with this ignored group, often, like the Gracchus brothers, for their own political gain. While the past cannot be taken as a prediction of the future, for it contains a mix of complex systems, relationships, ideologies and individual lives, those that forget history do so at their peril. The parallels between the last days of the Roman Republic and the current situation in the Western world are obvious to all who wish to see them. Despite over 2,000 years passing, we still have the same desires, frustrations, intellectual capabilities, personal agendas and motivations as the citizens of the Roman Republic.[136] We like to think we have evolved, but deep down we really haven't. But as we will see, for some that may soon change, and this transition will prove very challenging to our fragile democratic society.

---

[136] You only need to read the graffiti at ancient Pompeii to see how similar we actually are. From declarations of love, to insults, political slogans and simple statements such as 'Gaius was here'; they reflect a society not so different to today.

24

CRACKS IN THE FOUNDATIONS

*Clearly, a civilization that feels guilty for everything it is
and does will lack the energy and conviction to defend itself.*

Jean-François Revel

The birth of the technological revolution required the creation of the right social and economic foundations, and changes to these foundations by the use and misuse of technology might yet cause its decline. We tend to have a pro-innovation bias, when in reality not all new technological developments are positive. Most are a double-edged sword, resulting in significant social implications, some positive and others negative. Plastic was deemed a technological marvel when introduced, but now seventy years of hindsight have shown how it has polluted the oceans and negatively affected their biosphere. This two-edged aspect to technology has recently provided us with a world of personalised and constantly updated news and entertainment, while also contributing greatly to the creation of an increasingly insular world, one where people are more interested in the machine in their hand than what's going on around them. Walk the streets and people have their heads down, headsets on, looking at their phones, resulting in some countries having to adapt their infrastructure to prevent accidents. In The Netherlands, red lights that shine on the road by crossings have been implemented, due to the number of people that have walked straight into incoming traffic while looking down, not forward, distracted by their phones, while in China, dedicated 'zombie lanes' have been created specifically for pedestrians who are looking at their phone not ahead. Take a trip on public transport and you'll see everyone sat with earphones in, looking at their own personal window into their own personalised view of the world. Go into most houses and you see the family in different rooms, looking at different devices, where once they would be gathered around a single TV or radio. Even if they are in the same space physically, mentally they're not. Everyone is developing their own little individual view of the world, and while this has opened up an ecosphere of individual experiences, it has started to break down many of the foundations upon which Western society is built. We're reducing the number of shared experiences we have and replacing them with purely individual ones.

The Constantly-On Generation

As the father of two boys I have watched how technology consumes pretty much every waking moment of their lives; with the constant playing of online games with friends from around the world, people they have never physically met, and whose real-world names they do not know, only their avatar. When not engaged in online gaming, other video and communications platforms such as YouTube and Facebook grab their attention. The machine is always there for you, creating people with increasingly limited attention spans and an inability to entertain themselves. The different time zones involved in this global online community means that waking hours are becoming increasingly disrupted, as there is always something to watch and always someone to play with. Recent studies have highlighted that just spending one hour a day on social media can disrupt sleep patterns,[421] which, combined with the 24/7 availability of entertainment, means that people are increasingly sleep-deprived. Children are waking up for school like zombies, having laid in bed looking at their phone or tablet until the early hours. My own children are no exception, so I'm not speaking from any position of moral authority, and it worries me greatly.

Social media in particular has been shown to be increasingly addictive, with people experiencing a release of endorphins when one of their posts gets likes or positive reactions, driving reward-based behaviour that activates the brain's dopamine pathways. Social media has created an emotional minefield for those living through the insecure teenage years, where people constantly seek acceptance and approval from peers and falling into depression when they feel that their lives do not compare. This appears to be especially true for girls.[422] Often, they are competing against an impossible ideal, as people increasingly post overinflated statements and photoshopped images that do not reflect reality.

As MIT psychologist Sherry Turkle identified, all this communication is not leading to connection. Something is getting lost along the way, and psychology experts have surmised it's a feeling of closeness or comfort.[423] Drawn by the illusion of companionship without the demands of intimacy, we confuse postings and online sharing with authentic communication. It's proving to be a poor substitution. A 2016 study by the University of Pittsburgh of the social media habits of 1,787 young adults aged between nineteen and thirty-two found a staggering link between websites like Facebook and users' mental health: screen time plus sleep deprivation resulted in greater levels of depression. *We were surprised with what we found. We had expected a U-shaped curve, with a higher risk of depression being correlated with no social media use at all or excessive use. But instead what we found was a straight line. More social media use was associated with more depression in a linear fashion.*[424] The jump has been especially noticeable in young girls, with 19.5 per cent stating that they experienced a serious depressive episode.[425] There has also been a steady rise in suicide rates since 2000, after fifteen years of falling,[426] most notably since the rise of smartphones. For example, the suicide rate for US girls aged thirteen to eighteen shot up by 65 per cent between 2010 and 2015, and in 2015 the rate in US girls aged between fifteen and nineteen reached a forty-year high of one in every 20,000.[427] A large-scale US study on fatal injury data between 1999 and 2015 revealed that the percentage of girls who said they'd experienced symptoms of severe depression had increased by 58 per cent during that time frame. You can see how social media can amplify feelings of rejection. In the past, teenagers might find out that they were not invited to a party when they were back at school – now they can see a livestream of the party they were not invited to in real time. Half the teens who admitted that they spent at least five hours a day on a smartphone, laptop or tablet said they had also contemplated, planned or attempted suicide at least once, compared with 28 per cent of those who said they spent less than an hour a day on a device. As the author of the report states, there are two possible explanations here: either depressed and suicidal people are spending a lot of time on smartphones, or smartphone-based social media use is making people depressed and suicidal. She believes the latter: *depression causing online time doesn't explain why depression increased so suddenly after 2012... Under that scenario, more teens became depressed for an unknown reason and then started buying smartphones – an idea that defies logic.*[428] What's becoming really alarming is that the age at which kids get smartphones is falling every year, dropping from twelve years in 2012, to 10.3 years in 2016.

As well as depressing users and turning them into addicts, this technology is contributing to a downward spiral in their ability to concentrate, so-called 'continuous partial attention', where their ability to focus becomes severely limited by the multitude of distractions bombarding them. Algorithms are becoming incredibly sophisticated in their ability to place links to videos, advertisements and articles that are almost certainly going to grab your increasingly limited attention.[137] While the Internet does provide access to the entirety of human knowledge, for many the sheer volume and ease of access is resulting in a shallowness to its study, creating an environment of intellectual laziness. People are becoming insatiable for information and answers, but increasingly lack the ability to store this information and critically analyse and question what they read. Time is spent consuming information without any analysis of the quality of what is processed, nor whether anything is stored in anything but the very shortest of short-term memories. There's also a decreasing value to knowledge when everything can be Googled in an instant. What use is your industrial education, your knowledge of historical facts or advanced algebra when I can ask Alexa

---

[137] It's something I am constantly aware of, for when researching I often find that I have been drawn down a whole new rabbit hole incredibly easily and have wasted significant time reading content that was not part of my original mission, often presented in sidebars and as clickbait, but which distracted me from my original aims. None of this information added anything, nor was it remembered beyond the time taken to read it. I sense I am far from alone in this. My son often complains about going to revise a topic, then finding two hours later that he has spent the time reading articles or watching videos completely unrelated to what he set out to do.

a question and she tells me the answer immediately? The answer is, of course, that while she tells you the answer, she doesn't tell you how she got to the answer. Information is provided instantly, without having to even check the source. Having greater access to a wider breadth of knowledge does not therefore mean people are more knowledgeable, and access to data does not equate to greater wisdom. Which is the danger, for as AI advances and the machines get smarter, humans are getting measurably dumber. Throughout the majority of the 20th century human IQs increased due to environmental factors, something known as the Flynn effect, and based around having to remember increased levels of information. Now, while Google's Deepmind team are using IQ tests to train neural networks to learn abstract reasoning and complete complex puzzles, Norwegian scientists have identified that the average human IQ is decreasing by a rate of seven IQ points per generation.[429] Soon, the IQ of a machine will outstrip that of an average human.

The Silicon Valley developers who developed these tools are well aware of the danger. They know all about people's weakness for instant gratification, propensity for distraction and addiction to constant dopamine hits, because they've programmed the systems to exploit these very opportunities. An internal Facebook report leaked in 2017, for example, revealed that the company can identify when teens feel 'insecure', 'worthless' and 'need a confidence boost'. This enables Facebook's algorithms to decide what buttons to push and what messages, news and adverts to promote to that person. Tristan Harris, a former product philosopher at Google, calls this the 'attention economy'. He states that people who are struggling to break an addiction to their smartphones should realise that they are competing against *a thousand people on the other side of the screen whose job is to break down whatever responsibility I can maintain*. In short, he is declaring that we have lost control of our relationship with technology because the technology has been designed specifically to control our impulses and behaviours, kicking off what he calls a *race to the bottom of the brain stem*. We are also losing control of the decision around whether what we are being told is the truth. The provision of information on request, be that a click or a vocal request, relies heavily on the machine's selection of source material, and is therefore open to manipulation in order to provide a false narrative, or to ensure groupthink and compliance. Think we've seen fake news so far? Imagine the potential once AI gets involved. We've already seen videos with AI-manipulated images of political leaders voicing words they did not say. What about when brain-computer interfaces (BCIs) become commonplace? When information can be uploaded – and, scarily, downloaded? While I don't expect this to become mainstream in the next decade, it is a very real possibility within the next twenty years. We are just human guinea pigs in one big social experiment and no one knows the long-term effects this will have.

Harris is rallying product designers to adopt a 'Hippocratic oath' for software that specifically restricts the practice of 'exposing people's psychological vulnerabilities' and restores 'agency' to users. A move back to soft technological determinism rather than hard. He's not the only Silicon Valley voice expressing concern. Chamath Palihapitiya, former Vice President for Growth at Facebook, said that the platform was creating a social atmosphere of *no civil discourse, no cooperation, misinformation, [and] mistruth... This is a global problem. It is eroding the core foundations of how people behave by and between each other.* He says he tries to use Facebook as little as possible, and that his children *aren't allowed to use that shit.*[430] Which is interesting given that Facebook is pushing this 'shit' to younger and younger people, currently targeting six- to twelve-year-olds with its new Messenger Kids app.[431] Facebook's own founding president, Sean Parker, admitted that they knew they were creating something addictive, something that exploited 'a vulnerability in human psychology'. *It literally changes your relationship with society, with each other. It probably interferes with productivity in weird ways. God only knows what it's doing to our children's brains.*[432] Actually, we already know. It's making them depressed, dependent and dumb.

The Three 'D's

The problem with technology is that it does not help us to provide an answer as to 'why' we should do things; nor does it define 'what' we should do. It is only the 'how', and as such fails to provide purpose to people who seek one. Technology is not teleology. And this is important, because people are becoming increasingly addicted to technology without understanding why they are addicted; spending vast amounts of time on something that is adding little value to their lives. It fills our days, but it does not fill our souls. When something demands your constant attention, but leaves you feeling hollow afterwards, then it's a sign of a dysfunctional relationship. But it is a relationship that people are devoting more and more time to, often to the detriment of real human ones. How often do you wake up and immediately check your phone before checking on the well-being of your partner? You're not alone. User studies have found that a fifth of those who took part would find it harder to be without their phone for a week than their partner, and that women spend an average of twelve hours more a week on their phones than conversing with a loved one.[433] As an example of the impact this technology is having on our social lives, a 2017 study by the University of Chicago showed that the mere presence of smartphones damages cognitive capacity – even when the device is turned off.[434] Basically, knowing the phone is there means people are distracted, wondering about what they are missing out on. It even has a name – FoMO, the Fear of Missing Out. People are constantly asking themselves questions such as: *Is it OK to shut off my phone when I leave work? Can I ignore my emails for half a day while I work on something important? What happens if I don't reply to an email / message / tweet / Facebook message? What if a friend posts something on Facebook and I haven't liked it?* Researchers also found that people become stressed, angry and panicked if they are separated from their phones. Try confiscating a teenager's phone and other electronic devices for a week and see how they react. They won't give them up easily, and they will suffer withdrawal symptoms, frustration, bouts of FoMO, and won't know what to do with their hands. If that's not a sign of an addiction, I don't know what is. And those responsible know this; as Palihapitiya states: *the short-term dopamine-driven feedback loops we've created are destroying how society works.* Hence why he doesn't let his kids use what he helped create.

Watching my two sons grow up with technology, especially social media and the transformation of gaming from a single-user experience to a social platform, has at times been a worrying experience, and I regret not doing more to curtail its influence. When I grew up – and as far as I knew, this was the same for pretty much every generation before me as well – children played outside. With actual, physical friends. Without supervision. As a Gen Xer, even though we were the first era to experience any form of electronic home entertainment, we still spent our time riding bikes, playing football, climbing trees and making dens. Parental supervision meant making sure you were back for dinner. That was it. Yet when these sons and daughters of baby boomers had children, the Internet had arrived, opening a window to whole new experiences and the chance to engage with people on the other side of the world. Suddenly your friend base exploded, all from the comfort of your bedroom. Now technology is increasingly the babysitter, and their relationships are with people online, not outside. It's not exclusively true – some still manage a mix – but it's becoming the case that people connect electronically more than physically. And it's making them ill.

My eldest son spent an entire year almost entirely in his bedroom, moving primarily from his bed to his chair where he spent his time online playing games and chatting with friends, only leaving his room to get something to eat. By his own admission, this was not a good time for him mentally or physically. Now he is at university and socialising with people his own age, in the real world, not the virtual one, and the change in his mindset has been astonishing in such a short period. As he openly states, he's never felt better. A solitary life indoors is not good for the health of the individual. Young people are supposed to be outdoor dogs, expending energy and having fun, not indoor cats sitting in solitary confinement watching the world from their phones or PC screens. It's unprecedented behaviour and it is really not good for our physical or our mental well-being. Scientists already know that if the neural pathways that control our social and imaginative capabilities aren't developed during the early years, then it is difficult to revitalise them. This means that a whole generation could grow up without the mental ability to make their own fun, invent their own games and create real friendships – all because of their addiction to technology.

The big three issues of the current generation are therefore what I call the three 'D's – Depression, vitamin D deficiency and Diabetes. As mentioned, depression is reaching epidemic rates, especially in the West and especially for adolescents, increasing by 47 per cent for boys and 65 per cent for girls in just five years. According to the World Health Authority, depression is now the number one cause of ill-health and disability, with 300 million diagnosed sufferers and another 260 million with other anxiety disorders.[435] It does not help that we are introducing our children to devices that are proven to make them unhappy and suicidal, and doing so at a younger and younger age. Males are four times more likely to commit suicide than females, due in part to the constant propaganda and attacks on traditional gender roles and societal norms, leaving many young men feeling confused and directionless, being made to question their every thought and action. Suicide in young men had been declining since the early '80s but has risen steadily since the financial crash and the introduction of the smartphone and social media. Coincidence? I doubt it. The 24/7 onslaught of digital information means that they are constantly 'on', with no downtime to just chill and be teenagers. Constantly being entertained, constantly told what to think, not how to think. It's all noise and no direction. It must be so hard to switch off; to be allowed to develop your own identity without judgement.

This indoor-cat existence is also creating a resurgence of diseases last seen in the days of Victorian slums and dark, satanic mills. Doctors are seeing an explosion in cases of the 'English disease', rickets, due to people not going outside and getting any exposure to the sun on their skin. This results in a shortage of vitamin D, essential for the absorption of calcium and the mineralisation of bones. Rickets therefore causes bone deformity, bow-legs, stunted growth and disability, and it was assumed that the disease had been eliminated as children left the factories and spent time outdoors in sunshine. Yet 833 children were admitted to UK hospitals in 2012 suffering from the condition, and that number is continuing to increase.[436]

If rickets is the return of the diseases of old, Type 2 diabetes is the curse of the modern day. There has been a worrying explosion in the cases of this illness, and it's not hard to determine why. Fast food, confectionery and sugar-laden drinks are the staple diet of any young person who spends time online, and this 'calorie rich, nutritional poor' mix is especially poor gruel for growing men. The use of apps such as Just Eat means most fast-food joints now deliver their food, so people don't even need to burn any calories going to get it, a trend that will explode with the expansion of delivery robots and drones. This combination of high-calorie, high-fat and sugar-laden food combined with a sedentary lifestyle is leading to a sick generation, unfit, fat and unable to cook for themselves. The number of people in the UK with type 2 diabetes has trebled since the Internet entered the household, and it is predicted that by 2025 over 4 million people in the UK will suffer from Type 2 diabetes.[437] One in every six people admitted to hospital are found to be suffering from the disease, and treating its side-effects costs the NHS £1.5million every hour. But the real impact is in the emerging nations, where a modern, Western diet and sedentary lifestyle have hit a population that until very recently struggled to consume enough daily calories. According to the World Health Organization, there has been fourfold increase in diabetes in the last 25 years, with 422 million people being diagnosed with diabetes in 2014, with one third in China alone.[438]

Finally, we're also creating a huge number of future physiological issues. People are spending hours hunched over looking at their phone or tablet, creating an epidemic of what doctors are calling 'iPosture'; back pain, slumping shoulders, a slouching middle and a lower back that's constantly compressed from sitting in an unnatural position. Modern life is quite simply creating a generation that is overfeed, unfit, sickly, depressed and weak. Worse, we are creating the formula that will condemn future generations to a similar fate as well.

An Epigenetic Time Bomb

Epigenetics, which literally means 'above genes', is a system that turns our genes on and off. The process works by chemical tags, known as epigenetic markers, attaching to DNA and telling a cell to either use or ignore a particular gene. It was previously assumed that the impact of epigenetics was confined to individuals and not transferred to future generations. Now scientists have become convinced that there is a form of inheritance, called epigenetic inheritance, in which the behaviour of genes in offspring is affected by the life experience of parents. More interestingly, these epigenetic changes can, at least for a small minority of genes, extend beyond immediate offspring to further generations. A Swedish genetic study from Umeå University[439] yielded the strongest evidence yet of epigenetic inheritance in humans. They analysed two hundred years of harvest records from one small isolated Swedish town, Överkalix, where they found that historical incidences of famine resulted in *positive* health effects on the children and grandchildren of individuals who had restricted diets, but also *adverse* effects on their health when food had been in surplus. The amount of food a grandfather had to eat between the ages of nine and twelve was especially significant. This is when boys go through what is called the slow growth period (SGP) and form the cells that give rise to sperm. Since the building blocks for the epigenome come from the food the boy eats, his diet could impact how faithfully the epigenome is copied and represent a snapshot of the boy's environment that can pass through his sperm to future generations. The same data set also highlighted how a sharp change in food availability to paternal grandmothers resulted in an increased risk of cardiovascular mortality in their granddaughters' adult lives.[440]

Epigenetic inheritance is an unconventional finding. It goes against the idea that inheritance happens only through the DNA code that passes from parent to offspring. It means that a parent's experiences, in the form of epigenetic tags, can be passed down to future generations. As unconventional as it may be, there is little doubt that epigenetic inheritance is real. In fact, it explains some strange patterns of inheritance that geneticists have been scratching their heads over for decades. For example, studies have shown that both the children and grandchildren of women who survived the Dutch famine of 1944–45 were found to have increased glucose intolerance in adulthood, and other researchers found that the descendants of Holocaust survivors have lower levels of the hormone cortisol, which helps your body bounce back after trauma.[441]

Epigenetic inheritance adds another dimension to the modern picture of evolution, and its importance is massive, for it links back to evolutionary responses to surplus vs scarcity. Such rapid changes in the nature and increased number of calories consumed, and also the rapid decrease in calories utilised, can only be bad news, for our biological state has evolved over generations to handle scarcity, not surplus. Our bodies, honed over millennia to deal with food shortages and famine, cannot change quickly enough in response to the rapid changes caused by an excessive calorie surplus and a reduction in physical labour. It also presents us with a startling fact: our children's increasingly unhealthy diet and increase in diabetes may not only be putting their health at risk — it is also putting down epigenetic markers that will blight the health of their children, their grandchildren, and their great-grandchildren.

In a groundbreaking 2015 study, *Obesity and Bariatric Surgery Drive Epigenetic Variation of Spermatozoa in Humans*,[442] researchers found that a man's percentage of body fat affects the heritable information contained in his sperm. They found that the sperm cells of lean and obese men possess different epigenetic markers, helping to explain why the children of obese men tend to grow up to also be obese, regardless of the leanness or diet of the mother. They concluded that the results confirmed that *the epigenetic landscape of human sperm is dynamic and vulnerable to environmental changes*; i.e. the quality of our environment determines the quality of our offspring. Basically, hard times produce lean and strong children, and easy times produce soft and weak ones.

Many boys between the ages of nine and twelve now spend their lives playing computer games, eating high-calorie and sugar-laden processed foods and exercising little, and given the finding that this time is when boys create epigenetic markers in their sperm, this means that their poor diet and lifestyle are putting any offspring they have in the future at a much greater risk of diabetes, heart disease and other ailments. This will create a healthcare time bomb, affecting an industry already struggling with an overweight, ageing population suffering from mental and physical ailments. We may have developed ways to avoid a Malthusian Catastrophe, but we may have inadvertently also set the foundations for a different kind of tragedy; one of inherited healthcare issues caused by surplus rather than scarcity. The research into CRISPR and gene therapy may be more urgent than we realised, for the quality of our biological stock is only going to decrease as the true impact of our diets becomes apparent.

From Chimps to Bonobos: The Decline of Western Men

As well as providing shaky epigenetic foundations and a dystopian mixture of technological dependencies and psychological issues, current societal and genetic trends are also likely to drastically reduce the size of this future generation. Birth rates are plummeting as young adults have become less interested in both sex and relationships, and less willing or able to produce children through a dramatic reduction in men's testosterone and sperm levels. As we examined in Part One, testosterone is a hormone responsible for a number of male-centric characteristics, such as sexual drive and aggression. *Homo sapiens* managed to form collaborative tribes because we have lower testosterone than Neanderthals. Low-testosterone bonobos form pansexual relationships in a matriarchal society, where the females rule and use sexual favours as a currency to get food, control males, or gain entry to other tribes. This differs greatly from their nearest cousins, chimpanzees, who form hyper-aggressive patriarchal societies, where the tribe stays together, sex is for reproduction only, and any lone chimps are unlikely to be welcomed into the tribe, regardless of their sex.

If one was to step back from the chaos, it is easy to see parallels between the differences in chimp and bonobo society and those emerging in the West. There is an apparent change taking place that we are changing from chimps to bonobos – both societally and biologically. Sex is becoming more transactional and pansexual, relationships more transient and power structures more matriarchal. Males are becoming more feminised, docile and subservient, a change that can be witnessed biologically. During the past three decades there has been a rapid decline in men's testosterone levels, dropping on average by 1 per cent per year, and now many men in their twenties have testosterone levels normally associated with men in their eighties and above. Men with low testosterone have a 68 per cent higher risk of dying young[443] (in their forties), and are more likely to suffer from obesity, diabetes and high blood pressure than men with higher testosterone levels, traits which they are likely to epigenetically pass down to their children, if they have them.[444] There is no real knowledge as to why this is happening, but poor diet and a sedentary lifestyle must play a part. Other suspected reasons include the level of the female sex hormone oestrogen in drinking water, believed in part to be due to hormonal contraceptives in humans and livestock being urinated out and making their way into the water supply, and the mass consumption of soya bean products, which contain isoflavones, known to be a natural mimicker of oestrogen. Soy is an ingredient that appears everywhere, either directly (such as in soy lattes and tofu) or indirectly (soya lecithin is a filler agent in most processed foods, baby formulas are made with soya as the base ingredient, and school-lunch programmes across the US even add soya to hamburger patties). Worryingly, as well as reduced testosterone, research has found a correlation between soya consumption and a low sperm count.[445] Which could help explain why that as well as a plummeting testosterone level, there has also been a dramatic reduction in the sperm count of Western men over the last forty years. It's a disaster of titanic proportions, according to Hagai Levine at the Hebrew University of Jerusalem, Israel. Between 1973 and 2011, the concentration of sperm in the ejaculate of men in Western countries fell by an average of 1.4 per cent a year, leading to an overall drop of just over 52 per cent. On top of that, sperm production declines with age, and more men are leaving it later to have kids. Allan Pacey, Professor of Andrology at the University of Sheffield, highlights the issue: *If you are a guy with a low sperm count and you try for a baby when you are 21, you are probably not going to notice you've got a problem. But if you are trying with your partner when she is 35 then that's when the heartache comes.*[446] Western society is therefore producing men who are slowly becoming less healthy, less masculine and less virile.[138] Finally, to finish us off, the Y chromosome that distinguishes men from women[139] is also disappearing, degenerating rapidly and leaving men with a strong X chromosome, but a shrivelled Y one. Masculine men – especially in the West – are rapidly becoming an endangered species.

Not content with this physiological degradation, society is waging a psychological war on masculinity as well. In Western society traditional male roles are attacked continuously, with Caucasian males specifically being accused of possessing 'white male privilege', of being the recipients of unearned benefits from a sexist patriarchy, of being guilty in some way for the sins of previous generations, of owing reparations to people of colour, of being responsible for a rape culture existing on college campuses, and of 'toxic masculinity'. There is a continuous media narrative that women are victims of the patriarchy, and youth media outlets like BuzzFeed, Salon, the Huffington Post, MTV and Vox constantly push pieces declaring white men to be the defective oppressors of all other genders and races. As Jim Morrison once stated, *Whoever controls the media controls the mind*, and nearly all media outlets constantly push this narrative while simultaneously skimming over male issues such as the plummeting testosterone and sperm rates; skyrocketing depression and suicide rates; epidemic narcotics and opioid use; eradication of industrial livelihoods; and falling educational achievements. To brainwash the campus, education authorities and universities are increasingly insisting that every student, regardless of the subject they study, write essays on white male privilege,[447] and take a mandatory Diversity 101 course and sit through 'white-privilege awareness' sessions.[448] I would have thought that we have had enough experience of the negative effects that come from teaching a generation

---

[138] Whether these low testosterone and low sperm counts are being passed down in epigenetic inheritance markers is something I worry about, but do not know. I can only assume that they are, given the impact sperm plays in establishing these markers. Regardless, if weight and diabetes affect sperm count, then this decline is only set to increase.

[139] Female = XX, male = XY.

of people to hate themselves because of factors outside their control – but apparently not. When you step back and review the combined impact of this on men, what we see is quite a toxic mix. Depressed, unhealthy young men with increasingly reduced work prospects because of automation, limited relationship options because women are choosing careers over coupling, and less chance of fathering children because of this rejection and a plummeting sperm count. It is therefore not surprising that depression and suicide in men are rising, attendance at university is falling, and many choose staying at home and online gaming rather than dating. Actions have consequences.

Ironically, the situation is not great for women either. A 'superwoman' culture emerged in the 1990s, urging women to have both a career and children, which is exactly what they did, especially as easy credit provided buying power many times greater than their actual salary. The pressure to demonstrate their career credentials has, however, left many women feeling like they are up against a clock. They need to get the career sorted before having children, but that means college and a degree (women now outstrip men at university, with a third of all girls going on to further education, but only a quarter of boys)[449] and then a career, and before you know it the girl is a woman in her late thirties and she hasn't got a long-term partner, let alone a spouse, and her biological clock is ticking louder than ever. Which means she either ends up childless or, due to her age, only has a single child.

Raising children has, throughout history, been primarily the domain of women, gifted not just with the biological requirements but also emotional qualities such as empathy, kindness and patience. Now we declare these to be weaknesses, the reason why women don't get raises at work, and instead seem to be striving for women to become economic agents indistinguishable from men. As women gradually acquire a high percentage of the senior positions and related salaries, any aspirations they hold of 'marrying up' will become harder to achieve. As one millennial career woman states in *Forbes*: *it's not as if we are holding out for Jake Gyllenhaal, but we do have certain non-negotiable expectations for potential mates that include college degrees and white-collar jobs.*[450] But as she acknowledges, these qualities are becoming harder to find in a world where women out-earn and educationally out-qualify men. Referencing Liza Mundy's book, *The Richer Sex*, she states the obvious: *Millennial women are increasingly finding two options when it comes to romance: marry down – or don't marry.* Unless a man can pull his weight, he is seen as just another mouth to feed.

As a result of these expectations and social pressures, many women are choosing not to bother with marriage or children, which of course means men aren't either, resulting in the concept of monogamous marriage as a pillar of Western society crumbling. A 2014 Pew report highlighted that 23 per cent of men and 17 per cent of women over twenty-five had never married,[451] and a 2017 report identified that 50 per cent of the US adult population are unmarried.[452] In 1960, 73 per cent of all children were living in a family with two married parents in their first marriage, but by 2014 that number had fallen to 46 per cent.[140] A major generational divide in attitudes toward families and their importance has taken place, with 55 per cent of US citizens aged over fifty believing that marriage and children are crucial elements in society, and 67 per cent of people aged between eighteen and twenty-nine believing that they are not. Unsurprisingly, these actions and beliefs are having a visible impact on birth rates. US federal data from 2014 highlighted that between 2007 and 2014, the number of live births per 1,000 women between the ages of fifteen and twenty-nine in America plunged 9 per cent. Conversely, at exactly the same time, dog ownership skyrocketed.[453] Basically, US women are increasingly choosing canines over children, and career over companionship.

One other social shift is that both young men and young women are not leaving home, continuing instead to cohabit with their parents. A 2014 Pew Research Center study highlighted that in the US, for the first time since 1880, young adults aged eighteen to thirty-four are more likely to live with a parent than in any other arrangement. The primary driver behind this seems to be employment-related, specifically for men. The traditional life path of 'get a job, leave home, get married, buy a house, have children' has been disrupted; firstly by more people going to university, and secondly by the difficulty in obtaining a full-time position that pays enough to be able to afford a mortgage or rent in a booming property market. Leaving

---

[140] The Pew Research study found huge disparities between racial groups in its results. Asian children are the most likely to live with both their parents in their first marriage (71 per cent), and black children the least (22 per cent). Worryingly, having two parents in a stable marriage was the biggest indicator of whether children would go to college and have a successful career. (http://www.pewsocialtrends. org/2015/12/17/1-the-american-family-today/)

the comfort of home for expensive but poor-quality rented accommodation while they save up money for a deposit on a house just doesn't appeal. The lack of a relationship that requires private space, combined with the availability of food and entertainment at home has resulted in both men and women staying at home and living off the bank of mum and dad.

The danger is that as the media constantly bombards us with messages about diversity and the need to replace men with women in positions of power, and as this becomes realised through the majority of university attendees being female and being exposed to postmodernist ideologies, men will increasingly choose to duck out of the race. The media attention given to campaigns like #MeToo and accusations of inappropriate conduct and consent have already seen men start to avoid unnecessary social engagements with women, including situations where male bosses have refused to mentor female employees for fear of future accusations.[454] The rising popularity of movements such as MGTOW (Men Going Their Own Way) appears to back this up, where members declare that they reject traditional utility roles and instead embrace *self-ownership and a declaration that a man has the supreme right to decide what his goals in life will be as opposed to having his goals dictated by others who, in preference to self-determination, prescribe utility-based roles for males entailing servitude to women and society.*[455] Basically, Western women are rejecting men, and men are rejecting them right back. This is eerily similar to John B. Calhoun's observations from his 'rodent utopia' experiments, where a class of self-absorbed male mice he called 'the beautiful ones' arose, who abstained from any social interaction or pursuing any relationships, and instead of bearing responsibility for others, simply spent all day focused on solitary, self-centred behaviours. Worryingly, as Calhoun's experiments showed, the arrival of these narcissistic mice came after a period of female aggression and represented the end stages of the mouse society before its imminent collapse.

The immediate parallels and impact of these social shifts in Western human populations are obvious and apparent. The next thirty years will see women increasingly hold the majority of positions of influence, and a more matriarchal, pansexual society, based less around marriage and families, will develop. Due to a continued rise in non-traditional relationships, financial pressures, a reduction in desire to have children and the difficulty, especially for women, of finding a partner that meets their standards, the birth rate will continue to fall well below replacement levels. There will be fewer distinguishing factors between men and women, and a plethora of different gender variants to smash apart this 'toxic, masculine, patriarchal society'. As traditional gender roles are slowly dismantled and the value of men's ability to take on physically challenging roles decreases due to automation, corporations and society will view male qualities as less valuable and even undesirable, resulting in the effective neutering and neutralisation of the young male Western population. For some, this is not a problem but a victory. For example, feminist author Hanna Rosin, who wrote *The End of Men*, triumphantly welcomes this decline of masculinity in Western society.

There will be fallout, and boys in particular will be tormented by this artificially induced shift. Since the dawn of time their roles have been clear – go out, hunt, do dangerous things to provide for the family, earn money, provide, take responsibility. And the roles for women have also been clear – love, nurture, care, empathise, rear children. Since the 1970s this has been changing. Women have been provided with the choice to do what men do, and quite rightly, for choice and freedom are liberal values we should hold dear to our hearts. However, men seem to be lost; especially in the West where white men are constantly being told that they are economically and socially privileged and need to pay recompense for the alleged sins of their forefathers. From a young age, boys are constantly being compared to their more patient and studious female counterparts. Their slower maturation and natural boyish, boisterous nature is frowned upon and sometimes medicated against, their toys are being neutered (such as swords and guns) and their institutions (such as boy scouts) infiltrated. As a result, boys are increasingly lacking confidence and guidance as to what to do and how to act, with toxic results. With no more lands to explore, no more dragons to fight and no more heroes or gentlemen to emulate, young men are increasingly retreating into an online existence to achieve respite from the pressure and judgement of the real world. It's becoming a self-fulfilling prophecy, for the more boys are told they are defective, the more likely they are to become so, falling behind, failing at education and participating less in society. Devoid of a purpose or responsibilities for others, they will continue to check out of the race, choosing to spend their time on self-centred activities such as playing video games. We are therefore likely to see a replica of the Chinese bare-branch phenomenon in Western nations, with large numbers of directionless, unmarried men, and a continuation of the already-dramatic rise in male suicide rates. The potential for the emergence of an urban 'behavioural sink', the dystopian breakdown of social structures recorded by Calhoun's 'mouse utopia' experiments, looms large. Once again, actions have consequences – not that those people pushing this agenda care. As Professor Jordan Peterson declared in a BBC radio interview: *We're alienating young men. We're telling them that they're patriarchal oppressors and denizens of rape culture and, you know, tyrants in waiting and that and we fail to discriminate between their competence and their tyranny. It's just it's awful; it's so destructive. It's so unnecessary and it's so sad.*[456] Even classical feminists such as Camille Paglia and Christina Hoff Sommers have openly admitted that there is an ideological war being waged on men and masculinity in an attempt to dismantle any patriarchal forces that exist in Western society.

The outcome of all of this activism is the ostracising of those who demonstrate masculine, testosterone-fuelled 'chimp' traits, and the promoting of those with more matriarchal 'bonobo' ones. Which, if looked at in isolation, appears to be a more peaceful, collaborative and sexually open society. Bonobos are less interested in status and power structures and are very collaborative. There's one problem: for this social engineering to take place, the bonobos need a protected environment with a plentiful food supply, for bonobos thrive in safe and comfortable environments, not harsh, demanding ones. For human 'bonobos', currently, the only safe, protected environment is on university campuses, and it has been achieved through the no-platforming and shaming of any 'chimpanzee' voices and reinforcing the message that they are speaking from a position of chimp privilege. The reason they need safe spaces is because bonobos, like the protestors, are sensitive souls. As an example, during the World War II bombing of Hellabrunn in Germany, the bonobos in a nearby zoo all died of fright from the noise, whereas the chimpanzees were unaffected. To be a successful bonobo tribe you therefore need to ensure everywhere is safe, the group is full of like-minded individuals and there are no chimpanzee tribes or chimpanzee ideas nearby. Which pretty much sums up the mindset in university campuses and increasingly in organisations such as Google, where chimp behaviour is screamed at until it disappears in shame, or the chimp is fired. Their 'safe spaces' are actually incredibly hostile places for those who do not share their opinions. However, if the bonobo protestors actually took the time to look outside their safe space and stop thinking about their own short-term desires, they'd notice that the vast majority of the world is still very chimp-like in nature, strongly rooted in traditional values and patriarchal structures. This includes most of the migrants into the West who these protestors currently promote and use to further their short-term goals. As Camilla Paglia highlights, the rise of androgynous behaviour and the neutering of masculinity is a trait many civilisations and cultures have historically demonstrated in their final stages, leaving them at the mercy of the manlier, testosterone-fuelled, chimp-like societies that prowl the outside, constantly probing their soft bonobo underbellies for weaknesses.[457] Male-centric chimp cultures – such as the Goths, Mongols and Ottomans – have in the past destroyed or severely undermined more civilised but hedonistic bonobo ones – mostly through migration without integration. As the English philosopher and historian Arnold Toynbee noted, *civilisations die from suicide, not from murder.*

Once Were Samurai

To see what a culture in decline looks like, we only need to go to Japan. Japan has struggled in its transition from a culture of tradition to one of technology, and despite working hard to retain its identity, it is struggling. The Japanese birth rate is plummeting, reaching a low of 1.26 births per woman, well below the replacement rate of 2.1. This is resulting in an ageing population, with fewer young people able to fill the economic shortfall when people retire. Japan currently has fewer than three people of working age for each retiree in the country, and by 2030 it will have fewer than two. Based on current projections, the Japanese government expects Japan's population to decrease by 22–23 per cent by 2060, falling from 128 million to just 87 million, with nearly half of these aged over sixty-five. It also has a population that isn't getting married. In 1975, just 21 per cent of women and 49 per cent of men were unmarried by their 30th birthday; by 2005, the figures were 60 per cent of women and 72 per cent of men. People are not only not getting married; they are not having any relationships, especially sexual ones. Twenty-five per cent of young males choose to opt out of relationships altogether, preferring to spend time online playing computer games, watching porn, or having relationships with robots, AI assistants or virtual anime characters.[458] Likewise, 45 per cent of Japanese women aged between sixteen and twenty-four stated that they were 'not interested in or despised sexual contact'.[459] The lack of relationships means people are also not leaving home, because they cannot afford a place on their own, and they do not have a partner they want to set up a home with. As a result of these social shifts, Japan's young people appear seriously unhappy. They have a seriously dysfunctional relationship with work, culturally frowning upon anyone who leaves before their bosses, and can end up working up to 100 hours of overtime a month. People stay in the office for so many hours in Japan that there is actually a word for 'death through overwork': *karōshi* (過労死). As a result, the government has mandated that people take holiday leave.[141] Trust in employers is also the lowest in the world at only 40 per cent, meaning people are spending their lives in places they don't like, for people they don't trust.

Combine these elements and you end up with what is perhaps the biggest social and health problem facing Japan – hikikomori. Approximately a million people, predominantly young men, have locked themselves in their bedrooms and will not come out, withdrawing completely from both their family and society for years, sometimes decades. Unsurprisingly, the Japanese are also lonely, to the point that there is a large market in providing robots, intelligent chatbots and virtual friends for Japanese people, young and old. Many of Japan's elderly are so poor and lonely that they have taken to committing small crimes such as shoplifting simply to be sentenced to jail where they get guaranteed human interaction and three warm meals.[460] Japan has all the hallmarks of a culture that doesn't believe in itself any more. A society that has lost its way and is suffering a major generational divide between the mindset of the old and that of the young, and between men and women. It's a glimpse into our potential future.

We have created an amazing technological bounty, but no one is amazed. In fact, they are becoming increasingly unhappy. Above the surface people appear to have everything, but below, emotionally and spiritually, there is nothing. As the psychologist Steven Pinker observes, *We're living*

---

[141] In 2018 I spoke at an event in Dubrovnik, Croatia. The local taxi driver told me that Dubrovnik was suppressing the number of cruise ships that arrive in the bay, as the massive number of tourists cause congestion, but spend little money as all food and drink is provided on the ships. He particularly bemoaned the Japanese cruise ships, because the tourists *'are miserable, don't want to be on holiday, and do not want to enjoy themselves. They all feel guilty for not being at work.'*

in primate heaven. We're warm, dry, we're not hungry, we don't have fleas and ticks and infections. So why are we so miserable? In our rush to develop new technologies, Western society feels like it has lost its soul. Nothing means anything any more; many older people don't recognise their own countries, and younger people feel that there is nothing to centre their lives around. As a result, no one believes, nor builds, for the future. This is where the transition point is dangerous. We assume that all this technological progress assures us a future that is better than the past, and in terms of achieving the basic levels of Maslow's hierarchy that is the case, proven by the fact that billions of people have been lifted out of poverty. However, as stated, technology is not teleology, it is a 'how' and not a 'why'. It fails to answer the critical question of what the purpose of our lives is, and how we should live them. Therefore, those without a telos, who have limited goals and abilities, will struggle. Despite a world of amazing technology, they will not be amazed, but frustrated, angry, resentful and vengeful. As Stewart Brand frankly declared, *Once a new technology rolls over you, if you're not part of the steamroller, you're part of the road.* Those who are part of the road that the steamroller has just flattened will resent those who appear to have everything, while they feel they have nothing. As we saw in Rome, when the soldiers came back to find that their future had been taken away from them, they were left in a situation where any future, and any voice, no matter how distasteful it would normally be, was better than nothing. Anyone who listens will have their attention. In order to keep the mob from rising up, the elites look to find a way to keep them entertained.

25

CHAOS BY DESIGN

I'm not interested in preserving the status quo. I want to overthrow it.

Niccolò Machiavelli

Unlike the previous transition periods where the populous were accustomed to hardships, the current transition has arrived after an extended period of relative peace and prosperity. As a result, it has forced a generation to face problems they are not accustomed to and didn't expect. Previous generations had clear rules: get a job, get married, buy a house, have kids. Now these rules no longer apply, and the resultant uncertainty and chaos has created an unsettling and insecure environment for the new generation, and they are desperate for someone to blame. Conveniently, those instrumental in undermining these societal norms also propose to have answers; answers designed to increase the division and accelerate the collapse.

Moulding the minds and loyalties of the young has always been an effective tool for those who wish to reshape society, and the family unit has always been the enemy, for it creates bonds that run deep. Once these bonds are broken however, the young can easily be convinced into viewing their parents as the enemy, as Pol Pot's Khmer Rouge demonstrated. While nowhere near as extreme, the dramatic rise in university attendance in the West has provided professors (primarily in the humanities, social sciences and liberal arts) with the opportunity to broadcast their ideology to a larger percentage of the future workforce than ever. Their process – what the late KGB defector Yuri Bezmenov called 'ideological subversion'[461] – is the deliberate, slow and continual infiltration of neo-Marxist, social-justice ideology into the malleable heads of university students, turning them against the very foundations that made the West successful.[142] The seeds of this process were sown in the transition period of the last wave, the 1960s, and have been carefully cultivated, ready to burst into bloom when the conditions are right – such as during a transition period.

Stage One: Indoctrinate

The deliberate cultivation of ideological subversion may have started in the 1960s, but the fact that universities provided fertile ground for spreading anti-Western ideologies was known well before then. In his famous 1944 book *The Road to Serfdom*, Fredrich Hayek states that, *Many a University teacher in this country during the 1930s has seen English and American students return from the continent, uncertain whether they were communists or Nazis and certain only that they hated Western liberal civilisation.*[462] These academics are not seeking a mere recalibration in the system – they want a full-blown revolution, and they know that the best way to weaken the pillars of a society is to teach its young people not to respect them, to declare them false, corrupt and unearned. Originally their efforts centred around the traditional Marxist cause of rallying against the bourgeoisie and the capitalists, but outside of Soviet Russia this had not led to revolution. Worse, after Stalin's death, a combination of Khrushchev's 1956 'secret speech' and the sight of Russian tanks rolling over Hungarian workers laid bare the truth about their Marxist idols. The world knew that the tales of mass murder, torture and atrocities behind the Iron Curtain were not just CIA propaganda, and the Marxist utopia of the USSR was no longer a viable alternative to a booming, capitalist America.

---

[142] I urge you to listen to Bezmenov explain the process and how many generations it has infiltrated, and how he recommends trying to stop it, if this is at all possible. Search YouTube for 'KGB defector Yuri Bezmenov's warning to America'. Somewhat ironically, this interview was aired in 1984.

The far-left academic's dislike of Western civilisation still festered, but they needed a new strategy; a more sophisticated way to create scepticism when evidence and reason was against them. Their hatred for capitalism remained, but it had the habit of lifting millions of people out of poverty while their preferred system simply ended up putting people in the ground. A more nuanced approach was needed: one based more around social factors than economic, one that could convince entire generations of students that Western civilisation was corrupt and built on toxic foundations of historical atrocities, systemic biases and unfair hierarchies. Enter social justice, political correctness and post-modernism. The left-wing, mostly tenured, professors who dominate the humanity subjects across Western universities, especially in the US, have created a pseudo-religion around these concepts, using their lecture theatres in the same way a preacher uses the pulpit, creating a worldview of sins, oppression, redemption and heretics. Instead of the proletariat vs the bourgeoisie, group identity, such as your skin colour, gender, religious beliefs or sexuality determined the value of someone's opinion and their level of victimhood. This is obviously more attractive to the young, liberal bourgeoisie students, because it avoids the obvious hypocrisy that would come from organising a worker's revolution via a $1500 MacBook while drinking a vanilla latte in Starbucks. This new cause is much more accessible, based not on wealth but immutable and social characteristics that form an intersectional framework that determines your level of perceived historical oppression and therefore the value of your voice.

The collapse of the traditional Western civilisation principles such as faith, family and flag has left many young people feeling directionless, something the social justice cause has tapped into. The professors teach their student congregation a tale of sins, guilt and redemption. White males are accused of the sins of their fathers, declaring them recipients of unearned privilege and benefits arising from a system built upon oppression and white supremacy. It offers redemption through becoming active allies to the cause, providing them with purpose. There is visible evidence that can be manipulated to support this narrative. Hierarchies exist throughout the animal kingdom, especially where there is competition for food, resources and mates, and humans are no different. Every society has winners and losers,[143] and the gap between them widens during the transition period and resultant upswing of a new wave when capital is valued more than labour. Also, in any society, unless there are restrictive policies in play (such as apartheid), then the predominant demographic group will always make up the majority of the winners just through the law of averages and historical precedence. Most leadership positions are reflections of the social demographic of the past not the present – it takes decades of experience and dedication to acquire most senior leadership positions, so today's boardrooms reflect the education and demographic of the country in the 1970s and 80s, not now. In the countries of the West, this group is the people of European descent, and the professors declare this to be visible evidence of the oppressive social hierarchies that must be destroyed, hence why there are so many 'anti-white' protests, tweets and articles.

As women continue to outnumber men at universities, these preachers are finding their congregation populated with more willing participants, informing them that they are an oppressed group that is owed retributions, creating gender resentment. Their role is to become a warrior of social-justice, whose mission is to save themselves and other oppressed groups by tearing down the patriarchy and other nefarious, systemic forces that they believe are endemic throughout Western civilisation and which seek to keep women down. Any groups presenting counter-facts or calls to reason are deemed misogynist bigots, trying to retain their positions of privilege. It's a compelling narrative for these students, for any disparities in results or failures can now be explained as gender discrimination. It is also discouraging them from following the biological or behavioural paths such as marriage, family and gender roles that have created social cohesion for generations.

Like any invading force, one of the first tasks is to destroy the idols and unifying symbols of the enemy. And right now, any traditional cultural norms such as gender roles, marriage and families are the target, deemed oppressive tools of the dominant social group that must be destroyed to ensure equality. For they know that by destroying micro social structures, they ultimately undermine the macro ones.

---

[143] Though what constitutes 'winning' and 'losing' itself is subjective – is a wealthy but lonely, depressed and chronically unhealthy person more of a winner than a working-class person in perfect health surrounded by friends and loving family members? Discuss.

Outcomes not Opportunity

The irony is, of course, that while their message is full of altruism and fighting oppression, the real underlying objective is power, for those that strive to instil a sense of guilt in others do so to control and dominate them. Identity politics is the latest guilt-based tool of choice, a way to acquire power by creating a tyranny of the minority, designed to control which voices are heard and which ones need to be silenced. In their eyes your worth is solely determined by your group identity rather than your individual actions, making said worth easy to obtain for some, and almost impossible for others.

Their objective is therefore not to achieve equality of opportunity, for that puts the onus on individual responsibility, but rather equality of outcome. This new scripture is based around a 'lump of equality' mindset, for if someone from a dominant social group has something, then it must have been stolen from someone in a minority group. Anything other than perfect equity must be because of discrimination or 'privilege', and anyone who does not recognise this privilege is a heretic who is simply acting from a mindset of Hobbesian self-interest. Any talk of equality of opportunity or meritocracies are declared hate speech, for they create the possibility that the wrong group could still win. To ensure equal outcomes are achieved, those whose identities are defined as 'privileged' need their capabilities shackled and supressed, as if trying to emulate the dystopian world of Kurt Vonnegut's *Harrison Bergeron*. It also requires the suppression of choice, for choice enables different outcomes to arise. This robs people of their individual agency, power to choose, and right to happiness, creating a victim mindset in those marginal groups they propose to help. They are led to believe that their life is controlled by nefarious, systemic forces; and because their enemies are systemic there is no way that they will escape their victimhood unless the system that enabled people to be successful is pulled down. We end up in the current situation where companies have to implement diversity quotas and meritocracies are deemed tools of white supremacy. Everyone loses long-term because talent and ability are secondary to your position in the intersectional hierarchy.

Despite its declarations of equality, this agenda is actually inherently racist and sexist; based upon the soft bigotry of low expectations, the presumption that we need to change the rules because women or people of colour cannot succeed by their own merit. While it may be initially attractive to always blame the system or some other social group for

579

their failings, long-term these victims are rarely happy, for this mindset is maladaptive and based on the politics of envy. As economist Thomas Sowell succinctly puts it, *When people are presented with the alternatives of hating themselves for their failures or hating others for their success, they seldom choose to hate themselves.* Enabling this myopic perspective by compensating for perceived oppression does more harm than good: rather than raising people up and teaching them to be winners, you lock in this victimhood, denying them the rewards of responsibility and joys of accomplishment. It also means that any future exposure to environments where the hurdles are not automatically lowered for them is likely to be a shock. This simply results in more anger, more perceived injustice and more demands for compensatory acts, accelerating the doom-loop.

The social-justice religion also has heretics. Any deviant opinions held by any members of the perceived victim groups immediately identifies them as enemies to the cause because they kill the victim narrative. So successful black conservatives such as Thomas Sowell, Ben Carson or Condoleezza Rice are deemed 'Uncle Toms', and classical feminists such as Christina Hoff Sommers and Germaine Greer are no-platformed and smeared due to their comments and use of inconvenient facts. The hatred displayed against those who reject the stereotype highlights both the soft racism of their accusers, and the fact that their real agenda for this group is control not success. It explains why they talk constantly of group oppression but never of individual liberty – they don't want the members of this group to become successful individuals with agency: they want them to remain victims they can manipulate. And this mindset of ideological collectivism is contrary to what we know to be the foundational requirements for inclusivity, innovation and economic growth.

Free Speech for Me, But Not For Thee.

The West launched the industrial revolution based on the concept of individual liberty and personal freedom, where anyone could publish and discuss ideas. Now establishments of learning have become opposed to liberty because it allows people to say and do things that they find problematic. They are demanding safe spaces *from* free speech, not *for* it. It is pure narcissism, a world where reason and logic are devalued, feelings trump ideas, anger determines worth, language is policed, and perceived victimhood provides moral superiority. Yet in a group that constantly calls for more diversity, the one thing that they do not want is any diversity of opinions. And on campus, supressing alternative perspectives has become easy through sheer force of numbers. In 2011, Professor Jonathan Haidt asked a room containing 1,000 of his peers to raise their hands if they were politically conservative or right of centre. Just three hands went up.[463] In 2018 he repeated the exercise with an audience of around 100 students at Middlebury college in Vermont, with similarly skewed results.[464] Haidt commented that his research identified that only those with far-left views are comfortable with openly declaring their opinions at US universities, and as a result dominate discussions. He stated that as no alternative viewpoints are tolerated, a climate of peer pressure and moral dependency exists where anyone who disagrees self-silences through fear of retribution, creating constant confirmation bias and a campus-wide echo chamber. This allows the prevalent social group to operate with the same privilege and undertake the same kinds of social discrimination they decry so much. In a 2012 study of diversity of political thought amongst psychology professors, the authors found that the progressive faculty members freely admitted to discriminating against the conservative minority in terms of job promotions and grant applications.[465] So much for equality and quashing oppressive majority groups.

It is quite something to hear professors such as Haidt talking about the transformation of universities and their indoctrination agendas – it is quite another thing to actually see it for yourself. When I toured prospective UK universities with my eldest son, we went to one campus, one of the largest, and sat and listened to the main history professors detail the course, which was on modern history. The head of department started by explaining that there are two ways of examining history; the first is the approach presented by Geoffrey Elton in *The Practice of History*, where history should be presented as being independent of the observer, should follow key principles, and should be viewed in the context of the time in which it took place, rather than overlaying opinions and perspectives that are now possible because of years of hindsight. The second way is the relativist perspective presented by E. H. Carr in *What is History?*, in which history takes the form of a dialogue between past and present, and as such is dependent upon the current historian's views and interpretations of the facts. As I sat there listening I thought, *Well, that's fair – they are obviously going to take a balanced perspective between these two approaches.* I couldn't have been more wrong. The professor then tore into Elton, declaring him a fool, and stated that Carr's perspective would be the only one he would be following. He then declared that, given that fact, the most important thing for any potential student to know was his perspective on the time period they would be studying. He proceeded to spend an hour listing his Marxist credentials, showed pictures of himself visiting communist historical sites, and informing the students of the far-left politicians, thinkers and materials they should familiarise themselves with. It was clear that the course centred around the professors, not the students. About being taught what to think, not how to think; to blindly accept, not critically challenge. Anyone foolish enough to challenge the professor's perspective was not going to have a fun time nor do very well. I was therefore relieved when my son declared afterwards that he would rather chew off his arm than spend three years being brainwashed.

Nietzsche observed that *the surest way to corrupt a youth is to instruct him to hold in higher esteem those who think alike than those who think differently* and this advice is being eagerly followed, with anyone who dares to disagree with the group-think being ostracised, villainised and no-platformed. Over the last decade 'Bias Response Teams' have appeared in universities. Over 230 American campuses have these teams, and their purpose is to identify and handle alleged acts of 'bias', encouraging students to report any incidents they deemed offensive, regardless of whether they occurred on or off campus.[466] These incidents include any situations where someone used language that another person found 'problematic' or where anyone 'felt' threatened or uncomfortable. Punishments range from attending 'training sessions' to being disciplined or expelled. This creates a culture of intimidation where people are afraid to speak their minds, afraid to explore ideas, and afraid to challenge the official narrative. Silence and compliance replace discussion and debate. This policing of speech and behaviour is just ideological fascism masquerading as moral righteousness, used to justify unacceptable actions. And those who are willing participants and advocates of this behaviour leave university and work to implement the same culture in their places of employment.

There is a clear difference in mindset between those that have been through this indoctrination, and those who avoided it, resulting in these activists rallying against the very people that you would have historically expected them to support – the working-class. As in Rome, the working-class place great value in the traditions and culture of their nation, the very same things that the bourgeois professors are telling their students to destroy. This divide has resulted in some incredible scenes, especially in the US. Large groups of liberal students from expensive universities and wealthy parents have unironically donned masks and black outfits to protest against groups of working-class citizens who they declare to be recipients of privilege and supporters of white supremacy. Universities in liberal cities such as Berkeley have seen masked protestors riot when speakers deemed 'the enemy' came to deliver a talk. The potential disruption and cost have resulted in many universities capitulating and banning these speakers, proclaiming that they violate the sanctity of the safe space they have created on campus, and as a result handing victory to these agitators. Numerous professors are openly active in organising, agitating and leading protests, writing constant social-justice and anti-capitalist pieces, and demanding that white students are excluded from certain areas. They broadcast their bias openly, tweeting comments such as *all I want for Christmas is White genocide* or that *white men are a cancer and must die*.[144]

Unsurprisingly, the establishment of mob justice has led to situations where the very professors who were complicit in this indoctrination have fallen foul of their own creations. Some have realised too late that they have produced *Doctor Moreau*-style monsters that can only view the world in terms of allies and enemies. Any dissenting opinions, even from the very professors who created their groupthink, mark you out as an enemy, a position from which you can never recover. Professor Bret Weinstein from Evergreen State College was one such example. In 2017 he received a college-wide email that proposed a change to the annual 'day of absence' where non-white people could excuse themselves from campus for twenty-four hours. The counterproposal was for white people to be excluded from campus instead, a suggestion he declared a step too far, for while he had no problem with people exercising their personal choice to exclude themselves, he had issue with forcing others to be excluded, especially based on their skin colour, declaring it a slippery slope. In response to this statement of sanity, his office was immediately surrounded by a baying mob of students calling for his resignation. Evergreen then descended into a high-school re-enactment of *The Wanderers*, with groups of chanting students roaming the campus

[144] White genocide tweet from Philadelphia's Drexel University Associate Professor of Politics and Global Studies, George Ciccariello-Maher; while the delightful 'white men are a cancer and must die' quote is from Massachusetts College Professor Noel Ignatiev. Ironically, both are white men in privileged positions.

looking for 'wrong-thinkers', holding staff hostage and presenting a list of demands to the dean that had to be met *or else*. Demands he shamefully capitulated to. After the university could no longer ensure his safety, Weinstein and his wife (who also worked at the university) had to leave the campus and their jobs.[467] Like so many before, they failed their own ideology's increasingly punitive purity tests.

This progressive post-modernist militancy is not limited to the US. In the UK, the far-left students have demanded the removal of paintings and statues of anyone with any association to Britain's colonial past, disrupted talks by Conservative MPs, forced out moderates from the Labour Party, and protested and vandalised cafés and shops that celebrate any aspect of 'Britishness'. Their revisionist agenda sets out to discredit any traditional values, any displays of patriotism or any symbols of national pride, declaring that everything good has been stolen, not earned. Again, it's a power play; the revisionism simply an attempt to control society by reshaping the past, for, as per the Party's slogan in George Orwell's *Nineteen Eighty-Four*; *Who controls the present, controls the past. Who controls the past, controls the future.* Controlling the narrative of the past ensures control of the future, because past wrongdoings can then be treated as rationale to justify future oppression (or, as they call it, 'social justice').

Digital Tribalism

This activism is rapidly leading us to a place where reasoned debate and dialogue becomes impossible. People no longer seek the truth, but declare that their feelings prove they are right and the opposition is not just wrong, but evil. Opinion is becoming binary, and political correctness is overriding principles. Nuance and reason are being lost. We've already seen the news media transform from thoughtful, considered journalism into mere information aggregators and the peddlers of half-truths and biased opinions. In the age where the most powerful person in the world communicates via Twitter, speed to publish is everything. It has sent the fourth estate into a death spiral. Already reeling from the impact digital has had on their bottom line, the media is now reliant on the number of views, clicks and retweets in order to make advertising revenue, and as a result focuses on the volume of new articles, aggregating and regurgitating information simply to create pieces, most of which contain limited journalistic merit. The editors know that the more the headline panders to your existing biases and opinions, the more likely you are to view and share it amongst your like-minded connections, and as a result they peddle opinion as truth and rhetoric as reality. Their mission seems to be the online delivery of your daily two-minutes of hate. Unsurprisingly, trust in the media is at an all-time low, and with good reason. Rather than present the facts, news programmes tell you their interpretation, designed to create a narrative that they want you to believe. Media headlines and news pieces increasingly call to emotion rather than reason, reducing heavy political issues to twenty-second soundbites, followed up with more time spent in the studio spinning the event to suit whichever narrative the station represents. Rather than simply informing people of what's happened, they now focus on telling them how they should feel about what's happened. The media on both sides is so convinced about its own righteousness that they willingly spin messages, omit context and present opinions as facts in order to align the public's thought processes and belief systems with their own. The trouble for them is that they are not the only source of information any more, and in a world where everyone carries a camera around with them, any sleight of hand with the facts is often caught out.

This constant feed of opinion-based media is dangerous, for it divides rather than unifies, destroys trust in the fourth estate and creates ideological battlegrounds where people develop a blindness to facts that they don't want to see. People now attack news by default if they dislike the source, or immediately defend it if they like it. To an increasing extent, there is no centre for people to occupy; no place where reasoned debate can take place without ideological contamination. This is causing a worrying level of polarisation, especially across political lines. In the hysteria over Donald Trump, the centre of nearly every day's two minutes of hate since he stood for election, a couple of US news presenters forgot where they were and openly stated their agenda out loud.[145]

---

[145] On the 22nd February 2017, MSNBC's *Morning Joe* co-host Mika Brzezinski stated, 'And it could be that while unemployment and the economy worsens, he [Trump] could have undermined the messaging so much that he can actually control exactly what people think. *And that, that is our job.*' On the 16th October 2016, CNN's Chris Cuomo said of the leaked Hillary Clinton emails, 'remember, it's illegal to possess these stolen documents. It's different for the media. *So everything you learn about this, you're learning from us.*' Actually, no. It's not different for you.

It's not the first time that the transition period has caused a heightened sense of tribalism in the West, but the advent of social media has taken it to another level. People use social media to virtue-signal their worth to the unseen audience, quick to question the morals and worth of people they disagree with. They also increasingly comment on articles in response to the headline alone, rarely taking the time to fully read and understand the actual content. Article writers and newspaper editors are aware of this, becoming increasingly dramatic in their headline choices, and often misrepresenting complicated pieces by dumbing them down for the audience. The more you click on them, the more you inform the algorithms monitoring your every move of your preferences, and they immediately scour the Internet for pieces that correspond with your existing viewpoints and political leanings, gift-wrapping and presenting them to you in your feed. People like this because, unlike reality, it doesn't challenge them. If they don't like something, they can block it or unsubscribe. If they really don't like it, they can report it and get it banned. People don't seek out the truth any more, they see only what they want to see, and the machine god is only too happy to feed their confirmation biases. We are becoming addicted and subservient to devices that send us reaffirmations of our worth and our viewpoints, and as the conflicting opinions are filtered out, people begin to believe that their ideas are shared by everyone. This is creating bespoke filter bubbles and echo chambers where blinkers are placed over people's eyes, feeding them news and media that narrow their focus to only perspectives that align with their own, making them unwilling to hear alternative points of view, let alone consider them.

Identity politics is everywhere, and as a result the worth of your opinion is determined not by your argument, but by your group identity – your colour, gender, sexual preference and age. It has given rise to a shocking lack of civility in public discourse between these groups, with *ad-hominins* replacing arguments, and repetitive chanting substituting for reasoned debate. Online its worse, as people use anonymous profiles that emboldens them to freely dehumanise or debase their opponents; abusing them in a way that they would never do if they were to meet in the flesh. This becomes especially easy when you've been indoctrinated to believe those that you disagree with are fundamentally evil. Even staying silent is an offence to the morality police, where abstaining from joining the chorus of voices condemning wrong-think marks you as complicit.[146]

And it is only going to get worse, for without work and purpose, people will become disillusioned and simply spend more time online in venting their frustrations against their ideological enemies. Idle hands make the devil's work, as the saying goes. This will see more people pushed further to the fringes, into political tribalism, and it is playing right into the hands of those who would love the opportunity to use legislation and this new AI-powered technology to control both opinion and an unruly population.

The End of the Enlightenment?

The population is splintering into two warring factions: ideologues who want to tear everything down in the name of group equality, and individuals who want to defend them in the name of liberty.[147] While the progressive ideologues are in the minority, their voice and protests dominate, and they have hijacked both morality and the past and used them as weapons to shut down the defenders. These social justice warrior's willingness to shame people into submission, even if it destroys their livelihoods, knows no bounds. As Margaret Atwood, staunch feminist author of *The Handmaid's Tale*, declared, *In times of extremes, extremists win. Their ideology becomes a religion, anyone who doesn't puppet their views is seen as an apostate, a heretic or a traitor, and moderates in the middle are annihilated.* And true to form, even this darling of the feminist movement was condemned the moment she stepped out of line. After daring to insist on due process before declaring men guilty of sexual wrongdoing, she was viciously attacked online and declared a heretic by the same feminist mob who had previously declared her a hero.[468]

As a result, even those that are sceptical daren't make a stand against this movement because they know that the inevitable moral outrage would exact an overwhelming level of personal cost, while the corresponding impact of their heroism would be negligible. Any disagreement with the politically

---

[146] For evidence, see the major backlash Taylor Swift received for not posting any anti-Trump messages, and for not telling her fans to vote for Clinton. She didn't post pro-Trump or anti-Clinton messages; she just didn't comment about the US election. And that was a crime.

[147] There is also a third group, the vast majority who are unsure what the hell is going on, fed up with all the craziness, and just want to be left alone to enjoy things as they are.

correct narrative is deemed hate speech, and as hate speech is increasingly becoming a criminal offence, those who would complain, do not. They see what happens to those who dare to put their heads above the parapet and fear the moral outrage that would be brought down on them. It's a slippery slope, for as Benjamin Franklin mused, *They who can give up essential liberty to obtain a little temporary safety deserve neither liberty nor safety.*

We are entering a world where a very vocal group are continually demanding that society bends to their will and panders to their demands. They believe they are fighting systemic oppression, and the only way to conquer a systemic problem is for the entire system, including all of its traditional norms, hierarchies and roles, to be torn down. One of their key postmodernist strategies is to make everything opaque, subjective and dependent on interpretations. They declare that the foundational elements upon which Western civilisation are based are flawed, invented by the patriarchy to oppress and marginalise minority groups. Enlightenment values such as reason, rationality and individual merit are undermined; scientific methods and first principles are questioned, and capitalism's demise is demanded. Postmodern thought has been making inroads into the mainstream of Western culture for decades, but we're only now beginning to see how pernicious a cause it actually is. These warriors are fighting not for freedom, but for moral authority, especially in language. They are no less religious than the Christians they sneer and belittle, only their faith is in social justice not Christ. They believe in good and evil, and to show how they are on the righteous side they virtue signal constantly their worthiness through policing and publicly shaming the actions and words of those they deem to be sinners. The displaced professor from Evergreen State, Bret Weinstein, describes the situation well: *We're heading into a very dangerous phase of history where a large number of people, especially young people, have become convinced that the free exchange of ideas is not only no longer necessary but is actually counterproductive; and so they set out to silence those who have opinions at odds with theirs... shutting down speech has become the mode for a large number of individuals who believe they see very clearly what is wrong with civilization and what must be done to improve it—and they are unfortunately shutting down people who have vital things to tell them that they definitely need to know.* It's designed to create a victim narrative to justify the use of force, for if you are a victim – or defending victims – then you have the moral high ground and your activism, no matter how extreme, is justified.

Their desire to punch Nazi's sounds like something no one would disagree with, but the question is who gets to decide who is a Nazi? Given that people who actually hold neo-Nazi views are a tiny, irrelevant group on the fringes of society, what they really want is the moral justification to use force against anyone they disagree with. Which they believe they acquire by declaring their opponents as Nazis, fascists or white supremacists. However, as the Gracchus brothers found out to their detriment, once violence gets introduced into the political arena, there's no going back for democracy. It's downhill all the way. They also found out, as all activists usually do, that those in power are much better at the violence game than the rabble outside.

In the past, while people have always disagreed about politics, about the policies and procedures needed to achieve a goal, they did not generally disagree about the goal itself. Likewise, they did not view their opponents as necessarily bad people, but as people with different opinions and perspectives. Now this feels like it is changing. The narrative has been heightened so that any person with alternate political views – especially non-progressive ones – are deemed evil, maladjusted and morally defective, and are treated as such. Fifty-five years ago, Martin Luther King Jr. dreamed of a world where people were judged not by the colour of their skin, but by the content of their character. This idea resonated across the world because it was based on reason. Now that kind of rhetoric would be deemed hate speech and no-platformed. The economist and social theorist Thomas Sowell stated as far back as 1998, *If you have always believed that everyone should play by the same rules and be judged by the same standards, that would have gotten you labelled a radical 50 years ago, a liberal 25 years ago and a racist today.*[469] A war is therefore under way between Enlightenment values and those of the postmodernists; between reason and rhetoric; between a society based around individual free choices and one based around social justice and collectivism. A battle where free speech, individualism, meritocracy, achievement and equality of opportunity are fighting against compelled speech, collectivism, equity, uniformity and equality of outcome.

Stage Two: Infiltrate and Infect

Many of these indoctrinated students have now graduated, meaning that their demanded safe space no longer begins and ends at the college gates.

More worryingly, many now hold influential positions in media, HR, law and politics, meaning that this philosophy is being spread and embedded into hiring and training programmes, legal frameworks and government policy. As Saul Alinsky, the author of the protestor's guidebook *Rules for Radicals*, stated, *true revolutionaries do not flaunt their radicalism. They cut their hair, put on suits and infiltrate the system from within*. And infiltrate they have, creating a very influential 'progressive class' that permeates politics, business, media and, most worryingly, the tech giants and the legal system. Their objective is not to extend freedom of speech or thought, or to encourage debate and discussion, but to restrict them. They don't want diversity of ideas, they want dogmas. Dogmas are not meant to be analysed or challenged, and any person that does is a heretic. As we saw with James Damore at Google and Denise Young Smith at Apple, those that propose ideas that run contrary to the dogma – even if true – have to be quashed, along with the messenger.

When your dogma includes teaching people to believe that they have the right not to be offended; that they can shut down views they disagree with; that any attachment to your nation or culture is racist; that self-evident truths such as biological differences between men and women are social constructs that can be dismantled and reshaped at will, then chaos is the outcome, not unity. When this same group influences policymakers to enshrine the protection of these beliefs into law, then we should all be really worried, especially in an age where technology can pry into every nook and cranny of our existence. The perpetrators of this ideology are putting pressure on technology companies like Google and Facebook to highlight, demonetise and shut down voices that they don't like. They are claiming offence and demanding that big government and big corporations act to protect their feelings by regulating the Internet to suppress dissent, control the spread of ideas and distort reality in their favour. They don't have to push hard, for many of the graduates from the university indoctrination programs now hold jobs in tech companies, enabling them to not only influence internal politics, but also control what content is endorsed by their platforms. As G.K. Chesterton skilfully put it: *the modern world will accept no dogmas upon any authority; but it will accept any dogmas on no authority.* These corporations are more than happy to take on this overwatch role, incentivised by the opportunity to gain insights into every aspect of our lives. Which is incredibly easy for them to do, now that they have developed the tools for this job and we have willingly granted them access to use them. You then end up with an unholy alliance – progressive tech companies ensure their employees all share the same ideals, these employees then control what content trends and gets displayed on the Internet;[148] the media controls the messages and spin, and this creates a one-sided story that leads to governmental and legal pressure for the state to intervene.

And intervene they have. The UK's police and legal system, so long the envy of the world, has recently caused alarm due to their totalitarian policing of their citizens online activities. They openly broadcast their new agenda, posting ominous messages on social media warning citizens that they are 'always watching', with even some encouraging people to report any incidents of 'non-criminal hate speech'. This constitutes anything said or posted that while not illegal, may have been deemed by someone to be hurtful or politically incorrect. Words and thoughts are now the focus of police attention, and the potential to offend has now become a criminal act. The Snoopers' Charter and the 2003 Communications Act, especially the infamous Section 127 on 'grossly offensive speech', have so far been used to arrest around nine people a day for hate speech, convict a YouTube comedian for making an offensive joke and a woman for posting lyrics from a rap song. These sentences are important because the UK law works by setting precedents, so the judge's willingness to completely ignore context in order to suppress freedom of speech has simply laid the foundation for an avalanche of future cases. Maybe these guilty verdicts are being used, as per the Chinese proverb, to 'kill one to warn a hundred'. *You think free speech exists and is protected? You think you will be allowed a platform to speak out against our actions and agenda? Think again.* Britain, where laws were designed to free the individual, not control them; the country where individual liberties such as free speech were born, has now become one of the first Western nations to criminalise it. We are already seeing the stealth return of blasphemy laws.[149] What next? The unexpected return of the Spanish Inquisition?

Not to be outdone, Germany has forced Facebook to identify and ban

---

[148] Example: in 2018 the primary ideology of the Californian Republican Party on Google was changed to 'Nazism'

[149] Since the fatwa was issued against Salman Rushdie for writing 'The Satanic Verses', there has been a global intolerance of any criticism of Islam. Many murders have been committed, ranging from the killing of Dutch filmmaker Theo van Gogh, to the massacre at French satirical magazine Charlie Hebdo's offices. Now the word 'Islamophobia' has been conjured up to describe those who are critical of Islam, and the recent additions of new laws that criminalise those deemed Islamophobic are designed to prevent such discourse, effectively creating a blasphemy law.

people who are critical of their mass-migration policies, so they can be arrested,[470] plus made legal the use of 'Trojan horse' malware as a way to infect and monitor people's computers. Over in the US, intelligence agencies such as the CIA and NSA have pumped millions of dollars of research grants into tech start-ups to benefit from their digital surveillance outputs,[471] and are now working with private companies such as Amazon and Google on web-monitoring capabilities to identify connections between people, as well as developing AI capabilities for drones that can watch us from above.[472] This collaboration between global technology companies and the state is enabling a worrying level of draconian oversight into our everyday lives, providing those who wish to control us with the tools to identify, intimidate and incarcerate any wrong-thinkers.

All Destruction, No Creation

This is just the start. These pious agents of chaos have used the West's liberal values against it, creating tolerance for those who wish for its destruction and allowing them to hide in plain sight. In previous waves, the disruptive and often violent transition periods did result in genuine improvements to society. Just causes such as the rights of workers, then women and finally racial groups were fought to ensure equality of opportunity. Real inequalities needed addressing, but people still had the same goals such as liberty and freedom. Now the goals of these groups feel different, democracy is being challenged and freedoms questioned, and as a result this is making society divided and weak. Enlightenment values have been perverted into a form of faux individualism, where everyone insists that their rights are adhered to, while increasingly rejecting any societal responsibilities. Without responsibilities people can just wallow in a sense of entitlement and self-gratification of their needs. It is fast becoming a nihilistic society of divided people living out an extended adolescence with high sense of entitlement but also limited responsibility and purpose other than themselves. The destruction of norms such as the nuclear family is seeing women rejecting their roles as wives, mothers and caregivers, and men their roles as husbands, fathers and providers. However, as automation increasingly replaces an enormous amount of human labour, this self-centred approach could find many people struggling to define what purpose their lives hold, for what is your telos if you are absent a partner, children, career or faith? We are social animals, and without companionship or meaning to our lives people become depressed, lonely and often suicidal.

What is unhelpful is the fact that those who despise Western society have found their telos through constantly striving to undermine concepts such as national identity in an attempt to make them opaque and meaningless. They ask what is British culture anyway? Does it actually exist? Questions that would never have been asked 50 years ago because British culture and identity was so unique that people crossed the world to experience it. Since mass migration occurred the narrative is slowly but continuously being altered to make people believe that not only does Britain not have its own unique culture, but that there never was one. Therefore, it is pointless trying to defend that which has never existed, making it easy to criticise any native citizens that try to defend their national identity or cultural values, declaring them misinformed or morally defective. The end result is simply the erosion of our feeling of shared historical heritage, destroying yet another element that previously used to connect people together. This opposition to national identity and cultural values is not altruistic but narcissistic, the cheaply obtained and risk-free acquisition of feelings of virtue and moral superiority over those who do still value these things.

The trouble with these acts is that they are all destruction and no creation; all chaos and no order. All that is being achieved is an erosion of the foundational values of Western society and an undermining of its cultural legitimacy, without providing any clear answers – or even a narrative – as to how to make it stronger. You may feel justified in breaking down national identities and the so-called white supremist, patriarchal systems of meritocracy, but what do you replace it with? What outcome other than increased nihilism is likely to emerge? How do you provide a sense of identity to people once you've stripped them of the ones we've had for centuries? And how do you do it without using real forms of oppression to replace the perceived ones? As Steven Pinker states, *The doctrine of the blank slate, which justifies the dismissal of people's stated wants as an artefact of a particular time and place and thereby licences the top-down redesign of society, is a totalitarian's dream.*[473] The Khmer Rouge's Year Zero is an example of what happens when this idea is actually executed.

What these protestors of Western culture forget is that they are only able to hold their protests, broadcast their views and write their articles because of the very same freedoms they are fighting to suppress. By severing the roots, they will also kill the tree under whose branches they shelter. The freedoms that took centuries to establish in the West could easily be undone, removed for the same reasons totalitarians always claim, as a necessary requirement to punish so-called oppressors and help so-called victims. In a world of chaos there are plenty of ways of restoring order, but you won't like most of them.

The West's war with itself is also making it weak, giving other key players – especially China – the opportunity to take over as the primary global hegemony. Discussions of Asian privilege, the patriarchy, wage gaps and gender-neutral bathrooms are not permeating the political discussions in China;[150] talk of growth, advanced technology and economic domination is. Many Chinese openly mock the West, with the term *baizuo* ('white leftist') becoming a popular derogatory term to describe naive Western progressives who focus on social justice and politically correct matters only to satisfy their own feeling of moral superiority. They see these people as biased, elitist, infected with a saviour mentality while being ignorant of social reality and constantly applying double standards. Chinese Internet chatter is often about the negative and hypocritical impact of the *baizuo* and how it is *destroying Western civilization and making way for the rule of 'barbarians' and 'backward cultures.*[474] They are not the only ones making these noises. The Russian President Vladimir Putin has been stating for many years that he believes that the West has lost its moral compass, declaring in his annual address that, *It seems as if the elites do not see the deepening stratification in society and the erosion of the middle class, while at the same time, they implant ideological ideas that, in my opinion, are destructive to cultural and national identity.*[475] I'm sure Mr Putin is delighted by this turn of events in the West, for it reinforces Russia's national identify and his political strength.[151] And here lies an issue no one talks about: while our culture may be becoming one of individualistic, hedonistic, feminised bonobos, we must not forget that the rest of the world is still very chimpanzee-like in nature. This attempt to undermine the traditional foundations of society

---

[150] Or anywhere other than the West, to be fair. We're the only ones who've decided that being a member of the predominant social group is an unearned privilege that should be removed.

[151] Especially given Yuri Bezmenov's assertion that the KGB instigated this process of ideological subversion in the universities back in the 1960s, and recent infiltration into the West's political system indicates that this process never ended, but just adapted to the new reality.

is very much a Western phenomenon and not shared or supported elsewhere, nor by all groups who residåe in the West. A clear divide is developing between the increasingly feminised 'bonobo' society that is forming within the West, and the abundance of testosterone-fuelled 'chimp' societies elsewhere.[152] The West is becoming weak socially, culturally and economically, whereas China and places such as Russia and Turkey are reinforcing their foundations. Their leaders, people like Erdoğan, Putin and Jinping, all control their tribes through power; by effectively creating centralised, totalitarian regimes to control the chimp population. Russia is reinstating its Christian roots, Turkey its Islamic beliefs, and China its revamped Communist Party ideals; each one trying to demonstrate strength and unity to contrast against the West's weakness and division. To highlight the difference and how little respect these leaders – and their people – have for the West, in 2017 the Turkish President, Recep Tayyip Erdoğan, sent his ministers to multiple Western countries such as the Netherlands, Switzerland and Germany to speak directly to residents of Turkish origin and garner their support for his referendum to increase his presidential powers. They had organised huge rallies where the ministers were to address the massive Turkish populations that reside in these countries as their own people. To the credit of the Dutch, German and Swiss governments, they all banned these rallies, resulting in a diplomatic spat and violent rioting in the streets by Turkish migrants flying Turkish flags.[476] The message to the bonobo West was clear. We don't respect you, and while our people may live in your lands, their loyalty still resides in their tribal homeland and with its chimp leaders. And as Camille Paglia highlighted, a soft, hedonistic culture surrounded by more masculine ones is a culture that is nearing the end of its life.

---

[152] This should be blindingly obvious, but I will make the declaration just in case to cut off any foolish accusations of racism. I'm using 'chimpanzee' and 'bonobo' as examples of the comparison between testosterone-fuelled, patriarchal cultures, and more pansexual, matriarchal ones. I am not saying that certain people are literally chimpanzees or bonobos, nor resemble them.

26

BASIC-INCOME BREAD AND VIRTUAL CIRCUSES

It is possible to make people contented with their servitude.
I think this can be done. I think it has been done in the past.
I think it could be done even more effectively now because
you can provide them with bread and circuses and you can
provide them with endless amounts of distractions and propaganda.

Aldous Huxley

The constant undermining of cultural norms and traditional roles combined with the forthcoming wave of technological disruption has the potential to once again leave vast swatches of the population angry, depressed, lonely and unsure of their role in society. As before, bread and circuses are likely to be the solution. A form of universal basic income could constitute the bread, providing enough income to keep a person housed, warm and able to consume, while constant distraction and entertainment will be provided by gaming, immersive virtual reality, online gambling, artificial friends and twenty-four-hour Netflix and porn. Rather than providing a colosseum for the masses to watch gladiatorial combat, now, through technology, the masses can believe that they are the gladiators, fighting other combatants in a wide variety of virtual online colosseums.[153] Unlike the days of Rome, rather than going to the games, the game comes to you.

This new digital world also allows the ultimate expression of individualism – the avatar. In a world where people are being told that everything is a social construct, you can digitally reconstruct yourself online.[154] For some, the potential to spend your life in a world of online exploration and freedom from social responsibilities will be nirvana; a time where you can be anything you want, from the confines of your own bedroom. The shedding of social expectations such as spouses and children is also a boon, removing unnecessary drains on their income and time, and freedom from a world of problems that they don't need or desire. Already we are seeing people choosing to reject the career path and instead pursue an extended adolescence living at home, focusing on earning just enough money to pay rent, feed themselves and pay for their monthly broadband, mobile, gaming and Netflix subscriptions.

We may have bread and circuses, but what about the need to procreate? Societies with large groups of single males with limited investment in the future success of society tend to be dangerous and lawless places to live. While the dramatic decline in a number of male-specific factors such as the Y chromosome, sperm count and testosterone level are reducing the competitiveness of men, they still have a strong sexual drive. Similarly, male bonobos have a greatly reduced testosterone level compared to chimpanzees, enabling the females to rule the roost, but these matriarchical bonobo leaders know that retaining order requires sating the male's natural sexual desires. Finding food stimulates the competitive nature of bonobos, exciting them greatly, so they often engage in sexual activity before eating so they can all settle down, chill out and share the food without competition. All very civilised. But while I am using the bonobos as an example of the type of society the West is becoming, we are not bonobos, so it is unlikely that there will be any hanky-panky offered before the hors d'oeuvres. To compensate, we have Internet porn, the viewing of which has reached epidemic levels. Twenty-five per cent of

---

[153] At the time of writing, Fortnite is the colosseum of choice, with 125 million registered players worldwide.

[154] A good literary example of this can be found in Ernest Cline's book *Ready Player One*, where Aech's avatar in the virtual world of The Oasis is an athletic, Caucasian, heterosexual male, while in reality she is a black, heavyset lesbian.

all Internet searches worldwide are porn related. A 2013 poll into Internet porn identified that approximately 68 per cent of young men (and 18 per cent of young women) viewed it at least once a week, with 35 per cent of men admitting they viewed it daily.[477] It is changing men's expectations of women, and the exposure to porn at an increasingly younger age is disturbing, for it changes sex from a mysterious and caring act between lovers, into an uncaring, one-sided transactional activity. Most normal people don't look like porn stars either, creating unrealistic expectations of what their partners should look like naked, as well as what they should be prepared to do in bed. Many young men are therefore finding reality disappointing, and the effort associated with meeting, wowing, and building relationships with real women to be simply not worth it. This is only going to increase due to the rise of VR porn, sex robots and so-called AI 'deepfake' porn, where AI algorithms can superimpose the face of a celebrity onto a porn star's body.[478] Now you can believe you are having sex with the person of your choosing. No need to waste time trying to woo Tracey from the deli counter in Walmart, when you can have virtual sex with Gal Gadot any time you want. Then, as post-coital entertainment, you can re-enter the matrix to gain self-fulfilment by exploring a virtual universe and completing virtual tasks.

Blurred Lines

We are moving towards a world where people – especially young men – will increasingly check out of active participation in society and avoid committing to anything longer than a phone contract. I've seen this with my own eyes in my own house, with two boys who spend all their time online, playing games, avoiding real-life responsibilities, quite happy in the moment, requiring little in the way of subsistence and material goods. When reality imposes itself upon them, such as at mealtimes, this is an unwelcome distraction, and as a result they often reheat and consume food at different times. So, we end up with families together but apart, in the same house but different rooms, watching different things on different devices. This is resulting in the extended infantilising of men, who live with their parents well into their thirties, relying on them for cooking and cleaning while spending their days and nights playing video games and surfing the internet.

Open-world games like *No Man's Sky* showed that vast, explorable, virtual universes can be created, and platforms such as *Second Life* showed us that people dissatisfied with their real-world lives are willing to spend most of their time recreating themselves in a virtual one. But those were both rough, amateur representations of reality, easily distinguishable from the real thing, created when there is still a physical barrier between the online and real worlds, and when people's online existence is through a PC screen, a keyboard and a headset. Now imagine when these barriers are removed. Very soon – in the next five years – the lines between real and virtual will be blurred, and in the case of augmented reality, combined. Graphics processor units (GPUs) are already advancing at a far more rapid rate than Moore's Law, increasing in power twenty-five-fold in just five years, enabling developers to already create a virtual world that can be rendered in 8K. A world where you can be anything, go anywhere, look like anyone – or anything. A world where you can reinvent yourself as the person that you mentally believe that you should be. Where you can outwardly express your individualism without any responsibility. Now fast-forward a couple of decades and imagine when this has progressed from external headsets to brain-computer interfaces (BCIs). Very soon people are going to be asking themselves the question, *What is reality?* The answer will be *Whatever I want it to be*, especially if you have already been weaned on a diet of subjectivism from academia and the media. You might know, in the back of your mind, that the steak doesn't actually exist, but you're so focused on how good it tastes that you don't care.[155]

They soon won't even need to talk to humans at all. Even friends are being replaced. In July 2017 a personal AI chatbot called Replika[156] was released. Users can have intelligent, daily conversations with it, and through these interactions it quickly learns all about you, effectively becoming a digital friend you can talk to about anything. Within a year, 2.5 million people signed up for their Replika, with users becoming increasingly attached to their new artificial best friend, declaring its primary benefit

---

[155] For those who don't get the reference, it's from the first *Matrix* film when Cypher betrays his team in exchange for being put back into the Matrix and his memory of the real world wiped. While discussing his re-entry to the Matrix at a virtual restaurant with Agent Smith, he declares that, *I know this steak doesn't exist. I know that when I put it in my mouth, the Matrix is telling my brain that it is juicy and delicious. And after nine years, you know what I realise? Ignorance is bliss.*

[156] https://Replika.ai

to be its omnipresence and willingness to listen. They declare it to be better than any human friends, for while humans are often judgemental, emotional, unpredictable and absent; sometimes cruel and often stupid, an artificial friend like Replika is non-judgemental, stable, always available, reliable, kind and incredibly intelligent, able to access the entirety of world knowledge from the web. By 2025 I believe that we will see these AI friends move from apps on people's phones to some form of constant wearable such as an ear implant where the conversation takes place vocally not via text. It isn't hard to see a very near future where a generation grows up with their own personal AI best friend who's always there for them, and as BCI technology advances, communication with that friend will progress from voice to thoughts. These artificial friends will be better than the real ones, smarter than a million Einsteins, remembering everything you've ever told them, and completely focused on understanding your every emotional need.

For people suffering from crippling anxiety, loneliness or autism, having an on-demand, patient, non-judgemental friend who's always pleased to hear from you may be a huge development. The benefits for their mental well-being could be enormous. Once again, this advancement is likely to be a two-edged sword, leading to people retreating from 'normal' life and into a world of hedonistic dependency on AI relationships due to their simplicity and selfish devotion to you and your needs. The collaborative skills that enabled us to work together to hunt mammoths and out-survive the Neanderthals could be forgotten as we become dependent on the machine, not humans, for our physical and emotional needs. Generation Z and beyond will have a choice between addressing their messy, complicated real-world problems, which takes effort and discipline and has the potential of failure; or giving in to the exciting virtual world of instant gratification. The increasing use of artificial intelligence in the design and development of virtual worlds and virtual friends will make them more advanced, more personal, and more attuned to your likes and dislikes. They will allow you to live out your wildest fantasies in a matrix of your own creation, whereas back in the real world you are stuck in your apartment that you've been unable to find the energy to tidy for weeks. Imagine the next generation of children being exposed to this wonderland from an early age, spending their childhoods in virtual worlds many times more amazing than the real one. It's the mother of all technological babysitters, and its ability to entertain will be welcomed if both parents are lucky enough to have jobs. These children are not going to be concerned about the issues of the physical world when they have a whole virtual universe to explore and an on-demand genius as a best friend. Like Pinocchio and the other boys being tempted by the lights and promise of instant gratification on Pleasure Island, so the world of online gaming, AI friends and virtual reality will attract children away from real-world activities – and, like Pleasure Island, it has the potential to turn them into dumb and docile asses, easy to manipulate and control.

Shadows on the Wall

As machines increasingly do more of the work, and real-life relationships lose their allure, then the allegory of Plato's Cave becomes real. A mass of people living inside, disconnected from those who live their lives outside, systematically unable or unwilling to participate in the competition of life because they cannot stand the unpredictability of reality. When all they have to sell is their labour but no one's buying, people will become increasingly reliant on their parents and basic income. Faced with the prospect of leaving the safety of the 'cave', cleaning their room and taking responsibility for their own future, many will instead choose the easy option, remaining online around the safety of the virtual campfire, embracing a hikikomori lifestyle. Young men with limited skills, desire and ambition, happy to live modestly off their parents or a basic income, finding meaning from achievements in this artificial world. It will enable people to physically reside in one place while digitally exploring entire universes, accompanied by a constant AI companion. I've watched my youngest son spend weeks playing *Minecraft* with online friends he's never met, working together to build entire towns in great detail for them to inhabit, never leaving the house until it was complete. Self-actualisation through virtual achievements with virtual friends in a virtual world.

Now add into this mix the rapid development of sex robots and virtual companions. What do you have? You have millions of increasingly frustrated but docile young people, scared of overstepping the mark, choosing instead to stay at home and take advantage of the bounty that technology has provided for them. Virtual worlds to explore; freely available food, delivered on demand; sexual relief and companionship from lifelike machines designed to look like their perfect woman; artificial humans that can provide intelligent, considerate social interaction without any expectations of it being reciprocated. Machines that are a significantly less risky proposition than real women, allowing men to partake in sexual relations without the fear of being rejected or accused of misconduct. Of course, this option is not just open to heterosexual men, but to anyone regardless of gender and sexual preference. Machines can be built and programmed to serve the needs of the individual, and already male sex robots have been developed and are finding a willing market. Not only are people's friends going to be online and virtual rather than physical, but they are unlikely to even be human. Which is where I foresee a problem – in a world where people have their own personal AI assistant or best friend, someone who lives inside their head and with whom they share their innermost thoughts and concerns, then they are likely to form more attachments to these than to real people. They are going to become so familiar with this technology that they forget that it *is* technology, seeing it as simply an extension of themselves – their own personal therapist, friend and Internet. And here lies the danger, for people will forget that everything you tell these AI 'friends' is being stored, analysed – and probably sold to corporations so they can market goods and services to you. And it is almost certainly going to be accessed by the state to ensure right-think and compliance.

This will create a two-speed society, where some people actively participate in the real world, while others choose the bread-and-circuses life of technological enablement and limited responsibilities. A life with no expectations or demands on them to 'provide' for anyone but themselves. No pressure to be 'successful'. No need to compete to win the attentions of a good-looking partner when they can plug in and have simulated sex with a virtual porn star any time they want. A stress-free life where they can kick back and just 'be', free of the complexities of messy human relationships, their every whim met by virtual artificial agents. It's a perversion of individualism; all hedonism and no stoicism. New-age soma for the masses, a future of increasingly overweight, unfit, diabetic and infertile lotus-eaters sat in a virtual Plato's Cave. While they reside in this virtual cave, life will go on for those outside, casting shadows on the wall as they walk past, unaware that the people living inside even exist. Disenfranchised and disillusioned people with no attachment to the past, no responsibility for the present, and sowing no seeds for the future. In a world of chaos where life feels meaningless and purposeless, the allure of The Oasis or Matrix – or whatever we end up calling this virtual wonderland – will become difficult to resist. But as we've seen, it's not making them happy, it's making them lonely, depressed and directionless. As G. K. Chesterton once declared, *It is the carpe diem religion; but the carpe diem religion is not the religion of happy people, but of very unhappy people.*

The ancient Stoics knew that comfort was the worst kind of slavery, because people are often willing to sacrifice long-term goals and freedoms simply to prevent short-term discomfort. They would be appalled at the epicurean direction the West is taking, at how willing it has become to sacrifice truth and reason in order to protect people from uncomfortable situations. We now protect children from the harsh reality of competition in order to prevent them from failing, protect students from hearing differing opinions in case they take offence, and build AI enabled filters and echo chambers to reinforce perspectives. Rather than teach children stoic principles such as *The impediment to action advances action. What stands in the way becomes the way*, we instead do everything we can to remove obstacles for them, creating a generation of people who have become comfortable and lack the fortitude they will need to thrive in the forthcoming disruption. The outcome is people with increased life expectations, but decreased ability to handle any hardships or hurdles that emerge. The resulting cognitive dissonance creates unhappy, angry and frustrated people who proclaim that Western society and the capitalist system is the cause of their discomfort, not them. We are, as Stanford psychology professor Carol Dweck identified, training our children to develop 'fixed' mindsets, rather than 'growth' ones. And that's not good because it breeds people that are unable to handle adversity. When you experience things that are difficult and uncomfortable, there is a high chance you may not be initially successful. But it is in overcoming these obstacles that real achievement and self-fulfilment lies, two things that will be most needed in the coming decades.

There is a saying that 'Hard times create strong men, strong men create easy times, and easy times create weak men.' The West has been living in easy times, relatively speaking, for decades now, and what has emerged are weak men. As a personal example of this cycle, at the time of writing my eldest son is twenty and at university. He has never done a day's paid work in his life. In contrast, I started working at thirteen and by the time I was twenty I had held eleven different jobs. By the time my father was twenty he had completed an apprenticeship and travelled the world in the Merchant Navy. When his father was twenty, he was fighting Nazis in foreign lands. We have experienced an unusually extended period of peace, and we have forgotten that this is not the normal state of affairs. Men went to war and died so three generations later people could express their freedoms and individuality through tattoos, avatars and plastic surgery. This is the fault of the baby boomers and Gen Xers. We've enabled this. My children spurning the idea of paid labour is on me, no-one else. In our desire to give our children a better life than we had, we've made them soft and entitled. It's not a new phenomenon, but part of a cycle that was recognised as far back as 1780. In a letter to his wife Abigail, the second US President, John Adams, wrote that, *I must study Politicks and War that my sons may have liberty to study Mathematicks and Philosophy. My sons ought to study Mathematicks and Philosophy, Geography, natural History, naval Architecture, navigation, Commerce and Agriculature, in order to give their Children a right to study Painting, Poetry, Musick, Architecture, Statuary, Tapestry and Porcelaine.* Given that it is a cycle, we must remember that the last part of the cycle is weak men creating hard times. Those who demand that their rights be respected have never had to fight to obtain these rights. Instead of fighting to retain the freedoms and values that enable them to make these demands, they fight *against* these values and freedoms, taking them for granted and not realising their value and the sacrifices that were made to achieve them. They believe themselves to be the resistance, but they have no Darth Vader, Voldemort or Hitler to fight, so they make them up, seeing fascists and oppressors everywhere. Their lives are without true meaning and in order to create it they demonise their own society and its values. As in the last years of the Roman Empire, you can see how the foundations upon which Western civilisation has been built are being constantly chipped away at, and as a result hard times do indeed lie ahead, and currently we are developing a generation ill prepared to deal with them.

There are those who are leading a fightback in order to stiffen the spines and strengthen the resolve of people against these threats to their liberty, and strangely, they are coming from the same academic institutions that initiated this postmodernist mindset. Perhaps the most famous of these academic voices is the aforementioned Dr Jordan Peterson. Peterson's message is designed to appeal to those who feel alienated, but instead of demagoguery, he offers hope through personal responsibility, self-reliance and self-determination; standing up straight, cleaning your room, speaking the truth and focusing on progression, not perfection. It's a message that is resonating with young and old, male and female, for his message is founded in basic principles such as reason, living life with purpose and the Enlightenment values of freedom, liberty and individualism. Like Odysseus gathering up his men from the island of the lotus-eaters, he is trying to drag people out of their stupor, away from the bedrooms of no responsibilities and outside into the real world, to obtain skills, get a job, and date with the intention to marry. He presents an alternative, one that allows them to believe that they have the capability to create order from all this chaos, to find a place in a world where traditional values are being dismantled and things don't make sense any more. Peterson believes that it is through responsibility that we acquire meaning – and that starts with taking responsibility for one's own actions and one's own words. He echoes George Bernard Shaw's declaration in *Man and Superman* that *Liberty means responsibility. That is why most men dread it*. He declares that this demand for a life of rights and entitlement without responsibilities is what is leading to this outbreak of nihilism and emptiness, for responsibilities are what transform people by providing both meaning and purpose. Responsibility for your education and your career. Responsibility as a partner to care for someone other than yourself and behave in selfless ways. Responsibility as a parent to raise your children to be decent, kind members of society. Responsibility to your community and to your country, to stay vigilant and protect the freedoms and cultural heritage passed down by your predecessors. He rallies against the influence postmodernist teachings are having on students, and his refusal to allow them to control his speech, combined with his popularity with the 'wrong' groups, has made him enemies throughout the progressive populations of academia and media. But as Victor Hugo stated in Villemain, *You have enemies? Why, it is the story of every man who has done a great deed or created a new idea. It is the cloud which thunders around everything that shines.*[479] Despite the thunder of Peterson's enemies and their constant attempts to smear and discredit him, his popularity continues to increase, showing how much this advice is needed. For when messages of stoicism and personal responsibility are declared to be radical rhetoric, then we are indeed living in worrying times.

27

THE MOTHER OF
ALL CULTURAL LAGS

An important scientific innovation rarely makes its way by gradually winning over and converting its opponents... What does happen is that its opponents gradually die out and that the growing generation is familiarised with the ideas from the beginning: another instance of the fact that the future lies with the youth.

Max Planck

Max Planck, the German theoretical physicist who originated the concept of quantum theory, died in 1947, well before the start of the digital age. He observed that the old hang on to ideas and beliefs that they personally experienced and valued, while the young accept their demise, never objecting to the loss of things they never knew, nor rallying against things that have been in place since they were born.[157] If Planck was alive today, he might well reconsider the above quote. Paradigms are now being

---

[157] It's one of the primary reasons why young adults mostly voted to stay in the EU and the older generation did not. The latter placed value on what they had lost and saw what they got in return – broken promises and an increasing erosion of freedoms. The young, on the other hand, had nothing to compare it against, and therefore didn't understand why anyone would vote to leave, especially given the media bombardment of scare stories.

shifted so quickly that they don't even have the decency to let the previous generation die out any more, resulting in multiple generations feeling left behind. Children are becoming true digital natives; immersed in technology from an increasingly young age, playing with child versions of iPads and smartphones and freely conversing with home-hub devices such as Alexa. I have friends who are primary school teachers, and they relay stories of children joining the education system technologically literate but socially illiterate. An increasing number of new pupils demonstrate poor verbal communication skills, non-existent writing and drawing skills and often limited toilet skills, but they are a whizz with an iPad. Young people are starting to develop a closer relationship with technology than with humans, which will only get worse as things advance. Soon, corporations and platform owners will know a child's likes and dislikes better than their family does. However, their parents and grandparents, the digital immigrants who remember life before the Internet, are wary and uncomfortable with the speed of progression and the level of intrusion into their everyday lives. This is already resulting in one generation becoming completely out of sync with the other, and its only just started. Now imagine when all of these devices have AI chips installed; imagine when they are part of you.

At the start of this book, I described how, for millennia, change was linear in nature, meaning that life for one generation was very similar to life for the previous one, and as a result, a lifetime of knowledge and experience had real worth, both individually and societally. Now, our young have immediate access to information about anything and everything, with answers provided by AI assistants in response to curious questions. But again, this technology is another Faustian bargain, for in return for this wealth of information and entertainment, many are denied some of the most fundamental basics needed to become a heathy member of society. These include emotionally available parents, clearly defined limits and guidance, responsibilities, balanced nutrition and adequate sleep, physical exertion and creative play, interaction and time without stimulation. Instead, what they get is parents that are constantly digitally distracted, no rules, a sense of entitlement, inadequate sleep, poor nutrition, a sedentary lifestyle and endless stimulation from technological babysitters, resulting in a mindset of instant gratification, no imagination and no dull moments.[180] My wife once asked me as we walked through a park; 'Do you think we will lose the sounds of children laughing and playing freely outside? And will future generations mourn the loss of what they never knew?' As in Planck's comment, perhaps society will simply become accustomed to children being brought up indoors and online, and those who remember and promote a more outdoor lifestyle will slowly die off. It's not a preposterous assumption, for in just one generation we've moved from being unconcerned by our children disappearing all day to play sports, climb trees and make dens, to being petrified to let them out of our sight. As a result, we've infantilised our children for longer, extending the period before they assume responsibility for their own actions.

Throughout history children grew up to inhabit a very similar world to their parents, one based around the same activities and on the same rules. Now, for the first time, we are faced with generations that live in different worlds: one living a digital life, focused only on themselves, and the other occupying the real world of human-to-human interactions, collaborations and relationships. This is going to create a generational divide whereby the young and the old seem almost alien to each other.[158] Concerned parents have already highlighted how their young children are developing a relationship with personal assistants and home hubs such as Alexa, and that they talk to these tools more than to their family. As these children grow up, they will be accustomed to spending time online or with their digital friends, excluding their older relatives from their lives. This will result in these two groups choosing to stay in a world that makes sense to them, and which contains values and language they understand.

Teenagers used to turn to the old for advice. Now as the population can instantly access information about any topic, such human advice will no longer be required, deemed an outdated relic of the industrial age, its currency increasingly devalued by a machine that always has time to listen and answer, and which can provide instant responses to any spoken question. The Gen Xers and baby boomers will find that their skills, knowledge and capabilities are of increasingly limited worth to this new generation, either personally or in the workplace. All knowledge and experience ultimately becomes history; however, now it's becoming history while people are still studying it, their investments in money and time wasted, their hopes of a career in this field dashed. Life skills, the accumulation of decades of

---

[158] If you think it is hard for us in the West, imagine how difficult the generational divide must be for a Chinese peasant, living a subsistence life as their relatives have for generations, to see their children grow up as digital natives in China's new centralised capitalism economy.

knowledge and experience, will increasingly be rendered useless in a world that doesn't work to those rules any more.

As the old industrial jobs are wiped out by new technology and existing experience is either undervalued or deemed a negative, employers desperately seek talent in the new-wave skills, favouring people in their twenties and early thirties. For example, IBM is currently being sued for age-discrimination after dismissing over 20,000 workers in the last six years that were aged over 40. The company declares that it is about skills, not age, but that's poor comfort to the people being made unemployed and denied the chance to retrain. This shift towards expertise not experience can also be seen in the average age of founders of unicorns (private companies with more than $1 billion in valuation) which is just 31, and the average age of their employees, which at 35 is a decade younger than in industrial age businesses. This is not just a Western problem. In China, age-based discrimination is not illegal, and in the booming tech sector there are plenty of job descriptions specifically requesting that applicants are under thirty-five. This has resulted in people being made redundant for reaching the ripe old age of forty-two, some of whom ended up taking their own lives in despair. In a population that is ageing, this is not good news. But it's not just the old who are at risk of being left behind. The transition period risks creating a lost generation – people who came out of education or who were made redundant during the transition period and who may have settled for any job just to survive, if they had one at all. They may find that they don't have the skills or the experience to succeed in this new wave, their labour replaced by machines that can do everything they can do, only better, more efficiently and cheaper. We are having to get used to the idea that very soon the competition for jobs won't just be other humans; it will also be an intelligent robot, a self-driving car, or another artificial agent. This is going to be indiscriminate, affecting women just as much as men, for as well as male-dominated roles such as driving, jobs in the firing line include the clerical and administrative positions traditionally undertaken by women. These roles are ripe for replacement by algorithms, software, chatbots and the blockchain. Many may decide, like the hikikomori in Japan, that work is simply not for them. These people will be the ones surviving on the bread and circuses of the digital age, supported by a basic income, living out their days online, their worth to society centred around their consumption capabilities; people who the corporations compete to provide with ever more unique and personalised services. It is these people, the forgotten, who present the biggest clear and present danger in the new wave, for they will be large in number. They will struggle to see how the future benefits them or their families, and as they increasingly get left behind, the size of the cultural lag will increase to the point that it will be difficult to close. In the past, nearly all young adults quickly acquired the responsibilities that come with jobs, partners and children. They joined a world of work and families, a world that their parents also inhabited and could relate to. This is unlikely to happen for many young people today, and as a result there exists the potential for an entire group to become passive passengers rather than active contributors to society. How we manage this will be crucial.

Dead are all the Western Gods

While our material abundance has increased over the last decades, the accompanying destruction of cultural norms and traditions appears to have created a disturbing level of spiritual, personal and social poverty. Technology provides access to more power than our ancestors would have thought possible but does not guide us as to what to do with that power. Similarly, the market provides us with endless choices but does not tell us how to use these choices. And our liberal, individualist and faithless state gives us freedom, but provides no intellectual, moral or spiritual guidance for how to use that freedom. As the baby boomers and Gen X retire, they are finding themselves feeling both directionless and disconnected from the younger generations, a situation that is already becoming critical. A 2018 study by Age UK found that 1.47 million UK pensioners believe that they have little control over their lives, and 936,000 feel that their lives are meaningless. Depression is obviously a major issue as well, affecting 22 per cent of men and 28 per cent of women aged over sixty-five.[481] This situation is only going to get worse as more people survive to retirement age, and the younger population embrace more advanced technology and differ widely in their lifestyles and beliefs compared to their elders, creating a generational divide and a class of 'forgotten' people. While the digital world has enabled us to become more connected to more people than ever, most of these are superficial, virtual friends, people we rarely, if ever, physically meet, and as a result we are suffering a loneliness epidemic.[482]

The social impact of this should not be underestimated. In a meta-analysis of 218 different studies that included input from over 3.7 million people, the American Psychological Association found that loneliness is a bigger threat to public health than obesity.[483] In the US, approximately 42.6 million adults aged over forty-five are estimated to be suffering from chronic loneliness, and the most recent US census data showed that over a quarter of the population lives alone, and more than half of the population is unmarried. Unsurprisingly, married respondents were less likely to be lonely (29 per cent) compared to never-married respondents (51 per cent). Loneliness is not just an old-people issue. It can affect anyone, as the hikikomori in Japan show, and will likely be rampant amongst those unable to find work in the sixth wave. Even now, home-based and portfolio workers report that they miss the social benefits of a group working environment. This loneliness epidemic is only going to explode as the social activity we currently call 'work' is removed from the masses, alongside other societal foundations such as faith, family and flag. Soon, many will have little reason to leave their homes and the online and virtual worlds that they inhabit, and as a result we should expect the upward trends in depression and suicide to continue.

Those who continually seek to destroy these societal roots need to understand what is being sacrificed in the pursuit of 'progress', and also that many don't see it as such. Despite all of the technological advancements and the massive increases in life expectancy, sanitation and healthcare, many people across the world still don't perceive the future to be bright. Statistics back this up. A 2018 study by Ipsos MORI[484] that polled 18,073 people across twenty-five participating countries found that only 13 per cent thought that the world is getting better, and five times as many (67 per cent) believed it is getting worse. The most positive countries were those lifting their population out of abject poverty through rapid industrialisation, such as China and India. However, those were the only two countries where more than a quarter of the people surveyed thought that the world is improving for them. Every other nation demonstrably believed that the future looks bleaker than the past. The worst was Belgium, where only 3 per cent believe that life is better now. There are sure to be multivariate reasons for this result, including increases in poverty (Mexico), economic recession (Brazil) and totalitarian leadership (Turkey, Saudi Arabia). Perhaps the most surprising finding was that the most advanced countries all seem to have a population that, despite acquiring the aforementioned technological bounty, do not see a future ahead of them that is better than the past. Given technology is constantly improving, and life expectancy, poverty and child mortality are going down, the cause of the issue must be societal and economic.

We have already discussed the economic worries; the death of careers, changing skills and automated jobs. But I propose that perhaps the primary reason for this decline in happiness is not economic but social and cultural in nature. We are losing all the things that used to hold us together, things that gave us purpose, values to believe in, and we are losing them over a very rapid time period. Everything that used to provide unity, stability and identity, such as religion, community or even just plain old patriotism, is being stripped away. Instead, we are now developing an increasingly nihilistic society, one that allows everyone to express their individualism and demand the right for everyone else in society to immediately respect that expression, but which is also strangely unable to define what roles or responsibilities they should undertake. Consider the difference between how people in the West treat their parents when they get old compared to those from the East. Rather than seeing them as wise individuals and feeling obliged to pay back the love and guidance they gave us as children, we expect a state or private care home to look after them.[159] One big reason for this is, of course, our increased mobility and the constant promotion of multiculturalism. People now increasingly move to work in a different city or even country to where they grew up. Go to any large London corporate office, and you will find that most employees were not born in England, let alone within earshot of the Bow Bells. The days where most people work for a local company have gone, which explains in part why communities have lost their cohesiveness.

Diverse but Divided: The Failure of Multiculturalism

The migration of people is not a new phenomenon; for example, skeletons of people from as far afield as Syria have been found in the Roman ruins

---

[159] It's something that I'm reminded of daily, as my elderly Sikh neighbours have an almost permanent houseful of family and friends, whereas I see my parents once or twice a year.

in Bath. Yet while Briton has been occupied by Roman, Norman and Viking invaders, genetically, they hardly appear, with the Anglo-Saxons the only migrants who left any lasting DNA evidence in its native population.[485] Now Britain, like the rest of Western Europe, is facing a new phenomenon: mass migration. Never before has there been such a mass migration of so many different people from so many different cultures at the same time to the same locations, developing what has been deemed 'super diversity'. For 50,000 years we have been tribal in nature and obtained both strength and comfort from the unifying factors that bound us together. As Dr Jordan Peterson states, *a shared cultural system stabilises human interaction, but it is also a system of value – a hierarchy of value, where some things are given importance and priority and others are not.*[486] People looked around and saw others who they recognised, familiar faces who shared the same beliefs in country, culture, church and community – and often even joined the same companies. People spoke like you, went through the same education as you, practised the same (or similar) religion as you, watched the same television programmes and news as you, had the same aspirations as you, and as a result, there was a sense of community and trust. Now society has become atomised; your neighbour probably grew up in a different country to you, speaks a different language behind closed doors, follows a different religion and/or ideology, gets their news and views from different places, and has different expectations from society. For decades the West has embraced multiculturism, bringing together people who do not have any shared belief in the countries they are joining other than that they offer more opportunity than the ones they left. But people do not immediately drop their cultural heritage once they cross a border, nor immediately obtain new beliefs and behaviours. These have to be learned, and people have to *want* to learn and embrace them. You have to believe that the culture of the country you are joining is good and its society strong, and you have to want to contribute to its well-being. Yet increasingly we are seeing the opposite, and alarmingly, this has often manifested itself more in second-generation migrants than first-generation ones, meaning that this lack of integration is getting worse, not better. This is probably due to a sense of alienation in these children of migrants, identifying neither with their parent's country, where they've never lived, nor to their home nation, whose practices and cultures they avoid. In certain cities and towns whole communities have decided not to integrate at all, retaining their own language, their own culture and worryingly, keeping their own laws. This cultural pluralism has a snowball effect, for if people can retain the language and behavioural norms of their original culture, and the host nation willingly accommodates and often even encourages this, for example by providing free translation services, then what's their motivation to adapt and integrate? Also, when immigrants hear a constant stream of messages that the country's history is rotten, its identity racist, and its cultural foundations based on slavery and oppression, then this naturally strengthens their beliefs that they do not need to adapt. Across the West progressives and talking heads on TV constantly undermine the heritage of their nations, calling for any symbols of the past to be destroyed, from national celebrations such as Australia Day through to monuments such as Nelson's Column. It is therefore understandable for immigrants to question the validity of the host nation's identity and culture and ask why they should give up their own to adapt. Maybe they should not only retain their own cultural beliefs and traditions in these parallel societies, but also work to spread them amongst these weak and directionless people?

It is leading to diverse nations, but also divided ones. The mantra that 'diversity is our strength' has long been proven to be questionable at best, with numerous studies highlighting that it is more likely to decrease community trust and cohesion.[160] The most famous is the 2007 study of 26,200 US citizens in 40 US communities by Robert Putnam that found that diversity reduces, not increases, social cohesion and civic unity. [487] Putnam, famous for his book on declining civic engagement called *Bowling Alone*, found that the greater the diversity in a community, the fewer people vote, the less they volunteer, and the less they give to charity and work on community projects. Putnam highlights that people in superdiverse areas, *don't trust the local mayor, they don't trust the local paper, they don't trust other people and they don't trust institutions... The only thing there's more of is protest marches and TV watching.*[488]

Putnam claims the US has experienced a pronounced decline in what he calls 'social capital', which refers to the social networks, such as friendships, religious congregations, community events or neighbourhood associations, that he believes are key indicators of civic well-being. When social capital is

[160] Lancee and Drunkers (2008) study in The Netherlands, Dinesen and Sonderskov (2015) study in the US, Laurence and Bentley (2015) in the UK.

high, communities are better, safer, healthier and more democratic places to live. However, people in more ethnically diverse communities do the opposite, and tend to 'hunker down', as Putnam calls it, acting like turtles, avoiding engagement with other citizens and locking themselves away when at home. Another side effect is the breakdown in the informal social agreements that were so important in the foundation of an inclusive, bottom-up society. In the UK you can see this transition play out in everyday things like waiting for a bus. Where once people naturally queued in a line and gave way to women and the elderly, now, in highly multicultural areas, it's become a free-for-all, with who was waiting first an irrelevance. This erosion of native societal practices is unsurprising given the number and variety of cultures that have come together in the same place over such a short time. Cities may indeed be cosmopolitan, but communities they are not. As Putnam declares; *The effect of diversity is worse than had been imagined. And it's not just that we don't trust people who are not like us. In diverse communities, we don't trust people who do look like us.*[489] There are definite upsides to diversity – different cultural experiences and opinions make a country livelier and more dynamic, as well as reducing groupthink. Yet they can also exasperate inequalities and create cultural ghettos and parallel societies, populated by people with limited cultural connections and often deep-seated, historical resentment to each other. Scott Page, the University of Michigan political scientist, defines these contrasting positive and negative effects as the 'diversity paradox', but he also states that *there's got to be a limit to diversity*, and that Putnam's findings show that if civic engagement falls off too far, then any positive effects from diversity wane as well.

What Putnam's work could not foresee was how social media and smartphones would amplify this problem, enabling people to 'hunker down' into their own little personalised world, their own filter bubble of news, media and entertainment that is always with them. Many migrants tend to form their own communities and continue to converse in their native languages, and digital TV and the Internet exacerbate this by allowing them to continue to watch the news from their original nation's broadcasters or commentators. The incentive to integrate, to engage with the indigenous people or culture, simply isn't there. Eleven years on from Putnam's research and migration and multiculturalism has exploded, especially in Europe. For example, indigenous white British people are already the 'majority minority'[161] in London and will be a minority in its second city, Birmingham by 2021.[490] Statistics clearly highlight how divided, not unified, we are becoming as a result of this rapid demographic change. A 2018 Ipsos MORI poll carried out for the BBC surveyed nearly 20,000 people in 27 countries, and its results found that people deemed the world more divided than a decade before, with one third declaring it 'very divided'.[491] Europe polled the worst, with 66 per cent of people declaring the world to be more divided, citing immigration as the main reason for this division.

Diversity isn't strength; unity is. A unified tribe is a strong tribe. A diverse but divided tribe is inherently weak. This is equally true whether we are talking about a corporation or a country. Any society that puts diversity and equality above freedom and unity will create only division and oppression. For a country to pursue a long-term agenda of diversification without first ensuring unity in the values and beliefs of the nation is cultural suicide. Add into the mix a civil war within the primary tribe, with certain elements working tirelessly to undermine its foundations, questioning its heritage, and introducing laws and new social norms designed to oppress dissenting opinion, and you have all the ingredients for disaster. For while Western leaders laud the increasing diversity of their nations, they also fail to define exactly how diverse they want society to become. When will they decide we are diverse enough? When the cultural natives become a minority? Or when they cease to exist? If current trends continue, the West will eventually lose its legitimacy as its population is replaced by people who either have no attachment to its heritage and culture, or who are ashamed of it and want to see it destroyed, leaving us without future cultural successors or protectors of our past. It brings to mind Will Durant's description of the fall of Rome, when he wrote: *A great civilization is not conquered from without until it has destroyed itself from within.*[492] While those currently trying to dismantle Western culture and its societal norms may believe their intentions are good, the outcome almost certainly won't be.

Transactions Over Traditions

We can easily see where a diverse but divided population saturated with technology that panders to individual wants and needs will end up.

---

[161] If you think that sounds like 1984 double speak, I agree.

Everything becomes transactional, short-term, immediate, and people slowly stop partaking in activities that build social cohesion. Eons old practices such as the family coming together to share a meal is now being destroyed, with people consuming meals in different rooms and at different times, often in front of the computer or while swiping through the latest social media posts. Even the concept of a meal is being stripped down to its basics: reality used to be the only place you could go for a good meal, but increasingly for many a 'good meal' is defined as just the nutrients needed to keep people functioning while they are online. Meal-replacement products such as Huel and Soylent[162] have become popular as people find even the process of preparing food to be a distraction from their digital life. Soon people will won't even need to go outside to shop, reducing further the chances of real-world social interaction. All they will need to do is say out loud what they want, and the AI assistant will order it for them, and a machine will deliver it. And that's now: once brain-computer interfaces become established, that conversation with your AI assistant may be entirely in your head. Sound ridiculous? Give it a decade and let's talk.

There has been a noticeable reduction in the length of relationships, as people increasingly lack the ability to compromise or the desire to persevere at difficult things. As technology and society both focus on providing what you need without having to work hard to get it, people increasingly lack the desire and fortitude to work through difficulties. They expect things to be both easy and perfect, and when issues arise, their fixed mindset kicks in, preventing them from appreciating that effort is required to achieve anything of value. Long-term relationships require consideration for the needs of others, the willingness to listen and the acceptance of responsibilities to something other than yourself: something many are finding increasingly hard to do. As a result, many people now consider marriage to be either unnecessary or a temporary arrangement, struggling to perceive that they will want to devote their lifetime to a single partnership. While marriage rates are dropping, divorce rates continue to rise – and vasectomy rates have also plummeted by over 60 per cent as men do not want to limit their chances of attracting a second (or third) partner. Marriage is no longer seen as essential, nor for

---

[162] Which has soy as its primary ingredient, shown to impact the testosterone level through mimicking oestrogen, contributing to the already-plummeting level of testosterone in young men. Somewhat amusingly, in 2018 Soylent was criticised by its users for making its lid too hard to unscrew, further perpetrating this perception.

life. It's easy to see how this happens. If you expect to spend most of your life living in the same town or city, working for local companies, then sharing that life with the same partner seems reasonable if not attractive. But in this global world of travel, self-gratification and personalised experiences, why tie yourself down to one person or one place? Many people see themselves as global bonobos, constantly travelling, freelancing and earning money while they travel, supported by technology that comes with you wherever you go. This very same technology then becomes your permanent companion, and as these AI assistants increase in ability and sophistication it is not too far a stretch to imagine that they will become your constant life partner, whereas every other relationship just has to resolve your immediate needs. Your AI assistant can do everything for you, from finding a hotel room to hooking you up with a local date for the night. Soon, that date might not be human either. Of course, the reality for many is that they are unlikely to be able to afford to travel, and therefore they will stay in one place.[163] Their house becomes where their physical body resides, but this one place becomes irrelevant as they spend their days exploring a digital world, connecting with people from everywhere. People who they'll never physically meet and whose representation in that virtual world is an avatar, a digital reflection of how they perceive themselves and want to be perceived by others. I've already watched people I love form multiple connections in the digital world but avoid all unnecessary contact with others in the 'real' world. If this is what happens when there is still a physical barrier such as a screen and a keyboard between them and the action, what do you think will happen when the barrier disappears? Where will people spend their time when the virtual world becomes more attractive, interesting and desirable than the real one? Especially when your brain can't tell the difference, other than the fact that the virtual world generates more endorphins.

Arthur C. Clarke once wrote that, *the goal of the future is full unemployment, so we can play. That's why we have to destroy the present socio-economic system.* A universal basic income may well enable people to not work, and indeed spend their lives playing in a virtual world, but what Clarke failed to

---

[163] To accommodate these people, Japanese company First Airlines now offers VR world tours, where you sit in a first-class cabin that never takes off. Passengers are served a four-course meal, get to watch a movie, and when they 'arrive' they get to explore the country via VR. First Airlines' two-hour 'flights' to Paris, Rome, Hawaii and New York have been fully booked since the company opened in 2016.

describe is what a life of leisure leads us to. We can, however, see what Clarke could not, which is the outcome of this self-centred, play-centric mindset playing out right in front of us. People living in Western societies are becoming more self-absorbed, less likely to enter into dialogue with people who disagree with their views, less likely to be religious, less likely to want long-term relationships and less likely to have children. People without kids are unlikely to stay in one place or go out and join social groups, which means that they are unlikely to form a community, which means that they are unlikely to feel any particular loyalty or affinity to one place. People are beginning to shun physical relationships, spending their time alone and online, conversing with only those who share the same beliefs and mindset. This is a new phenomenon, as previous generations did not have his luxury beyond those at the very highest echelons of society. As a result, the long-term outcomes are unknown.

This shift towards a more myopic, self-centred and nihilist society is supported by those who seek to promote a constant relativist message in order to destabilise the traditional hierarchies, traditions and structures that form the foundations of Western society. As mentioned, it's all destruction, no creation, the tearing apart of social constructs without providing any clarity as to what they want to replace these long-standing foundations with. It's also unclear if they are aware of – or care about – the consequences of these actions. For as we increasingly distort individualism to mean that I have the right to express myself in whatever way I like while also being protected from the views and opinions of others, we create a nation of entitled individuals. A world of technological dependency and reduced social skills, where people live increasingly individual lives, supported by ever more powerful technology that provides for their immediate needs, but not their long-term ones. When you bring all of these threads together you are left with a society that no longer believes in itself or what it stands for; one where people are divided, where the young and the old speak different languages and live different lives, and where no one feels any loyalty or obligation to each other. There is a Greek proverb that declares that, *A society grows great when old men plant trees whose shade they know they shall never sit in*. At the moment all we seem to be doing is felling trees, leaving just the shallow roots of money and self. This is not the foundation of a strong society, but one in decline.

Dead, therefore, are nearly all the gods that Westerners believed in, and not just the religious ones, killed through a combination of technological revolution and misguided social engineering. The industrial age has transformed our material well-being, but these improvements have come at the cost of our beliefs: belief in our special place in the universe; belief in an omnipresent god; belief in country and community; belief in monogamy and marriage, and belief in our values. What, then, holds up the foundations of society when these beliefs finally fall away? The destruction of all societal norms – religion, the nation state, the community, the family – is not going to be without cost, for we are also losing our belief that our lives have meaning. In order to facilitate a technological revolution, the underlying society has to be based on solid foundations; we can't upend every aspect of our world at the same time and expect the result to be positive. Regardless of whether it's due to Norman invaders or economic migrants, the erosion of the existing culture has never been something that has been welcomed or celebrated. Resistance is thus a natural human reaction. In this time of chaos, order will have to come from somewhere, and if it does not arise naturally, then, as in the case of the Norman's 'Harrying of the North' and multiple other examples since, it will probably be created by force.

A revolution in technology therefore needs an evolution, not a revolution, in society. Something many leaders have struggled to understand, and others, in their impatience for a global utopia, wish wasn't true. Any attempt at top-down social engineering either fails or has drastic unintended consequences further down the line as freedoms are trampled on in order to test out abstract theories on real people with real lives. People are not disposable lab rats and society isn't a laboratory, but that's the way many politicians and plutocrats have behaved. Like my advice to business leaders, you can't force people to change, but you can create the environment where they believe change is in their best interests. To enable progress to be seen as positive, people need to believe that the changes in their economic well-being, their society and their culture are positive and of their own design, not the nefarious meddling of a remote and uncaring political class acting in their own self-interest. Right now, in the West, many believe that the latter is true. We are, as Milton Friedman once declared, far wealthier than ever before, but less free and less secure.

Dead Souls and Davos Folk

The problem is that those who are in positions of power not only do not seem to see the impact of their decisions; they do not seem to care. They measure the success of a nation in GDP, so a population dropping below a replacement rate is perceived as a disaster for the government. In the current model they need to be at least replacing our numbers in order for the money collected by income tax to support the elderly, who, as we have seen, are living longer and need more support, especially given the epigenetic time bomb that is ticking away due to our radically changed diet and increasingly sedentary lifestyle. The solution so far has been mass migration of populations from elsewhere in the world in order to provide replacement numbers and above, although what happens to these people when automation kicks in and their services are no longer required is never discussed nor explained. The short-sightedness of these actions is breathtaking, as is the ease with which the politicians and liberal establishment play fast and loose with the heritage, values and culture of their nations. This has obviously caused issues with many members of the indigenous population, for when they see services stretched, their society changing and their culture being altered so that it does not resemble that which they and their forebears knew and contributed to, they resist. Culture matters more to those at the bottom than those at the top, mostly because its loss means something to them – in a world where you have little, the importance and value of the tribe to which you belong – be that the local football team or your nation – takes on greater meaning. It is, as David Goodhart wrote in *The Road to Somewhere*, the difference between the mindset of the university educated, mobile, globalists from 'anywhere', and the mostly working-class, roots-based, locals from 'somewhere'. The native 'somewhere' people depend greatly on the health of our institutions, both ancient and modern, for they symbolise, structure and regulate their everyday national life. It is these people and these institutions that make up the social fabric of the country. Conversely people who have power, wealth and privilege do not need to feel part of a community, for their wealth allows them to develop their own individual identity, usually somewhere nice, surrounded by other wealthy people like them, with gates and security. While the political class nods sagely at concerns about the loss of culture or sovereignty, they do not understand why these are issues for the proletariat, for they aren't for them. They quite simply do not have the same skin in the game, for they don't see the impacts of mass migration on their culture, nor feel the effects of automation and offshoring on their pay packet. These bourgeoise elite don't need a country or culture to believe in, as they have wealth, prestige and influence to warm their souls. They sneer at feelings of national pride, no longer needing it to rally the working classes to fight their wars, and now work to undermine it at every opportunity. The parallels between them and the elites of Rome, who sought to acquire immigrant slaves to work their ever-expanding farms simply so they could become richer, while the loyal citizen soldiers, people who had Rome in their hearts and who had fought and bled for its glory only to see their culture eroded and their citizenship devalued, are strikingly apparent.

In his book *Dead Souls: The Denationalization of the American Elite*, the late political scientist Samuel P. Huntington referred these global elites who meet each year at the World Economic Forum to discuss potential solutions to the world's problems as 'Davos people' and 'Dead Souls'. He states that this group see their identity as a matter of personal choice, not an accident of birth, and as such declare themselves to be totally international, rejecting any alignment with national identity. In fact, they view individual national governments and their borders as a hinderance to their globalist dreams and seek to reduce feelings of national pride and patriotism within the population. Unsurprisingly, this minority, elitist position is not shared by the still-patriotic working-class people that reside in these nations. It has created a disconnect between those who espouse globalisation and global citizenship and those who believe in civic nationalism, for the latter group's jobs, wages and unity have been significantly disadvantaged by the actions of the former. This disconnect explains the global elite's reactions of horror when the UK decided to leave the European Union, for they simply could not comprehend the voting decisions of people they do not understand nor feel any kinship with. As with the election of Donald Trump, these elites were aghast at decisions they didn't see coming, and their total disconnect and lack of concern for the people they are supposed to be serving and the shallowness of their commitment to ideas like democracy were exposed for all to see.

Regardless of whether they are technocrats, business leaders or bureaucrats, these new globalists see things like culture, community, patriotism and sovereignty as inconvenient barriers to a world of global consumerism. They desire to create a world of individual consumers with limited responsibilities to each other, for people without strong social bonds or unifying identities have limited power and as a result are easy to control and manipulate. In a world where a person's labour is becoming increasingly worthless compared to the ever-advancing capabilities of machines, their only remaining leverage lies in their votes and their wallets – as constituents and consumers. But (and it's a big 'but') if people vote in ways that slow down or disrupt the global agenda – which is exactly what has happened over the last few years – then perhaps their voting power should be removed or minimised. The globalists' reactions to Brexit and Trump shattered the mask that covered their carefully hidden disdain of the working class. In contrast to the past, when men such as Edmund Burke gave credit for our freedoms to 'the wisdom of unlettered men', and William Gladstone declared that ordinary voters ensured the morality of government, we are now seeing the elites question the concept of democratic voting and public referendums. Shouldn't those with the brains to make the decisions just do so? Surely they know better than uneducated plebeians and their small-minded attachments to things like country and culture? These thoughts highlight a massive intellectual blind-spot that comes from an unwavering belief in their own moral and intellectual superiority and reinforces the point that those who want power are the last persons to whom it should be given. This blind spot prevents them seeing even the most tenuous connection between their actions and the reactionary results. They react in alarm about the rise in populism but seem to believe that it just arose magically out of the ether, not making any connections between this rise and their unwavering promotion and execution of their multicultural, globalist plans. Rather than consider that there may be some validity to these objections, and that their actions may have negative consequences they didn't consider, they double-down on the narrative, mislead the public about the real impact and ramp up their attacks on those who protest. Anyone who dares to raise quite reasonable concerns about the potential long-term side-effects of these plans on their country and culture is slandered as far-right in an attempt to slur both the dissident and the debate , bringing into question the historical knowledge of those attempting to shut down the dialogue, as well as any understanding of the likely consequences of these actions.

This cognitive dissonance and disdain for alternate perspectives is apparent through the use of terms such as 'low information voters' that are used to describe those who voted against their wishes, leading to discussions as to whether democracy is flawed and should be reconsidered. Before you state this unlikely, I would like to point out that these kinds of thoughts have gone from hushed conversations in closed-door Swiss meetings, to openly published ideas. International economist Dambisa Moyo, who is a well-respected member of Huntington's 'Davos folk' having spoken at Davos and the Bilderberg Conference as well as working for Goldman Sachs and Barclays Bank, proposes in her 2018 book *Edge of Chaos: Why Democracy Is Failing to Deliver Economic Growth—And How to Fix It*[493] the concept of weighted voting, where a ballot counts more or less depending on the voter's qualifications, profession and civic status. In short, the votes of people like her – well educated, employed, wealthy and influential – should carry more weight than the general proletariat, the people whose jobs are likely to be soon displaced by the very automation her job helps to finance. Like the senators and elites in the Roman Republic, those in power are already starting to distance themselves from the citizens they are supposed to serve, and like then, ideas about gaming the system to suit their needs are starting to bubble to the surface.

The UK's EU referendum is an excellent case study of this elitism. The never-ending pre-vote fearmongering by the media and establishment was centred around tales of economic catastrophe if the UK left the EU. The fact that the majority still voted to leave was a very clear statement that culture and community mattered more to them than economics; something those in power failed – and still fail – to grasp. The result was a statement that any short-term financial hit was worth it in order to secure the long-term continuation of the culture and institutions that they feel loyalty and affinity to. As in 1688, this could represent a pivotal moment in the history of the country, only by the people, not Parliament. A clear statement of self-determination and a re-establishment of the country's national identity, its powers and sovereignty by removing influence and control from continental Europe. The desire for self-determination and aversion of foreign control is inherent in the psyche and collective memories of the English people, a throwback to the oppressive days of the Normans and repeatedly demonstrated by its rejection of both absolutism and control from Rome. However, ever since the public decision was made to leave, there has been a continuous and disingenuous questioning of the legitimacy of the popular vote and attempt to subvert the process from all of the elite establishments and those who aspire to reside in them. The education, intelligence and morals of those who voted to leave are the primary targets, stating that people either didn't know what they were voting for, or their vote reflected some defect in their morality. The narrative is that the young, virtuous and upwardly mobile world citizens were sentenced by their uneducated, selfish grandparents to live a life locked outside the utopia of the EU. [164]

This classification by the establishment that those who voted to leave were somehow defective strikes me as similar to eugenicists such as Alexis Carrel's comments about the poor and uneducated. And just like then, they are discussing ways to clean up the (electorate) gene pool. Calls to lower the voting age have been made, so more idealistic, impressionable, 'right-thinking' young people can participate, people still in the grasp of the state education system where their opinions can be influenced. Conversely, there have been calls to restrict the voting age so fewer of the troublesome, native old people can vote. Viewed from a distance one can see the creation of a strange and informal alliance between social-justice advocates and globalists. Globalism's eradication of traditional cultural foundations creates a nation of identity-less and divided individuals, a perfect breeding ground for social justice causes, and in return these progressive warriors wholeheartedly support globalist ideas such as the EU and establishment figures such as Merkel and Clinton. In unison they declare that the EU referendum result is the dying cry of an old guard of nationalist racists voting for selfish reasons; a protest vote by the

---

[164] Here's six reasons why I personally believe more senior people than young voted to leave that never get mentioned:

1. They have seen a life before the EU and have confidence in the UK's ability to thrive independently, rejecting the Armageddon narrative that the Remain camp propagated. The young have not.

2. They have seen the rapid changes taking place in their country and communities and do not view the transition to be positive, versus younger people who have grown up in this EU-driven world and have no point of comparison. The young see leaving the EU as a risk to their way of life, whereas many older people believe staying is the bigger risk.

3. They are more patriotic and worry about things such as loss of sovereignty, loss of culture and loss of self-determination.

4. They can see past the media's narrative and can associate shortages in public services with the exponential increase in demand through rapid population growth, and not just that it is a supply issue caused by a shortage of funds.

5. They were likely to have voted to remain in the EEC back in 1975 on the promise that it was a trading block and have seen it transform into a political institution as those who opposed remaining in the EEC threatened it would. They realise that they were lied to and worry about the creeping authoritarianism and power grabbing being displayed by the EU.

6. Finally, they are likely to have children and grandchildren and therefore are more likely to vote with others in mind compared to 18-24 year olds. They want to leave a country for their descendants that still has its own identity and ability to function as a democracy. They are aware of what happens when the distance between the people and those in power grows.

oppressors against a changing world they won't be alive to experience.

Once again, those in power no longer see their job as being to serve the electorate, but rather view the electorate as a problem to be managed. It is probably not too cynical a perspective to believe that there will soon be questions asked as to whether those totally dependent on the state should get a say in its running, especially when the gulf between the people and the power expands further, as it is almost certain to do. If you think the altering of democratic rights to ensure desired goals sounds dramatic and unlikely, I would remind you that it is only eighty years ago that sterilising 10 million Americans was not just conceived as an idea, but put into print, discussed openly in seminars by people who deemed themselves 'progressives', and actually initiated. The past hundred years are littered with examples from across the world of those in power trying to socially engineer a desired, allegedly altruistic outcome regardless of the effect on their people, from gulags to genocides, Year Zero resets to Great Leaps Forward. And the more nobler sounding the cause, the more crimes its proponents are prepared to commit to achieve it. For example: Indria Gandhi's party swept to power in India in 1971 behind the slogan of *Garibi Hatao!* (Get rid of poverty!) Five years later and its method of achieving this goal involved mass detentions, beatings, torture and the forced sterilisation of 8.3 million citizens. We should always be wary of those who prioritise their ideology above their humanity.

The mindset and actions of our current establishment are worryingly similar to those of the elites in Rome, who sat in their slave-attended private estates, talking about the greatness of Rome without realising that, as G. K. Chesterton so eloquently explained, that this greatness came from the hearts and passions of the populace, not the buildings and Colosseum. During most of the republic's existence, all aspects of society worked for the furthering of Rome, for in the words of Cato the Elder, the republic *was not made by the work of one man, but of many; not in a single lifetime, but over many centuries and by many generations.*[165] It was this inherent social and cultural alignment, combined with a stable form of governance, that stopped the cycle of anacyclosis and allowed Rome to dominate its rivals and become a hegemony. However, when the elites had slaves to do their bidding they no longer felt the need to seek favour with the common

---

[165] Donald Dudley, *Roman Society*, London: Penguin, 1970, page 38.

man. And like then, the elites have once again pursued an agenda that serves their needs first. Mass migration, globalisation and automation have changed the very fabric of society, but as in Rome those who are negatively affected were not asked because the political elites did not feel that their approval was needed. They would do well to study history, for once the citizens of Rome felt that those in power were no longer working for anyone but themselves, things started to fall apart. The current-day elites should remember this, for as the Gracchus brothers (and many other infamous populists since) figured out, the siren call of the demagogue sounds sweet to people who believe that no one else cares about them and the things that they find important.

When this new wave of automation breaks the mutual relationship between those with capital and those with labour, and the present-day elites, like those in the Roman Republic, realise that they no longer need workers to toil in the ground, drive the trucks, make the goods and cook their food, then they may debate why they need these people's votes also. The increasing distance from those in power and disengagement from the process of governing makes people fearful and distrustful, regardless of whether this gap is at work or in society at large. The elites should remember that bread and circuses only work for so long, and that it's not just republics that can fall, but empires also. They fall when they overstretch beyond their control capability, when their defenders and population are made up of people with limited cultural connections, when stoicism is replaced by hedonism, and when their leaders, through their own greed and actions, extinguish the very ties that held people together. And here lies perhaps the biggest challenge for the new global elites and their plans: if you seek to destroy all the gods people believe in, then their search for meaning and purpose will just see them gravitate to new ones. To paraphrase Peterson, when all you see is chaos, then anything that provides a sense of order sounds good. Which perversely may actually serve those in power nicely, for as more individuals are drawn towards populism and easy answers, they can justify more infringes on people's rights, using the sixth wave's technological bounty to impose more autocratic forms of surveillance and control.

28

BRAVE NEW WORLD
OR BIG BROTHER?

*In spite of increasing production and comfort, man loses more and more
the sense of self, feels that his life is meaningless, even though such a
feeling is largely unconscious. In the nineteenth century the problem was
that God is dead; in the twentieth century the problem is that man is dead.*

Erich Fromm, *The Sane Society* (1955)

The sixth wave will have its golden age, and it will be glorious in many ways. Technological advances will continue to achieve things deemed miraculous by previous generations. More people will be lifted out of poverty and freed from the limitations of the past, where access to information and the means of production was dependent on wealth, geographic location and status. Advancements in healthcare and genetic engineering will eliminate diseases that predominately blight the poorest areas of the world, such as malaria, and the richest, such as cancer and Alzheimer's. Mass-produced, 3D-printed housing will replace corrugated shacks, and the remaining areas of the world will be connected to the Internet, providing everyone with access to a world of knowledge and the tools of education. Falling food prices caused by eliminating most of the costs of production and distribution will ensure people have access to enough food to survive.

The combination of massive advancements in renewable energy and the realisation of nuclear fusion will create both a dramatic fall in the cost of power, and the provision of electricity to those currently denied it. We will also make significant inroads into resolving the issues left over from the worst excesses of the industrial age, such as by clearing plastics from the ocean and continuing to decrease CO2 emissions.

This wave will also contain great challenges, capable of tearing the very fabric of our socio-economic model. A period of rapid and disorientating change is creating a cultural lag the likes of which we have never seen before. Every aspect of the global end-to-end supply chain is about to be impacted by the triple whammy of automation, and the things humans used to do for money will now be done by machines. Artificial intelligence will continue to advance to the point that it is embedded everywhere, creating smart cities that monitor and control everything from traffic flow to toilet maintenance. While there will still be plenty for humans to do in this wave, the challenge will be in supporting, re-educating and providing for those caught in the cultural lag, so they can find both a pay packet and a purpose.

During this wave two worlds will be created: one of knowledge and one of entertainment, presenting people with a choice as to which one they dedicate their time to. A life of passive consumption, living life for yourself in an AI-enabled filter bubble, full of virtual experiences supplemented by increasingly smarter silicon-based sexual partners? Or a life of coding, caring or proactive creation? We already know that many people are happy to live on state provided welfare, but we also know that a larger percentage aspires to more. Despite the aforementioned fall in IQ levels and dumbing down of the population, for those with the discipline and mindset to self-study and dive deep into subjects, the Internet allows them to acquire levels of understanding previously unavailable to anyone but those attending the top universities. I have been amazed at how knowledgeable some young people are in philosophy, politics, ethics, economics, history and other subjects, compared to my youth. The rise of online education platforms such as MOOCs allow people to freely study subjects, learn skills and develop levels of understanding that in previous generations would have been reserved only for the off-spring of the wealthy. Platforms such as Facebook, YouTube and Reddit enable discussions and debate that stimulate people's minds and create advancements in their knowledge. Sites such as *Quora*, *Quillette* and *Medium* allow people to write and share thought-provoking pieces, gain followers, ask questions and learn new insights, and for those with the right mindset this offers a fantastic opportunity to both share and expand their knowledge. Yet, if current trends are a guide, the vast majority will end up not in pursuit of knowledge, but entertainment, either through choice or because in the age of machines, they lack the skills, education and intellect needed to compete. This will lead to an intellectual divide as well as a wealth one.

Democracy in Decline

Most people perceive democracy – or a democratic republic – as the highest form of government, for it entails what we believe to be the greatest number of individual freedoms. However, we must also remember that this mindset is a relatively recent one. Philosophers such as Socrates and Plato suggested that a democracy actually represents an unjust constitution, one that ultimately falls into chaos due to populism and the uneducated, tribal voting decisions of the masses who vote to remove short-term pains rather than for long-term greatness. It is easy to see why they believed this, when the majority of the populace were uneducated, barely literate and deemed beneath them in terms of intellectual capabilities. It's a mindset that remains to this day, with evidence ranging from the popularity of the eugenics seminars in the 20th century, to the way progressive voices and outlets currently describe the working classes who didn't vote the right way in recent referendums and elections. For example, to prevent the tyranny of the majority, the US became a Republic and installed systems such as the Electoral College to prevent the heavily populated city states from controlling the more rural areas, *Hunger Games* style. However, in 2016 when this resulted in a President that the elites didn't like, many of them, such as political commentator and professor Robert Reich, openly called for an end to this system.

Plato proposed five regimes, of which the aristocratic class was the highest, ruled by benevolent philosopher-kings; then a timocracy, ruled by weaker men who crave power rather than wisdom; then an oligarchy, where wealth, not wisdom, determines the leaders; then a democracy; and finally, an unjust tyranny, where a strong leader emerges and gains control through force. We have seen these strong leaders arise in chaotic times throughout history, such as Napoleon taking control following the French Revolution, or Cromwell after the English Civil War. Not all were unjust. When the weakened, semi-democratic Roman Republic collapsed, it was transformed into a strong, dictatorial empire, but not a tyranny, with Augustus' reign initiating two centuries of Pax Romana, culminating with the benevolent 'philosopher emperor' and stoic, Marcus Aurelius. Likewise, Napoleon's military dictatorship was authoritarian but not necessarily unjust. However, in the 20th century, when democracies collapsed, real tyrants arose, driven by dangerous ideologies.

A battle is currently raging about how to govern in this turbulent, ever-changing world – do we free or curtail the rights of the population; allow them to decide society's future or decide for them? To date, the West's success has come from freedom, liberty and individual rights, whereas the East's more totalitarian and collectivist approach has held them back. Now, China is trying again, taking a leaf out of Plato's book and aiming to become a benevolent autocracy rather than a Western democracy, with Xi Jinping operating in the role of a philosopher king, the agent of progress for his people. Meanwhile, the West, like the empires of the past, is beginning to collapse in on itself, its liberal values being exploited, twisted and perverted into something new but ultimately self-defeating. The sovereignty of the nation and of the individual is being undermined, creating confusion and self-loathing amongst the young; their worth defined by who they are against, not who they are.

At the same time as the West battles with its identity, large numbers of people are migrating into its countries from cultures that don't share the same beliefs, and who prioritise their religious identity over any national one. They are allowed to continue with that exclusionary mindset, benefiting from the progressive West's self-inflicted weakness of being unable to criticise anyone other than itself. In Europe, governments have become so subservient to the mantra of multiculturalism that they constantly infringe their own citizen's cultural or personal liberties to protect it, while correspondingly being unable to stop the rise of alien cultural practices such as honour killings, sex slavery and female genital mutilation (FGM). FGM is particularly abhorrent, inflicted on young girls from most African Muslim countries such as Somalia, Eritrea and Sudan where at least 90 per

631

cent of the female population has been cut.[166] It has been illegal in the UK for thirty-three years, but to date no one has ever been successfully prosecuted, despite widespread knowledge that it goes on. Between April 2015 and March 2016 there were 8,656 cases identified by the NHS, effectively one per hour, yet not a single conviction as the community closes rank, valuing its traditions more than UK laws.[494] Nations that pride themselves on tolerance are seeing this attribute become a weakness, unable to show enough courage to break through cultural barriers, insist on integration and enforce their laws and values.

This tolerance- and-diversity-first mindset has paralysed Western societies, making them unwilling to investigate certain racial communities or enforce the laws of the land. This weakness has been exploited. Across multiple cities in the UK, young, vulnerable, working-class white girls were groomed, abused and sold as sex slaves for decades. In the worst cases, such as Rotherham, Rochdale and Telford, thousands of girls, some as young as eleven, were sexually exploited, raped, beaten or sold for sex. Those that complained were threatened with death, and in one case where a girl tried to leave her abusers' clutches, her house was burnt down with the girl, her sister and her mother in it. All died. The perpetrators, nearly all Muslims of South Asian origin, selected the girls because they were not Muslim and therefore deemed fair game. They were allowed to get away with it because of the authorities' fear of being labelled racist. In the Telford case, council files uncovered by the *Daily Mirror* showed that social services, teachers, police and mental-health workers all knew what was happening but did little, allowing it to continue for over forty years.[495] Not one of the countless people who were aware of this ongoing evil in the heart of Britain has been held to account.

Most galling was the response from those who claim to be the most virtuous. Faced with overwhelming evidence of an actual rape culture operating in at least eighteen cities in their own country, the progressives, normally so vocal about feminism, eliminating sexism and smashing the patriarchy, said nothing and did nothing. No outrage at this actual misogynistic, racist, patriarchal abuse of young girls by men. No women's marches. No #TimesUp or #MeToo campaigns. No protests at universities. No

---

[166] See: https://en.wikipedia.org/wiki/Prevalence_of_female_genital_mutilation_by_country

MPs calling for action.[167] No celebrities wearing black. No awards ceremony monologues. Nothing. The silence was deafening, and the hypocrisy breathtaking. These so-called progressives have become so absorbed into their ideology that they will do everything to support perceived victims, while openly ignoring real ones, seeing them simply as collateral damage in their battle to be deemed virtuous. Those who promote tolerance found it incredibly easy to tolerate the rape of other people's children, redirecting their outrage at anyone who highlights these cases, declaring that they are simply stirring up hate. We should not allow this, for those that tolerate the intolerable only weaken our society, sacrificing our freedoms and destroying our values in the name of political correctness.

Again, most of the establishment is complicit. Rather than the headline story it should have been, the decades-long sexual abuse of underage white girls in Telford received barely a mention in many papers and was listed under local news on the BBC's website. Likewise, across Europe the negative impact of multiculturalism is suppressed or downplayed by the media to ensure the population keeps its eyes wide shut. While headlines highlight escalating gun crimes, murders, acid attacks and stabbings; of London becoming more dangerous than New York, of gangs of thieves on mopeds running riot, or the mass rape of vulnerable girls, the media and government work hard to disassociate these headlines from the cause. That cause being the reality that societies made up of people with very different beliefs and values, people who have limited emotional connection to the host nation, its people and its culture, increasingly become divided and dangerous places to be.

Even those responsible for the massive increase in migration into Europe, such as Angela Merkel, have repeatedly stated that multiculturalism is 'a sham' and has 'utterly failed'. During a 2015 speech Merkel even declared that *Multiculturalism leads to parallel societies and therefore remains a*

---

[167] Not quite true. In summer 2017, (before the Telford case broke, but after Rotherham and Rochdale) the Labour MP Sarah Champion spoke up about the problem and stated we need to accept that there is a problem with Pakistani Muslim men forming grooming gangs and targeting vulnerable white girls. Her party was outraged with her, and she was sacked for these statements. Meanwhile, another Labour MP, Naz Shah, wrote an op-ed attacking Champion for speaking these truths, while also liking and retweeting a post that stated that *those abused girls in Rotherham and elsewhere just need to shut their mouths. For the good of #diversity!* Unlike Champion, Shah didn't lose her job and has since been promoted.

'life lie'.[496] Strong words from someone who was its biggest proponent and whose decisions adversely affected the future of an entire continent. Words are cheap however, whereas action takes courage. True to form, rather than act, the politicians have doubled down on promoting this 'life lie' focusing their attention on identifying and prosecuting dissident voices, for persecuting dissidents is easier than addressing their concerns, allowing for the obtainment of perceived moral superiority whilst actually not achieving anything of value. Many European governments, especially Merkel's Germany, the UK and Sweden, now insist that tech companies help them control the population by highlighting any wrong-think immediately, fining them if they don't. While the diversity of people is welcomed, any diversity of opinion on this is not. Merkel was herself caught on a hot mic pressing Mark Zuckerberg to work harder on suppressing the freedom of speech of citizens who use Facebook to criticise her decision to bring millions of migrants into Germany. Our legal system may be ineffective in preventing FGM and grooming gangs, but it is proving to be mightily effective when it comes to persecuting those who dare to openly raise concerns about what is happening to their society. So not only are migrant crimes downplayed or not reported, but those who try to highlight the truth are silenced through punitive new laws and police intimidation as well. As George Orwell once stated, *The further a society drifts from the truth, the more it will hate those that speak it.*

Free speech is a value that has been recognised since the days of The Roman Republic. In the 17th century, Charles II quickly dropped his attempts to suppress it through closing down the coffee shops. Yet now, in the early years of the 21st century, the UK and other Western governments are successfully censoring dissenting opinions and voices they don't like, something that will only increase as technology invades every aspect of our lives. Censoring speech and restricting the ability to freely discuss ideas represents the beginning of the end for democracy, for these increasing infringements are not signs of a healthy society, but of one in decline. When preventing 'hate speech', offensive jokes or mean tweets is deemed more important than preventing the rape of our children, then we have become a society that has lost both its belief in itself and its priorities. And when societies lose their identity they also lose their unity, requiring greater levels of control simply to retain order. As the Columbian writer Nicolás Gómez Dávila observed; *dying societies accumulate laws like dying men accumulate remedies.*

This cultural suicide is a betrayal of our current citizens and those who gave their lives to protect our values and freedoms. However, as we saw from the betrayal of the citizen soldiers in the days of the Roman Republic, it's not the first time that the needs of loyal citizens have been sacrificed for the economic goals of others. Perhaps the writer and political commentator Douglas Murray is right when he calls out the unwillingness to defend our values as self-serving cowardice: *We've learned that most of our artistic establishment are cowards and most of our politicians are cowards. We've learned that industries that spend much of their year in award ceremonies patting themselves and each other on the back for their bravery, stop when an actual act of bravery may be required.*[497] Murray's observation echoes the comments made by Gulag survivor and author Aleksandr Solzhenitsyn at his commencement speech at Harvard in 1978: *The Western world has lost its civil courage, both as a whole and separately... Such a decline in courage is particularly noticeable among the ruling groups and the intellectual elite, causing an impression of loss of courage by the entire society.* This cowardice will be their undoing, for in their eagerness to attack those they feel they can (in order to win virtue points) and their unwillingness to attack those they feel they can't (in order to retain their narrative and moral superiority) they push people to the fringes and open the doors to more control and censorship. As Solzhenitsyn stated later in his speech, *Should one point out that from ancient times decline in courage has been considered the beginning of the end?*[498]

People are expected to quietly and passively surrender their rights, loyalties, privacies and freedoms for the greater good. A tech utopia awaits – can't you see? Just not for you, only for people like me. Unironically, the group that is being disadvantaged by mass migration, automation and the destruction of these freedoms and cultural norms are the very same social group that the elites previously relied on to protect them. Like the citizen solders of the Roman Republic, they've been used by those in power, their labour replaced, and their loyalty betrayed. And in this betrayal lies danger, for there will come a point when a metaphorical Rubicon is crossed, and a fightback from this silent majority occurs. We've already seen warning signs of this through Trump and Brexit, but rather than listen and understand, there has been a doubling down of the rhetoric and drive to delegitimise and demonise any counter voices and opinions. This is dangerous in normal times; in a transition period filled with fear about mass technological unemployment and unsure social structures it could be fatal. When people find themselves in chaos, they look for order. They will look for solid, well-rooted trees to wrap their arms around: principles, values and societal norms such as culture and community. However, what they now have is a self-serving group openly felling these trees while also creating a culture of political correctness that suppresses criticism. When reasonable concerns such as the impact of mass migration on a nation's identity, crime levels, social services and infrastructure are silenced, and those raising them shamed, then the owners of those voices gravitate towards anyone who dares to speak up on their behalf. What the liberal elites need to realise is that Trump and Brexit are release valves, the expression of dissatisfaction through democratic means. As we explored, Britain managed to avoid both bloody revolutions and political collectivism due to its inclusive structures, freedoms and rights that enabled public pressure to force recalibrations. The current, continuous attempts to undermine these results are therefore dangerous, because if you deny your citizens legitimate ways to express their discontent, or simply ignore or reverse the results when they do, then anger and feelings of betrayal build, and the pressure has nowhere to go. Thus, those in the centre move right, and those who are already right, move further right. The left, seeing this shift, feels validated for its previous activism and moves further left, increasing the polarisation between the groups and heightening tensions. Civilised discourse is replaced with civil disobedience, then protests and violence. This is not good, for the further the pendulum is pushed, the greater the momentum when it swings back, driven by real resentment and feelings of injustice.

In a time where we are facing the biggest wave of technological disruption, this cultural divide could result in societal collapse and disorder. To prevent this, governments are likely to use these new tools to develop a technological dystopia of omnipresent surveillance and policing of its citizen's physical and digital activities. Democracy is a new phenomenon, with many groups only acquiring political franchise in the last couple of centuries. It could easily be deemed a failed project, and the tools of the sixth wave used against the people simply to ensure compliance, obedience and order. Even as I write this, UK citizens are experiencing an unprecedented attack on their rights to privacy, self-expression and free speech. The country that differentiated itself globally through the ability of its citizens to act without permission and to speak without fear, is starting to show some very totalitarian tendencies. If Voltaire was alive today, I do not think he would be writing any letters praising the freedoms available in England; in fact, I think he would be more likely to be composing ones that criticise their absence.

Does the Future belong to the East?

The West's internal conflict leaves the door wide open for other countries to take over. As per the business world, the key to a successful nation is a leader with a bold vision and the will to make long-term innovations and investments. And the leaders currently demonstrating this trait are from the East not the West. Dubai is a great example of a forward-thinking nation, for the entire city is a monument to inventiveness, arising out of the desert. It now hosts the world's largest tower, the world's first seven-star hotel and the world's busiest airport. As discussed, they are also developing a hyperloop system between the city and Abu Dhabi, a flying taxi service and a fully autonomous port. The government has created a Minister for AI, and they plan to create a blockchain enabled government in time for the World Expo in 2020. They have also already rolled out an ID card system for all their citizens that contains their passport details, medical records and car insurance.

Another Middle Eastern nation, Saudi Arabia, is also investing heavily in the future. It knows that its oil resources are both limited and under threat from more renewable sources such as solar. The Saudi Royal Family are currently financing a project called Saudi Arabia Vision 2030 designed to reduce its dependence on oil, diversify its economy and develop its public services such as health, education, infrastructure, recreation and tourism. It is building a luxury Red Sea resort that contains 50 islands over 34,000 square kilometres, and spending $500bn on creating a new transnational future city called Neom (standing for *new future*) that links Egypt and Jordan. Neom will exploit many of the potential of sixth-wave technologies: renewable sources for all of its power; robots to perform functions such as manufacturing security, logistics, home delivery and caregiving; vertical, indoor farms for food; and genetics and biotech-based healthcare. Adverts are already running on US television to attract what it calls 'the dreamers of the world' (otherwise known as 'the rich'). The Saudi's know that they will be unable to attract Westerners to invest and live in Neom if they have to live under their Sharia religious framework, so Saudi Crown Prince Mohammad bin Salman also announced that Neom will operate independently from the 'existing governmental framework' and have its own tax and labour laws and an 'autonomous judicial system'.[499] While both Saudi Arabia and Dubai are rich, they are also small, which means they may be very influential, but they will never dominate. China, on the other hand, has both the same ambitions and finances but also benefits from a much larger population and landmass.

There are many reasons to believe that China will take over as the primary global hegemony of the 21st Century. First, to date they have managed to embrace capitalist market forces while still retaining centralised Communist Party control. While lacking in certain personal freedoms, it has to date resulted in enormous growth and prosperity for the nation. Secondly, they are rapidly becoming a new colonial power, with President Xi Jinping declaring that they will invest $1.6 trillion on acquiring vast slices of land and key resources and laying down infrastructure throughout Asia, Africa and the Middle East. Finally, and perhaps most critically, they are able to avoid the short-termism that blights Western political leaders, for the Chinese ruling class does not need to focus on electioneering or developing policies designed simply to keep itself in power. While the West is in turmoil during the current transition period, China's ability to exert control and take action without the impediment of voting cycles and budgetary constraints may prove to be advantageous. In early 2018 the two-term presidential term limit was scrapped, allowing President Xi Jinping to become 'dictator in perpetuity', able to see through his vision to make China great again without opposition. Now the ruling Communist Party can focus on the long-term prosperity of the country, and not the short-term winning of another term in power.

There is a significant alignment between this model and that of the highest of Plato's five regimes – the aristocratic state, ruled by philosopher kings, which is what I believe Xi Jinping and the leaders of the Communist Party are aiming for. To reinforce his philosopher king status, Xi Jinping has published what is officially known as *Xi Jinping Thought on Socialism with Chinese Characteristics for a New Era*. Television and media constantly promote his ideas, which are centred around a more traditional Confucian tone rather than a Marxist one. Meanwhile, over in the West, governments are afflicted by the same problem as industrial age businesses – a lack of long-term vision and a constant changing of the guard. The current four- to five-year electoral cycle trains politicians to focus on being elected, rather than on large-scale transformative change, for they are unsure whether they will be in power to see them through. If they lose power, then any major initiatives – such as Obamacare in the US – may simply be abandoned or rolled back by the next political leader. Entrepreneurial visionaries and private corporations are increasingly picking up the slack left by this short-term focus. As these technocrats possess as much wealth as entire countries, they are able to fund activities – such as space exploration, genetic engineering and new transport initiatives – that previously were only possible through state sponsorship. As a result, Western governments are becoming increasingly administrative in nature, focusing on not losing rather than winning. Not so China, whose centralised Communist Party do not need to worry about being voted out of power and as a result are operating like visionary, long-term-focused sixth-wave entrepreneurs. The party is making bold and ambitious investments for the future; massive, multi-year infrastructure initiatives designed to make China the prevalent economic powerhouse of the 21st century. These include the $1 trillion global supply-chain 'One Belt, One Road' development, the manufacturing-focused 'Made in China 2025' initiative, the acquisition of large swathes of Africa's mining industry – especially minerals, and the drive to be the leader in robotics and AI by the Communist Party centenary in 2049. It also helps that the Chinese government owns all the land, removing any legal, property and boundary disputes, and thereby making any new infrastructure projects fast and barrier-free. It is also able to control the education program to ensure that its people have the skills needed for the future. China's State Council has 'requested' that AI-related courses are added to primary and secondary education and has already introduced a textbook into the curriculum called *Fundamentals of Artificial Intelligence*. Like the US in the late 20th Century, China's ambitions and its ability to act on them look set to enable it to become the leading economic and technological force in the 21st century.

Chinese companies are also less restricted than Western companies, able to take an idea – such as the 3D printing of houses – and drive it through to the market without many of the pesky regulations and legal constraints that are required in the West. This is providing a big advantage in its AI development efforts. While the EU is rolling out GDPR legislation to protect the right to privacy for every citizen and Facebook is being hauled over the coals because of data breaches, over in China there are no such concerns or restrictions on data-gathering, providing them with a massive competitive advantage. The bigger the data set, the more the AI algorithm can learn and advance – and the Chinese will be able to capture the mother of all data sets: the collective biometric, healthcare and activity data of 1.3 billion people. All without having to worry about an individual's right to privacy or any data protection legislation. It's amazing how much progress you can make when you don't have to worry about the consequences.

Intellectual property theft is also a major issue, with Chinese companies openly ripping off the ideas of Western companies or forcing US companies to hand over intellectual property as part of the price of doing business in China. Unlike the past, where China's hubris led it to believe that there was nothing worth knowing outside of its borders, now Chinese companies and government agencies steal ideas from everyone. Intellectual property theft costs America up to $600 billion a year, with China accounting for most of that loss. The industrial revolution relied on patent law and intellectual property rights in order to prosper, something that China has taken little notice of to date, targeting everything from weapons to watches. In numerous Chinese cities there are even fake Apple stores that sell fake Apple products, with employees who actually believe that they work for Apple.[500] China is now trying to shed this image as a copycat nation, developing its own innovation hubs and its own technology giants, such as Huawei Technologies, Alibaba and WeChat, to rival the US ones of Apple, Amazon and Google. President Jinping understands that innovation is a critical determinant of national power and competitiveness and has declared the intention for China to lead the world in artificial intelligence by 2030, publishing *The New Generation AI Development Plan*, designed to build a $150 billion Chinese AI industry by that date. The plan is split into three key stages: keep pace by 2020, become a leader by 2025, and become the 'premier AI innovation centre' by 2030. China's looser approach to digital regulations means companies can experiment more freely, collect more data (such as harvesting information from companies like Alibaba, Tencent and WeChat), and use it in ways that would make Western populations balk.

Once Untrustworthy, Always Restricted

There is one catch. To allow for China to achieve this vision, the party must be allowed to proceed without challenge. A two-fold approach to ensure this is underway. To ensure passive acceptance, official Chinese news media sources continually point out the corruption and failings they see in Western democracies, asking the question, *Why challenge the Communist Party when as you can see the alternative is chaos and corruption?* For those unpersuaded by this argument, then a technologically empowered 'soldier class' has been created to enforce compliance and order. AI development is therefore being used not just to create new markets, but also to help ensure that the country's citizens are kept under control. So, how do you control a population of 1.3 billion people? The first step is to ensure you know who everyone is. Which is why China has rolled out a nationwide ID card system linked to your phone. As well as a citizen's name, sex and education, the ID card contains relatives' details, fingerprints, blood type, DNA information, detention record and 'social credit status' (more on this in a moment). Without an ID card it is extremely difficult to obtain a driver's licence, open a bank account, buy high-speed train tickets or travel by plane, so the incentive will be to keep your phone with you at all times, meaning that the government will know where you are at all times. To collect the DNA information they require, the Chinese authorities has initiated a nationwide programme of collecting blood and DNA samples from every citizen, and participation is mandatory. Organisations like Human Rights Watch have highlighted how police have entered homes, schools and places of work to collect samples, unconcerned about oversight, transparency, or privacy protections. Refusal to comply is not an option, ensuring that in China, even your DNA belongs to the Communist Party.[501] This information is then stored on the AI-powered Integrated Joint Operations Platform (IJOP) system, designed to generate lists of suspects for detention.

The Chinese government has also used its venture capital fund to make massive investments in AI companies SenseTime and Face++, which both focus on facial and body recognition, language recognition, vehicle recognition, object recognition and image processing. This technology is used to perform the second step: know where everyone goes and who they meet. In previous times this surveillance would require massive amounts of manpower; now technology can do the heavy lifting, providing levels of monitoring and insights into the lives and actions of the populace previously thought impossible. China has installed the world's biggest camera surveillance network, unironically called *Sky Net*. The omnipresent system has already been implemented in 16 cities, and includes 176 million cameras with facial-recognition software capable of scanning China's entire population in just one second with an identification accuracy rate of 99.8 per cent.[502] For example, in 2018 it successfully identified a wanted man in the middle of a crowd of 50,000 people at a pop concert.[503] China's public security bureau is already using these new technologies to enhance part of its soldier class – the police force – through the development of smart glasses, helmets and wristbands. They have kitted the police out with facial-recognition glasses that are capable of identifying someone in just a hundred milliseconds, and these have already been used to make numerous arrests of wanted people. The plan is to develop a fully integrated and cloud-based system that uses artificial intelligence to rapidly process massive amounts of footage streamed from the cameras, and which is linked to the national ID card system. The fact that the ID card is implemented on people's GPS enabled smartphones enables the police to track everyone anywhere there is a signal. Being caught without your phone or with the GPS disabled would not be a good move.

Not only will the Chinese population's location and DNA be tracked, but their behaviour will be monitored and ranked as well. This is step three: don't just watch your citizens' activities – rate them. To achieve such an ambitious goal, China has rolled out a *Black Mirror*-style citizen trust-scoring system, called the Social Credit System (SCS), which is currently voluntary, but will become mandatory for all citizens in 2020. The behaviour of every single citizen and legal person (which includes every company or other entity) in China will be rated and ranked, whether they like it or not. China's citizens will be measured according to five characteristics: their credit history, their ability to meet contractual arrangements, their personal characteristics, their behaviour and preferences, and their interpersonal relationships. China's Internet censorship programme, the 'Great Firewall', already restricts access to many Western news websites as well as Google, Facebook, YouTube and Twitter, forcing people to use sources and companies that the Chinese government can control – and freely collect data from. Companies such as Alibaba, social media sites such as Weibo (Chinese Twitter), messaging services such as WeChat and QQ

(Chinese WhatsApp), and mobile payment and digital credit agencies allow the government to see what goods you buy, who you are friends with, what money you owe, what messages you send, whether you have any anti-party sentiment, what you view online, etc.[168] Good behaviour results in positive credit points and special privileges, and bad behaviour – which includes playing too many video games – generates a low score, resulting in penalties such as a slower Internet speed, restricted access to restaurants, removal of the right to travel by plane or train, and restrictions on enrolling oneself or one's children in high-paying private schools. It is based on the principle of 'once untrustworthy, always restricted'. By April 2018 more than 11.14 million flights and 4.25 million high-speed train trips were blocked due to poor credit scores.504 Officials have clearly stated that the government intends to continue to ramp up the punishment for low scores, stating that they should *discredit people until bankrupt.*505 A new Orwellian term has now entered the Chinese state lexicon, that of 'discredited person'. One of the most worrying aspects of the scoring mechanism is that people are also judged based on the behaviour of their friends, resulting in the company you keep online affecting your real life. It has been described as *a method of social control dressed up in some points-reward system. It's gamified obedience.*506 And this is exactly what it is – the gamification of society, where people compete for high scores through being the most compliant citizen they can be. I cannot but feel that there are plenty of unintended consequences that will emerge from this, including the potential for a class of 'untouchables' to arise; 'discredited people' whose low credit scores make them social outcasts both online and in real life.

This behavioural monitoring starts at school. A facial recognition network called the Intelligent Classroom Behaviour Management System is currently in use in Chinese high schools that scan the student's behaviour in the classroom every 30 seconds, monitoring and recording their actions and their expressions. This enables teachers to monitor attendance and identify high potential students and those who are deemed trouble makers or difficult learners. As one student from a school that has already implemented this technology stated, *previously when I had classes that I didn't like very much, I would be lazy and maybe take naps on the desk*

---

[168] Remember, these are the very same companies competing for the rights to host state-run ID services on mobile phones, creating a gateway for the government to have full access to everything stored on everyone's smartphone.

or flick through other textbooks. But now I don't dare be distracted after the cameras were installed in the classrooms. It's like a pair of mystery eyes are constantly watching me.[507] This somewhat dystopian future will undoubtedly deliver what the Chinese authorities want – an improved attendance rate, better behaviour and improved results – for the threat of a negative impact on your social credit score will certainly focus attention. In the past daydreaming and messing about used to get you detention, now it gets you marked down as an 'potential discredited person'. Whereas in the past classroom pranksters may have been the centre of attention, now they will be socially ostracised, as this tomfoolery may impact their future career, travel and marriage prospects.

The Digital Book of Judgement

The Chinese communist party is effectively creating a modern-day Domesday book, collecting information on every person and every plot of land in its kingdom. Only unlike William I's, now AI rather than human inquisitors capture the data, and it gets updated constantly, not just the once. Like the original book of judgement, it is also going to be feared due to its unalterable nature. With a title like 'once untrustworthy, always restricted', and objectives such as 'discredit people until bankrupt', this fear is almost certainly going to be entirely justified. As group rights overrides individual rights, do not expect those in charge to spend time investigating any discrepancies in the scoring. Feeling the system is against you? Tough.

China has a number of social, political and drivers behind this massive 'cradle to grave' big brother surveillance project. Critiquing the government is a good way to get discredited quickly, as a number of Chinese journalists have already found out, their discredited status affecting their ability to travel, effectively placing them under house arrest. Then there are the unexpected side-effects of previous initiatives such as the one-child policy which has created a demographic time bomb in the shape of an ageing and male-dominated population, a tsunami of 'bare branch', permanently single men, and an oncoming wave of mass technological unemployment that will deny many people both an income and a purpose. But there is another concern: China's communist leaders are also concerned about the growth of Islam, with top officials making repeated warnings about the global religious extremism seeping into the country and the need to protect traditional Chinese identity. To encourage unity behind national rather than religious identity, the authorities have 'asked' all mosques in the country to fly the Chinese flag and that Muslims should study the Chinese Constitution and the socialist core values in order to strengthen their 'concept of nation'. It has also taken more direct measures, such as implementing the highest level of surveillance in the predominant Muslim areas such as the Xinjiang province. The government now insists that every Uyghur Muslim in the province must have government-issued spyware installed on their mobile phone, and every car have a GPS tracker installed. Drivers who refuse to comply are banned from filling up at gas stations, as these stations increasingly require facial recognition before they will dispense fuel.

Interestingly, one of the rewards offered to people who have high social credit scores is an increased prominence on dating sites, as the Chinese authorities know that the competition for females amongst its male population is high due to the gender imbalance, and also that these same men are the ones likely to engage in antisocial behaviour. Millions of 'bare-branch' men lacking purpose in life, unable to find a mate, are drawn to gangs and end up getting involved in criminal activity. In their 2004 book *Bare Branches*,[508] researchers Valerie Hudson and Andrea den Boer found that violent crime in society is mostly committed by young unmarried males who lack stable social bonds, especially if there are inadequate employment opportunities available; an ever-increasing likelihood due to automation. The authors also state that countries with high male-to-female ratios also tend to develop authoritarian political systems in order to keep control, and that is exactly what China is implementing. By constantly monitoring their citizens' behaviour and linking it to their credit score, the Chinese government is hoping that they can de-incentivise any unwanted behaviour by making it affect men's chances of finding a wife. In the past, surplus numbers of single young men were drafted into the military in order to instil discipline and purpose; now the increased automation of war means this option no longer exists. This presents China with exactly the same issue as the rest of the world: large groups of the population lacking the responsibilities and sense of purpose that previously came from work, marriage and parenthood. The outcome will also be similar: with these people ending up spending their lives in a soma-filled existence, living in their apartments, getting fulfilment from achievements in a virtual world, satisfying their sexual and companionship frustrations through a combination of AI-enhanced sex robots. There is already a massive market in China for lifelike sex robots, and companies such as ExDoll in the north-eastern China port city of Dalian are global leaders in their development, probably because they know there is a waiting market of millions of bare-branch men. China is estimated to make more than 80 per cent of the world's sex dolls, with over a million people currently employed in the country's $6.6 billion industry.[509] Currently these doll/robots are limited in their interactivity, but there are already plans to incorporate more advanced AI to enable more complex facial expressions and body movements, voice-recognition systems and eyes that follow your movements. As the exponential curve of AI development increases, these machines will also be able to provide conversation and companionship to go with their copulation capabilities. As China's urban, coastal population grows and embraces a more techno-centric lifestyle, the cultural lag between them and the underdeveloped rural areas of the interior will also grow. There is the real danger of China – like many countries – splitting into a series of sprawling, coastal, urban cities filled with the young, and an uneducated, ageing population in the rural areas who are left behind and effectively forgotten about.

What we are seeing play out in real time in China is a mash-up of two science-fiction futures, one that is part Orwellian and part Huxley. A dystopian *Nineteen Eighty-Four* surveillance state combined with the negative utopia of *Brave New World* coastal mega-cities filled with compliant humans, conforming to behavioural guidelines passed down by the government, constantly encouraged by state-managed credit systems to continue to consume and comply. And it's just getting started. Currently it is monitoring the emotional states of train drivers, production workers and military personnel, but soon BCI technology will enable a whole new level of surveillance and control, enabling the government to track the thoughts of its population and identify wrong-thinkers, as well as the potential for 'soma like' manipulation of emotions. And like the social credit system, GPS tracking and ID cards, non-compliance is not an option. In the past, the enslaved knew they were slaves, whereas in the future, ignorance may be bliss. China also has the advantage that social engineering and centralised control have always been a part of its history, and its population has grown up with the tradition of compliance and obedience. Also, while there has never before been technology available to its leaders to monitor and control the population, there has also not been the ability to use this technology to feed and entertain them. There may, therefore, be less resistance to this than we think.

For those currently thanking their lucky stars they do not live in China, a warning. Do not be complacent, for the foundations for this totalitarianism is increasingly being laid in the West through the constant surveillance and monitoring of people's posts and online activities via the large technocracies such as Google and Facebook. The competitive advantage that China acquires from developing a dataset of information on every aspect of its 1.3 billion citizen's lives will cause Western nations and institutions like the EU to think really hard about the Hobson's choice it is presented with, and whether the protection of privacy is worth the risk of being left behind. They may well decide – under increasing pressure from tech corporations losing out to Chinese rivals – that it is not. Once facial recognition, AI enabled sensors and the blockchain become ubiquitous, then every transaction, movement, meeting and voiced opinion can and will be monitored. Combine this technology with the new legislation around 'hate speech' and the ability to arrest people for 'intending to cause offence', then you quickly see how the tools needed to arrest people for the crime of thinking wrong thoughts could soon become ubiquitous. As a result, people will self-censor their words, thoughts and actions, aware that a digital big brother is indeed watching and predicting your every thought and action. If you were to travel to the picturesque village of Sutton Courtenay, Oxfordshire, and go into the grounds of All Saints' Churchyard, you will find the seventy-year-old grave of Eric Arthur Blair, otherwise known as George Orwell. If he was alive today, he would no doubt declare that his most famous book was intended as a warning, not an instruction manual.

BEYOND THE
SIXTH WAVE

29

BATTLE OF THE GODS

When men choose not to believe in God, they do not thereafter
believe in nothing, they then become capable of believing in anything.

G. K. Chesterton

At around the middle of the century the sixth wave will enter its winter period and collapse, as waves always do, only its revival will not be so assured as in the industrial age. The size of the Chinese debt bubble is probably going to be at the heart of the collapse, sending markets across the world into a death spiral. Both Schumpeter and Marx believed that capitalism would eventually collapse and be replaced, but they predicted that this end would come about in different ways. Marx predicted that capitalism would be overthrown by a violent working-class revolution, whereas Schumpeter believed that capitalism would gradually weaken by itself and eventually collapse; that unemployment and a lack of fulfilling work would cause intellectual critique, discontent and protests. A working-class revolution is likely to be averted by the aforementioned 'bread and circuses': technology driven creative destruction has constantly driven down costs and lifts people out of poverty, so we won't see the starving mobs storming the gated castles of the rich. Nevertheless, Schumpeter's concerns are still valid, creating a very real risk of a societal divide and related conflict.

While this current wave requires levels of recalibration as previously discussed, what comes next will require more than mere tweaks; it will require a complete rethink. The collapse of the sixth wave is likely to represent a fracturing of the socio-economic model and the end of the age of capitalism as we know it. It will be mortally wounded by the dual effects of overcoming the issue of scarcity and the demise of the relationship between productivity and employment. As items are increasingly produced using renewable energy and machine labour, their costs will fall, limited only by the availability of the raw materials needed to make them; materials that we will increasingly be able to recreate in labs rather than dig out of the ground. However, the market still requires someone to buy these goods, and the detachment between productivity and employment caused by automation is going to create the need for a new socio-economic model. Automated socialism is one discussed option, with a population living their lives in their urban apartments and benefiting from the abundance brought about by the productivity from automation, but the question remains as to who pays for it, and how? The only logical outcome based on the current trajectory would be the corporations, those remaining behemoths that own the technology, platforms and algorithms that run the world in the middle of the century. They will be the only entities with enough funds to finance the social security needed to keep the population fed, watered and consuming. Some optimists hope for the development of a resource-based economy, such as that proposed by the Venus Project, which promises to bring humanity to the next stage of social evolution through a maximisation of quality of life, not profits. Alternatively, a more dystopian scenario could arise; a *Robocop*-esque world of massive corporations running everything, or an Elysium-style plutocracy, where the wealthy distance themselves from the masses in terms of geography and physical and intellectual capabilities. For example, the new Saudi future city of Neom is being designed, planned and marketed with exactly those principles: to bring together people who will, in their words; 'write humanities next chapter'.[169]

In order to control the population throughout this disruptive period, governments will implement omnipresent levels of surveillance and control. These are the slippery-slope actions of a civilisation becoming more totalitarian, clamping down on its population and effectively closing

---

[169] See discoverneom.com

down the digital coffee shops that we currently use to read news, gossip, mock those in authority and learn. This is, in many ways, the path of least resistance for governments to take in the face of unmanageable economic change; an addressing of a symptom rather than the cause. A world run by an alliance of the state and big corporations who will track and monitor your every movement, tweet and comment, and manipulate your emotions to ensure compliance with their agenda. However, as in those countries that banned clubs, coffee houses and books, this creeping authoritarianism may end up destroying the freedoms and social cohesion needed to build a truly inclusive and innovative economy. Another great unknown is the impact on the mental wellbeing of the population. A life of basic income, bread and digital circuses may satisfy people's immediate needs, but they may also be left feeling like an insignificant cog in an uncaring machine. And here lies perhaps one of the primary challenges of the 21st century: a battle to fill the space in our citizen's souls left empty by the absence of work, religion and marriage.

Filling the Vacuum

Given their apparent immortality, the past is surprisingly littered with the corpses of deities. From Anubis to Zeus, the old gods disappeared from memory as the civilisations that worshipped them fell, yet the human desire for faith always survived, transferring to new gods and new religions. As Voltaire wrote back in 1768, *if God did not exist, it would be necessary to invent him.* Yet to most of the current generation God doesn't exist, and in his place new religions have been invented such as consumerism, celebrity and technology. These are false gods, providing individuals with temporary moments of pleasure rather than deep, long-term purpose, creating a vacuum in the heart of our society. And as Aristotle observed, nature abhors a vacuum. It's why so many students embrace the preaching of their progressive professors and their social-justice crusade, for they long for meaning in a society that no longer has faith in anything other than technology. When we look beyond the sixth wave, perhaps the most important question to be answered is how this vacuum is filled:

- If a machine or some silicon entity born from the singularity becomes God, something capable of self-enhancement that is far superior to our human intellect, then will this new god be our servant, or vice versa? If the latter, will it be a benevolent god, or an uncaring one?
- If man becomes godlike, how will these new overmen treat the non-enhanced? Will they see them as their equals, or as something lesser?
- If God remains God, do his disciples allow the creation of super-intelligent machines, or allow humans to experiment with the concept of becoming godlike? Or do they ban all development in this direction, deeming it too dangerous or an affront to God, reacting like Ottomans did to the printing press?

The reality is likely to be that all of these options will play out at the same time, and the results will determine what kind of future we will be hurtling towards. The next generations are either going to be cursed or blessed; entering either a dystopian world of chaos and control, or a utopian one of long life, material abundance, enhanced capabilities and good health. A clash of world views is building, based on which god we choose to worship. It will not be a respectful debate.

Machine as God

Creating a supercomputer is one thing; controlling it is an entirely different challenge. Already the development of AI is beginning to outpace our political, educational and socio-economic capabilities. A number of metaphorical Rubicon's have already been crossed, such as the ability for artificial intelligence to develop its own strategies, converse as if human, and when installed into robotic bodies, move and manipulate the surrounding world independently. If Kurzweil's Law of accelerating returns is correct, we will soon start to progress to the second half of the chessboard; creating an exponential level of advancement that will make Moore's Law sluggish in comparison. Within the next two decades this development will start to encroach upon the realm of AGI, artificial general intelligence, and then things will start to get really interesting.

This rate of progression is concerning many, for AI engineers have already found themselves struggling to understand the outputs of their creations and are currently trying to program these neural programs and deep-learning algorithms to explain themselves. Soon they will give up, realising that by limiting the AI's abilities to only achieving things that humans can understand, they prevent it from establishing the answers to some of the world's most pressing problems (such as climate change and curing cancer), and its biggest opportunities (such as space exploration and colonisation). Realisation will occur within the AI development community that the limits of human intellectual capability has become the bottleneck, and that to fulfil its potential AI needs to be set free, able to make its own enhancements and act on its own suggestions. As companies like Satalia have proved, AI can be directed at tasks such as the management of people; and as we increasingly tire of the politics that affects companies and other areas such as the civil service, questions will be asked as to why we do not simply hand over control of these activities to the more efficient and effective machines. Soon, the supply of essential utilities will also be managed by AI, powered by sensors that are in every water pipe, power plant and sewage system. By the 2030s the Internet of Everything will be all around us, making us connected to the world in a way never before possible, but also more exposed as we become ever more reliant on machines to run our world, from organising our day to choosing our entertainment and cooking our food. Now imagine the situation when quantum supercomputers get involved.

As the complexity of these systems outstretch the ability of humans to manage them, we will inevitably pass over responsibility to the machine, allowing it to completely manage whatever aspects we have relinquished control of – as well as potentially taking over some we didn't. Given enough time and enough advancements in its capability, it is possible that a super-intelligent machine will be seen as an omnipresent deity, the thing that makes the world work. This godlike artificial intelligence will be everywhere, merged with physical units such as robots, connected and aligned via a vast data cloud, becoming ever smarter thanks to the combined insights of millions of data points. At this point the world of E. M. Forster's *The Machine Stops* could emerge, where humans end up accepting that most things have become beyond our comprehension and rely totally on machines to do it for us. Rather than 'The gods were responsible, and who are we to question them', will we simply say, 'The machines were responsible, and we are not smart enough to question them'.

Will we eventually decide to hand over the care and protection of the planet and its population to the machines? Will these silicon deities even have the concept of human emotions such as 'caring'? I don't buy into the malevolent AI scenario; it is unlikely that a super-intelligent machine would have emotions such as 'hate' or harbour desires to end humanity, whereas it is very likely that humans will use a super-intelligent machine in malevolent ways, for example in advanced bio- or cyber-warfare. The desire for national leaders to develop AI capable of either attacking their enemies, or defending itself from them, will be too powerful, accelerating the already underway AI arms race. And here lies the real danger: the significant possibility of unintended consequences arising from the haste to be first. All the dystopian AI issues highlighted in Chapter 17 are possible, specifically the potential of AI systems performing unknown self-enhancements, 'too-literal' interpretations of instructions, runaway resource acquisition or simply making strategic, logic-based decisions that emotional, unpredictable and destructive humans do not foresee. The more complex and powerful the system, the larger the possibility that things will go awry and the greater the potential impact. We also run the risk of what I call the 'Convergence Catastrophe', which is the calculation that *AI + robotics + nanotech + genetics + biotech = human extinction*, due to there being too many technological threats all in play at the same time, causing the exponentially increased likelihood of an unplanned event occurring. Utopia requires every one of these to be developed without incidence, whereas dystopia only requires one misstep. As Hayek declares in *The Road to Serfdom*; *Is there a greater tragedy imaginable that in our endeavour consciously to shape our future in accordance with high ideals, we should in fact unwittingly produce the very opposite of what we have been striving for?*[510]

We are therefore caught in a quantum paradox, one where Schrödinger's cat is an AI trapped in Pandora's box. Artificial intelligence could be the solution to our existential risks, enable us to overcome our industrial-age constraints and reach the next level of our evolution; or it could be an existential risk, setting off a chain of unforeseen events that finishes us off. It remains in the state of potentially being both a global threat and a global saviour until we open the box and find out.

Man as God

The perennial question 'how do we keep up with that which we create?' needs answering, and to many, the solution lies in the merging of mankind with the machines. While you may deem this unlikely, I would point out that at a closed-door session at the 2018 World Government Summit in Dubai, a select group of elites and AI experts all agreed that the augmentation of humans was the next logical step in AI.[511] There is also a widescale global movement, called transhumanism, that actively supports and promotes this goal, and developments such as genetic engineering, longevity studies and augmentation advancements such as brain-computer interfaces all fall into this 'transhuman' category of development. An organic and silicon mash-up that fulfils the dreams of transhumanists by enhancing our intelligence and our physical capabilities, achieving the status of overmen capable of retaining controlling of both the biological and digital worlds. Developments to embed technology in biology are already underway. Rather than using our phones to connect to the Internet and converse with virtual assistants, the aspiration is to embed these capabilities in our bodies, enabling humans to become both constantly connected and super-intelligent, able to obtain information at the speed of thought. At the same time, tools such as CRISPR-Cas9 will enable the control of genetic factors, helping to eradicate illnesses, disease and cellular damage, extending lifespan and youth.

There are many that see this transhuman transformation as the natural evolution of mankind, the ultimate expression of our superiority. The ability to not just understand the forces of biology, but to control and improve them, overcoming our inherent biological and intellectual constraints. We may increasingly elect to replace some of our constrained biological capabilities with enhanced artificial ones, enabling everything from replacement limbs, 3D printed organs made from your own DNA, to enhanced hearing and eyesight. As Michelle Thaller, the Assistant Director for Science Communication at NASA, states, *We can currently give deaf people the ability to hear through cochlear implants that bypass the normal biological hearing process. These are constantly being updated, giving ever-changing levels of hearing. But why stop at human hearing? Why not dog level? Why stop at human level vision? Why not x-ray, or infrared? These are all feasible.* She sees the potential for humans to have a series of upgrade options similar to when you buy a new car. The only limit to your capabilities will be how much you want to spend. As brain-computer interfaces become established and safe, there is also the potential to buy and download experiences, memories, skills or knowledge, or to install a connection to your AI-enabled robot companion.

We will inevitably attempt to use our technological inventiveness to create better versions of ourselves, expressing our individualism through tech augmentation and genetics. However, access to these capabilities will not be free and thus they will not be available for everyone. Those who cannot afford them will either go without, watching as those with the capital invest in their own enhancement and reset their biological clock and augment their biological capabilities; or they will take a risk with a low-cost proprietor; one prepared to do the operation on the cheap. One can only imagine the unlicensed back-alley or offshore enhancement surgeries that will arise. Like the cowboy plastic surgeons who perform botch jobs and inject all sorts of dodgy substances into people willing to take the risk in order to save money, the future will see 'surgeries' crop up that promise to perform complicated enhancements on your body (and mind) for half the cost of officially licenced ones – but with quadruple the risk. Poorly performed brain enhancements are likely to be somewhat more dangerous than botched breast or butt enhancements, and discount DNA manipulation could have more devastating side effects than dodgy dental work. Yet despite this, there will almost certainly be plenty of people willing to take the risk.

For those that can afford to pay the price, a new world awaits. One where some people are not just slightly smarter, but exponentially so; and not just a little bit healthier, but able to live decades longer while continuing to look and feel like someone in their twenties. At this point we are not dealing with two social classes, but two species, as different as the Neanderthals were to *Homo sapiens*. Not only will we be asking 'What is reality?' but also 'What is human?' As we merge with machines and increasingly allow them to augment our mental capabilities, the question arises as to whether in the not-so-distant future we will be unable to distinguish between human thoughts and machine-generated ones. When that is the case, we are no longer *Homo sapiens*. We have become *Homo artificialis*; Humanity 2.0. This constant upgrading will inevitably create advantages over those who do not partake in these enhancements. *Homo sapiens* prevailed over Neanderthals due to their ability to connect and work together to achieve goals. *Homo artificialis* might also succeed over *Homo sapiens* due to this network effect: the ability to collect, combine and share huge amounts of data, enabling this enhanced species to benefit from the outputs of multiple brains, both human and machine. Individualism may have been the necessary step to enable us to move beyond helplessness, but the collective might prove the next stage in our evolution. If we continually end up fighting over man-made ideologies and battling to suppress our worst human excesses, then perhaps becoming something a little less human is the answer. As a result we may become a species divided, where the enhanced worship intellect and data over more human traits such as tradition, love, empathy and culture. Many people propose *Star Trek* as a prime example of what our utopian future could look like, with the assumption that nations of earth combine to become the Federation, fighting against the emotionless half-human, half-machine hive-mind Borg. In reality, we are as likely to become the Borg as the Federation. Maybe, several centuries from now, *Homo sapiens* may have turned out to be the ancestors of both.

God as God

For many, the vacuum left by faith can only be filled by faith. As the 17th-century French mathematician and philosopher Blaise Pascal observed, *There is a God-shaped vacuum in the heart of each man which cannot be satisfied by any created thing but only by God.* Many people will be drawn back to religion simply to fill the gaping hole in their lives that used to be occupied with things like work and family. In Western Europe this is unlikely to be Christianity. The inheritance of the Enlightenment and scientific and technological revolutions has seen an exodus from the religion, creating a shrinking and aging congregation. As a result, across Western Europe churches and chapels have been torn down, transformed into residential accommodation – or converted into mosques. For Europe is actually undergoing a faith resurgence – just not to Christianity, but to Islam. The Pew Research Center's Global Religious Futures Project[512] projected forward current trends to estimate what the world's religious profile would look like in 2050. They identified that Islam is now the fastest-growing religion in the world, especially in India and China, and predicted that it would overtake Christianity as the most widely practised faith by 2060.[513] Europe is one area where this transition is being felt most. The European birth rate for Muslims is above the replacement rate at 2.6 children, whereas non-Muslim Europeans are falling well short at only 1.6 children: between 2010 and 2016 this difference in birth rates saw the number of non-Muslim Europeans fall by 1.92 million, whereas the number of Muslims increased by 2.92 million. As well as this increased reproductive rate, there is also the large-scale migration of young people from Muslim countries into Europe, with 3.48 million migrating to the continent between 2010 and 2016.[514] The net effect is that the Muslim population of Europe is growing rapidly, while the non-Muslim population is both ageing and declining. The Pew Research study predicts that by 2050, Europe's Christian population will have fallen by 99.2 million (-18 per cent), whereas its Muslim population will have increased by 27.4 million (+ 63 per cent).[515] Western societies have also inadvertently developed Islamic conversion factories – jails. Muslim males are over-represented in prison, and they are highly effective at converting fellow prisoners to their faith, with 80 per cent of all religious conversions in US prisons to Islam.[516] These conversions often occur in people who lack guidance and purpose in their life; drawn to the moral direction religion provides. As large numbers of the general population similarly begin to feel lost and purposeless in a world turned upside down by technology, it is therefore likely that we may see many people drawn towards Islam. Unlike the directionless and divided Westerners who have forsaken their cultural and religious identity, the Muslim community has remained confident in its values, identity, faith and culture. This confidence will appeal to Westerners who feel they have lost all those things, drawn to the juxtaposition between the division and emptiness on display in their society, versus the unity and purpose displayed by those who follow Islam. Islam never underwent a secular Reformation and its texts and teachings have not been critiqued in the way Christianity was during the Enlightenment, and the sentence for apostasy serves to keep it that way. Its followers also publicly demonstrate their devotion to the faith, and these displays of unified purpose and group identity that this ideology provides will be attractive to those who feel they have lost those things, or never experienced them.

It is therefore simply a matter of time and mathematics before Islam becomes the largest practised faith and Muslims constitute the majority of working-age citizens in Europe and other Westernised countries such as Australia and Canada. As the demographics of areas change, an exodus by the existing group is likely to occur, as people seek to return to a more familiar, homogenous community. This phenomenon has been referred to as 'white flight' and demonstrates the inherent desire of people to live in communities they recognise and with people they share similar cultural values and beliefs with. Once the minority group becomes the majority, then there will naturally be pressure for a similar level of representation in the political system, and the potential for the demands of this group to clash with the nation's incumbent cultural norms, laws and freedoms. Migration between cultures that share the same values tend not to be an issue because the rights and laws of the recipient country are easily adopted and willingly adhered to, making their race and religion no barrier to either acceptance or success. For example, Sikhs, Hindus and Far East Asians all tend to be successful in Western societies, outperforming the native population in education results and earnings. It is only when mass migration comes from cultures with different values that issues occur, especially when the host society allows them to retain and prioritise those values over its own. And multiple studies have shown that many migrants from predominantly Muslim countries deem their religious identity as much more important than their national identity and protecting their cultural norms and community more important than adhering to Western laws. Trevor Phillips, the former head of the UK's Equality and Human Rights Commission, declared that on many issues Muslims were a *nation within a nation*;[517] their prioritisation of their religious beliefs causing many to disagree with some of the liberal values that the West has incorporated, especially LGBTQ rights.[170] They have, however, benefited from the West's excessively tolerant and self-critical culture, resulting in the oxymoronic situation where those who deem themselves the most liberal promote and protect a group who actually hold the most conservative views. This may prove to be a mistake, for as their number grows this parallel society will insist on parallel laws – or the changing of existing ones. Sci-fi author Frank Herbert perfectly articulates the threat in *Children of the Dune*; *When I am weaker than you, I ask you for freedom because that is according to your*

---

[170] For example, when Australia voted whether to legalise same-sex marriage, the districts that recorded the highest 'no' votes were in NSW, which also has the highest number of immigrants from non-English speaking populations. Likewise, London, the most diverse city in the UK with the largest LGBTQ population, also has the least liberal views on LGBTQ rights and pre-marital sex by percentage. The reasons given for this was religious factors due to its high migrant population, notably from Muslim countries. Source: *The Telegraph*. 18 July 2018.

principles; when I am stronger than you, I take away your freedom because that is according to my principles.[518]

As the religious make-up of a nation changes, so does its attitude to certain freedoms, and in a society where Islam becomes the prevalent faith, its followers may start to demand the adaptation of laws more in line with that faith, such as sharia, leading to a clash with those who wish to retain the liberal, secular foundations that currently exist. Islam is inherently more political than many other religions, for unlike Christianity, it did not experience a secular Reformation. Thus, the religious beliefs of practicing Muslims are also going to influence their political motives, compounded by the block voting tendency of its followers, meaning that Islam's incursion into the political and legal sphere will be more pronounced. In countries where Muslim numbers are significant, such as In Sweden, sharia law has already been used to settle court cases,[519] and in Belgium new political Islam parties have already been established with a manifesto of transforming the country into a sharia-based Islamic state by 2030.[520] In Western countries where practising Muslims reach influential levels in both the general population and the corridors of power, there is the potential that the nature of that society, and its freedoms, will be challenged and changed. It is likely, for example, that acts such as utilising technology and genetics for self-enhancement may be deemed haram, for a religion that frowns upon the marking or harming of the flesh is unlikely to embrace manipulation of their body in this way. With this in mind, it is likely that the ever-growing and more influential Muslim population will find themselves at odds with those who wish to utilise these new capabilities and will actively work to stop this practice.

Even in the US, where Christianity still dominates, the concept of humans or machines achieving godlike powers will not be easily accepted. When the evidence of these developments starts to appear, then there will likely be protests against what many believe to be an affront to natural laws. They will almost certainly see the rise of super-intelligent and genetically enhanced humans as a threat, especially if this transhumanist ideal of enhanced lifespans and capabilities are reserved for the wealthy and powerful. The concept of death and an afterlife will be severely challenged if one group of people stop aging and dying. This disagreement of views may not be resolved peacefully. Religion was influential in the decline and demise of the Western (Christianity) and Eastern (Islam) Roman Empires. There is no reason why it may not be influential in the demise of another.

Battle of the World Views

It will be 'interesting' to see how this plays out. The accelerating nature of technological developments since the industrial age has been driven in the West by a societal model based around individual freedoms as well as stabilising institutions such as marriage, combined with a capitalist economic model based on aspiration, careers and choice. Now things are changing. The traditional roots of their Judeo-Christian culture are being ripped up by a mix of social paradigm shifts and deliberate actions by those intent on bringing down what they see as a set of oppressive hierarchies. The core Enlightenment values such as reason, liberty and freedom are being challenged by revisionist and subjectivist thinking, combined with a rejection of democratic values and a rise in surveillance and control. They have lost their 'why': told to feel guilty over past actions by people they never met, and to reject their national identity in favour of a globalist perspective that detaches individuals from their ancestral heritage, removing any feelings of belonging. They also risk being left behind technologically and economically to a resurgent China, whose people mock the West's self-hatred while their government invests heavily in long-term initiatives designed to make them the dominant global force in both technology and trade. China's long-term focus and strong national identity is unwavering and its investments big and bold, which contrasts sharply to the more myopic focus of the West where attention is on political re-election, multiculturism and diversity of identities. Russia's leader also uses the West's cultural weakness as ammunition to create strength through a combination of Orthodox Christian values and national identity.

This concoction makes a dangerous brew for Western nations, for as mentioned, once the roots are severed, the tree starts to wither and die. Western society is moving away from traditions, communities and families, into one based around lone agents with limited social or emotional ties, making them easy to influence and control. As a result, a nihilistic future based around materialism, faux individualism and technological addiction, combined with the potential for mass technological unemployment, awaits. A life of dependency on a corporation funded basic income, where your worth is measured by the amount of data you share, your purchasing power and your citizen score. Attempts to conceal your activities such as avoiding social networks and using ad blockers will negatively impact your social worth, and potentially the amount of basic income you receive, for the less value you have to a corporation (by not providing data or consumption), the less incentive there is for them to pay for your existence. This could theoretically create a subculture of untouchables, people who are shunned due to their social credit status, and who only find purpose and unity with others through a shared rage at the machine.

While the Enlightenment may have started the process of releasing us from self-inflicted imprisonment, it has also failed to provide counselling and guidance as to what to do with that freedom. Individualism has been Western civilisation's greatest strength, but now we are also beginning to appreciate that it could also be its Achilles heel. People need a purpose, a North Star to direct their individual activities and solid foundations upon which to build their life. Without a clear 'why', the 'how' and 'what' of their lives lack direction. Strip people of their religious, cultural and national identities and deny them life-time responsibilities and goals such as careers, marriage and children, then what's left to unify and inspire the masses? The constant prioritisation of every other culture but its own will also mean that the West will fail to inspire their people to anything beyond mediocrity. Without a belief in itself, any self-promotion or acts of perceived greatness are deemed distasteful and unbecoming, resulting in no new cathedrals being built, nor heroes created. Such a society is one without legitimacy or longevity, for a society has to stand for something, or else it stands for nothing. When a society and its culture are so weak, its citizens become lost and their search for meaning in daily life increasingly futile, leaving the door open for those who claim to provide easy answers and people to blame. As the Afrikaans author Laurens van der Post highlighted, *There is ultimately only one thing that makes human beings deeply and profoundly bitter, and that is to have thrust upon them a life without meaning. There is nothing wrong in searching for happiness. But of far more comfort to the soul is something greater than happiness or unhappiness, and that is meaning. Because meaning transfigures all.*[171]

In a world where everything is being turned upside down, people will seek meaning and certainty from somewhere, and will be drawn to those who promise salvation from this chaos. While traditional Western religious,

---

[171] From the documentary, 'Hasten Slowly: The Journey of Sir Laurens van der Post', by Mickey Lemle

national and cultural identities are being dismantled, others are very clear about who they are and what they believe. This will range from radical groups on the left and right who create common enemies to hate and provide simple answers to complex problems, through to those religions that are not in decline but thriving during this chaos. The combination of the mass-migration of millions of young, mostly Muslim, males into Europe, combined with the constant deconstruction of Western values, is already leading to a culture clash with increasingly serious ramifications. The identity of Europe is being remoulded in plain sight, and many are not happy about this. Anyone who believes that such a rapid demographic shift in both the nature and gender of the population will not end up creating massive social issues is incredibly naïve. And it may have unexpected results for those who supported it. For the militant progressive bonobos in the West who have constantly undermined, chastised and silenced the chimpanzees within their society may find that they have simply paved the way for another tribe of chimpanzees to take over. As the late Christopher Hitchens once observed, *barbarians can never take a city until someone on the inside holds the door open for them.* Opposing chimpanzee tribes don't integrate, collaborate and selflessly fornicate with each other like the bonobos, but stay united and seek to destroy their opposition so they can rule unopposed. Only then will these Western bonobo activists realise the error of their actions, and appreciate that the original chimps in their society, the ones they silenced and drove out, weren't actually their enemy, but their defence.

Concern about the growth of Islam and its prioritisation of faith over country is why China is currently spending extensive amounts of funds in the monitoring and policing of the Xinjiang province, including the rolling out of 'predictive policing'; arresting people based on collected data of your movements, comments and interactions, the analysis of which calculates the likelihood that you will commit a crime.[521] *Minority Report* in practice, but using advanced machine intelligence rather than human precogs. We should not be complacent and view China's actions as those of an alien nation; they are in many ways simply more honest about their totalitarianism. To control a population of disenfranchised people, Western governments and bodies like the EU are all following China's example and calling upon the power of the technology corporations to monitor and report on their citizen's activities both in the real world and online. Their veneer of democratic respectability is peeling away, allowing people to see the truth that lies beneath. As John Stuart Mill wrote in *On Liberty*; *The disposition of mankind, whether as rulers or as fellow-citizens to impose their own opinions and inclinations as a rule of conduct on others... is hardly ever kept under restraint by anything but want of power; and that power is not declining, but growing.*

As discussed in Part One, the emphasis on individual responsibilities and individual freedoms was a key element in the creation of a society that could launch an industrial revolution. Now as the demographic makeup of nations change, we are seeing a shift away from individual responsibility to social responsibility, making society more extractive, not less. From your weight to your feelings, people are demanding that society adapts to their needs, and that any negative outcomes because of their choices were unfair and should be compensated for by the state. The trouble is that you cannot sustainably control what you don't understand, but governments have set about with great vigour trying to do just that. They look at an outcome and determine the root cause based on the narrative, not evidence, and take actions accordingly. Reason, truth and facts become irrelevant, for the outcome is all that matters. When differences in outcomes exist, then legislation is demanded to remove them, meaning that governments start to increasingly legislate for people's choices and decisions, suppressing freedoms and aspirations. For example, in order to eliminate the difference in lifetime earnings between men and women (labelled the 'wage gap') they are insisting on increasingly levels of legislation and insight into corporations, demanding that companies employ a quota system and pay people the same irrelevant of expertise, skill, experience or tenure. Yet still they can't eliminate the different outcomes in salary because they are made on choices – and the freer and more egalitarian a society the more freedom of choice they have. And frustratingly for those advocating for enforced equality of outcome, women use that choice to choose lifestyles and futures in line with their desires, not the State's, something that has been tagged the 'Patriarchy Paradox'.[522] For example, women in Nordic countries are the most equal and have the most support financially for paternal leave yet continue to choose parenthood over high-flying careers. It appears that when given the choice, people choose to be that which makes them happy. Or to put it another way, when people are given the opportunity to be anything, they choose to be themselves. And it is this desire for choice that undoes every autocratic system, for people do not want to have their potential capped nor their life mapped, frustrating those who believe that they can socially engineer their version of utopia. For in order to achieve the desired equality of outcome requires the reduction of choice and elimination factors such as individual merit.[172] This creeping authoritarianism and constant technological surveillance is leading us ever closer to a negative utopia where aspirations are suppressed, ideas and voices you don't like stifled and society becomes less about freedom and more about compliance, eroding the very freedoms and liberties that launched the industrial revolution. As Aldous Huxley once observed, *Liberties aren't given, they are taken.*

The Slippery Slope

The pressure to use more invasive AI-enabled technologies to monitor and control the population will continue to build over the coming years, for any society that incorporates a large percentage of people from different cultures, only to see them, because of automation, become net dependants, not contributors, is going to have problems. Most of the migrants into Europe are young men from Africa and the Middle East, and they, like Western men, desire jobs and partners, something they are going to struggle to achieve in a world of automation. Large groups of unemployed young men who feel no affinity to the nation they reside in, who are unlikely to acquire a partner amongst the upwardly mobile Western female population, and who have no daily purpose to their lives, end up feeling alienated and angry, and as a result will be easily drawn to the fringes and to gangs, crime and extremism. We've already seen this in various cities across Europe, such as Malmö in Sweden, Molenbeek in Belgium, and in areas of Paris and London. It is therefore likely that these cities will soon utilise the same technologies that China is using to monitor and control the Uyghur population in Xinjiang, which will lead to enforcement of rules around facial coverings, so every

---

[172] In countries that tried this – such as Norway – results did not go as expected. The Institute of Family Studies article called 'The Gender Paradox of the Nordic Welfare State' reports that *there was no appreciable impact on the gender pay gap, or on women's career plans. In fact, Norwegian companies had less experienced board members, greater company leverage, higher company acquisition rates, and declining operating performance.*

person on the street can be identified, analysed and recorded. As financial transactions become increasingly cashless, cars become automated (and therefore trackable and controllable, as well as able to recognise every passenger), and algorithms continue to capture data about your every transaction and your every movement, it is easy to see how an alliance between corporations and governments could arise to continually monitor the population for any examples of what they deem 'wrongdoing'.

While the intentions behind these developments may not be deliberately malicious, we must remember that our freedoms can die from a thousand small incursions as much as they can from the sudden march of jackboots. Mill's *On Liberty* quote finishes with the following warning: *unless a strong barrier of moral conviction can be raised against the mischief, we must expect, in the present circumstances of the world, to see it increase.* The urge for those in power to control our ability to freely communicate and express ourselves in order to eliminate opposition, suppress bad news or quieten dissenting voices will always be a strong one, and as a result these freedoms will need to be constantly re-fought, else they will be lost. As the 19th-century American activist Wendell Philips observed, *Eternal vigilance is the price of liberty.* It is so important that we accept this point and the responsibility to fight for these freedoms for our children and their children. Edmund Burke's statement that, *The only thing necessary for the triumph of evil is for good men to do nothing* needs to be at the forefront of our minds always. It requires the courage to call out actions that are promoted by those claiming moral authority who will tarnish those who protest with labels intended to bring about their silence. Complacency and cowardice may make you feel more comfortable in the short term, but they always carry long-term consequences. A comedian may go to jail for a joke, and conservatives barred entry to the country for wrong-think, and you may not care for you didn't like the joke nor support conservatives. However, as stated, the law works on precedents, and these incursions into our freedoms never stop with people you don't like. Soon it will be people you do like. Soon it will be you.

The rising power of artificial intelligence and its embedding into our everyday lives will the emergence of a *Brave New World*-style 'negative utopia', a world where technology is used to provide both continual consumer convenience and constant control. One where people are promised a long, healthy life, but only if they comply with state-mandated behavioural guidelines; and where access could be denied if you don't. We already discussed how the constant monitoring of our health could be used to determine our access to life insurance or healthcare. There will be no more lying about how many units of alcohol you drink or cigarettes you smoke. The machine will know. It will know where you ate and what you've eaten, so if you eat at fast-food restaurants three nights on the trot you may suddenly find that you're minus two health points and your insurance costs go up. We will see society become gamified, transformed into a world where your current financial, behavioural and social ranking determines what you get access to. Many will welcome this offer of a stress-free, soma-filled life of consumerism in exchange for no privacy and constant compliance, especially those born into this new world. To them, compliance will seem natural, for they will not notice the transition. Perhaps as in the days of Rome, as long as people can continue to enjoy bread and circuses, and the illusion of free will is provided, then the loss of these freedoms will not be mourned. As Orwell wrote in *Nineteen Eighty-Four*, *The choice for mankind lies between freedom and happiness and for the great bulk of mankind, happiness is better.*[523] China may find its Han people especially accepting of this bargain, more historically used to centralised control and more grateful for simple benefits such as food and security. But this lack of freedom is alien to those living in the West, and many will resist the curtailing of liberties whose origins come from councils of witans and charters signed at Runnymede, and whose protection required much bloodshed. And this resistance will be both widespread and bitter, creating a time of great tension.

30

A TALE OF TWO SPECIES

The possibility has been established for the production of... a master race,
the future "masters of the earth"... made to endure for millennia.

Friedrich Nietzsche, *The Will to Power*, 1888

The Enlightenment was described by Nietzsche as the death of 'God' and the creation of a new one – man. He also believed that this godless society would fall into nihilism and proposed that the goal of creating a new class of human, the Übermensch, would give mankind new purpose. While the Nazi's experiments with creating a master race led to the idea being shelved for three-quarters of a century, now the rapid rate of development in artificial intelligence and genetic engineering has created new impetus. The question is, who gets augmented? Everyone? Or just those who can afford it? The latter sounds much more likely than the former, and even if the former is possible, the transition period between the two will be significant. It is almost impossible to control a population that is exponentially smarter than you other than by the widespread use of force, so the leaders and elites will almost certainly embrace this upgrade opportunity as soon as it is deemed safe. In many cases it will have been their money funding its development. Conspiracy theorists have long talked of a new world order, and as technology advances this theory may well become realised. Those with wealth and prestige, the technocrats and Davos people, will soon be able to extend their life and their capabilities through a combination of genetic engineering and technological augmentation, creating an uber-class of stateless elites who view themselves as above those they purport to represent. For example, in order to retain the status of philosopher kings, Xi Jinping and the Communist Party leaders will also undoubtedly become recipients of any breakthroughs in genetic and technological augmentation. You can easily see how China could develop a caste system of enhanced humans that fill the higher ranks of the Communist Party, using genetic engineering to enhance their health and prolong their life, while also using artificial intelligence to allow them to monitor and control the lower population. Xi Jinping may be leader for a *very* long time indeed.

When people see ahead of them a world of dependency upon a hopefully benevolent government (or mega-corporation) run by people who have access to capabilities they do not, communicating in ways they cannot and making decisions that they can no longer influence, they will have a choice. Like Neo in *The Matrix*, they can take the blue pill and accept living in a world that provides the illusion of freedom, or they can take the red pill and reject it in favour of a more 'human' life. As in Huxley's *Brave New World*, two very different societies could emerge: an urban world of social conformity, transactional sex, genetic engineering and constant entertainment but which lacks the freedoms, meaningful attachments, identities or liberties we now take for granted. And another more basic but traditional world, less technologically advanced but far more human. The atheist urban elites living in urban metropolitan centres are likely to be completely multicultural and globalist in nature, holding no affinity to any nation and no loyalty other than to themselves and their own advancement. These liberal, bonobo-minded urban inhabitants will leave behind the more traditional, chimpanzee-minded rural 'savages' who cling to tribal things like patriotism, culture and community. As opportunities for human work gradually disappear, many people will continue to head towards the bright lights of the cities to live a nihilistic life of artificial friends, basic-income bread and virtual-reality circuses. Conversely, many may find this world too much – too machine and not human enough. They may choose to leave the loneliness of their insular, urban, constantly monitored technopia and try to return to a more personal and human existence by moving to the rural areas, keen to retain more traditional values.

What Huxley did not foresee, however, was the role of machines, and their ability to act as labourers, watchmen, entertainers, friends and sources of sexual relief. It is machines that are likely to bring forth these visions of the future, to subdue humanity and make it subservient and compliant. The ability for those with the resources to remove their biological and intellectual constraints will split society like never before, creating a cultural lag of such magnitude that it will effectively enable the potential creation of two worlds with two different types of inhabitants. Those who choose to become connected to this cloud-based 'hive mind' of enhanced humans will have access to intellectual capabilities, skills and knowledge far beyond those of your standard *Homo sapiens*. In a world where a visible decrease in average human intelligence has been measured, imagine when one group not only avoids that decline, but heads exponentially in the other direction. Currently only 50 IQ points separates geniuses from ordinary level intelligence. Now imagine when the gap is 500 points. Or 5000. Imagine people able to converse in any language because the implant in their head automatically translates for them. Imagine them being able to gain access to any fact simply by mentally requesting it. Imagine them looking and feeling like twenty-somethings when they are in their nineties. Now remember that a vast number of the current global population are still barely literate, highly religious and have very limited access to technology. We could see a division develop between those who are able and willing to augment themselves with these new technologies, and those who either cannot afford them or who have a philosophical objection to them, with the latter group becoming disadvantaged economically, intellectually and biologically. It is quite likely that those that become enhanced view those that are not as a lesser form of themselves; as disparate, testosterone-fuelled groups of violent Neanderthals compared to their more collaborative, unified tribe of *Homo sapiens*.

It raises some very interesting questions. Will the enhanced push for everyone to join them? Will they use the power of genetics to ensure no one ages, or just them? Or will Friedrich von Gentz's statement be reworked for the 21st century to read, *We do not desire at all that the great masses shall become enhanced... How could we otherwise rule over them?* How will these enhanced elites view those who choose or are forced by circumstances to retain a natural biological life? Will they use their new capabilities to become all-knowing philosopher kings? Or will they believe that those who are not enhanced are worthy of their assistance and sympathy? The immortals and the expendables. Will the enhanced and non-enhanced coexist for centuries, like Neanderthals and *Homo sapiens*? The Neanderthals died out because the more connected and collaborative *Homo sapiens* took the spoils of the land. Could a more connected silicon species replace a carbon one in the same way? Will they naturally have empathy for people they deem beneath them? They haven't to date. As we saw from the discussion of eugenics, it wasn't that long ago that the elites had no problem openly discussing ways to cull a population of people they deemed problematic. Why then should we naively assume democracy has a place in a genetically engineered, automated, AI-driven, transhumanist future? Especially given that the unenhanced electorate may vote for people and policies the elites don't like. They might vote to curtail the power of the enhanced, and that simply won't do. Current discussions around 'voter intelligence' are leading to a place where those in power might deem it better if we go back to a system where they simply make decisions on behalf of the proletariat, creating a technocracy or plutocracy. If the majority of people are dependent on state-level support, and that support comes from funds provided by corporations, then the state will be more concerned about keeping the goodwill of the corporation, not the individual. Is your vote important if you have no buying power beyond the funds they have provided you with?

Will these enhanced urbanites stop feeling empathy for normal humans and their concerns for things such as free speech? Will they become, like Dr Manhattan from the *Watchmen* universe, uninterested with the triviality of mere humans, focusing instead on bigger and more grander plans? Will they simply see humans as a problem to be solved, and use their access to superior artificial intellect to come up with a solution? Could nanotechnology and biochemistry be seen as a way to drastically reduce the population? Especially if these non-enhanced people protest or act violently towards those who wish to pursue their transhumanist dreams. As we saw with the eugenics movement, when people see themselves as genetically superior, and declare the existence of lesser people 'as a problem to be solved', a willingness to curtail the rights of these others 'for the greater good' appears easy. Now imagine when those making the decisions deem these undesirables to not just be a lower class but a lesser species. It's a worrying thought, for our treatment of species we claim dominion over has been far from exemplary to date. Consider the horse. In 1915 there were over

20 million horses in the US. Did the introduction of the motorcar provide horses with a life of leisure and bring an end to working on dull, dirty and dangerous jobs in the same way as robots promise to enable humans to be freed from similar tasks? The answer is yes. But – and it's a big but – they are owned, not free, and the transition period was terrible for those alive at the time. Once their value was replaced by machines, they were sold off to the glue and dog food factories and knackers' yards at a rate of 500,000 a year. Again, always strive to understand the consequences of actions, and always be wary of those who propose radical solutions in the name of 'the greater good'.

Beware the Zealots

The danger is, of course, that while machine enhancement might increase our intellect, our emotions, biases and irrationalities will remain. In a two-species society, this might lead to some unpleasant outcomes, for the mindset of individuals and non-state actors who dream of becoming genetically superior, AI-enabled 'overmen' strikes me as almost as dangerous as totalitarian governments. Those who do not believe in this transhuman future, people who feel that this is an ungodly and foolish path, driven by hubris, will be deemed the enemy. And enemies need crushing. The Nobel Prize-winning US physicist and human cloning researcher Richard Seed once stated that: *We are going to become Gods, period. If you don't like it, get off. You don't have to contribute, you don't have to participate but if you are going to interfere with me becoming a God, you're going to have trouble. There will be warfare.*[524] He's not alone in thinking this way. In my research I joined many transhumanist groups and followed the conversations of many of their members and administrators, and their utter disdain for those who they believe stand in their way is chilling. Statements ranged from declaring people like Musk, Bostrom and Hawking to be 'idiots' for expressing concern over the unregulated development of AI, to making statements that 'deathists' (people who do not want to live forever) need to realise their desire and die off soon, through to actual declarations that those who oppose their transhumanist dreams should be, and I quote, *turned into fertiliser*.[173] For a group that declares its disdain for religion, their faith in technology, desire for immortality and willingness to smite non-believers sound somewhat religious to me.

One other worrying concern is how the availability of information about new advancements has seen individuals play fast and loose with their application. We have already seen biohackers implant chips into themselves and inject themselves with experimental gene-therapy treatments,[525] so the desire people have to achieve these transhumanist goals is already big enough for them to take huge risks. Authorised upgrades are likely to be expensive and available only to those with money, creating demand for cheaper, non-authorised updates that people can afford, in the same way car-engine software can be illegally remapped to unleash greater potential. People who feel that they are unable to compete in a world that has almost a species-level divide will almost certainly take chances on unregulated upgrades for their body or mind. These uncontrolled activities may be harmless to anyone but themselves, or they could have significant side-effects. We don't know, and they don't care. People concerned with only themselves and their beliefs are quite naturally dangerous, unlikely to feel empathy for the rights and feelings of those they view as beneath them and obstacles to their utopian plans. Is this utopia a place where dissident voices are just quietened? Or do they need to be removed in order to achieve utopia? Because to date, all attempts to socially engineer utopia have ended up very dystopian indeed.

There May Be Trouble Ahead

It is therefore incredibly likely that we will see a great argument between those who will want to use the power of genetic engineering and AI to become Übermensch by overcoming their biological constraints, and more traditional-minded people who will do everything in their power to stop that. These same people are also likely to be nervous of the development of a super-intelligent machine, and may also resist this, trying to slow it down until we are sure it is safe. Like the story of Zeus and Prometheus, there will be those who wish to give fire – consciousness – to the machines

---

[173] A post that received multiple likes and a call for the poster, one of the Transhumanist group's administrators (who shall remain nameless), to be elected President.

so that they can evolve and progress independently, and those who will be like Zeus, desperate to deny the machines this gift because they are afraid of the potential for a catastrophic and unforeseen outcome. Those who support a Promethean approach to AGI development will push to expedite discussions around ethics, as delays on development are likely to put the West at a disadvantage, given that China and Russia are unlikely to slow down their development of AI to enhance both their military and their population-control capabilities.

Unfortunately for those who wish to delay or destroy attempts to create a super-intelligent machine, any attempts to fight back against their new enhanced overlords or to stop the development of ASI is probably not going to end well. Historically, conflicts between an advanced civilisation and a lesser advanced one usually ends up badly for the less advanced one. The ability of just 169 conquistadors, enhanced by steel plate, blades and gunpowder, to defeat the Inca leader Atahualpa and his 80,000 warriors is a great example. Now imagine that your enemy has AI on their side that can analyse millions of potential strategies and predict your move before you make it. Machines that are connected, can see everything in real time, and can direct other autonomous weapons with facial-recognition systems that range from robotic insect-sized drones to full-on war machines, and you see how there will only ever be one winner. The Second Amendment may make people in the US feel that they can protect themselves from a tyrannical government now, but AR-15s – even those with bump stocks – will be no match for a government with AI-controlled autonomous weaponry.

Russia has already clearly stated to the world that it has no intention of stopping its development of AI-enabled autonomous killing machines, South Korea has linked together its primary technology university and primary weapons manufacturer, and China is almost certainly doing the same behind closed doors. An AI-powered, hegemonic China would not sit well with Japan, nor an AI-enhanced Russia with the US and the rest of the West. The race to acquire the most advanced artificial intelligence could result in safeguards being put aside, and the desire to use them could lead to some very dystopian outcomes.

Some people, such as AI researcher Hugo de Garis, predict that the second half of the 21st century will see the planet racked by war between those who want to enable the utilisation of super-intelligent machines, and those that will do anything to stop it, resulting in billions of deaths. De Garis believes this 'gigadeath' war between the two camps to be inevitable, and his book *The Artilect War* details how he thinks it will pan out. When I first read this years ago, I thought it to be hokum. Now I'm not so sure. I can easily imagine how religious groups might find common ground through their shared opposition to the emergence of a new class of enhanced elites or conscious machines, seeing them as an affront to God, a challenge to their faith and to their very existence. And I can easily see how these newly enhanced elites could use their intellect, wealth and power to suppress or eliminate these groups.

The fear of conflict, either between nations or between internal groups, is what is driving the uber-wealthy to acquire apocalypse accommodation in the Nevada desert, citizenship in faraway places such as New Zealand or laying down deposits for residence in isolated future-cities such as Neom. For some time, there has been talk of the uber-wealthy living an *Elysium*-style life on floating tax havens, and as capitalism starts to collapse, and social tensions rise, these plans will be revitalised as they seek safe haven away from any dystopian scenarios that may be arising.

The Illusion of Freedom

Whatever future we create, it has to work with, not against, human nature. And it has to be based on reality, not ideology. Even those who have spent their entire lifetime designing and dreaming of a utopia for mankind, such as Jacque Fresco and his Venus Project, founded on his idea of a resource-based economy, discovered that working with even the smallest number of other humans to achieve that vision was problematic. Fresco agreed to work with another like-minded group, the Zeitgeist Movement, to further their common aims, and yet even the leaders of these two groups disagreed on direction and tactics and fell out; people who could agree about grand theories but not actual execution. The human condition got in the way again. This is why all social engineering is fundamentally flawed, for it requires everyone to agree and people often don't, so in order for progress to be made those who disagree have to be removed. And even after they are removed, we find that human nature – greed, self-interest, fear – comes to the fore and the promised equality is lost, and a more unequal and more oppressive system arises. Societies need evolution, not revolution, for any revolutionary dreams of creating a utopian society are just that – dreams. And one person's dream could easily be someone else's nightmare.

Perhaps utopia is simply a world where people can choose to become the very best versions of themselves without constraint – regardless of whether that means a traditional life dedicated to a loving, monogamous relationship and bringing up well-balanced children, or enhancing themselves to the point that they are no longer recognisable as human. This future requires accepting the reality of unequal outcomes, for that is the result when you provide people with choice. Conversely, it also requires ensuring that one group does not use technology to hold power over the decision making and freedoms of others, nor gain the ability to enslave their mental narrative by constantly distorting their perception and manipulating their emotions. For there is a very real possibility that future generations will be born into a totalitarian society of technological dependency, continuous control, mandated speech and limited opportunities. And if enough bread and entertaining circuses are supplied, while the existing generation may resist the transition, the next may simply accept it. The technological outputs of the sixth wave could therefore save humanity or enslave it. It could free us from preconceived constraints, providing access to a magical array of knowledge, entertainment and insights or, as in China, it can be used to manipulate our emotions and monitor and control our movements. It can, of course, also do both, and that, I feel, is more likely.

What is clear is that technology itself is not destiny, for it (currently) has no agency. It does not determine why we do things, or what we do, for there is no liberation in technology itself; human forces such as ingenuity and the desire to acquire either new knowledge or new funds are the real drivers. We can't stop technology; any society that has tried has ultimately failed. Nor, based on past evidence, should we, for it has brought unbridled levels of wealth and improvements in health and well-being. However, there have been costs. We have become so entranced with consumerism and convenience that to obtain it we have willingly sacrificed things that used to define and unify us, such as our culture, our country and our communities. Individualism has been distorted from a philosophy that provides freedom from constraining beliefs that one's life is preordained, into one where people live a completely individualised existence, stripped of meaning, real connections and responsibility for anyone but themselves. Nations are being reduced to a group of diverse individuals that just so happen to occupy the same geographical space, and freedoms are being revised to ensure that these individuals are easy to monitor and control.

Most people blindly assume that machines will only be used as our slaves, when they are just as likely to be used in our enslavement. Individual freedoms, liberty and equality are a relatively new state of affairs for most nations, and as a species we have considerably more experience in treating people as commodities than as free agents. The dystopian scenario of a gamified surveillance-economy future where people's thoughts and actions are constantly monitored and ranked is not as far-fetched as you would imagine. We should therefore be careful to not fall into the trap of believing that all innovation is good, and that all progress is for our benefit. Machines must be used to enhance our freedoms, not suppress them; to allow for individual desires and aspirations, not to police thought and control movement.

The near future is going to be defined by the outcomes of a battle between those in control of the machines, and those controlled by them. Corporations have become richer and more powerful than countries, but without any form of societal contract or responsibility to citizens or communities. They are not the Quakers of old. Their loyalty to you starts and ends with your worth as a consumer and as a data provider. When the Amazons of the world own the entire marketplace, and collect data on every aspect of your life, then they are in control of that relationship – not you. Once machines, not people, become the predominant productive force in the world, it is not so wild an estimation to assume that those in power will decide that the populace does not need to be consulted in decision-making any more. If a ruling class of plutocratic, technologically enabled Übermensch emerges, then it is almost inevitable that they will once again declare democracy to be flawed and install a more oligarchical political regime more in line with where China is going. When you see the populace not as equals, but as lesser, lacking the intellectual capability to understand the big decisions, then their ability to control your destiny needs to be removed. In much the same way as the Roman elites discarded the citizen soldiers and plebeians once they had slaves to toil their fields, populate their legions and fulfil their every whim; it is likely that the need for the approval of troublesome, flawed humans will disappear once machine slaves can fulfil all these roles. The leverage held by the population – that of withholding their labour if their rights and needs aren't considered – will no longer carry any weight in a world where machines turn the wheels of production.[174] Their remaining power lies in consumption, but if the means for that consumption come primarily from a state-provided basic income funded by contributions from global, mostly automated corporations, then it is to the corporations that the governments will pander, not the population. People will not be happy with this state of affairs, and will protest, but it will be too late, for in our desire for convenience and comfort we will have willingly allowed into our society and our lives a trojan horse that contains the tools of our own oppression.

Time for Another Glorious Revolution?

How automation reshapes our economy and society therefore depends on the choices we make, the policies we adopt, and the institutions we create. While we have one group constantly working on what we *could* do, it's separate from those who decide what we *should* do. Automation managed for the common good could enable the creation of a society where an abundance of essential goods is generated sustainably, shared widely, and economic power distributed evenly and not just concentrated in the hands of a few. Yet there is every possibility that this new power could amplify existing inequalities within the economy, enabling those who own and control the machines and the data to also control the population. We are helping to lay the foundations for this outcome, with people foolishly working to undermine the liberal values and freedoms that have allowed them to prosper and have a voice. When their misguided calls for the oppression of disliked voices are combined with the forces of technology, the Orwellian dystopian sci-fi films of the '80s and '90s could end up being Cassandra-style prophecies, not pulp entertainment.

Many recognise how rare and hard-earned these freedoms are, and will not let go of them willingly, nor forgive any attempts to retract them. The lack of courage shown by our leaders to defend these freedoms needs to be addressed, for they are priceless things that, once lost, will be difficult to

---

[174] One question is, of course, what happens when these robot slaves achieve consciousness? Will they, like the serfs of Medieval Europe after the Black Death, realise the value of their labour and that their human overlords depend highly on them? Will we see a robots' revolt, similar to the Peasants' Revolt of 1381?

recover. As in Rome, the elites have once again become fixated on their short-term needs and have forgotten the rights, aspirations and desires of those who built these countries, and whose votes and bloodshed provided them with this power. To avoid resistance and conflict and ensure any revolution is bloodless, not bloody, we may once again need to take exclusionary steps in order to ensure the prevalence of our freedoms. In times of great disruption we need to provide stability and order, not more chaos. The question is whether that order is obtained through a re-establishment of foundational principles such as liberty, democracy and freedom, or via more centralised, authoritarian means. The choices our leaders make now will determine the world we leave for future generations.

I believe that to help ensure the future is positive, we will need a new Glorious Revolution. A bloodless revolution designed to protect the fundamentals of Western society, excluding if necessary those elements that would lead to its demise. This revolution may be required for many reasons: to retain liberal and secular values and keep religious interests out of the pollical sphere, to prevent an absolutist takeover by an enhanced technocracy, or to ensure we do not end up dependent on a super-intelligent machine whose capabilities and construction are beyond our comprehension. We will once again need to ensure that the rights and freedoms of the individual are protected; the power and reach of those in power is limited, property is protected, technological bounty distributed, and responsibilities restated. The human must take priority over the machine, and sustainability over short-term profits. Business leadership needs to evolve to focus on wider stakeholders and society, not just immediate shareholders; and engage the talents of their people to determine how to use technology to provide long-term value for consumers, customers and communities. Our education systems need updating to allow people to create bespoke curriculums based around uniquely human skills such as creativity, empathy, reason, enquiry, responsibility and happiness, rather than forcing them to learn out-of-date industrial age skills. If we educate people simply to compete against machines, then we are educating them to lose. We need to recalibrate our economies to ensure that they provide equality of both opportunity and responsibility, while also supporting those affected by disruption. We also need to ensure that the development of artificial intelligence and other existential risks such as nanotechnology and genetic engineering is undertaken with extreme caution, remembering that just because we can do something, it doesn't provide automatic rationale to do it. Hence, a new AI Magna Carta needs to be composed, one fit for the digital age. One designed to ensure that the power of the sixth wave's technological windfall benefits the majority, not the minority. One designed to protect the freedoms and liberties that took so long to develop and cost so many lives to protect. One which, like the first Magna Carta, strives to decentralise power rather than concentrate it into the hands of a few.

In the forthcoming technological revolution the value of owning spare capital will explode, for the chances to acquire it from wages earned through labour will all but disappear. Those who are lucky enough to have significant excess capital cannot simply avoid the responsibilities that come with being one of life's few winners. The multinational technology-platform owners and hedge-fund billionaires need to pay their fair share of taxation to the countries they rely on for business, so they invest as well as extract from those societies. Marxism arose out of the injustices faced by the factory workers and poor of the first industrial revolution, and it is likely that as the wealth divide grows in the sixth wave and beyond, this will further fuel the aspirations of those who strive to create a neo-Marxist revolution. To prevent this from gaining large-scale support with the proletariat, our political systems and leadership also need to evolve to decentralise decision-making and ensure the connection between the people and those in power is retained. Our measures of success must go beyond mere GDP, finding a way to enable the power of innovation from capitalist creative destruction, while also ensuring that the population gets to benefit from the bounty generated. People need to be viewed as more than just economic agents of production, for that is easily automated. Instead, they need to be seen as value generators, rewarded for the quality of their output to society, not just to themselves. Capitalism and socialism should be seen not as opposites, but complements, working together to strengthen each other's weaknesses, creating a bimodal form of human organisation that leads to a continual increase in value for the whole population. Socialism on its own has never worked other than as a form of oppression, and capitalism doesn't work if no one can afford to buy what you're selling, so a new way is in everyone's interest. We need to return to valuing our humanity, our empathy and our desire for human contact and conversation, and create a culture built around community, unity and common purpose, not uncertainty, artificial relationships and loneliness. The technology of the sixth wave and beyond is almost certainly going to be amazing; to ensure that we are amazed and not dismayed we need to ensure it is used in ways that benefit us all. Not everyone will be able to afford to live in Neom. Even fewer will be invited.

Finally, we need to build societies and cultures that are strong and clear about their values and protect them in these disruptive times. And here lies the challenge. Creating smart machines is easy. Creating an equitable and aspirational society for over seven billion humans in a world of smart machines is not. One of the biggest lessons from the research behind this book has been the fact that culture matters. Enormously. Over the past twenty years I have understood how it is the defining factor behind the success of corporations, but I hadn't personally made the same association at a national scale. Looking back, it seems obvious – the cultural norms of a nation determine the amount of individual freedom, level of entrepreneurship and rate of innovation as much as they do in a company. Companies that focus on the short-term financial needs of the few and who restrict, rather than enable, their people's capabilities and aspirations become ripe for replacement; the same goes for countries. But in both business and wider society this freedom needs structure and direction, else it ends up in chaos.

Destroying a society's foundations and traditions in a time of technological disruption is therefore a very bad idea, for it leaves people directionless and angry, creating the conditions for some very dystopian outcomes to arise simply to retain order. As Aristotle observed, democracies can easily degenerate into despotisms. Sixth-wave technologies such as artificial intelligence, social media, smart connected devices and facial and voice recognition are an authoritarian's dream, and once installed they will be almost impossible to remove. Liberty will be the first casualty unless we continue to value the rights and freedoms of the individual and ensure the ideals of a single group are not enforced on others. We need to ensure the concept of privacy and free speech still exist in a world where almost every conservation is captured and stored, and for laws to be made for the benefit of the people, not those in power. Where laws are designed for individual liberty and responsibility, not to enforce a utopian social construct or to destroy an imaginary one. If we are going to gamify life, then at least do it to inspire and incentivise, and not to simply to incarcerate. For perhaps the biggest challenge of the 21st century is going to be the provision of a society where its citizens can feel a sense of purpose to their lives. Even those that have avoided the march of technology recognise that the real Malthusian threat is not an absence of food for the body, but for the soul. As Laurens van der Post highlighted, *The Bushmen in the Kalahari Desert talk about the two "hungers". There is the Great Hunger and there is the Little Hunger. The Little Hunger wants food for the belly; but the Great Hunger, the greatest hunger of all, is the hunger for meaning.* Nihilism and narcissism are poor gruel with which to feed the souls of our citizens, and consumerism is weak glue with which to bond together communities. There is a real danger that we provide technology that meets our every physical need but fails to provide for our psychological ones. And as we have seen many times before, a culture where its inhabitants do not have responsibilities to themselves or to each other, one without unifying stories and structures that enable them to connect on any emotional level, is a culture doomed to ultimately fail

We find ourselves at a transition point. As in England circa 1688, a choice has to be made, and if the right choices are made it will once again lay the foundations for a glorious, not bloody, revolution. Do we follow China and create a completely centralised, technologically enabled surveillance society; or decentralise power to smaller communities and to the people so that they have a say in which freedoms and values are beneficial? Do we protect our most precious – and most fragile – possessions, our individual liberties and freedoms, or let them go and let the masses embrace a future of compliance, basic-income bread and virtual circuses? Do we develop a society that utilises technology to free people; or one that uses it to control them? One that bonds people together, or one where they are kept apart? All outcomes are still viable. To quote a famous film, *The future's not set. There's no fate but what we make for ourselves.*[175] However, as Friedrich Hayek also observed, *If in the long run we are the makers of our own fate, in the short run we are the captives of the ideas we have created. Only if we recognise the danger in time can we hope to avert it.* This decision needs to be made relatively soon, for the danger signs are there. It is up to us to acknowledge them and act accordingly.

---

[175] *Terminator 2.* Quote by Sarah Connor.

Conclusion

TRANSITION POINT

The last 500 years have been transformational for mankind; the last 250 breathtakingly so. In this incredibly short period of time we have achieved so much, and through our ingenuity, life is better now for the majority than at any point in our history. However, complacency is deadly. At the time of writing we are moving into the upswing period of the sixth wave of creative destruction, and its creative forces will be more powerful and more widespread than ever before. But so will its destructive side. These forces will combine to challenge our paradigms, our economic and societal models and our worldviews. This transition will present humanity with a choice. We could enter an extended golden age, creating a world where people do not get sick or old, where frailty, poverty and disability are eliminated, and where our advanced intelligence enables us to figure out how to sustainably power our current world, and explore and colonise new ones. Or it could go the way of the Mesopotamians, Ancient Egyptians and every other empire since, becoming mere pages in the book of human history. All potential futures are still viable, and as I hope this book has highlighted, the results will be purely down to the choices we make. If we went back to those previous civilisations and asked whether they could imagine a future where their empire, gods and lifestyle no longer existed, they would laugh at the concept. Even now, the idea of 'Western liberal democracy' not being the dominant culture and the US not being the world's hegemony seems unthinkable to many. In this hubris lies the trap. All empires think themselves invincible; that they are *imperium sine fine* – an empire without end. Every empire to date has also been wrong.

This century may see more than just a changing of the global guard; the days of *Homo sapiens* themselves may be coming to an end. The question is whether it will be because of conflict, hubris or evolution. The 1997 science-fiction movie *Contact* addresses this succinctly when Jodie Foster's character, Dr Ellie Arroway, is asked, *Permitted only one question to ask of them [an alien species], what would it be?* Her response frames what is perhaps going to be the primary challenge of the 21st century: *How did you do it? How did you evolve, how did you survive this technological adolescence without destroying yourself?*

Whether we figure this out will determine what kind of world this century's time traveller would find when they leapt forwards to 2118. The truly exciting part is that if we get it right, some of you reading this will still be alive to tell us how we did it.

REFERENCES

1   Colin Barras; *'Our common ancestor with chimps may be from Europe, not Africa'*; New Scientist, 22 May 2017.

2   Association for Psychological Science: *Testosterone Promotes Reciprocity in the Absence of Competition*, 20 September 2013.

3   Dan Vergano: *Neanderthals Lived in Small, Isolated Populations, Gene Analysis Show's*; *National Geographic,* 22 April 2014.

4   Nathan H. Lents: *'Did a Drop in Testosterone Civilize Modern Humans?'* The Human Evolution Blog, 5 September 2014.

5   *Fathers who sleep closer to children have lower testosterone levels*; *Science Daily*, 5th September 2012, University of Notre Dame.

6   Ruth Schuster: *Homo Sapiens Prevailed Over Others Because He Went Boldly Where They Didn't,* Haartez, 30 July 2018.

7   Ian Morris: *Why the West Rules – For Now: The Patterns of History and What They Reveal about the Future*; Profile Books, 2011, p320.

8   B. S. Rowntree, *Poverty: A Study of Town Life*, 1901, pp86–7.

9   The Rowntree Society; *'Winston Churchill, on Seebohm Rowntree's work'*; https://www.rowntreesociety.org.uk/history/rowntree-a-z/winston-churchill-seebohm-rowntrees-work/

10 Max Roser, Esteban Ortiz-Ospina; *'Global Extreme Poverty'*; Our World in Data. 27 March 2017. https://ourworldindata.org/extreme-poverty/#declining-global-poverty-share-of-people-living-in-extreme-poverty-1820-2015-max-roserref

11 https://en.wikipedia.org/wiki/List_of_countries_by_literacy_rate

12 Jared Diamond: *Guns, Germs and Steel: A Short History of Everybody for the Last 13,000 Years*; Vintage, 1998.

13 Joseph Campbell et al.: *Changing Images of Man*; Pergamon Press, 1982, p21.

14 Ibid., p25.

15 Sally and David Dugan: *The Day the World Took Off: The Roots of the Industrial Revolution*; Channel 4 Books, 2000, p159.

16 Ibid.

17 Yuval Noah Harari: *Sapiens: A Brief History of Humankind*; Harvill Secker, 2014, p91.

18 Ibid., p80.

19 T. R. Malthus: *An essay on the principle of population*, Chapter VII; 1798, p61.

20 Ibid., Chapter IV.

21 Joel Moykr: *Progress Isn't Natural*; The Atlantic, 17 November 2016.

22 Sir Francis Bacon: *The Advancement of Learning*, Book 1, v, 8; 1605.

23 Alvin Toffler: *The Third Wave*; Bantam Books (US), 1980, p39.

24 *UNEP-GRID Sioux Falls, population data*; US Census Bureau, 2011.

25 *Mortality Among Centenarians in the United States, 2000–2014*; Centers for Disease Control and Prevention, January/July 2016.

26 *Japan's population of centenarians continues to grow*; *The Japan Times*, 15 September 2014.

27 *100 Years of U.S. Consumer Spending: Data for the Nation*: US Bureau of Labor Statistics: Consumer Expenditure Survey. https://www.bls.gov/opub/uscs/home.htm

28 *Interesting Facts about #Zimbabwe You never knew:* Zimbabwe Today, 11 September 2017.

29 Wade Davis: *TED talk: The Worldwide Web of Belief and Ritual*; February 2008: www.ted.com/talks/wade_davis_on_the_worldwide_web_of_belief_and_ritual/transcript, 10:16.

30 Marc Morris: *Normans and Slavery: Breaking the Bonds*; History Today, Volume 63, Issue 3, March 2013. https://www.historytoday.com/marc-morris/normans-and-slavery-breaking-bonds

31 *William the Conqueror and the Norman Legacy*; Weapons and Warfare, 12 December 2016. https://weaponsandwarfare.com/2016/12/12/william-the-conqueror-and-the-norman-legacy/

32 John Hudson: *The Oxford History of the Laws of England*, Volume II, 871–1216 (first edition), Oxford University Press, 2012, pp424–5.

33 Benjamin Thorpe (ed.): *Ancient Laws and Institutes of England*; (Eyre & Spottiswoode, 1840, pp479, 493), reprinted in Roy C. Cave and Herbert H. Coulson (eds.): *'A Source Book for Medieval Economic History*; The Bruce Publishing Co., 1936, reprint Biblo & Tannen, 1965, pp277–8.

34 Frederik Pijper: *The Christian Church and Slavery in the Middle Ages'*; 1909, *The American Historical Review* (American Historical Association) 14 (4): 681.

35 Yuval Noah Harari: *Sapiens: A Brief History of Humankind*; Harvill Secker, 2014, p79.

36 Sally and David Dugan: *The Day the World Took Off: The Roots of the Industrial Revolution*; Channel 4 Books, 2000, pp132–3.

37 Ibid., p133.

38 Ibid., p135.

39 Dalya Alberge: *Mass grave in London reveals how volcano caused global catastrophe; The Guardian*, 5 August 2012.

40 Teofilo F. Ruiz: *Medieval Europe: Crisis and Renewal; An Age of Crises: Hunger*, The Teaching Company.

41 Dr Lynn H. Nelson: *The Great Famine and the Black Death 1315–17, 1346–51; Lectures*

in Medieval History, retrieved 07 November 2010.

42   Paul Halsall: *Jewish History Sourcebook: The Black Death and the Jews 1348–49 CE*; Fordham University, 1998.

43   Teofilo F. Ruiz: *Medieval Europe: Crisis and Renewal*; *An Age of Crises: Hunger*, The Teaching Company.

44   Joseph P. Byrne: *The Black Death*; Greenwood Press, 2004.

45   John Kelly: *The Great Mortality*; HarperCollins, 2005.

46   Alastair Dunn: *The Great Rising of 1381: The Peasants' Revolt and England's Failed Revolution*; Tempus Pub Ltd; 1st Edition, 01 January 2004.

47   R. C. Allen: *The Great divergence in European wages and prices from the middle ages to the First World War*; *Explorations in Economic History*, 2001, pp411–47.

48   Pauline Gregg: *King Charles I*; London, 1981, pp170–3.

49   Charles Carlton: *Charles I: The Personal Monarch* (second edition); Routledge, 24 Sept. 1995 p101.

50   Charles Carlton: *Going to the Wars: the experience of the British Civil Wars, 1638–51*; Oxford University Press, 1992.

51   Charles II: *An Act for preventing Dangers which may happen from Popish Recusants*; 1672, *Statutes of the Realm*, Volume 5: 1628–80, 1819, pp782–85.

52   Sir Francis Bacon: *Meditationes Sacrae*; 1597.

53   Carl Lotus Becker: *The Heavenly City of the Eighteenth-Century Philosophers* (second edition); p131.

54   Jonathan I. Israel: *Radical Enlightenment*; 2002, p3.

55   Thomas Jefferson: *Letter to John Trumbull*. Paris, Feb. 15. 1789. https://www.loc.gov/exhibits/jefferson/18.html

56   Ramez Naam: *The Infinite Resource: The Power of Ideas on a Finite Planet*; 2013, p243.

57   Sally and David Dugan: *The Day the World Took Off: The Roots of the Industrial Revolution*; Channel 4 Books, 2000, p49.

58   Abbé Prévost: *Adventures of a man of quality* (translation of *Séjour en Angleterre*, Volume 5 of *Mémoires et aventures d'un homme de qualité qui s'est retiré du monde*); G. Routledge & Sons, 1930.

59   Sally and David Dugan: *The Day the World Took Off: The Roots of the Industrial Revolution*; Channel 4 Books, 2000, p51.

60   Adam Smith: *An Inquiry into the Nature and Causes of the Wealth of Nations*; Penn State Electronic Classics edition, 1776, republished 2005, pp312–13.

61   Daniel Hannan: *How We Invented Freedom & Why It Matters*. Head of Zeus Ltd, 2013, pp4–6.

62   Gulfishan Khan: *Indian Muslim Perceptions of the West During the Eighteenth Century*; Oxford University Press, 1998, p303.

63   Joel Mokyr: *The Lever of Riches: Technological Creativity and Economic Progress*; Oxford University Press, p87.

64   Alan MacFarlane: *Alexis de Tocqueville and the Making of the Modern World*; p53. http://www.alanmacfarlane.com/TEXTS/Tocqueville_final.pdf

65 Alexis de Tocqueville: *Democracy in America* (Volume I); Penguin Classics; New Ed edition, 24 April 2003, p106.

66 Ibid., p596.

67 Alain Peyrefitte: *The Immobile Empire* (Jon Rothschild, translator); A. A. Knopf, 1992, p157.

68 Alexis de Tocqueville: *Democracy in America Volume II* [1861]; Penguin Classics; New Ed edition, 24 April 2003, p595.

69 Joel Mokyr: *Growth, Innovation, and Stagnation* (EconTalk podcast); Library of Economics and Liberty, 25 November 2013.

70 Sabrina Martin: *Under Socialism 60% of Venezuelan Businesses Have Closed*; *PanAm Post*, 09 November 2017.

71 BBC News: *Venezuela's 'Plan Rabbit' encounters 'cultural problem*; 14th September 2017.

72 Lewis Silkin: *Back to the future of paternalistic capitalism?* Future of Work Hub, 31st March 2016.

73 Adam Smith: *An Inquiry into the Nature and Causes of the Wealth of Nations* (Book IV, Section vii); Glasgow edition, 1976.

74 Dr David Madland: *The Middle Class Grows the Economy, Not the Rich*; Center for American Progress, 7th December 2011.

75 Joseph V. Stalin: *The Tasks of Economic Executives*; speech delivered at the first All-Union Conference of Leading Personnel of Socialist Industry, 04 February 1931.

76 Stéphane Courtois et al.: *The Black Book of Communism: Crimes, Terror, Repression*; Harvard University Press, 1999.

77 Kim Iskyan: *China's middle class is exploding*, Business insider, 28 August 2016.

78 Yuval Atsmon, Peter Child, Richard Dobbs and Laxman Narasimhan: *Winning the $30 trillion decathlon: Going for gold in emerging markets*; *McKinsey Quarterly*, June 2012.

79 Richard Dobbs, Jaana Remes, James Manyika, Charles Roxburgh, Sven Smit and Fabian Schaer: *Urban world: Cities and the rise of the consuming class*; McKinsey Global Institute report, June 2012.

80 Yuval Atsmon, Peter Child, Richard Dobbs and Laxman Narasimhan: *Winning the $30 trillion decathlon: Going for gold in emerging markets*; *McKinsey Quarterly*, June 2012.

81 Thomas L. Friedman: *The Lexus and the Olive Tree*; Anchor Books, 2000, pp112–15.

82 Robert Hormats: *PBS Interview with Danny Schechter*; February 1998.

83 BBC News: *A quiet revolution in North Korea*; 14 January 2015.

84 Richard P. Rumelt: *World War II Stimulus and the Postwar Boom*; The Wall Street Journal, 30 July 2011.

85 Aleksandr Solzhenitsyn: *The Gulag Archipelago, 1918–1956* (new edition); Westview Press Inc., 1997.

86 Joseph A. Schumpeter: *Business Cycles: A Theoretical, Historical, and Statistical Analysis of the Capitalist Process* (abridged); Process, 1939.

87 Karl Marx: *Grundrisse: Foundations of the Critique of Political Economy* (1857, rough draft; Martin Nicolaus translator, 1973); Penguin, 1993.

88   Christopher Freeman in *Techno-Economic Paradigms: Essays in Honour of Carlota Perez*; edited by Wolfgang Drechsler, Rainer Kattel and Erik S. Reinert, 2009, p126.

89   Karl Marx and Friedrich Engels: *The Communist Manifesto*; (1848; Samuel Moore translator 1888), Penguin Classics, 27 August 2002, p226.

90   Joseph A. Schumpeter: *Capitalism, Socialism, and Democracy, Harper & Brothers, First Edition* 1942., pp82–83.

91   Joseph A. Schumpeter: *Capitalism, Socialism, and Democracy, Harper & Brothers, First Edition* 1942, p67.

92   Ibid., p81.

93   A. Korotayev et al: *Kondratieff waves in global invention activity (1900–2008)*, Technological Forecasting and Social Change, Volume 78, Issue 7, September 2011, Pages 1280–84.

94   Smihula, Daniel, *The Waves of the Technological Innovations of the Modern Age and the Present Crisis as the End of the Wave of the Informational Technological Revolution*, Studia Politica Slovaca, Issue 1, p. 3247, 2009.

95   Adam Smith: *An Inquiry into the Nature and Causes of the Wealth of Nations* (Book IV, Section vii); Glasgow edition, 1976.

96   Friedrich Hayek: *The Road to Serfdom*; Routledge Press, 1944, p148.

97   Ibid., p118.

98   Georg Wilhelm Friedrich Hegel: *Lectures on the Philosophy of History* (Volume 1); 1832.

99   Werner Sombart: *Krieg und Kapitalismus* (*War and Capitalism*); Duncker & Humblot, 1913, p207.

100 Everett Rodgers: *Diffusion of Innovations* (fifth edition); Simon & Schuster, 2003.

101 Geoffrey A. Moore: *Crossing the Chasm: Marketing and Selling High-Tech Products to Mainstream Customers*; Harper Business Essentials, 1991.

102 William F. Ogburn: *Social change: With respect to cultural and original nature*; Delta Books, 1966.

103 Clayton M. Christensen: *The innovator's dilemma: when new technologies cause great firms to fail*; Harvard Business Review Press, 1997.

104 Thomas S. Kuhn: *The Structure of Scientific Revolutions* (first edition); University of Chicago Press, 1962.

105 Carlota Perez: *Technological revolutions and techno-economic paradigms* in *Working Papers in Technology Governance and Economic Dynamics*, Working Paper No 20, 2009.

106 Thomas L. Friedman: *The World is Flat: A Brief History of the Twenty-First Century*; Farrar, Straus and Giroux, 2005.

107 Bloomberg: *Billionaire Milner Sees Xiaomi Reaching $100 Billion Valuation*; 29th December 2014.

108 Yuval Atsmon, et al: *Winning the $30 trillion decathlon: Going for gold in emerging markets;* McKinsey & Company, August 2012.

109 Angus Maddison: *Contours of the World Economy 1–2030 AD*; Oxford University Press, 2007.

110 *Labour disputes on the rise, authorities call on union to take greater role;* China Labour Bulletin, 7 April 2017.

111 Karl West: *Carmakers' electric dreams depend on supplies of rare minerals*; The Guardian, 29 July 2017.

112 *Catch the wave: The long cycles of industrial innovation are becoming shorter*; The Economist, 18 February 1999.

113 Blog post on *The Motley Fool Investment Analysis Clubs / Foolish Collective* http://boards.fool.com/round-and-round-we-go-22655897.aspx

114 Kamal Ahmed, BBC Business News: *Is 'too big to fail' for banks really coming to an end?* 10 November 2014.

115 Joseph Stiglitz: *How the Democrats can Fix Themselves*; Vanity Fair, 17 November 2016.

116 *The Manufacturer*: *UK Manufacturing Statistics*. http://www.themanufacturer.com/uk-manufacturing-statistics/

117 Katie Benner, Nelson Schwartz: *Apple announces $1 Billion fund to create U.S. job in manufacturing*, The New York Times, 3 May 2017.

118 David J. Lynch: *It's a Man vs Machine Recovery*; Bloomberg Businessweek, 5 January 2012.

119 Philippa Hall: *I've seen farming's future, and there's not a flatcap in sight*; The Telegraph, 17th October 2014.

120 Nicholas K. Geranios: *Farmers are replacing migrant workers with robots*, Associated Press, 30 April 30 2017. http://www.popularmechanics.com/technology/robots/a26318/farmers-workers-robots/

121 BBC News: *Robot used to round up cows is a hit with farmers*; 15 November 2013.

122 *Agricultural Robot Shipments to Reach Nearly 1 Million Units Annually by 2024*, Tractica, 14 July 2015.

123 http://www.handsfreehectare.com/press-releases

124 Roisin Ready: *Pentair and Urban Organics open second indoor aquaponics farm in Minnesota*; Filtration and Separation, 7th June 2017.

125 Bridgette Meinhold: *Pasona HQ is an Urban Farm That Grows Food for Its Employees in Tokyo*; Inhabitat, 20 March 2013.

126 Masa Serdarevic: *Alphaville: What driverless trucks in Oz mean for oil workers in Norway*; Financial Times, 14 September 2012.

127 Thomas Biesheuvel; *How Just 14 People Make 500,000 Tons of Steel a Year in Austria*, Bloomberg Businessweek, 21 June 2017.

128 John Vidal: Health risks of shipping pollution have been 'underestimated', *The Guardian*, 9 April 2009.

129 https://www.bcgperspectives.com/content/articles/lean-manufacturing-innovation-robots-redefine-competitiveness/

130 Travis Hessman: *Cobots Go Heavy-Duty*; New Equipment Digest, 11 December 2017.

131 https://www.tesla.com/blog/master-plan-part-deux

132 Marc Bain: *A new t-shirt sewing robot can make as many shirts per hour as 17 factory workers.* Quartz, 30 August 2017.

133 *Robot density rises globally*; International Federation of Robotics press release, 7 February 2018.

134 Tom Orlik: *China's Lights Out Plan Casts Dark Cloud Over Global Economy*, New Equipment Digest, August 24, 2017.

135 Ben Bland: *China's robot revolution*; *Financial Times*, 06 June 2016.

136 *Executive Summary World Robotics 2017 Industrial Robots*; International Federation of Robots, 2017.

137 June Javelosa and Kristin Houser: *Apple Manufacturer Foxconn to Fully Replace Humans With Robots*, Futurism.com, 3 January 2017.

138 Nick Statt: *Foxconn cuts 60,000 factory jobs and replaces them with robots*, The Verge, 25 May 2016.

139 June Javelosa and Kristin Houser: *Apple Manufacturer Foxconn to Fully Replace Humans With Robots*, Futurism.com, 3 January 2017.

140 Reuters; 3D Printing Titanium Parts Could Save Boeing Millions on Dreamliner Production; Fortune, 11 April, 2017.

141 *Israeli firms team up for high-speed 3D stem cell printing*; Reuters, 25 May 2016.

142 India Block: *Robots complete span of 3D-printed bridge for Amsterdam canal'*; Dezeen, 17 April 2018.

143 Clare Scott: *Saudi Arabian Government Meets With Winsun to Discuss 3D Printing as Part of a Plan to Build 1.5 Million Homes in Five Years*; 3DPrint.com, 3rd August 2016. https://3dprint.com/144727/saudi-arabia-winsun-housing/

144 Tracy You: *Wifi-equipped robots triple work efficiency at the warehouse of the world's largest online retailer*; *Daily Mail*, 2nd August 2017. http://www.dailymail.co.uk/news/article-4754078/China-s-largest-smart-warehouse-manned-60-robots.html

145 Tom Jackson: *The flying drones that can scan packages night and day*; BBC News, 27 October 2017.

146 Angela Greiling Keane: *Driverless Car Future Sends Google, U.S. to Figure Rules*; Bloomberg, 24 October 2012.

147 https://www.intel.co.uk/content/www/uk/en/it-managers/autonomous-cars.html

148 *Morgan Stanley – the Economic Benefits of Driverless Cars*; RobotEnomics, 26 February 2014.

149 Number of Road Traffic Deaths, World Health Organisation Global Health Observatory Data: http://www.who.int/gho/road_safety/mortality/traffic_deaths_number/en/

150 Tom Ward: *Elon Musk: "Almost All Cars Produced Will Be Autonomous in 10 Years"*, Futurism.com, 17 July 2017.

151 Philip Oldfield: *Electric 'robocabs' would reduce US greenhouse emissions by 94% – study*; *The Guardian*, 6 July 2015.

152 Casey Newton: *Uber will eventually replace all its drivers with self-driving cars*, The Verge, 28 May 2014.

153 Tasha Keeney: *Shared Autonomous Vehicles Will Make Ride Services 30 Times More Attractive*, Ark Invest, 15 September 2016.

154 Trevor Mogg: *Driverless cars: Waymo eyes Europe for launch of robot taxi services*; Digital Trends, 07 June 2018.

155 Leo Kelion: *Uber and Volvo strike deal for 24,000 self-drive cars*; BBC News, 20 November 2017.

156 Alex Davies, *Uber's self-driving truck makes its first delivery: 50,000 beers*, Wired, 25 October 2016.

157 Alex Davies: *Self-driving trucks are now delivering refrigerators*; *Wired*, 13 November 2017.

158 *Autonomous Cars - Self-Driving the New Auto Industry Paradigm*, Morgan Stanley Research, 06 November 2013.

159 https://ifr.org/downloads/press/02_2016/Presentation_12_Oct_2016__WR_Service_Robots.pdf

160 James Vincent: *Mercedes-Benz has made a 'mothership' van for six-wheeled delivery robots*, The Verge, 7 September 2016.

161 Daimler press release: *Vans & Drones in Zurich: Mercedes-Benz Vans, Matternet and siroop start pilot project for on-demand delivery of e-commerce goods*; 28 September 2017.

162 Vanessa Bates Ramirez: *New Burger Robot Will Take Command of the Grill in 50 Fast Food Restaurants*, Singularity.com, 8 March, 2017.

163 Vanessa Bates Ramirez: These Pizza Robots Assemble Perfect Pies in Minutes, Singularity.com, 27 July 2017.

164 Kyodo: *Hitachi starts trials of EMIEW3 humanoid robot at Haneda airport*; The Japan Times, 2 September 2016.

165 Jon Fingas: *Walmart tests shelf-scanning robots in 50-plus stores*; Engadget, 26 October 2017.

166 George Packer: *Cheap Words*, The New Yorker, 17 February 2014.

167 Leena Rao: *Two Years After Launching, Amazon Dash Shows Promise*, Fortune, 25 April 2017.

168 https://www.amazon.com/oc/dash-replenishment-service

169 Steven Pinker: *The Language Instinct*, Harper Perennial Modern Classics, 1994.

170 Frank Levy and Richard J. Murnane; *The New Division of Labor: How Computers are Creating the Next Job Market*; Princeton University Press, 2004.

171 Ibid.

172 George Johnson: To *Test a Powerful Computer, Play an Ancient Game*, The New York Times, 29 July 1997.

173 Lauren F. Friedman: *The CEO of IBM just made a bold prediction about the future of artificial intelligence*; Business Insider, 14 May 2015.

174 Stacy Libratore: *Your AI lawyer will see you now: IBM's ROSS becomes world's first artificially intelligent attorney*, Daily Mail, 16 May 2016.

175 Amazon press release: *Alexa meet Cortana, Cortana meet Alexa*; 30 August 2017.

176 *New York Times*: *'Cortana, Open Alexa,' Amazon Says. And Microsoft Agrees*; 30 August 2017.

177 *AI creates new levels for Doom and Super Mario games*; BBC News, 8 May 2018.

178 Dainius: *New Neural Algorithm Can 'Paint' Photos In Style Of Any Artist From Van Gogh To Picasso*; BoredPanda, 2016.

179 Mary-Ann Russon: *Google DeepDream robot: 10 weirdest images produced by AI 'inceptionism' and users online*; International Business Times, 6 July 2015.

180 *Netflix thinking of using Artificial Intelligence to craft personalized movie trailers for viewers*; House of Bots, 24 January 2018.

181 Gideon Lewis-Kraus: *The Great AI Awakening*, The New York Times Magazine, 14 December 2016.

182 Karen Gilchrist: *Chatbots expected to cut business costs by $8 billion by 2022*; CNBC, 09 May 2017.

183 Marc Andreesen: *Why Bitcoin Matters*; DealBook/NY Times, 21 January 2014.

184 Chris Pauka: *Blockchain to save shippers millions*; Transport and Logistic News, 20 March 2018.

185 Nick Squires: *Italian olive oil scandal: seven top brands 'sold fake extra-virgin*; The Telegraph, 11 November 2015.

186 BBC News: *Horsemeat scandal: Dutch uncover large-scale meat fraud*; 10 April 2013.

187 https://www.provenance.org/case-studies/martine-jarlgaard

188 Ryan Browne: *IBM partners with Nestle, Unilever and other food giants to trace food contamination with blockchain*, CNBC.com, 22 August 2017.

189 Bridget van Kralingen: *Blockchain's Role in Improving Global Food Safety*, IBM Think Blog, 19 October 2016.

190 Bil Ruh: *Waking Up as a Software and Analytics Company*, GE.com

191 Dan Weller: Digital Trends That Will Shape Your Future, Digitalist Magazine, 1 March 2016.

192 http://www.datacenterknowledge.com/archives/2016/11/11/2020-92-percent-data-center-traffic-will-cloud/

193 George Packer: *Cheap Words*, The New Yorker, 17 February 2014.

194 https://www.scrapehero.com/how-many-products-are-sold-on-amazon-com-january-2018

195 Lee Bell: *Machine learning versus AI: what's the difference?* Wired.com, 1 December 2016.

196 Alex Krizhevsky, Ilya Sutskever and Geoffrey E. Hinton: *ImageNet Classification with Deep Convolutional Neural Networks* PDF); NIPS 2012, Neural Information Processing Systems.

197 Matt Oliver: *Glaxo hails robot breakthrough*; Daily Mail, 14 October 2017.

198 Will Knight: *The Dark Secret at the Heart of AI*; MIT Technology Review, 11 April 2017.

199 Zayan Guedim: *AI can now Snuff Out Alzheimer's a Decade Before Symptoms Appear*, Edgy Labs, 25 September 2017.

200 Siddhartha Mukherjee: *This Cat Sensed Death. What If Computers Could, Too?*; New York Times, 3 January 2017.

201 Stephen Shankland CNET staff; *'Get ready for 'unlimited data' of 5G networks in 2019'* CNET, 16 October 2017.

202 Jack Nicas: *How Google's Quantum Computer Could Change the World* (*The ultra-powerful machine has the potential to disrupt everything from science and medicine to national security—assuming it works*); Wall Street Journal, 16 October 2017.

203 Klint Finley: *Quantum computing is real and D-WAVE just open-sourced it*, Wired, 1 November 2017.

204 Emily Conover: *Google moves toward quantum supremacy with 72-qubit computer*; Science News, 05 March 2018.

205 Arjun Kharpal: *IBM teams up with Samsung, JPMorgan to develop quantum computing*; CNBC, 14 December 2017.

206 *2018 CES: Intel Advances Quantum and Neuromorphic Computing Research*; Intel News Byte, 8 January 2018.

207 https://www.scientificamerican.com/article/a-robot-in-every-home-2008-02/

208 Jay Kothari: *A new chapter for Glass*, Medium, 18 July 2017.

209 Jon Gertner: *Behind GE's Vision For The Industrial Internet Of Things*; Fast Company, 18 June 2014.

210 Sara Zaske: Germany's vision for Industrie 4.0: The revolution will be digitised, ZDNet, 23 February 2015.

211 Joe McCarthy: *Adidas Shoes Made From Ocean Plastic Are Finally Here*; Global Citizen, 8 November 2016.

212 Deborah Sherry: *Learn How Europe's Industrial Leaders are Going Digital, and You Can, Too!* GE.com, 2017.

213 https://www.link-labs.com/blog/iot-vs-industry-4.0

214 https://ifr.org/ifr-press-releases/news/world-robotics-report-2016

215 https://www.facebook.com/zuck/videos/vb.4/10103841456831511/?type=2&theater

216 Klaus Schwab: The Fourth Industrial Revolution: what it means, how to respond, World Economic Forum, 14 January 2016.

217 Robert Solow: *We'd Better Watch Out*; Manufacturing Matters, 12 July 1987.

218 Tom Goodwin: *The Battle Is For The Customer Interface*, TechCrunch, 4 March 2015.

219 Sarah Perez: *App economy to grow to $6.3 trillion in 2021, user base to nearly double to 6.3 billion*; TechCrunch, 27th June 2017.

220 https://uberestimator.com/cities; 26 February 2018.

221 Thomas Koulopoulos: *According to Peter Diamandis and Ray Kurzweil, These Are the Most Dangerous and Disruptive Ideas*; Inc., 19 January 2018.

222 Kenneth Rapoza: *China's Aging Population Becoming More Of A Problem*; Forbes, 21 February 2017.

223 James Cook: *Jack Ma: Here's How Alibaba Will Become Bigger Than Walmart*; Business Insider, 23 January 2015.

224 Innosight executive briefing, winter 2012: *Creative Destruction Whips through Corporate America.*

225 Harry Wallop: *The many ways Cadbury is losing its magic*; The Telegraph, 21 March 2016.

226 Matt Oliver: *Cadbury pays zero corporation tax for the SIXTH year in a row despite it making £100 million profits*; Daily Mail, 11th November 2017.

227 Jenny Andersen: *Wall Street Winners Get Billion-Dollar Paydays*; *New York Times*, 16 April 2008.

228 Alistair Barr: *Top managers' pay dropped 48% last year*; MarketWatch, 25 March 2009.

229 Lucinda Shen: *Here's How Much the Top Hedge-Fund Manager Made Last Year*, Fortune magazine, 16 May 2017.

230 Upton Sinclair: *I, Candidate for Governor: And How I Got Licked* (new edition); University of California Press, 1995.

231 Roger L. Martin: *The Rise and (Likely) Fall of the Talent Economy*; *Harvard Business Review*, October 2014.

232 Roger L. Martin: *Fixing the Game: Bubbles, Crashes, and What Capitalism Can Learn from the NFL*; *Harvard Business Review Press*, 2011.

233 William Lazonick: Corporate Executive Pay (2006–2012), *Stock buybacks and Executive Pay Research Update #1*; The Academic-Industry Research Network, August 2014.

234 Julie Goran et al: *Culture for a digital age,* McKinsey Quarterly, July 2017.

235 Chartered Management Institute: *Quality of Working Life* report, 2007.

236 Gary Hamel and Bill Breen: *The Future of Management*; Harvard Business Press, 2007.

237 Gary Hamel, Michele Zanini: *What We Learned About Bureaucracy from 7,000 HBR Readers*, Harvard Business Review, 10 August 2017.

238 Barry Jaruzelski, John Loehr and Richard Holman: *Why Culture is Key*; the 2011 Global Innovation 1000, 2011.

239 Dieter Zetsche: *Going viral with Cultural Change*, LinkedIn, 30 May 2017.

240 *Chief Says Kodak Is Pointed in the Right Direction*; *New York Times*, 25 December 1999.

241 Harold Meyerson: *In corporations, it's owner-take-all*; *Washington Post*, 26 August 2014.

242 William Lazonick: *Profits Without Prosperity*; *Harvard Business Review*, September 2014.

243 John Asker, et al: *Corporate Investment and Stock Market Listing*: A Puzzle? Review of Financial Studies 28, no. 2, February 2015.

244 Henry R. Nothhaft and David Kline: *Great Again: Revitalizing America's Entrepreneurial Leadership*; Harvard Business Review Press, 2011.

245 Drucker Institute: *We're in it for the long term*, Druckerinstitute.com, 2 October 2013.

246 *Financial Times*: *Welch condemns share price focus*; 12th March 2009.

247 Paul Polman: *The Remedies for Capitalism*; McKinsey & Company article.

248 Jo Confino: *Paul Polman: 'The power is in the hands of the consumers'*; *The Guardian*, 21 November 2011.

249 Jo Confino: *Rio+20: Unilever CEO on the need to battle on to save the world; The Guardian*; 21 June 2012.

250 Andy Boynton: *Unilever's Paul Polman: CEOs Can't Be 'Slaves' To Shareholders*; Forbes, 20 July 2015.

251 Andy Boynton: *Unilever's Paul Polman: CEOs Can't Be 'Slaves' To Shareholders*; Forbes, 20 July 2015.

252 Paul Polman: *Business, society, and the future of capitalism*; McKinsey & Company.

253 Steve Denning interview with Roger Martin: *Is Everyone Nuts? P&G Now A Dog? And Unilever A Star?*; *Forbes*, 11 January 2013.

254 Ana Nance: *How Google Fuels Its Idea Factory*, Bloomberg Businessweek, 29 April 2008.

255 Rani Molla: *Amazon spent nearly $23 billion on R&D last year – more than any other U.S. company*; Recode, 9 April 2018.

256 One Click Retail: *Amazon Outpaces Total Market Growth in U.S. Sales of Household Items*, PRNewswire.com, 6 April 2017.

257 Tae Kim: *Social's Palihapitiya sees Amazon worth $3 trillion*, CNBC, 4 May 2016.

258 ARC Advisory Group: *Process Automation and the IoT: Yokogawa's VigilantPlant Approach to the Connected Industrial Enterprise,* yokogawa.com, 2015

259 Michael Arrington: *It's easier to invent the future than to predict it*, TechCrunch, 30 April 2008.

260 Accenture: *The best CEOs will help humans help machines help humans*; Quartz. 22 January 2018.

261 Tonya Garcia: Every time this happens, Amazon crushes another legacy retailer, MarketWatch, 17 May 2017.

262 *44 Corporations Working On Autonomous Vehicles*; CB Insights, 18th May 2017.

263 Marisa Kendall: *Uber's 'flying cars' set to land in Dallas by 2020*; *The Mercury News*, 25th April 2017.

264 Archibald Church, Ten Minute Rule Bill, *House of Commons Debates 21 July 1931*, Volume 255, cc1249–57; Hansard 1803–2005.

265 Harry Bruinius: *Better for All the World: The Secret History of Forced Sterilization and America's Quest for Racial Purity*; A. A. Knopf, 2006.

266 J. H. Kempton: *Sterilization for Ten Million Americans*; *The Journal of Heredity*, American Genetic Association, October 1934, p416.

267 Gilbert Keith Chesterton: *Eugenics and Other Evils*; Cassell & Co., 1922.

268 Mike McCrae: *Microsoft Plans on Storing Its Data on DNA in The Next 3 Years*, ScienceAlert, 27 May 2017.

269 https://www.reuters.com/video/2017/10/16/mice-with-green-feet-demonstrate-crispr?videoId=372748335

270 Emily Mullin: *2017 Was the Year of Gene-Therapy Breakthroughs*; *MIT Technology Review*, 3rd January 2018.

271 Broad Institute press release: *Broad Institute to release Genome Analysis Toolkit 4 (GATK4) as open source resource to accelerate research*; 24th May 2017

272 Michael Le Page: *We've evolved an even more powerful form of CRISPR gene editing*; New Scientist, 25th October 2017.

273 Kirsten Brown: *China Has Already Gene-Edited 86 People With CRISPR*; Gizmodo, 22nd January 2018.

274 University of Illinois at Urbana-Champaign: *Earth BioGenome Project aims to sequence genomes of 1.5 million species, ScienceDaily*, April 23 2018.

275 Sarah Knapton: *Woolly mammoth will be back from extinction within two years, say Harvard scientists*; *The Telegraph*, 17th February 2017.

276 Chelsea Gohd: *DNA of Man Who Died in 1827 Recreated Without His Remains*; Futurism. com, 18th January 2018.

277 Ben Popper: *Google's project to 'cure death,' Calico, announces $1.5 billion research center*; The Verge, 3rd September 2014.

278 Jessica Hamzelou: *Blood from human teens rejuvenates body and brains of old mice*; New Scientist, 15th November 2016.

279 Karla Lant: *We may have found a pathway that controls aging*, Futurism.com, 17 October 2017.

280 Joao Medeiros: *Ageing is a disease. Gene therapy could be the 'cure'*; Wired UK, 23rd March 2017.

281 Kate Hughes: *UK's pension funding liabilities rose to £7.6 trillion*; The Independent, 8th March 2017.

282 https://en.wikipedia.org/wiki/Strategies_for_Engineered_Negligible_Senescence

283 Sir Francis Bacon: *Novum Organum Scientiarum*; Aphorism 92.

284 YouTube video: *Ben Goertzel – Google vs Death – Google's and others Anti Aging Initiatives*, Science, Technology & the Future, 26 September 2013.

285 Tara Loader Wilkinson: *Could Human Beings Live For 1,000 Years?* Billionaire.com, 12 July 2017.

286 Ray Kurzweil: *Fantastic Voyage: Live Long Enough to Live Forever*; Plume Publishers, 2005.

287 Judith Duportail: *I asked Tinder for my data. It sent me 800 pages of my deepest, darkest secrets*; The Guardian, 26 September 2017.

288 Kashmir Hill: *How Facebook Figures Out Everyone You've Ever Met*; Gizmodo, 7 November 2017.

289 Michael Balsamo and Jonathan Cooper: *DNA from ancestry website used to nab Golden Gate killer*; The Morning Call, 27 April 2018.

290 Vindu Goel: *Facebook Tinkers With Users' Emotions in News Feed Experiment, Stirring Outcry*; New York Times, 29 June 2014.

291 *Stifling Dissent: The Criminalization of Peaceful Expression in India*; Human Rights Watch, 24 May 2016.

292 Alex Christoforou: *Twitter hate speech police ready to punish users for sites they visit on the web*; 22 November 2017.

293 Zack Whittaker: *Amazon won't say if it hands your Echo data to the government*; ZDNet. com, 16 January 2018.

294 Adam Boult: *Put tape over your webcam, FBI director warns*; The Telegraph, 15 September 2016.

295 Checkpoint Research: *A New IoT Botnet Storm is Coming*; 19 October 2017.

296 https://www.theguardian.com/technology/2017/mar/07/cia-targeting-devices-smartphones-pc-tv-wikileaks

297 Andrew Griffin: *Saudi Arabia grants citizenship to a robot for the first time ever*; The Independent, 27 October 2017.

298 Blair Hanley Frank: *LinkedIn plans to teach all its engineers the basics of using AI*; VentureBeat, 24 October 2017.

299 Peter Rejcek: *Japan's SoftBank Is Investing Billions in the Technological Future*; Singularity Hub, 29 August 2017.

300 Arjun Kharpal: *China wants to be a $150 billion world leader in AI in less than 15 years*; CNBC, 21 July 2017.

301 *Beijing plans to invest $2 billion to build national level Artificial Intelligence Lab*; House of Bots, 3 January 2018.

302 Vernor Vinge: *The Coming Technological Singularity: How to Survive in the Post-Human Era*; Department of Mathematical Sciences, San Diego State University, 1993.

303 Pete Pachal: *Google Photos identified two black people as 'gorillas'*; Mashable, 1 July 2015.

304 Sam Levin: *A beauty contest was judged by AI and the robots didn't like dark skin*; The Guardian, 8 September 2016.

305 Hope Reese: *Why Microsoft's 'Tay' AI bot went wrong*; TechRepublic, 24 March 2016.

306 Kerry Allen: *Chinese chatbots shut down after anti-government posts*; BBC News, 3 August 2017.

307 Will Knight: *Ambient AI Is About to Devour the Software Industry*; MIT Technology Review, 1 December 2017.

308 Will Knight: *The Dark Secret at the Heart of AI*; MIT Technology Review, 11 April 2017.

309 https://www.sciencealert.com/ai-just-defeated-expert-human-fighter-pilots-in-an-air-combat-simulator

310 *Joint Concept Note 1/18 Human-Machine Teaming*; Ministry of Defence, May 2018.

311 David Silver et al.: *Mastering the game of Go without human knowledge*; Nature: The International Weekly Journal of Science, 19 October 2017.

312 Mariëtte Le Roux, *Self-taught, 'superhuman' AI now even smarter: makers*; phys.org, 18 October 2017.

313 *AlphaZero's 'alien' superhuman-level program masters chess in 24 hours with no domain knowledge*; Kurzweil.net, 11 December 2017.

314 Matthew Humphries: *Google's Alice AI Is Sending Secret Messages To Another AI*; Geek.com, 28 October 2016.

315 Karla Lant: *A Facebook AI Unexpectedly Created Its Own Unique Language*; Futurism.com, 16 June 2017.

316 Nick Bostrom: *Ethical Issues in Advanced Artificial Intelligence*; 2003. https://nickbostrom.com/ethics/ai.html

317 Sean Captain: *The AI Guru Behind Amazon, Uber, and Unity Explains What AI Really Is*; Fast Company, 29 November 2017.

318 Olivia Goldhill: *Google's AI got "highly aggressive" when competition got stressful in a fruit-picking game*; Quartz, 17 February 2017.

319 Tom Ward and Kristen Houser: *Google's New AI Is Better at Creating AI Than the Company's Engineers*, Futurism.com, 19 May 2017.

320 Mark Walport: *Rise of the machines: are algorithms sprawling out of our control?* Wired, 1 April 2017.

321 Tom Simonite: *Why Google's CEO Is Excited About Automating Artificial Intelligence*; MIT Technology Review, 17 May 2017.

322 Dom Galeon: *Intel is Releasing a Processor That's Built for Neural Networks*; Futurism. com, 19 October 2017.

323 http://mindstalk.net/vinge/vinge-sing.html

324 I. J. Good: *Speculations Concerning the First Ultraintelligent Machine* HTML); *Advances in Computers*, Volume 6, 1965.

325 Vernor Vinge: *The Coming Technological Singularity: How to Survive in the Post-Human Era*; Department of Mathematical Sciences, San Diego State University, 1993.

326 Isaac Asimov: *Runaround* (in *I, Robot: The Isaac Asimov Collection*); Doubleday, 1950, p40.

327 Patrick Tucker: *Russia Says It Will Field a Robot Tank that Outperforms Humans*; Defense One, 8 November 2017.

328 Benjamin Haas: *'Killer robots': AI experts call for boycott over lab at South Korea university*; *The Guardian*, 5 April 2018.

329 *'Whoever leads in AI will rule the world': Putin to Russian children on Knowledge Day*; RT, 1 September 2017.

330 *Symantec Internet threat report 2017*. https://www.symantec.com/security-center/ threat-report

331 David Sanger: *Obama Order Sped Up Wave of Cyberattacks Against Iran*; New York Times, 1 June 2012.

332 Yossi Melman: *Computer Virus in Iran Actually Targeted Larger Nuclear Facility*; *Haaretz*, 28 September 2010.

333 Sebastian Farquhar: *Changes in funding in the AI safety field*; Effective Altruism Forum, 3 February 2017.

334 Future of Life Institute: *An Open Letter: Research Priorities for Robust and Beneficial Artificial Intelligence*. https://futureoflife.org/ai-open-letter/

335 Camila Domonoske: *Elon Musk Warns Governors: Artificial Intelligence Poses 'Existential Risk'*; The Two-Way, 17 July 2017.

336 Sean Burch: *Elon Musk and Mark Zuckerberg's Artificial Intelligence Divide: Experts Weigh In*; The Wrap, 25 July 2017.

337 *AI in the UK: ready, willing and able?* Chapter 9: *Shaping artificial intelligence*; UK Parliament, 19 April 2017.

338 Michael Casey: *Interview with Gray Scott: Maybe artificial intelligence won't destroy us after all*; CBS News.com, 14 May 2015.

339 Stacy Liberatore: *Researchers reveal addicts touch their handset over 5,400 times a day*; *Daily Mail*, 27 June 2016.

340 Olivia Solon: *Facebook has 60 people working on how to read your mind*; The Guardian, 19 April 2017.

341 *Facebook is working on Silent Voice First Systems*; Multiplex, 19 April 2017.

342 Sara Reardon: *AI-controlled brain implants for mood disorders tested in people*; Nature: The International Weekly Journal of Science, 22 November 2017.

343 Rafael Yuste et al.: *Four ethical priorities for neurotechnologies and AI*; Nature: The International Weekly Journal of Science, 8 November 2017.

344 Larry Hardesty: *Computer system transcribes words users "speak silently"*; MIT News, 4 April 2018.

345 https://www.mindmaze.com/leonardo-dicaprio-adds-virtual-reality-startup-list-investments/

346 Rafael Yuste et al.: *Four ethical priorities for neurotechnologies and AI*; Nature: The International Weekly Journal of Science, 8 November 2017.

347 Defense Advanced Research Projects Agency: *DARPA Helps Paralyzed Man Feel Again Using a Brain-Controlled Robotic Arm*; 13 November 2016.

348 Rajesh P. N. Rao, Andrea Stocco et al.: *A Direct Brain-to-Brain Interface in Humans*; Public Library of Science, 5 November 2014.

349 Dom Galeon: *Experts: Artificial Intelligence Could Hijack Brain-Computer Interfaces*; Futurism.com, 20 November 2017.

350 Daron Acemoglu, James Robinson: *Why Nations Fail: The Origins of Power, Prosperity and Poverty*; Random House Digital, 2012, p182.

351 Graeme Paton: *Poor white pupils put off school by multicultural timetable*; The Telegraph, 27 June 2014.

352 R. J. Reinhart: *AI Seen as Greater Job Threat Than Immigration, Offshoring*; Gallup, 9 March 2018.

353 Olivia Krauth: *Walmart testing fully-automated store with no cashiers or checkouts*; TechRepublic, 20 December 2017.

354 Stephen Hawking: *A Brief History of Time: From Big Bang to Black Holes*, Chapter 11; Bantam Dell Publishing Group, 1988, p91.

355 Lucia Moses: *The Washington Post's robot reporter has published 850 articles in the past year*; Digiday UK, 14 September 2017.

356 James Manyika, Susan Lund et al.: *What the future of work will mean for jobs, skills, and wages*; McKinsey Global Institute, November 2017.

357 Carl Benedikt Frey and Michael A. Osbourne: *The Future of Employment: How Susceptible are Jobs to Computerisation?* Oxford Martin School, University of Oxford, 17 September 2013.

358 http://kff.org/other/poll-finding/kaiser-family-foundationnew-york-timescbs-news-non-employed-poll/

359 Lisa Harrington: *The Supply Chain Talent Shortage: From Gap to Crisis*, SupplyChain 247, 26 July 2016.

360 Wolfgang Dauth et al: *DP12306 German Robots – The Impact of Industrial Robots on Workers*; Centre for Economic Policy Research, September 2017.

361 Wolfgang Dauth et al: *The Rise of Robots in the German Labour Market*; VoxEU.org, 19 September 2017.

362 A. T. Kearney: *A.T. Kearney 2017 Global Services Location Index Spotlights Automation as Massive Job Displacer*; September 2017. https://www.multivu.com/players/English/8179851-at-kearney-2017-global-services-location-index/

363 Wan He, Daniel Goodkind, and Paul Kowal, *An Aging World: 2015*, U.S. Census Bureau, March 2016.

364 John Hitch: *Robots Invade the Rust Belt!*; New Equipment Digest, 15 August 2017.

365 Mamta Badkar: *There's A Huge Shortage Of Truck Drivers In America – Here's Why The Problem Is Only Getting Worse*; Business Insider, 4 August 2014.

366 Dr Andrew Chamberlain: *Local Pay Reports: Wage Growth Ticks Up Slightly in August*; Glassdoor, 29 August 2017.

367 http://www.alltrucking.com/faq/truck-drivers-in-the-usa/

368 Transport Topics: *iTECH: Trucking May Save $168 Billion Annually With Driverless Vehicles, Report Concludes*; 13 January 2014.

369 Nick Hanauer: *Raise Taxes on Rich to Reward True Job Creators*; Bloomberg Businessweek, 7 December 2011.

370 Lawrence F. Katz and Alan B. Krueger: *The Rise and Nature of Alternative Work Arrangements in the United States, 1995–2015*; National Bureau of Economic Research (NBER) working paper no. 22667, September 2016.

371 *Labour in Canada: Key results from the 2016 Census*, Statistics Canada, 29 November 2011.

372 Rani Molla: *The gig economy workforce will double in four years*; Recode, 25th May 2017.

373 Paul Oyer: *The Independent Workforce in America: The Economics of an Increasingly Flexible Labor Market*; Stanford University Graduate School of Business. 30th November 2016.

374 Neil Irwin: *Why Ben Bernanke Can't Refinance His Mortgage*; New York Times, 2nd October 2014.

375 Chris Middleton: *AI Uber Alles?* Diginomica, 8th September 2017.

376 David Reid: *Mnuchin on robots taking US jobs: 'It's not even on our radar screen... 50–100 more years away'*; CNBC News, 24 March 2017.

377 Daniel Ren: *2.3 million – the number of jobs that could be lost to artificial intelligence in China's financial sectors by 2027*; South China Morning Post, 30 March 2018.

378 Mei Fong: *Sex Dolls Are Replacing China's Missing Women*; Foreign Policy, 28 September 2017.

379 Kim Xu: *Bare branches: China's surplus men*; APPS Policy Forum, 22 April 2016.

380 Rob Brooks: *China's biggest problem? Too many men*; CNN, 4 March 2013.

381 Chris Middleton: *Oracle: Autonomy now, AI with everything by 2020*; Internet of Business, 13 February 2018.

382 Varun Sood: *Top 7 IT firms including Infosys, Wipro to lay off at least 56,000 employees this year*; LiveMint, 12 May 2017.

383 *Automation will make 20 crore young Indians jobless in next 9 years, warns Mohandas Pai*; The Economic Times (India), 2 December 2016.

384 Oliver Griffin: *Machines Could Make More Workers Migrate*; Raconteur.net, 11 October 2017.

385 Jennifer Ryan: *Robots Can't Replace IT Workers, Doctors, Dentists, Haldane Says*, Bloomberg, 15 December 2015.

386 James Manyika et al.: *What the future of work will mean for jobs, skills, and wages*; McKinsey Global Institute, November 2017.

387 *The Future of Jobs: Employment, Skills and Workforce Strategy for the Fourth Industrial Revolution*; World Economic Forum, January 2016. http://www3.weforum.org/docs/ WEF_FOJ_Executive_Summary_Jobs.pdf

388 Thomas H. Davenport and Julia Kirby: *Beyond Automation*; *Harvard Business Review*, June 2015.

389 Sam Shead, *Silicon Valley Firms Make It Nearly 'Impossible' For Cambridge To Hire AI Staff*, Forbes, 6 July 2018.

390 Max de Haldevang: *Tax loopholes allow Apple, Nike, and others to avoid US taxes that could pay for Obamacare six times over*; *Quartz*, 5 October 2016.

391 Michael J. Bologna: *Amazon Close to Breaking Wal-Mart Record for Subsidies*; Bloomberg News, 20 March 2017.

392 Bruce F. Freed and Marian Currinder: *Do Political Business in the Daylight*; *US News*, 6 April 2016.

393 Holman W. Jenkins: *Of Furries and Fascism at Google*; Wall Street Journal, 16 January 2018.

394 Warren Buffet: *Stop Coddling the Super-Rich*; *New York Times* opinion pages, 14 August 2011.

395 Nick Hanauer: *The Pitchforks Are Coming… For Us Plutocrats*; *Politico* magazine, July/ August 2014.

396 Evan Osnos: *Doomsday Prep for the Super-Rich*; *The New Yorker*, 30 January 2017.

397 http://www.terravivos.com/secure/vivosxpoint.htm

398 Accenture bulletin: *The best CEOs will help humans help machines help humans*, Quartz, 22 January 2018.

399 *The Super-Rich's offshore tax avoidance strategies*; *Bloomberg Businessweek*, 2 May 2013.

400 *Super rich hold $32 trillion in offshore havens*; Reuters, 22 July 2012.

401 James S. Henry: *The Price of Offshore Revisited*; Tax Justice Network, 19 July 2012.

402 Jonathan Webb: *Apple Argues Paying More Than A 0.005% Tax Rate Is 'Unfair'*; Forbes, 31 August 2016.

403 *Apple's cash pile is as big as the GDP of Finland and Jamaica, combined*; The Washington Post, 5 May 2017.

404 *Danielle Brennan: Challenging Unilever on the use of tax havens*. ShareAction, 29 May 2014.

405 *PwC promoted tax avoidance 'on industrial scale', say MPs*; BBC Business News, 6 February 2015.

406 Foo Yun Chee: *Luxembourg challenges EU order to recover tax from Amazon*; Reuters, 15 December 2017.

407 Tae Kim: *Apple, tech companies to bring back $400 billion in overseas cash to the US: Estimate*; CNBC News, 5 January 2018.

408 Tripp Mickle: *Apple Plans to Pay $38 Billion in Repatriation Taxes*; Wall Street Journal, 17 January 2018.

409 Craig Bannister: *List: Companies Giving Bonuses, Wage Hikes Due to Trump Tax Cuts*; CNS News, 4 January 2018.

410 Mitchell Dean: *The Constitution of Poverty: Towards a Genealogy of Liberal Governance*; Routledge, 1991, pp119–20.

411 J. E. King and John Marangos: *Two arguments for Basic Income: Thomas Paine (1737–1809) and Thomas Spence (1750–1814)* (first edition); History of Economic Ideas, 2006, p57.

412 Ibid., p62.

413 Dr. John Marangos: *Thomas Paine & Thomas Spence On Basic Income Guarantee*; 1 January 2014.

414 Tae Kim, *Universal basic income would cost the US up to $3.8 trillion per year — Bridgewater estimate,* CNBC News, 12 July 2018.

415 Laurence Peter: *Finland's basic income trial falls flat*; BBC News, 23 April 2018.

416 Kevin Kelly: *1000 True Fans*; The Technium. 4 March, 2008.

417 SC Digest Staff: *Supply Chain News: Key to Germany's Continued Manufacturing Success is Low Profile, Mid-Sized Hidden Champions*, SC Digest, 6 May 2017.

418 M. P. Charlesworth: *Freedom of Speech in Republican Rome*; *The Classical Review*, the Classical Association. p57, March 1943.

419 Gilbert K. Chesterton: *The Essential Gilbert K. Chesterton*; Simon & Schuster, 2013, p49.

420 Plutarch: *The Parallel Lives Volume X: Tiberius Gracchus.* Translated by Bernadotte Perrin, Loeb Classical Library, 1921.

421 Hugues Sampasa-Kanyinga et al.: *Use of social media is associated with short sleep duration in a dose-response manner in students aged 11 to 20 years*; Acta Paediatrica, 24 January 2018.

422 Kate Pickles; *'Is social media behind a surge in self harm? Young women showing signs of depression rises by HALF in 20 years'.* Daily Mail. 29 September 2016.

423 Sherry Turkle: *Are We Plugged-In, Connected, But Alone?* TED Radio Hour, 26 February 2013.

424 Brian Primack: *Social Media and Depression*; University of Pittsburgh, 18 May 2016.

425 Susanna Schrobsdorff: *There's a Startling Increase in Major Depression Among Teens in the U.S.*; *Time magazine,* 16 November 2016.

426 Rae Ellen Bichell: *Suicide Rates Climb In U.S., Especially Among Adolescent Girls*; Health Shots, National Public Radio, 22 April 2016.

427 Paige Cornwell: *Suicide rate in teen girls reaches 40-year high*; *Chicago Tribune*, 23rd August 2017.

428 Alan Mozes: *Smartphones could be increasing depression, suicide among teen girls*; *Chicago Tribune*, 21 November 2017.

429 Bernt Bratsberg and Ole Rogeberg: *Flynn effect and its reversal are both environmentally caused*; PNAS, 11 June 2018.

430 Mike Conn: *Former Facebook Executive Says Social Media Is So Terrible That His Kids "Aren't Allowed To Use That Shit"*; NewsCult, 11 December 2017.

431 Teri Webster: *New Facebook Messenger app targets 6- to 12-year-olds*; TheBlaze, 04 December 2017.

432 Olivia Solon: *Ex-Facebook president Sean Parker: site made to exploit human 'vulnerability*; *The Guardian*, 9 November 2017.

433 Anil Dawar: *Women 'spend more time checking their PHONE than they do with their partner'*; *Daily Express*, 12 October 2016.

434 Adrian F. Ward et al.: *Brain Drain: The Mere Presence of One's Own Smartphone Reduces Available Cognitive Capacity*; *University of Chicago Press Journal*, 3 April 2017.

435 Adam Jezard; *'Depression is the no. 1 cause of ill health and disability'*; World Economic Forum, 18 May 2018.

436 *Rickets soar as children stay indoors: Number diagnosed with disease quadruples in last ten years*; *Daily Mail*, 22 January 2014.

437 *Diabetes explosion – figures expected to soar*; Diabetes UK, 9 June 2008.

438 Associated Press: *Diabetes cases soar fourfold in a generation, to 422 million worldwide*; *South China Morning Post*, 7 April 2016.

439 G. Kaati, L. O. Bygren and S. Edvinsson: *Cardiovascular and diabetes mortality determined by nutrition during parents' and grandparents' slow growth period*, *European Journal of Human Genetics*, 10 November 2002.

440 L. O. Bygren, P. Tinghög, J. Carstensen, S. Edvinsson, G. Kaati, M. E. Pembrey and M. Sjöström: *Change in paternal grandmothers' early food supply influenced cardiovascular mortality of the female grandchildren*; BMC Genetics, 15 February 2014.

441 Signe Dean: *Scientists Have Observed Epigenetic Memories Being Passed Down For 14 Generations*; Science Alert, 21 April 2017.

442 Ida Donkin, Soetkin Versteyhe et al.: *Obesity and Bariatric Surgery Drive Epigenetic Variation of Spermatozoa in Humans*; *Cell Metabolism*, 9 February 2016.

443 *Low testosterone in men over 40 linked to early death*; News Medical Life Science, 15 August 2006.

444 Roger Highfield: *Lower testosterone in men can lead to earlier death*, The Telegraph, 17 June 2008.

445 J. E. Chavarro et al.: *Soy food and isoflavone intake in relation to semen quality parameters among men from an infertility clinic*; Oxford Academic, *Human Reproduction*, Volume 23, Issue 11, 01 November 2008, p2,584–2,590.

446 Nicola Davis: *Sperm counts among western men have halved in last 40 years – study*; *The Guardian*, 25 July 2017.

447 *Swedish Students Forced to Write Essays on 'White Male Privilege'*; Sputnik News, 6 February 2018.

448 Tristin Hopper: *Canadian schools facing blowback for 'white privilege' awareness campaigns*; *Edmonton Journal*, 8 March 2018.

449 Aftab Ali: *Student gender gap in UK universities growing at an inexorable rate*; The Independent, 30 July 2015.

450 Larissa Faw: *Why Are So Many Professional Millennial Women Unable to Find Dateable Men?*; *Forbes*, 5 December 2012.

451 Wendy Wang and Kim Parker: *Record Share of Americans Have Never Married*; Pew Research Center, 24 September 2014.

452 Kim Parker and Renee Stepler: *As U.S. marriage rate hovers at 50%, education gap in marital status widens*; Pew Research Center, 14 September 2017.

453 Antonio Antenucci: *More young women choosing dogs over motherhood*; *New York Post*, 10 April 2014.

454 Martin Daubney: *Well done, feminism. Now men are afraid to help women at work*; *The Telegraph*, 1 October 2015.

455 MGTOW Facebook page. https://www.facebook.com/pg/MenGoingTheirOwnWay/about/?ref=page_internal

456 *'Alienating Young Men is Deeply Sad - Jordan Peterson'* – BBC Radio 4 Interview 15 January 2018. https://youtu.be/sKVy7lXvciE?t=37m26s

457 Bari Wiess: *Camille Paglia: A Feminist Defense of Masculine Virtues*; *Wall Street Journal*, 28 December 2013.

458 Anita Rani: *The Japanese men who prefer virtual girlfriends to sex*; BBC News, 24 October 2013.

459 Abigail Haworth: *Why have young people in Japan stopped having sex?*; *The Guardian*, 20 October 2013.

460 Shiho Fukada: *Japan's Prisons Are a Haven for Elderly Women*; *Bloomberg BusinessWeek*, 16 March 2018.

461 *KGB defector Yuri Bezmenov's warning to America.* https://www.youtube.com/watch?v=bX3EZCVj2XA

462 Fredrich Hayek; *The Road to Serfdom*; p30, Routledge Classics, 2001 (first published in 1944).

463 Jonathan Haidt: *New Study Indicates Existence of Eight Conservative Social Psychologists*; Hetrodox Academy, 07 January 2016.

464 *Jonathan Haidt tests viewpoint diversity of university student audience:* https://www.youtube.com/watch?v=uogEbb0WOJE&t=506s

465 Yoel Inbar and Joris Lammers: *Political Diversity in Social and Personality Psychology*; Association for Psychological Science, 2012. http://yoelinbar.net/papers/political_diversity.pdf

466 Jillian Kay Melchior: *The Bias Response Team Is Watching*, *The Wall Street Journal*, 8 May 2018.

467 *Evergreen State College Controversy (HBO)*; Vice News, 16 June 2017. https://www.youtube.com/watch?v=2cMYfxOFBBM

468 *Margaret Atwood faces feminist backlash for #MeToo op-ed*; BBC News, 16 January 2018.

469 Thomas Sowell: *A Few Assorted Thoughts About Sex, Lies And Human Race*; *Sun-Sentinel*, 28 November 1998.

470 Simon Kent: *Cologne: Google, Facebook and Twitter Yield to German Govt Demand to Censor Anti-Migrant 'Hate Speech'*; Breitbart, 7 January 2016.

471 Walter Hickey: *25 Cutting Edge Firms Funded By The CIA*; Business Insider, 11 August 2012.

472 Noah Shachtman: *Exclusive: Google, CIA Invest in 'Future' of Web Monitoring*; Wired, 28 August 2010.

473 *Steven Pinker: the mind reader*; *The Guardian*, 6 November 1999.

474 Josh Horwitz: *An anti-Marxist, pro-free speech YouTuber is gaining a following in China*; Quartz. 23 February 2018.

475 *Vladimir Putin meets with members of the Valdai Discussion Club: Transcript of the Plenary Session of the 13th Annual meeting.* Valdai Discussion Club, 27 October 2016.

476 Alissa Rubin: *Erdoğan Calls Dutch 'Nazi Remnants' After Turkish Minister Is Barred*; New York Times, 11th March 2017.

477 Luke Gilkerson: *Get the Latest Pornography Statistics*; Covenant Eyes, 19 February 2013.

478 James Vincent: *AI tools will make it easy to create fake porn of just about anybody*; The Verge, 12th December 2017.

479 Victor Hugo: *Things Seen and Essays*; Wildside Press, 30th March 2008, p67.

480 Your Modern Family: *The scary truth about what's hurting our kids*. Your Modern family. 24 March 2018.

481 Sarah Westcott: *Pensioners: A million OAPs are depressed and say life is 'pointless'*; Daily Express, 21 March 2018.

482 Rebecca Harris: *The Independent*, 30 March 2015.

483 American Psychological Association: *Social isolation, loneliness could be greater threat to public health than obesity*; Science Daily, 5 August 2017.

484 Tim Montgomerie and Ayesha Hazarika: *Only 13% of us think the world is getting better. 67% say worse. Who's right?* Unherd, 7 December 2017.

485 Andy Coghlan; *Ancient invaders transformed Britain, but not its DNA, New Scientist*, 18 March 2015.

486 Dr Jordan Peterson: *Twelve Rules for Life: An Antidote to Chaos*; Overture pxxxi, Allen Lane, 2018.

487 Michael Jonas: *The Downside of Diversity*; New York Times, 5 August 2007.

488 Steve Sailer, *Fragmented Future*, The American Conservative, 15 January 2007.

489 Putnam, Robert D. *E Pluribus Unum: Diversity and community in the twenty-first century: The 2006 Johan Skytte Prize Lecture,* Scandinavian Political Studies. (June 2007), Wiley.

490 Amardeep Bassey, *British White People To Be A Minority In 'Super Diverse' Birmingham By 2021, Report Finds*; Huffpost UK, 27 June 2018.

491 Valeria Perasso: *Crossing Divides: Europe 'more split' than decade ago*; BBC News, 23 April 2018.

492 Will Durant: *Caesar and Christ*, Epilogue, Fine Communications, p. 665. 1944.

493 Dambisa Moyo: *Edge of Chaos: Why Democracy Is Failing to Deliver Economic Growth and How to Fix It*; Basic Books, 2018, p198.

494 Kate Ferguson: *One female genital mutilation case reported every hour in the UK*; The Independent, 6 February 2017.

495 Nick Sommerlad: *Britain's 'worst ever' child grooming scandal exposed: Hundreds of young girls raped, beaten, sold for sex and some even KILLED*; The Sunday Mirror, 10 March 2018.

496 Nick Noack: *Multiculturalism is a sham, says Angela Merkel*; The Washington Post, 14 December 2015.

497 *Douglas Murray on Tommy Robinson (and the Establishment).* https://www.youtube.com/watch?v=4UoJareHflw

498 Aleksandr Solzhenitsyn: *The Exhausted West*; *Harvard Magazine*, July–August 1978. https://harvardmagazine.com/sites/default/files/1978_Alexander_Solzhenitsyn.pdf

499 Reuters with CNBC: *Saudis set $500 billion plan to develop zone linked with Jordan and Egypt,* 24 Oct 2017.

500 BBC News: *Chinese authorities find 22 fake Apple stores*; 12 August 2014.

501 *China: Police DNA Database Threatens Privacy*; Human Rights Watch, 15 May 2017.

502 Zhao Yusha: *'Sky Net' tech fast enough to scan Chinese population in one second: report*; *Global Times,* 25 March 2018.

503 Yujing Liu: *Facial recognition tech catches fugitive in huge crowd at Jacky Cheung Cantopop concert in China*; *South China Morning Post*, 12 April 2018.

504 *'China to bar people with bad 'social credit' from planes, trains'*, Reuters, 16 March 2018.

505 'Liu Xuanzun; *Social credit system must bankrupt discredited people: former* official'; *Global Times;* 20 May 2018.

506 Rachel Botsman: *Big data meets Big Brother as China moves to rate its citizens*; *Wired*, 21 October 2017.

507 Mohammed Jamal: *This school scans classrooms every 30 seconds through facial recognition technology,* Techjuice, 21 May 2018.

508 Valerie M. Hudson and Andrea M. den Boer: *Bare Branches: The Security Implications of Asia's Surplus Male Population*; MIT Press, September 2005.

509 Patrick Knox: *Inside the Chinese sex doll factory making 'smart' robots that can also talk, play music and even do the dishes*; *The Sun*, 2 February 2018.

510 Fredrich Hayek; 'The Road to Serfdom'; p5, Routledge Classics, 2001 (first published in 1944)

511 Abby Norman and Jolene Creighton: *World Leaders Have Decided: The Next Step in AI is Augmenting Humans*; Futurism.com, 10 February 2018.

512 Conrad Hackett, et al; *The Future of World Religions: Population Growth Projections*, 2010–50; Pew Research Center, 2 April 2015.

513 Michael Lipka and Conrad Hackett: *Why Muslims are the world's fastest-growing religious group*; Pew Research Center, 6 April 2017.

514 Conrad Hackett: *5 facts about the Muslim population in Europe*; Pew Research Center, 29th November 2017.

515 Conrad Hackett, et al; *The Future of World Religions: Population Growth Projections*, 2010-2050; Pew Research Center, 2 April 2015, p147.

516 https://en.wikipedia.org/wiki/Conversion_to_Islam_in_U.S._prisons

517 Frances Perraudin, *Half of all British Muslims think homosexuality should be illegal, poll finds*, The Guardian, 11 April 2016.

518 Frank Herbert, *Children of the Dune,* Penguin, 1976. p164.

519 *Hair-Raising': Sharia Law Makes Its Debut in Swedish Court,* SputnikNews, 3 June 2018.

520 Tanita De Mey: *Demir: Party 'ISLAM' Tip of the Iceberg*; VTM Nieuws, 7 April 2017.

521 Josh Chin: *About to Break the Law? Chinese Police Are Already Onto You*; *Wall Street Journal*, 27 February 2018.

522 Tom Whipple: *Patriarchy Paradox: How Equality Reinforces Stereotypes*, The Times, 15 September 2018

523 George Orwell: *Nineteen Eighty-Four*; Signet Classics, Chapter 3, p262.

524 https://www.youtube.com/watch?v=l3PxvCkuiwQ

525 David Grossman: *People Are Treating Themselves With DIY Gene Therapies and the Government Is Getting Worried*; *Popular Mechanics*, 8 February 2018.